SUSTAINABLE DEVELOPMENT STRATEGIES

SUSTAINABLE DEVELOPMENT STRATEGIES

A RESOURCE BOOK

Compiled by

Barry Dalal-Clayton and Stephen Bass
of
The International Institute for Environment and Development

Earthscan Publications Ltd
London • Sterling, VA

First published in the UK and USA in 2002
by Earthscan Publications Ltd

Citation: Sustainable Development Strategies: A Resource Book. Organisation for Economic Co-operation and Development, Paris and United Nations Development Programme, New York

DISCLAIMER

The views expressed in this resource book are those of the compilers and should not be taken to represent those of the Organisation for Economic Co-operation and Development, the United Nations Development Programme, the International Institute for Environment and Development, or any of the agencies that have provided financial support for this document (listed in Acknowledgements).

The International Institute for Environment and Development (IIED), 3 Endsleigh Street, London WC1H 0DD, **www.iied.org**

ISBN: 1 85383 946 9 hardback
          1 85383 947 7 paperback

Page design by S&W Design Ltd
Typesetting by PCS Mapping & DTP, Gateshead
Printed and bound in the UK by Thanet Press, Margate, Kent
Cover design by Danny Gillespie

For a full list of publications please contact:

Earthscan Publications Ltd
120 Pentonville Road
London, N1 9JN, UK
Tel: +44 (0)20 7278 0433
Fax: +44 (0)20 7278 1142
Email: earthinfo@earthscan.co.uk
Web: **www.earthscan.co.uk**

22883 Quicksilver Drive, Sterling, VA 20166-2012, USA

Earthscan is an editorially independent subsidiary of Kogan Page Ltd and publishes in association with WWF-UK and the International Institute for Environment and Development

A catalogue record for this book is available from the British Library

Library of Congress Cataloging-in-Publication Data

Sustainable development strategies : a resource book / compiled by Barry Dalal-Clayton and Stephen Bass.
     p. cm.
Includes bibliographical references.
   ISBN 1-85383-946-9 -- ISBN 1-85383-947-7 (pbk.)
   1. Sustainable development. 2. Economic development--Environmental aspects. I. Dalal-Clayton, D. B. (D. Barry) II. Bass, Stephen, 1958-
HC79.E5 S8649 2002
338.9'27--dc21

                                                                                          2002009561

This book is printed on elemental chlorine-free paper

Acknowledgements

This resource book is a product of a project on sustainable development strategies initiatied by the OECD DAC Working Party on Development Cooperation and Environment. It builds on and complements an earlier output – *DAC Guidelines on Strategies for Sustainable Development* – published in 2001.

Members of the Working Party are Australia, Austria, Belgium, Canada, Denmark, European Commission, Finland, France, Germany, Greece, Ireland, Italy, Japan, Luxembourg, The Netherlands, New Zealand, Norway, Portugal, Spain, Sweden, Switzerland, the United Kingdom and the United States. The International Monetary Fund, the World Bank and the United Nations Development Programme participate as permanent observers. The Club du Sahel, Development Centre, International Institute for Environment and Development, United Nations Environment Programme, World Conservation Union and World Resources Institute participate regularly in the work of the Working Party.

The project has been undertaken by a special Task Force of the Working Party co-chaired by the UK Department for International Development (DFID) and the European Commission (EC-DG8) with strong support by the German Agency for Technical Cooperation (GTZ), and coordination and technical support provided by the International Institue for Environment and Development (IIED). The Capacity 21 initiative of the United Nations Development Programme and the United Nations Department of Environmental and Social Affairs actively supported the project.

The Task Force was led by Adrian Davis, Paula Chalinder and Jonathan Hobbs (DFID), Artur Runge-Metzger and Liselotte Isaksson (EC-DGVI), and Stephan Paulus and Kathrin Heidbrink (GTZ). Remi Paris of the DAC Secretariat provided guidance and advice throughout.

Financial support

Generous financial support for the work on which these guidelines are based, and for their preparation and publication, has been provided by, in alphabetic order:

- Department for International Development (DFID), UK
- European Commission (EC DG8)
- Finnish Ministry of Foreign Affairs
- French Ministry of Foreign Affairs
- German Agency for Technical Cooperation (GTZ)
- Japanese Ministry of Foreign Affairs
- Royal Norwegian Ministry of Foreign Affairs
- Spanish International Cooperation Agency (AECI)
- Swiss Development Cooperation
- United Nations Development Programme (UNDP) (Capacity 21)

Sources

This resource book draws from multiple sources:

- Status reviews, dialogue reports and commissioned papers prepared by the lead teams from developing country partners involved in the DAC project on NSDSs (see Preface) (Bolivia, Burkina Faso, Ghana, Namibia, Nepal, Pakistan, Thailand, Tanzania);
- UNDP made available a wide range of country-based and synthesis documents arising from the Capacity 21 programme. Grateful thanks are due to Penny Stock (Capacity 21);
- Materials developed and provided by IIED programmes;
- Publicly available information on a large number of websites.

Chapter reviews

Grateful thanks are due to the following people for reviewing individual chapters:

Chapter 2	Professor Michael Carley (Herriot Watt University, Edinburgh)
	Stephan Paulus (GTZ Germany)
Chapter 3	Professor Michael Carley (Herriot Watt University, Edinburgh)
	Maheen Zehra (IUCN Pakistan)
	Carol James (consultant, Trinidad)
	Paul Steele (DFID, UK)
Chapter 4	Ralph Cobham (consultant, UK)
	Jorge Reyes (UNDP Philippines)
	Joseph Opio-Odongo (UNDP Uganda)
Chapter 5	Jon Lindsay (FAO)
	Pippa Bird (consultant, USA)
	Duncan Macqueen and Josh Bishop (IIED)
	Robert Prescott-Allen (Padata, Canada)
Chapter 6	Carol James (consultant, Trinidad)
	Duncan Macqueen (IIED)
Chapter 7	Saneeya Hussain (consultant, Brazil)
	Dafina Gercheva (UNDP, Bulgaria)
	Penny Stock (Capacity 21, UNDP)
	Lilian Chatterjee (IIED)
Chapter 8	Ralph Cobham (consultant, UK)
	Professor Michael Carley (Herriot Watt University, Edinburgh)
Chapter 9	Tariq Banuri (Stockholm Environment Institute, Boston Center)
	Nicola Booregaard (consultant, Germany)
Chapter 10	Robert Prescott-Allen (Padata, Canada)
	Henk van Trigt (DGIS, The Netherlands)

Materials and information

The following people provided helpful materials, information and comments on various aspects of the resource book:

- Ashok Chatterjee, National Institute of Design, India;
- Mercie Ejigu, Partnership for African Environmental Sustainability;
- Fayen d'Evie, Earth Council;
- Kathrin Heidbrink, GTZ;
- Cees Moons, Ministry of Housing, Spatial Planning and Environment (VROM), The Hague;
- Ali Raza Rizvi, IUCN-Pakistan;
- Adrian Reilly, Brunel University;
- Clara Rodrigues, Environment Canada;
- Bansuri Taneja, Kalpavriksh, New Delhi.

Individual contributions

A large number of individuals made significant contributions to the learning on which this Resource Book draws, through their involvement in the national teams and in the international workshops:

Therese Adam (Swiss Development Cooperation); Anibal Aguilar (Bolivia); Jamie Aranibar Del Alcázar (UDAPE, Ministry of Treasury, Bolivia); Marco Balderrama (Bolivia); Bernardo Valdivia Baldomar (Bolivia); Sylvia Bankobeza (UNEP); Abihudi Baruti (Planning Commission, Tanzania); Mario J Baudoin (Ministry of Sustainable Development and Planning, Bolivia); Inger-Marie Bjonness (Royal Norwegian Ministry of Foreign Affairs); Ignacio Cabria (Spanish International Cooperation Agency); Ken Campbell (Natural Resources Institute, UK); Paula Chalinder (Department for International Development, UK); Patchaneeboon Charpoenpiew (Thailand Development Research Institute); Marcela Clavijo (Bolivia); Sambou Coulibaly (CONAGESE, Burkina Faso); Jürgen Czermenka (GTZ, Bolivia); Djiri Dakar (CONAGESE, Burkina Faso); Adrian Davis (Department for International Development, UK); Philip Dobie (UNDP); Nicolaj Draminski (consultant, Bolivia); Jairo Escobar (UNDP, Bolivia); Rosalind Eyben (UK Department for International Development, Bolivia); Angela Brown Farhat (National Development Planning Commission, Ghana); Gustavo Suarez de Freitas (Pro Naturaleza, Peru); Daniel Gantier (Ministry of Sustainable Development and Planning, Bolivia); Miguel Gonzalez (Bolhispania, Bolivia); Willi Graf (Swiss Development Cooperation, Bolivia); Hum Gurung (National Planning Secretariat, Nepal); Kathrin Heidbrink (GTZ, Germany); Alicia Herbert (Department for International Development, UK); Jan-Jilles van de Hoeven (UNDP Capacity 21); Saleemul Huq (IIED); Liselotte Isaksson (EC, DG8); Adis Israngkura (Thailand Development Research Institute); Brian Jones (Namibia); Saada K Juma (AGENDA, Tanzania); Utis Kaothien (National Economic and Social Development Board, Thailand); Peter de Koning (DGIS, The Netherlands); Karen Kramer (Royal Netherlands Embassy, Tanzania); Ronald Maclean (Minister for Sustainable Development, Bolivia); Ram C Malhotra (Nepal); Oswald Mashindano (University of Dar es Salaam, Tanzania); Sylvester Mbangu (National Planning Commission, Namibia); Artur Runge-Metzger (EC DG8); Paul Mincher (IIED); Giovanna Parolini de Mollinedo (Bolivia); Lucian Msambichaka (University of Dar es Salaam, Tanzania); Ali Mufuruki (Infotech Investment Group, Tanzania); Charles Mutalemwa (Planning Commission, Tanzania); Viroj Naranong (Thailand Development Research Institute); Anita Nirody (UNDP Capacity 21); Ndey Njie (UNDP Capacity 21); Matti Nummelin (Ministry of Foreign Affairs, Finland); Ernestine S Okoko (recif, Burkina Faso); Krishna Prasad Oli (IUCN Nepal); Arturo Lopez Ornat (Pangea consultants, Spain); Badre

Dev Pande (IUCN Nepal); Remi Paris (OECD, Paris); Stephan Paulus (GTZ, Germany); Mogens Pedersen (Danish Embassy, Bolivia); Nipon Poapongsakorn (Thailand Development Research Institute); Jagdish Pokharel (National Planning Commission, Nepal); Jesus Quintana (Spanish Agency for International Development, Bolivia); Prakash Raj (consultant to IUCN Nepal); Kirsten Rohrmann (Division for Sustainable Development, UN); Somkiet Ruangchan (Thailand Development Research Institute); Claudia M B Sánchez (Vice Ministry of Public Investment and External Finance, Bolivia); Cynthia M Yañez Sánchez (Ministry for Economic Development, Bolivia); Maimouna Sondzo Sangare (Ministry of Economics and Finance, Burkina Faso); Salif Sawadogo (Coordination Against Desertification, Burkina Faso); Gyan Sharma (National Planning Commission, Nepal); Uday Sharma (Ministry of Forests and Soil Conservation, Nepal); Pete Shelley (Department for International Development, UK); Fred Smidt (Netherlands Embassy, Bolivia); Serge Snrech (OECD); Penny Stock (UNDP); Krystyna Swiderska (IIED); Ferdinand Tay (National Development Planning Commission, Ghana); Carlos E Chávez Terán (Sustainable Development Commission, Bolivia); Daniel Thieba (GREFCO, Burkina Faso); Oussouby Touré (CSE, Senegal); Henk van Trigt (DGIS, The Netherlands); Aree Wattana Tummakird (Ministry of Science, Technology and Environment, Thailand); Gerardo Velasco (Cámara Nacional de Industria, Bolivia); Joachim Tres Vildomat (Bolhispania, Bolivia); Cámara Nacional de Industria (consultant, Bolivia); Guillermo Vivado (European Union, Bolivia); Terry Vojdani (Bolivia); Seth Vordzorgbe (Devcourt Ltd, Accra, Ghana); Taizo Yamada (JICA, Philippines); Mai Yamamoto (Ministry of Foreign Affairs, Japan); Asif Ali Zaidi (IUCN Pakistan); Maheen Zehra (IUCN, Pakistan).

Finally, the compilers are grateful to several IIED colleagues for their inputs and help:

- Joshua Bishop (contributed to Chapters 5 and 8);
- Lilian Chatterjee (contributed to Chapter 7);
- Maryanne Grieg-Gran (developed the first draft of Chapter 9);
- Paul Mincher (contributed to Chapter 7);
- Krystyna Swiderska (contributed to Chapter 5);
- Devyani Gupta and Sue Mylde researched information on websites and prepared materials.

Contents

Acknowledgements   *v*
Contents   *ix*
List of figures, tables and boxes   *xvi*
Preface   *xxii*
Acronyms and abbreviations   *xxiii*

1   About the resource book   1
    Aims   1
    Target audience   2
    Layout   2
    How to use this resource book   4

2   Sustainable development and the need for strategic responses   5
    The opportunity for a strategic approach to national development   5
        Organization of this chapter   6
    The challenges of environment and development   7
        Trends and major challenges   7
            Economic disparity and political instability   7
            Extreme poverty   8
            Under-nourishment   8
            Disease   8
            Marginalization   8
            Population growth   8
            Consumption   8
            Global energy use   9
            Climate change   9
            Nitrogen loading   9
            Natural resource deterioration   9
            Loss of diversity   10
            Pollution   10
            Growing water scarcity   10
            Other urban problems   10
            Interactions between social, economic and environmental problems   10
        International responses to the challenges of sustainable development   11
            The emergence of sustainable development as a common vision   11
            Multilateral environmental agreements (MEAs)   14
            Environmental monitoring and assessment   15
            Economic instruments   15
            Engaging the private sector   16
            New technologies   17

Financing sustainable development | 18
Governance – and the twin trends of decentralization and globalization | 18
Decentralization | 20
Globalization | 22
Focus on national strategies for sustainable development: a Rio commitment and one of the seven international development goals | **23**
Guidance to date on strategies for sustainable development | **25**
Why a strategic approach to sustainable development is needed | **27**
The need for structural changes | 27
Difficulties in introducing changes | 28
What being strategic means | 28

3   The nature of sustainable development strategies and current practice | 30
Introduction | **30**
What are sustainable development strategies? | **31**
Key principles for developing sustainable development strategies | **33**
Learning from current practice: existing strategy frameworks | **35**
Building on national level strategies | 38
National development plans | 38
Sector and cross-sectoral plans and strategies | 42
Plans and strategies related to conventions | 42
National forest programmes (NFPs) | 47
National conservation strategies (NCSs) | 50
National environmental action plans (NEAPs) | 50
National Agenda 21s and National Councils for Sustainable Development | 52
National visions | 53
Comprehensive development frameworks | 54
Poverty reduction strategies | 56
Sub-national strategies | 63
Decentralized development planning | 66
Village and micro-level strategies | 66
Convergence and links between national, sub-national and local strategies | 69
Regional approaches to developing strategies | 70

4   Key steps in starting or improving strategies for sustainable development | 74
Harnessing effective strategic mechanisms in a continual-improvement system | **74**
Scoping exercise | **77**
Establishing or strengthening a strategy secretariat or coordinating body | **77**
Establishing or strengthening a strategy steering committee or equivalent forum | **81**
Seeking or improving political commitment for the strategy | **82**
Establishing or confirming a mandate for the strategy | **85**
Ensuring broad ownership of the strategy | **85**
Securing strategy 'ownership' and commitment by all ministries | 87
Securing strategy 'ownership' and commitment by civil society and the private sector | 88
Mobilizing the required resources | **90**
Harnessing the necessary skills | 91

Bringing institutions and individuals on board 93
Raising the financial resources 94
Identifying stakeholders and defining their roles in the strategy **96**
Typical roles of the main actors in strategy processes, and constraints faced 98
Politicians and leaders 98
Public authorities 98
The private sector 99
Civil society 100
Donor agencies 100
Mapping out the strategy process, taking stock of existing strategies and other planning processes **102**
Seeking to improve coherence and coordination between strategy frameworks at all levels **104**
Coherence, coordination (and convergence) of national strategic frameworks 104
Focusing strategic objectives at the right level – from regional to local, and between sectors – and ensuring coherence and coordination there 105
Establishing and agreeing ground rules governing strategy procedures **110**
Establishing a schedule and calendar for the strategy process **112**
Promoting the strategy **112**
The role of experiments and pilot projects **112**
Establishing and improving the regular strategy mechanisms and processes **113**

5 Analysis 114
Approaching and organizing the tasks of analysis **114**
Introducing the main analytical tasks in NSDS processes 114
Challenges in analysis for sustainable development strategies 115
Effective strategies depend on sound information 115
Sustainable development is complex and difficult to analyse 115
Capacities to analyse sustainable development are often weak 115
There are dangers in relying on narrow, non-local, out-of-date or unreliable information 116
Basic principles for analysis 116
Engage and inform stakeholders within democratic and participatory processes 116
Use accessible and participatory methods of analysis 117
Include roles for independent, 'expert' analysis 117
Develop a continuing, coordinated system of knowledge generation 118
Agree criteria for prioritizing analysis 118
Ensure the objectives of the analysis are clear 119
Agree the types of output from the analysis, and who will get them 120
An introduction to methods available for analysis 120
Analysing stakeholders in sustainable development **120**
Why stakeholder analysis is important 120
Identifying stakeholders 124
Using an issues-based typology 124
Ways to identify stakeholders 125
Stakeholder representation 125
Identifying stakeholder interests, relations and powers 126
Identifying stakeholders' interests 126
Analysing the relationships between stakeholders 127

Analysing stakeholders' powers 127
Comparing stakeholders' powers with their potential for sustainable development 129
Limitations of stakeholder analysis 130
Approaches to measuring and analysing sustainability **132**
Accounts 133
Narrative assessments 135
Indicator-based assessments 135
Contributing measurements and analyses 138
Spatial analysis 138
System of national accounts 141
Genuine domestic savings 142
Ecological footprint 142
Natural resource, materials and energy accounts 144
Human Development Index 145
Sustainable livelihoods analysis 145
Policy influence mapping 148
Problem trees and causal diagrams 148
Strategic environmental assessment 149
Community-based issue analysis 153
Deciding what to measure: a framework of parts and aims 154
Deciding how to measure: choosing indicators 158
Seeing the big sustainability picture: generating indices 159
Identifying priority sustainability issues: using a rigorous, routine system 160
Analysing sustainable development mechanisms and processes **161**
Steps in analysing the component mechanisms 162
Analysing the legal framework for sustainable development 162
Analysing the economic context 169
Describing how the mechanisms link up 170
Scenario development **171**
The purpose and limitations of scenarios 171
Organizing scenario development 171
Some illustrations of sustainable development scenarios 173

6   Participation in strategies for sustainable development 177
Introduction **177**
Understanding participation **178**
Multiple perceptions, expectations and definitions of 'participation' 178
Typologies of participation – and associated dilemmas 178
'Horizontal' and 'vertical' channels for participation – and associated dilemmas 182
Why participation is needed in strategies for sustainable development **186**
Ensuring effective participation – issues and planning requirements **193**
Scoping the basic requirements 193
Consideration of costs and benefits of participation 193
Clarity of expectations 193
Consideration of scale and links 197
Representation, selection and intermediaries 198

Infrastructure, organization and legal framework for participation   201
Planning for participation in strategies   204
Methods for participation in strategies   **207**
Participatory learning and action   207
Community-based resource planning and management   211
Participation in decentralized planning systems   211
Multi-stakeholder partnerships   213
Focusing on consensus, negotiations and conflict resolution   217
Working in groups   218
 Facilitation   220
 Participants' responsibilities   222
 Rapporteurs   222
 Meeting agendas   222
Market research, electronic media and other remote methods   225

7 Communications   226
Introduction   **226**
Shifting values, attitudes and styles   **227**
Establishing a communications and information strategy and system   **230**
An information, education and communications strategy and action plan   233
Coordination of information   234
 Internal coordination – focus on creating a shared information base   235
 External coordination – using a wide range of methods   235
Choosing the medium, and developing complementary information products   236
Documents and audio-visual material   238
Events   240
 Managing dialogue and consensus-building during meetings   242
Establishing networks, or making links with existing networks   242
Establishing databases, or making links with existing databases   245
Use of electronic media   246
 Electronic democracy   247
Mass media   249
Monitoring the communication process   250

8 Strategy decision-making   253
The scope of strategy decisions   **253**
Strategic vision   254
Strategic objectives   254
Targets   254
Triggers   254
Action plan   255
Institutional plan   255
Challenges, principles and useful frameworks for making strategy decisions   **258**
Challenges for decision-making   258
 Getting a good grasp of the problems being faced   258
 Dealing with a wide range of integration and trade-off challenges   258

Dealing with 'real-world' issues and avoiding 'planners' dreams'   259
Achieving consensus on the vast range of sustainable development issues   261
Principles and frameworks for decision-making   261
Good decisions should be based on acknowledged values   261
Strategy decisions should reflect locally-accepted values   262
Strategy decisions should reflect global values   263
Strategy decisions should reflect risk and uncertainty   265
Formal methodologies for decision-making can help, but have limitations   265
Decision theory   265
Decision support tools   267
'Strong' and 'weak' sustainability   269
Institutional roles and processes for strategy decisions   **270**
Multi-stakeholder structures for decision-making   270
Facilitating decision-making through workshops   272
Consensus   272
Negotiations and conflict resolution   276
Negotiations   276
Conflict resolution   280
Policy coherence – a step-wise approach   280
A challenge: strengthening relations between decision-developers and the ultimate decision-takers 282
Selecting instruments for implementing strategy decisions   **283**
The range of sustainable development instruments   284
Legislative/regulatory/juridical instruments   284
Financial/market instruments   285
Educational/informational instruments   286
Institutional instruments   286
Guidance on selecting instruments   287

9   The financial basis for strategies   288
Introduction   **288**
Mobilizing finance   **290**
Financial requirements of the strategy   290
Formulation and review   290
Implementation   292
Sources of finance   292
Donor finance   292
Government   293
Other in-country sources of finance   293
International transfer payments   294
Global Environmental Facility   294
Carbon offsets and the Clean Development Mechanism   295
Debt swaps   295
National environmental funds   296
Trust funds   296
Mobilizing finance at the local level   297

Using market mechanisms to create incentives for sustainable development   **298**

Market mechanisms at the national level   299

Removing perverse incentives   299

Adapting existing market mechanisms   300

New market mechanisms   300

Market mechanisms at the local level   302

Mainstreaming sustainable development into investment and financial decision-making   **303**

Motives for addressing sustainable development   303

Company level   304

The business case from the financial institution viewpoint   305

Crucial factors in the business case   306

How can financial institutions mainstream sustainable development?   306

Challenges for Northern financial institutions   306

Challenges for national finance and investment institutions   307

10   Monitoring and evaluation systems   309

Introduction   **309**

Elements of a monitoring and evaluation system   309

Principles of successful monitoring and evaluation   310

Who should undertake monitoring and evaluation?   **311**

Formal internal and external monitoring   311

Internally-driven monitoring (conducted by local strategy stake-holders)   311

Externally-driven monitoring and evaluation (conducted by agreed independent bodies or donors)   313

Linking internal and external monitoring   314

Participatory monitoring and evaluation   315

When should monitoring and evaluation be undertaken?   **318**

The 'pressure–state–response' framework for monitoring – its utility and limitations   **318**

Use in state-of-the-environment reporting   318

Use and limitations for monitoring sustainable development   320

Monitoring the implementation of the strategy and ensuring accountability   **321**

Monitoring the performance of strategy stakeholders, and mutual accountability   322

Monitoring and evaluating the results of the strategy   **324**

Disseminating the findings of monitoring exercises and feedback to strategy decisions   **325**

Appendix   *327*

References   *331*

Index   *348*

List of Figures, Tables and Boxes

Figures

1.1	User's road map to the resource book chapters	3
2.1	Interactions between watershed management problems in the Densu River and Weija Reservoir area, Ghana	11
2.2	The systems of sustainable development	12
3.1	Rationale for a systematic approach to sustainable development strategies	32
3.2	Constellation of mechanisms contributing to a sustainable development strategy	32
3.3	Developing Malawi's National Forestry Programme	49
3.4	Bombardment by strategic planning requirements: illustrative examples of international conventions and initiatives, and national frameworks, that typically challenge a country	70
4.1	Constellation of mechanisms contributing to a strategy for sustainable development	75
4.2	The continuous improvement approach to managing sustainable development strategies	75
5.1	Stakeholder groups' size, potential and power to contribute to sustainable development	131
5.2	Gross domestic product versus Genuine Progress Indicator: United States 1950–1999 (in 1996 US dollars)	134
5.3	Environmental weight declines as the number of human 'subsystems' increases	137
5.4	Group Barometer of Sustainability, showing the well-being of North and Central America	139
5.5	Individual Barometer of Sustainability, showing the well-being of Canada	139
5.6	The Dashboard of Sustainability: an example for Canada	141
5.7	Sustainable livelihoods framework	147
5.8	Simple policy influences map concerning deforestation	148
5.9	Problem tree	149
5.10	Causal diagram of cause and effect linkages relating to poverty	151
5.11	Example of a systemic arrangement of parts	157
5.12	Sustainability components arranged hierarchically	158
5.13	Mechanisms for sustainable development: an analytical framework	161
5.14	Mapping the type/intensity of participation in strategy mechanisms	168
5.15	Institutional mapping: relationship chart of the entries involved in the implementation of the Sarhad Conservation Strategy	172
6.1	The leadership continuum	182
6.2	National and local participation experience	183
6.3	The sustainable development 'triad'	186
6.4	Identifying partners for stakeholder and working groups	199
6.5	Land use map made by an indigenous surveyor and villagers of the Marwa sub-region, Panama	210
7.1	The communication pyramid	227
8.1	Decision tree for a strategy to reduce women's time spent in gathering fuelwood	269
8.2	Rights- and risks-based negotiation process	279
8.3	Annual plans for integrating sustainable development into business	285
10.1	The driving force–state–response monitoring framework as applied to sustainable agriculture	321

Tables

2.1	Commercializing environmental services	16
2.2	Classification of national and regional government authorities (in Box 2.5)	19
2.3	Sub-national/local government authorities	20
3.1	Basic comparisons between developed and developing country strategy processes	37
3.2	Examples of National Councils for Sustainable Development and similar multi-stakeholder fora for sustainable development	54
3.3	Example of a draft CDF matrix from Vietnam	57
3.4	Comparison of strategies at different levels in Pakistan	65
4.1	Scoping some of the main benefits of preparing a national conservation strategy in Barbados	80
4.2	Checklist of key stakeholder groups in an national sustainable development strategy	86
5.1	Information-gathering and analytical tools to help strategy decision-making	121
5.2	The limits of participatory and economic analysis	123
5.3	Stakeholder power analysis of a particular issue (or policy or institution): suggested table for comparisons	129
5.4	Mapping power and potential of stakeholders: Malawi's National Forestry Programme	130
5.5	Three main approaches to measuring and analysing sustainability	134
5.6	Indicator-based assessments of sustainability	136
5.7	Genuine domestic savings: accounting for depletion of human, physical and natural capital. An example from Pakistan.	143
5.8	Calculating annual consumption of biotic resources: Costa Rica (1995)	144
5.9	Comparing SEA and EIA	150
5.10	Illustrative framework of parts and aims for indicator-based assessment (human subsystem only)	156
5.11	Illustrative performance criteria for the indicator, life expectancy at birth	160
5.12	Component mechanisms in NSDS, and how to analyse them	163
5.13	Questions asked about strategy quality by the OECD DAC initiative	166
6.1	Types of participation in local-level development	180
6.2	Levels of participation in policy processes	181
6.3	Examples of institutional channels for decision-making and action by sector and level	184
6.4	Illustrative comparison of strategies with high and low intensities of participation	197
6.5	Stakeholder interests and roles: the case of Guyana's National Biodiversity Action Plan	201
6.6	Examples of likely existing structures/institutions and methodologies for participation	202
6.7	Rights and obligations of OTBs (in Box 6.14)	203
6.8	Examples of participatory methodologies for strategy tasks	206
6.9	Techniques of participatory learning	209
6.10	Potential resources from organizations in the development triad	217
7.1	Examples of mass and alternative media forms	236
7.2	Public concern survey on the environment in St Helena	241
7.3	The choice of electronic media will be determined by access costs and speeds to the internet	247
7.4	Users of the internet (February 2000)	247
7.5	Examples of possible indicators to use in monitoring and evaluating a strategy website	251
8.1	Examples of the framework of linked strategic decisions	256
8.2	Choicework table for mobility	281
8.3	Diagnostic for alignment of business processes with sustainable development principles	284
8.4	Annual plans for integrating sustainable development into business	285
10.1	Example matrix for linking impacts with strategy mechanisms	326
10.2	Data for monitoring, sources and timing: examples from a poverty alleviation strategy	327
10.3	CSD list of indicators of sustainable development (September 1996)	328

Boxes

1.1   The OECD DAC donor-developing countries dialogues project   1
2.1   The Global Environment Outlook project   7
2.2   Sustainable development – a guiding vision to tackle interacting problems   12
2.3   Agenda 21 on national strategies for sustainable development   13
2.4   Key multilateral environmental agreements   14
2.5   Governance structures in flux   19
2.6   Decentralization   21
2.7   Decentralization in Indonesia   22
2.8   Some challenges of globalization for sustainable development   23
2.9   International development goals   24
2.10   The millennium development goals   25
2.11   Selected reviews of, and guidance on, strategic planning for sustainable development   26
2.12   Affirming the need for a strategic approach to sustainable development.   29
3.1   Key principles for sustainable development strategies   33
3.2   Elements of a national sustainable development strategy   36
3.3   Five-year planning in India and China   39
3.4   Civil society involvement in recent national plans in Thailand – and their alternative agenda   40
3.5   Harmonizing national development plans in Morocco   40
3.6   The Bangladesh Flood Action Plan   40
3.7   National human development reports   41
3.8   National Biodiversity Strategy and Action Plan, India   43
3.9   Examples of effective principles in national action programmes to combat desertification   45
3.10   Experience of non-Annex 1 (developing) countries in developing national communications for climate change   47
3.11   The tropical forest action plan – a non-strategic approach   48
3.12   The National Forestry Programme, Malawi   51
3.13   Pakistan's NCS – a strong basis for a national strategy for sustainable development   52
3.14   National Councils for Sustainable Development   53
3.15   National Visions   55
3.16   Progress with PRSPs: key points of the comprehensive review by the World Bank and IMF   59
3.17   Civil society opposition to PRSPs and NGO views   62
3.18   The DEAP mechanism in Zimbabwe   63
3.19   Local Agenda 21   64
3.20   Relations between Pakistan's national, provincial and district conservation strategies   65
3.21   Decentralized planning in Ghana   67
3.22   Village level planning in Iringa Rural District, Tanzania   68
3.23   The Uganda PRSP   71
3.24   The Eastern Caribbean Environmental Charter: principles relevant to strategies for sustainable development   72
4.1   Illustrative steps for starting, managing and continually improving a strategy for sustainable development   78
4.2   Membership of steering committee for Balochistan Conservation Strategy, Pakistan   82
4.3   The Netherlands' National Environmental Policy Plan – a response to public pressure   83
4.4   Strategy survival through changes of government   84
4.5   Covenants with industry in The Netherlands   89
4.6   Checklist of skills required to manage and coordinate a strategy   91
4.7   Capacity requirements for an effective NSDS   92

4.8	Unimplemented state environmental action plans in Nigeria: a failure of undefined roles	97
4.9	The role and functions of NGOs	101
4.10	The development of El Salvador's National Sustainable Development Strategy: a diversity of contributing mechanisms	103
4.11	Building on what exists: links between poverty reduction strategies and other strategic planning processes	106
4.12	Initiating bottom-up strategy approaches in Pakistan: complementing provincial and district strategies	107
4.13	Departmental strategies for sustainable development, Canada	109
4.14	Sarhad Provincial Conservation Strategy: coordination through 'Focal Points'	110
4.15	Linking strategies to budget processes	111
5.1	Poverty of environmental information in Southern Africa	116
5.2	Future of the Environment Survey Office – providing analysis for The Netherlands' Environmental Policy Plan	118
5.3	Signals that an issue might be a priority for analysis and action	119
5.4	Basic steps in stakeholder analysis	124
5.5	Policy communities in Pakistan	128
5.6	'Who counts most?' The tricky issue of stakeholder priority	132
5.7	What is an indicator?	136
5.8	The quest for a single indicator of sustainable development	138
5.9	Examples of sustainable development indicator initiatives	140
5.10	The use of GIS in achieving Regional Forest Agreements, Australia	142
5.11	Ecological footprints: some examples	143
5.12	The Human Development Index	146
5.13	Some principles for strategic environmental assessment	152
5.14	Strategic environmental analysis (SEAn): the AidEnvironment approach. The main step.	152
5.15	Lessons from strategic environmental analysis (SEAn) in Benin and Nicaragua	153
5.16	Agenda 21 as a basis for analysis	158
5.17	Selecting indicators	159
5.18	SWOT analysis (strengths, weaknesses, opportunities and threats)	168
5.19	Futurology: experience from India	172
5.20	Global scenarios	174
5.21	European scenarios	175
5.22	South African scenarios	176
6.1	Participation traditions in Central and South America	178
6.2	Participation – a loaded term	179
6.3	Some perceptions of participation in the Bangladesh Flood Action Plan and in rural planning in Tanzania	179
6.4	Community-based Turtle Conservation Programme, Trinidad	183
6.5	Structures for 'horizontal' and 'vertical' participation	185
6.6	Why existing strategies continue to be mainly top-down	188
6.7	The political dimensions of participation	190
6.8	Agenda 21 on participation	192
6.9	The benefits of participation in strategies	194
6.10	The costs of participation	195
6.11	Key constraints to participation: the experience of Joint Forest Management, India	196
6.12	Checklist for partner selection in Local Agenda 21s	200
6.13	Transparency in the selection of stakeholder representatives	200
6.14	The Popular Participation Law, Bolivia	203
6.15	Enshrining participation in legislation: principles of the Eastern Caribbean Environmental Charter	205
6.16	Sectoral collaboration for environmental management in Trinidad and Tobago	207

6.17	Principles of participatory learning and action	208
6.18	RRA and PRA compared	210
6.19	Some examples of participatory rural planning	212
6.20	Planning for Real: neighbourhood planning in urban Britain	212
6.21	Decentralized planning systems	214
6.22	Partnerships – a loaded term	214
6.23	Principles of multi-stakeholder processes	215
6.24	The multi-stakeholder approach of Canada's *Projet de société*	216
6.25	Involving the public and Maoris in developing New Zealand's Resource Management Act	218
6.26	Search conferences and nature tourism strategies in the Windward Islands	218
6.27	National Economic Development and Labour Council, South Africa – an example of a public sector-led partnership initiative	219
6.28	The dynamics of group work	220
6.29	Facilitation skills	221
6.30	Illustrative ground rules for group working	222
6.31	Example timetable for a cross-sectoral workshop	224
6.32	Market research clinches participatory forest policy, Grenada	225
7.1	The Aarhus Convention	228
7.2	The Access Initiative	229
7.3	Principles of effective communication	230
7.4	Sustainable development – a communications challenge	231
7.5	How can sustainable development be communicated successfully?	232
7.6	Communication strategy for the Pakistan National Conservation Strategy	232
7.7	Educating for sustainable development	233
7.8	Key questions for developing an information, education and communications plan	234
7.9	Sustainable development and desertification: a public awareness campaign in Burkina Faso	237
7.10	Outline of the prospectus for the Canadian *Projet de société*	239
7.11	Support services for journalists and NGOs, Sarhad Provincial Conservation Strategy, Pakistan	240
7.12	Ground rules for meetings	243
7.13	Some existing networks in Bolivia	244
7.14	Benefits and problems of networks	245
7.15	Some examples of strategy practitioner networks	246
7.16	Some examples of strategy websites	248
7.17	The website of the National Assembly for Wales	249
7.18	Some benefits and limitations of electronic communication	250
7.19	The internet for communication, awareness raising and problem solving: UNDP's Sustainable Development Networking Programme. Examples from Pakistan and China	252
8.1	Flaws in the conventional route of strategy decision-making	260
8.2	The emerging universal normative framework	263
8.3	What some Southern African constitutions say about the environment	266
8.4	The decision-making framework of the World Commission on Dams	267
8.5	Risk-based priority setting	268
8.6	Diverse mandates, structures and composition of National Councils for Sustainable Development (NCSDs)	271
8.7	Best practice decisions in NCSDs	273
8.8	Workshops as a means to find decisions, not pre-determine them	274
8.9	Consensus – a loaded term	275
8.10	100 per cent consensus or less – which is better?	276

8.11 Experience of multi-stakeholder mechanisms to build consensus in Canada   277
8.12 Target setting in The Netherlands   278
8.13 Rights- and risk-based negotiation process for decision-making on dams   279
8.14 Conflict resolution and mediation in a river basin strategy, USA   281
8.15 Promoting policy coherence in the United Kingdom   283
9.1   Financing the Pakistan National Conservation Strategy   291
9.2   Assessing the impact of new environmental regulations   291
9.3   Examples of debt swaps   296
9.4   PROFONANPE – Peru's Conservation Trust Fund   297
9.5   The Funds of the Americas   298
9.6   Integrating sustainable development objectives into the tax system – Belgium   300
9.7   Market mechanisms for meeting sustainable development objectives   301
9.8   Financial mechanisms for environmental objectives at the local level: the ICMS Ecologico   302
9.9   Types of institution involved in private sector investment decisions in developing countries   304
9.10 UNEP Financial Institutions Initiative   307
9.11 Sustainability ratings for companies   308
9.12 Examples of sustainable investment initiatives in developing countries   308
10.1 A strategy without regular monitoring and evaluation – Pakistan   310
10.2 The Bellagio principles for assessing progress towards sustainable development   312
10.3 The use of Commissions to hold government to account – Ghana and Canada   313
10.4 Development agency performance in supporting strategy processes: 20 questions   314
10.5 The process to review Pakistan's National Conservation Strategy   315
10.6 Guidelines for participatory monitoring and evaluation   316
10.7 Community-based monitoring and indicator development   319
10.8 State of the environment reporting   320
10.9 Internal audits for implementing Local Agenda 21   323
10.10 The value of 'quick and dirty' monitoring   323
10.11 Annual Sustainability Day: Hamilton-Wentworth, Canada   324

Preface

In 1992, Agenda 21 called for all countries to develop national sustainable development strategies (NSDSs). These are intended to translate the ideas and commitments of the Earth Summit into concrete policies and actions. Agenda 21 recognized that key decisions are needed at the national level, and should be made by stakeholders together. It believed that the huge agenda inherent in sustainable development needed an orderly approach – a 'strategy'. But Agenda 21 stopped short of defining such a strategy, or even of guidance on how to go about it.

The United Nations (UN) held a Special Session to review progress five years after the Earth Summit. Delegates were concerned about continued environmental deterioration, and social and economic marginalization. There have been success stories, but they are fragmented, or they have caused other problems. Sustainable development as a mainstream process of societal transformation still seems elusive. Strategic policy and institutional changes are still required.

The Rio+5 assessment led governments to set a target of 2002 for introducing NSDSs. The Development Assistance Committee (DAC) of the OECD, in its 1996 *Shaping the 21st Century* publication, called for the *formulation and implementation* of an NSDS in every country by 2005 (as one of seven International Development Targets). It also committed DAC members to support developing countries' NSDSs. But, again, no attempt was made to set out what a strategy would include or involve – in spite of growing experience with a number of international and local strategic models. 'How would I know one if I saw one?' one minister asked.

During 1999-2001, members of the OECD/DAC Working Party on Development Cooperation and Environment worked in partnership with eight developing countries to assess experience of country-level sustainable development strategies: Bolivia, Burkina Faso, Ghana, Namibia, Nepal, Pakistan, Tanzania and Thailand. Through dialogues involving stakeholders from government, the private sector and civil society, past and existing strategic planning experiences were analysed, key issues and challenges identified, and principles for best practice developed. An iterative process involving in-country discussions and three international workshops in Tanzania, Thailand and Bolivia, led to consensus on the final text of the Policy Guidance (*Strategies for Sustainable Development: Guidance for Development Cooperation* (OECD DAC 2001a)). This Resource Book is the companion to the Policy Guidance. Both publications draw from international experience of many strategic approaches to sustainable development over the past two decades.

The Policy Guidance sets out best practice in developing and operating strategic processes for sustainable development, and on how development cooperation agencies can best assist developing countries in such processes, and includes a set of principles which underpin the development of effective strategies in many developing countries (Chapter 3, Box 3.1).

In November 2001, a UN International Forum on National Strategies for Sustainable Development (held in preparation for the 2002 World Summit on Sustainable Development, WSSD) agreed guidance on NSDSs which confirms almost identical 'elements' of successful strategies (Box 3.2) for both developed and developing countries alike.

This resource book provides in-depth information on processes and methodologies. It was prepared by the International Institute for Environment and Development (IIED), working in collaboration with members of the partner country teams (see above) and a number of other organizations and individuals. It will be of value to a wide range of organizations, institutions and individuals in both developed and developing countries aiming to bring about sustainable development.

Acronyms and Abbreviations

AIDS	auto immune deficiency syndrome
AKRSP	Aga Khan Rural Support Programme
CAMPFIRE	Communal Areas Management Plan for Indigenous Resources, Zimbabwe
CBO	community-based organization
CBD	Convention on Biological Diversity
CDS	city development strategy
CSD	Commission for Sustainable Development
CDF	comprehensive development framework
CILS	Permanent Committee for Drought Control in the Sahel
DA	district assembly
DAC	Development Assistance Committee (of OECD)
DANIDA	Danish International Development Agency
DEAP	district environmental action plan
DFID	Department for International Development (UK)
EC	European Commission
EIA	environmental impact assessment
FAP	Flood Action Plan, Bangladesh
GDP	gross domestic product
GEF	Global Environmental Facility
GNP	gross national product
GTZ	German Agency for Technical Cooperation
HDR	human development report
HIMA	*Hifadhi Mazingira* (Swahili, meaning 'conserve the environment')
HIPC	highly indebted poor country
HIV	human immuno-deficiency virus
ICLEI	International Council for Local Environmental Initiatives
IDA	International Development Agency
IDG	international development goal
IDT	international development target
IEC	information, education and communication
IFC	International Finance Corporation
IIED	International Institute for Environment and Development
IPF	Inter-Governmental Panel on Forests
IMF	International Monetary Fund
IPCC	Inter-Governmental Panel on Climate Change
IT	information technology
IUCN	World Conservation Union
LA21	Local Agenda 21
LCA	life cycle assessment
LGO	local government organization

MEA	multilateral environmental agreement
	millennium ecosystem assessment
MDG	millennium development goal
MoEF	Ministry of Environment and Forests, India
MSP	multi-stakeholder process
MTEF	medium term expenditure framework
NAP	national action programme
NBSAP	national biodiversity strategy and action plan
NCS	national conservation strategy
NCSD	National Council for Sustainable Development
NEAP	national environmental action plan
NEDLAC	National Economic Development and Labour Council, South Africa
NEPP	National Environmental Policy Plan, The Netherlands
NFAP	national forestry action plan
NFP	national forest programme
NGO	non-governmental organization
NPACD	national plan of action to control desertification
NRTEE	National Round Table on the Economy and the Environment, Canada
NSDS	national sustainable development strategy
ODA	official development assistance
OECD	Organisation for Economic Co-operation and Development, Paris
PRS(P)	poverty reduction strategy (paper)
4Rs	rights, responsibilities, returns/revenues and relationships
RAP	regional action programme
REC	Regional Environment Centre, Budapest
RMA	Resource Management Act, New Zealand
SADC	Southern Africa Development Community
SD	sustainable development
SEA	strategic environmental assessment
SIA	social impact assessment
SL	sustainable livelihoods
SLF	sustainable livelihoods framework
SWOT	strengths, weaknesses, opportunities and threats
TFAP	tropical forestry action plan
UNCED	United Nations Conference on Environment and Development (1992)
UNDESA	United Nations Department of Environmental and Social Affairs
UNDP	United Nations Development Programme
UNEP	United Nations Environment Programme
UNFCC	United Nations Framework Convention on Climate Change
UNSO	UNDP Office to Combat Desertification and Drought (formerly UN Sahelian Office)
WBCSD	World Business Council for Sustainable Development
WCED	World Commission on Environment and Development
WWF	World Wide Fund For Nature
WRI	World Resources Institute
WSSD	World Summit on Sustainable Development
WTO	World Trade Organization

CHAPTER
1

About the Resource Book

Aims

This resource book provides guidance on how to develop, implement and assess national sustainable development strategies (NSDSs). It is based on an analysis of past and current practice, in both developed and developing countries, to undertake comprehensive approaches to sustainable development. In particular, it builds on dialogues and learning in the eight countries directly involved in a project on NSDSs undertaken by the Development Assistance Committee (DAC) of the Organisation for Economic Co-operation and Development (OECD) (Box 1.1), as well as on the work of a wide range of organizations, such as the Capacity 21 initiative of the United Nations Development Programme (UNDP), the UN Department of Economic and Social Affairs (DESA), the World Bank, World Conservation Union (IUCN), International Institute for Environment and Development (IIED) and many other groups (see the extensive References chapter at the end of the book and sources of further information at www.nssd.net).

This guidance is based on experience of past and current practice in the North and South ...

There is a particular focus on tried, tested and practicable approaches that have been used successfully in strategic planning processes. As such, the book's basis is 'real world' conditions rather than presenting approaches that could only be realized in an idealized or dream world. But it is well recognized that many previous approaches to strategies have failed – and even the successful ones have not worked well in all areas. We can learn from this: strategies need to experiment, wherever possible, with new ways of working; experience is evolving rapidly; and new methods for some strategy elements are being developed or tested. For instance, methods of participation, policy and scenario analysis and methods of monitoring and

... emphasizing tried and tested approaches

> **Box 1.1 The OECD DAC donor-developing countries dialogues project**
>
> During 1999–2001, members of the Working Party on Development Cooperation and Environment of the OECD DAC worked in partnership with eight developing countries to assess experience of country-level strategies for sustainable development. In Bolivia, Burkina Faso, Ghana, Namibia, Nepal, Pakistan, Tanzania and Thailand dialogues were held involving stakeholders from government, the private sector and civil society, past and existing strategic planning experiences were analysed, key issues and challenges identified, and principles for best practice developed. An iterative process involving in-country discussions and three international workshops led to consensus on the final text of Policy Guidance on strategies for sustainable development, endorsed by aid ministers at the DAC in April 2001
>
> Source: OECD DAC (2001a)

evaluation, which have been used successfully in other contexts, seem to hold promise for strategies as well. Innovative and cutting-edge approaches and methodologies that have potential are also included, although examples of their successful use may not yet be available. In practice, in many countries, unsettled political and social circumstances, difficult economic conditions and/or limited skills and capacity will determine what is actually practicable.

Each country's approach to developing its NSDS will be very different. In many countries it is likely to require the coordination of a suite of different processes, some existing and others new. Other countries may choose to prepare a single umbrella strategy. Whatever its format, a strategy will need to suit the nation's individual set of ecological, socio-cultural, economic and institutional conditions. Any form of straitjacket is inappropriate, especially if imposed by external agencies. Governments should work in partnership with civil society and the private sector to establish the right system.

Each country will need to adopt an approach tailored to its own needs

Target audience

This resource book is intended for a wide range of organizations and individuals in both developed and developing countries concerned with sustainable development at national, sub-national or local levels. These are likely to include the stakeholders in making strategy decisions – for example, people in government, NGOs, citizens' and community-based groups, educational institutions and business – as well as external individuals in development cooperation agencies, multilateral development banks, international organizations and multinational companies.

A wide range of people and organizations involved in sustainable development will find this book relevant to their work

Layout

A flexible approach has been taken to the material in the resource book. It is intended to be informative and not prescriptive. It sets out principles and ideas on process and methods, and suggests how these can be used. Each chapter has been written so that it can be read, as far as possible, as a stand-alone section and used independently of others. This is a response to many requests for briefing notes and 'how to' guides on particular issues and methodologies. However, there is also considerable cross-referencing throughout the book to related materials in other chapters.

This resource book contains a wealth of information and ideas in an extensive volume. No summary is provided since, to be effective, this would have required another substantial section of text. Instead, throughout the book, there are 'summary' comments in the margin. They aim to signal the essence of the text and enable the busy user to navigate quickly through chapters and sections, and find particular issues or discussions, which may be of interest and use. The 'road map' in Figure 1.1 shows how the different chapters relate to each other.

A non-prescriptive approach is followed – with principles and ideas on processes and methods, and guidance on the main tasks

The 'road map' figure shows the relationships between chapters

Following this Introduction, Chapter 2 offers background on the rationale for strategies for sustainable development. It discusses the nature and challenges of sustainable development and the need for strategic responses to them, amplifying much of the OECD DAC policy guidance on NSDSs – and is aimed at those making policy decisions on them.

The rest of the resource book covers the practice of NSDSs. It offers guidance on the main tasks in strategy processes, with individual chapters dealing with:

- the nature of sustainable development strategies and current practices (*Chapter 3*);
- key steps in starting, managing and improving sustainable development strategies (*Chapter 4*);
- methods of analysis (*Chapter 5*);
- participation in strategies (*Chapter 6*);

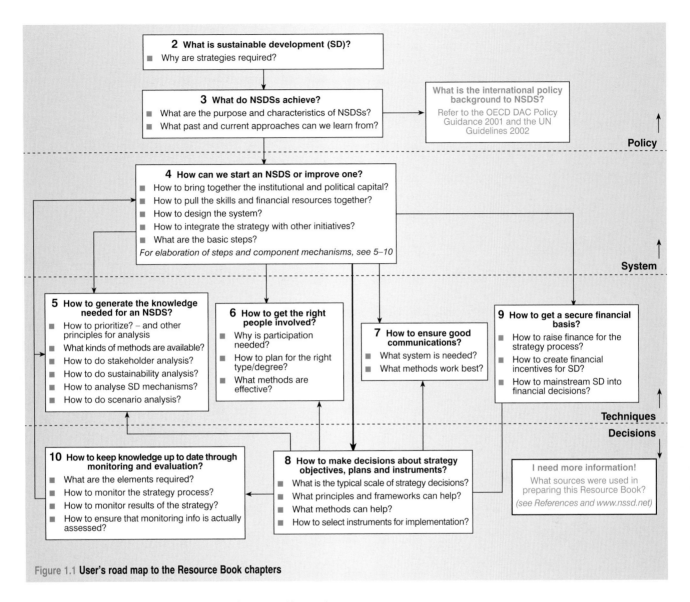

Figure 1.1 **User's road map to the Resource Book chapters**

- communications, information and education (*Chapter 7*);
- strategy decision-making and linkages (*Chapter 8*);
- the financial basis for strategies (*Chapter 9*);
- monitoring and evaluation systems (*Chapter 10*).

Chapters 3–10 are aimed at anyone engaged in planning, managing or reviewing a strategy process. For ease of presentation, they assume a logical sequence of steps, which might be followed if commencing a strategy process from an absolute beginning. In practice, very few, if any, strategies will need to start from scratch but should build on existing strategic planning processes and stages they have reached.

Finally, an extensive list of references is provided. Other sources of materials, as well as useful contacts with addresses and websites, are provided on the strategies website (www.nssd.net) and will be of use to those involved in NSDSs on a day-to-day basis as well as academics and researchers wishing to explore NSDSs further.

How to use this resource book

The resource book is not a rigid manual – use it flexibly to suit your particular needs

The resource book offers material to inspire and assess specific local and national approaches. It is not a complete 'construction' manual. Nevertheless, it is recommended that users explore each chapter in sequence if they have not been involved in developing a strategy before, are in the early stages of preparing a new strategy or are considering revising an existing strategy to cover a more ambitious remit. Other users may find it more helpful to concentrate on chapters of particular interest or on particular elements of the strategy process, to consider their relevance and utility and the implications for their own conditions and available resources, and then to design an approach suitable for the purposes at hand.

CHAPTER
2

Sustainable Development and the Need for Strategic Responses[1]

The opportunity for a strategic approach to national development

There has been unprecedented progress in development over the past 30 years. Life expectancy in developing countries has risen by more than 20 years, infant mortality rates have been halved and primary school enrolment rates have doubled. Food production and consumption have increased around 20 per cent faster than population growth. Improvements in income levels, health and educational attainment have sometimes closed the gap with industrialized countries. Advances have been made in the spread of democratic, participatory governance, and there have been forward leaps in technology and communications. New means of communication support opportunities for mutual learning about national development processes and for joint action over global challenges.

Much progress on many development fronts …

Notwithstanding this remarkable progress, there are also pressing constraints on development, and entrenched negative trends. These include: economic disparity and poverty; the impact of diseases such as HIV-AIDS and malaria; over-consumption of resources in the industrialized countries, contributing to climate change; and environmental deterioration and pollution of many kinds, including the impacts of intensive farming, depletion of natural resources and loss of forests, other habitats and biodiversity. The trends, and important international responses to them, are discussed in more detail later in the chapter.

… is compromised by entrenched poverty and environmental degradation, and other challenges

Negative trends – and the complex, dynamic and, therefore, difficult-to-grasp interactions between them – represent a vast range of challenges to efforts at national development in all countries, whatever their current level of economic development. Nations have agreed, through processes such as the 1992 Earth Summit, that development should be *sustainable*. This means, in a straightforward definition, that nations are able to achieve positive economic and social development, without excess environmental degradation, in a way that both protects the rights and opportunities of coming generations and contributes to compatible approaches elsewhere.

---

1 This chapter has benefited from review comments and additional material provided by Professor Michael Carley, Herriott Watt University, Edinburgh

The achievement of sustainability in national development requires a strategic approach, which is both *long-term* in its perspective and *integrated* or 'joined-up' in linking various development processes so that they are as sophisticated as the challenges are complex. A strategic approach at the national level implies:

- linking long-term vision to medium-term targets and short-term action;
- 'horizontal' linkages across sectors, so that there is a coordinated approach to development;
- 'vertical' spatial linkages, so that local, national and global policy, development efforts and governance are all mutually supportive; and
- genuine partnership between government, business, and community and voluntary organizations, since the problems are too complex to be resolved by any group acting alone.

Over the last decade, governments, the private sector and civil society in countries across the world have struggled to meet the challenges of sustainable development through a wide array of approaches to develop such visions, linkages and partnerships at national and local levels.

This resource book draws from this broad experience, assessing what has worked well and less well, setting out principles and characteristics for a more permanent, coordinated approach to strategies for sustainable development – on which there is growing international consensus among practitioners. It presents, for the first time in a consolidated way within a comprehensive volume, the mechanisms, processes and tools which can be used to support the development and implementation of national sustainable development strategies (NSDSs). It emphasizes coordinated, multi-stakeholder approaches providing for continuous learning and improvement. It is increasingly clear that NSDSs can facilitate the creation of 'win–win' opportunities in national economic and social development while also helping efforts to preserve the enormous diversity of ecosystems on which economies and social systems depend. Examples are offered of good practice in the various tasks required to achieve sustainable development. However, as efforts have so far been largely ad hoc, discontinuous and uncoordinated, there are not yet examples of strategies that combine good practice on *all* fronts.

The World Summit for Sustainable Development (WSSD), to be held in Johannesburg in August/September 2002, is focusing minds and attention once again on the challenges of sustainable development. It will take stock of progress since 1992 and seek ways in which to make progress through real behaviour change – and not merely in aspirations and exhortations. NSDSs offer a key set of processes and mechanisms to help achieve this goal.

The WSSD, its preparatory process and associated events and activities provide an unprecedented opportunity to recognize the difficulties and grasp the chance to make a serious commitment to sustainable development through NSDSs. But just negotiating agreed accords and communiqués – as in the past – will be insufficient. Given the progressively deteriorating environmental and social trends discussed in the next section, there is an urgent need for genuine political commitment for taking action: to establish in each country the environment in which stakeholders can engage effectively in debate and action; to develop real partnerships between government, the private sector and civil society; to agree roles and responsibilities for sustainable development; to establish effective coordination mechanisms; and to work together on agreed priorities. Now is the time to commit to a new systematic and strategic approach to sustainable development.

Organization of this chapter

The next section (page 7) looks in more detail at the trends and major challenges that stand in the way of achieving sustainable development. Recent attempts to achieve sustainable development are examined, ranging from global initiatives to technological advances and economic instruments (page 11). The subsequent sections look at the different governance contexts and contemporary twin processes of decentralization (which can empower local groups for sustainable development) and globalization (which presents potentials for involvement of the private sector in sustainable development) (page 18). Next, recently available guidance on integrated national strategies is explored (pages 23 and 25). The final section (page 27) provides a fuller explanation of what we now know to be effective, strategic approaches to sustainable development.

The challenges of environment and development

Trends and major challenges

The many urgent challenges and negative trends which remain to be overcome are well reviewed by regular, global assessment initiatives. Although these tend to focus on either environmental, social or economic concerns, they increasingly adopt a more holistic approach. Useful resources include:

- *Global Environment Outlook 2000*; *Global Environment Outlook 3* (UNEP 1999, 2002) (Box 2.1).
- *World Resources Report* (WRI/UNDP/UNEP/World Bank 2000).
- *DAC Development Report 2000* (OECD DAC 2001b).
- *Human Development Report 1999* (UNDP 1999, 2001a).

These reports, and many others, reveal a range of pressing and interrelated challenges to the achievement of sustainable development:

ECONOMIC DISPARITY AND POLITICAL INSTABILITY

The economic fortunes of most nations have risen steadily in the past 20 years, but still too many nations have experienced economic decline and falling per capita incomes. The recent downturn in Asian economies demonstrates how growth may be fragile. Disparity in incomes between the rich and poor within nations, between wealthy and poorer nations, and between many multinational companies and the countries in which they operate (or avoid), continues to widen. This means that a relatively small percentage of the world's people, nations and corporations control much of the world's economic and natural resources. This, as well as the marginalization of ethnic and other minorities from processes of governance and economic opportunity, contributes to instability. Political instability, sometimes leading to violent conflict, further hinders socio-economic progress in many countries and regions.

Box 2.1 The Global Environment Outlook project

The Global Environment Outlook (GEO) project was launched in 1995 by UNEP with two main components:

1. A participatory and cross-sectoral global environmental assessment process, incorporating regional views and perceptions and involving studies by a coordinated network of collaborating centres (multidisciplinary institutes with a regional outlook, which work at the interface of science and policy) around the world, and associated centres. Advice and support is provided by expert working groups on modelling, scenarios, policy and data.
2. GEO outputs in printed and electronic formats.

Global Environment Outlook 2000 reports on a comprehensive integrated assessment of the global environment at the turn of the millennium (UNEP 1999). *GEO-2000* draws from a participatory process involving the work of experts from more than 100 countries. It also provides a vision for the 21st century and documents many policy successes in the recent past, and stresses the need for more comprehensive, integrated policy-making, especially given the increasingly cross-cutting nature of environmental issues. *Global Environment Outlook 3* offers a more forward-looking perspective, setting out a range of environmental scenarios and their possible consequences (UNEP 2002). The report is accompanied by a CD-ROM containing the full GEO-3 text and a compendium of data from 249 countries and aggregations used in preparing it.

EXTREME POVERTY

Even in these prosperous times, extreme poverty still ravages the lives of one out of every five persons in the developing world. In 1993, more than 1.3 billion people were living on less than US$1 per day (UNEP 1999) – nearly 1 billion of these in the Asia and Pacific region. The highest proportion of the poor and the fastest growth in poverty are both in sub-Saharan Africa where half the population was poor in 2000. The social ills associated with poverty are on the rise in many countries with high rates of poverty. These include disease, family breakdown, endemic crime and the use of narcotic drugs.

UNDER-NOURISHMENT

Currently, global food production is adequate to meet overall human nutritional needs, but problems with the distribution of economic resources and foodstuffs mean that some 800 million people remain under-nourished. Although world food production is still rising, several trends will make it more challenging to feed a growing world population. The rate of increase in the yields of major grain crops is slowing down, and post-harvest losses remain high. Soil degradation from erosion and poor irrigation practices continues to harm agricultural lands, jeopardizing production in some regions. In general, without a transition to more resource-efficient and less polluting farming methods, it will be difficult to meet world food needs in the future without increasing the environmental burden that stems from intensive agriculture.

DISEASE

HIV-AIDS and malaria are serious diseases that erode both the productive capacity and the social fabric of hard-hit nations. In the worst affected countries, HIV has already had a profound negative impact on infant, child and maternal mortality. In addition, nearly 500 million people suffer from acute malaria every year, of whom 1 million die.

MARGINALIZATION

Many countries are struggling under the combined pressures of slow economic growth, a heavy external debt burden, corruption, violent conflict and food insecurity. These problems can be exacerbated by actions taken in the North, such as trade protectionism. Many of the residents of these countries suffer from a lack of access to social services, energy supplies and infrastructure. Their ability to develop their potential economic assets is also hampered by lack of access to resources, to credit or to the means for influencing national policy. At best, some become refugees or economic migrants. As a result of these processes, poor countries and poor people are continually marginalized from the opportunities presented by the global economy.

POPULATION GROWTH

Population growth is expected to exacerbate these pressures, although it is usually people's localized concentration or their resource consumption levels that matter more than their mere numbers. World population now stands at nearly 6 billion and, while it is growing more slowly than predicted a few years ago, it is still expected to increase substantially before stabilizing. Ninety-seven per cent of the estimated increase of 2 billion people over the next 20 years will live in the developing world.

CONSUMPTION

The demands of people in high-consumption, developed economies can have a more dramatic environmental impact than in countries with low levels of per capita resource consumption. Consumption of natural resources by modern industrial economies remains very high – in the range of 45–85 metric tons per person annually when all materials (including soil erosion, mining wastes and other ancillary materials) are counted. It currently requires about 300 kilograms of natural resources to generate an income of US$100 in the world's most advanced economies. Given the size of these economies, this volume of materials represents environmental alteration on a massive scale. Consequently, if the emerging economies of developing countries were also to be based on such an intensive use of resources, this would put extreme environmental pressure on the world's resource base.

GLOBAL ENERGY USE

Since 1971, global energy use has increased by nearly 70 per cent and is projected to continue to increase by over 2 per cent per year over the next 15 years – despite the fact that 2 billion people are still largely unconnected to the fossil fuel-based economy. While this increase will mean that more people will have access to energy services, it will raise greenhouse gas emissions by 50 per cent over current levels, unless there are serious efforts to increase energy efficiency and reduce reliance on fossil fuels. Although there has been considerable growth and technical progress in the use of renewable energy sources such as wind, solar, geothermal, hydro-electricity and others, public infrastructure and the convenience of fossil fuels and their low prices seriously inhibit any large-scale switch to the use of such clean energy sources in the foreseeable future.

CLIMATE CHANGE

In the late 1990s, annual emissions of CO_2 were almost four times the 1950 level with atmospheric concentrations of CO_2 reaching their highest level in 160,000 years (UNEP 1999). According to the Intergovernmental Panel on Climate Change, 'the balance of evidence suggests that there is a discernible human influence on global climate change' (IPCC 2001). This is expected to result in shifts of climatic zones, changes in the productivity of ecosystems and species composition, and an increase in extreme weather events. This will have substantial impacts on human health and the viability of natural resource management in agriculture, forestry and fisheries – with serious implications for all countries. Developing countries, and notably the least developed, are expected to be the most vulnerable to the impacts of global climate change, although their current contribution to the problem is minimal.

NITROGEN LOADING

Intensive agriculture, dependent on high levels of fossil fuel combustion and the widespread cultivation of leguminous crops, is releasing huge quantities of nitrogen to the environment, exacerbating acidification, causing changes in the species composition of ecosystems, raising nitrate levels in freshwater supplies above acceptable limits for human consumption, and causing eutrophication in freshwater and marine habitats. Nitrogen oxide emissions to the atmosphere also contribute to global warming. There is growing concern among scientists that the scale of disruption to the nitrogen cycle may have global implications comparable with those caused by disruptions of the carbon cycle.

NATURAL RESOURCE DETERIORATION

Environmental deterioration continues to increase with serious depletion of natural resources, including soil erosion, and loss of forests and fish stocks. Deforestation (most often due to conversion to farms, pastures, human settlements or for logging) continues to reduce the extent and condition of world forests. Some 65 million hectares of forest were lost between 1990 and 1995 (UNEP 1999). In the Amazon and Indonesia, recent forest fires have caused extensive forest loss and damage. Fragile aquatic environments such as coral reefs and freshwater wetlands are under considerable threat from land-based pollution, destructive fishing techniques and dam construction, as well as climate change. It is estimated that almost 60 per cent of the world's reefs and 34 per cent of all fish species may be at risk from human activities.

Current patterns of production and consumption, and global climate change, raise questions about the continued capacity of the Earth's natural resource base to feed and sustain a growing and increasingly urbanized population, and to provide sinks for wastes. As a result of environmental degradation, the biodiversity of the Earth's ecosystems and the availability of renewable natural resources have declined by 33 per cent over the last 30 years while demands on these resources have doubled.

LOSS OF DIVERSITY

Biologically derived products and processes account for an estimated 40 per cent of the global economy. Much of this production is based on the cultivation of an increasingly narrow range of species and genes, with many large-scale production processes in agriculture and forestry dependent on eradicating local biodiversity and replacing it with mono-cultural production. However, there is also growing realization of the value of biodiversity, both for providing insurance in case of failure of given species and genes (due to disease, climate or economic change), and for providing 'intellectual property' to develop new uses. Yet that same pool of biodiversity is increasingly coming under the control of the powerful companies that have been reducing its extent. At the livelihood level, many poor groups may be very dependent on a diversity of habitats, species and genes, especially for dealing with changed circumstances – and they may be good managers of biodiversity. However, there are often few institutions to integrate livelihood and biodiversity needs, and to look after local rights.

At the same time, cultural diversity (which has evolved alongside biodiversity) is reducing. The globalization of production, communication, knowledge generation, work and leisure patterns brings with it a loss of tradition which could have been a valuable resource for resilience.

POLLUTION

Most countries now experience anything from moderate to severe levels of pollution, which places a growing strain on the quality of water, soil and air. Despite clean-ups in some countries and sectors, a massive expansion in the availability and use of chemicals throughout the world, exposure to pesticides, heavy metals, small particulates and other substances all pose an increasing threat to human health and the environment.

GROWING WATER SCARCITY

Global water consumption is rising rapidly, and availability of water is predicted to become one of the most pressing and contentious issues in the 21st century. One-third of the world's population lives in countries already experiencing moderate to high levels of water shortage. That number could rise to two-thirds in the next 30 years, unless serious efforts are made to conserve water and coordinate watershed planning among water uses. Some 30–60 per cent of the urban population in low-income countries still lacks adequate housing with sanitary facilities, drainage systems and piping for clean water.

OTHER URBAN PROBLEMS

Continuing urbanization and industrialization, combined with a lack of resources and expertise, and weak governance, are increasing the severity of environmental and social problems, which reinforce one another in densely populated areas. Air pollution, poor solid-waste management, hazardous and toxic wastes, noise pollution and water contamination combine to turn these urban areas into environmental crisis zones. Children of poor households are most vulnerable to the inevitable health risks.

INTERACTIONS BETWEEN SOCIAL, ECONOMIC AND ENVIRONMENTAL PROBLEMS

Environmental, social and economic problems interact in complex ways

There are extensive interactions between many of the challenges described above, which make it necessary to take a strategic approach to sustainable development. Figure 2.1 is just one illustration, from a relatively well-defined area, of just how complicated the interactions are.

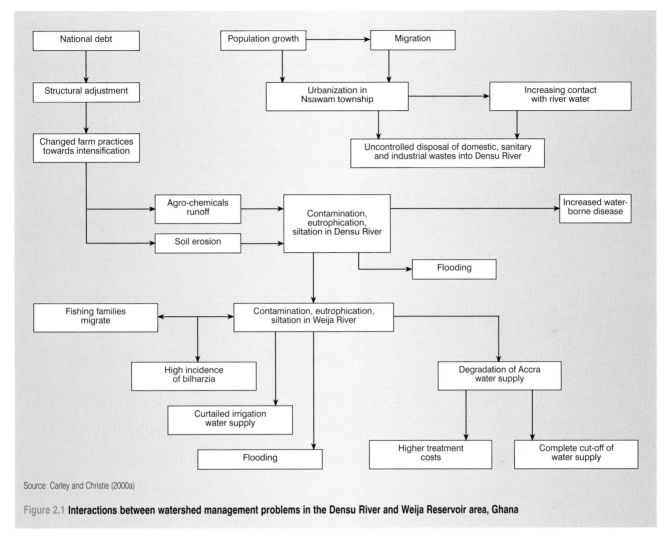

Source: Carley and Christie (2000a)

Figure 2.1 **Interactions between watershed management problems in the Densu River and Weija Reservoir area, Ghana**

International responses to the challenges of sustainable development

THE EMERGENCE OF SUSTAINABLE DEVELOPMENT AS A COMMON VISION

Recognition of deteriorating environmental trends led to the 1972 UN Conference on the Human Environment in Stockholm which, in turn, led to the creation of UNEP and IIED. Since then, worldwide acceptance of the importance of environmental issues has grown enormously. The World Conservation Strategy (IUCN/UNEP/WWF 1980) and, subsequently, the report of the World Commission on Environment and Development – the Brundtland Commission (WCED 1987) – were developed in response to increasingly informed analyses of the links between environment and development. The World Conservation Strategy emphasized the need to 'mainstream' environment and conservation values and concerns into development processes.

The report of the Brundtland Commission emphasized the social and economic dimensions of sustainability, revealing links between, for example, poverty and environmental degradation. The follow-up to the World Conservation Strategy, *Caring for the Earth: A Strategy for Sustainable Living* (IUCN/UNEP/WWF 1991) went further, elaborating principles for the practical integration of environmental, social and economic concerns (Box 2.2).

'Sustainable development' means more than 'environmentally sound'

Box 2.2 Sustainable development – a guiding vision to tackle interacting problems

The 1987 Brundtland Report defined sustainable development as '*development which meets the needs of the present without compromising the ability of future generations to meet their own needs*'. At the heart of the concept is the belief that social, economic and environmental objectives should be complementary and interdependent in the development process. Sustainable development requires policy changes in many sectors and coherence between them. It entails balancing the economic, social and environmental objectives of society – the three pillars of sustainable development – integrating them wherever possible, through mutually supportive policies and practices, and making trade-offs where it is not (Figure 2.2).

This includes taking into account the impact of present decisions on the options of future generations. However, sustainable development has often been mistakenly interpreted in a narrow sense as an environmental issue. This ignores the power and utility of the concept in its integration of economic and social development in the context of high quality environmental management. Given these complexities, however, it is understandable that the concept of sustainable development presents a challenge to communicate (see Box 7.4).

Approaches to sustainable development have been varied, reflecting the diversity of challenges faced by individual countries. Thus, while sustainable development is a universal challenge, many practical responses can only be defined nationally and locally. For example, in Thailand, sustainable development is defined as holistic development which involves six dimensions: economic, social, environment, politics, technology and knowledge, and mental and spiritual balance.

Reaching agreement on how to address the challenges requires a degree of pluralism and room for negotiation. This depends on factors such as peace and security, prevailing economic interests, political systems, institutional arrangements and cultural norms. In Bolivia, for example, good governance is seen as a central component of sustainable development – and is not just a 'means to achieve' it.

The practical outcomes of sustainable development processes tend to be described in two categories:

1   *Institutions and mechanisms* which produce decisions to balance social, economic and environmental objectives, and which ensure they are implemented. For example: particular planning and policy processes and procedures such as EIA and stakeholder fora.
2   *Activities on the ground* which add good environmental, social and/or economic practice to what might otherwise have been narrower goals. For example: new forms of natural resource management or integrated development projects.

There is a common, but mistaken, perception of 'environmental sustainability' as synonymous with 'sustainable development'. It is understandable how this has arisen: it has most often been the environmental 'pillar' of sustainable development that has been missing to date, and there has had to be considerable attention to this area.

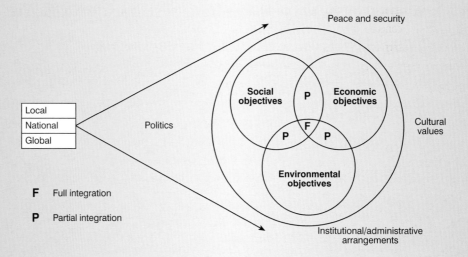

Sustainable development will entail integration of objectives where possible; and making trade-offs between objectives where integration is not possible.

Source: Dalal-Clayton et al (1994), modified from Barbier (1987)

Figure 2.2 **The systems of sustainable development**

Box 2.3 **Agenda 21 on national strategies for sustainable development**

Preamble

[Agenda 21's] successful implementation is first and foremost the responsibility of governments. National strategies, plans, policies and processes are crucial in achieving this. International cooperation should support and supplement such national efforts.

Chapter 8

Governments, in cooperation, where appropriate, with international organizations, should adopt a national strategy for sustainable development based on, inter alia, the implementation of decisions taken at the Conference, particularly in respect of Agenda 21. This strategy should build upon and harmonize the various sectoral economic, social and environmental policies and plans that are operating in the country. The experience gained through existing planning exercises such as national reports for the Conference, national conservation strategies and environment action plans should be fully used and incorporated into a country-driven sustainable development strategy. Its goals should be to ensure socially responsible economic development while protecting the resource base and the environment for the benefit of future generations. It should be developed through the widest possible participation. It should be a thorough assessment of the current situation and initiatives.

Source: Agenda 21 (UNCED 1992)

Agenda 21 and the conventions and agreements reached at the Earth Summit in 1992 comprise a global programme of action for sustainable development.[2] They cover 40 different sectors and topics and pay particular attention to national legislation, measures, plans, programmes and standards, and the use of legal and economic instruments for planning and management.

Arguably, Agenda 21 has become the most prominent and influential – but non-binding – instrument in the environment and development field and is a guiding document for sustainable development in most regions of the world. Its most important impact has been to focus attention on the core concept of sustainable development, providing policy-makers with a point of reference for linking environmental, social and economic issues. It stresses the importance of NSDSs and supporting policy instruments for giving these effect, although little guidance is given on NSDSs (Box 2.3).

Apart from the Earth Summit, the 1990s also saw a number of UN conferences on a variety of issues concerned with sustainable development and the challenges that need to be overcome to achieve it (see Box 2.4). Despite this concern, however, commitment and knowledge of best-practice instruments for NSDSs remain elusive. International initiatives on NSDSs have been based largely on international institutions' ideas of the agenda and methods to be applied, tempered by political constraint, rather than on locally proven practice.

'Sustainable development' unites environmental, social and economic concerns and initiatives

---

2 Agenda 21 – the action plan of UNCED: Chapters which describe the need for national plans: Preamble 1.3; Social and Economic Dimensions 2.6; Combating Poverty 3.9; Changing Consumption Patterns 4.26; Demographic Dynamics and Sustainability 5.31, 5.56; Protection and Promotion of Human Health 6.40; Promoting Sustainable Human Settlement Patterns 7.30, 7.51; Integrating Environment and Development in Decision-Making 8.3, 8.4, 8.7; Protection of the Atmosphere 9.12; Integrated approach to the planning and management of land resources 10.6; Combating Deforestation 11.4, 11.13; Fragile Ecosystems, Desertification and Drought 12.4, 12.37; Sustainable Agriculture 14.4, 14.45; Biodiversity, objectives (b); Biotechnology 16.17; Oceans 17.6, 17.39; Freshwater and water resources 18.11, 18.12, 18.40; Toxic Chemicals 19.58; Solid Wastes 21.10, 21.18, 21.30; Local Authorities 23.2; Financial Resources 33.8, 33.22, 33.15; Science 35.7, 35.16; Education 36.5; National Capacity Building 37.4, 37.5. 37.7. 37.10; International Institutions 38.13, 38.25, 38.36, 38.38, 38.39, 38.40; Information 40.4; Rio Declaration – Principle 10; Convention on Biodiversity – Article 6; Convention on Climate Change – Article 3, 4, 12.

Box 2.4 **Key multilateral environmental agreements**

Biodiversity

Convention on Biological Diversity (CBD), Nairobi, 22 May 1992 [www.biodiv.org]

Climate

United Nations Framework Convention on Climate Change (UNFCC), New York, 9 May 1992 [www.unfcc.de/]

Desertification

United Nations Convention to Combat Desertification in those Countries Experiencing Serious Drought and/or Desertification, Particularly in Africa (CCD), Paris, 17 June 1994 [www.uncod.de/]

Endangered species

Convention on International Trade in Endangered Species of Wild Fauna and Flora (CITES), Washington, 3 March 1973 [www.wcmc.org.uk/cites/]

Hazardous waste

Basel Convention on the Transboundary Movements of Hazardous Wastes and their Disposal (Basel), Basel, 22 March 1989 [www.unep.ch/basel/index/html]

Heritage

Convention Concerning the Protection of the World Cultural and Natural Heritage, 23 November 1927 [www.unesco.org/whc]

Migratory species

Convention on the Conservation of Migratory Species of Wild Animals (CMS), Bonn, 23 June 1979 [www.wcmc.org.uk.cms]

Ozone

Vienna Convention for the Protection of the Ozone Layer, Vienna, 22 March 1985; and
Montreal Protocol on Substances that Deplete the Ozone Layer, Montreal, 16 September 1987 [www.unep.org.org/ozone/]

Sea

United Nations Convention on the Law of the Sea (UNCLOS), Montego Bay, 10 December 1982 [www.un.org/depts/los/losconv1.htm]

Wetlands

Convention on Wetlands of International Importance especially as Waterfowl Habitat (Ramsar Convention), Ramsar, 2 February 1971 [www.ramsar.org/]

MULTILATERAL ENVIRONMENTAL AGREEMENTS (MEAs)

Multilateral environmental agreements promote some aspects of sustainable development, but can compromise social and economic objectives

A few historic international environmental treaties were signed many decades ago, such as the 1900 Convention for the Preservation of Animals, Birds and Fish in Africa. But it was concern about pollution and the depletion of natural resources in the 1960s that gave rise to the negotiation of a series of binding MEAs. The first generation of these were mainly single-issue, sectoral agreements and legislation, addressing allocation and exploitation of natural resources such as wildlife, air and the marine environment.

Overlapping with, and supplementing these, a second generation of agreements is more cross-sectoral, system-oriented and holistic. Some of the key MEAs are listed in Box 2.4.

Through these MEAs and other instruments of international law, a number of sustainable development legal principles are emerging: for example, polluter pays, prior informed consent and the precautionary principle. These are discussed in Chapter 8. There is, however, growing concern about the implementation, compliance with and effectiveness of the MEAs – and about their coherence with each other and with multilateral economic and trade agreements, notably the World Trade Organization (WTO). The increase in the number of uncoordinated MEAs and non-binding instruments has led to more and more onerous reporting requirements and bureaucratic burdens.

ENVIRONMENTAL MONITORING AND ASSESSMENTS

In the last two decades, a wide array of monitoring regimes have been established to track environmental change, some connected to the MEAs described above such as UNEP working in partnership with various UN organizations to coordinate terrestrial, oceanic and climate observing systems. Periodic reviews and assessments of trends and conditions are undertaken by the UN and other international organizations (some on a global basis, others regional or sectoral). There are also regular, independent assessments of global and regional trends and progress on international agreements, such as the annual *State of the World* reports of the Worldwatch Institute (Brown 2001) and the *Yearbook of International Co-operation on Environment and Development* (Bergesen et al 1999).Given the many serious constraints on sustainable development described in the section on trends and major challenges (pages 7–11), a major challenge for the 21st century is to understand the vulnerabilities and resilience of ecosystems so that ways can be found to reconcile the demands of human development with the tolerances of nature. Responding to this need, the Millennium Ecosystem Assessment is an important effort organized and supported by a wide range of governments, UN agencies and leading scientific organizations. It was launched at the UN in June 2001 and is a global scientific assessment of ecosystems, taking into account regional, national and local assessments. In addition to its assessment function, it aims to build capacity at all levels to undertake integrated ecosystem assessments and to act on their findings. The Millennium Ecosystem Assessment followed a year-long Pilot Analysis of Global Ecosystems (PAGE), which assessed five major ecosystem types: agro-ecosystems, forests, freshwater, grasslands, and coastal and marine systems. The results were reported on in the *World Resources Report 2000–2001* (WRI/UNDP/UNEP/World Bank 2000). It is now moving on to assess the effectiveness of different response options.

There have also been a number of regional assessments of the state of the environment, and of challenges to sustainable development. A good example is *State of the Environment in Southern Africa* prepared by Southern African Research and Documentation Centre in collaboration with IUCN and Southern African Development Community (SADC) (SARDC 1994). This report examined the natural resources of the region – particularly ecological zones shared by countries – provided details of the most serious environmental issues, and discussed the impacts of global warming and scenarios for the future of the region.

At the national level, the 1980s and 1990s saw a plethora of different kinds of environmental studies and reports, many prepared in response to the requirements of international agreements. Examples include profiles, strategies and action plans covering biodiversity, climate, conservation, environment and forestry; state-of-the-environment reports; UNCED national reports; Agenda 21 national reports; and OECD environmental performance reviews. Many of these are listed in the *World Directory of Country Environmental Studies: An Annotated Bibliography of Natural Resources Profiles, Plans and Strategies* (WRI/IIED/IUCN 1996).

ECONOMIC INSTRUMENTS

Sustainable development entails private individuals, corporations and communities behaving in ways that will balance private benefits with public benefits such as securing environmental services, or improving equity. Regulations are only partially effective in this. The 1992 Earth Summit stressed the need for economic incentives to promote more sustainable patterns of production and consumption and to generate resources to finance sustainable development. But economic reform has been slow and there has been

International environmental monitoring programmes have improved awareness of sustainability problems

Governments are increasingly using economic instruments to secure environmental benefits where regulations lack impact

Table 2.1 Commercializing environmental services

Environmental service	Commodities	Sources of demand
Watershed protection (eg reduced flooding; increased dry season flows; reduced soil erosion; reduced downstream sedimentation, improved water quality)	Watershed management contracts; tradable water quality credits; salinization offsets; transpiration credits; conservation easements; certified agricultural produce	*Domestic/regional* – hydroelectric companies; municipal water boards; irrigators; water-dependent industries; domestic users
Landscape beauty (eg protection of scenic 'view-scapes' for recreation or local residents)	Ecotourism concessions; access permits; tradable development rights; conservation easements	*Domestic/international* – local residents, tourist agencies; tourists; photographers; media; conservation groups; foreign governments
Biodiversity conservation (eg conservation of genetic, species and ecosystem diversity)	Bio-prospecting rights; biodiversity credits; biodiversity management contracts; biodiversity concessions; protected areas; development rights; conservation easements; shares in biodiversity companies; debt-for-nature swaps; land acquisition	*Domestic/international* – pharmaceutical, cosmetic and biotechnology companies; agri-business; environmental groups; foreign governments; the global community (eg Global Environment Facility)
Carbon sequestration (eg absorption and storage of carbon in vegetation and soils)	Carbon offsets/credits; tradable development rights; conservation easements	*Domestic/international* – major carbon emitters (eg electricity, transport and petrochemical companies); environmental groups; foreign governments; consumers

Source: Landell-Mills (2001)

limited use of market-oriented instruments, despite proposals in many (mainly developed) countries for 'green taxes', for example on emissions, mineral oils and pesticides for the purpose of internalizing social and environmental costs in market mechanisms. Only a few countries have so far introduced such taxes (eg Sweden and the UK). Promising new economic instruments involve markets in environmental services (Table 2.1). Market-based approaches can permit service provision to be concentrated where it is most cost-effective – which would often benefit developing countries. Attention is also being given to the removal of 'perverse' governmental subsidies that move society away from sustainability rather than towards it. Examples of such subsidies include support for intensive, environmentally degrading agricultural practices in many OECD countries and tax breaks for fossil fuel energy production. Chapter 9 discusses economic instruments in more detail.

ENGAGING THE PRIVATE SECTOR

In many countries, the last decade has seen some progress towards more sustainable business, with companies committed to sustainable development strategies through partnerships with customers, suppliers, government, NGOs and the general public. More openness is evident, for example, in publication of company environmental reports and implementation of voluntary environmental self-regulation schemes in some countries. But such appropriate policy responses remain few and more concerted action is still required to begin to achieve sustainable production and to encourage consumers to embrace sustainable consumption patterns.

Business is organizing itself to benefit from sustainable development …

Thus the goal of sustainable development has also become a concern of the private sector. For example, the World Business Council for Sustainable Development (WBCSD) was formed during the Earth Summit preparations to ensure business played a part. It now has over 130 fee-paying member corporations, mainly from industrialized countries. Membership is by invitation to companies committed to the concepts of sustainable development and responsible environmental management. Members are expected to provide in-kind and personnel support, including financial backing for individual working groups, and the active participation, including secondment, of their staff in the WBCSD work programme. Participation is sought at the highest level, normally from the chief executive officer or equivalent.

The WBCSD has four objectives:

1 *Business leadership:* to be the leading business advocates on issues connected with the environment and sustainable development.
2 *Policy development:* to participate in policy development in order to create a framework that allows business to contribute effectively to sustainable development.
3 *Best practice:* to demonstrate progress in environmental and resource management in business and to share leading-edge practices among its members.
4 *Global outreach:* to contribute through its global network to a sustainable future for developing nations and nations in transition.

The views of the WBCSD on sustainable development are now actively sought in many international negotiations (eg on climate change). It has made policy prescriptions on various issues such as trade and environment, financial markets, the paper industry, freshwater access and sustainable forestry. For a review of the role and impact of the WBCSD, see Najam (1999).

Speaking at the 1999 World Economic Forum in Davos, the UN Secretary-General, Kofi Annan, called for a new 'global compact of shared values and principles' between business leaders and the UN, particularly on environment. The Global Compact is a value-based platform to promote and showcase good corporate practices and learning experiences in the three areas of human rights, labour and environment (for which it upholds nine principles). It provides an entry point for the world business community to work in partnership with UN organizations. The Compact asks business leaders to:

... and is engaging with the United Nations

■ Make a clear statement of support for the Global Compact and the core values set out in its nine principles, and engage in public advocacy for the Compact.
■ Post once a year on the Global Compact website [www.unglobalcompact.org] a concrete example of progress made or lessons learned in implementing the principles. This can take many forms; for example, changes in internal management policies or concrete operational experiences.
■ Engage in partnership with UN organizations by undertaking activities that further the implementation of the principles, or by entering strategic partnerships in support of broad UN goals, such as the eradication of poverty.

NEW TECHNOLOGIES

In some cases, industry has found it financially profitable and environmentally beneficial to adopt the concept of cleaner production, involving re-designed products and production processes intended from the outset to minimize resource use, waste and harmful emissions. Many industries in developed countries have established clean production methods on a voluntary basis. UNEP is a good source of advice for governments on how to encourage cleaner production strategies and policies in domestic industry (UNEP 1994).

Sustainable development policies are too commonly viewed as constraints, but they also can be drivers of innovation – for new technologies ...

A similar approach, called eco-efficiency, has been promoted by the WBCSD. This is defined as:

the delivery of competitively-priced goods and services that satisfy human needs and improve
quality of life while progressively reducing ecological impacts and resource intensity, throughout
the life cycle of the product, to a level at least in line with the Earth's estimated carrying
capacity (WBCSD 1995).

Life cycle assessment (LCA) is now being used to evaluate the 'cradle-to-grave' effects of a product on the environment over its entire life cycle. LCA is being used for a range of purposes, such as comparing the environmental performance of new and older products, setting eco-labelling criteria, and in developing business strategies and investment plans.

FINANCING SUSTAINABLE DEVELOPMENT

... and new financing
mechanisms

At the 1992 Earth Summit, it was agreed that new, additional sources of funding were required to implement Agenda 21. Some resources might be provided by each country's public and private sectors, but it was agreed that low-income countries would require substantial additional funding through Official Development Assistance (ODA) or foreign capital investment. The UNCED Secretariat estimated, at the time, that the full implementation of Agenda 21 would cost low-income countries, on average, more than US$600 billion annually between 1993 and 2000.

In practice, ODA has been declining in recent years, owing to budgetary pressures in donor countries and other reasons. Only four nations consistently attain the UN target for ODA of 0.7 per cent of GNP (Denmark, The Netherlands, Norway and Sweden) – a target re-affirmed by high-income countries at the Earth Summit. However, this decline in aid may have been partially balanced by the rapid increases in private capital flows to low-income countries – by over 300 per cent since 1992. According to the World Bank's Global Development Finance 2000 report, net long-term flows to developing countries totalled US$291 billion in 1999. Of this, only US$52 billion took the form of official aid, while private flows amounted to US$238 billion (US$192 billion of this was foreign direct investment). However, private flows have been concentrated on a few countries with dynamic economies (mainly in Asia, Europe, and Central and South America). The poorest countries continue to struggle to attract resources for development. They face a continuing need for aid to help them create the conditions that will promote market investment, self-sustaining growth and reach the internationally agreed goals for development (Boxes 2.9 and 2.10).

At the same time, however, the international finance community has begun to correlate good corporate financial performance with corporate provisions for sustainable development. Various sustainability indices have emerged, and there is evidence that finance houses are beginning to use them (Chapter 9).

Governance – and the twin trends of decentralization and globalization

Sustainable
development balances
needs from local to
global levels

The challenges discussed on pages 7–11 are primarily about making decisions on social, environmental and economic priorities, and on new forms of investment, production and consumption. They must be dealt with by governance systems at local, national and global levels. It is important to recognize that the architecture and operation of governance systems at different levels differs between countries, as well as the meaning of terms such as national, provincial and district, and that the processes of governance are changing (Box 2.5). Moreover, two major trends, which can be either complementary or contradictory, are increasingly relevant for governance: decentralization and globalization. While it is being increasingly recognized that many social and environmental issues are most effectively dealt with on a decentralized basis, issues arising from globalization processes require, by definition, global rules and governance systems. The challenge for strategies for sustainable development is therefore threefold:

Box 2.5 **Governance structures in flux**

Trends in governance: The term governance refers to the *process or method by which society is governed*, or the *'condition of ordered rule'* (Rhodes 1997). It reflects the structures and processes of regionalization and decentralization, which have tended to build on previously informal interactions between government and other actors.

In this regard, the position of sub-national governments is changing. For example, elected local authorities find themselves 'sharing the turf' with a whole range of bodies also exercising governmental powers at the local level. Local governance, barely discernible a decade ago, has become a reality (Wilson 2000). It is now the *active inclusion of a wide range of public, private and voluntary sector actors in carrying out policy on the ground*.

For many sub-national governments, the innovative nature of many of their partnerships and mobilization efforts is a direct response to the attempts to control the policy process by the national government. As Stoker (2000) puts it, the challenge is in 'achieving collective action in the realm of public affairs, in conditions where it is not possible to rest on recourse to the authority of the state'.

Thus, paying too much attention to formal governmental structures ignores the policy capacity that now exists for a range of actors – governmental and non-governmental – in developing sustainable development strategies.

Principles: The European Union has defined principles of good governance: openness, participation, accountability, effectiveness and coherence (CEC 2001). These principles are echoed by the World Bank, which operates a set of aggregate governance indicators based on: voice and accountability; political instability and violence; government effectiveness; regulatory burden; the rule of law; and graft (Kaufmann et al 1999).

Typology: Countries can be classified relatively simply according to the nature of their national and regional governance (Table 2.2).

Table 2.2 **Classification of national and regional government authorities**

Nation-state form	Regional level characteristics	Examples
Federal	▪ Wide ranging powers ▪ Elected parliament ▪ Budgetary powers ▪ Legislative rights ▪ Right to levy taxes	Germany: Länder Canada: Provinces Belgium: Provinces
Regionalized states	▪ Advanced powers (political regionalization) ▪ Elected parliament ▪ Limited budgetary powers ▪ Limited right to levy taxes	Spain: Autonomous communities India: States Italy: Regions
Devolving unitary states	▪ Limited powers (regional decentralization) ▪ Elected parliament ▪ Limited budgetary powers ▪ Substantial financial transfers from central government ▪ Limited right to levy taxes	Mexico: States France: Regions Netherlands: Provinces
Classic unitary states	▪ No powers (regionalizing without creating a Regional level) ▪ No elected parliament ▪ No budgetary powers ▪ All financial resources transferred from central government ▪ No right to levy taxes	UK: Local authorities Sweden: Counties

Authorities at a more local level exhibit a much wider degree of variety than at the regional level, and the meaning of terms differs. For example, the French *commune* is a self-administering community of local inhabitants rather than an organization controlled by elected representatives, and is thus similar to the German *Gemeinde*. Examples of basic and intermediate-level local authorities are shown in Table 2.3. However, the powers and status of each of these levels can only be understood within their specific contexts.

Table 2.3 **Sub-national/local government authorities**

Country	Basic level	Intermediate level	State or region
Australia	Local Councils		States
Brazil	Municipalities		States
Canada	Towns/Cities	Metropolitan and Regional Municipalities, Counties and Regional Districts	Provinces
France	Communes	Departements	Regions
Germany	Gemeinden	Kreise/Kreisefreie Städte	Länder
India	Panchayats		States
Spain	Municipios	Provincias	Communidad Autonomas
Switzerland	Communes		Cantons
UK	Non-Metropolitan Districts/ Unitary Authorities/ Metropolitan Councils	Non-Metropolitan Counties/ Greater London Authority	Devolved States (Wales and Scotland)
USA	Municipalities/Towns	Counties/City Councils	States

Source: Adrian Reilly, Brunel University (personal communication)

■ to determine which issues are best addressed at which level;

■ to ensure coherence between policy options pursued at different levels; and

■ to find ways of ensuring local people are involved, even where it appears the policy agenda is best focused at national or international initiatives.

DECENTRALIZATION

Decentralization is under way almost everywhere, but with contrasting perspectives on what it should achieve

Decentralization aspires to foster development policies and strategies suited to local social, economic and environmental conditions. Done in an appropriate manner, it can promote localized governance structures responsive to citizens' needs and allow the downsizing and streamlining of centralized government institutions. As such, decentralization provides an opportunity to establish effective mechanisms for sustainable development.

However, the underlying principles of decentralization are as yet poorly understood and capacities for managing the process are frequently inadequate. Successful decentralization depends on a clear definition of the respective roles of local, regional and national-level authorities and the development of effective institutions at each level for planning and decision-making, involving actors at those levels. Unless these requirements can be put in place, the risks of inappropriate decentralization include the reinforcement of local elites, socio-political fragmentation along ethnic lines, marginalization of less dynamic regions, the weakening of national cohesion, and associated conflicts. A major problem is that decentralization, like participation, means different things to different people (Box 2.6).

Box 2.6 Decentralization

Decentralization is the transfer of the locus of power and decision-making either downwards (vertical decentralization) or to other units or organizations (horizontal decentralization). The power that is transferred can be political, administrative or fiscal. Five aspects of decentralization are commonly recognized: devolution, deconcentration, delegation, deregulation and privatization; though, in reality, most situations entail a mixture of all types. French usage is more specific: decentralization corresponds to the English devolution.

Devolution or *'democratic decentralization'* is the transfer of power from a larger to a smaller jurisdiction; for example, from national to sub-national political entities such as states or local government. This transfer may be total (eg to make all decisions) or partial (eg transfer to local communities of the powers needed to manage the renewable resources on their village lands).

Deconcentration or *administrative decentralization* is the vertical decentralization of the power to act – but not to decide or, ultimately, control – within the administration or technical institution (eg from the ministry of interior to a governorship or from the national directorate of a service to the regional directorate).

Delegation may be vertical or horizontal transfer of limited executive – but not decision-making – authority from an administrative service to local government, parastatals or private companies.

Deregulation is the lifting of regulations previously imposed by a public authority.

Privatization is the transfer of the ownership and/or management of resources, and/or the transfer of the provision and production of goods and services, from the public sector to private entities (commercial or non-profit).

Governments often intend *administrative decentralization* – a transfer of activities within the structure of governance to local outposts – but without ceding any real authority over decision-making or resource allocation. NGOs, on the other hand, feel that decentralization should be about *devolution* of powers from central to more local authorities, so that local people have a real stake in making decisions which affect their lives and the local environment.

Administrative decentralization has often been tried in response to the failure of centrally controlled rural development and service provision but has enjoyed only limited success, since problems encountered centrally are merely displaced to the local level without any increase in local accountability or management effectiveness. Nowadays, *devolution* is being promoted as a panacea for local development, on the basis of institutional evidence. At best, devolution can redress legitimate concerns about the constraints and inefficiencies of centralized government, but at worst it is never completed beyond a mere public relations exercise to sweeten the sometimes bitter pill of structural adjustment. In Indonesia, new decentralization laws provide real devolved authority as well as substantial financial resources, but they were hastily introduced and have many flaws. It remains to be seen how they will be implemented (Box 2.7).

Moreover, decentralization, even with the best intentions, can fail if it does not address 'invisible' institutional problems such as: individuals seeking financial gain from assets they control but do not own; patronage; personal power struggles; negative attitudes to participation, and so on. More recent attempts at devolution show promise, especially in socially homogeneous areas with poor natural resources. Priority is best given first to social issues and providing infrastructure for education and health, rather than attempting immediately to devolve control over income-generating activities or the management of natural resources.

Examples of successful local development initiatives, which do include the management of natural resources, are as yet rare with lessons seldom fed into wider processes of development. One reason is that natural resource management requires that politically sensitive issues are addressed before devolution, such as land tenure and control over resources. Often, these issues are highly contentious and seen as threatening

> **Box 2.7 Decentralization in Indonesia**
>
> Under the rule of President Suharto, Indonesia was unusually centralized for a country of its size and diversity. The central government allocated natural resource concessions in the regions, without consulting local governments and without regard for existing land uses or local customary rights. Local governments received only a small share of revenues from natural resource exploitation.
>
> Under the post-Suharto governments, central government authority in the regions largely collapsed and illegal exploitation of resources and environmental degradation were proceeding apace.
>
> In 1999, new decentralization laws were introduced hastily by the government of President Habibie, fearing that the process would run out of steam if prolonged. The legislation provides for the transfer of real authority for local public works, infrastructure and services and substantial funding increases to the regions. However, it mainly empowers district (city and *kabupaten*) governments, which are now entitled to receive 80 per cent of government revenues from forestry, fisheries, non-oil and non-gas mining. But there is a severe deficiency of skills and capacity in some local governments to make use of such powers. The provincial governments, which generally have greater capabilities, have been by-passed by the new legislation.
>
> Noting the anomalies in the system, World Bank experts argued that decentralization should first be undertaken to provincial level, with associated constituency- and capacity-building, prior to decentralizing further to district level; and also that it should occur in a phased manner among the provinces, according to their capacity.
>
> Source: Aden (2001) *Asia Environmental Review*, vol VI, no 1, May 2000

by local and national elites. In short, while decentralization might have a facilitating role, it is neither a prerequisite nor a guarantee of good local management.

To be effective, decentralized systems must have:

- sufficient devolved power for the exercise of substantial influence over political affairs and development activities;
- provision of sufficient financial resources to accomplish important tasks;
- adequate capacity (both technical and institutional) to accomplish those tasks;
- reliable accountability mechanisms.

Two factors seem key in designing support programmes to meet these requirements:

1 They should be realistically tailored to the local context rather than idealized, desired outcomes or imported principles.
2 They need to acknowledge the highly political dimension of local development processes, and thus place special emphasis on means to address the 'invisible institutions problem' in a pragmatic and non-antagonistic fashion.

GLOBALIZATION

Globalization brings new technology, and rising incomes and influence, to some people ...

The process of globalization is being driven by factors such as trade liberalization, rapidly improving and cheaper communications, the consequent growth and spread of multinational corporations with increasing levels of foreign investment, technological innovation, and the proliferation of multilateral institutions and agreements. On the positive side, globalization is fuelling economic growth, creating new income-generating opportunities, accelerating the dissemination of knowledge and technology, and making possible new international partnerships.

But globalization may also have profound and worrying implications for sustainable development in developing countries. These include:

- the external political, cultural and economic shocks associated with globalization;
- the vulnerability of national economies;
- the marginalization of knowledge, individuals, businesses and indeed whole countries and cultures that this may cause.

For example, the continuing Asian economic crisis has had serious social and environmental impacts, which have affected the poor disproportionately. The achievement of sustainable development will require a good understanding of the effects of globalization in relation to national and local governance, assets and vulnerabilities. It calls for appropriate policy responses in many areas; for example, structural adjustment, trade, foreign investment, development assistance and policy coherence (see Box 2.8).

Globalization has thus far only been weakly addressed in strategies for sustainable development. There is a particularly urgent need for a new approach to the international dimension of national strategies, and for helping to develop resilience to external economic shocks – fostering inclusion, not marginalization. The private sector (both big and small) needs to be involved in meeting this challenge.

... but also social and economic shocks, vulnerability and marginalization to weaker groups

Decentralization and globalization both determine sustainable development prospects, yet sustainable development plans and policies tend not to get to grips with them

---

Box 2.8 Some challenges of globalization for sustainable development

Globalization has profound implications for sustainable development. But the impacts of globalization have been weakly addressed in strategies for sustainable development so far, and there is a particularly urgent need for a new approach to the international dimension of national strategies.

Trade and investment provide a critical source of capital for driving economic growth in developing countries, and are becoming increasingly important with the decline in aid flows. Increased trade and investment could have a significant impact on the environment if increased productive activity (such as mineral extraction and new manufacturing processes) is not accompanied by robust social and environmental controls. Inequalities within developing countries could also widen, as poor people find themselves less able to exploit new economic opportunities and become more vulnerable to a loss of access to resources and environmental degradation associated with privatization and industrialization.

Steering globalization towards the objectives of sustainable development depends on the capacity of governments to stimulate and regulate market access arrangements that prevent environmental degradation, and ensure that economic benefits are widely distributed. Critical policy areas include:

- **Structural adjustment:** Stabilization and adjustment can exacerbate unsustainable use of natural resources and environmental degradation, due to weak institutional capacity and regulatory frameworks and lack of clear tenure over resources. In many cases, the poor are the worst affected by these impacts. This is a central issue for national strategies for sustainable development.
- **Trade:** Export-led development is now regarded as a major route to prosperity for poor nations, but the least developed countries are still constrained by barriers to trade, notably in agriculture and textiles. To date, developing countries have been wary of attempts to link trade and environment in policy-making, fearing a new wave of 'green protectionism'. The challenge is to find ways in which developing countries can make positive links between export growth and sustainable development.
- **Foreign investment:** Recent OECD negotiations for a Multilateral Agreement on Investment have highlighted the need for developing country governments to balance the need for a secure investment regime (to attract and retain foreign capital) with mechanisms to encourage corporate responsibility for social and environmental performance.

Focus on national strategies for sustainable development: a Rio commitment and one of the seven international development goals

We have noted how, at the 1992 Earth Summit, governments made a commitment to adopt NSDSs (see page 13). Such strategies were foreseen as highly participatory instruments intended 'to ensure socially responsible economic development while protecting the resource base and the environment for the benefit of future generations' (Agenda 21, UNCED 1992).

An NSDS can provide a conduit between Agenda 21 commitments and changed stakeholder behaviour, by mobilizing capacities and rethinking governance

---

Box 2.9 International development goals

In 1996, the Development Assistance Committee (DAC) of the OECD selected an integrated set of goals for sustainable development which aim to provide indicators of progress. These goals were based on targets formulated and agreed by the international community over the last decade through UN conferences, which addressed subjects important to sustainable development: education (Jomtien 1990), children (New York 1990), environment (Rio de Janeiro 1992), human rights (Vienna 1993), population (Cairo 1994), social development (Copenhagen 1995) and women (Beijing 1995).

Economic well-being

■ The proportion of people living in extreme poverty in developing countries should be reduced by at least one half by 2015 (Copenhagen).

Social and human development

■ There should be universal primary education in all countries by 2015 (Jomtien, Copenhagen and Beijing).
■ Progress towards gender equality and the empowerment of women should be demonstrated by eliminating gender disparity in primary and secondary education by 2005 (*Cairo, Beijing and Copenhagen*).
■ Death rates for infants and children under 5 years should be reduced in each developing country by two-thirds of the 1990 level by 2015 (*Cairo*).
■ Rate of maternal mortality should be reduced by three-quarters between 1990 and 2015 (*Cairo, Beijing*).
■ Access should be available through the primary health care system to reproductive health services for all individuals of appropriate ages no later than 2015 (*Cairo*).

Environmental sustainability and regeneration

■ There should be a current national sustainable development strategy (NSDS) in the process of implementation, in every country, by 2005, so as to ensure that current trends in the loss of environmental resources are effectively reversed at both global and national levels by 2015 (derived from a commitment agreed at UNCED in *Rio de Janeiro*).

At the meeting of the DAC on 11–12 May 1999, aid ministers endorsed a note clarifying the role of development cooperation in assisting partner developing countries in the formulation and implementation of NSDSs. This note was based on lessons emerging from the DAC project to develop policy guidance on NSDSs, which are amplified in this resource book. It accepted that the timeframe set out in the above goal should be interpreted as one for achieving progress, rather than as a strict deadline.

Source: OECD DAC (1997a)

NSDSs were expected to provide focal points for integrating environment and development in decision-making, and for defining and implementing sustainable development priorities. The importance and value of such strategies is a strong theme throughout Agenda 21 (Box 2.3).

The OECD's *Shaping the 21st Century* strategy (1997a) called for the formulation and implementation of a sustainable development strategy in every country by 2005. This is one of the seven international development goals (IDGs) agreed by the OECD (Box 2.9).

In 1997, the Special Session of the UN General Assembly met to review progress since the Rio Summit, and noted that there had been continued deterioration in the state of the global environment under the combined pressures of unsustainable production and consumption patterns and population growth. This assessment led governments to set a target date of 2002 for *introducing* national sustainable development strategies.

More recently, 147 heads of state signed the Millennium Declaration in September 2000. The associated Millennium Development Goals (Box 2.10) include one relating to environmental sustainability, with a target (but no date) to: 'integrate the principles of sustainable development into country policies and programmes and reverse the loss of environmental resources' (UNGA 2001). Initiatives towards sustainable development strategies should, therefore, also contribute to the achievement of this particular target.

Box 2.10 **The millennium development goals**

Each goal is accompanied by various targets and a range of indicators. Only those for Goal 7 are shown.

Goal 1   Eradicate extreme poverty and hunger
Goal 2   Achieve universal primary education
Goal 3   Promote gender equality and empower women
Goal 4   Reduce child mortality
Goal 5   Improve maternal health
Goal 6   Combat HIV-AIDS, malaria and other diseases
Goal 7   Ensure environmental sustainability
Goal 8   Develop a global partnership for development

Goal 7   Ensure environmental sustainability – the targets:

(9) Integrate the principles of sustainable development into country policies and programmes and reverse the loss of environment resources

Indicators
- Proportion of land area covered by forest
- Land area protected to maintain biological diversity
- GDP per unit of energy (as proxy for energy efficiency)
- Carbon dioxide emissions (per capita)*

(10) Halve by 2015 the proportion of people without sustainable access to safe drinking water

Indicator
- Proportion of population with sustainable access to an improved water source

(11) By 2020 to have achieved a significant improvement in the lives of at least 100 million slum dwellers
Indicators
- Proportion of people with access to improved sanitation
- Proportion of people with access to secure tenure

* Plus two figures of global atmospheric pollution: ozone depletion and the accumulation of global warming gases

Source: UNGA (2001)

Guidance to date on strategies for sustainable development

It is nearly ten years since the UNCED agreement, but very little official guidance has emerged on how to fulfil the NSDS commitments. Nevertheless, a body of literature has described the activities to date of developing and developed countries in respect of NSDSs and similar initiatives.

Agenda 21 promoted NSDSs in 1992, but official guidance on NSDSs has only just been released

Most notably, in 1994, IIED and IUCN published a handbook on the planning and implementation of NSDSs, drawing from international experience of conservation strategies, environmental action plans and similar processes, the result of both independent analysis and discussions at regional meetings of practitioners. This document was widely distributed and used (Carew-Reid et al 1994), but had no official status. This, and other key reviews, have been used to compile the current resource book; they are listed in Box 2.11. Abstracts and full texts of many documents can be found on the NSDS website [www.nssd.net].

More recently, in policy guidance endorsed by aid ministers in April 2001, the OECD DAC has sought to clarify the purposes and principles underlying effective national and local strategies for sustainable development; to describe the various forms they can take in developing countries; and to offer guidance on how development cooperation agencies can support them (OECD DAC 2001a). Following from this commitment, this resource book provides a more detailed elaboration of this policy guidance. It draws

Box 2.11 **Selected reviews of, and guidance on, strategic planning for sustainable development**

Bass, S M J and Dalal-Clayton, D B (1995) *Small Island States and Sustainable Development: Strategic Issues and Experience*, Environmental Planning Issues no 8, International Institute for Environment and Development, London

Bass, S M J, Dalal-Clayton, D B and Pretty, J (1995) *Participation in Strategies for Sustainable Development*, Environmental Planning Issues no 7, International Institute for Environment and Development, London

Bernstein, J (1995) *The Urban Challenge in National Environmental Strategies*, Environmental Management Series Paper no 012, Environment Department, The World Bank, Washington, DC

Bressers, H and Coenen, F (undated) *Green Plans: Blueprints or Statements of Future Intent for Future Decisions*, Center for Clean Technology and Environmental Policy, CSTM, University of Twente, Enschede, The Netherlands

Carew-Reid, J (ed) (1997) *Strategies for Sustainability: Asia*, IUCN in association with Earthscan, London

Carew-Reid, J, Prescott-Allen, R, Bass, S and Dalal-Clayton, D B (1994) *Strategies for National Sustainable Development: A Handbook for their Planning and Implementation*, International Institute for Environment and Development (IIED), London, and World Conservation Union (IUCN), Gland, in association with Earthscan, London

Carley, M and Christie, I (2000a) *Managing Sustainable Development*, 2nd edn, Earthscan, London

Coenen, FHJM (1996) *The Effectiveness of Local Environmental Policy Planning*, CSTM Studies and Reports, University of Twente, Enschede, The Netherlands

Dalal-Clayton, D B (1996) *Getting to Grips with Green Plans: National Level Experience in Industrial Countries*, Earthscan, London

Dorm-Adzobu, C (1995) *New Roots: Institutionalizing Environmental Management in Africa*, World Resources Institute, Washington, DC

EAP Task Force (1998) 'Evaluation of Progress in Developing and Implementing National Environmental Action Programmes (NEAPs) in CEEC/NIS', paper produced for *Environment for Europe*, Aarhus, 23–25 June 1998, OECD, Paris

Earth Council (2000) *NCSD Report 1999-2000: National Experiences on Multi-Stakeholder Participatory Processes for Sustainable Development*, Earth Council, San José, Costa Rica

ERM (1994) 'Developing Plans and Strategies', paper II prepared for the Ministry of Housing, Spatial Planning and Environment in The Netherlands and presented to the *First Meeting of the International Network of Green Planners, 30 March–1 April 1994, Maastricht, The Netherlands*, Environmental Resources Management, London

Falloux, F, Talbot, L and Christoffersen, L (1990) *National Environmental Action Plans in Africa: Early Lessons and Future Directions*, AFTEN, Technical Department, Africa Region, World Bank, Washington, DC

Falloux, F, Talbot, L and Larson, J (1991) *Progress and Next Steps for National Environmental Action Plans in Africa*, The World Bank, Washington, DC

Falloux, F and Talbot, L (1993) *Crisis and Opportunity: Environment and Development in Africa*, Earthscan, London

Hill, J (1993) *National Sustainability Strategies: A Comparative Review of the Status of Five Countries: Canada, France, The Netherlands, Norway and the UK*, The Green Alliance, London

Hill, J (1996) *National Sustainability Strategies: A Guide to Drafting and Ensuring Participation*, 1st edn, The Green Alliance, London

IPPF, UNFPA and IUCN (1993) 'Strategies for Tomorrow's World', *People and the Planet*, vol 2, no 4

IUCN (1984) *National Conservation Strategies: A Framework for Sustainable Development*, IUCN, Gland, Switzerland

Jänicke, M and Jörgens, H (1997) *National Environmental Policy Plans and Long-term Sustainable Development Strategies: Learning from International Experience*, Forschungsstelle für Umweltpolitik, Berlin

Lampietti, J A and Subramanian, U (1995) *Taking Stock of National Environmental Strategies*, Environmental Management Series Paper no 010, Environment Department, The World Bank, Washington, DC

Lopez Ornat, A (ed) (1997) *Strategies for Sustainability: Latin America*, IUCN in association with Earthscan, London

OECD (1992) *Good Practices for Country and Environmental Surveys and Strategies*, OECD Development Assistance Committee, Guidelines on Environment and Aid, no 2, OECD, Paris

OECD (1995a) *Planning for Sustainable Development: Country Experiences*, OECD, Paris

OECD DAC (2001a) *Strategies for Sustainable Development: Practical Guidance for Development Cooperation*, DCD/DAC(2001)9, 21 Mar 2001, Development Cooperation Committee, OECD, Paris

REC (1994a) *Summary of the Environmental Action Programme for Central and Eastern Europe*, document endorsed by the Ministerial Conference in Lucerne, Switzerland, 28–30 April 1993, Regional Environmental Center for Central and Eastern Europe, Budapest (March 1994)

REC (1995a) *Report on the Stage of Advancement of the Central and Eastern European Countries in Development and Implementation of the National Environmental Action Programs (NEAPs)*, draft, Regional Environmental Center for Central and Eastern Europe, Budapest (March 1995)

REC (1995b) *Status of National Environmental Action Programs in Central and Eastern Europe*, Regional Environmental Center for Central and Eastern Europe, Budapest

REDDA-NESDA (1993) *Proceedings of the Fourth Regional Workshop on National Strategies on Environment and Sustainable Development*, Network for Environment and Sustainable Development in Africa, Abidjan, Côte d'Ivoire, 15–19 May 1993

UN-DESA (2002b) *Guidance on Approaches to Developing a National Sustainable Development Strategy*, Department of Economic and Social Affairs, UN, New York

Wood, A (ed) (1997) *Strategies for Sustainability: Africa*, IUCN in association with Earthscan, London

World Bank (1995a) *National Environmental Strategies: Learning from Experience*, World Bank, Washington, DC

heavily on the experience of eight developing countries in developing and implementing such strategies, based on reviews by country teams commissioned as inputs to the OECD DAC policy guidance.[3]

Building on the OECD DAC policy guidance and other experiences (including strategies in industrialized countries), UN DESA (2002b) has also produced guidance on approaches to developing NSDSs, in preparation for the World Summit on Sustainable Development.

Why a strategic approach to sustainable development is needed

The need for structural changes

Achieving sustainable development will require deep structural changes and new ways of working in all areas of economic, social and political life. Economic growth patterns that actively favour the poor should be promoted. Fiscal policies that negatively affect the poor or promote environmental damage will need to be reformed. In the longer term, countries will want to ensure that their net wealth, including natural, man-made and human capital, remains constant or increases. Innovation and investment in actions that promote sustainable development should be encouraged. Among other things, this will require the development of a market pricing structure in which prices reflect the full social and environmental costs of production and consumption.

Issues of inequity and inequality of access to assets and resources need to be confronted in a more open and progressive manner. For example, in many countries it will be necessary to reform land tenure policies so as to increase access to resources for disadvantaged and marginalized groups. Equally, it will be important to build and strengthen social capital, and to devise formal 'safety nets' to enable vulnerable economies and groups of citizens to better cope with both external and domestic shocks.

Achieving sustainable development requires deep structural and governance changes on many fronts. A strategic framework can help to organize this ...

3 Bolivia, Burkina Faso, Ghana, Tanzania, Namibia, Pakistan, Nepal, Thailand

Sustainable development therefore has important governance implications. At the national and local level, it requires cross-sectoral and participatory institutions and integrating mechanisms which can engage governments, civil society and the private sector in developing shared visions, planning and decision-making, a topic addressed in subsequent chapters. Governments, corporations and development cooperation agencies will also need to be more open and accountable for their actions. More generally, economic planning and policy-making will have to become more participatory, prudent and transparent, as well as more long term so as to respect the interests of future generations. The difficulty of these challenges does not mean they can be shirked. A strategy can offer a framework to organize and coordinate action to address them.

Difficulties in introducing changes

There are many technical and political difficulties in integrating social, economic and environmental objectives and in adequately addressing the intergenerational dimension of sustainable development. In general there is little documented experience in most countries of developing such mechanisms, and no tried and tested methodologies. Integrating and making trade-offs between sustainable development objectives will therefore require experimental approaches, learning and backing by strong legislative and judicial systems. These institutions are often very weak in developing countries.

... by coordinating plans and activities at different spatial levels ...

As suggested earlier, different challenges need to be addressed at different spatial levels. Some challenges must be addressed at the global level, such as climate change and ozone depletion; some challenges are most effectively addressed at the national level, such as economic, fiscal and trade policy, and legislative change; and some challenges can only be addressed at the local level, such as alterations in patterns of resource use. The impacts of decisions taken at different levels need to be taken into account in an integrated and coherent way. Their consequences must be considered, particularly implications across different sectors and for different interest groups.

There will certainly be short-term conflicts between global, national and local sustainable development priorities, but there will also be complementarities. For example, the conservation of global biodiversity requires the preservation of local habitats, while the need to feed growing populations implies their conversion to agriculture. However, for long-term sustainability, the need to preserve habitats for ecosystem services such as crop pollination, flood controls and water purification ultimately benefits agricultural production. Another example is improved energy efficiency leading to reduced local air pollution, with corresponding health benefits and reductions in greenhouse gas emissions.

... and by uniting the required mechanisms – of participation, communications, information, investment and monitoring ...

Often there are costs involved in establishing or harnessing mechanisms to move towards sustainable development, such as establishing regular fora for participation, taking time and effort to engage in the process, establishing mechanisms for collecting information, investment screening, and monitoring achievement on a range of sustainable development indicators. Costs for such mechanisms may be high in the short term, a particular problem for developing countries and poor groups of residents. But the costs of taking no action are likely to be much greater and assistance must be made available.

All these issues need to be taken into account in steering a track towards sustainable development. They cannot be effectively dealt with on an ad hoc or piecemeal basis. They require a strategic approach.

What being strategic means

The need for such a strategic approach is increasingly being recognized as countries assess why past efforts towards sustainable development have been less effective than desired, and as young nations and states – latterly East Timor – seize the concept of sustainable development as an opportunity to chart the direction of nation-building. More and more strategy documents now contain language which acknowledges the need to build national capability in strategic policy-making and planning (Box 2.12).

Box 2.12 Affirming the need for a strategic approach to sustainable development

Truly sustainable development must systematically provide for linkages among social, economic and environmental concerns, so as to fit them together into coherent strategies … The Federal Plan for Sustainable Development is designed to promote the effectiveness and internal coherence of government policy with respect to sustainable development. (The Federal Plan for Sustainable Development, 2000–2004, Belgium (SSESD 2000))

The policy choices and solutions provided in this document are the guidelines for the years to come. Transitions require vision, courage and perseverance from everyone involved. The question is not whether it is possible, but how it is possible. An on-going re-evaluation will occur as new circumstances present themselves. Accordingly, the approach must not be rigid, but flexible, not dogmatic, but creative, while learning to deal with uncertainties. (4th National Environmental Policy Plan, The Netherlands (VROM 2001))

We must strengthen our working relations to overcome shared problems. This means talking with one another constructively and analytically, and sharing information on what has been done and what is planned… In a country the size of East Timor, we have to ensure that we are all working together to address some of the considerable development hurdles before us … To achieve a stronger partnership, we need to improve communication and coordination between us all. (Emily Pires National Planning and Development Agency, East Timor (in Anderson and Deutsch 2001))

Being strategic is about developing an underlying vision through a consensual, effective and iterative process; and going on to set objectives, identify the means of achieving them, and then monitor that achievement as a guide to the next round of this learning process.

Being strategic requires a comprehensive understanding of the concept of sustainable development and its implications, but not necessarily a comprehensive set of actions – at least at any one time. More important than trying unsuccessfully to do everything at once, is to ensure that incremental steps in policy-making and action are moving towards sustainability – rather than away from it, which is too frequently the case.

A strategic approach to sustainable development therefore implies new ways of thinking and working so as to:

… into an adaptive system for continuous improvement

- move from developing and implementing a fixed plan, which gets increasingly out of date … towards operating an adaptive system that can continuously improve;
- move from a view that it is the state alone that is responsible for development … towards one that sees responsibility with society as a whole;
- move from centralized and controlled decision-making … towards sharing results and opportunities, transparent negotiation, cooperation and concerted action;
- move from a focus on outputs (eg projects and laws) … towards a focus on outcomes (eg impacts) and the quality of participation and management processes;
- move from sectoral planning … towards 'joined-up' or integrated planning;
- move from a focus on costly 'projects' (and a consequent dependence on external assistance) … towards domestically driven and financed development.

Taking a strategic approach will assist countries to participate more effectively in international affairs – providing opportunities to consider both the adverse social and environmental effects of globalization and how nations might benefit from its advantages. It should also enable improved dialogue with other governments, to negotiate new ways of working towards, and supporting, the process of sustainable development at both national and international levels.

An NSDS can help a country's fitness for dealing with globalization and international relations

CHAPTER

3

The Nature of Sustainable Development Strategies and Current Practice[1]

Introduction

This chapter describes the nature and scope of national sustainable development strategies (NSDSs), articulates key principles and common elements, and provides examples of current practice in a range of countries. It offers guidance to understand the linkages that are needed between the array of national level mechanisms that can contribute to an NSDS.

An NSDS requires coordinated mechanisms and participatory processes, with monitoring, learning and continuous improvement

Recent policy guidance on NSDSs developed by the OECD DAC, notes that our perception of a strategy has evolved over the last decade. It was once seen as a single, new, master plan for sustainable development. Today there is increasing consensus that it comprises a set of coordinated mechanisms and processes that, together, offer a participatory system to develop visions, goals and targets for sustainable development, and to coordinate implementation and review. It is also accepted that a strategy cannot be a one-off initiative but needs to be a continuing participatory process, with monitoring, learning and continuous improvement. These and other characteristics are discussed in the key principles section on page 33. They provide a useful frame of reference for a country to structure its own approach according to its individual needs, priorities, existing mechanisms and processes, and available resources.

Existing strategic planning approaches include elements of good practice

'Learning from Current Practice' on page 35 introduces the existing integrated frameworks that can be built upon, including domestic ones such as national development planning and national budgetary exercises as well as externally stimulated or driven frameworks such as national environmental action plans (NEAPs), national conservation strategies (NCSs) and poverty reduction strategies (PRSs). International organizations and development cooperation agencies have invested heavily in shaping and driving a number of these national level strategic planning frameworks. Elements of good practice can be found in such existing approaches, but usually they have not been coordinated appropriately as an integrated NSDS, and national ownership may have been lacking.

---

1 This chapter has benefited from review comments and additional material provided by Professor Michael Carley, Herriott Watt University, Edinburgh; Carol James, Trinidad; and Maheen Zehra, IUCN-Pakistan.

Research, analysis and international sharing of experience on the systems, processes and practices of past and current strategic planning frameworks has contributed to building consensus on a range of key principles (Box 3.1) and common elements (Box 3.2), as well as other lessons and guidance, for the development and implementation of NSDSs. Together, these describe desirable characteristics that are sufficiently flexible to allow for the incorporation of local perspectives. Although not intended as a prescription, it is hoped that these principles and elements, cross-referenced throughout this Resource Book, will provide a useful template for fashioning individual NSDSs.

Lessons and guidance are illustrated by concrete examples of approaches and practice from a range of countries, both North and South – from national through sub-national to village and micro-levels – and opportunities for convergence and linkages between these various levels are highlighted. Comparisons are made between the aims of, and approaches to, strategic planning in both developed and developing countries.

Ten years after the Earth Summit, there are still few examples of truly home-grown, successful sustainable development strategies. This underscores the need for the guidance and lessons for practitioners at all levels provided by this Resource Book.

What are sustainable development strategies?

To meet the challenges of sustainable development, discussed in Chapter 2, strategic policy and planning mechanisms need to become more participatory, integrated and flexible. They also need to be recognized as learning processes, in which information about progress towards sustainability, or lack of progress, is used constructively to revise the mechanism and the means of realizing objectives. Rigid, standardized or blueprint approaches are best avoided, usually being at best irrelevant and, at worst, counter-productive. So also is the production of an 'encyclopedia' or a long 'wish list' of unrealistic possible actions, which have little chance of being implemented. Instead, there is a pressing need to structure a strategic approach to national sustainable development according to each individual country's own needs, priorities and resources. In light of this, the DAC policy guidance on strategies for sustainable development (OECD DAC 2001a) defines a strategy as comprising:

Blueprint approaches are best avoided

> *A coordinated set of participatory and continuously improving processes of analysis, debate, capacity-strengthening, planning and investment, which integrates the economic, social and environmental objectives of society, seeking trade-offs where this is not possible.[2]*

Figure 3.1 illustrates the logic behind the NSDS approach.

Each country's strategy should be structured to meet its own needs, priorities and resources …

The learning generated by the country dialogues, carried out as part of the development of the OECD DAC policy guidance, confirmed that putting a sustainable development strategy into operation would, in practice, most likely consist of building on, and improving, existing strategic planning frameworks and their coordination. Improvements are needed in:

- mutual consistency;
- actual implementation;
- the political attention given to strategic planning frameworks;
- the leadership of these frameworks;
- understanding of, and commitment to, them.

This is preferable to trying to establish a new, time-bound approach, which is not recommended.

---

2 This definition also reflects the indicator for sustainable development strategies agreed in IMF/OECD/UN/World Bank (2000) which focuses on the importance of effective (strategic planning) processes.

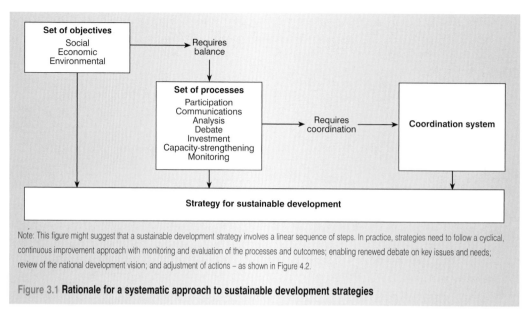

Note: This figure might suggest that a sustainable development strategy involves a linear sequence of steps. In practice, strategies need to follow a cyclical, continuous improvement approach with monitoring and evaluation of the processes and outcomes; enabling renewed debate on key issues and needs; review of the national development vision; and adjustment of actions – as shown in Figure 4.2.

Figure 3.1 **Rationale for a systematic approach to sustainable development strategies**

The country dialogues also identified a number of specific mechanisms and processes that could strengthen the effectiveness of countries' development strategies. These are outlined in Figure 3.2 and discussed in Chapter 4. The manner in which these existing and new mechanisms and processes are implemented needs to be consistent with a set of basic strategic principles, discussed below. Where these principles are successfully applied, the result will be progress towards a NSDS, although the planning framework might be given another label. National development plans, poverty reduction strategies, national conservation strategies and other approaches all provide a basis on which to build in moving towards the goal of an effective NSDS (OECD DAC 2000d; UN DESA 2000b).

... and should build on existing frameworks

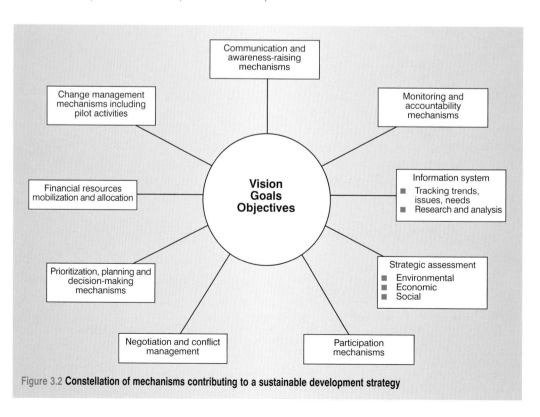

Figure 3.2 **Constellation of mechanisms contributing to a sustainable development strategy**

Key principles for developing sustainable development strategies

Differing national circumstances and priorities among countries result in varied approaches to strategic planning. These are reviewed on page 35. But consultations with developing countries during the OECD DAC dialogues, and wider international experience emerging from the UN regional consultative workshops on sustainable development and experience of comprehensive development frameworks and poverty reduction strategies, have shown that there are common features of good practice. These are presented as a set of principles which underpin the development of effective strategies in many developing countries (Box 3.1). These principles have been endorsed by the DAC in its policy guidance on strategies for sustainable development (OECD DAC 2001a). In November 2001, a UN international forum on national strategies for sustainable development (held in preparation for the 2002 World Summit on Sustainable Development) confirmed almost identical principles – which the Forum termed 'elements' (Box 3.2) – these were defined as being applicable to both developed and developing countries alike (UNDESA 2002b).

Common principles or elements underpin effective strategies

Many of these principles represent good, common-sense development practice and many are already being implemented at the project level. But putting these principles into practice in strategic planning and policy processes is more of a challenge. A cautionary note is indicated by the fact that many existing and past strategic planning processes, such as NEAPs and NCSs, have not had a lasting impact in terms of moving countries towards sustainable development. This is because they were not focused on the full set of key principles.

They are applicable in both developed and developing countries

Traditional development often tends to generate severe competition over resource allocation and use, and this leads invariably to conflict among stakeholders. Strategy development needs to address this issue for genuine partnership and participation. Thus, resolving conflicts, averting potential ones, facilitating and building capacity for negotiation, bargaining and effective inclusion must be central elements of the strategy process.

Many past strategies were not focused on the full set of NSDS principles

---

Box 3.1 Key principles for sustainable development strategies

These are principles towards which strategies should aspire. They are all important and no order of priority is implied. They do not represent a checklist of criteria to be met but encompass a set of desirable processes and outcomes which also allow for local differences.

1   **People-centred.** An effective strategy requires a people-centred approach, ensuring long-term beneficial impacts on disadvantaged and marginalized groups, such as the poor.

2   **Consensus on long-term vision.** Strategic planning frameworks are more likely to be successful when they have a long-term vision with a clear timeframe upon which stakeholders agree. At the same time, they need to include ways of dealing with short- and medium-term necessities and change. The vision needs to have the commitment of all political parties so that an incoming government will not view a particular strategy as representing only the views or policies of its predecessor.

3   **Comprehensive and integrated.** Strategies should seek to integrate, where possible, economic, social and environmental objectives. But where integration cannot be achieved, trade-offs need to be negotiated. The entitlements and possible needs of future generations must be factored into this process.

4   **Targeted with clear budgetary priorities.** The strategy needs to be fully integrated into the budget mechanism to ensure that plans have the financial resources to achieve their objectives, and do not only represent 'wish lists'. Conversely, the formulation of budgets must be informed by a clear identification of priorities. Capacity constraints and time limitations will have an impact on the extent to which the intended outcomes are achieved. Targets need to be challenging – but realistic in relation to these constraints.

5   **Based on comprehensive and reliable analysis.** Priorities need to be based on a comprehensive analysis of the present situation and of forecasted trends and risks, examining links between local, national and global challenges. The external pressures on a country – those resulting from globalization, for example, or the

impacts of climate change – need to be included in this analysis. Such analysis depends on credible and reliable information on changing environmental, social and economic conditions, pressures and responses, and their correlations with strategy objectives and indicators. Local capacities for analysis and existing information should be fully used, and different perceptions among stakeholders should be reflected.

6   **Incorporate monitoring, learning and improvement.** Monitoring and evaluation need to be based on clear indicators and built into strategies to steer processes, track progress, distil and capture lessons, and signal when a change of direction is necessary.

7   **Country-led and nationally-owned.** Past strategies have often resulted from external pressure and development agency requirements. It is essential that countries take the lead and initiative in developing their own strategies if they are to be enduring.

8   **High-level government commitment and influential lead institutions.** Such commitment – on a long-term basis – is essential if policy and institutional changes are to occur, financial resources are to be committed and for there to be clear responsibility for implementation.

9   **Building on existing mechanism and strategies.** A strategy for sustainable development should not be thought of as a new planning mechanism but instead build on what already exists in the country, thus enabling convergence, complementarity and coherence between different planning frameworks and policies. This requires good management to ensure coordination of mechanisms and processes, and to identify and resolve potential conflicts. The latter may require an independent and neutral third party to act as a facilitator. The roles, responsibilities and relationships between the different key participants in strategy processes must be clarified early on.

10 **Effective participation.** Broad participation helps to open up debate to new ideas and sources of information; expose issues that need to be addressed; enable problems, needs and preferences to be expressed; identify the capabilities required to address them; and develop a consensus on the need for action that leads to better implementation. Central government must be involved (providing leadership, shaping incentive structures and allocating financial resources) but multi-stakeholder processes are also required involving decentralized authorities, the private sector and civil society, as well as marginalized groups. This requires good communication and information mechanisms with a premium on transparency and accountability.

11 **Link national and local levels.** Strategies should be two-way iterative processes within and between national and decentralized levels. The main strategic principles and directions should be set at the central level (here, economic, fiscal and trade policy, legislative changes, international affairs and external relations, etc, are key responsibilities). But detailed planning, implementation and monitoring would be undertaken at a decentralized level, with appropriate transfer of resources and authority.

12 **Develop and build on existing capacity.** At the outset of a strategy process, it is important to assess the political, institutional, human, scientific and financial capacity of potential state, market and civil society participants. Where needed, provision should be made to develop the necessary capacity as part of the strategy process. A strategy should optimize local skills and capacity both within and outside government.

Source: OECD DAC (2001a)

Notes:

Principle 1:

(a) Particular attention must be paid to youth to ensure nurturing of long-term attitudinal changes in society – educational reform is central to this process.

(b) While many past strategies have been about development, they have often had mixed effects on different groups.

Principle 8:

(a) It is crucial that the lead institutions are truly representative and reflect the many publics in the country, to ensure national buy-in. There is a tendency to assume that NGOs, CBOs and market-oriented interest groups from the private sector and industry represent civil society. More care is needed to ensure the inclusion also of organizations/leaders drawn from academic, religious, political, cultural and grass-roots levels.

To the above list of principles endorsed by the OECD DAC, can be added:

Principle 13: Incorporate effective conflict and negotiation management systems.

Traditional development often tends to generate severe competition over resource allocation and use, and this leads invariably to conflict among stakeholders. Strategy development needs to address this issue for genuine partnership and participation. Thus, resolving conflicts, averting potential ones, facilitating and building capacity for negotiation, bargaining and effective inclusion must be central elements of the strategy process.

Problems included:

- many were not, and did not aim to be, *integrated* into a country's mainstream strategic planning system;
- very many were 'wish-lists', lacking clear objectives and achievable targets; or
- there was often a very narrow base of *participation* which did not represent a partnership of key stakeholders; or
- they were not supportive of *existing processes, strategies and capacities* but attempted to start something new without building on existing strengths and capabilities;
- a large number were not *country-led* but were induced and/or imposed by external agencies;
- finally, in developing countries, external agencies pushed their own strategy initiatives and there was often competition between these 'brands'.

This record of poor quality strategic planning mechanisms has given the concept of 'strategies' a bad name. Despite this, these examples also provide us with useful 'lessons of experience' on which to build more robust approaches, discussed in the next section.

Learning from current practice: existing strategy frameworks

In most countries, there is a range of past and current strategic planning approaches at both national and decentralized levels. In developing countries, many of these have been externally conceived, motivated and promoted by multilateral development banks, development cooperation agencies, UN organizations, international non-governmental organizations (NGOs) and other external organizations – often as planning mechanisms to implement international agreements (see Box 2.4) or as conditions for securing financial assistance. Few of these external organizations have adopted or built on the systems, mechanisms and practices that were operating in the country for some time, such as national development plans, local plans and traditional participation mechanisms.

In developing countries, many strategic planning approaches have been externally conceived, motivated and promoted ...

Research and analysis, the DAC dialogues and international experience captured through numerous workshops show that a number of principles and elements appear to be common to the more successful strategies (Boxes 3.1 and 3.2). This is not so surprising since many have followed a basic framework developed in the 1980s for NCSs.

The common approach has then been built upon for NEAPs, tropical forestry action plans and similar initiatives as experience has grown (see the section on building on national level strategies, page 38). Furthermore, these approaches have been promoted in developing countries as time-bound projects, rather than ongoing policy mechanisms, mainly by donors who have provided financial support and technical assistance, partly as a framework for planning aid support. In many cases, expatriate technical experts and advisers worked on strategies in several different countries and then translocated their experience and approaches. In any case, the World Bank was at the centre of NEAP guidance and learning, as was IUCN in the case of NCSs (although there were some attempts at South–South exchange, eg the Bank supported an African network on NEAPs, and IUCN supported regional NCS reviews and workshops).

... often as time-bound projects, rather than ongoing policy mechanisms

The outputs of many of these initiatives remain paper plans which, at best, have been only partly implemented. This is due in large measure to the limited emphasis placed by their sponsors on generating national ownership and establishing participatory processes for their elaboration. However, valuable lessons have been drawn from these failures in developing the NSDS principles in Box 3.1 and elements in Box 3.2. Analysis of past and existing approaches (see Chapter 5) can inform effective strategy decision-making (Chapter 8).

The main outputs have often been only partly implemented plans, but they provide valuable lessons

---

Box 3.2 **Elements of a national sustainable development strategy**

Recent UN guidance on preparing a national sustainable development strategy (drafted by a consultant) features a range of recommended elements of an NSDS. These were finalized by a UN-organized international forum on NSDSs held in Ghana in November 2002 (UN DESA 2002a) and presented formally in January 2002 to PrepCom2 for the World Summit on Sustainable Development. The strategy elements are based mainly on the OECD DAC principles in Box 3.1, drawing also from the experience of UNDP's Capacity 21 programme, the Earth Council's work with national councils for sustainable development and discussions at the forum:

a) *Integration of economic, social and environmental objectives, and balance across sectors, territories and generations*

- linking local, national, regional and global priorities and actions;
- linking the short term to the medium and long term;
- linking the national, regional and global levels;
- linking different sectors;
- coherence between budgets and strategy priorities.

b) *Broad participation and effective partnerships*

- institutionalized channels for communication;
- access to information for all stakeholders and effective networking;
- transparency and accountability;
- trust and mutual respect;
- partnerships among government, civil society, private sector and external institutions.

c) *Country ownership and commitment*

- strong political and stakeholder commitment;
- sound leadership and good governance;
- shared strategic and pragmatic vision;
- strong institution or group of institutions spearheading the process;
- continuity of the national sustainable development strategy process.

d) *Developing capacity and enabling environment*

- building on existing knowledge and expertise;
- building on existing mechanisms and strategies.

e) *Focus on outcomes and means of implementation*

- the means to assess and agree priority issues in place;
- coherence between budget, capacity and strategy priorities;
- realistic, flexible targets;
- linked to private sector investment;
- anchored in sound technical and economic analysis;
- integrated mechanisms for assessment, follow up, evaluation and feedback.

Source: UN DESA (2002b)

In developed countries, approaches have been fashioned by domestic agendas

The situation in developed countries has been substantively different. Approaches have been fashioned by domestic agendas, following national government styles and cultures – and sometimes those of business and the networks of civil society – rather than the dictates of external agencies (Dalal-Clayton 1996). Although this means they have been more realistic in terms of existing policy processes, many have been prepared as one-shot processes with little in the way of monitoring and no follow-up revision.

In light of this experience, some basic comparisons can be made between experience in developed and developing countries (see Table 3.1).

In approaching the challenge of developing national strategies for sustainable development, it is apparent that the countries of the North and those of the South have much to learn from each other's experience. For example, in many developed countries, the response to Agenda 21 has been to develop plans

Table 3.1 Basic comparisons between developed and developing country strategy processes

Developed Countries	Developing Countries
Approach	**Approach**
Internally generated	External impetus (IUCN, World Bank, etc)
Internally funded	Donor-funded
Indigenous expertise	Expatriate expertise frequently involved
Political action	Bureaucratic/technocratic action
Brokerage approach	Project approach
Aims	**Aims**
Changing production/consumption patterns	Increase production/consumption
Response to 'brown' issues (pollution)	Response to 'green' issues/ rural development
Environment focus	Development focus
Means	**Means**
Institutional re-orientation/integration	Creation of new institutions
Production of guidelines and local targets	Development of project 'shopping lists'
Cost-saving approaches	Aid-generating approaches
Links to Local Agenda 21 initiatives	Few local links
Awareness-raising	Awareness-raising

Source: Dalal-Clayton (1996)

and strategies focusing narrowly on environmental concerns. Such 'green' plans could take a step towards becoming genuine sustainable development strategies if they were to adopt the approaches being promoted in the South and address social and economic issues as well as the environment in an integrated manner. In developing such strategies, Northern countries also need to review those policies and practices which lead to over-exploitation of natural resources in developing countries (their 'environmental footprint').[3]

Southern countries, on the other hand, would benefit from better analysis, the development of market-based instruments, efforts at cost-savings, and better use of existing government structures, with Northern countries showing ways forward here. In both North and South, most approaches need to improve the basis of their participation, and need to be periodically revised to take into account feedback and lessons from review following implementation. In this way, they would become genuine, cyclical, 'learning by doing' processes.

A notable example of a country that has taken this constructive approach to sustainable development is The Netherlands, where the National Environmental Policy Plan (NEPP) is revised every four years through a dialogue between the government, industry and the public. NEPP (1989), NEPP2 (1993) and NEPP3 (VROM 1997) set out the broad policy, the latter for the period 1999–2002, taking 2010 as a horizon year. NEPP4 was completed in mid-2001 extending the horizon to 2030.

Countries of the North and South have much to learn from each other's experiences

Strategies in all countries need to improve participation and become learning processes

---

3 In recent years, widespread concern about links between trade and environment/sustainable development have fanned large-scale and often violent protests at major global meetings (notably, WTO and the World Economic Forum, but also a few other economic fora). Analysis of the negative impacts of trade and foreign direct investment on sustainable development is outside the scope of this resource book.

The Netherlands illustrates a constructive approach

Through the rolling NEPP process over the last decade, The Netherlands has succeeded in reducing its environmental burden (particularly reducing pollution levels) while enjoying improved living standards and economic growth (a process the NEPP calls 'decoupling', which means achieving economic growth while reducing material use and pollution). A particular achievement of the NEPP process is that it has involved representatives of government at all levels, business and voluntary organizations, including environmental activists, in dialogue, visioning, planning and setting objectives and targets for the country's short-, medium- and long-term future.

In early 2001, the Dutch Cabinet established an interdepartmental body, guided by a ministerial group led by the Prime Minister, to develop a National Strategy for Sustainable Development. This group decided that the government would first publish an overview of sustainable development policies on five subjects (population, climate, water, biodiversity and developing an economy based on know-how), indicating which dilemmas would influence further policy debate over the next decade. Furthermore, all policy areas should be embedded within the notion of sustainable development, and experiments will be started to apply the integration of economic, socio-cultural and environmental aspects of major government investments.

Each ministry has been requested to give an overview of its contribution to sustainable development in its annual budget to be discussed in Parliament. Selected indicators will be used to show whether The Netherlands is moving towards sustainable development, with targets set for the next 5–10 years. The Cabinet decided to start the process of reviewing the strategy in public, while making an inventory of the many initiatives of municipalities, provinces, business and citizens which was to be submitted to Parliament in spring 2002. The process to prepare a revised strategy has started with the aim that the next government (following elections in May 2002) would continue the process.

Building on national level strategies

NATIONAL DEVELOPMENT PLANS

Many developing countries have a strong tradition of preparing periodic national development plans, often covering a five-year span and setting out grand objectives (see the examples of India – which is typical of many Commonwealth countries – and China in Box 3.3). Usually, line ministries prepare sector chapters for national plans following guidance issued by a national planning commission or equivalent coordinating body. This body normally undertakes the tasks of screening against financial and political concerns, usually a very influential factor, and environmental and social concerns. It is often the case that finance ministries are in charge of development planning, with the all-too-frequent implication that the quality of environmental and social screening, and accountability for it, are weak. At best, the general approach is to screen out potential bad impacts, rather than to screen for the most positive environmental and social outcomes. The development planning body also usually integrates the sector plans. Sometimes, the task of integration is supported by inputs from the decentralized levels (Box 3.21 on Ghana).

The quality of environmental and social screening is often weak in national development plans

The national plans derived from this process tend to set out broad goals and include projects and activities to be funded from the annual recurrent and development budgets. Economic, or only occasionally social, imperatives have been predominant, with minimal inclusion of environmental concerns. These plans tend to be linked into the annual budget or to the medium term expenditure framework (MTEF) – a three-year rolling budget mechanism. Often, the plans have been linked weakly to institutional or procedural changes which could foster strategic, sustainable development.

There has been little civil society or private sector involvement in the past

In the past, there has been little civil society or private sector involvement in developing or monitoring such national plans. But there is increasing evidence of stakeholder participation in these mechanisms in a number of countries, for example, in Thailand (Box 3.4). There is also greater use of environmental screening mechanisms (although usually to screen out certain bad impacts, rather than to optimize

Box 3.3 **Five-year planning in India and China**

India

Planning in India derives its objectives from Directive Principles of State Policy enshrined in the Constitution. The Planning Commission was set up in 1950 to prepare the blueprint of development, taking an overall view of the needs and resources of the country. To date there have been nine five-year plans: beginning in the period 1951–1956 with the latest, ninth plan covering the years 1997–2002. In the past, economic planning envisaged a growing public sector with massive investments in the basic and heavy industries. Now the emphasis on the public sector is pronounced and current thinking on national planning is that, in general, it should increasingly be of an indicative, rather than prescriptive, nature.

The objectives of the Ninth Five-Year Plan evolved from the Common Minimum Programme of the government and the Chief Minister's Conference on basic minimum services. They include:

- priority to agriculture and rural development with a view to generating productive employment and eradication of poverty;
- accelerating the growth rate of the economy with stable prices;
- ensuring food and nutritional security for the vulnerable section of society;
- providing the basic minimum services of safe drinking water, primary health care facilities, universal primary education, shelter and connectivity to all in a time-bound population;
- containing the growth rate of the population;
- ensuring environmental sustainability of the development process through participation of people;
- empowerment of women and socially disadvantaged groups (eg minorities);
- promoting and developing Panchayati Raj (the lowest unit of local self-government – at district, block and village level), cooperatives, etc;
- strengthening efforts to build self-reliance.

Source: www.travel-india.com/stat/economics/five_year_plans

China

In China, the five-year planning mechanism is a long-term programme at the heart of the country's economic development. The aim of this mechanism is to provide a detailed plan for major construction projects, distribution of productive forces, and proportional development of the national economy, as well as to set an orientation for the future development of the country. Since the founding of the People's Republic of China in 1949, nine five-year plans have been developed. The first covered 1953–1957 with the latest, ninth plan, covering the years 1996–2000.

The major objectives of the Ninth Five-Year Plan are:

- complete the second phase of the strategic plan for the modernization drive; and quadruple the per capita gross national product of 1980 under the condition that the population in 2000 will have increased by 300 million over that in 1980;
- raise living standards to that of a fairly comfortable life with poverty practically eradicated and expedite the formulation of a modern enterprise system and establish a socialist market economy.

The major tasks set are to:

- ensure sustained and stable growth in agriculture and the rural economy as a whole;
- actively promote readjustment in industrial structure;
- promote the coordinated development of regional economies;
- strive to maintain macro-economic stability;
- continuously raise the people's living standards in both urban and rural areas.

Source: www.afrchn.com

environmental potential), and progress in mainstreaming environmental concerns in national development plans, as in Morocco (Box 3.5).

Box 3.4 Civil society involvement in recent national plans in Thailand – and their alternative agenda

Since 1961, Thailand has implemented successive National Economic and Social Development Plans. The country is currently operating under the Eighth Plan (1997–2001) and the Ninth Plan is under development with civil society involvement. Hundreds of NGOs and community-based organizations (CBOs) and thousands of people from all walks of life were invited by the National Economic and Social Development Board (NESDB) to engage in formulating the eighth National Economic and Social Development Plan by voicing their concerns and providing inputs. The process was very successful and many NGOs began to feel that they were gaining for the first time some ownership of the Plan.

However, many issues they raised were subsequently left out in the synthesis process. The plan mentioned sustainable development, but in an unfocused way, along with a wide array of other ideologies. As a result, some NGOs, notably the national NGO network, and various people's organizations, subsequently refused to participate in the development of the Ninth Plan and instead launched their own alternative National Agenda for the Free Thais. This consisted of issues covering 16 key areas (eg politics, agriculture, marine resources and fisheries, AIDS and education). It did not specifically refer to sustainable development but the issues covered, taken together, effectively addressed the concept.

At the same time, another NGO network and many CBOs continued to work with the NESDB on drafting the Ninth Plan, trying to correct the earlier problems by emphasizing the need for parallel local/community plans as a complement to the national plan. In this context, they raised issues such as the need for decentralization and community rights.

Source: Poapongsakorn et al (2001).

Box 3.5 Harmonizing national development plans in Morocco

In Morocco, attempts have been made to integrate environmental concerns and priorities into mainstream economic and social development plans, and to provide synergy between sectors.

Supported by UNDP's Capacity 21 programme, multi-stakeholder workshops on such integration have been organized around the country. Two inter-sectoral workshops have also been organized: one on legislation, regulations and finance; the other on information, education and communication. Participants included key stakeholders from development sectors such as industry, population, energy, soil, agriculture, water, health, land management, urbanization and habitat – each providing information about their sector and lobbying for it to be considered.

The goal was that this process would produce a set of integrated action plans and raise awareness of the potential for synergies towards sustainable development. The hope was to avoid a sense of confrontation and stalemate between environmental and economic priorities.

Through an integration workshop, key recommendations from each of the sectoral workshops were brought together to produce a cohesive, integrated Environmental Action Plan. In turn, this plan was then linked with Morocco's three other national development plans: the Economic and Social Development Plan; the Plan to Combat Desertification; and the Land Management Plan.

Each Plan was prepared while taking the other plans into account. There are no redundancies or repetitions, but there is synergy. The whole point is to protect the environment and natural resources while fighting poverty, and each plan makes its contribution to this common goal.

Source: www.undp.org/capacity21

Box 3.6 The Bangladesh Flood Action Plan

The Bangladesh Flood Action Plan (FAP) was developed with international support, as a response to periodic and devastating floods. But those institutions and individuals driving the FAP viewed water management rather narrowly without taking account of the complex nature of the issues and interrelationships. Consequently inadequate attention was paid to environmental issues and to the necessary participation of floodplain communities in the FAP process. Critics pointed to the need for strategic planning to provide for integrated water resource management, and the FAP was subsequently replaced by a national water plan developed in a more participatory manner.

Source: Hughes et al (1994)

Most national development plans have now shifted from a philosophy of central planning to one of 'creating enabling conditions', to accommodate a degree of voluntary and civil society action, which contributes to partnership and the implementation of strategy. This approach, and some of the planning infrastructure set up for it, is conducive to NSDSs. Applying the principles and elements of NSDSs (Boxes 3.1 and 3.2), and bringing together the systems in Figure 3.2, could result in national development plans offering much that is required for NSDSs. Attention would especially have to be paid to developing shared, multi-stakeholder visions of development goals, and to broader criteria for making trade-offs.

Plans are now shifting to creating enabling conditions and building partnerships

---

Box 3.7 National human development reports

National human development reports (HDRs) are powerful tools for national policy analysis. They generally compare data from regions, provinces or localities on indicators such as education, life expectancy, gender disparities and income, pointing to achievements and disparities.

More than 350 national, sub-national or regional HDRs have been issued in 130 countries since 1992. The reports have introduced the human development concept into national policy dialogues through country-led processes of consultation, data collection and report writing. Preparation of the reports brings experts from different fields together, often helping to build a national consensus on key issues.

Since the first national HDRs were published, in Bangladesh and Cameroon, the concept has spread rapidly. The reports are prepared by national teams assembled by UNDP's country offices, led by an independent national coordinator – usually an independent think tank, an NGO, an academic institution, or a semi-public or governmental institution.

Most national HDRs share the following key elements:

- *Advocating human development* and highlighting a more people-centred approach to policy-making. They fill an important niche within the policy dialogue among development partners, complementing other government-led planning as well as civil society initiatives and donor-supported studies and reports.
- *Highlighting critical concerns:* In most countries the first national HDR provides a general profile of the state of human development; subsequent reports address specific themes. Bangladesh, Benin, Cambodia, Cameroon, Madagascar, Namibia, Nigeria, Sierra Leone and the Indian state of Madhya Pradesh, among others, have all prepared reports focusing on poverty. Many of the reports in Eastern Europe and CIS have focused on the transition from centrally planned to free market economics, and are now beginning to focus on issues related to governance and human rights. The 1997 report from Namibia focused on HIV/AIDS and poverty. The Philippines and Bangladesh have prepared reports focusing on women and development, while Armenia, Lithuania and Poland, among others, have focused on human settlements.
- *Providing a tool for development planning:* By providing comprehensive human development indicators and indices (see Box 5.12), the national HD reports help to monitor progress and setbacks in human development and poverty. One of the most exciting features of many of the national HDRs is the disaggregation of human development indices (human development index, gender-related development index, gender empowerment measure, and human poverty index) by region or groups within the country. Measuring human development by region, province, gender, urban/rural populations or ethnic groups has provided a useful planning tool for governments to target development programmes and public expenditure to areas where human deprivation is the most critical. This approach helps governments to focus on *equity* when planning for development and, in some cases, when conducting public expenditure reviews. This is the case in, for example, Brazil, Bolivia, Turkey, Namibia and Egypt. Through the use and analysis of human development indicators and indices, disaggregated by region or group, the reports can be used as an essential input for developing human development strategies and action plans.
- *Articulating people's perceptions and priorities:* Some HDRs provide interesting insights into people's perceptions of human development and their concerns and priorities, and have incorporated them into the policy analysis. A good example is the 1996 Bangladesh report which gives equal weight to two different approaches to assess human development and poverty: an analytical study by academics, using data and survey results, and a comprehensive participatory appraisal by poor people themselves.

Source: www.undp.org

SECTOR AND CROSS-SECTORAL PLANS AND STRATEGIES

Associated with these national development planning instruments, line ministries frequently prepare sector-wide plans and investment strategies in policy areas such as transport, agriculture, health and education. However, no matter how good a sector plan appears on paper, it can suffer from the weak integration, and the lack of sustainability criteria, inherent in the overall national planning process. There is a great challenge, however, in defining sustainability criteria and timeframes for a national plan that suit the different conditions facing individual sectors. The NSDS approach represents an organized mechanism for addressing these issues.

A good example of a progressive approach to building on sectoral planning is provided by Jamaica. Here, the Planning Institute of Jamaica has developed strong capacity for systematic data collection and analysis, presenting comprehensive reports which facilitate the integration of sectoral plans into an holistic national planning framework (see www.pioj.gov.jm).

Many countries also prepare cross-sectoral or issues-based strategies such as those for reducing HIV/AIDS, for food security or for improving rights for women. Examples of cross-sectoral strategies for environment include coastal zone management plans, and plans for freshwater management (Box 3.6).

Since the launch by UNDP of the annual Human Development Report in 1990, many countries have prepared national human development reports. These are cross-sectoral and focus on analysis of key national or sub-national issues and priorities. The reporting processes vary from country to country but most share common key elements, which can be built on in developing an NSDS (Box 3.7).

PLANS AND STRATEGIES RELATED TO CONVENTIONS

Many environmental strategies have been developed as a response to the Rio Conventions (Box 2.4). Responsibility for the preparation of these plans has usually been given to national environment ministries, which carries the risk of isolating the strategy process from key aspects of policy controlled by the ministries for finance, economic development and social affairs.

Convention on Biological Diversity   National biodiversity strategies and action plans (NBSAPs) have been prepared by many countries. Usually, these plans include a systematic analysis of issues and problems, as well as the establishment of agreements among public and private organizations on how to implement various provisions of the Convention on Biological Diversity (1992). They are then the basis of detailed programmes setting out how individual countries propose to manage their biological resources. A number of guidelines have been prepared to assist countries in preparing such plans (eg Hagen undated; Fernández 1998; Prescott et al 2000).

The Global Environment Facility (GEF) has provided grant support to some countries for developing NBSAPs and, according to UNDP's Biodiversity Planning Support Programme (www.undp.org/bpsp), by March 2001, 80 of these countries had completed plan documents.

The approach being taken in India is briefly described in Box 3.8. Such strategies and plans may suffer from a lack of integration, especially with other national institutions and planning mechanisms. A notable exception is Jamaica where the NBSAP has been used to integrate biodiversity concerns into other planning mechanisms (see www.nrca.org; and www.nepa.gov.jm).

They may also tend to favour global biodiversity objectives (protecting species that are rare and threatened at global level) over local biodiversity objectives (people-centred goals for conserving biodiversity for cultural reasons, or for use in times of hardship, etc). This is partly because the institutions that have been developed to address biodiversity issues have been heavily influenced by global institutions concerned with biodiversity. Currently there are few institutions capable of integrating local biodiversity and livelihood concerns, and these tend to be weak in terms of their influence on policy and local action.

Box 3.8 **National Biodiversity Strategy and Action Plan, India**

In 1999, India's Ministry of Environment and Forests (MoEF) prepared a national policy and macro-level action strategy on biodiversity through a consultative process. It identified the need to prepare more detailed action plans building on this framework document. It was recognized that the preparation of such a detailed micro-level plan for the conservation of the country's biodiversity was part of India's obligations under the Convention on Biological Diversity, and funds were accessed from the GEF to prepare a national biodiversity strategy and action plan (NBSAP).

The NBSAP is being managed by a national project directorate in the MoEF, and executed by a technical and policy core group (TPCG) headed by Kalpavriksh, an environmental NGO, and comprising experts from various fields and parts of India. The administration of the project is coordinated by the Biotech Consortium India Ltd.

The NBSAP process will result in the formulation of about:

- 20 local-level action plans;
- 30 state-level plans;
- 10 inter-state ecoregional plans;
- 14 national thematic plans.

All of these plans will then be built into an overview national plan, but will also remain independent action plans, capable of being implemented at the level for which they are prepared.

The guidelines to the executing agencies preparing these plans indicate that each Strategy and Action Plan (SAP) should consist of the following:

- statement of the issue or problem;
- identification of ongoing initiatives regarding the issue, key actors involved and major gaps in coverage;
- delineation of steps needed to plug gaps and enhance the effectiveness of ongoing initiatives;
- list of measures and strategies needed to implement these steps;
- identification of key elements needed for implementation: institutional structures, funds, expertise/human resources, policy/legal measures, monitoring, etc;
- timeframe for implementation.

The NBSAP is being developed in a highly *participatory* way, involving a large number of village-level organizations and movements, NGOs, academicians and scientists, government officers from various line agencies, the private sector, the armed forces, politicians and others who have a stake in biodiversity. This approach aims to encourage wide ownership of the process and the product (the NBSAP) so as to ensure implementation of its recommendations.

The NBSAP sets out to assess and take stock of *biodiversity-related information* at various levels, including distribution of endemic and endangered species, site-specific threats and pressures, social/political/economic issues, ethical concerns and ongoing conservation initiatives by various sections of society. All agencies are required to keep in mind two bottom lines: ensuring the ecological security of the country and the area they have responsibility for, and ensuring the livelihood security of communities most dependent on biological resources.

The NBSAP *builds on existing expertise and information* and involves no new field research. The process emphasizes gender sensitive decentralized planning and the use of inter-disciplinary working groups involving all sectors concerned with biodiversity conservation. The detailed action plans (at sub-state, state, regional and national thematic levels) will be consolidated to produce the national-level action plan.

Source: www.sdnp.delhi.nic.in/nbsap/index-main.html

NBSAPs have tended to deal inadequately with the reality that people have always used biodiversity to sustain themselves. While these plans flag the issue of unsustainable patterns of biodiversity use, they seldom include analyses of patterns of use (by communities, countries, multinational companies, etc), or assess practical applications of indigenous know-how on sustainable resource use, which could provide lessons to shape mechanisms for reversing such trends. Recommendations concerning unsustainable use of biodiversity tend to be too prescriptive and focus on projects.

They seldom analyse patterns of biodiversity use or assess indigenous people's know-how

Funding constraints and time limitations have often hampered progress, and many plans have failed to arouse much political interest and remain on the shelf. However, in some countries, the plans have led to further action; for example, in Guyana, where the NBSAP evolved from a participatory formulation process and stimulated ongoing actions two years after it was completed (www.sdnp.org/gy).

Convention to Combat Desertification   In response to the Convention to Combat Desertification (CCD) (1994), many dryland countries have prepared National Action Programmes (NAPs). In addition, some regional and Sub-Regional Action Programmes (RAPs and SRAPS) have also been developed. During 1985–1988 (sponsored by CILS, the Permanent Committee for Drought Control in the Sahel), some countries in the Sahel region had already prepared National Plans of Action to Combat Desertification (NPACD) prior to the adoption of the Convention. They adopted these plans into the NAP process and identified concrete field-level activities. As stated in articles 9 and 10 of the Convention, the purpose of a NAP is:

> *'to identify the factors contributing to desertification and practical measures necessary to combat it and/or mitigate the effects of drought'. The NAP is expected to 'incorporate long-term strategies to combat desertification and be integrated with national policies for sustainable development. In addition, preventive measures should be fundamental in NAPs'.*

By taking a problem-based approach, rather than a sectoral focus, NAPs have tended to be strategic from the start. But they still face the challenge of having to integrate a variety of policies and the actions of a broad range of local institutions in order to move natural resource management towards a more sustainable basis. A preliminary overview of progress in developing and implementing NAPs sets out the envisaged broad scope and process of a NAP (UNSO 1999):[4]

National Action Programmes (NAPs) to combat desertification should include policy and institutional measures

> *The actions under a NAP should entail policy and institutional measures that facilitate the establishment of an enabling environment at national level for sustainable resource use. The process should follow a bottom-up approach and therefore should build on local level development activities to preserve and/or restore the resource base and improve livelihood security of affected populations. As highlighted in the Convention, the NAP is process-orientated, bottom-up, iterative and decentralized. Through it, a set of integrated measures should be identified. The process itself could continue beyond the identification of these elements to provide for implementation and continuous review and adjustment. In formulating and implementing the NAP, maximum flexibility is called for to take into account variations in the circumstances of the affected countries.*

The overview noted 'significant progress' in the first four years after the adoption of the CCD, although the stages of implementation and approaches differ from country to country. It also reported some shortcomings.

NAPs have made significant progress, but also show some shortcomings

> *For example, in some countries, the involvement of some key stakeholders (civil society, external partners) may not have been satisfactory; some of the approaches may not necessarily be in conformity with the spirit of the Convention; and some of the support arrangements are either not*

---

4 For report, see www.undp.org/seed/unso/prog/prog.htm

*yet in place or their potentials have not been fully realized (eg partnership arrangements,
enabling policies and legal frameworks, funding sources and mechanisms, etc). Still the issue of
the way forward in programme development (ie 'stand-alone' NAPs or integrate into sectoral
programmes) is not yet fully addressed ... The failures ... should serve as lessons to guide future
action.*

Others have also criticized shortcomings in the NAP process. For example:

*Ministries of Environment have been preparing NAPs while other policy and legislative changes
– such as decentralization and land reform – of enormous relevance to the desertification agenda
are taking place, yet with no link made between them.* (Toulmin 2001)

Some 50 countries have received UNDP/UNSO funding to help with their NAPs. Most have adopted a
three-phased approach: (1) launching of the NAP process; (2) implementation of agreements at the first
forum; and (3) full implementation of the NAP and continued monitoring with periodic reviews in
subsequent stakeholder fora.

NAP-related activities in participating countries during recent years have focused primarily on
launching the process, community-based activities and efforts to convene and follow-up on the first forum.
A national coordinating body or focal point is usually within a government ministry or agency. A steering
committee is responsible for the overall organization, developing a vision, a 'road map' of objectives and a
timetable for involving the relevant parties and ensuring timely inputs and actions.

No single country process typifies the NAP approach – the realities in affected countries are different
not only between the regions but even within the regions. However, the examples of approaches being
pursued outlined in Box 3.9 demonstrate some important common features and elements of the process.
These have much in common with the principles in Box 3.1.

*Country NAP
approaches vary
considerably, but
have some common
features*

Box 3.9 Examples of effective principles in national action programmes to combat desertification

Good preparations through effective participation: In Burkina Faso 30 Provincial and 10 Regional Committees
have been set up to facilitate consultation at the local level. The stakeholders were able to identify the problems, set
priorities, determine their responsibilities and decide who would represent them. Such consultations are vital for
effective participation and bargaining in the forum in order to elaborate national strategies for local needs.

Demand for decentralization: In Cape Verde, the first African country to ratify the Convention, local participants at
the National Forum insisted that people on each island be trained to facilitate the preparation of action programmes
and to work to build partnerships directly between government and donors. The issue of decentralization surfaced in
Botswana where participants at the National Forum called for provincial action programmes complementary to the
national process, to govern local activities.

Participation of civil society: There has been positive participation by members of Swaziland's civil society where
the NAP process is gaining priority status in government circles. Consultations among specific stakeholder groups in
Senegal involved religious leaders.

Clear responsibilities: Niger, a Sahelian country that has been wrestling with democracy, held its first Forum
meeting in March 1998 which was distinguished in that the 517 participants sought to define not only what
programmes they thought were necessary, but also to clarify the responsibilities of the various stakeholders.

Quick action: Eritrea, Kenya, Lesotho, Malawi, Sudan, Swaziland, Tanzania, Uganda and Zimbabwe are participating
in a pilot programme to support local initiatives, aimed at promoting access to small grant resources to address their
priorities and make communities responsible for the programming and monitoring of resources. Cape Verde has
identified eight community pilot projects. Niger decided on 'urgent actions' that would provide concrete, short-term
results, which would give the process visibility.

Building on existing frameworks: Several countries such as Bolivia, Chile, Mexico and Peru had already adopted an approach to address land degradation issues prior to the development of the CCD, and efforts focus on strengthening these initiatives in response to the principles of the CCD. In Kazakhstan, Pakistan, Turkmenistan, and Uzbekistan, the current emphasis is on improving participation in existing frameworks. The Sahelian countries can generally build on the strategic frameworks that many of them had prepared with UNSO support.

Role of the private sector: The private sector has started to join forces in a number of countries, such as Brazil and Peru, and representatives of the private sector and NGOs are on the national steering committees of many African and Latin American countries.

Integration with national policies and strategies: The Zimbabwean Government has chosen a 'bottom-up' approach, whereby the District Environmental Action Plans (DEAPs) provide the framework in which the NAP has been integrated. In Burkina Faso the NEAP Secretariat has been designated as the focal point for the NAP process and also in Mali, Senegal, Togo and Uganda. In Botswana and Ethiopia, the National Conservation Strategy provides the framework for the NAP.

Harnessing local expertise: A number of countries, such as China, Kazakhstan and Turkmenistan, already possess some expertise on the scientific issues concerning desertification, and emphasis is now placed on building operational and management capacity at the local level, as well as to promote participatory processes.

Source: www.undp.org/seed/unso/prog/nap.htm

Developed countries must submit a National Communication within 6 months of ratifying the Climate Change Convention

Framework Convention on Climate Change   Under the UN Framework Convention on Climate Change (Article 12, UNFCC), industrial countries (including Eastern Europe and the Former Soviet Union, also known as Annex I parties) are required to submit a 'national communication' to the Secretariat six months after ratification. These require a considerable amount of assessment and planning in their development and are to include:

I An inventory of all greenhouse gas emissions in the country from different sectors (eg transport, energy, industry, agriculture, etc) following the methodology prescribed by the Intergovernmental Panel on Climate Change (IPCC).[5]

II A projection of future expected emissions of greenhouse gases using a business-as-usual economic growth scenario and identification of ways to reduce expected emissions in future.

III An assessment of the vulnerability of the country (including both natural ecosystems and human systems) to the impacts of climate change, highlighting the most vulnerable areas and groups within each country.

IV An assessment of possible options for adaptation to climate change in order to reduce the expected impacts.

These are independently audited to determine coherence with other policies

In preparing these national communications, Annex I Parties must follow guidelines, which have been revised several times. The communications, once submitted to the UNFCCC secretariat, are then subject to independent audit. Auditors examine such issues as coherence with other national policies and the degree of stakeholder involvement (cf NSDS principles). The majority of Annex I Parties submitted their first national communication in 1994 or 1995.

Non-Annex I Parties (developing countries) must make similar national communications, but have three years to do so from entry into force of the Convention for that Party, or from the availability of financial resources. They are also eligible for financial and technical assistance to prepare their national communications – provided by the GEF through its implementing agencies (UNDP, UNEP and the World

5 The IPCC Task Force on National Greenhouse Gas Inventories oversees the National Greenhouse Gas Inventories Programme. http://www.ipcc-nggip.iges.or.jp/

Bank) and following specific guidance from the COP. The same issues are reported, but there is no obligation to make formal commitments to the policies and programmes described, although a number of countries have made commitments, notably on energy, and many have emphasized greenhouse gas inventories and mitigation plans (Box 3.10). Small island developing states (SIDS) have focused particularly on vulnerability and adaptation. Least developed country Parties may make their initial communication at their discretion.

By the end of 2001, 77 non-Annex I Parties had submitted their initial national communications. The external support has, however, tended to focus on gas inventory and projections, and the developing countries are now asking for resources to assess vulnerability, to make adaptation plans and to improve integration – specifically with NSDSs. Methodologies for these tasks, however, are currently lacking.[6] So far, over 100 countries (including both developed and developing countries) have submitted their national communications on climate change to the UNFCCC Secretariat. These communications can be accessed on the UNFCCC website (www.unfccc.de/resource/docs/natc).

> *Developing countries have 3 years to submit a National Communication, and GEF support is available*

> *They have overemphasized greenhouse gas inventories and mitigation plans*

Box 3.10 Experience of non-Annex 1 (developing) countries in developing national communications for climate change

A common experience of many developing countries in preparing their National Communications on Climate Change has been an overemphasis on preparing the greenhouse gas inventories and mitigation plans (in many developing countries, their emissions of greenhouse gases were very small in the first place) in comparison to assessments of vulnerability and especially of adaptation options. Many countries felt that more resources and effort should have been allocated to the latter.

In many developing countries, there was a perception that the National Communication for Climate Change had not been linked at the national level with other environmental plans required by the Rio conventions (eg Biodiversity or Desertification Action Plans) as well as with national sustainable development strategies.

The exceptions to this tended to be those countries where the adverse impacts of climate change were expected to be very severe, including some of the small island developing states (SIDS). An example of one such country that was able to carry out its National Communication for Climate Change with some integration into the other environmental national plans, as well as the national development planning mechanism, was Jamaica (www.unfccc.de/resource/docs/natc/jamnc1.pdf).

The lesson seems to be that national communications for climate change (as well as plans prepared under the other Rio conventions) will tend to be better integrated into national planning and strategy processes where their importance to the development path of the country can be clearly demonstrated.

Source: Saleemul Huq (perssonal communication)

NATIONAL FOREST PROGRAMMES (NFPs)

The experience of developing tropical forest action plans (TFAPs) in the late 1980s and early 1990s revealed a number of lessons for mainstreaming social, environmental and economic concerns in the sector. But it was more notable for revealing what was not required for a national strategic approach (Box 3.11).

During the mid-1990s, the Intergovernmental Panel on Forests (IPF) concluded that, in spite of the incomplete success of the TFAP, some kind of NFP was still desirable. However, such a programme was relevant to all countries, and not just those in the tropics. The IPF also concluded that national forest programmes should be country-led, rather than following a formula developed by outside agencies, and should pay close attention to the integration of forestry policies with other economic and social policies and strategies. A general *definition* of NFPs was given in the IPF Final Report (IPF 1997). It suggested that 'national forest programme' be used as a generic expression for a wide range of approaches to sustainable forest management within different countries, to be applied at national and sub-national levels:

> *Tropical Forestry Action Plans were a top-down, bureaucratic, technical fix approach*

> *Now, country-led National Forest Programmes are being promoted …*

---

6 The development of methodologies for vulnerability/resilience assessment, and integrated adaptation planning, is currently being undertaken by IIED, among other groups.

Box 3.11 The tropical forest action plan – a non-strategic approach

A sense of crisis has often been a principal catalyst for policy change. The TFAP could be characterized as a top-down, quick – but none the less comprehensive – fix to the perceived tropical forest crisis, the perception being promoted by NGO and media concern about 'deforestation'. The response was essentially a bureaucratic and technocratic one, led by professional foresters, and lubricated by development aid. The product of FAO, UNEP, World Bank and World Resources Institute thinking in the mid-1980s, TFAP set a 'standard' for a balanced forest sector for the next decade, and defined a new liturgy for forestry aid planning.

While the TFAP set out a broad set of worthy areas for aid intervention, in practice it resulted in fewer improvements in forestry than had been hoped. Because it was closely associated with the government-to-government aid system, the TFAP was not able to challenge the inequities and perverse policies that underlie deforestation, and then to build the necessary trust between governments, NGOs, local people and the private sector. Its very standardization, within a global framework, and the exigencies of the aid system that supported it (which often meant that expatriates actually led the in-country planning), meant that the TFAP did not adequately recognize diverse local perceptions, values, capacities and needs. Finally – and despite efforts to house TFAP exercises in powerful but 'neutral' bodies such as planning ministries – the TFAP failed to generate real extra political support to the broad range of forest values, and thus to appropriate aid and investment.

Source: Mayers and Bass (1999)

National forest programmes are comprehensive forest policy frameworks for the achievement of sustainable forest management, based on a broad inter-sectoral approach at all stages, including the formulation of policies, strategies and plans of action, as well as their implementation, monitoring and evaluation. They should be implemented in the context of each country's socio-economic, cultural, political and environmental situation. They should be integrated into the country's sustainable development strategies and into wider programmes for sustainable land use, in accordance with chapters 10 to 15 of Agenda 21.

In this context, the national forest programme is a technical process in the sense that the identification of goals, policies, strategies and mechanisms for implementation are based on accurate information. It is a political process in the sense that the choices between the available options are the outcomes of debates, negotiations and compromises of relevant stakeholders. This means participation of all actors, starting from a process of clarification of their roles and responsibilities, defining their rights of intervention, ways and means of collaboration and cooperation and, eventually, arriving at joint implementation and sharing of inputs and benefits.

NFPs are to be based on the following *principles*:

... based on defined principles and main elements

- national sovereignty and country leadership;
- consistency with the constitutional and legal frameworks of each country;
- consistency with international agreements and commitments;
- partnership and participation of all interested parties in the NFP process;
- holistic and inter-sectoral approach to forest development and conservation;
- long-term and iterative process of planning, implementation and monitoring.

The *main elements* of NFPs, in practical terms, are intended to be:

- *National Forest Statement:* a political expression of a country's commitment towards sustainable forest management within related commitments and obligations at the international level.
- *Sector review:* a process to establish an understanding of the forest sector and its relations and linkages to other sectors to identify key issues and priorities for further action; depending on

existing information this could be a major exercise or a continuous process.

- *Policy and institutional reform:* a process of change in favour of sustainable forest management, based on the sector review and dialogue with all actors.
- *Strategy development:* definition of strategies to implement policies towards sustainable forest management, including financing strategies.
- *Action plan:* a bundle of measures, based on needs assessment and jointly agreed prioritization, defined for one planning cycle according to the national development plan (eg five-year plan).
- *Investment programme:* prioritized public sector investments, and incentives for private and non-governmental sectors and partnerships.
- *Capacity-building programme:* to assist stakeholders in fulfilling their roles and mandates.
- *Monitoring and evaluation system:* multi-layered monitoring of the NFP and decentralized forest programmes to provide continuous feedback.
- *Coordination mechanisms:* effective vertical and horizontal coordination within the forest sector and with other sectors, at all levels and in interaction with the international level with regard to donor involvement and forest-related agreements and commitments; for example, through specific fora and consultative groups, inter-sectoral working groups and task forces.

An NFP implementation support facility is being set up by FAO, but, as yet, there are no detailed guidelines for these programmes beyond a 'Practioners' Guide' to the IPF Proposals for action. This also offers a framework for screening the relevance of the more than 130 proposals for action to the national context, and for prioritizing them. A few NFPs have been developed according to the new approach. A particularly interesting exercise was in Malawi (Figure 3.3 and Box 3.12).

A support facility is being established

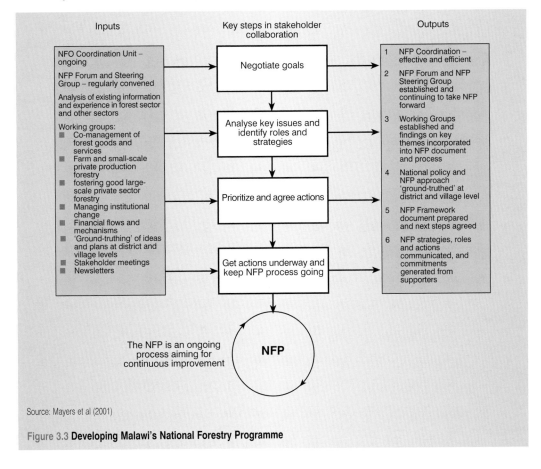

Source: Mayers et al (2001)

Figure 3.3 Developing Malawi's National Forestry Programme

Most SIDs have a limited natural resource base, and forestry, as a sector producing traditional timber-based marketable products, is less relevant. Here, NFPs must centre on the values and benefits of ecological services and other potential benefits of non-timber forestry. Some SIDS provide good examples of comprehensive forest policy, articulated through participatory processes, which encompass the full range of forestry services, eg Grenada and St Vincent.

NATIONAL CONSERVATION STRATEGIES (NCSs)

Conservation strategies were popular in the 1980s/1990s

NCSs were proposed by the World Conservation Strategy (IUCN/UNEP/WWF 1980) to provide a comprehensive, cross-sectoral analysis of conservation and resource management issues. They were popular in the 1980s and early 1990s when NCSs were prepared in over 100 countries, many with technical support from IUCN. 'Conservation for development' was the 'spin' on NCSs, with the occasional call also for 'development for conservation'. Promoted by IUCN, NCSs harnessed much creativity in their early stages, as there was little precedent for linking the 'weak and soft' concerns of conservation with the powerful, hard systems of development. But they suffered from a lack of commitment from the powerful development and financial interests.

They linked environmental needs and development issues

NCSs aimed to identify urgent environmental needs, link them to development issues, stimulate national debate and raise public consciousness, assist decision-makers to set priorities and allocate resources, and build institutional capacity to handle environmental issues. Information was often obtained and analysis undertaken by cross-sectoral groups. NCSs sought to develop political consensus around the issues identified and resulted, inter alia, in policy documents approved at high level and the establishment of cross-sector coordinating groups. An extensive review was made of NCS experience in three continents, Asia, Africa and Latin America – albeit by IUCN, the organizers of the NCS processes and their close collaborators (Carew-Reid 1997; Lopez 1997; Wood 1997). These reviews found a strong set of common factors: NCSs which could be considered to be successful were characterized by 'legitimacy', 'ownership', 'commitment', 'equity' and good 'networking' – all functions of participation (Bass et al 1995).

Many conservation strategies evolved to address economic growth and poverty alleviation

While most NCSs did not begin with an overt focus on economic growth and poverty alleviation, many evolved to address these issues. This was especially the case where the NCS process successfully raised environmental awareness in key economic and social sector agencies, or in agencies at intermediate and local levels which already had a high level of engagement with community groups and businesses. Some NCSs are now providing a valuable platform for the development of more holistic strategies for sustainable development, for example, in Pakistan (Box 3.13).

NATIONAL ENVIRONMENTAL ACTION PLANS (NEAPs)

National Environmental Action Plans were promoted by the World Bank

In contrast to NCSs, NEAPs were promoted by the World Bank – a much more powerful body, economically and politically. Undertaken from the mid-1980s, NEAPs were primarily developed under the umbrella of a host-country organization (usually a coordinating ministry) with technical and/or financial assistance from the World Bank and other donors. The first generation of NEAPs were strongly criticized as a form of conditionality – if a country wanted to secure soft loans (under IDA-10), it was required that a NEAP be completed by June 1993 at the very latest. Pakistan managed to get its NCS accepted as an equivalent, but most countries were not able to convince the Bank that they had a NEAP in place. The requirement was subsequently relaxed and, under its current Operational Directive on NEAPs (OP 4.02, Feb 2000), the World Bank encourages and supports efforts of borrowing countries to prepare and implement 'an appropriate environmental action plan and to revise it periodically as necessary'. According to this directive:

The first generation of NEAPs was criticized as a form of conditionality

An EAP describes a country's major environmental concerns, identifies the principal causes of problems, and formulates policies and actions to deal with the problems. In addition, when

Box 3.12 **The National Forestry Programme, Malawi**

The Malawian government's decision to put together an NFP signalled both its intention to meet its international commitments and its need to redress some of the poor relationships between stakeholders stemming from the autocratic approach to forest management prior to the 1990s. The Forestry Department's dialogue with several international organizations and with some of the donor representatives in-country was slowly persuasive in moving the department away from earlier ideas of an NFP as a comprehensive 'master plan' for the sector. It accepted that a thick master plan document with a 'wish-list' of project proposals which poorly reflected the real priorities and motivations of key stakeholders, and quickly went out of date, was not going to get the forest sector to where it needed to be. The department was also painfully aware of its limited financial and human resources and, while increased donor funding was keenly sought, needed an approach that would not demand a level of resources simply beyond its reach.

Actions emerging from the NFP thus needed to be genuinely viable, building on existing capacities and motivations and avoiding the temptation to try everything at once and thus do nothing well. A process that focused on prioritization of issues and actions, and pulled people in to work together, became the agreed need.

A small group of senior staff in the Forestry Department, in contact with key players in some other government departments and several NGOs, reflected on their various international experiences and information available to them related to national forestry programme approaches. Material included personal experiences from previous donor-supported study tours of forest sector programmes in Zimbabwe and South Africa, published NFAP guidance booklets from FAO, and IIED's lessons-learned series on 'policy that works for forests and people'. There was a determination to engage with political and economic reality to show not only what needs to change, but also how it can change.

International emphasis on participation and dialogue, for example, encouraged the government to promote the inclusion of key stakeholders and avoid a top-down and largely irrelevant plan likely to occupy shelf space rather than demand attention. Its highlighting of the strong extra-sectoral influences that could well override forest policy or forestry interventions was also seen as key to ensuring that the fine words laid out in the forest policy actually delivered better lives and forests.

NFP supporters recognized the need for a process which concentrated on agreeing and adopting new roles and responsibilities for all stakeholders, as well as one that brought the then estranged players together so that they might begin to forge meaningful partnerships. The Malawi NFP was therefore seen as one means to break down barriers and to start to dissolve the high level of distrust between partners with very different powers and potentials – most notably the government, the private sector, traditional authorities and local communities.

The ongoing *process* of the NFP can be seen as a 'cycle' – aiming at continuous improvement. The cycle connects the core elements in the process:

- Negotiating goals and roles – stakeholders understanding each other and hammering out core aims and positions.
- Building institutions and prioritizing actions – developing and organizing the capacity around the agreed roles and deciding the relative importance and urgency of all the actions needed.
- Implementing practical actions for sustainable forestry and livelihoods – securing support for the prioritized actions and carrying them out.
- Monitoring and learning – tracking and reviewing implementation to ensure learning and adaptation (which in turn should enable goals and roles to be refined and further developed).

This NFP document can thus be seen as capturing the thinking in the initial round of the cycle – harnessing the results of 'one round' of negotiating goals and roles and one round of prioritizing actions. The process should continue to complete this first cycle and to ensure further rounds of improvement take place.

Source: Mayers et al (2001)

environmental information is lacking, the EAP identifies priority environmental information needs and indicates how essential data and related information systems will be developed. The EAP provides the preparation work for integrating environmental considerations into a country's overall economic and social development strategy. The EAP is a living document that is expected to contribute to the continuing process by which the government develops a comprehensive national environmental policy and programs to implement the policy. This process is expected to form an integral part of overall national development policy and decision-making.

Box 3.13 **Pakistan's NCS – a strong basis for a national strategy for sustainable development**

In Pakistan, the National Conservation Strategy was prepared through an elaborate, high-level participatory process spanning six years, gained widespread support in government, among political parties, NGOs and civil society, and received cabinet approval in 1992. Despite political upheavals and changes of government, the NCS retains a high level of support and is still being implemented.

A mid-term review of the NCS was undertaken in 2000. It found that, during eight years of implementation, the (quite coherent) strategic objectives and early debate and visioning processes had fragmented into hundreds of unconnected component activities with no feedback mechanism. There was a lack of routine monitoring of project impacts and sustainability indicators, and a lack of policy links between the NCS coordinating body and NCS-inspired projects. As a result, the possibilities for learning were far fewer than there could have been. The NCS review therefore tried to provide a simple base line and framework for correlating sustainability outcomes with strategic processes in future. The review found that the NCS had generated much awareness about the links between environment and development, and had inspired spontaneous innovation and investment in the private sector. The NCS recognized its broad scope, and called for provincial and district conservation strategies to deal with local trade-offs. These local strategies have incorporated economic and livelihood issues more firmly – and indeed, some are seen as sustainable development strategies (Box 3.20).

Given that the NCS retains considerable recognition in the country, it is proposed to retain the label and prepare an NCS-2, although the purpose would be sustainable development. The mid-term review suggested that the NCS-2 should address *national-level concerns, and national institutional roles*, rather than prescribing everything right down to the village level. But it should also recognize, encourage and support the provincial, district and other demand-driven strategic approaches based on local realities consonant with the current devolution plan. This contrasts with the national policy/intellectual push of the original NCS. Finally, recognizing that limited government capacity and weak government–civil society relations had limited the NCS to date, NCS would emphasize the development of *systems* – of participation, information, investment and coordination – rather than the previous 'shopping list' of desirable projects.

Source: Hanson et al (2000)

Most NEAPs included a package of environmentally related investment projects

NEAPs have recommended specific actions, outlining the required policies, legislation, institutional arrangements and investment strategies. But the typical outcome of most NEAPs was not so much institutional change as a package of environmentally related investment projects, many intended for donor assistance. Progress with NEAPs is still reviewed by the Bank and forms a part of its Country Assistance Strategies, but the Bank is now placing more emphasis on Comprehensive Development Frameworks and poverty reduction strategies (see below). NEAPs can therefore be seen as an eclipsed planning tool in the Bank's relations with its member countries, although most of the lessons from NEAP practice have been taken on board in the way the Bank approaches comprehensive development frameworks (CDFs) and poverty reduction strategy papers (PRSPs).

NATIONAL AGENDA 21S AND NATIONAL COUNCILS FOR SUSTAINABLE DEVELOPMENT

National Agenda 21s have been prepared by a range of countries, often with support from UNDP's Capacity 21 programme. A common intention has been to set out how Agenda 21 will be translated into action at a country level. These strategies have frequently been developed by National Councils for Sustainable Development (NCSDs), multi-stakeholder participatory bodies set up in more than 80 countries (Box 3.14). The Earth Council has supported the development of many NCSDs in developing countries.

National Councils for Sustainable Development are multi-stakeholder bodies, but vary in form and function

The status of NCSDs varies from region to region (they are very active in Latin America, moderately so in Asia, and limited in Africa) but, where they exist, NCSDs have sometimes played an important role in promoting dialogue among stakeholders in participatory decision-making processes. Many have been used as ad hoc think tanks for government, as and when issues arise, although others play more routine roles in development planning. Most importantly, NCSDs have the potential to play a facilitating role in developing strategies for sustainable development. This is often within their mandate, as described in the decrees or acts by which they were established (Table 3.2).

Box 3.14 National Councils for Sustainable Development

Although NCSDs vary widely in form and function, common roles are:

- facilitating participation and cooperation of civil and economic society and governments for sustainable development;
- assisting governments in decision-making and policy formulation;
- integrating economic, social and environmental action and perspectives;
- looking at the local implications of global agreements such as Agenda 21 and other international conventions related to sustainable development;
- providing a systematic and informed participation of civil society in UN deliberations.

Since the creation of first NCSD in the Philippines in September 1992, the Earth Council has facilitated and supported the establishment and strengthening of NCSDs in some 70 (especially developing) countries. The Council's NCSD Sustainable Development Report is a progress report that documents successful NCSD practice and problem areas, and assesses the effectiveness of NCSDs in influencing policy decisions in several key thematic areas.

With funding from GEF-UNDP, a prototype project is under way to develop methodologies to integrate global environmental priorities into sustainable development plans. Participating in the project are NCSDs of Burkina Faso, Costa Rica, the Dominican Republic, Mexico, the Philippines and Uganda. The project is founded on the concept of 'multi-stakeholder integrative sustainability planning' (MISP) – an approach to development planning that appears to have much in common with the principles for strategies for sustainable development in that it is:

- built on people's participation and action;
- multi-stakeholder, and seeks to reconcile divergent interests of stakeholders;
- flexible and adaptable;
- promotes coordination and vertical and horizontal integration and empowerment;
- dynamic and iterative.

See Box 8.7 for further details on NCSD mandates, structures and composition; and Box 8.8 for a review of their decision-making processes.

Source: Earth Council (2000); www.ncsdnetwork.org

To move towards sustainable development, NCSDs will usually need to broaden their initial environmental focus to cover more fully the concerns of social and economic stakeholders. They may also need to improve their links to decentralized levels of governance and administration, and local action by voluntary organizations and CBOs (the Mexican and Philippines NCSDs provide good examples of this).

They need to broaden their initial environmental focus

NATIONAL VISIONS

National visions for sustainable development are being developed by an increasing number of countries, many supported by UNDP's Capacity 21 programme. National visions bring together different groups of society, including those of different political parties, to agree common development objectives. Examples include Ghana, Pakistan, Tanzania and Thailand (Box 3.15). Their advantage is the opportunity they present for many stakeholders to take a forward view on national development and work towards broad, shared objectives for their country's future. Their success depends very much on the degree to which stakeholders participate, the durability of the vision between successive political administrations, its widespread promotion among those who make key decisions, and its transferability to standard developmental and administrative procedures.

National visions set out common development objectives of different groups of society

Table 3.2 Examples of National Councils for Sustainable Development and similar multi-stakeholder fora for sustainable development

Country	Multi-stakeholder mechanism	Date of creation	Instrument of establishment
Burkina Faso	National Council for Environmental Management	June 1998	Decree
Canada	National Round Table on Environment and Economy	1994	Law
Estonia	National Commission on Sustainable Development	1996	Decree
Finland	Finnish National Commission on Sustainable Development	June 1993	Council of State decision
Hungary	Commission on Sustainable Development	April 1993	Decree
Jamaica	Sustainable Development Council of Jamaica	June 1996	International agreement
Mexico	National Consultative Council for Sustainable Development	April 1995	Law
Mongolia	National Council for Sustainable Development	April 1996	Government resolution
Philippines	Philippine Council for Sustainable Development	September 1992	Decree
Romania	National Center for Sustainable Development	June 1997	Project
Senegal	National Committee for Sustainable Development	May 1995	Decree
South Korea	Presidential Commission on Sustainable Development	August 2000	Decree
Uganda	National Environmental Management Authority	January 1996	Law
United States of America	President's Council on Sustainable Development	June 1993	Decree

Source: Earth Council (2000)

COMPREHENSIVE DEVELOPMENT FRAMEWORKS

CDF principles are consistent with those of NSDSs

The CDF concept was introduced by the World Bank President, James D Wolfensohn, in 1999, as a holistic approach to development in the Bank's client countries. World Bank programming must be consistent with the CDF, which is based on four interrelated principles and objectives to be pursued at the country level. These are consistent with the basic principles for sustainable development strategies, outlined in Box 3.1:

- a long-term vision and strategy;
- enhanced country ownership of development goals and actions;
- more strategic partnership among stakeholders;
- accountability for development results.

The CDF encourages the use of a long-term strategic horizon of, say, 15–20 years. It seeks a better balance in policy-making by highlighting the interdependence of all elements of development – social, structural, human, governance, environmental, economic and financial. It emphasizes partnerships among governments, development cooperation agencies, civil society, the private sector and others. Of particular importance is a stress on country ownership of the process and direction of the development agenda, with bilateral and multilateral development cooperation agencies each defining their support for their respective plans.

Box 3.15 National Visions

Ghana-Vision 2020 was developed by the government of former President Jerry Rawlings as a policy framework for accelerated growth and sustainable development in Ghana. It gave a strategic direction for national development over 25 years from 1996 to 2020. Its main goal was to transform the country from a poor, low-income country into a prosperous middle-income country within a generation. The goals of Ghana-Vision 2020 were expected to be accomplished through a series of medium-term development plans based on the routine, decentralized, participatory planning framework which requires priority-setting at the district level. Ghana-Vision 2020 was the product of an extensive consultation and collaborative effort over some four years involving many groups and individuals from the universities, the public sector, the private sector and civil society, coordinated by the National Development Planning Commission.

The change of government in late 2000 was followed by initial uncertainty about how it would treat Vision 2020 and the accompanying 2000–2005 policy framework. In May 2001, the new government rejected Vision 2020 as a framework for formulating economic policies as well as the goal to achieve middle-income status by 2020, reasoning that this goal could not be achieved in the planned timeframe, given the major slippages in achieving targets under the First Medium-Term Development Plan (1995–2000). In its place, an alternative vision has been proclaimed – to develop Ghana into a major agro-industrial nation by 2015, propelled by a 'golden age of business'.

The government is currently fashioning a new economic policy framework to enable the nation to achieve this new goal and the specifics are yet to be made public. A National Economic Dialogue (NED) was held in May 2001, with participation by several stakeholder groups, around six themes: poverty reduction strategy; a golden age of business; education, labour market and human resource development; resources for growth; economic policy; and development of the financial sector. It was the first national consensus-building exercise for stakeholders to discuss the new government's economic policies, including its approach to poverty alleviation within the context of its new vision for long-term economic growth and the decision to participate in the HIPC programme. Several of the thematic thrusts of the newly evolving economic policy framework cover the same ground as under the Vision 2000 (Seth Vordzorgbe, personal communication).

Pakistan's 2010 Programme and the 25-year Perspective Plan were developed in the pursuit of defining a long-term vision for the country's development. The goals were to achieve economic growth through technological development and sustained human development. The Planning Commission of the federal government was the main coordinating body with inputs from, and implementation through, other sectoral ministries and departments. A government-coordinated committee organized a consultative process for both initiatives, which included representatives from the civil society and public sector.

Tanzania's Vision 2025 sets targets to achieve a nation characterized by a high quality of life for all citizens; peace, stability and unity; good governance; a well-educated and learning society; and a diversified economy capable of producing sustainable growth and shared benefits. Implementation is to be through short- and medium-term strategies such as the National Poverty Eradication Strategy, Poverty Reduction Strategy and the Medium Term Plan.

Thailand's National Vision was developed over 18 months as part of a participatory process, involving 50,000 people, to prepare the Ninth Economic and Social Development Plan. A draft vision emerged from a first round of consultations in the People's Forum on Development Priorities. This was then subjected to research-based analysis of internal strengths and weaknesses and external opportunities and threats. A revised draft was amended further by the People's Forum, operational elements related to institutional improvements were added, and the vision finalized.

The CDF was initiated in 12 pilot countries[7] and also by some non-pilot countries under their own initiative. Early progress in implementing the CDF was uneven, which was not surprising given the different starting points and varying circumstances of the participating countries. By July 2000, after 12–18 months of the initiative (World Bank 2000), more than half of the pilots had made progress with the majority of CDF elements. Greatest progress was made on long-term vision and strategy development, while least progress was in establishing open, transparent management information systems. Nearly all

Progress with CDF has been uneven, but most participating countries have developed long-term visions and engaged in debate on development aspirations

---

7 CDF pilot countries include: Bolivia, Côte d'Ivoire, Dominican Republic, Eritrea, Ethiopia, Ghana, Kyrgyz Republic, Morocco, Romania, Uganda, Vietnam, West Bank and Gaza.

pilots were focusing on governance issues, and many were implementing projects to improve their justice systems. Romania, for example, had embarked on a major reform of public administration. Several countries were emphasizing the importance of 'knowledge sharing and transparency' through country-based CDF websites.[8]

The latest review (World Bank 2001c; www.worldbank.org/cdf) reports that sustained progress is being made. The PRSP initiative (see next sub-section) has substantially expanded the number of countries seeking to develop strategies based on CDF principles. Nevertheless, implementation of the CDF principles has been difficult and uneven. The review looked at progress in implementing CDF principles in 46 countries that were either part of the original CDF pilot group or that have prepared interim PRSPs or full PRSPs. It reports that:

- a majority of the 46 countries are developing long-term country visions;
- 80 per cent of these countries are developing strategies based on internal debate around domestic aspirations;
- progress in building partnerships among stakeholders has been slow;
- least progress has been made on accountability development results.

The CDF proposal suggested the use of a regularly updated matrix showing the activities of all partners across all sectors (part of the matrix for Vietnam is set out in Table 3.3). The aim of the matrix is to give all players a framework of information to ensure openness and a basis for coordinating efforts and judging the effectiveness of programmes and strategies. The review uncovered a mixed experience of the use of such matrices. Some countries felt that a matrix should be a regular output of the CDF process, while others have relied on more familiar ways to share information.

The City Development Strategy (CDS) is an application of the CDF at the urban level, and is being implemented in 27 cities, 21 of which are in Asia, including three in pilot countries.

The CDS is part of the Bank's response to the need for decentralization and associated changes in the structure and roles of governments.

Positive aspects of the CDF programme include country ownership, enhanced accountability, and development of long-term vision. Its principles are consistent with the NSDS approach, and CDFs could therefore form a basis for a country's NSDS. However, it is also clear, at this stage, that an intention of the CDF programme as a whole is to enhance the World Bank's role in sustainable development.

POVERTY REDUCTION STRATEGIES

The strategic planning mechanisms of many developing countries have focused on *strategies to reduce poverty*. For example, Tanzania developed a Poverty Alleviation Action Plan in 1996, Uganda's Poverty Eradication Action Plan followed in 1997, and Zambia prepared a poverty alleviation strategy towards the end of the decade. Such plans were of varying quality. The best were truly cross-sectoral strategies to address poverty – with clearly budgeted priorities. Others, however, tended to be no more than a list of social sector investment projects.

To receive debt relief, poor countries must prepare a Poverty Reduction Strategy Paper (PRSP) …

Within the CDF framework, the World Bank and the IMF launched *Poverty Reduction Strategies* for low-income countries in 1999. PRSPs are country-written documents detailing plans for achieving sustained reductions in poverty.

Initially required as a basis for access to debt relief in Highly Indebted Poor Countries (HIPC), PRSPs are required by all International Development Agency (IDA) countries as of 1 July 2002.

---

8 Bolivia, Côte d'Ivoire, Ghana, Kyrgyz Republic, Romania and Vietnam.

Table 3.3 **Example of a draft CDF matrix from Vietnam**

| | Structural | | | | Human | | | Physical | | | | | | Specific Strategies | | |
	(1) Good and Clean Govern-ance*	(2) Justice System	(3) Financial System	(4) Social Safety Net and Social Programs	(5) Education	(6) Health and Popul-ation	(10b) Cultural Issues	(7) Water and Sanitation	(8) Power	(9a) Transport	(9b) Telecoms	(10a) Environ-ment	(11) Agriculture/ Rural Dev't (not forestry)	(12) Urban Dev't	(13) Private Sector Dev't	(14) Forestry
Lead External Agencies	UNDP SIDA DANIDA	UNDP (with Danish $)	WB SAC team with IMF	WB SAC team	WB with ADB	WB with SIDA & UN Agencies	Sweden	ADB, with WB & UN	WB with ADB, Japan, Sweden	Japan with ADB, WB	Telstra (Australian part state-owned company)	UNDP	WB with ADB	ADB UNDP Japan WB	WB (IFC)	Netherl. WB ADB
Multi-lateral	UNDP ADB	UNDP	WB IMF UNDP	UNFPA UNDP WB	WB ADB	UN WHO WB WFP		WB UN ADB	WB ADB	WB ADB		ADB UNDP WB	WB FAO ADB	UNDP ADB WB	WB (IFC) UNIDO UNCDF UNDP	WFP ADB
Bilateral	Sweden Germany EC Canada Denmark	Denmark Australia Sweden France Germany	Canada Japan Germany Switzerl. France	Netherl. UK	Australia Japan France Sweden Belgium	Sweden Japan Netherl. Australia Germany	Sweden France Finland Netherl.	Finland Japan Australia Netherl. Denmark	Japan Sweden	Japan Denmark Korea France Australia	Canada France Japan	Netherl. Sweden Canada Denmark Norway	Australia Denmark Belgium France Netherl.	Switzerl. Japan Belgium	Australia Switzerl. Sweden Denmark New Zealand	Japan Germany
Civil Society	Oxfam UK	Radda Barnen, Asia Found-ation		Actionaid, Oxfam UK, Save the Children UK			Ford Found-ation					WWF IUCN			CECI	
Private Sector											Telstra (1/3 private)					

Note: First draft indicated to be completed gradually by the end of 2000 (title: The prerequisites for sustainable growth and poverty alleviation)
* Donors considering new programming in governance include Denmark, Canada, Australia, Sweden, the EC and the ADB

Source: www.worldbank.org.vn/partner/part2.htm

The activities of partners who can assist in the development process

The stated principles of poverty reduction strategies are that they should:

*... following CDF
principles ...*

*be country-driven, be developed transparently with broad participation of elected institutions,
stakeholders including civil society, key development cooperation agencies and regional
development banks, and have a clear link with the agreed international development goals –
principles that are embedded in the Comprehensive Development Framework.* (Development
Committee Communiqué, September 1999)

According to the IMF, PRSPs take the following form:

*They are prepared by the member country in collaboration with the staffs of the World Bank and
the IMF as well as civil society and development partners. Updated annually, they describe the
country's plan for macroeconomic, structural, and social policies for three-year economic
adjustment programmes to foster growth and reduce poverty, as well as associated external
financing needs and major sources of financing. Interim PRSPs (I-PRSPs) summarize the current
knowledge and analysis of a country's poverty situation, describe the existing poverty reduction
strategy, and lay out the process for producing a fully developed PRSP in a participatory
fashion.* (www.imf.org/external/np/prsp/prsp.asp)

*... and building on
pre-existing decision-
making processes*

World Bank guidance for CDFs and PRSPs explicitly supports building on pre-existing decision-making
processes. Governments developing PRSPs and external partners supporting them have taken advantage of
this in many cases, although in some it has taken time for the implications of this inclusive approach to be
understood.

   The Bank and the IMF have prepared guidelines for the preparation and assessment (Joint Staff
Assessment) of I-PRSPs and PRSPs (annexes in IMF 2001). These reflect the principles of the CDF and
embody a three-part approach to poverty reduction, based on creating economic opportunity, empowering
the poor and addressing vulnerability (as set out in the World Development Report 2000/2001). A PRSP

*A PRSP sourcebook is
available*

Sourcebook has been developed as a compendium of reference material to help countries in preparing their
own country-specific strategies, bringing together information on international best practices and policies
for poverty reduction. The Sourcebook is an evolving document that will be revised in the light of
comments and country experience. It is presented in two volumes: the first covers core techniques (eg
poverty measurement and analysis, monitoring and evaluation) and cross-cutting issues (eg participation,
governance, environment); the second volume deals with macro and structural issues (eg pro-poor growth,
trade), rural and urban poverty, human development, and private sector infrastructure (available at
www.worldbank.org/poverty/strategies/sourctoc.htm).

*Interim-PRSPs are
road maps to full
PRSPs*

*A comprehensive
PRSP review reveals
growing country
ownership, more open
dialogue, but the
need for realistic
targets*

   By March 2002, the World Bank and IMF boards had considered a total of 42 interim PRSPs, which are
'road maps' to forthcoming PRSPs intended to reduce delays in debt relief and concessional lending. Ten full
PRSPs had also been considered for Albania, Bolivia, Burkina Faso, Honduras, Mauritania, Mozambique,
Nicaragua, Niger, Tanzania and Uganda (www.worldbank.org/prsp). Three first annual PRSP
implementation progress reports had been submitted (Tanzania, Uganda and Burkina Faso). The boards also
received a report on a comprehensive review of the PRSP approach (started in mid-2001), which provides
descriptions of good practice for countries and partners, numerous country examples and coverage of
sectoral issues. The boards endorsed its main findings: the need for realism of targets and choosing
appropriate indicators; ensuring timely monitoring of progress; good public expenditure management; and
focusing on growth, sources of growth and the role of the private sector
(www.worldbank.org/poverty/strategies/review) (Box 3.16).

Box 3.16 Progress with PRSPs: key points of the comprehensive review by World Bank and IMF

It is clear that the development of PRSPs is a major challenge for low-income countries, in terms of both analysis and organization. Besides managing a complex policy dialogue with development partners, low-income governments have to put together an integrated medium-term economic and poverty reduction strategy, complete with short- and long-term goals and monitoring systems; these are a set of tasks few industrial countries could systematically do well. And in many countries, these tasks must be managed with limited technical and institutional capacity and in ways that reinforce – rather than undermine – existing national institutions, processes, and governance systems. Thus, there is a need to have realistic expectations about the PRSPs that are being developed.

The central message is that there is broad agreement among low-income countries, civil society organizations and their development partners that the objectives of the PRSP approach remain valid … and that there have been improvements over time in both process and content … There is widespread agreement on four key achievements of the PRSP approach to date:

- a growing sense of ownership among most governments of their poverty reduction strategies;
- a more open dialogue within governments and with at least some parts of civil society than had previously existed;
- a more prominent place for poverty reduction in policy debates;
- an acceptance by the donor community of the principles of the PRSP approach.

While it is premature to draw any firm conclusions about the development impact of the PRSP approach, there are nonetheless a range of good practices by countries and their development partners … In reality, there are only a few concrete cases where such practices are in place.

Interim PRSPs

The requirements for an I-PRSP were deliberately minimal, although this was evidently not widely understood by all stakeholders. The I-PRSP was to describe the existing situation (with respect to poverty: the existing poverty reduction strategy and macroeconomic and policy framework) and set out a plan for developing the full PRSP (including the participatory processes; plans for identifying and developing appropriate policies, targets and indicators; and a system for monitoring and evaluating implementation). Policy commitments and targets for the outer years were to be revised in the full PRSP.

While the quality of I-PRSPs has varied, their preparation has served a useful purpose by encouraging countries to take stock of existing data and policies, to launch a broader process of rethinking current strategies, and to produce time-bound road maps for the preparation of their first full PRSP. In many cases (eg Mongolia and Nicaragua), I-PRSPs were longer than expected, as countries put forward quite comprehensive documents. At the same time, however, the road maps were sometimes relatively weak with respect to plans for participatory processes (eg Senegal); plans to fill data gaps (eg Sierra Leone) and the proposed institutional arrangements for the PRSP (eg Moldova and Tajikistan). This appears to have been due to both an unclear understanding about the intended nature of an I-PRSP, coupled with pressures imposed by HIPC and/or PRGF timetables.

Although I-PRSPs were initially viewed as a transitional device, they may still be useful in many of the nearly three dozen low-income countries that will need to prepare PRSPs for access to Bank/Fund concessional lending and/or debt relief.

In order to qualify for debt relief, many countries prepared their I-PRSPs too hastily. In fact, the push by many countries to reach their Decision Point at the earliest possible date came at the expense of the quality of some I-PRSPs road maps, for example, participation plans and proposed institutional arrangements.

Full PRSPs

Ten countries have now finalized their first full PRSPs. These varied considerably in form and content, reflecting each country's own starting point, capacities and priorities. Each of the documents included the four elements proposed in the joint Bank/Fund paper on PRSPs (Operational Issues, SM/99/290, 12 Dec 1999): (a) a description of the participatory process used in preparing the PRSP; (b) a poverty diagnosis; (c) targets, indicators and monitoring systems; and (d) priority public actions. However, the PRSPs varied considerably in the relative weight given to the treatment of the core elements and to key areas within these elements, and in style and format of presentation. Key points raised about PRSP documents and the approach include:

- PRSPs have generally built on existing data and analyses and on prior strategies;

- they reflect considerable improvement in both process and content relative to their corresponding I-PRSPs;
- they have received attention at the highest political level in almost all countries, and many provide useful information about the institutional arrangements for preparation and implementation;
- in some cases, documents have clarified the linkages between PRSPs and existing governmental plans and decision-making processes – especially budget formulation.

Participation

- PRSPs have established a presumption in favour of openness and transparency and broad-based participation – the approach has often led to an improved dialogue within the various parts of government and between governments and domestic stakeholders, and has brought new participants into the policy dialogue;
- however, some concerns have been expressed about inadequate engagement by certain groups or institutions seen as key to successful poverty reduction efforts;
- sectoral ministries generally are less fully involved than core ministries, such as the Ministry of Finance or the Ministry of Planning;
- the role of parliaments in the PRSP process has generally been limited, although individual parliamentarians have been involved in some countries;
- in most countries, bringing civil society organizations into the process has improved with time;
- in some cases, there have been constraints to deepening and widening the process to all constituents to meet their expectations;
- there is some evidence that civil society's efforts have affected PRSP content, particularly in drawing attention to problems of social exclusion and the impoverishing effects of bad governance;
- in some countries, there may be a risk of 'participation fatigue'.

Poverty diagnostics

- despite the significant advances in poverty data and analysis in PRSPs relative to pre-existing government strategies and policy frameworks, analysis of the impact of the policy actions on the lives of the poor appears to have been limited;
- poverty and social impact analysis of major policies and programmes has typically not been undertaken as part of PRSPs.

Targets, indicators, monitoring and evaluation (M&E)

- many PRSPs set long-term targets that seem overly ambitious relative to prior achievements and/or likely available resources;
- PRSPs often lack good indicators of intermediate processes that would help track the implementation of public programmes;
- many PRSPs have detailed plans for improvement of M&E capacities, but the institutional structure for monitoring has not always been clearly defined.

Priority public actions

- PRSPs are generally weak regarding the prioritization and specificity of public actions;
- some early PRSPs have made progress in identifying pro-poor growth policies;
- there were various shortcomings in the macro-economic frameworks put forward in the early PRSPs, both in terms of presentation and content. All included ambitious growth targets and could have benefited from a sharper analysis of the likely sources and levels of growth;
- key cross-cutting issues (eg gender, HIV/AIDS, good governance, rural development) have been addressed to varying extents;
- all PRSPs have emphasized access to services as a key concern, with improved access to education a priority;
- in general, the primacy of the private sector for growth is acknowledged;
- most PRSPs have dealt with issues concerning trade openness in only a limited way.

EXAMPLES

Tanzania's *poverty reduction strategy is anchored within a macroeconomic framework designed to raise the GDP growth rate while maintaining macroeconomic stability. It focuses on reducing income poverty and on enhancing human capabilities, survival, and well-being. Reduction of income poverty is to be achieved through rural/agricultural* *development and export growth. The government also places special emphasis on improving primary education, access to health services and water (especially in rural areas), and governance (including anti-corruption and better access to the judicial system). At the same time, the PRSP candidly acknowledges gaps in poverty analysis, in some strategy components, and in the comprehensiveness of participatory processes. The PRSP spells out plans to rectify these gaps in the coming months.*

While acknowledging the positive aspects of the strategy, the Joint Staff Assessment of the PRSP and comments from the Executive Boards identified a number of areas where additional work will be needed, including: statistical information on poverty; programme costing, monitoring and evaluation; added attention to specific areas such as gender, environment, and the impact of HIV/AIDS; and, critically, fleshing out Tanzania's agricultural development strategy. Work already undertaken by the government and civil society on the integration of gender issues into the budget planning process should provide an opportunity for ensuring that gender is fully integrated into Tanzania's poverty reduction strategy.

__Mauritania's__ anti-poverty strategy preceded the PRSP approach. It has included the introduction and expansion of participatory processes with civil society, as well as consultations with development partners. Building on these processes, the PRSP recognizes the multidimensional nature of poverty, and offers an integrated vision for poverty reduction based on four inter-related elements — accelerating economic growth with macroeconomic stability; stimulating pro-poor economic growth (ie rural development, support for small and medium enterprises); developing human resources by improving education and health services and access to basic infrastructure; and strengthening institutional capacity and governance (including civil service and judicial reform, decentralization, enhancing partnerships with civil society, and developing effective and transparent public expenditure management and impact monitoring systems). The PRSP sets ambitious targets for halving income poverty by 2010, and reducing it to about one-third of its estimated current level by 2015. The boards of the World Bank and IMF strongly endorsed the strategy, while noting that it is subject to certain risks, including possible shortfalls in economic growth targets, in budgetary revenues and external financing, and in the efficient and timely delivery of services to the poor.

Both Executive Board discussions and Joint Staff Assessments of PRSPs have been frank in noting gaps in countries' analyses of the complex mix of policies and priority actions needed to secure both broad-based economic growth and specific poverty reduction outcomes. Not surprisingly, those countries able to build on prior experience with poverty reduction programmes have been able to elaborate initial strategies more successfully than those lacking such experience. But even in the more successful cases, basic problems, such as capacity constraints and lack of adequate data, have made it hard for countries to prepare fully worked out strategies. For example, the full PRSPs for Mauritania and Tanzania had to rely on poverty data that were 5–10 years old. To some extent, existing Bank and Fund work — such as core Bank economic and sector work (ESW) — can help provide countries with the material they need in preparing their strategies, but additional technical assistance and support for capacity building, including from development partners, is likely to become increasingly needed, especially as countries make the transition to full PRSPs.

Note: This box is based on extracts drawn from the main review report and the separate summary of main findings (available on: www.worldbank.org/poverty/strategies/review)

Source: IMF (2001)

Despite the intensive role played by the Bank and IMF in PRSPs, and their relative lack of attention to date on key issues of environmental sustainability, economic growth and diversification, these approaches are capable of taking on the broader role of NSDSs.

Improvements to the basis of participation and analysis of environment/poverty links would help, as stressed by the World Bank/IMF review. A separate World Bank study of participation in PRSPs by the Participation Group of the Bank's Social Development Department has brought together a synthesis of external assessments of participation in the PRSP process with the in-house review of participation in 33 I-PRSPs and 9 full PRSPs (World Bank 2002). The report concludes that 'almost all countries are on the lower half of the spectrum' and information-sharing and consultation is largely confined to capital cities. Furthermore, the process is driven by finance and planning ministries, with other ministries such as health and education playing minor roles. On participation by civil society organizations, the report concludes that NGOs are assuming an increasingly important role. However, non-conventional NGOs such as community

PRSPs need improved participation

groups and women's organizations are given little attention. Other weaknesses highlighted include the poor quality of data and a lack of gender analysis. The study suggests joint learning and assessment across countries and greater focus on the participation of local government.

NGOs are sceptical and critical

The development of PRSPs has gained momentum, but considerable scepticism remains about their underlying intentions. Two statements in 2001 by participants representing civil society concluded that the PRSP approach is simply delivering re-packaged structural adjustment programmes rather than poverty-focused development plans. They were also said to have failed to involve civil society and parliamentarians in discussions of economic policy. More recently Asian NGOs have commented on the problems they face with PRSP processes in their region (Box 3.17).

Box 3.17 Civil society opposition to PRSPs and NGO views

In May 2001, 39 organizations and regional networks from 15 African countries agreed a statement at a meeting in Kampala that PRSPs were:

> simply window-dressing to improve the IMF and World Bank's declining legitimacy. The content of PRSPs continues to put corporate rights before social, human and environmental rights. Rather than enable local people to decide their content, PRSPs means more IMF and World Bank control not only over financial and economic policies but over every aspect and detail of all our national policies and programmes. The macro-economic programme is still not open for discussion and anti-poverty programmes are expected to be consistent with the neo-liberal paradigm including privatization, deregulation, budgetary constraints and trade and financial liberalization. Yet these ignore the role of international/global factors and forces in creating economic crises and poverty.

The statement details how problems with the process limit civil society participation, and notes that southern NGOs have been distracted from the task of opposing structural adjustment programmes (SAPs) and the HIPC debt initiative. It calls for NGOs to 'return to our own agendas and reinvigorate and further strengthen our engagement and work with people at the grass roots' (for statement, see afrodad@samara.co.net.zw).

Another statement signed by 19 French NGOs in March 2001 points to the 'illusion' of ownership. It calls for the international financial institutions (IFCs) and their major shareholders to cancel poor countries' debts, ensure the full participation of national parliaments and civil society organizations in macro-economic reform discussions, and engage in a thorough reform of the IFCs (for statement, see agirici@globenet.org and www.globalnet.org/ifi).

Source: Bretton Woods Project (2001)

Focus on the Global South has issued a report assessing PRSP processes in Lao PDR, Cambodia and Vietnam. Drawn from interviews with NGOs and World Bank missions, the report concludes that the interim PRSPs produced for these countries are not about poverty eradication. While Vietnam has been better able to direct the process, in both Lao PDR and Cambodia, interim PRSPs conflict with existing medium-term development plans. The report criticizes the level of participation in the drafting process. While prominent NGOs were consulted, a failure to translate the papers into either Khmer or Lao marginalized the majority of civil society actors. Focus researchers believe that the World Bank is repeating errors of the past, as policy recommendations are similar to previous structural adjustment measures. The report reveals that none of the three governments had been informed of the results of the Structural Adjustment Participatory Review Initiative assessments of the impact of SAPs in their countries.

In Bangladesh, at a national convention on the poverty reduction strategy (PRS) on 9 March 2002 organized by the People's Empowerment Trust (PET) and Action Aid Bangladesh, participants condemned the lack of transparency in the PRS drafting process. Criticism was made that the timeline set by the World Bank and IMF for people's participation in the process threatened to lead to the 'abandonment of the very principles of poverty reduction'. A declaration by participants called on the World Bank and IMF to remove PRSP conditionality for receipt of further funds, and develop a transparent 'route map' to guide the process (www.focusweb.org).

Source: Bretton Woods Project (2002)

Box 3.18 **The DEAP mechanism in Zimbabwe**

District Environmental Action Plans (DEAPs) were launched as a pilot exercise in 1995. This was a follow-up to the National Conservation Strategy developed with support from IUCN and UNDP. DEAP is being implemented by the Department of Natural Resources (DNR) in the Ministry of Environment and Tourism. The objective of DEAP is to prepare environmental action plans for all rural districts in Zimbabwe. The first phase concentrated on one ward in each of eight pilot districts – including budgeted portfolios for the sustainable development of the natural resource base in the district and one activity to be implemented immediately to tackle an environmental issue identified by villagers in the district.

Following an earlier critical review, the initiative was extended in 1999 – overall there are now two districts covered per province. The focus of the DEAPs is on poverty alleviation, socio-economic improvement and environmental degradation. The overall programme is overseen by a steering committee of senior officials. Provincial strategy teams are responsible for the training of district, ward and community strategy teams. In each district, a district strategy team is responsible for facilitating the process and reports to the relevant sub-committee of the Rural District Development Committee.

Activities in each district include:

- participation with villagers to identify environmental problems, set priorities and initiate action;
- collecting relevant environmental, economic and institutional data in all wards;
- scanning all environment projects/programmes;
- mobilizing technical inputs in developing the plans;
- documenting relevant institutions and expertise, and defining their roles in plan implementation;
- identifying and designing projects/programmes to constitute the main elements of each plan;
- documenting requirements for implementing each plan;
- disseminating each plan among institutions and groups and building consensus on its appropriateness.

The entry level for activities is now at the ward rather than community level – the latter was judged to have failed and the training in the use of participatory methods introduced in the first phase has ceased. This initiative is very much on a pilot, experimental basis. The transaction costs of scaling up such a comprehensive approach are considerable, especially given a tendency to weak institutional capacity in local councils. It is also the case that the achievement of strategic objectives at the municipal level can be conditioned by the integration of sustainable development policy and practice at the national level, and by determination of appropriate spatial levels of governance for various actions. For example, the success of recycling processes at the village or neighbourhood level can be conditional on support from higher-level strategies and economic instruments.

Source: Munemo (1998)

Sub-national strategies

Many countries have strategic planning frameworks at different sub-national levels, including urban and regional planning. Some of these frameworks are inspired by national mechanisms. A series of boxes set out experiences in this regard. In Box 3.18, the district environmental action plans in Zimbabwe are described. Local Agenda 21s have been developed in many countries and are described in Box 3.19. The experience in Pakistan of preparing, in sequence, national, provincial and district conservation strategies is set out in Box 3.20. This reveals growing attention to stakeholder participation, which can be correlated with increasing attention to a broad range of developmental (as opposed to environmental) affairs. But it also suggests a capacity limit to intensive conservation strategy approaches at 'lower' levels. The prospects in both Pakistan and Zimbabwe for such strategies in all districts are slim at present – there is much institutional development to be undertaken first. However, as the tentative plans for NCS-2 in Pakistan suggest, local institutional development, under the devolution plan currently being implemented, can in part be achieved *through* the strategic exercise – if it is carried out in ways consistent with the principles and elements in Boxes 3.1 and 3.2.

Applying NSDS principles can help local institutional development

Box 3.19 **Local Agenda 21**

The Local Agenda 21 (LA21) concept was formulated and launched by the International council for Local Environmental Initiatives (ICLEI) in 1991 as a framework for local governments worldwide to implement the outcomes of the United Nations Conference on Environment and Development (UNCED). ICLEI, along with partner national and international local government associations and organizations (LGOs), championed the LA21 concept during the 1991–1992 UNCED preparatory process.

Following UNCED, local governments, national and international LGOs, and international and UN organizations began experimenting with implementing the LA21 concept. Some local governments, often supported by national municipal associations, developed LA21 planning approaches appropriate to their circumstances.

LA21 gets to grips with the capacity problem, which has limited other approaches (Boxes 3.13 and 3.15). It can help to address many weaknesses or limitations in local development planning and environmental management – they have increased the willingness of citizens, community organizations and NGOs to 'buy in' to planning and environmental management where they are organized in such a way as to encourage and support their participation. They also have some potential to integrate global environmental concerns into local plans.

LA21s represent a major innovation in local planning for sustainable development. They have an international identity and an international network, but are (meant to be) locally driven and implemented. At their best, Local Agenda 21s:

- are grounded in a broad inclusive process of consultation, coordinated by a local authority and drawing in all key stakeholders;
- ensure that environmental concerns, from the very localized to the global, enter the mainstream of urban planning and management;
- provide an efficient and equitable means of identifying common goals, reconciling conflicting interests and creating working partnerships between government agencies, private enterprises and civil society groups.

Experience with ten years of LA21s indicates that local leadership and commitment are critical, but that the success of a LA21 is also very context dependent. Their effectiveness depends on the accountability, transparency and capacity of local government, although they can also become a means for promoting these qualities. Thus, most examples of successful and influential LA21s come from cities where there have been major improvements in the quality of local government, only a few of which can be ascribed to the LA21 process itself. Similarly, the capacity and incentives for LA21s to integrate global environmental concerns into local plans depends on supportive national and international networks, although they can also help to strengthen such networks.

According to ICLEI (2002), LA21 processes are expanding worldwide: 6416 local authorities in 113 countries have now either made a formal commitment to LA21 or are actively undertaking the process; and national campaigns are under way in 18 countries accounting for 2640 processes.

The most successful LA21s can provide a source of inspiration for strategic planning for sustainable development, not only at the local level, but also at the national and international levels, where the establishment of associations of local authorities can help to provide collective voice and influence. They have helped to create new and better ways of managing local environments, and engaged a wide range of stakeholders in the process. There is also much to learn from the less successful examples, which illustrate some of the key obstacles to local sustainable development planning – including the dangers of staying at the margins of urban planning (and initiating a few minor projects but steering well clear of the major policy issues) or of underestimating the resistance to new ways of doing things (and going through the motions, without really changing the standard operating procedures of local government).

Several assessments can be found at www.iclei.org. They show that one of the most important challenges for effectiveness has been harmonizing national and local regulations and standards. Unless local actions and regulations are supported by national policy and regulatory frameworks, they cannot be effective. The establishment of a national association of local authorities can help to provide a collective voice and influence.

LA21 has actively encouraged city governments to share their experiences. This led LA21 practitioners to identify five key factors for success – which also accord with the principles and elements of strategies for sustainable development in Boxes 3.1 and 3.2.

- *Multi-sectoral engagement* in the planning process, through a local stakeholder group which serves as the coordination and policy body for preparing a local sustainable development action plan.
- *Consultation* with community groups, NGOs, business, churches, government agencies, professional groups and unions, in order to create a shared vision and to identify proposals and priorities for action.
- *Participatory assessment* of local social, economic and environmental conditions and needs.
- *Participatory target-setting* through negotiations among key stakeholders to achieve the vision and goals set forth in the action plan.
- *Monitoring and reporting procedures*, including local indicators, to track progress and to allow participants to hold each other accountable to the action plan.

Source: ICLEI (1997, 2000); Hardy et al (2001); Gordon McGranahan, personal communication

Box 3.20 Relations between Pakistan's national, provincial and district conservation strategies

Pakistan's National Conservation Strategy (NCS) called for more specific provincial strategies (PCSs). North West Frontier Province (NWFP or Sarhad) was the first to respond. It took participatory and integrating approaches a step further than the NCS, being the first province to:

- adopt multi-stakeholder round tables (informed by a Canadian model, through CIDA support);
- adopt district conservation strategies (DCSs) – in Chitral and Abbotabad;
- attempt to define 'indicators for sustainability' to measure progress;
- adopt provincial Sustainable Development Funds;
- attempt liaison between a PCS and private sector bodies.

Much experience in conservation strategies has accrued over time in Pakistan, in the NCS, then SPCS, and now via the DCSs. While the NCS lost the momentum of a learning process within government due to weak management at the centre, there has been continued learning during SPCS and DCSs. It is principally IUCN-Pakistan and some foreign donors that are actively monitoring that learning. A 1999–2000 Mid Term Review of the NCS (Hanson et al 2000) had this to say:

We have been struck by the extent to which most strategy activities operating at local levels have been demand-driven, while those operating at higher levels, especially at the NCS level, are supply-driven. The NCS deals with a worthy set of concepts that have an influence on the lives of people, but in the complex and abstract way in which they are presented, they represent an abundant supply of new thinking that appears to be beyond the grasp of institutions to implement properly. At very local levels, people and local institutions are reasonably clear in what they demand in the context of their particular community, household, etc. Pollution control objectives, waste management, clean drinking water, access to irrigation water of sufficient quality and abundance, income from wildlife protection, are examples. At the provincial level there is a mix of practical demands and an extensive supply of theoretical constructs about adequate natural resource and environmental management. This is abundantly clear in both the Sarhad and Balochistan Conservation Strategies.

[Thus we] conclude that the closer strategies operate to clients—the people of Pakistan and their local institutions—the more likely they are to reflect actual interest and demand, and therefore the more influential they are likely to be. Of course, there is still a need to have a continuing supply of ideas that may go beyond current demand, but as long as these are so far beyond the capacity and perhaps even interest/knowledge levels of people, it will be difficult to implement them. In essence, this means placing much greater emphasis on development of local level implementation and understanding of demand. It reinforces the need for the whole conservation strategy process to work in ways that are consistent with the government efforts at devolution, and to be able to monitor the demand side of sustainable development as carefully as possible in order to be reasonably certain of current concerns within specific districts and at the community level.

[There are] three interesting points in addition to the supply/demand issue. One is the flow from conservation principles to developmental priorities in moving from NCS to DCS. Secondly, the NCS still needs to deal with macro policy and international links as a set of concerns that may affect the other two levels. Third, the issue of scale-up and resource mobilization will be huge concerns at the district level, likely with a high degree of provincial intervention for both.

Without a coherent set of provincial strategies throughout the country, it will be more difficult for a revitalized NCS to be as effective as it should be. The NCS should be allowed to focus on national and international issues, and on supporting provincial strategies—the latter being driven largely from the provinces and, in turn, the districts.

The characteristics of the various strategies are compared in Table 3.4.

Table 3.4 **Comparison of strategies at different levels in Pakistan**

National Conservation Strategy	Provincial Conservation Strategy	District Conservation Strategy
Guidelines	Policy/ plan in progress	Plans
1980s concerns	1990s concerns	Current concerns
Intellectual push	Round tables freely discussing and promoting SD	Demand pull through village planning—asking for demonstration and action
Natural resource conservation principles	Broad mix of conservation and development issues	Developmental priorities
MISSING STILL?	*MISSING STILL?*	*MISSING STILL?*
Macroeconomic integration/ arguments International links Federal policy Linking PCSs together Information support Monitoring, learning	Prioritization Institutional reform and capacity Provincial policy change Support to private sector	Local governance and institutional capacity Resource mobilization Means for scale-up to cover many districts

DECENTRALIZED DEVELOPMENT PLANNING

Decentralized participatory planning is hampered by limited skills and capacity

Where governance is being decentralized, districts and municipalities increasingly assume devolved responsibility for sustainable development and are therefore required to prepare and implement development strategies and plans. There is a growing movement to do this through participatory processes, which can be backed by new legal requirements, as in Bolivia. However, the skills, attitudes and methods to undertake decentralized participatory planning are frequently lacking or weak, and the finances to implement plans inadequate. Often such plans are constrained by high-level policies – and at very least need to be passed upwards for harmonization and approval at regional and national levels, as in Ghana (Box 3.21) and Tanzania. In short, policy and institutional challenges need to be addressed if decentralized sustainable development planning is to be effective.

Village and micro-level strategies

Local institutions are the basis for participatory planning

Successful local strategies share a common focus on strengthened local institutions, whether villages, user groups or stakeholder organizations. These local institutions are the basis for participatory planning, joint action, 'striking deals' with service providers, monitoring and review, and – critically – for ensuring more effective coordination by higher-level authorities. In developing countries, there is considerable experience of village planning. Increasingly, such planning is undertaken in a strategic, participatory and transparent manner. In Tanzania, the HIMA (*Hifadhi Mazingira*, conserve the environment) programme and the *Tanzakesho* (Tanzania tomorrow) programmes help wards (of 3–5 villages) to prepare plans through identifying major problems, solutions and sources of required resources (Box 3.22). In Nepal, under the Sustainable Community Development Programme, CBOs have been trained to develop community plans reflecting shared economic, social and environmental priorities.

A variety of other local-level strategies are developed through mechanisms which are largely ignored by central government, but which could potentially provide important local pillars for a sustainable development strategy and a supporting coordination system. Some involve *traditional fora* in which communities and local groups are able to express concerns and agree actions to create culturally appropriate

---

Box 3.21 Decentralized planning in Ghana

The previous, highly centralized government planning system in Ghana marginalized local government. Now, a decentralized system has been introduced which is avowedly participatory and 'bottom-up'. Each of Ghana's 110 districts now has full responsibility to develop and implement its own medium-term (5 year) and annual District Development Plans that should address sustainable development, following guidelines prepared by the National Development Planning Commission (NDPC 1995). This responsibility lies with the District Assemblies (DAs) whose members are elected every four years from people ordinarily resident in the district. In addition, the President, in consultation with traditional authorities, can appoint one-third of the members – in practice from individuals nominated by the districts to ensure the inclusion of people with skills and expertise so that the business of local government is properly conducted. The District Chief Executive is also appointed by the President, subject to approval by the Assembly.

Bottom-up and integrated procedures: The base level for planning lies in Unit Committees for groups of settlements with a population of 500–1000 in rural areas and 1500 for urban areas. Community problems are identified here and goals set out and passed to the DA. Committees of the DA prioritize problems and opportunities. Departments of the DA together with sectoral specialists and NGOs collaborate to distil the ingredients of the District Plan. The District Planning Coordinating Unit integrates the district sectoral plans into long-term, medium-term and short-term and annual plans/budgets for consideration by the DA. District Planning Officers have received training to facilitate community meetings, through which communities can identify their concerns and needs. This process has led to some unexpected requests. One village, for example, wanted funds for a brass band, reasoning such a band at their weekly village market would attract other villages and enhance economic growth.

Each District Plan must be subjected to a public hearing. District Development Plans are harmonized at the regional level by Regional Coordinating Councils, and these regional plans are then consolidated with individual sector plans (prepared by line ministries and also subject to hearings) by the National Development Planning Commission (NDPC) into a National Development Plan. The NDPC undertakes this task through cross-sectoral planning groups that have representatives from the public sector, business, university, districts, trade unions and farmers. The first of these rolling medium-term development plans covered the period 1997–2000 (Ghana NDPC 1997). A second, covering 2001–2005, is under preparation.

Power and resources have been accorded to the districts: At least 5 per cent of internal government revenue is allocated by Parliament to the District Assemblies Common Fund, and legislation has given power to the DAs. Each year, Parliament agrees a formula for the distribution of the Fund. This takes into account the population of each district, weighted by its development status (judged pragmatically by indicators such as the number of pupils attending school, the presence of commercial banks) and its revenue mobilization effort (the percentage increase over the amount collected in the previous year). DAs are able to use these funds for capital expenditures in implementing their development plans. For example, five districts are currently implementing a poverty reduction programme under which targeted communities decide on what action is to be taken.

But capacity is weak – too few staff and too many demands: DAs have limited capacity to undertake these new responsibilities as districts still lack decentralized departments of many line ministries. In the past, line ministries operated centrally determined programmes and many had district-based staff. Under the Local Government Services Bill, district offices of line ministries will become departments of the DAs answerable to the DCE. However, there is resistance to the new arrangements and lingering allegiance of district level staff to their regional and national headquarters. Some staff have been reluctant to accept postings, particularly to deprived districts. The quality of district staff is generally poor, although it has improved following training courses and postings of national/regional staff to districts. As a result, some DAs have turned to consultancy firms to assist in the preparation of their plans.

The DAs have also become burdened by pressures from line ministries to establish a variety of district committees; for example, for environmental management, disasters and health. The new system also faces continuing logistical problems (inadequate accommodation, equipment, vehicles, etc) despite the establishment of the District Assemblies Common Fund.

---

sustainable societies, such as the traditional *khotla* system of village meetings in Botswana, and Maori *hui* meetings in New Zealand.

NGOs often mobilize local energies to combine socio-economic development and environmental conservation at the grass-roots level. For example, in Northern Pakistan, the Aga Khan Rural Support

Box 3.22 Village level planning in Iringa Rural District, Tanzania

HIMA (*Hifadhi Mazingira*, a Swahili phrase meaning 'conserve the environment') is a natural resource programme, funded by the Danish International Development Agency (DANIDA) since 1989, which operates in several districts in Iringa Region in Tanzania's southern highlands. The programme collaborates closely with central government, local government and local communities through research, extension and training to promote the sustainable and equitable use of resources by preventing and controlling the degradation of land, water and vegetation. Awareness raising and participation are central elements of the strategy. HIMA is supporting village institutions in allocating land to its most productive use, and is supporting the improvement of farming systems within given sub-catchments (watersheds). Since about 70 per cent of farmers in villages are women, the programme pays special attention to the needs of poor women and female-headed households, especially those who are involved in programme activities.

Within Iringa Rural District, HIMA-Iringa operates in three Divisions aiming to cover all 94 villages covering some 7000 km² and accounting for over half of the district. The approach involves:

- *Developing a logical framework* as a collaborative exercise by ward and division representatives, village-based extension staff, selected representatives of villages (progressive farmers, knowledgeable people).
- Preparing *guidelines for holistic studies*.
- *Training workshops* for HIMA staff in the divisions (especially extension officers) to elaborate the procedures and information to be collected.
- *Initial visits to villages* to explain the forthcoming activities and to determine dates for holistic studies; followed by development of a work programme.
- *Holistic studies in villages:* Teams of three district government officers spend about one week in each village to capture a broad balance of information (originally teams were as large as 22 people and spent 2 weeks in each village – but this proved too costly). The team works on particular themes (eg socio-economic data, land use planning, forestry demarcation, etc) using a mix of approaches (eg participatory rural appraisal, questionnaires, interviews, surveys, etc) and works with different groups of villagers (eg youth, women, farmers, etc) to compare ideas. This interactive process enables problems, priorities and possible solutions to be identified in partnership between HIMA and the villages. This is followed by data analysis and report writing. The output of the holistic studies, called a village profile report, sets out possible areas that might be supported in the village by HIMA. The information is also used by HIMA to monitor progress and achievement of goals.
- *Annual village planning:* Over time, as villages gain experience, they begin to prepare their plans alone. Each annual village plan is prepared by a village 'team' comprising the village government (20–25 members), progressive farmers selected by the village government and the village extension workers. In the first year, the plan is prepared through the holistic study process. In subsequent years, there is no such study but rather an evaluation and update process taking 4–5 days. This also involves preparing sub-plans for sub-villages by sub-groups (chaired by sub-village chairmen). These sub-plans are compiled by each of the village standing committees, which constitute the village government (usually: planning and finance, social welfare and self-reliance, and defence and security, but sometimes additional ones – each dealing with the issues under its responsibility). This produces the annual village plan and a budget is prepared.

  The plan is then submitted for approval to the Village Assembly, which all members of the village can attend. Village work plans list activities to be undertaken, from brick-making and a day-care centre to bridge-building and training in soil fertility, soil and water conservation, improvement and establishment and care of fruit tree nurseries; each with timing, place, target group and supervisor identified.
- *Submission of plans to HIMA and the District Council* (via Ward and Divisional Committees): A copy of each village plan is submitted to the Ward Development Committee to be passed upwards through the Divisional Committee to the District Council. The plans are consolidated and may be modified at each stage. Independent of this formal process, HIMA identifies the elements of individual village plans that it is able to support (ie those which fall within its remit, excluding roads, bridges, schools, hospitals and other similar infrastructure). This is undertaken through a district planning meeting attended by district heads of department, divisional secretaries, representatives of divisional extension staff and HIMA staff. Following this meeting:
- Implementation of activities.

Source: Kikula et al (1999)

Programme is now the leading organization supporting rural development, through catalysing, strengthening and linking together village organizations and ensuring their bargaining power is strong in relation to government, NGOs and private service providers. Resource user groups can also play an important role. For example, in Nepal, over the past 40 years, some 9000 forest user groups have assumed responsibility from government for the sustainable management of parcels of national forests and play an important role in sustainable development in remote villages.

NGOs can mobilize local energies

Much can be learned from the myriad approaches (coping strategies) of indigenous people, traditional societies and grass-roots organizations in many countries to sustainably meet their survival needs – approaches which have often worked effectively for centuries until disturbed by external influences which have interfered with their rights, access to resources, knowledge systems or social organization. Some assessments have shown that some of these approaches appear to have worked well, others less well or not at all sustainably (eg case studies undertaken under the Caribbean Capacity 21 programme, UNDP 1997). Deeper studies are needed to assess what can be learned from such micro-level strategies and how they can influence the treatment of risk and the building of resilience, through upstream policy formulation.

There is much to learn from indigenous approaches

Convergence and links between national, sub-national and local strategies

A range of initiatives such as the CDF, PRSP, national visioning, Local Agenda 21 and local-level planning initiatives can all encompass many of the principles set out in Box 3.1 and related elements in Box 3.2. They may also demonstrate potential for convergence between these different approaches and with the concept of a unified strategy for sustainable development.

Often there are several such initiatives ongoing in a particular country and most countries are faced with having to develop strategies and action plans in response to international obligations (eg under MEAs) and other external political or technical demands, ideas and initiatives as illustrated by Figure 3.4. This bombardment of both similar and conflicting requirements can be bewildering and place great strains on institutions, especially where capacities are weak. There are similar challenges of coherence between strategic initiatives at different levels within a country.

Countries are bombarded by international initiatives

Only occasionally have the different levels been deliberately linked. Box 3.20 provides an example from Pakistan, which shows such linkage, but it also demonstrates that initiatives can drift apart after an initial integration. It therefore can be critical to find ways of improving convergence around the principles of strategic planning, ensuring complementarity and coherence between:

Complementarity and coherence are needed between strategies across sectors and between national and sub-national levels

- national level strategies for different sectors and different international obligations;
- national, sub-national and local level strategies.

Based on the experience described above, convergence could be improved through:

- tiered participatory fora, leading up to a national council for sustainable development or a similar national forum (Box 3.14);
- frequent constructive reviews and participatory learning exercises cutting across several strategies – to identify what works and what doesn't (page 161);
- common strategic principles shared by all initiatives (Box 3.1);
- common facilities and functions (notably information, participation and coordination systems), and points for mutual reinforcement (Chapter 4);
- exposure of high-level policy-makers to a variety of approaches, and involvement in them, to begin the 'unfreezing' of key institutions enabling them to take a key role in sustainable development;

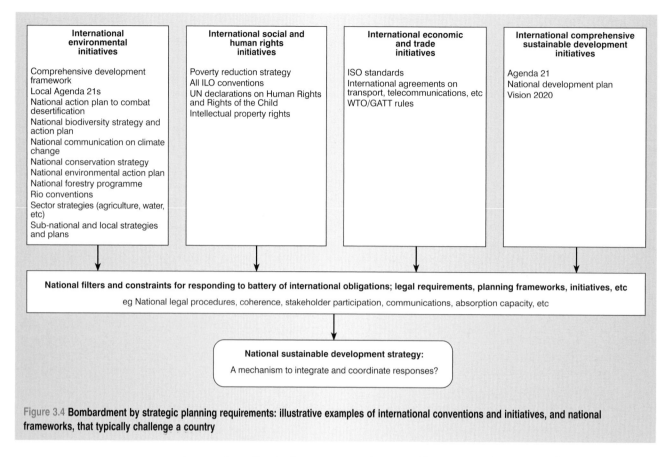

Figure 3.4 Bombardment by strategic planning requirements: illustrative examples of international conventions and initiatives, and national frameworks, that typically challenge a country

■ improved coordination between external partners (donor agencies) supporting these initiatives in developing countries, in order not to overwhelm national institutions with planning processes.

Strategies can evolve to integrate NSDS principles

Key principles for a NSDS are that it should provide a means for continuous learning and improvement, building on existing mechanisms and strategies. A number of examples illustrate how strategies can evolve to integrate NSDS principles. In Pakistan, following a mid-term review, the NCS framework is being built on to develop a NSDS (Box 3.12). In Uganda, the evolving approach to develop the PRSP demonstrates increasing incorporation of NSDS principles (Box 3.23).

Regional approaches to developing strategies

Regional strategies can help countries deal with some issues

In some parts of the world, regional strategies and overviews on the theme of sustainable development have been prepared. Countries have found this valuable particularly to deal with issues and priorities of a regional nature.

Examples from before UNCED include the Mediterranean Blue Plan (MBPRAC 1988) and 'Our Own Agenda' of the Latin American and Caribbean Commission on Development and Environment (LACCDE 1990). In 1993, the comprehensive Environmental Action Programme for Central and Eastern Europe spelled out a process to equalize environmental conditions in the East and West, with an emphasis on the urban environment.

In December 1999, the Helsinki meeting of the European Council invited the European Commission to prepare a proposal for a long-term strategy to integrate policies for economically, socially and ecologically sustainable development. In March 2001 the European Commission issued a consultation paper (SEC(2002)517) providing initial views on the challenges and opportunities for such a strategy, discussing

Box 3.23 **The Uganda PRSP**

In 1995, Uganda started a process of developing a comprehensive sustainable development strategy with an overall objective of wiping out abject poverty in the country. By 1997, this process had produced the draft Poverty Eradication Action Plan (PEAP), which aims at reducing the population living in absolute poverty by 10 per cent in 2017. In 2000, this was revised to incorporate new information generated from widened consultations and analysis, particularly from the pilot Participatory Poverty Assessments (PPAs) undertaken and analysed over the past three years. The revised PEAP also reflects progress in various sectors in terms of elaborating on their policies, investment plans, outcomes and performance indicators. Besides roads and education, the major additions relate to health, modernization of agriculture, private sector competitiveness, water, sanitation, and justice, law and order. The PEAP therefore offers a fairly comprehensive development framework (CDF) and the PEAP summary was adopted in 2000 as Uganda's Poverty Reduction Strategy Paper (PRSP).

Based on the PEAP as the guiding policy framework, Uganda has pursued the development and implementation of sector-wide policies, investment plans and programmes, with the participation of representatives of as many stakeholders as possible. It is a genuine partnership, which involves the government, both at the centre and in the Districts; external funding agencies (development partners); civil society and NGOs; and the private sector. Uganda's strategic action plan for mass poverty eradication is based on four interrelated pillars for ensuring: sustainable economic growth and structural transformation; good governance and security; the ability of the poor to raise incomes; and improvement of the quality of life.

In Uganda, the focus of economic planning has moved away from the forecasting and management of macro-economic aggregates. Instead, it has turned to the process of refining and implementing a Poverty Reduction Strategy (PRS) which is sustainable in terms of policies, plans and programmes, ensuring proper resource management, and operating within a fully comprehensive development framework. The aim is to transform Uganda into a modern economy in which all agents, in all sectors, can participate in economic growth, keeping in mind the needs of future generations.

Analysis shows that many of the NSDS principles and elements (Boxes 3.1 and 3.2) have been applied successfully during the development of the PRSP as described above:

- strong political leadership;
- shared strategic and pragmatic vision;
- nationally owned and country-driven processes;
- built on existing knowledge, expertise and capacity;
- built on existing mechanisms and strategies;
- spearheaded by a strong institution;
- the widest possible participation;
- process anchored in sound technical analysis;
- short-term linked to the medium- and long-term;
- coherence between budget and strategy priorities;
- continuity of the strategy development process.

while other principles have presented major challenges:

- integrated and balanced strategy;
- setting realistic but flexible targets;
- linking national and local priorities and actions;
- building mechanisms for monitoring, evaluation and feedback.

Source: Muduuli (2001)

important trends and presenting a policy toolkit to tackle them. A European strategy for sustainable development was then prepared and adopted in June 2001 at the European Council meeting in Gothenbrg. This strategy builds on a series of previous five-yearly environmental action plans. Under the new strategy, major European policy proposals are to include:

- sustainability impact assessments;
- EU institutions improving internal policy coordination between different sectors;
- Member States developing national sustainability plans.

Headline indicators are being developed to allow annual reviews of progress.

Small island states have found it particularly useful to work together to share experience and design common approaches, particularly because of their many shared characteristics, challenges and vulnerabilities – notably to external influences. For example, the South Pacific Regional Environmental Programme (SPREP)[9] coordinates the preparation of four-year action plans for managing the environment of the Pacific Islands region. The latest plan (2001–2004) was developed through a highly participatory process and embodies the vision of SPREP members and key stakeholders for the long-term management of their shared environment.

It is the main planning document which identifies broad priorities and key result areas of the regional agenda and associated capacity-building processes and interventions. It is intended to be implemented by SPREP member governments and administrations in conjunction with organizations and individuals who are active in the protection of the environment and natural resources of the region. (www.sprep.org.ws/)

During the 1990s, guided by the regional action plan, SPREP coordinated a programme to facilitate the development of national environmental management strategies (NEMs) in 14 Pacific region island countries. The countries worked together, through SPREP, to a broadly common format and strategy process. Building on the NEMs, SPREP is now coordinating a regional capacity-building programme for sustainable development.

A similar regional approach has been taken by the Organization of Eastern Caribbean States (OECS) – a political grouping of eight member states that has developed a common approach to address developmental problems. This arrangement helps to overcome problems such as limited capacity and resources in individual countries, and members of the OECS have benefited from economies of scale. The OECS states used a participatory process to fashion an Eastern Caribbean Environmental Charter, which provides a legal framework for action – enshrining the principles of sustainable development – as well as a progressive management tool for 'island systems management'. Box 3.24 summarizes those principles of the Charter that are of relevance to NSDSs.

Box 3.24 The Eastern Caribbean Environmental Charter: principles relevant to strategies for sustainable development

---

Principle 1: Foster Improvement in the quality of life

Each contracting state should develop and promote programmes to address poverty, health, employment, education, social development and provision of basic human needs to improve the quality of life within the carrying capacity of its natural resources, and giving due consideration to levels of acceptable change.

Principle 2: Integrate social, economic and environmental considerations into national development plans and programmes within the concept of island systems management (ISM)

---

9 SPREP is the regional technical and coordinating organization responsible for environmental matters in the Pacific region. SPREP works on behalf of its 26 members, which include all 22 islands and territories, and four developed countries with direct interests in the region: Australia, France, New Zealand and the United States of America.

Each Contracting State agrees to:

- pursue sustainable development policies aimed at poverty and its alleviation, the general improvement of social, economic and cultural conditions, the conservation of biological diversity, the mitigation of adverse effects of climate change and the maintenance of essential ecological processes and life support systems;
- formulate integrated development plans and programmes to ensure that environmental management is treated as an integral component of the planning processes in pursuit of sustainable development;
- ensure that any action likely to impact significantly on the environment, shall only be taken subject to a prior assessment of the effects of such action on the environment, and subject further to the requisite authorization, following on that assessment;
- take steps to ensure the sustainable use of natural resources which recognize the intricate linkages between ecological systems in small island states, and between these systems and human activity, consistent with the concept of ISM.

Principle 3: Improve on legal and institutional frameworks

Each Contracting State agrees to:

- create or strengthen existing national agencies with responsibility for environmental management to achieve effective management of natural resources;
- rationalize the roles of national environmental agencies to maximize efficiency in managing the use of natural resources;
- collaborate in the rationalization of regional environmental agencies, networks and institutions to reduce duplication, and to realize maximum cost effectiveness;
- support and enhance the capacity of non-governmental and community-based organizations for environmental management;
- strengthen and enforce environmental legislation to effectively implement the principles contained in this charter and reflect the precautionary approach to environmental management;
- create legal and institutional frameworks that allow for the effective participation of the relevant public, private, non-governmental and community-based organizations in environmental management.

Source: OECS (2001)

CHAPTER

4

Key Steps in Starting or Improving Strategies for Sustainable Development[1]

Harnessing effective strategic mechanisms in a continual-improvement system

The guidance in this chapter is based on practical experience

In each country that participated in the OECD DAC project on strategies for sustainable development, stakeholder dialogues were organized to examine current and past strategic planning processes and to assess how they had been conducted, what had worked well or less well, and the reasons for this. These dialogues and wider experience from around the world suggest a number of steps that will assist a country in strengthening its strategic planning processes and moving them in the direction of a sustainable development strategy. This entails the identification, coordination and continuous improvement of mechanisms that can help towards balancing the economic, social and environmental concerns of multiple stakeholders. Figure 4.1 illustrates the types of mechanisms that usually will be needed. The way that these mechanisms are coordinated must be consistent with the principles and elements in Boxes 3.1 and 3.2 – most notably, that of continual improvement, the only practical way to deal with large change agendas in situations of uncertainty and limited resources.[2]

A continuous improvement approach is most practical

To achieve a continual improvement process, the mechanisms need to work together as an action-learning system. A continuous improvement approach is broadly cyclical (illustrated in Figure 4.2). Priorities

1 This chapter has benefited from review comments and additional material provided by Ralph Cobham, UK; Jorge Reyes, Philippines; and Joseph Opio-Odongo, Uganda.

2 This premise is supported by two decades of experience of quality/environmental management systems in progressive corporations and government agencies; and also by the experience of pioneering efforts by some segments in wider society (especially civil society organizations): to revitalize or help to create new institutional mechanisms, to change the rules of engagement for stakeholders, to build infrastructure to link initiatives and learn from each other, and to encourage greater participation to allow the vision of sustainable development to flourish across society.

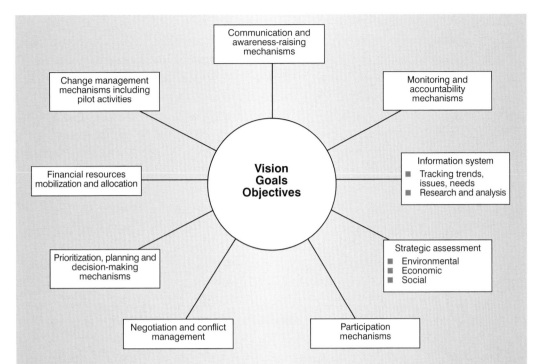

Explanation: This figure visualizes suggested basic elements of a system for developing and implementing a strategy for sustainable development. The system should encourage and facilitate the building of consensus in society about a vision, goals and objectives for sustainable development (the centre circle). It should provide a coordinated set of information and institutional mechanisms to deliver these (the satellite boxes). In establishing such a system, there is a need to look at precedents, recent trends and improvements in mechanisms beyond branded and packaged approaches that might provide examples on how to make progress – adhering to the basic principles and elements set out in Boxes 3.1 and 3.2. Note that this figure does not cover the particular relationships between the different elements: these should be designed for a particular case. Figure 4.2 suggests a basic 'continuous improvement' approach to such relationships.

Figure 4.1 **Constellation of mechanisms contributing to a strategy for sustainable development**

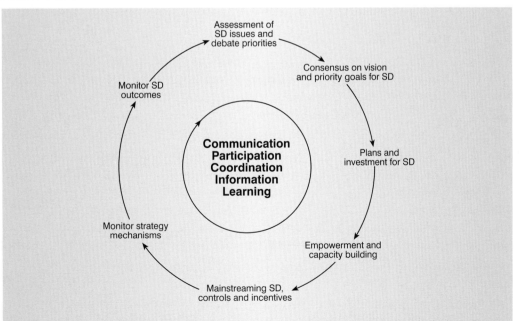

Note: The figure shows some of the more important relations between the mechanisms shown in Figure 4.1. As portrayed, it suggests that the overall process involves a rigid sequence of steps. However, in practice, these are ongoing and necessarily overlap. Key features of the central tasks are stakeholder identification, strengthening capacity, collaboration and outreach

Figure 4.2 **The continuous improvement approach to managing sustainable development strategies**

are dealt with first; experiments are incorporated; lessons learned are shared; time is taken for people to realize the need for change and to change attitudes and approaches. The idea is to achieve key targets to build both the capacity (especially analytical and problem-solving skills) and the commitment that will enable even more challenging targets to be addressed. The process and its outcomes (whether institutional changes, legal reforms, particular initiatives or action programmes, etc) are monitored and evaluated to provide lessons and feedback for review and revision. The strategy, through an iterative process, thus operates as a knowledge system that coordinates the collection of information, analysis, monitoring and communication.

In contrast, unsuccessful strategies have usually been linear processes, that is, designing, implementing and (sometimes) monitoring a new strategy as separate phases. This has usually resulted, at best, in only partial implementation (see section on learning from current practice, page 35). The agenda has been too big to deal with over the strategy 'project's' short life; there has been inadequate time for experimentation, feedback, debate and attitudinal change; the component activities are seen as 'outside' day-to-day reality and are given less attention; and there is no way of dealing with changed circumstances such as economic difficulties – the actual realities that strategies should accommodate. In other words, there has been very limited room to manoeuvre.

Usually, there will be many possible 'entry points' to the strategy process

Figure 4.2 is not intended to describe strict phases in a strategy 'cycle', with an obligatory starting point and sequence. A key task (described in detail in the section on mapping out the strategy process, page 102) is to take stock of which of the strategic mechanisms shown in Figure 4.1 already exist, especially those that have effective stakeholder engagement processes and collaborative structures. These mechanisms and elements, and their associated tasks, are likely to be spread among a variety of local and national strategic planning frameworks as well as one-off initiatives such as the more recent NCSs and NEAPs. Taking stock might involve national debate and analysis among a wide range of stakeholders on what the different strategic approaches have to offer and whether prerequisites for effective strategies are in place; for example, whether the country is in peace, with democratic systems, freedom of speech and the rule of law.

A strategy system must improve synergies and encourage participation

Bringing together 'what works' can be cost-effective and credible, ensuring 'buy-in': This would enable a strengthened strategy system or framework to be constructed, using the best of what currently exists to improve synergies, remove inconsistencies, avoid conflicts and fill gaps. The system would not *plan* everything, but would largely aim to *guide* change in circumstances of uncertainty, and to encourage a culture of experimentation and innovation. This 'framework' approach is conducive to wide ownership, as it can accommodate many thematic, regional, decentralized and local strategies, some of which may have been around for some time, as well as others which will be developed in the future.

Sometimes it may be desirable to develop a new comprehensive strategy. This could be the case where stakeholders agree that a new identity is required, either because of problems with past approaches or to signal a fresh vision and major investment in strategy mechanisms. Care must be taken in introducing a new initiative, as it is then all too easy to ignore existing approaches, to compete with them and to cause confusion, if not resentment. Even if a new identity is required, it should be presented and promoted as building on what has been achieved so far – especially if this involves learning the lessons from previous failures.

It is essential to use and strengthen existing capacities

Whether an 'evolved' or a brand new approach is adopted, it is essential from the outset to use and strengthen capacities to plan and implement on a nationwide scale. These are challenging tasks because the resultant strategy will need to address all of the main development issues that confront society: health, transport, energy, water and food supply, natural and cultural resource conservation, and so on. In short, the goal is to 'mainstream' sustainability into administrations, sectors and livelihoods. Strategies do this through processes of debate, agreement, learning and ultimately behaviour change. This can only work if stakeholders are involved in the strategy. As processes that promote continuous improvement, strategies themselves are an efficient way to build capacity. Usually adequate national/local resources will be available to keep a strategy process alive if there is enough understanding about its importance, and if the process is designed continually to improve efficiency and effectiveness.

Bearing these points in mind, illustrative steps for identifying, coordinating and developing strategy mechanisms are summarized in Box 4.1, and explored further in the rest of this chapter. Further details on operating the component mechanisms – analysis, debate, communication, planning, strategic decision-making, financing, implementation, monitoring, evaluation and review – are offered in Chapters 5–10.

Scoping exercise

One of the earliest tasks involves conducting a 'scoping' exercise. This is likely to test and ideally capture the interest of multiple stakeholders. It would entail an initial assessment of the need for, and approach to, sustainable development (see Chapter 2), looking at which actors might be affected by a strategy process and its possible outcomes, and considering the notional costs and benefits. It would also involve a preliminary examination of the opportunities and challenges of undertaking the steps suggested in Box 4.1 and the likely actors. In particular, it would entail:

An early task is to identify stakeholders' views on sustainable development priorities and benefits of a strategy

- First, identifying what stakeholders consider to be the top priority economic, social, institutional, environmental and technological **issues** (problems and opportunities). Chapters 5 and 6 cover the analytical and participatory tasks required to do this.
- Second, estimating the net **benefits** that stakeholders can expect to derive from all of the resources required to provide the solutions. This component will need to embrace both quantitative and qualitative dimensions. An example from Barbados is provided in Table 4.1. Chapters 5, 6 and 8 also cover aspects of the methods involved in quantifying benefits, costs and risks.

Not until such a 'scoping' exercise is either well advanced or completed is it usually possible to achieve the required commitment to the whole strategic planning process from a country's prime decision-makers. Furthermore, the determination and weighing of priority issues[3] can serve as an extremely helpful way of identifying the nature and composition of the institution that should be commissioned to coordinate the overall process. The 'scoping' exercise itself can, if necessary, be facilitated either by an existing multi-disciplinary development planning unit within a lead ministry or by an ad hoc team specifically established for the purpose.

The scoping exercise can help to build high level commitment

Establishing or strengthening a strategy secretariat or coordinating body

The steps and functions suggested in Box 4.1 and the mechanisms shown in Figure 4.1 will require careful management and coordination for effective progress to be made. It will, therefore, be necessary to establish some form of secretariat or coordinating body. A strategy secretariat is needed for the following *key tasks*:

A secretariat is needed for key tasks …

---

3 Experience has repeatedly shown the need for such priority issues to be addressed in the 'macro' rather than the narrow or 'micro' context. A classic example relates to the development of a multi-sectoral strategy designed to conserve and use sustainably the tropical high forest resources of a country. There has been a tendency by some international agencies (particularly the bilateral aid agencies) to seek to address the issue in relation to forestry alone. However, in reality, it calls for an integrated multi-sectoral approach, involving such dimensions as good governance; poverty alleviation; rural infrastructure development; community value systems; agricultural and population pressures; the non-timber values of forests (eg wildlife, water catchment, tourism); international and local trading patterns and markets; institutional capacities and reforms; certification and sustainable management tools; national parks and biodiversity management.

Box 4.1 Illustrative steps for starting, managing and continually improving a strategy for sustainable development

The following steps apply in full to strategy development tasks, that is, those needed to scope out and establish the strategy by building on existing mechanisms, and/or initiating new mechanisms if necessary. But the same or similar tasks are then iterative during strategy coordination and continuous improvement.

A useful first step is to undertake an initial *scoping exercise* to identify stakeholders' views on priority issues that need to be addressed, and to estimate the benefits that might derive from developing and implementing a strategy. Such an exercise would involve a preliminary examination of the opportunities for, and challenges of, undertaking the steps suggested below (page 77).

It should not be assumed that the subsequent steps should be undertaken as a rigid sequence. In practice many of them will need to be pursued in parallel and some might best make use of opportunities as they arise.

(a) Establish or strengthen a *secretariat or coordinating body* acceptable to stakeholders, with sufficient authority and resources to coordinate the steps outlined in this box, and the continuing strategy mechanisms (page 77).

(b) Establish or strengthen a *steering committee or equivalent multi-stakeholder forum* (eg National Council for Sustainable Development) with a broad balance of representation from government, the private sector and civil society acceptable to stakeholders (page 77).

(c) Seek or improve *political commitment* to the strategy preparation and implementation process from the highest levels as well as all other levels (page 82).

(d) Secure or confirm a *mandate* for the strategy. The more this represents domestic public demand with high-level support, rather than external mandates, the better (page 85).

(e) Identify the *stakeholders* that will own the preparation and implementation of an integrated sustainable development strategy, and encourage discussion of their (potential) roles (page 85).

(f) Ensure *broad-based ownership* by key ministries and agencies, civil society and the private sector (pages 87–90).

(g) Mobilize the *required resources*. Identify, secure, and allocate in a timely and accountable manner, the required:
   - skills, and sources of knowledge and learning;
   - management, legal and institutional support;
   - financial resources (page 90).

(h) Define and seek agreement on the roles of *stakeholders* (ie their rights, responsibilities, rewards, and relations) – private sector, civil society (eg NGOs, local communities), donors, national and local government, the Secretariat, etc (page 94).

(i) *Map out the strategy process*, taking stock of *existing processes and mechanisms*:
   - catalogue the range of existing strategies related to sustainable development;
   - identify the issues covered, vision, goals and responsibilities;
   - identify mechanisms and processes used by existing strategies (see Figure 4.1);
   - review achievements of these mechanisms in terms of synergies, clashes and gaps, and their outcomes;
   - determine the existence/extent of sectoral policy conflicts and inconsistencies, and the work necessary to resolve them;
   - identify what is required to improve synergies and plug gaps (page 102).

(j) Develop or improve *coherence* and *coordination* between strategy frameworks at all levels from international to local; and between and within sectors (page 104).

(k) Establish or improve the *ground rules* governing the strategy process:
   - debate and agree how all decisions will be made and agreed, and uncertainty dealt with;
   - coordinate means for negotiation of trade-offs and conflict management (page 110).

(l) Establish and promote a *schedule or broad calendar* for the strategy process – determine activities, responsibilities, capabilities and resources needed, and their timing (page 112).

(m) *Promote* the strategy as a unified concept. Possibly publish a 'prospectus' for the strategy outlining all the above (page 112).

(n) Establish or improve provisions for *regular analysis, debate, communication, planning, implementation, monitoring and review*; to ensure that all stakeholders are best able to play their part in the strategy. These processes are the 'heart' of the strategy and are discussed in detail in separate chapters. They will involve establishing or improving:

- *means for analysing* sustainability, stakeholders, mechanisms and processes, and scenarios (Chapter 5);
- *regular stakeholder fora and other means for participation* (thematic, national, decentralized and local) to reach and improve consensus on basic vision, goals, principles, system components, pilot activities, targets and responsibilities, and to review progress (Chapter 6);
- *communication and information systems* to ensure regular flows of information concerning both the strategy and sustainable development between stakeholders and between fora. This will include development of key information products to improve awareness and stimulate action, and the establishment of knowledge management systems to ensure sharing of experience and facilitate collective learning (Chapter 7);
- *major decision-making arrangements*, notably: structures and roles; handling global and local values and risk; means of delivering consensus and handling negotiations; and ways of linking those involved (Chapter 8);
- *implementation services and control mechanisms* – means for selecting policy implementation instruments (regulations, incentives and voluntary mechanisms) and applying them (Chapter 8);
- *means for planning investments* – tasks involved in making the case to different investment sources, and the criteria that should be used (Chapter 9);
- *monitoring and accountability mechanisms* to assess both strategy processes and their results. These will include: developing and reviewing sustainability indicators, baselines, standards and codes of practice; identifying and encouraging innovative processes to promote the culture of action-learning; independent monitoring; and feedback to decision-making (Chapter 10).

Source: Modified from OECD DAC (2001a)

- Organizing and coordinating the overall strategy processes.
- Gaining confidence and support for the process from key political groups, statutory bodies and (where needed) donor organizations.
- Planning specific activities, meetings and events.
- Facilitating the setting of agendas at all stages of the strategy process, and follow-up of decisions/agreements.
- Budgeting for and procuring expertise and resources.
- Ensuring that the roles of participants in strategy processes are clearly established.[4]
- Supporting working groups and other committees.
- Acting as a communications focal point for information and enquiries.
- Ensuring adherence to timetables.

Thus the secretariat does not make the key decisions on strategy goals, policies, and so on, nor is it expected to undertake everything itself, but to fulfil an organizing, anchoring and support role to provide day-to-day coordination on a continuing basis within a broadly agreed timescale. The secretariat needs to command the respect and trust of stakeholders and to discharge its functions in an open and neutral way. Past experience shows that a secretariat works best if it is located centrally within government; for example, within the office of the president or prime minister or within a body which has recognized authority for cross-government and cross-sectoral coordination such as the ministry of finance and development planning or a national planning commission (often the latter are directly responsible to the president or prime minister). Where a secretariat is placed within a line ministry, there is the danger that the strategy will become, and be seen as, an activity of that ministry and will cease to command the wider acceptance and support that is needed. Alternatively, a secretariat can be established in an independent body – or one with

... fulfilling an organizing, anchoring and support role ...

4 Sometimes it may be required to identify and resolve potential conflicts between stakeholder groups, or to engage neutral and independent third parties for this task.

Table 4.1 **Scoping some of the main benefits of preparing a national conservation strategy in Barbados**

A.1 Generic benefits applying to all or most stakeholders and sectors of society	1 Generation of increased GNP through resource restoration, implementation of sustainable development programmes and new resource use opportunities (eg recycling of wastes) 2 Generation of employment
A.2 Generic benefits to decision-makers that also apply to most other stakeholders	1 Establishment of the linkages between environment and sectoral economic development policies and integration programmes (eg the tourism and craft industries) 2 Identification and removal of the policy gaps 3 Formulation of policies and programmes for pollution prevention, control and 'clean-up' 4 Identification and use of appropriate performance indicators
B.1 Specific benefits for the 'educators': formal and non-formal sectors	1 Identification of issues, practices and linkages to be communicated 2 Modification of curricula to include sustainability dimensions 3 Procurement of the necessary funding
B.2 Specific benefits for NGOs and community groups	1 Clarification of priority sustainable development actions required 2 Coordination of research and training programmes to avoid duplication and to achieve optimal benefits 3 Assistance with procurement of donor funding support
B.3 Specific benefits for the media	1 Identification of the main sustainable development issues likely to be newsworthy over the next 3–5 years and the potential roles of different sectors of the media 2 Assistance with the procurement of funds to assist in raising the standards and levels of public awareness about sustainability issues and practical solutions
B.4. Specific benefits for the business community and property developers	1 Identification of the potentially most helpful sustainability contributions that this sector can make 2 Provision of greater opportunities to achieve accreditation as a 'green or sustainable company' 3 Increased access to incentives to participate in resource conservation and enhancement 4 Improved scope for opportunities to win customer/public acclaim for sustainability performance improvements
B.5 Specific benefits for the general public	1 Introduction of measures which result in the reduction of all forms of pollution and environmental degradation, plus enhancement of the living environment 2 Enhanced opportunities for gaining stakeholder recognition and awareness about the key improvements that are required

Source: Cobham (1990

a broad mandate – acceptable to all stakeholders and especially to government (for example, a parastatal, or a national research council as was the case in Zambia where stakeholders agreed that the council was sufficiently independent and objective to run an effective forum).

At the outset, when the strategy is being designed and support sought from different constituencies, it might only need a few staff. More may be required later when analyses and facilitation functions are needed. But, in general, a secretariat should limit what it undertakes itself and rely, wherever possible, on bringing together and commissioning others to work together on tasks, or on tapping into the capabilities of existing affiliated networks. For this to succeed, it will be essential for all those involved to demonstrate an ability to relate to multi-sectoral perspectives rather than to single sector needs.

To command confidence, respect and support from all stakeholders, the secretariat will need to operate in an open and transparent way. It will also need highly skilled staff with experience of coordinating multi-stakeholder processes (see Box 4.6).

... and it must operate in an open and transparent way

Although best located centrally within government (for coordination purposes), the secretariat should not be established as a formal organ of government. Rather it has been found best for a secretariat to be responsible to a broadly based and formally mandated steering committee or equivalent forum (see below).

Establishing or strengthening a strategy steering committee or equivalent forum

A multi-stakeholder steering committee, comprising representatives of the private sector and civil society as well as government, has generally been found necessary to ensure equitable governance of the strategy processes and to make the key decisions. This body needs to be seen both to have, and to be able to exercise, the powers required to formulate a strategy, achieve consensus on its scope and content, and monitor its development, implementation and impacts.

A multi-stakeholder steering committee should have overall responsibility for the strategy process

Its *key tasks* include:

- promoting acceptance (in political circles) of the need for, and benefits of, the participation of stakeholders in the strategy process;
- encouraging the sustained participation of key stakeholder groups in the development, implementation, monitoring and evaluation of the strategy, its outcomes and impacts;
- providing general oversight of the strategy process, and particularly representation of stakeholders within it;
- taking responsibility for the appointment and conduct of the secretariat;
- approving process design and revisions;
- reviewing major evidence on sustainable development problems and potentials;
- reviewing technical and policy options;
- making policy decisions (or recommendations to higher authorities where needed);
- obtaining (when required) timely decisions from higher authorities that enable strategic planning and implementation processes to be seen to be working;
- reviewing and approving major strategy documents and progress reports, and formal submission of such documents to government, where needed;
- providing appropriate advocacy for the process among respective constituencies (government, private sector, civil society and, where appropriate, the donor community) to engender confidence.

It is the membership and procedures of this committee or forum that form the 'heart' of the strategy process. As such, they will largely determine the credibility of the strategy – whether it is perceived as a venture reflective of society at large, and not merely another government project or donor-driven initiative. For similar reasons, it is preferable for the chairperson of such a steering committee/forum to be an independent, eminent person not beholden to any particular interest group. The steering committee/forum needs to meet regularly. Where an NCSD has been established as recommended by Agenda 21 (see Box 3.14),[5] this can serve as a ready-made NSDS steering committee. Box 4.2 provides an example of a specially convened steering committee for Balochistan in Pakistan.

Preferably, the chairperson should be independent

---

5 Box 8.7 gives even more detail on NCSD mandate, structure and composition, and Box 8.8 on decision-making approaches.

Box 4.2 Membership of steering committee for Balochistan Conservation Strategy, Pakistan

Government of Balochistan

Additional Chief Secretary (Development), Planning and Development Department (Chairman)
Secretary, Environment, Wildlife, Livestock, Forests and Tourism Department
Secretary, Education, Culture, Sports and Youth Affairs Department
Secretary, Finance Department

Civil society

Chief Executive, Balochistan Rural Support Programme (an umbrella organization focusing on institutional, vocational capacity-building of CBOs)
Country Representative, IUCN Pakistan
Chairman, Society for Torghar Environmental Protection (a community-based project)
Chairperson, Female Education Trust

Private sector

President, Balochistan Chamber of Commerce and Industries

Note: The NGO sector in Balochistan is extremely weak. Given this fact, the inclusion of two organizations operating at the grass-roots level was considered to be most balanced

Source: Government of Balochistan and IUCN Pakistan (2000); Maheen Zehra (personal communication)

Seeking or improving political commitment for the strategy

Political commitment is vital

Political commitment at the higher levels (eg parliamentary, cabinet or head of state) and at decentralized levels (eg members of parliament) is central to an effective strategy, notably to:

- ensure that priority sustainable development issues can be addressed from multi-sectoral dimensions rather than narrow sector standpoints;
- underpin appreciation that in order to progress towards sustainable development, a magnitude of interrelated issues need to be addressed in terms of their physical, social, economic, financial, technical and environmental implications;
- enable the strategy coordinating system to work (the secretariat and steering committee will rely on political support for their formation and operation);
- ensure that the principles and elements set out in Boxes 3.1 and 3.2 are followed throughout the strategy process;
- ensure that the NSDS vision and objectives incorporate political goals consistent with sustainable development;
- conversely, ensure that the NSDS vision and objectives are reflected in political aspirations, developments, plans and policy statements;
- ensure that the policy implications of the strategy are followed and considered throughout the process, and not merely at some formal end-point (to allow a continuous improvement approach to work);
- make decisions on recommended policy and institutional changes;
- ensure that changes are introduced and followed through;
- instruct government departments that relevant policies, plans and procedures should be coordinated with the strategy;
- commit government funds (and, if necessary, donor assistance);
- keep the strategy process open and inclusive, and not confidential and closed – encouraging

participation in the strategy, giving participants ready access to information, and encouraging them to adopt critical approaches.

Sustainable development is about making key decisions for transforming society. This is very close to the realm of politics. But the two have been viewed separately: previous sustainable development plans have too often been seen as technocratic dreams, and the political support essential to sustainable development has been missing. They need to come together in non-partisan ways, by dealing with real stakeholder needs, and with real constraints in a step-by-step (continual improvement) process.[6]

Sustainable development is a political process – it requires key decisions

The pioneering first Netherlands' National Environmental Policy Plan (NEPP) was, to a large extent, a response to public concerns about pollution (Box 4.3). Similarly, political demand for Canada's Green Plan (1990–1996) grew out of increased environmental awareness in the late 1980s, particularly concern about local air quality following accidents involving polychlorinated biphenyls (PCBs). In the run up to the UN Conference on Environment and Development (UNCED) in 1992, the environment became the number one public issue with demands that the federal government 'do something'.

Box 4.3 The Netherlands' National Environmental Policy Plan – a response to public pressure

The main motivation behind The Netherlands' first National Environmental Policy Plan (NEPP) and subsequent plans was a desire to bring about a shift from a sectoral to a theme-based approach to environmental planning and management. The report of the Brundtland Commission (WCED 1987) was very influential and 'provided a strong tail wind'. Public opinion was strongly in favour of the government playing a more active role on the environment. This had come about for various reasons, including the Chernobyl accident in 1986, the coming to light in the 1980s of domestic scandals concerning soil pollution in the 1970s, and the high public expenditure needed to deal with the pollution created by attempts to clean up the water. In the 1970s and 1980s, it was possible to smell polluted air and see waste heaps grow.

The Cabinet, which wanted to 'take a lead', established the NEPP process in 1987. But there was also strong leadership from key individuals in the Ministry of Housing, Spatial Planning and the Environment (VROM), who saw the need for NEPP, were not 'afraid of other influential ministries' and who 'made possible the enormous jump forward represented by NEPP'.

Source: Dalal-Clayton (1996)

In some cases, strategy development has followed a decree by the head of state or the prime minister because of their commitment to a particular cause or development approach. For example, preparation of Zambia's NCS was launched in 1981 on the instruction of former President Kenneth Kaunda who had long been committed to conservation. He was much persuaded by the goals of the World Conservation Strategy (IUCN/UNEP/WWF 1980) and committed his country to developing the first NCS. Similarly, Ghana's Vision 2020 (Ghana NDPC 1994) was the idea of former President Gerry Rawlings who had a vision that Ghana could become a middle-income country within a generation. The weight given to strategies by such presidential involvement can give the bodies charged with coordinating them (the NCS Secretariat in

---

6 Politicians have found it relatively easy to make speeches on sustainable development, which offers good buzzwords and easy-to-use phrases that can be used rather vaguely and without serious commitment; for example, 'developing an integrated response to global threats' and 'involving stakeholders in a partnership with government'. The concept of sustainable development and what it really implies for governance is still rather intangible to politicians. It has been far easier to make election promises and commitments over sectoral or stakeholder-specific concerns, especially when these have clear political advantage. Equally, sustainable development planners have too easily seen their work as separate from the 'messy' world of politics and too often blame failure on 'a lack of political will'. In reality, political commitment is generated by social forces and dynamic balancing of interests – and NSDS processes are designed to help this materialize in a positive way.

Zambia, the National Development Planning Commission in Ghana) considerable 'authority' to bring government departments together.

But political support can also mask negative trends and realities

Yet political support and other excellent features of a strategy process can mask the march of negative trends. There is a danger that success in 'process' terms can provide false security that outcomes are being achieved; that is, the very resources that the process seeks to sustain are still being lost. For example, in Ghana's case, substantial depletion of the country's tropical rainforest took place during the period when the Vision 2020 was being prepared (Vordzorgbe et al 2001). In Malawi, there was an even more acute gulf between aspiration and reality. Here, while an exemplary suite of sustainable development documents was being developed, the country continued to suffer major loss of forests and soil erosion. This points to the need to ensure good monitoring and to keep in mind the possible need to establish 'emergency or contingency management procedures and powers'. Otherwise, the key components of a vision, strategy and action plan (which can take between two and six years to develop and secure widespread acceptance) may represent little more than 'paper tigers'.

In some countries, such as Lesotho and Botswana, these practical difficulties have been tackled directly either by commissioning independent, special rapid appraisal studies or by conducting strategic environmental assessments led by impartial international consultants. In all cases, field developments have been suspended until the outcomes of the investigations have been concluded and publicized.

Cross-party support, focused on a compelling vision, can underpin long-term commitment

Political commitment also needs to be long term, and should therefore involve longer-term stakeholders such as the range of political parties and younger generations of commentators and decision-makers. Otherwise, there is the danger that an incoming government will see a particular strategy as representing the views or policies of its predecessor and so will either ignore it or even initiate a new strategy process more in line with its own thinking (see Box 4.4). The conclusion from reviewing strategies in Ghana (Vordzorgbe et al 2001) is that a strategy for sustainable development needs to focus on a compelling vision to which all parties will aspire, and on basic mechanisms (of the types illustrated in Figure 4.1), to allow continuous improvement to take place. If the strategy is too strongly associated with the details of individual regimes and programmes, it may not survive any changes in political administration.

Box 4.4 Strategy survival through changes of government

In Pakistan, the National Conservation Strategy was prepared through an elaborate participatory process spanning six years. It gained widespread support in government (at high level), among political parties, NGOs and civil society, and received cabinet approval in 1992. Despite political upheavals and changes of government, the NCS retains a high level of recognition and support and is still being implemented.

The Ghana Vision 2020 was an initiative of the president and ruling party and became the country's guiding development policy, recognized across government and among stakeholders. A new government was elected in December 2000 and rejected the vision as unachievable in the planned timeframe. It replaced it with its own alternative vision (see Box 3.15).

Cabinet commitment can cement support across government and departments

It is probable that early commitment to a strategy for sustainable development will lie with individuals. We have noted the case of presidential leadership above, but leaders might also be civil servants, or work with NGOs, academic institutions, the private sector or in civil society. However and wherever this initial inspiration arises, an early step should be to gain political support and, given the importance of the agenda and weight of the task, to seek cabinet commitment so as to cement such cross-government support and bind in line agencies. It is also helpful to seek the support of parliamentarians and lower level political bodies, as noted in Namibia (Jones 2001). A useful way to introduce the idea is to provide information or make a presentation to the parliamentary committee responsible for sustainable development, or indeed to the cabinet. Such presentations have usefully been made through videos; for example, in Botswana, Nigeria, St Lucia and Pakistan.

NCSDs (Box 3.14) will often be the most appropriate vehicle through which to first raise and then promote the notion of a strategy for sustainable development with government and politicians. Moreover, although their membership is usually drawn from a mix of sectors, NCSDs are public institutions through which the influence of the public, private and civil society sectors can be channelled.

Finally, political commitment should not be seen solely in terms of a 'prerequisite before starting a strategy', although clearly a certain level is needed. The continual improvement approach helps to generate and raise political commitment through the involvement of politicians in the NSDS process at key stages, and through providing them with relevant information.

Establishing or confirming a mandate for the strategy

If it is to be effective, a strategy should be a national initiative that will need broad support across government as well as the private sector and civil society. As we have seen, this will often entail setting up new bodies (eg steering committee/council and secretariat) perhaps with little precedent. In order for them to be able to promote the concept and process, they will need a clear mandate:

- to engage with stakeholders, encouraging and negotiating their support and involvement;
- to call for information;
- to organize analysis and debate on major topics concerning sustainable development;
- to make recommendations to identified bodies (cabinet or other high-level bodies);
- to make certain decisions (within agreed limits – cabinet will usually make the major decisions).

Such a mandate needs to be provided by a trusted, powerful body that also reflects public demand. This can be a tall order in some countries: the mandate might come from government at a high level (see page 82), or from parliament or a decentralized system such as a panchayat. Mandates similar to those of parliamentary or people's commissions have been used.

The mandate should be made public and signal the authority given to the steering committee/council and secretariat to carry out their functions and clearly indicate that the process has high-level support in government. One way would be for the mandate to be provided through legislation. This provides the committee/council with permanent status and insulates the process from the vagaries of politics or changes in political regimes, reducing the problem that support for a sustainable development strategy can change as governments and administrations change (a serious problem in a number of countries, eg Ghana – see Box 3.16).

A clear public mandate will authorize and help to sustain the strategy process

Ensuring broad ownership of the strategy

Central to the NSDS approach is the notion that people and institutions alike do not change because someone else tells them to – they have to be involved in understanding and realizing the need for change, making decisions about change, and then going through the process themselves. An NSDS, however, involves a broad range of stakeholders who all need to undertake change towards sustainable development. NSDS 'ownership' is therefore not a simple task. It implies that stakeholders from the private sector and civil society, as well as government, are involved in all stages of the process of developing and implementing the strategy, and in making decisions about its scope, the process and the outcomes (Table 4.2).

A strategy needs the broad support of civil society and the private sector as well as government

Table 4.2 **Checklist of key stakeholder groups in a national sustainable development strategy**

GOVERNMENT	CIVIL SOCIETY	PRIVATE SECTOR	REGIONAL AND INTERNATIONAL AGENCIES
■ President	■ Independent academic and research institutions	■ Banking and financial institutions	■ Multilateral development banks
■ Cabinet	■ NGOs and NGO coalitions	■ Industry associations	■ Bilateral development cooperation agencies
■ Line ministries	■ Community-based organizations/groups	■ Major companies	■ Multinational/global organizations (eg UN agencies)
■ Government agencies	■ Private voluntary organizations	■ Small and medium enterprises	■ International NGOs
■ Sub-national authorities at all levels	■ Resource user associations (farmers, hunters, fishers, tourism operators, etc)	■ Informal enterprises	■ Regional aid organizations
Government-supported bodies	■ Community groups	■ Chambers of commerce	■ Regional coalitions of countries (eg SADCC, ASEAN, EU)
■ Research establishments	■ Environment organizations	■ Business round tables	
■ Educational institutions	■ Human development and rights organizations	■ The media	
■ Armed forces	■ Indigenous peoples' organizations	■ Enterprise development agencies	
■ The judiciary	■ Professional associations		
■ Parliament	■ Political parties/groups		
■ Resource management authorities and agencies	■ Relief and welfare organizations		
■ QUANGOS (Quasi autonomous NGOs)	■ Churches and religious groups/institutions		
	■ Schools, teachers and parent-teacher associations		
	■ Trades unions		
	■ Women's groups		
	■ Campaign groups		

Note: Non-government stakeholders are very diverse – only examples can be given. Stakeholder analysis (page 120) can be used to 'map' the key groups who should be engaged in a strategy process (Chapter 6)

Real 'ownership' of the NSDS is achieved by:

- all stakeholders (particularly those making key contributions to policy development and decision-makers) having a comprehensive understanding of the multi-sectoral strategic planning and implementation process involved;
- balanced participation of the above stakeholders, and the widespread perception of this;
- stakeholder representation that takes good account of how well representatives are accountable to the group they are required to represent, and how clear their identity is with that group;
- clarity in expectations about what stakeholder involvement can and cannot achieve;
- an agreed level of shared control of the NSDS process;
- all stakeholders having adequate access, time, resources and incentives to be involved in those parts of the NSDS process that they believe are relevant to them;
- transparency in decision-making;
- reliable and relevant information about the ongoing process and its outcomes, and effective means of communication;
- clearly defined and bounded roles of external parties such as development agencies.

In many countries there is a tangible lack of ownership of strategic planning processes. The primary reason for this is the perceived lack of balanced participation and excessive control by government or influence of external agencies. To confront this problem, seminars and training programmes have an important role to play in building both a common understanding of sustainable development processes and the management capacities of stakeholders.

Building common understanding of sustainable development processes can encourage broader strategy ownership

Many country planning frameworks are externally driven as a consequence of conditionality and time pressure and are therefore seen as being owned by international and bilateral development cooperation agencies. For example, in the past, NEAPs were required by the World Bank if countries wanted to secure soft loans under IDA and, currently, the IMF requires poor countries to prepare PRSPs if they are to receive debt relief. Strategies driven by such external pressures can result in a lack of coordination between different frameworks, and a tendency for responsibilities to be left to a particular government institution. These are often ministries of environment when environment and natural resources issues are the focus, and ministries of finance where budget support is involved. This can result in a lack of policy coherence and the alienation of others who might also have legitimate interests or could make important contributions. In some cases, discontent with national processes has led private sector and civil society stakeholders to develop their own parallel strategies (see, for example, Box 3.4). In order to increase country ownership it is crucial to build on strategies that already exist and to ensure the continued development and improvement of such strategies through monitoring and evaluation.

Building on existing strategies increases country ownership

Securing strategy 'ownership' and commitment by all ministries

We have seen that government 'ownership' of a strategy must not be too strong in relation to civil society and private sector stakeholders. Nor must it be too skewed in the sense that it is perceived as the 'property' of narrow or weak interests (commonly an environment ministry). But perhaps more strategies have failed because of weak government understanding, leadership and overall commitment.

As discussed in Chapter 3, a strategy for sustainable development should only rarely involve a completely new or stand-alone strategic planning project. Instead, there are likely to be several existing strategies, programmes and processes covering, for example, health, poverty, population, economic development, water and energy supply/conservation, housing and environment, and combinations thereof (the main ones are discussed in Chapter 3). Taken together, a number of these existing frameworks could meet the definition of an NSDS in Chapter 3 (page 31), meet the principles and elements in Boxes 3.1 and 3.2, be combined in the strategy system illustrated in Figure 4.1 – and thereby increase the basis of ownership.

Ministries should be brought together to scope a shared vision and agree on coordination

Doing this is especially important where there is strong ownership of some of the component processes – although this may not be the case (see section on mapping out the strategy process, page 102). Lead responsibility for existing processes is usually vested in particular line ministries and government agencies. So an early step will be to bring these departments and agencies together to assess the degree of ownership, express aspirations, scope out a shared vision, and consider how to deal with coordination and rationalization. Working in this way requires a preparedness to work in different ways from those that have generally prevailed to date. Some existing strategy mechanisms may have shown more promise and could be used for this exploration.

Bringing existing initiatives closer to an effective strategy for sustainable development might involve complementing them with a broad *'umbrella' vision, goals and objectives* to give a common purpose. It will certainly mean coordinating or rationalizing them as an integrated set of mechanisms and processes – improving their complementarity, smoothing out inconsistencies and filling gaps when needed (activities which need to be done judiciously if they are not to destroy a sense of ownership).

Regular, informal meetings can maintain interest and commitment

Another key challenge is to maintain the interest and commitment of government ministries throughout a strategy process. Scheduling regular meetings to take stock of progress can help, especially if they are informal and relaxed. For example, in Zambia, in the early 1980s, the development and coordination of the NCS process was greatly enhanced by a monthly lunch for permanent secretaries (hardly anyone ever missed a meeting!). The regular but informal exchange of information and ideas, and reviews of progress, became a powerful 'fuel supply' for the NCS process. A further approach is to ensure that NSDS processes and activities become integrated into the work plans and targets of government organizations and individual officers. In North West Frontier Province, Pakistan, ministry focal points have the job of improving information flows and developing incentives for ministry officers to stay involved in the provincial conservation strategy (Box 4.14).

Securing strategy 'ownership' and commitment by civil society and the private sector

Many civil society and private sector organizations are committed to fostering sustainable development

It is very important to secure the commitment of the civil society and the private sector. Many community-based and civil society organizations are sometimes more aware than line ministries of problems resulting from decisions taken by central government. In Thailand, for example, many such organizations have become environmental watchdogs with a continuous commitment to monitor new and existing projects for compliance with rules and regulations. This has led to better feasibility and impact studies, public hearings and the cancellation of some projects with adverse impacts.

In response to the challenge of globalization, the private sector is addressing its role in fostering sustainable development, for example, through the work of the WBCSD (see Chapter 2, page 17) and initiatives such as the new UN-Private Sector Global Compact on responsible business behaviour. Many multinationals are working vigorously to understand the implications of sustainable development for their businesses and clients and to develop their own policy responses.

There is increasing dialogue between governments and the private sector …

Throughout the last decade there has been increasing dialogue in many industrial countries between governments and the private sector, particularly industry, in strategic planning. In The Netherlands, for example, this led to the agreement of voluntary covenants between the government and industry (Box 4.5). Other examples are to be found in Egypt (via the successful environmental pollution abatement programme) and the UK (through the Eco Management and Audit Scheme and ISO 14001 environmental management system).

Box 4.5 **Covenants with industry in The Netherlands**

In The Netherlands, there has been a long tradition of cooperation between the government and industrial associations which enabled the second National Environmental Policy Plan (NEPP2) (1993) to move away from direct (top-down, command and control) economic and environmental management instruments to more socially negotiated and participatory instruments: for example, voluntary covenants with target groups such as industry. Initially, covenants were essentially 'gentlemen's agreements', with a highly uncertain status and degree of enforceability. But they are now generally standardized and formalized with regard to procedure and content. The government sees them as a way of expressing joint responsibility. By 1996, over 100 covenants had been concluded between the government and the private sector.

Covenants are generally seen as complements to existing legislation rather than as alternatives; they have a special role in meeting NEPP targets. While authorities still prefer to use laws and regulations to exercise control, covenants are used to speed up environmental improvements pending legislation, if there are too many uncertainties regarding the content of legislation to be drafted, if government intervention is needed only temporarily, or if covenants are likely to be less costly in terms of implementation or enforcement. Under NEPP2, some 26 environmental covenants were signed with industry, dealing, *inter alia*, with products, packaging, waste and emissions in general. With the advent of the NEPP, the focus changed from products and packaging to production of waste and emissions.

The main requirements for covenants between industry and the central government are laid down in a code covering procedural arrangements (especially information to politicians) and the content of covenants (objectives, requirements, period of validity, consultation, monitoring of compliance, evaluation and settlement of disputes). The legal status of covenants is generally that of an agreement under private law. If need be, the authorities can turn to the civil courts for enforcement.

Consultation started in 1990 on environmental policy guidelines for the construction industry. After three years of discussion, the government and the industry adopted key objectives and signed an environmental policy plan:

Covenant with the construction industry (policy lines and selected targets)

A   Reduction in use of non-renewable raw materials:
- 2.5 per cent reduction by 2000 and 5 per cent by 2005 with respect to 1990.
B   Stimulation of reuse of raw materials:
- Reuse of construction and demolition waste to rise from 60 per cent in 1990 to 90 per cent in 2000.
C   Reduction in volume and separate collection of construction and demolition waste:
- 5 per cent quantitative prevention of demolition waste in 2000.
- 80 per cent of demolition operations to use selective demolition techniques and separate collection by 1996.
D   Stimulation of use of renewable resources:
- Tropical hardwood to be used only from sustainably managed forests from 1995.
- Use of non-tropical wood to increase by 20 per cent between 1990 and 1995.
E   Reduction of use of harmful materials and substances:
- At least 50 per cent of paint used by construction industry to be low-solvent paint by 1995.
- Emissions of polycyclic aromatic hydrocarbons (PAH) to be reduced by 50 per cent in 1995 with respect to 1990 levels.
F   Promotion of energy saving heating systems and water efficient installations in new and renovated buildings:
- Energy consumption of buildings to be decreased by 8 per cent by 1995 with respect to 1989/90.
- Water efficient installations to be fitted in defined percentage of new and renovated buildings by 1995 (eg 50 per cent with water-saving shower heads).

Considerable progress has already been achieved concerning some of the targets. For instance, recycling of construction waste has reached about 60 per cent.

Under NEPP3, the core policy remained that companies are responsible for improving their environmental performance – industry having, to a large extent, achieved its environmental targets (VROM 1997). The covenant approach was continued. As part of its response to the Kyoto climate change agreement, the government identified the potential to negotiate a CO_2 covenant with electricity producers about changing over from coal to gas-fired power stations.

Source: OECD (1995b)

In developing countries, there has been some engagement of the domestic private sector in strategic planning processes, but there are few cases where the international private sector has been involved. Given that financial flows to developing countries through private investment now dwarf official development assistance, this is a challenge that needs to be addressed in developing and implementing strategies for sustainable development.

... about their concerns, and constraints to innovation and investment

Private sector involvement is more productive if the strategy process is open to voluntary agreements and market-based instruments, balanced with regulatory and fiscal instruments: for example, covenants in The Netherlands (Box 4.5). To engage effectively with the private sector requires dialogue about their concerns in order to understand the constraints they face to be innovative and to invest, and the factors that are likely to bring about improved ways of working. In Pakistan, since 1996, the Federation of Chambers of Commerce and Industry has supported a programme of audits of a wide range of industrial units to examine how compliance can be achieved with National Environmental Quality Standards (NEQS) – designed to promote effective pollution control and to carry forward recommendations in the NCS. The constraints and opportunities identified enabled industry to negotiate revised, and more achievable, NEQS with the Environmental Protection Agency in 1999. The same approach has been adopted successfully in Egypt by the Environmental Affairs Agency

It is important to understand motivations and incentives to engage in a strategy process

The commitment and involvement of both private sector and civil society is dependent on how well the strategy responds to the motivations of these groups and on what incentives they have to engage in the strategy process. Thus, in designing a strategic process, stakeholder analysis should be employed at an early stage. This can provide important information on the motivations and interests of stakeholders, the means they use to secure their interests, the pressures on them to change and the constraints to making changes.

Stakeholder commitment may be improved by working with the fora in existing 'policy communities'

It can be particularly useful to identify how stakeholders are already interacting through concerned 'policy communities'. This is because the most effective approach for improving stakeholder commitment to a strategy may not be through their individual organizations, but through existing 'fora' that have already been trying to influence sustainable development. Policy communities are likely to be issues-based and involve more than one stakeholder type, if not yet fully multi-stakeholder. They might take the form of formal or informal groups, networks or movements concerned with, for example, poverty alleviation or biodiversity conservation. The key point is that they are already communities for interaction, often with strategic functions. They will be committed to – indeed 'own' – particular causes, but may be frustrated by their lack of mainstream influence and impact. Some of them would be potential NSDS 'clients' who could become committed to – and joint 'owners' of – the NSDS. One example is the work of the Centre for Russian Environmental Policy, a leading NGO, which coordinated the inputs of all Russian NGOs to the second All-Russia Congress on Nature Protection in 1999, and published recommendations on the priorities for Russia's National Environmental Policy (Zakharov 1999a, b, c). In some countries, NCSDs bring together a number of theme- or issues-based 'policy communities' under their coordinating umbrella – each relating to sustainable development issues identified as priorities for the country. These communities may be represented on specific NCSD sub-committees (eg biodiversity conservation, sustainable agriculture). Although the NCSD provides policy coordination, the sub-committees retain a certain level of independence and initiative within their thematic areas.

Mobilizing the required resources

A strategy process should harness a country's skills and capacities for dealing with change

A strategy will require a range of resources: the necessary skills, the support of various institutions, and the financial means to undertake the process and coordinate the resulting policies and plans. In essence, these are resources for participation, coordination and project management, information and analysis. They will rarely amount to a large proportion of the costs of concerned institutions. But they can be demanding of skills – of good analytical skills and creativity – and of the time and attention of senior policy-makers.

Many of the resources will usually be available but there are two problems: of opportunity cost and of getting resources mobilized. Hence the importance of securing commitment (page 82). In the absence of such local commitment, external interests have been able to deal with these problems at a stroke, by offering external resources. However, as we have seen in Chapter 3, such external resources (common to NEAPs, for example) can distort the relevance and ownership of local strategies.

Harnessing the necessary skills

Members of a secretariat team will not be able to, nor should they be expected to, do everything themselves. They will need to identify and draw upon skills and capacity throughout the country, wherever they exist – in individuals or within institutions, in the public or private sector. But, as a minimum, the secretariat team should encompass individuals who have the skills listed in Box 4.6, or at least a basic

The secretariat team needs skills to manage the strategy process

---

Box 4.6 Checklist of skills required to manage and coordinate a strategy

Those *managing the strategy process* will require skills in:

- identification and quantification of priority sustainable development issues;
- stakeholder analysis;
- facilitation – of meetings, workshops, round tables at national to local levels, and for technical and lay groups;
- participatory methodologies – suitable to employ at different levels (national to local), and for different purposes: for example, meetings, research and opinion-gathering;
- strengthening the planning and management capacities of all the main stakeholders, including, for example, the skills required to conduct impartial cost-benefit appraisals;
- harnessing local, national and international data (eg concerning environmentally friendly production, distribution, consumption, and resource conservation and recycling processes);
- exploring the range of technical, institutional, human resource, economic, financial and other options available for addressing sustainable development issues;
- designing synergistic packages of policy-support mechanisms, comprising legal, economic, institutional and public awareness instruments;
- networking and knowledge management – among stakeholders and internationally with those managing similar processes in other countries;
- negotiation – of agreements on roles and responsibilities between interest groups;
- conflict management/resolution and consensus-building;
- diplomacy and empathizing with different people's perspectives and positions;
- communication:
    - writing, both technical reports and simple pieces for the press;
    - use of mass media (and traditional media);
    - presentations and public speaking;
    - IT skills;
    - awareness-raising about sustainable development and the purpose and role of the strategy process;
- programme management – commissioning and managing research, consultations and pilot projects, with associated financial and reporting skills;
- monitoring and evaluation (first of the strategy development process and subsequently of its implementation).

Those *undertaking strategic analysis* will require skills in:

- evaluation of potential technological solutions and systems for addressing environmental infrastructural service issues: for example, solid waste management, energy generation and conservation, and transport;
- understanding the linkages between disciplines (environmental, social, economic) and sectors, as well as vertical interactions (eg between international, regional, national, sub-national and more local levels) including cross-border issues;
- understanding the institutional, legislative and administrative dimensions and dynamics of development;
- being able to summarize key trends and actual or potential impacts, and produce syntheses and options for debate;
- specific technical expertise in different forms of analysis: environmental, social/stakeholder, economic, institutional, policy, multi-criteria and scenario development – preferably in interdisciplinary contexts.

knowledge of those they lack in order to be able judge how and when such skills are required, know where they are available, and assess how effectively they are being deployed. They will primarily require skills in managing multi-stakeholder research and consensus-building processes, preferably from a position of independence. Such skills will often be in short supply, and may be closely associated with previous or current strategy models. Bringing staff together from more than one approach can improve the process. The secretariat should be given the opportunity to reflect on those models and make improvements.

Wherever, possible, secretariat staff should be drawn from within the country. The necessary skills and capacities can be in short supply in developing countries, and those which exist are usually already heavily committed and overstretched. Capacity building is, therefore, a critical component of NSDS processes. Box 4.7 summarizes the key capacity requirements for an effective NSDS. Where it is necessary to involve skills

The strategy process is an efficient way to build and coordinate capacity for sustainable development

---

Box 4.7 Capacity requirements for an effective NSDS

The capacity needs of a national sustainable development strategy are manifested at the human, institutional and systemic levels.

The human dimension of capacity building relates to a variety of abilities, with an emphasis on interdisciplinary and process skills. It includes the acquisition of technical skills on both an individual and a collective basis. It encompasses abilities for negotiation, conflict resolution and consensus building, through teamwork and effective communication ('demystifying' the complex codes, symbols and jargon that are often associated with sustainable development). It also includes the capability to internalize diverse experiences and perspectives, to enable effective learning. The dynamics associated with this level of capacity development are often influenced by subjective determinants such as attitude, perception, cultural orientation and intuitive faculty.

Institutional capacity requirements focus on collective learning and institutional change. In addition to tangible skills associated with programme and project development, the principal requirements include institutional capacities to:

- understand and deal with multiple perceptions;
- develop a common vision and sense of purpose that binds stakeholders;
- catalyze internal change processes;
- encourage innovative behaviour;
- encourage incentive mechanisms to enhance capacity development;
- develop effective monitoring and evaluation capabilities for learning purposes;
- coordinate and mobilize activities at different levels;
- adapt to new contexts and challenges.

The systemic dimension of capacity building is closely associated with the 'enabling environment', that is, appropriate policy and legal frameworks, a clear definition of institutional roles and mandates, widespread access to information, upstream/downstream linkages, the availability of a 'culture of dialogue' and enhanced networking capabilities linking diverse stakeholders. These attributes are essential to sustain the growth of institutions and individuals, as well as to generate learning dynamics.

Innovation is important. The testing of new approaches at the local level can often assist learning processes through validation, and thus facilitate integration at the policy level.

Indigenous knowledge needs to be taken into consideration. Indigenous knowledge systems, as growing bodies of locally relevant experience and means for resilience, can also make positive contributions to a NSDS, and institutional processes need to be able to value and encourage them.

Whereas conventional tools such as manuals, guidelines, and formal training and research are of key importance, other means of education and awareness should also be promoted. Different approaches and entry points can be utilized to achieve such improvements. This will include the promotion of 'built-in' performance-based incentive mechanisms that encourage continuous improvement. Traditional organizational models based on hierarchy and compartmentalization should be complemented by more inclusive approaches in order to stimulate greater interaction and shared learning. Institutions should focus on learning from failures as well as from successes. Finally, time and patience are key ingredients – it takes time for capacity building to evolve and mature into capacity retention.

Local governments, private sector and civil society need to play a stronger role in national sustainable development strategy development and implementation. Capacity-strengthening exercises and resources that are made available need also to be relevant to the local levels – and not only be confined to the national level.

Source: UN DESA (2002a)

from outside the country, such individuals can provide useful international experience – knowledge of, and links to, processes elsewhere. Outsiders should be careful to play a supporting role for the process (eg using their skills and knowledge to help the process, providing training where needed) and avoid influencing the content of the strategy or its outcomes. In an age of globalization, the international dimensions are becoming increasingly important in developing strategies, and so external expertise might be brought in to improve understanding of the international context and dynamics.

The secretariat should map the tasks and skills required

An early step for the secretariat should be to map out the tasks to be undertaken and the skills required, and then to identify those skills available in the country (individuals and institutional). This can be done through the use of questionnaires and perhaps by using or creating a skills database. Where particular skills are lacking or unavailable, contacts with sister secretariats in other countries in the region might indicate where help can be found. The assistance of donors can also be sought. Various international and donor-supported capacity-building programmes are working to support NSDS processes: for example, UNDP's Capacity 21 programme, and the German Agency for Technical Cooperation (GTZ) Rioplus programme.

Bringing institutions and individuals on board

An early step for the secretariat should be to identify all those institutions (government and non-government) that should play a role in the strategy process (the timing of their possible inputs may vary). Then, through meetings or briefings – initially of individual stakeholders and later in groups of compatible stakeholders – the purpose of the strategy should be explained along with initial ideas for the approach to be followed. These early consultative exercises should seek to gain feedback and support and commitment either to engage, or to permit or provide staff capable of undertaking particular tasks when needed. (See page 85 for more information on building ownership and commitment.) Careful consideration needs to be given to the appropriate timing for meetings to be convened for different stakeholders. If such meetings are held too early in the process (ie before there is a mature understanding of the issues to be addressed and the participatory nature of the planning procedures), they may prove to be counter-productive.

Early consultative meetings can encourage stakeholders to engage in a strategy process

Many stakeholders will be able to engage through their existing jobs and roles, but where individuals are likely to devote a significant proportion of the time to working on strategy issues, it may be necessary for their job descriptions or terms of reference to be amended. For others, there will be short-term opportunity costs, particularly where individuals need to take time from their livelihood activities (eg those in civil society and particularly those from local communities where involvement can mean, for example, time lost to harvesting crops). Women may find it particularly difficult to engage in participatory processes due to the multiplicity of tasks they perform. So ways of compensating for this or for providing assistance may need to be found if they are to participate effectively. These ways will need to be defined in the context of normal practice in the country concerned. Examples of mechanisms that have been used include:

Some groups may need financial help to engage in the proces

- reimbursing travel and other out-of-pocket expenses;
- meeting the legitimate costs of NGOs in organizing meetings, preparing responses, and so on;
- paying honoraria for contributions (eg commissioned work);
- providing attendance fees to those serving on committees and, in some countries, for participating in meetings and workshops.

At the same time, extreme care needs to be taken to avoid meeting and conference allowances forming an essential component of monthly emoluments. This situation has arisen in some countries where civil service salaries are extremely low, and has led to government officers devoting considerable efforts to attending countless meetings and conferences in order to 'harvest' the honoraria. This problem can severely constrain the time available for regular duties and implementation activities.

Raising the financial resources

A stable and sustainable source of funding for a NSDS is vital. It is preferable that financial provision for supporting a strategy is made within the country's recurrent budget. This will give it more chance to become a continuing process. Securing a legislated mandate for the steering committee/council increases the chance of such budget provision. Many past strategies have failed because they have been funded by government or development cooperation agencies as one-off initiatives or projects. This has tended to sideline them so that they cannot influence budget decisions; and has constrained timeframes for developing and implementing strategies, undermining the establishment of participatory, multi-stakeholder processes (as it takes time to build trust, confidence and commitment to engage, as well as to consult stakeholders' constituencies). Also, in the past, there has been limited appreciation of the realistic timescales required to establish and sustain effective strategic planning processes.

Although a continuous improvement approach has been identified as desirable for strategies, in practice it will be possible to identify discrete 'phases', depending, for example, on what new mechanisms need to be established, studies or reviews done. Typically, the first stage would be to establish a secretariat with a 'start-up' budget to enable it to undertake a scoping exercise. This would involve tasks such as initial consultations with a range of stakeholders (to build support and constituency for the process), developing a plan or 'prospectus' for the strategy, and preparing a budget for the full process. The budget for this initial stage will need to meet such costs as the salaries of a small team (say three people), operating an office and administration, travel to visit each of the provinces to explain the proposals for a strategy process and to identify priority issues as well as potential solutions, and meetings – especially a significant national meeting to finalize key process decisions and to sign off on the strategy process and its scope (if not yet the final objectives and responsibilities involved). This type of 'process scoping and prospectus' approach was used successfully during the 1980s by IUCN in a number of developing countries; it allowed time for the 'externally introduced' NCS concept to become internalized and redefined.

The costs of undertaking the full strategy process will vary in different countries and will be influenced by a wide range of factors, such as:

- the area and population size of the country;
- the extent of the natural resource base;
- whether it takes place in a unitary or federal state (ie whether parallel processes need to be pursued in each province);
- the complexity of the process to be adopted;
- the timescale involved;
- prevailing salary and travel costs;
- how many of the component mechanisms of the strategy are already covered by other (recurrent) budgets, and how many need to be set up.

But in preparing a budget, the secretariat will need to consider the costs of a range of key functions and tasks (this an illustrative list only):

- salaries (secretariat staff);
- fees to consultants (eg for commissioned papers and analysis);
- honoraria to participants attending formal meetings (if this is usual practice);
- meetings, workshops, round table events (meeting room hire, lunches, travel costs, accommodation when necessary);

Preferably, a strategy should receive government budget funding

A phased approach is desirable

A range of tasks and functions need to be financed

- travel for staff and others to attend events and meetings;
- steering committee/council meeting costs;
- preparation of audio-visual aids to explain the strategy process and its outcomes, for the benefit of the main stakeholder groups, especially local communities;
- publicity through a prospectus and use of local print and broadcast media;
- publication of key background papers, reports, draft and final strategy documents (typesetting, printing, dissemination, website);
- office costs, secretarial support and administration, communications (post, phone, fax, e-mail);
- a fund for trials, demonstrations and pilot activities (see page 112);
- monitoring and evaluation.

Development of a strategy is a challenge for society as a whole and all sections should be expected to play a part. While the government should meet the costs of the secretariat and the key processes for stakeholder engagement (meetings, consultations, etc), the private sector as well as non-governmental institutions and organizations can all provide support in kind (providing skills, organizing meetings, etc, or sponsoring art and essay related competitions, environmental clean-up campaigns, tree planting programmes, etc). Consideration needs to be given to establishing demonstration projects to provide a practical 'shop-front' for the overall process and the range of benefits that it can generate.

The private sector, NGOs and other organizations can also provide support

Development cooperation agencies are often prepared to support strategy processes but, following the adoption of the DAC guidelines on strategies (OECD DAC 2001a), they are likely to require that the government demonstrates a financial commitment as well by providing counterpart funding. Some development cooperation agencies follow the principle that external funding should be catalytic; that is, it should aim to generate (eventually if not immediately) domestic sources of support consistent with the goal of national ownership.

It is impossible to prejudge the costs of implementing the outcomes of strategy processes. These might involve changes to legislation, policies, institutions and administrative arrangements, or a range of particular targeted initiatives. In the spirit of partnership, opportunities to involve the private sector in the latter should be explored early on. In developing countries, development cooperation agencies will often be prepared to discuss with governments how they can support the implementation of strategies.

Chapter 9 examines the financial basis of NSDSs in detail.

Identifying stakeholders and defining their roles in the strategy

Starting, managing or improving the NSDS process requires that time is taken to identify the key participants from among the relevant stakeholders, as well as defining their respective roles. The first task, identifying the participants, consists of two steps: identifying the interests and then identifying the appropriate representatives of those interests. To identify the interests, there is need to concentrate on groups likely to be affected by the strategy and those with the power to implement or frustrate potential outcomes. To identify the representatives, focus should be on:

A first task is to identify the participants

- consulting with various agencies, organizations, businesses, and so on, to develop a sense of who is viewed with credibility as an accountable leader or accepted spokesperson strongly identified with the group concerned;
- identifying existing or potential mechanisms that will enable participants to represent their constituencies;
- confirming that the participants are accountable if they represent groups or constituencies.

Table 4.2 provides a checklist of potential key stakeholder groups. Methods for identifying stakeholders and their interests, dynamics, relations and powers are discussed in detail in Chapter 5 (see page 125).

Various stakeholders must think in terms of re-negotiating their roles to make and sustain the changes required in the transition to sustainable development:

- from domination by government, private operators' interests and professionals in policy/planning processes, to exploration and integration of different interests;
- from management based on evidence, to a learning process that manages uncertainty and experimentation;
- from reliance on technical expertise and opinion, to the inclusion of local knowledge and proposals from stakeholders, and the need for people-oriented skills;
- from a narrow focus on sectoral economic development and physical planning of resource/land user, to multiple objectives including environmental management and social development;
- from loose ideas of 'participation', to concrete actions for empowerment.

There are two issues here: one, an NSDS should offer the right processes to negotiate such changes in roles; and two, roles in the strategy itself need to be both agreed and conducive to the negotiation process. We address the second issue in this section.

Not all stakeholders need or want to be involved in all tasks associated with the NSDS. One purpose of stakeholder analysis (page 120) is to ensure that the secretariat, and others involved in managing the strategy process, adequately understand the stakes of different interest groups, where they wish to participate, and what their expectations and skills are. This is so that the principle of participation is not watered down by an unrealistic and unnecessary pressure to get all stakeholders to participate at every stage (Box 3.1).

Central government will not be able to shape a strategy for the sustainable development of a country on its own, let alone implement the outcomes. It is but one partner in a network that also includes regional and local government, and a wide array of interest groups in the private sector and civil society, as

illustrated in Table 4.2. So it is important to clarify early on the roles of the key participants in strategic planning processes and relationships between them, as defined in the formal roles and mandates of institutions and organizations in the process, and as promoted by the different policy communities. Sustainable development will require effective cooperation between the partners in this network. Failure to define roles can lead to conflicts, lack of strategy implementation and gaps between aspirations and realities, as illustrated by environmental action plans in Nigeria (Box 4.8)

A useful approach to addressing stakeholder roles is offered in work by the International Institute for Environment and Development (IIED) on developing capacity for sustainable forestry in Africa, which assessed stakeholders' roles as combining their *Rights, Responsibilities, Returns/Revenues and Relationships* (summarized as the 4Rs) (Dubois et al 1996). Applications of the 4Rs approach are discussed in Chapter 5. It can be used as a framework to assess current roles, to negotiate new roles and to monitor change, and is conducive to participatory approaches.

Several aspects of stakeholder roles and relations are particularly important and will require change:

- It is important to *dispense with some traditional 'strategic planning' roles*; for example, that only 'experts' do the analysis, and that only senior bureaucrats and politicians make the major decisions. The roles in an NSDS process need to be able to 'rehearse' some of the likely roles that an NSDS will recommend.

- Vigorous efforts will need to be made to *interest citizens in the strategy process* and to encourage them to become increasingly involved in both analysis and defining solutions to societal issues. Good communication between government and the general public during the development and implementation of a strategy is a prerequisite for its success.
- *NGOs and interest groups will need to be encouraged to* (and be allowed to) assume an increasing role; they can mobilize policy communities, assess public opinion about key problems and make good use of the media, as well as act as watchdog of the NSDS process.
- In many countries, an increasing number of jobs traditionally done by government are now 'privatized' to *commercial or semi-commercial organizations*. Resource survey, market research and opinion polling are all NSDS jobs that can be done by the private sector. In some cases, the self-regulating interplay of supply and demand can be successfully harnessed to find ways to tackle the problems which face sustainable development; for example, in The Netherlands, cooperation between the public and private sectors is increasing (see Box 4.5).
- The trend towards globalization, with less freedom to manoeuvre for national government, is being accompanied by another towards decentralization, and responsibilities for policy development and implementation will need to pass to lower levels. *'Tiered' systems of participation* and good information flows between them will make for a better NSDS. In most cases, decentralized levels have merely been 'consulted' on NSDSs, or have been empowered to make compatible action plans, or been given an information dissemination role. More attention to rights and powers will be needed. Frameworks established by central government must leave some room for manoeuvre for the other partners.
- It can be useful to distinguish between *the broad group of stakeholders* who participate in the strategy process, the *'decision-developers'* who have the responsibility to forge recommendations and options based on analysis and consultation (eg a steering committee) and the *'decision-takers'* who are ultimately responsible for decisions and their impacts (see page 270).

The various organizations and interest groups that need to be engaged in a strategy process each have their own interests that they will seek to promote and defend. They can become involved in the process in different ways and contribute at different levels: for example, to identify and find solutions to problems, to build a vision and goals for the future, and to debate policy options and possible actions. Involvement in a strategy process may be seen as a right, but it also carries with it certain responsibilities, and it is therefore important to establish and agree roles as early in the process as is agreed to be appropriate. Some roles

Roles need to be agreed early in the process

Box 4.8 Unimplemented state environmental action plans in Nigeria: a failure of undefined roles

Gulfs can sometimes arise during strategic planning. A review was undertaken in 1999–2000 of environmental management systems in Nigeria at the federal level and in three states. This revealed that Environmental Action Plans had been developed in each state with abundant stakeholder consultations. But they had not been implemented due a lack of 'ownership' by the State Environmental Protection Agencies (EPAs). Both the consultation and plan preparation exercises had been carried out by the Federal EPA. A huge gap was evident between the aspirations set out by the plans and reality. A number of key strategic components that should have been provided by state agencies were absent from the plans: the formulation of state policies on the management of natural resources and environmental services; the development of packages of supporting measures (incentives and disincentives); the provision of achievable/realistic standards and targets, as well as transparent monitoring and evaluation of annual performance; and the enhancement of public participation through effective communication and awareness campaigns. This case exemplifies the need for the respective roles of federal and state agencies to be properly defined and monitored.

Source: Ralph Cobham (personal communication)

might be obvious or reasonably evident, as discussed in the next section, others might be assessed by answering such questions as:

- Who has the right to do what, and how?
- Who has the required skills, resources and capacity to deliver the agreed outcomes?
- Who does what, and when?
- Who is committed and willing?
- Who pays for particular actions or services?
- What is the best alternative to a negotiated agreement on aspects of policy or particular actions, especially for the most powerful stakeholders?
- What are the means and capacities of different stakeholders?
- What is the procedure in case agreements cannot be reached or, once reached, are breached?

Typical roles of the main actors in strategy processes, and constraints faced

POLITICIANS AND LEADERS

Providing leadership

Politicians and leaders in the private sector and civil society will be expected to provide leadership and to endorse and promote the strategy as an initiative in the nation's interest and of importance to society as a whole.

PUBLIC AUTHORITIES

Providing resources, shaping regulations and setting standards

Public authorities (ie central government, sub-national authorities at various levels, resource boards/agencies) play an important role in putting economic, social and environmental problems on the agenda. They must also provide resources for tackling problems (eg money and information); create the framework for economic, political and social rights; shape the regulations to realize goals; establish mechanisms to set standards and to adhere to international obligations; and ensure that policies, plans and programmes are implemented and applied, and that legislation and regulations are complied with. The authorities are also expected to act in the general interest (eg protecting wildlife and landscape).

Establishing mechanisms

The *central government* needs to take the lead in establishing the mechanism(s) for the strategy and creating the necessary enabling conditions – notably an open and transparent, participatory process. Government tends to be bureaucratic and intransigent but can/should:

- resist taking full ownership of and operation control of the process, but play an enabling role – acting as a facilitator of a wider process, creating the broad framework and supporting participation, seeking to engage and empower stakeholders (see Table 4.1) so as to foster a partnership approach between the different levels of government, the private sector and civil society, and promoting the development of a long-term vision for national development;
- use/build on existing forms of participatory structure available within government which have been used in strategic planning (eg the planning systems, decentralized administrative systems, education systems), establish new structures (eg special committees, round tables) and build capacity;
- encourage/promote participation throughout the vertical hierarchy – provinces/states and different types of lower-level divisions;
- ensure the committed engagement of all sectoral departments and agencies and key individuals within them (notably those who have cross-sectoral expertise/vision and are open to change);
- ensure the strategy is not affiliated strongly with particular political parties (to help it to survive a

change of government), is not in the hands of politicians or civil servants who could be moved by a new government, and promote strong support outside government.

Sub-national authorities (eg at regional, provincial, district and municipal levels) play a parallel role to national government, promoting the development of strategies at these levels. They can/should act as a broker between national policy and the specific demands of different groups on the ground, establishing links and dialogue with the general public (resource user groups, local communities, NGOs, etc) and private sector businesses.

Acting as a broker between national policy and local demands

But these more local authorities will need to be given more 'policy space' – more ability to develop policy that is relevant at their geographic levels. Thus, they will need to consider how to transform and translate any national-level strategy(ies) into more detailed or comprehensive approaches relevant at their levels and addressing more local concerns – this may mean taking the lead in establishing a more local strategic planning process (eg a Local Agenda 21). Conversely, such authorities (and other stakeholders) will be able to build on already existing sub-national strategies (eg the approaches they have followed, the issues and problems addressed, and the solutions and outcomes agreed) in contributing to a national process.

Regional and local authorities will also have to assume and discharge (formal and legal) responsibilities for which they are (or will be) accountable to central and other government bodies and others. They will have to assume responsibility for reporting, monitoring and providing quality assurance, and make clear agreements with one another on these matters. Partnership implies mutual accountability, first horizontally, to the authorities' own management board and the local community, and thereafter vertically to the government level which sets the framework. As monitoring and reporting becomes more integrated, less policing by central government of policy implementation and enforcement will be necessary.

Responsibility for reporting, monitoring and quality assurance

Local rural and municipal authorities are the layer of government closest to the general public, and this gives them a special responsibility for getting ordinary citizens involved in the strategy process (working with NGOs wherever possible – see below).

Getting citizens involved

Resource boards/agencies (eg water boards) play a key role in coordinating resource use, increasingly on an integrated resource management basis (this is now acknowledged as more appropriate to sustainable development). They can make valuable contributions to fostering debate and coordinating actions related to natural resources at national to local levels.

Coordinating resource use

THE PRIVATE SECTOR

The private sector is responsible for creating goods and services, generating profit for investors and providing employment opportunities, innovation and economic growth. It can nominate representative, accountable members of the sector to engage in the strategy process. Leaders of large businesses responsible for making new patterns of investment and operation can play an effective role. But there should also be representatives of smaller-scale industries, which are important for employment, and smaller businesses with particularly high resource requirements (eg small-scale mining, agricultural processing) or industries that have sensitive impacts (eg tourism).

Both large and small businesses should be involved

Organizations and businesses in particular economic sectors or in other homogeneous groups – sometimes referred to as target groups (eg agriculture, industry, retail trade, transport) – can be the source of particular problems (eg pollution) and, as a consequence, can contribute to their solution (eg by improving production processes). They also benefit from the good social, economic or environmental conditions (eg the food industry needs clean water). Often, the organizations and companies in these sectors have considerable in-house know-how. The private sector (from large multinationals to domestic, small and medium-sized enterprises) also has a major role to play in identifying how it can ensure that it invests in activities and ventures that promote and underpin, and not undermine, sustainable development.

Investment should support sustainable development

CIVIL SOCIETY

Some of the more prominent civil society groups tend to be combative and territorial, but can/should:

- Elect/appoint organizations/people to participate in strategy meetings, workshops and so on, ensuring that they are accountable and aware of/reflect the views of the groups they represent, and have a mandate to voice particular views. Accountability can better be achieved when an interest group is represented by an association with democratic procedures (eg chambers of commerce, professional association).
- Resist being compromised by any support provided to enable their participation (eg to meet the costs of attending meetings or preparing informed positions).

NGOs play varied roles and are important partners. Their involvement in strategy processes in developed and developing countries has differed

NGOs can play an important role in drawing attention to particular issues and problems, mobilizing public opinion and advancing knowledge. In developing countries, NGOs play a vital role undertaking development programmes in poor urban and rural communities, have much better knowledge of community problems and concerns than government and can play a key catalytic role in engaging communities in voicing their concerns. In developed countries, the NGO movement is very sophisticated and maintains a dialogue with industry and government. Environmental NGOs, for example, play a major role in nature and environmental education and take action, often through the courts, to defend conservation and environmental interests. NGOs and interest groups must therefore be important partners in any strategy process. Unlike public authorities or target groups, NGOs seldom have any formal responsibilities for implementing or applying government policies, and are free to choose their own roles (the role of NGOs is discussed in more detail in Box 4.9).

The public put sustainable development into practice by making choices

The public ultimately determines how ambitious policy can be and which measures are acceptable. A societal support base is therefore a prerequisite for a successful strategy. It is the public that puts into practice the notion of sustainable development – by making choices in which they trade off economic and social factors against environmental considerations. The public will play a key role in bringing about desired socio-cultural, administrative and technological breakthroughs and achieving society-wide changes; for example, changing consumption patterns, greening tax systems or moving to environmentally friendly transport systems.

The *public* are particularly significant as consumers. Individuals demand and purchase durables. They respond to financial instruments and price incentives and have their say in local policy-making and planning. They undertake their livelihoods, use resources, produce and dispose of waste (even separating it), pursue recreation, drive vehicles and continually make choices that affect the environment or other citizens and therefore influence sustainable development. But the public also fulfils other roles and they have rights and obligations. They form part of the immediate living environment and comprise employees, employers, self-employed workers, voluntary workers, recreationists, members of householders, those raising children and so on.

Citizens' groups can communicate with the public

Other, more general, organizations such as *citizens' groups* (eg trade unions, motorists' associations, councils of churches, consumers' associations, youth groups) can play a key role in communications with the public. Emphasis needs to be placed on action as much as knowledge. The citizen needs to know what he or she can do him or herself, and both 'desire and be able' to change. It is difficult for the government to gain access to private citizens. Specialist organizations are better placed to do this.

DONOR AGENCIES

Donors can support and assist strategy processes

In developing countries, development cooperation agencies have a role to play in providing support (when requested) to assist the development and implementation of strategies. Donors can support strategies in four main ways:

Box 4.9 **The role and functions of NGOs**

The way in which NGOs have been involved in strategic planning processes in developed and developing countries differs markedly. In industrial countries, they have been consulted extensively in strategic planning processes, although their inputs have mainly involved providing information, gathering data and commenting on strategies. In contrast, in developing countries, NGOs tend to have been viewed more as vehicles for strategy implementation in the field. With notable exceptions, they have been canvassed less frequently for their views and information for the strategy process – and still more rarely involved in policy formulation, monitoring and the other elements of strategies. But it is now recognized that NGOs in all countries have a vital role to play in strategies.

NGOs form a very diverse group, covering a spectrum from long-established, major international and national institutions to fragile, local operations with no staff or guaranteed funding. They may work on single issues or broad-spectrum development concerns. Almost all of them operate through organizing groups of people to make better use of their own resources. Their expertise and views encompass many practical functions which can be enormously important in both developing and implementing strategies:

- mobilizing the public, or certain groups;
- detailed field knowledge of social and environmental conditions;
- delivery of services: disaster relief; education, health;
- encouraging appropriate community, organization and capacity building;
- research, policy analysis and advice;
- facilitation and improvement of social and political processes;
- mediation and reconciliation of conflict;
- awareness raising and communications;
- watchdog, warning and monitoring;
- advocacy and challenging the status quo; promoting alternatives;
- training in, and use of, participatory approaches.

NGO coalitions can complement and buttress governments where the latter are weak, such as in welfare and in engagement with local communities, and where governments are limited in their capacity to use participatory methods. Working with government can help to 'scale up' the contribution of NGOs, which otherwise can remain parochial. On the other hand, NGO coalitions can act as a check and critic where governments and the private sector are too strong (eg in appropriating natural resources and causing adverse social and environmental impacts).

It must be remembered that NGOs do not act as one group. With respect to sustainable development, they cover a spectrum of approaches:

- 'interest-based' NGOs, for example, natural history societies and professional association;
- 'concern-based' NGOs, for example, environmental and animal welfare campaigning and advocacy groups;
- 'solution-based' NGOs, for example, education and rural development groups.

It is the type of approach, as much as the functions of the NGO, that will really determine how it can participate in a strategy. As Bass et al (1995) note:

Many NGOs, particularly the 'solution-based' groups, are comfortable with ideas of participation and consensus – and actively promote them. Others, who work through lobbying and advocacy, tend to see their role as one of 'disagreeing', not seeking compromise. Consequently, a few of these NGOs (particularly from environmental and welfare campaigning interests) take approaches, which appear to be incompatible with sustainable development – which depends upon negotiated trade-offs. Normally, such NGOs are likely to stay on the margins of a participatory strategy – where the debate and consensus usually will take place within a middle ground which none the less should cover all sectors and major groups.

Often, NGOs have been successful at organizing participation locally. Occasionally, NGOs can play central roles in sustainable development in a government 'vacuum'. For example, in Kenya and Tanzania, NGOs operate a major proportion of the health system. In Northern Pakistan, the Aga Khan Rural Support Programme is the leading actor in rural development support. The Bangladesh Rural Advancement Committee (BRAC) runs a large proportion of primary schools.

These major operations are the exception. Yet their much-publicized success tends to have resulted in NGOs being viewed principally as 'delivery mechanisms'. This view – or worse, viewing NGOs merely as amateurs, rather than as development organizations with lessons to teach – is a serious error.

In the past, NCSs and NEAPs tended to involve environmental NGOs more than other types of NGO. But strategies for sustainable development need to deal more extensively with the social dimension, in which development NGO/CBOs have much experience. This is particularly the case because NSDSs will need to address the common policy/planning system failure to: link government to local communities and resource users; understand and act on local complexity; and enlist local resource users in implementation. All of these are areas where NGOs have comparative advantages – at the 'meso' level between central government and local communities.

- in changing their *internal* procedures and practices to support the principles and elements of NSDSs (Boxes 3.1 and 3.2);
- at the *international level* in discussions and negotiations on issues of relevance to sustainable development strategies;
- at the *national level*, in the policy dialogue with partner country governments;
- at the *operational level* in the projects and programmes which development agencies support.

These roles and donor involvement in monitoring strategies are considered in detail in the OECD DAC policy guidance for development cooperation on NSDSs (OECD DAC, 2001a) (see also the section on formal internal and external monitoring, page 311).

Mapping out the strategy process, taking stock of existing strategies and other planning processes

It is usually best to build on existing strategic planning processes

As noted in the section on harnessing effective strategic mechanisms in a continual-improvement system on page 74, the DAC policy guidance on strategies for sustainable development (OECD DAC 2001a) does not generally recommend a strategy to be a completely new or stand-alone initiative, but strongly recommends building on existing strategic planning processes in a country – at national to local levels – and seeking convergence between them (see page 104). Chapter 3 (pages 30–73) describes the main types of strategy framework likely to be found in most countries. Box 4.10 illustrates how a diversity of mechanisms can contribute to the development of an NSDS.

So a key task is a stocktaking exercise to identify and analyse past frameworks ...

In designing the processes and coordination system(s) that will be required to develop a strategy for sustainable development, a key task will be to map out existing strategic planning processes, as well as any past ones which can provide important lessons – identifying the key features of the processes followed, the mechanisms used, and analysing what has worked well or less well. This will help to suggest which processes and mechanisms can be built upon, which approaches might best be avoided, where there are synergies to be forged and where there are gaps that need filling. Such a mapping and stocktaking exercise is considered in detail on page 161. It may be summarized in two basic steps:[7]

1 *Identify* all existing and past strategic planning frameworks, mechanisms and processes, and gather a collection of all key documents (covering: process followed, background materials, major reports and outputs).

   It will be necessary to contact all line ministries, government agencies and sub-national authorities to identify those official processes they are leading and/or involved in as participants. In addition, similar information in respect of unofficial and project-related processes should be sought from NGOs such as key NGOs and NGO coalitions, and private sector organizations.

2 *Analyse* the different existing strategy frameworks, processes and mechanisms, setting out their main features according to a common set of parameters and undertake a comparative analysis of their strengths and weaknesses. This will include an assessment of both process and content, as explored further in Chapter 5.

   This should include: mandate; principles followed (from Box 3.1); main stakeholders and their responsibilities; functions employed (analysis, debate, communication, decision-making, planning investments, implementation and control, monitoring and review – see Figure 4.2); types of

---

7 These steps will need to be undertaken in parallel to assessing the net benefits of a strategy as part of the initial scoping exercise – see page 77.

Box 4.10 The development of El Salvador's National Sustainable Development Strategy: a diversity of contributing mechanisms

---

Following the end of civil conflict in 1992, El Salvador has been in transition to democracy. It provides a concrete example of a country where a variety of mechanisms emerged and were used to help develop a NSDS. Different sectors and levels of society debated and promoted a wide range of proposals, mechanisms and initiatives aimed at greater participation and decentralization in order to consolidate democratic processes and generate inclusive, sustainable development (**vision and goals** for the country).

Converging towards a unified objective, a variety of mechanisms were initiated or drawn upon.

- Several institutions/organizations provided channels for **communication and awareness–raising**. An advocacy campaign – using consensus documents as a platform – was pursued by the National Association of Private Enterprises (ANEP), together with two prestigious national research institutes: the Salvadoran Fund for Economic and Social Development (FUSADES) and the El Salvador Centre for Democratic Studies (CEDES).
- ANEP drew up the 'Entrepreneurs' Manifesto to the Nation' and FUSADES/CEDES presented 'The Salvadorian challenge: from peace to sustainable development'.
- The NGO Network for Local Development promoted decentralization and local development, laying the groundwork for **participation** mechanisms.
- At the invitation of the country's President, the National Commission on Development promulgated the 'Basis for the National Plan' (a **strategic assessment**).
- Subsequently, the Commission presented 'Initial Actions in the National Plan', following extensive consultations with citizens and the participation of numerous national professionals as part of **planning, prioritization and decision-making** mechanisms.
- The 'Proposal for a National Strategy for Local Development' (ENDL) was developed and presented by the Social Investment Fund for Local Development (FISDL) and the Consultative Group (formed by other organizations representing civil society and government). This set out a comprehensive and integrated approach to development, including **institutional change management** mechanisms.

Among the numerous processes and proposals formulated, various **coordination mechanisms** can be identified. For example, in 1997, government and donor agencies collaborated in:

- forming the National Council for Sustainable Development (CNDS), created by decree;
- supporting amendments to the Law on the Fund for Economic and Social Development (FODES) that allocates 6 per cent of the national budget to municipal development (**financial resources mobilization and allocation**);
- advocating and supporting the 'Proposed Guidelines for a Rural Development Strategy' by the Rural Development Committee (CDR) based on three fundamental pillars: (1) establishment of the basis of development; (2) adoption of policies to benefit rural areas; and (3) co-responsibility of civil society in rural development (**negotiation and conflict management**);
- backing the citizens' consultative process at the local level under the framework of the National Plan, as well as the establishment of the National Mechanism for Follow Up on the National Plan for Reconstruction and Transformation (**monitoring and accountability**).

Source: Jorge Reyes (personal communication)

---

participation used; resources actually employed; links to other processes (including regional and international links); where and how decisions are made; and stakeholder opinions, differences and contentions regarding the strategy processes. This should be supplemented by a stocktaking of the scope/content of each strategy to include: major issues covered by theme and sector; strategy objectives; schedule of resulting vision, policies and programmes or recommendations for these; and stakeholder opinions, differences and contentions regarding the strategy contents.

Questionnaires can be used, but experience shows that more useful information and materials can be elicited through semi-structured interviews with key individuals (those responsible for managing individual processes and key stakeholders who participated – or were excluded from – these processes), and by convening small stakeholder workshops.

... leading to a status
review report as a
baseline ...

The outcome of such a stocktaking should be synthesized in a 'status review' report, which can be used as a baseline for further work and as a means to inform potential stakeholders about the status of existing processes and where there are gaps (eg issues not being addressed) or critical opportunities for making progress. This report would be submitted to the steering committee as one of the first outputs of the strategy process.

As a 'map' of the country's key strategic planning experience emerges, depending on the number of frameworks involved, it might be necessary to prioritize which ones should be the focus of deeper analysis. It will also be necessary to decide how far back (in time) the search and analysis should reach. It is probably worth undertaking a general sweep back over the last decade in the first instance. As a rough guide:

- If there is *one clearly dominant strategy process* which initial review and discussions indicate is by far the most important and has had great influence on development in the country, then it would make sense to focus mainly on this, but still to devote some effort to examining other processes which it is felt will yield important lessons. It will probably be useful to focus the analysis from a clear turning point (eg a major shift in government policy, or the establishment of a new cross-cutting institution with influence and power).
- If there are *several strategies* which are seen as being of broadly similar importance and influence, then it might be worthwhile covering all of these, at least at first, and then selecting which one(s) to focus on (based on an assessment of importance, influence and likelihood of deriving important and useful lessons).

... identifying key
cross-cutting issues

The initial assessment of these strategic planning processes will identify key cross-cutting process and content issues that are going well. It will also show which need to be tackled further through a strategy for sustainable development. This all helps to establish a useful agenda for an early steering committee meeting, which should be focused on *where do we want to go, what might our strategic objectives be, and what processes will best take us there?*

Seeking to improve coherence and coordination between strategy frameworks at all levels

Coherence, coordination (and convergence) of national strategic frameworks

There is insufficient
convergence of
planning frameworks
at and between all
levels

Currently, there is insufficient convergence between different planning frameworks at both national and decentralized levels as well as between these levels and between sectors. This is not surprising, as these frameworks are often based on fundamental differences in the motivations and mandates of the 'driving' institutions, stakeholder power bases, concepts, ideologies and funding. It follows that these strategic frameworks have different intentions, stakeholders and objectives, and use different mechanisms. Where they all impact on sustainable development aspirations and outcomes, there is a need to strengthen coordination and coherence. Multiple strategies that are *not* united by a basic common vision or use the same processes for continuous improvement will risk duplication, conflict, waste of scarce administrative and intellectual resources, and rapidly decreasing goodwill.

Coherence and
coordination of
planning frameworks
is essential

It is not feasible to merge all frameworks, although some may converge. It is feasible, however, to work towards coherence and coordination so that different strategic planning frameworks are mutually supportive. The key here will be to encourage (or require) those responsible for the different frameworks to adhere to the principles and elements outlined in Boxes 3.1 and 3.2. The process of convergence could be enhanced by better information. Governments (in partnership with key stakeholders in the private sector and civil society, as well as with development agencies) should ideally develop and maintain a matrix framework of all the existing and new strategic planning processes in their countries, highlighting linkages, differences and relationships between them, and how they adhere to the principles and elements in Boxes 3.1 and 3.2. This would focus attention on what needs to be done for complementarity. The mapping and stocktaking exercise discussed on pages 102–104 would produce the baseline matrix (the CDF aims to promote this approach – see page 54). Such a matrix would help to ensure that new planning frameworks build on what already exists and create links between frameworks. This is a simple informational approach – the advantage being that it would encourage the different frameworks to come together for certain operations, such as visioning and monitoring. It would save costs and unite efforts. Eventually, it should become clear where stronger management of the coherence process is needed; for example, through regulation or by establishing some elements as formal policy.

Where such links have been made and strategies have built on what exists, progress has been good and resulting strategies have broader ownership, as evidenced by different experiences of developing poverty reduction strategies (Box 4.11).

One practical measure to enhance coherence would be to invest in the capacities to implement and enforce.[8] This applies particularly where effort is spent on upgrading and consolidating laws and regulations as part of the strategic planning process. Through parallel investment in legal revision and enforcement improvements, the merits of coherence become self-evident (page 162). The fact that they remain obscure to many participants in many countries indicates that there is still a long way to travel.

Focusing strategic objectives at the right level – from regional to local, and between sectors – and ensuring coherence and coordination there

As we noted in Chapter 3, many previous national strategies have, in fact, been 'encyclopedias' covering all kinds of possible actions from national institutional reform to local technical issues (eg proposing particular soil conservation technologies). Many strategies have been rather insular, and have not particularly touched on international political objectives (eg to improve ocean management) – although others have included this in the mix. Pakistan's experience has shown quite how unstrategic this is. In contrast, the intention for the next iteration of Pakistan's NCS is for it to focus on what can only be done at the national level to mainstream sustainable development. This primarily means improving federal policy on, for example, finance, growth and poverty, and developing strategic, supportive links to local strategic mechanisms that work well or are promising: for example, provincial and district strategies, major rural development programmes and the new political devolution process (see below). But it also means improving trade and foreign policy so that the international 'rules of the game' can begin to favour sustainable development in Pakistan. Box 4.12 gives further details on this development. Ghana's Vision 2020 is a good example of where such national issues as finance, trade and foreign policy were explicitly considered and the responsible ministries have all been heavily involved in developing the medium-term policy frameworks to operationalize the vision.

It is important to be clear about what a 'national' strategy should do

Decentralization potentially offers an effective mechanism for the convergence of different planning frameworks. Integration can often be more successfully achieved through bottom-up demand rather than top-down reorganization. Strong local institutions, accessible information, fora to allow debate and

Strategic links should be established between national and local levels

---

8 The strengthening of enforcement capacities needs to extend beyond the recruitment and training of additional legal staff (police or administrators), as well as beyond the changing of public attitudes and acceptance of codes of behaviour. It should also include the education and training of judges, magistrates and related staff to appreciate the full nature of the environmental and social impacts that violations of the law can have. This should enable proportional corrective penalties to be determined and administered. Unfortunately, to date, many activities which are detrimental to sustainable development remain largely 'beyond the law'. See page 162 for discussion on legal mechanisms.

Box 4.11 Building on what exists: links between poverty reduction strategies and other strategic planning processes

Uganda

The Poverty Reduction Strategy Paper (PRSP) was based on a revision of Uganda's own 1997 Poverty Eradication Action Plan. It also drew on other existing strategic assessment work including a Poverty Status Report, a Participatory Poverty Assessment and a Plan for the Modernization of Agriculture. This inclusion of previous work has apparently greatly increased country ownership of the PRS.

Bolivia

The Biodiversity Strategy and Action Plan was developed through a highly participatory process that ensured an emphasis on poverty alleviation through economic activities related to the sustainable use of biodiversity. Following lobbying by the Minister for Sustainable Development in the Economic Policy Council, this strategy has now been incorporated as part of the Poverty Reduction Strategy.

Burkina Faso

When the PRSP was developed, efforts were made to incorporate its intentions into existing sectoral policies, plans and reform programmes (eg basic education and health). This integration needs to continue, particularly to ensure that sectoral policies and plans specifically address the linkages between poverty and environment, and define indicators to track these linkages.

The process of integration could have been strengthened by drawing on the country's National Action Programme (NAP) to combat desertification. The NAP was developed in a participatory manner, with nearly 50,000 people involved in its development, and was based on considerable analysis. But those responsible for the NAP were not involved in the PRS process, and the experience and lessons from undertaking the NAP were not drawn into it. The updating of the PRSP provides an opportunity to address this.

In developing the OECD DAC policy guidance, development agencies supported a dialogue process in Burkina Faso, which played a catalytic role in fostering this convergence of frameworks. The dialogue ensured that recommendations to government reflected the views of stakeholders. These included proposals for the sustainable development strategy for the country to be prepared not as a document with new policy assessments but rather as an umbrella for the main legal instruments, principles for intervention and institutional reforms. In this way, the strategy would aim to ensure sustained growth, taking into account and responding practically to issues such as:

- sustainable human development;
- equity in the distribution of the benefits of growth;
- transparency in the management of public affairs and the provisions of help;
- efficiency and sustainability of development programmes;
- reinforcement of capacities at the national level.

The dialogue proposed measures for improving the PRS which are being used as a reference framework by the Ministry of Economy and Finance, namely:

- to present the PRSP more widely as the only framework which the cooperation programmes of development assistance agencies should follow;
- to make the PRSP more widely available and to prepare shorter and more simple versions;
- to update the PRSP, with a view to integrating all sectoral plans within a single framework. This will involve close collaboration between all the ministries, the private sector and civil society so as to ensure harmonization and coherence among existing or planned coordination mechanisms, indicators, and mechanisms for monitoring and evaluation;
- to generate new financial resources for the national budget to implement the strategy.

Ghana

In contrast to the above cases, a domestic poverty eradication strategy had been prepared in Ghana. This was subsequently transformed into an interim PRSP. The preparation of the full PRSP is being undertaken as part of the preparation of the Second Medium-Term Development Plan to implement Ghana's Vision 2020 – a broader, longer-term framework. This plan will also incorporate the core development objectives of Ghana's Comprehensive Development Framework (developed through separate institutional arrangements) and the UN Development Assistance Framework. The convergence of these strategic planning processes attests to the common principles that underpin them.

Source: OECD DAC (2001a)

consensus/conflict management mechanisms can all forge integrated solutions – if they really have the power to influence intermediate-level and national decisions. Hence there is an imperative to link top-down and bottom-up approaches. This needs to be accompanied by:

- the transfer of financial resources and the empowerment of appropriate organizations to raise such resources locally;
- capacity building (this is a key component of Tanzania's Local Government Reform Programme, 2000–2003);
- a clear delineation of government roles in planning, financial management, coordination and so on, at various hierarchical levels;
- comprehensive legislation and administrative actions to bring about integration of the decentralized offices of government agencies into local administrative structures;
- coordination of development agency support.

Box 4.12 Initiating bottom-up strategy approaches in Pakistan: complementing provincial and district strategies

Following the National Conservation Strategy (NCS), provincial strategies were developed in most provinces. These adopted many process innovations such as round table workshops, contact focal points in line agencies, and much more consultation with resource user groups and 'policy communities'. Subsequently, this led to district strategies in Sarhad (North West Frontier) Province. The nearer to the level of direct resource management, the more clearly are sustainable development and livelihood trade-offs having to be addressed. The challenge recognized in Pakistan is now to develop channels for information and demand to be expressed from district, to provincial, to national levels.

It is therefore proposed that NCS-2 should focus on *national-level concerns, and national institutional roles*, rather than prescribing everything right down to the village level. But it will also recognize, encourage and support provincial, district and other demand-driven strategic approaches based on local realities consonant with the devolution plan. This contrasts with the national policy/intellectual push of the original NCS. Thus the scope includes:

International issues

- Pakistan's position and contribution in relation to global environmental issues and conventions;
- sustainable development aspects of globalization;
- regional issues such as river basins, shared protected areas, transboundary and marine pollution.

National issues

- need for an overarching framework for the preparation, implementation, monitoring, evaluation and updating of regional and provincial strategies, including the national coordination of research and development programmes relating to sustainable development;
- bringing together the most useful and effective mechanisms required for developing and implementing a strategy (eg information systems, participatory mechanisms, packages of supporting measures, economic instruments, etc – see Chapter 8);
- continued guidelines for provincial and sectoral policies for mainstreaming sustainable development through policies, principles/criteria, standards, indicators and monitoring;
- coordinating major national programmes aimed at sustainable development;
- promoting sustainable development within macro-policy concerns, notably structural adjustment loans, poverty reduction, national environment and security issues;
- assessing and monitoring sustainable development and environmental standards.

Supporting provincial, urban and district issues

- supporting provincial sustainable development strategies and initiatives – especially so that local (urban, district and community-related) institutions are able to drive the strategy from the bottom up;
- controls and incentives for increased private sector innovation and investment in sustainable development, and for responsible practice.

Source: OECD DAC (2001a)

*Coherence can be
forged through
'sectoral/thematic'
processes*

In Canada, a slightly different approach has been followed to develop a 'national' strategic response to sustainable development challenges. Individual ministries/departments in government are expected to take a lead in integrating sustainable development into sectors and policy communities. There is no single national strategy for sustainable development. Nor does one institution 'strategise' for the others.[9] Instead, parliament has established a 'Commissioner of the Environment and Sustainable Development' to hold all of government accountable for 'greening' its policies, operations and programmes, and for ensuring sustainability is central to all of these. Thus, its prime responsibilities include monitoring, evaluation and coordination. Legislation requires all federal ministries (including finance, trade and foreign affairs) to table departmental sustainable development strategies in parliament. An advantage of this approach is that it enables a greater clarity on what sustainable development means for a particular sector. The departmental strategies are prepared under the guidance provided by a 1995 government policy statement on sustainable development, *A Guide to Green Government* which gives direction on broad objectives, priority areas and how the strategies are to be structured and prepared (Box 4.13). However, it remains to be seen how effective this singularly different approach proves to be. Much will depend on the extent to which parliament is required to act upon the advice and recommendations provided by the Commissioner. One area where government departments have determined that more work needs to be done is in developing more coordinated approaches to sustainable development issues that cut across departmental mandates. To this end, departments have agreed to work closely together on a number of theme areas and to reflect them in their individual strategies.

Work is currently under way to synthesize the 28 individual departmental strategies in order to present a more comprehensive view of sustainable development effort across the federal government. The shared jurisdiction and responsibility between the federal and provincial and territorial governments makes moving towards a 'national' sustainable development strategy particularly challenging (Clara Rodrigues, Environment Canada, personal communication).

*Coherence can also be
built through 'link'
officers*

In the Sarhad Provincial Conservation Strategy (SPCS) in Pakistan, coherence between government departments is being attempted in a different fashion – Focal Point staff link that department to the provincial strategy secretariat and to thematic round tables connected to the provincial strategy process (Box 4.14). Similar institutional arrangements were established in the Governorate of Sohag, Egypt, as part of the provisions for effective implementation of the Environmental Action Plan in 1997/98; they have also been advocated, and are variously being applied, in Botswana, Kenya and Cross River State, Nigeria.

*Coherence and
coordination with
finance and
development
authorities needs
extra attention*

We have stressed that NSDSs need to involve all key ministries, and that one ministry should not dominate. But the fact is that, in all countries, major development decisions tend to be taken by ministries responsible for finance and economic planning, and their major stakeholders such as banks and corporations. Special efforts must be made to involve these, and to ensure coherence and coordination with their policies and procedures. However, sustainable development has usually been made the responsibility of environment ministries, which have limited influence in government, and have therefore not been seen as of interest in other sectors. At best, this has enabled the formation of a community or network concerned only with environmental policy. At worst, this undermines progress towards sustainable development through lack of integration in these key sectors. For key finance and economic stakeholders to become

---

9 In the past, a particular ministry has often initiated discussion on a strategic planning process. There has rarely been effective engagement with other line ministries to build cross-government support, and seldom has the issue been introduced in cabinet so as to gain broader political commitment at an early stage. Experience shows that when lead responsibility for a strategy lies within a particular line ministry (especially where it controls the process and budget), this creates a perception that the strategy is a project of that ministry or a sectoral matter. This results in limited involvement and cooperation from other ministries (OECD DAC 2001a).

Box 4.13 Departmental strategies for sustainable development, Canada

The Canadian government's *A Guide to Green Government* is designed to assist all federal departments in preparing sustainable development strategies. It comprises three parts:

I. The Sustainable Development Challenge translates the concept of sustainable development into terms that are meaningful to Canadians, underscoring its important social, economic and environmental dimensions. A series of sustainable development objectives are presented (for example, using renewable resources sustainably, preventing pollution, fostering improved productivity through environmental efficiency) that represent a starting point for the preparation of departmental strategies.

II. Planning and Decision-making for Sustainable Development sets out the policy, operational and management tools that will facilitate the shift to sustainable development. It encourages an integrated approach to planning and decision-making, based on the best available science and analysis, and visions and expectations of Canadians. The approaches discussed include: promoting integration through the use of tools such as full-cost accounting, environmental assessment and ecosystem management; developing strategies by working with individuals, the private sector, other governments and Aboriginal people; using a mix of policy tools such as voluntary approaches, information and awareness tools, economic instruments, direct government expenditure and command and control.

III. Preparing a departmental Sustainable Development Strategy presents the main elements that departments could consider as the basis of their strategies. It is recommended that 'strategies should all be results-oriented, showing in clear, concrete terms what departments will accomplish on the environment and sustainable development; comprehensive, covering all of a department's activities; and prepared in consultation with clients and stakeholders'. Six steps are suggested for the preparation of strategies:

1   Preparation of a **departmental profile**, identifying what the department does and how it does it.
2   **Issues scan:** assessment of the department's activities in terms of their impact on sustainable development.
3   **Consultations** on the perspective of clients, partners and other stakeholders on departmental priorities for sustainable development and how to achieve them. It is suggested that a brief report 'on the nature of the consultations and how views contributed to the final product would be useful for partners and stakeholders, and contribute to openness and transparency in the preparation of strategies'.
4   Identification of the department's **goals and objectives and targets** for sustainable development, including benchmarks it will use for measuring performance.
5   Development of an **action plan** that will translate the department's sustainable development targets into measurable results, including specifying policy, programme, legislative, regulatory and operational changes.

   Because sustainable development is a shared responsibility among departments, governments, Aboriginal people and other stakeholders, implementation of action plans will likely require cooperation and partnership. In these instances, departmental strategies should describe the cooperative mechanisms and partnerships that will help them achieve the targets, objectives and, eventually, their goals.

6   Creation of mechanisms to monitor (measurement and analysis), report on and improve the department's performance.

Source: Government of Canada (1995)

---

major participants in a strategy, there must be high-level commitment and relevant economic and risk analyses available. In some countries, this has been enhanced on a regular basis by linking strategies to budget processes (see Box 4.15).

Regional issues are important for a nation's sustainable development, and regional processes can be supportive. The NSDS process needs to incorporate a consideration of the issues (notably an ongoing analysis of the impacts on neighbouring countries – and vice versa – and of past strategies and new development options and proposals), and links to key regional processes. Regional approaches need to address, for example, the concerns of indigenous peoples where they are located across international borders, and problems of cross-border refugees. Regional coordination and management is also important

Regional coherence is likely to be increasingly important

Box 4.14 **Sarhad Provincial Conservation Strategy: coordination through 'Focal Points'**

Pakistan's National Conservation Strategy (NCS) has relied on a couple of centralized units in the Ministry of Environment, Local Government and Rural Development to promote the NCS to provinces and other ministries. In contrast, the Sarhad Provincial Conservation Strategy (SPCS) recognized the need to establish 'insider' posts within the various departments. Some of these 'SPCS Focal Point' posts are filled by government staff, others are IUCN staff.

The job of the Focal Points is to link together the departments, the SPCS Support Unit in the provincial planning department, and thematic round tables (RTs) of the SPCS. They gain intelligence about the plans and progress of the various departments. Thus they can improve communication between the departments and the SPCS Support Unit, and improve coordination in planning. They also aim to encourage full participation by the department in the RTs, and thus integration with the plans of other departments, the private sector and NGOs (each Focal Point's technical agenda more or less corresponds to one of the RTs – see Box 3.20). This is a simple way of trying to improve links, but it is certainly improving information flows and many Focal Points are gaining respect. However, they face constraints that derive from norms in the Pakistani civil service:

- *Inadequate administrative powers:* Until recently, the Focal Points were not of a high enough status. With few bureaucratic powers, they have been obliged to use expert and persuasion powers (and occasionally links to donors) to encourage a greater mainstreaming of sustainable development concerns in that department. However, the departmental counterparts to the Focal Point are now more senior – the Additional Secretary.
- *'Cult of the boss':* Irrespective of the value of the Focal Point's contribution, it is the interest and motivation of the department head which tends to set the tone for the department, not an 'outsider/insider'. This is a general observation in Pakistan – thus the conservation strategies aim for change, demonstrating that real leadership is shared.
- *Few resources for change:* One person with no administrative support does not command 'hierarchy'-related respect or resources, and is overburdened. He or she has to rely on a variety of tactics at various levels in the relevant department to get anything done, sometimes causing delays and upsetting people in the process. Focal Points need training as facilitators, to get the best out of others.
- *Poor links to federal level:* Since there are many aspects of change at provincial level that are still subject to control at federal level, the work of the provincial departmental Focal Points is constrained by poor links between the provincial SPCS Unit and the federal NCS Coordinating Unit.

Source: Hanson et al (2000)

when a number of countries share natural resources and ecosystems (eg a river basin or watershed) or suffer transboundary pollution. If global governance has so far failed to help countries with many international issues, regional approaches appear more promising. Common problems are more apparent, common resources may be available, and similar cultural or political values may be employed in making trade-offs. For example, the Andean Biodiversity Strategy developed by several South American countries provides a shared regional vision and identifies common interests. The Central American Forest Convention provides a framework for individual national forest programmes.

Establishing and agreeing ground rules governing strategy procedures

We have established the principle that an NSDS best builds on what exists already. However, as this approach brings together different initiatives, as well as many actors, there will be multiple ways of working, precedents and expectations. This is particularly the case with expectations relating to participation and consensus processes, and what impact this will have on decisions. Stakeholders need to know that there is an orderly approach to participation (see Chapter 6).

While the strategy principles and elements in Boxes 3.1 and 3.2 provide generic guidance, they need to be given substance when developing and implementing a particular strategy. It may, therefore, be advisable to formalize clear and distinct 'ground rules' (operating rules) governing the strategy process and procedures

---

Box 4.15 Linking strategies to budget processes

New Zealand: The annual budget and planning cycle includes a strategic phase for establishing the government's priorities in the short-, medium- and long-term. These strategic priorities are 'bedded in' through budget appropriations, purchase agreements and strategic and key result areas in chief executive's performance agreements. Chief executives of government departments that affect the environment are required to take into account in their annual planning the relevant goals of the country's Environment 2010 Strategy.

Canada: The Green Plan (1990–1996) was linked to the federal budget process and had built-in targets and schedules as a mechanism for public accountability.

Botswana: Over the past decade, the National Conservation Strategy Coordinating Agency has been drawn into the national planning and budget review processes of the Ministry of Finance and Development Planning. Professional linkages have been established although multi-sectoral reform has yet to be achieved.

---

involved. These will enable those with responsibility for coordinating or managing particular processes to know exactly how to proceed, and within what parameters. It will help all stakeholders to know what can be expected. It will also be helpful to gain agreement from component processes and institutions to adjust their own ground rules to accommodate the strategy.

NSDS 'ground rules' can clarify how processes should proceed and what stakeholders can expect

Ground rules will also be needed to give rigour to the strategy process, ensuring that it is comprehensive, and protecting it from becoming one-sided or inequitable. Nevertheless, ground rules should encourage experimentation.

The ground rules will need to be consistent with the principles and elements in Boxes 3.1 and 3.2, and a discussion of these principles will be a useful starting point. Agreement will be needed on which will be obligatory and which will be merely aspirations. The NSDS ground rules should be simple, and could cover:

- *Membership* of the various steering committees, working groups and secretariat – procedures on representation and attendance – and similar rules on selecting stakeholders for consultations.
- How *decisions* will be made. Where a recognized existing body is used to take decisions, for example, cabinet, the precedent will be clear. Where powers are given to special NSDS groups, rules would cover the development of decisions; for example, the use of consensus (page 272), voting, conflict management and arbitration in relation to different types of decision (major policy decisions versus, for example, programme development or project decisions, etc). Clarity will be needed on the scope and limitations to participation in the strategy. Consensus has generally been found to be a useful approach, since it incorporates principles of equity and learning (see Chapter 8).
- *Conduct of meetings* – their timing, recording, reporting and attribution of ideas and opinions to named groups.
- *Communication and public disclosure* – the channels that will be used, how they can be accessed by stakeholders, and timing.
- *Financial rules* regarding fees and expenses.
- *Monitoring, review and accountability* – it may be helpful to establish some ground rules at the beginning about when, how and by whom the NSDS processes and outcomes will be assessed, and who will be accountable, especially if independent reviews are required.
- The *schedule and timing* (see next section).

Establishing a schedule and calendar for the strategy process

A strategy calendar can specify tasks, products and targets

The secretariat will need to determine activities to be undertaken in developing and operating the strategy, as well as identify responsibilities, capabilities and resources needed, and their timing. A generic strategy 'calendar' can be scheduled, based around existing component calendars, such as those of government (budgetary) processes and other key strategies. This could cover, for example, regular 'state of the environment and livelihoods' reports, major NSDS review meetings and annual national conferences. Three- to five-year cyclical calendars have commonly been used (although the cyclical element may not subsequently have taken place in practice). Specific targets related to the NSDS objectives and major programmes would then be inserted into the first regular 'cycle'; for example, passing a new law, launching a new programme or removing a specific causal problem.

Clear and reasonable limits for working towards a conclusion of the process and reporting on progress or results should be established. Such milestones bring a focus to the process, mobilize key resources and mark progress towards consensus. Sufficient flexibility, however, is necessary to embrace shifts or changes in timing.

Promoting the strategy

A 'prospectus' sets out the aims, objectives, procedures and mechanisms for the strategy

At any stage, it is important for both the purpose and approach of the strategy to be widely known. Once a new approach to an NSDS has been decided, it has been common to prepare a 'prospectus' which combines the timetable/calendar with:

- the broad *purpose* of a strategy – why it is needed, how it can help and what it would aim to achieve;
- the scope of or (later) the specific *strategic objectives* of the strategy – linked to a brief problem/opportunity statement for each;
- the basic *principles and ground rules* governing the strategy;
- an overview of the *component mechanisms* (participation, information, monitoring, decision-making, investment and the various committees, etc) and how they will work;
- the schedule of *steps and actions* for the regular NSDS 'calendar', and to tackle specific strategic objectives;
- an indication of *who needs to be involved* and how they can do so;
- an overview of the types of *indicators* of achievement;
- an assessment of the key *skills and resources required*, how those which are lacking will be found, and the order of cost;
- *achievements to date* where relevant – stories from, for example, pilot projects (see next section) and policy changes. Include a brief overview of past approaches (including their key strengths and weaknesses) when a new approach is being promoted.

A summary version of this should be published for use as a promotional tool and press releases provided regularly to the media to promote the strategy. Chapter 7 provides more details on community approaches.

The role of experiments and pilot projects

Strategy pilot projects can demonstrate implementation and tangible benefits

Many outcomes of strategies take time to prepare, and delays can lead to an apparent vacuum of on-the-ground activity and consequent loss of interest, trust and support. It has been found helpful to undertake pilot projects during the strategy process as a 'shop window' to show how the strategy might be implemented in practice, and to demonstrate some tangible and practical benefits and results early on (eg better public health facilities, efficient solid waste management, the regular provision of clean drinking water, conservation of natural resources). For example, in 1986, the Zambia NCS supported the Luangwa Integrated Resource Development Project (one of Africa's earliest, and now longest running and most successful, community-based natural resource management initiatives) as a rural pilot, and a poverty-and-environment peri-urban squatter settlement upgrading pilot project (Human Settlements of Zambia). Budget provision needs to be made for such pilot initiatives. Obviously, pilots and demonstrations should continue and not be confined to the early stages of a strategy.

Practical demonstration through such pilot initiatives has a vital role to play in both developed and developing countries – in showing that it is possible to deliver at least some components of sustainable development.

Establishing and improving the regular strategy mechanisms and processes

Certain mechanisms (Figure 4.1) and processes (Figure 4.2) provide the 'lifeblood' of the strategy. They ensure that all stakeholders are best able to play their part, and they enable a continuous improvement approach to take place.

Each mechanism or process will have been mapped out as described on pages 102–104. They will be discussed in detail in separate chapters, covering:

- analysis (Chapter 5);
- stakeholder fora and means for participation (Chapter 6);
- communication between stakeholders and between fora (Chapter 7);
- major decision-making procedures (Chapter 8);
- means for planning investments (Chapter 9);
- monitoring, evaluation and accountability mechanisms (Chapter 10).

Great stress has been placed on how important it is that strategy processes are participatory and transparent. It is imperative, therefore, that they are perceived by all stakeholders to be both demand-led and oriented to the achievement of results, whether process improvements or tangible lifestyle and resource conservation improvements.

CHAPTER

5

Analysis[1]

Approaching and organizing the tasks of analysis

Sustainable development is knowledge-intensive

If strategies for sustainable development are genuinely to get to grips with priority problems and produce innovative solutions, good analysis is essential. The term 'analysis' is used in this chapter in a 'catch-all' sense to include identifying and applying relevant *existing knowledge* to the challenges of sustainable development, identifying *gaps in knowledge*, and filling them through research.

The questions and steps involved in conducting the analyses required for effective strategies for sustainable development are set out, and some of the main analytical methodologies are introduced. Analysis does not, however, take place in isolation.

Introducing the main analytical tasks in NSDS processes

Stakeholders need several types of analysis

Analysis of several types may be needed for an NSDS, including:

- *Stakeholder analysis:* Objective identification of stakeholders in the transition to sustainable development, their interests, powers and relations. This helps in constructing committees, working groups and consultation processes. As a continuous process, it should bring in those that matter but might otherwise not have come forward (page 120).
- *Sustainability analysis:* Assessing human and environmental conditions, major strengths and weaknesses, key relationships between human and ecosystem elements and between the country (or locality) and the larger system, how close the society is to sustainability, and the direction of change. This is crucial for deciding what the NSDS should address and the actions it should propose as well as for monitoring its implementation (page 132).
- *Strategy process/mechanism analysis:* Identifying and assessing the potential component systems and processes that could be used in an NSDS, by analysing their effectiveness, reliability, equitability and performance (outcomes) to date. This can apply to information, participation, investment and other component processes. It is needed to improve the quality of NSDS performance (page 161).

1 This chapter has benefited from review comments and additional material provided by Robert Prescott-Allen, Canada; Pippa Bird, USA; Jon Lindsay, FAO; and Duncan Macqueen and Joshua Bishop, IIED.

- *Scenario analysis:* Developing plausible pictures of the future, as a means to explore possible strategic options and test their robustness or sensitivity (page 171).
- *Analysis and ranking of options:* Assessing the costs, benefits and risks of optional instruments or programmes to implement the strategy, to submit to subjective decision-making – in this way avoiding biased trade-offs. Decision-making without the advantage of good analysis runs a huge risk of prejudice and misjudgement (Chapter 8).
- *Reviewing strategy achievements:* Assessing how far sustainable development outcomes have been achieved and how they can be correlated with NSDS processes. Many of these tasks are those of routine monitoring and evaluation (considered in Chapter 10).

Challenges in analysis for sustainable development strategies

EFFECTIVE STRATEGIES DEPEND ON SOUND INFORMATION

National strategies for sustainable development should be 'based on comprehensive and reliable analysis', as stated in Principle 5 of the OECD DAC Policy Guidance on strategies (OECD DAC 2001a) (see Box 3.1). Analysis should power the transformation towards sustainable development: all stakeholders need the opportunity to reflect and learn in ways which are suitable to them individually and to society as a whole – what Capacity 21 (UNDP 2000) has called the 'analysis-action-reflection' concept. 'Country-driven', participatory, integrated, continuous improvement approaches to achieving sustainable development called for by the agreements reached at the 1992 Earth Summit (NSDSs, Local Agenda 21, national forestry programmes, etc) place heavy emphases on understanding the local context, on integrating social, environmental and economic goals at local levels, on experimentation and review, and on forming local partnerships. All of this is information-intensive.

Strategies need to be based on a reliable and accurate understanding of local realities

SUSTAINABLE DEVELOPMENT IS COMPLEX AND DIFFICULT TO ANALYSE

If the challenges inherent in sustainable development are not fully explored, any strategy to promote sustainable development will remain nothing more than a bland set of exhortations, unconnected to local realities. Sustainable development requires that a large number of interacting factors be addressed and, since it also requires value judgements, there is a need to involve many groups so that multiple perspectives can be heard. These are major challenges given that multiple factors make correlations and causations difficult to prove. It may be necessary to separate out issues at field, enterprise, landscape, region, national and global levels, as different trade-offs are found at each level. Furthermore, sustainable development demands the ability to anticipate change and assess optional scenarios.

Addressing interacting factors and multiple perspectives is a challenge ...

In earlier attempts at strategic approaches to sustainable development, 'analysis' often consisted merely of assessments of the status of various sustainability issues. Acknowledged 'experts' (but not always local professionals) would be enlisted to write papers assessing, for example, the status of soil erosion or pollution. Good synthesis papers have proved particularly useful if they present what is known about the strengths and weaknesses, opportunities and threats of an issue, and also set out the uncertainties and what is not known – and if they were able to kick off useful debate. But, frequently, these analyses repeated information from long ago, did not challenge assumptions and were done only in the early stages of 'preparing the strategy'.

CAPACITIES TO ANALYSE SUSTAINABLE DEVELOPMENT ARE OFTEN WEAK

This lack of experience in analysis for sustainable development is compounded by local research and analytical capacities, particularly in developing countries, often being severely constrained. Analytical mandates, frameworks and methods for analysis have tended to be narrow or focused on priorities set in the past. The lack of access to good analysis is often worst where it matters most (in poor countries and communities).

... where analytical experience and capacity is not strong

The experience of countries that have tried to analyse their current situations has demonstrated the grave shortage of tools available, and the serious weaknesses of Agenda 21 as a planning or predictive instrument. Ideally, it should be possible to build on the rigor of economic analysis and extend similar approaches to the inter-related domains of sustainable development. In practice, our ability to understand all the social and physical interactions involved is limited. We do not have accepted analytical techniques that bring together all of the interactions of development.
(UNDP 2000)

In practice, in the absence of formal analytical capacity, other democratic processes have fulfilled part of the assessment role – the 'vote' does, after all, capture public perceptions of issues. With so many sustainable development issues being of high political concern, however, the electorate deserves better information.

THERE ARE DANGERS IN RELYING ON NARROW, NON-LOCAL, OUT-OF-DATE OR UNRELIABLE INFORMATION

Reliable, up-to-date information is important

If non-local data are used, other people's myths can become the basis of change (or they merely reinforce the status quo). Out of date analysis (or, more insidiously, the recycling of unchallenged 'facts') is also clearly a poor basis for an NSDS – a problem exemplified by the case of environmental information in Southern Africa (Box 5.1). Even if analysis offers projections of current trends, this can be dangerous if scenarios are not also developed to identify possible major shifts and the consequent problems of vulnerability.

Box 5.1 Poverty of environmental information in Southern Africa

Whilst there is a wealth of documentation on the environment in the countries of Southern Africa, a major problem is that, all too often, a significant proportion of the data which they report has not been 'ground truthed' by field observations, but is based on or summarizes information from other existing sources, much of which is itself repeated from elsewhere. Furthermore, there is often uncertainty about the reliability of data in the original sources. This means that questionable information continues to be given currency without checking, and various 'environmental myths', which they are used to support, such as the extent and seriousness of land degradation in the region, are perpetuated.

In practice, for many environmental factors for which reliable data are required to assess trends meaningfully and to predict future positions, the available data are either questionable or not sufficiently available. Another example is the difficulty of making comparisons between data for rural and urban populations.

The poverty of information in Southern Africa is a serious impediment to predicting future environmental trends. However, whilst there is an undoubted problem with data availability, in some cases the problem is more one of 'invisible information' – ie information exists, but it is dispersed, inaccessible (even kept secret) or unrecognized. A key challenge in addressing many sectoral and cross-sectoral information issues is to think creatively about accessing hidden and unconventional information sources as well as making obvious existing information more useful.

Source: Dalal-Clayton (1997)

Basic principles for analysis

ENGAGE AND INFORM STAKEHOLDERS WITHIN DEMOCRATIC AND PARTICIPATORY PROCESSES

It is interesting that most of the reviews and guidance on strategic approaches have heavily stressed participation, but have barely tackled analytical methods and quality – as if the need for enhanced knowledge were over and all that is needed now is to convince people to change their behaviour and make them feel part of the process (Carew-Reid et al 1994; Dobie 2000; World Bank 2000; UNDP 2000; IMF 2001).

Good analysis is integral to democratic processes, in which governments are trusted with developing the machinery to make complex and difficult decisions. It is also needed where there is a perceived democratic deficit, where special 'participatory mechanisms' may have been set up to help do this: for example, by development assistance agencies and multi-stakeholder initiatives (Chapter 6).

Democratic processes require good analysis …

Analytical inputs are required that can be made available for decision-making through routine and acknowledged systems, that are acceptable to stakeholders, and that produce a ranking or distributional analysis, to help with questions of significance and winners and losers.

Thus, it is not a case of *either* analysis *or* participation – analytical tasks cannot be divorced from stakeholder inputs. Where groups are affected by key issues, they should be able to engage in analysis themselves. This can ensure that NSDSs are demand-driven, rather than the intellectual construct of bureaucrats and professional analysts. Thus, the analytical tools used in an NSDS should enable participation – to encourage wide ownership and to obtain information from a broad range of perspectives that might otherwise remain 'hidden'.

… and analytical tools themselves should enable participation

It is true that there is still prejudice against information generated through participatory techniques. As Dalal-Clayton et al (2000) note, findings from participatory assessments are still commonly greeted with the question 'but how do they compare with *real* data?' Participatory methods of analysis are becoming available which are more accessible to non-'expert' stakeholders and which do not require advanced skills, yet, if used well, cannot be accused of compromising the rigour and quality of findings.

USE ACCESSIBLE AND PARTICIPATORY METHODS OF ANALYSIS

Such action research and participatory analysis methods are becoming available. They offer the 'learning by doing' approach required for sustainable development. Certain methods help to bring multiple dimensions together. Some are more influential than others in terms of engaging decision-makers: for example interdisciplinary processes and action learning. But many are not widely known and/or require further improvement.

Participatory analysis fosters 'learning-by-doing' …

INCLUDE ROLES FOR INDEPENDENT, 'EXPERT' ANALYSIS

While the general approach to NSDSs is a participatory one, this should not obscure the need, in many cases, for specialist expertise. This might be where:

… but specialist expertise can also be needed …

- particular issues may be contentious (when independent commissions and/or specialized expertise may be required);
- there is a large analytical task to be undertaken (such as when it is agreed that a strategy process requires a significant baseline of information which hitherto has been absent);
- highly technical skills and equipment are required: for example scientific measurements, computer analysis of data.

Where an independent institution is selected for conducting the analysis, it should show evidence of maintaining a careful balance between:

… sometimes via an independent body

- relative independence from the policy process (in order to be able to view the big picture, critique policy and innovate without undue fear);
- active engagement with policy actors (so that analysis is, to some extent, demand-driven and gets a good hearing);
- engagement with other stakeholders (so that the institution is seen as credible and not viewed as a servant of higher powers only);
- multiple disciplines and interdisciplinary methodologies (to ensure a holistic approach).

> **Box 5.2 Future of the Environment Survey Office - providing analysis for The Netherlands' Environmental Policy Plan**
>
> In 1988, RIVM published a National Environment Survey – an independent scientific analysis that demonstrated the scale of The Netherlands' environmental problems and the major policy changes required to implement sustainable development. The survey was used to develop the National Environment Policy Plan (NEPP), which indicates how the government intends to deal with the problems. In 1991, RIVM published a second survey, the National Environment Outlook, examining progress with the implementation of the NEPP, the likely effect of policies, and the extent to which these policy measures would be sufficient to reach the objectives set for 2000 and 2010. It was based on the latest scientific developments and expectations about changes in society.
>
> The NEPP is published every four years (see Boxes 4.3 and 4.5). RIVM has been requested to publish an environment survey every two years to provide an assessment and forecasting of the quality of the environment. One year after publication of the NEPP, the survey sets out the expected future quality of the environment when current policies are implemented. One year before the next NEPP, a survey of possible additional policy options is prepared. For this purpose, RIVM has set up a Future of the Environment Survey office, which coordinates the contributions from RIVM laboratories and institutes, and integrates the information and model calculations, including geographical information system (GIS) maps.
>
> Source: RIVM (1992)

This can be a tall order, and some countries have had to support the development of such independent bodies to organize and conduct some of the larger analytical tasks. For example, the National Institute of Public Health and Environmental Protection (RIVM) conducts much of the analysis for The Netherlands Environmental Policy Plan (Box 5.2). The Sustainable Development Policy Institute in Pakistan was established to serve the NCS with policy research support, and has grown in scope and influence.

DEVELOP A CONTINUING, COORDINATED SYSTEM OF KNOWLEDGE GENERATION

Continuous and coordinated knowledge generation ...

In this chapter, we propose a coherent, continuing programme of knowledge generation for sustainable development (comprising data centres, analysis and research capabilities) – and not just a one-off exercise. This should be an integral part of the NSDS process. There are several related principles here:

- Multi-stakeholder groups should design the information gathering, analysis and research process themselves, to ensure *ownership* of the strategy and its results.
- All the 'analysis' tasks laid out in this chapter are best implemented by bringing together, and supporting, *existing centres* of technical expertise, learning and research.
- Since analysis is central to strategy development, it should be *commissioned, agreed and endorsed at the highest level* (ie by key government ministries or by the strategy steering committee). This will increase the chance that analysis will be well focused and timely in relation to the strategy's evolution and timetable, and that its results will be used.
- In the same way, analysis needs *good coordination*. It is logical for the strategy secretariat or coordinating team to coordinate the analysis. However, the secretariat should not undertake all the analyses itself and, indeed, not necessarily any of it. Many players need to be involved. Through their active involvement in reflection and analysis, the strategy will help in building learning institutions.

AGREE CRITERIA FOR PRIORITIZING ANALYSIS

... keeps analysis focused on things that really matter

Without a focus on priorities, the number and type of issues addressed in the strategy process are likely to expand beyond any ability to handle them, and the process may become discredited. It is therefore important to channel attention and thought into what matters, and into what can be done with the best effect for the resources and political will currently available – and not provide a forum for unending debate.

It is important to agree criteria by which analysis – and especially expensive new research – might be prioritized. This is best assessed by reference to criteria for human and ecosystem well-being and practicality. Sustainability assessments described in "Approaches to measuring and analysing sustainability" on page 132 (eg the 'barometer of sustainability' and 'sustainable livelihoods analysis') use such criteria and will be able to reveal this.

In their absence initially, a basic checklist of criteria might be developed (Box 5.3). Among conventional techniques, such checklists are by far the most widely used and practical, and are often combined with some form of cost benefit analysis or econometric approach. This can be qualified by estimates of the chance of success, the likely rate of adoption of results and the probable time needed to complete the project (Macqueen 1999).[2] The development of strategy options and plans should also directly address these criteria, to help stakeholders to make decisions in an informed and accountable manner.

Develop a checklist of criteria for analysis ...

Special interest is now placed on the approach of causal diagrams (or problem trees, see page 148) based on the capital assets in the sustainable livelihoods framework. Here, resources are allocated to research on the basis of the maximum likely impact on the five capital assets of poverty, in turn based on cause and effect linkages of poverty for specified groups of poor people. They offer an attempt to deal transparently with multiple facets of sustainable development.

ENSURE THE OBJECTIVES OF THE ANALYSIS ARE CLEAR

Analysis is least effective where it deals with 'themes' or 'subjects'. Formulating questions will provide direction to the analysis and developing solutions. For example, 'watershed degradation' is a less useful formulation than 'what incentives have encouraged watershed conservation? How can we remove perverse incentives to degrade key watersheds? And who should make the changes?' Questions should:

... and frame the analysis in terms of questions

- address a priority issue (Box 5.3);
- also address contextual issues, where possible;
- exhibit and enable the scope for policy responsiveness.

Box 5.3 Signals that an issue might be a priority for analysis and action

The issue is a priority if it:

- is an opportunity/threat to poor people's livelihoods;
- is an opportunity/threat to key economic sectors;
- is an opportunity/threat to key ecosystem assets and processes (especially where they are critical to livelihoods and sectors as above);
- is possible to act without extra finance;
- presents a major learning opportunity;
- is visible to the public;
- has an extension/ multiplier effect;
- is an international obligation;
- is timely in relation to a pending decision;
- is linked to current political concerns, other initiatives and skills.

An analysis of recent policy decisions could impute some criteria as a basis for debate and definition of a more formal set.

---

2 Macqueen (1999) lists the advantages and disadvantages of particular tools for prioritizing research for poverty alleviation: historical precedence; arbitrary 'armchair' subjectivity; checklists, simple or weighted; CBA, econometric analysis; and causal diagrams. Their most prominent drawback is their inability to rank interventions, which aim to tackle very different facets of poverty or sustainable development.

AGREE THE TYPES OF OUTPUT FROM THE ANALYSIS, AND WHO WILL GET THEM

It is important that the analysis should not be a complete surprise once it has been produced, and so stakeholder expectations and political/legal procedures and implications for conducting the analysis need to be discussed and agreed beforehand. The hierarchy of possible outputs might first be discussed, to get expectations right. These may be ranked, from least to most ambitious, as: data, findings (correlating key factors), conclusions (identifying causal links), recommendations and design. For example, will the output be 'evidence', 'proposals' for a policy or initiative, or a draft policy or project design itself?

An introduction to methods available for analysis

Table 5.1 offers a very basic listing and assessment of the various analytical methods and tools that might be found useful in generating knowledge for NSDSs. Particular methods are described in more detail later in this chapter where they are recommended as especially relevant to the particular analytical task being discussed. Some of the more technical approaches (eg cost-benefit analysis, macro-economic forecasting, sector analysis and project evaluation) and detailed planning approaches (eg EIA and strategic environmental assessment) are professional fields in themselves with their own vast literature, and cannot be covered in full detail in this resource book. Table 5.2 explores some of the limitations of economic approaches compared with participatory approaches.

In essence, the more that the technical tools try to accommodate many dimensions and help predict outcomes, the hungrier they are for good data, and the more assumptions they tend to include. This means that they may not reflect the real world well, and may be inaccessible by non-technical stakeholders. Many analytical approaches are weak in identifying the distributional effects of different policy options – the winners and losers. This is one very good reason why analysis should be accompanied by participatory processes to consider such questions, although the impacts of policies may not always be clear even to those who are directly concerned. Note also that the division of approaches into 'expert' and 'participatory' is becoming blurred in practice.

Analysing stakeholders in sustainable development

Why stakeholder analysis is important

Stakeholders are those people, groups or institutions who have specific rights and interests in an issue or system, and related powers, knowledge and skills. With a national strategy for sustainable development, every citizen is effectively a stakeholder. But, in practice, it is impractical to involve everyone individually, and not all people will wish to participate in the process. Table 4.1 lists a range of key stakeholder interest groups from government, the private sector and civil society that might need to be involved and that should be represented in the strategy process.

Stakeholder analysis can help to:

- draw out the interests of stakeholders in relation to problems which the strategy is seeking to address;
- identify conflicts of interests (actual or potential) between stakeholders which will influence the riskiness of the strategy, before efforts and funds are committed;
- identify positive relations between stakeholders which can be built upon, and which may enable coalitions of sponsorship, ownership and cooperation;
- identify negative relations between stakeholders which may limit the scope of the strategy or which may influence the design of participation;

Table 5.1 Information-gathering and analytical tools to help strategy decision-making

A: Some tools typically associated with technical 'experts'

Tool/approach	Description/purpose	Advantages	Disadvantages
Land suitability classification	Distinguish and map areas in terms of characteristics that determine suitability for different uses	Distils a mass of physical, biological and (sometimes) economic information into a single index of relative suitability for various land uses	Economic comparisons are rarely made explicit and the relative importance of different factors in calculating the final index may be arbitrary
Impact assessment	Detailed documentation of environmental and social (including health) impacts, adverse effects and mitigation alternatives (see Table 5.4 comparing EIA and SEA)	Explicitly requires consideration of all environmental effects; ability to monetize does not pre-empt enumeration of all benefits and costs of an action	Difficult to integrate descriptive analyses of intangible effects with monetary benefits and costs; not designed to assess trade-offs among alternatives. Reactive/project-focused
Cost-benefit analysis	Evaluates investment projects, based on monetization of net benefits (benefits minus costs)	Considers the value (in terms of willingness to pay) and costs of actions; translates outcomes into commensurate terms; consistent with judging by efficiency implications	No direct consideration of distribution of benefits and costs; significant informational requirements; tends to omit outputs whose effects cannot be quantified; tends to reinforce status quo; contingent on existing distribution of income and wealth
Cost-effectiveness analysis	Selects option that will minimize costs of realizing a defined (non-monetary) objective	No need to value benefits; focus on cost information often more readily available; provides implicit values of objectives (eg marginal cost of increasing by one unit)	No consideration given to relative importance of outputs; degree to which all costs are considered will be important to judgements on 'best' approach
Macroeconomic and behavioural models	Econometric programming models used to simulate linkages between supply and demand, within or across sectors	Dynamic and price-endogenous models allow explicit simulation of feedback effects and price movements; best for sector-level or macro-economic analysis, or very large-scale projects	Tend to require much data and analysis; may be expensive to build and run; often difficult to interpret; opaque to many stakeholders
Multi-criteria analysis	Mathematical programming selects option based on objective functions including weighted goals of decision-maker, with explicit consideration of constraints and costs	Offers consistent basis for making decisions; fully reflects all goals and constraints incorporated in model; allows for quantification of the implicit costs of constraints; permits prioritizing of projects	Results only as good as inputs to model; unrealistic characterization of decision process; must supply the weight to be assigned to goals; large information needs for quantification
Risk-benefit analysis	Evaluates benefits associated with option in comparison with risks	Framework is left vague for flexibility; intended to permit consideration of all risks, benefits and costs; rather than an automatic decision	Too vague; factors considered to be commensurate often are not
Decision analysis (decision trees)	Step-by-step analysis of the consequences of choices under uncertainty	Allows various objectives to be used; makes choices explicit; explicit recognition of uncertainty	Objectives not always clear; no clear mechanism for assigning weights

Tool/approach	Description/purpose	Advantages	Disadvantages
Scenario development and foresighting	Used to consider the likely environmental, social and economic consequences of current and possible future trends	Helps to illustrate the consequences of taking (and not taking) particular actions or implementing particular policies in the short, medium and longer-term future	Difficulties arise when data are poor and unreliable and trends are disputed. Longer-term scenarios are problematic since there are likely to be many unpredictable changes

B. Tools explicitly designed for stakeholder participation

Tool/approach	Description/purpose	Advantages	Disadvantages
Community-based analysis	Uses a series of exercises to help community stakeholders to share knowledge, review and participate in technical assessments, set priorities and jointly develop options for action	Fundamental to a truly participatory planning effort. Takes the process to the local level where action will need to take place. Serves to engage local inhabitants, focus planning on their needs and gather local information and views	May not provide a sufficiently rigorous/comprehensive analysis and should preferably be combined with technical assessments
Participatory appraisal	Communities actively engage in analysis of local conditions, share knowledge and plan activities, using visual tools such as mapping, matrices etc, with outsiders acting as facilitators	Serves to engage local inhabitants and enables them to 'own' the results and hence assume responsibility for actions identified; seeks out the voices of the poorest people. Often provides more accurate information than conventional surveys and is speedy and cost effective	May not work in every situation. Requires a facilitator who understands the approach, and is trusted by the local people
Key informant interviews	Usually conducted one-to-one and structured around a set of questions to glean insights on a particular issue or policy. Semi-structured interviews are used in participatory appraisal alongside visual tools to improve the level of information and understanding	People are not constrained by the presence of others and can put forward information in their own way. Can be a useful approach with politicians, whose formal engagement can cause problems for others	Does not allow for group debate. Very sensitive to interviewees selected
Market research	Surveys or consultations used to analyse market trends, demand, opinions and opportunities. By telephone, website, interview or at community level using participatory appraisal tools	Can be used to forecast trends, public/consumer opinion and preferences, assess markets for environmental goods and services, and identify options for income generation and enterprise development	Costly if done in-depth
Focus groups	Usually conducted with small groups representing particular neighbourhood/ resource/ policy 'communities' and interests to gain insights about people's perceptions and values	Useful information-gathering tool that can be used to understand particular issues and concerns, good for obtaining qualitative rather than statistical information, and refining preliminary ideas	Setting up a focus group process, including selection of the sample group and facilitation of sessions, requires trained facilitators. Problems associated with nomination/ access to that group. Subject to bias if group small or dominated. Generates 'norms' rather than reality

Table 5.2 **The limits of participatory and economic analysis**

Economic methods	
Limitations	**Effect on analysis**
Concepts, terms and units imported from Western experience, and are defined and interpreted in different ways by different disciplines	The definitions are critical as they structure how information is both gathered and analysed. For example, the 'household' is frequently the basic unit of analysis, but this means that intra-household and inter-household interactions, which may affect the way a particular resource is valued, are overlooked
Dominated by a set of assumptions that present a limited reflection of 'reality'	Underlying assumption is that individuals and households are driven by welfare (or utility) maximization. This ignores other rational motives such as maximizing chances of survival or fulfilling social duties and rituals
Simplified analysis can be especially misleading in dealing with non-marketed natural resources	For example, during droughts, wild foods may mean the difference between life and death, so their value increases compared with other periods. How can these values be incorporated in long-term planning?
Assumes everything can be valued. Important economic role of some resources may be lost or underestimated	For example, certain species may play a vital role in rituals and so be irreplaceable. Many ecological functions are too difficult or costly to estimate reliably
Data collection methods can result in biases and inaccuracies (even when assumptions are relatively realistic). Interview-based questionnaires are notoriously prone to bias and inaccuracies	If data collected through questionnaires is fed uncritically into analysis, the results may be highly misleading
Participatory methods	
Limitations	**Effect on analysis**
Micro-level detail and local-level diversity combine with an emphasis on social processes	Information generated is too detailed for policy-makers and is difficult to analyse for policy implications (although detailed case-study approach can enrich policy analysis). Some type of sifting process will be necessary to understand the policy implications
Information is frequently context specific. Relative, rather than absolute values are commonly emphasized	This makes quantification difficult as well as comparison between regions or communities
Requires strong facilitation skills	The dependence of the methodologies on good quality facilitation to provide trustworthy and representative findings means that, if good facilitators are absent, the methodology may not provide good quality data
Group discussion generates 'group think' or reversion to conventional wisdom and social norms (similar to focus groups)	Minority opinion and/or 'unpalatable' facts may be neglected
Conclusions may take the form of 'wish lists' with limited attention to conflicts, trade-offs and individual behaviour	Insufficient assessment of the constraints on alternative courses of action, or the extent to which they match individual motivations

Source: Adapted from Dalal-Clayton et al (2000); based on IIED (1998a)

■ identify which type of participation is most appropriate for different stakeholders, and the role(s) each might play, at successive stages of the development and implementation of the strategy.

It is, obviously, best if stakeholder analysis is undertaken at the beginning of the strategy process or component activity, to maximize these benefits.

The basic steps in stakeholder analysis are set out in Box 5.4.

Box 5.4 Basic steps in stakeholder analysis

1   Draw up a stakeholder table on an issues basis – identifying the stakeholders (primary and secondary) according to their interests (overt and hidden). Each stakeholder may have several interests in relation to the problems being addressed by the project or process.
2   Develop a relationship matrix – 'mapping' each stakeholder's importance to resolving the issues and their relative power/influence, and indicating what priority should be given to meeting their interests.
3   Identify risks and assumptions affecting the design and success of the strategy. For example, what is the assumed role or response of key stakeholders if the strategy is to be successful? Are these roles plausible and realistic? What negative responses might be expected, given the interests of particular stakeholders? How probable are they, and what impact would these have on the activity?
4   Identify appropriate approaches to stakeholder participation in the strategy; for example, partnership in the case of stakeholders with high importance and influence, consulting or informing those with high influence but with low importance.

Source: Adapted from ODA (1995)

Identifying stakeholders

USING AN ISSUES-BASED TYPOLOGY

An initial stakeholder analysis needs to be conducted at the scoping stage of a strategy, closely related to the issues identified by the scoping process (see Chapter 4 page 77). An issues-based typology will group, for example, all the stakeholders with interests in moving from an over-dependence on fossil fuel, or in tackling deforestation. This approach helps the analysis to be strategic, rather than be too comprehensive. But it helps move an issues analysis on to defining who really must be involved in the strategic process to tackle each issue.

Primary and secondary stakeholders can be distinguished ...

Accepting an issues-based typology, it is then helpful to classify the stakeholders with interests in each issue as primary or secondary:

■ *Primary stakeholders* are those who are likely to be affected by the issue or a potential response to it, either positively or negatively; for example, farmers, urban dwellers, landless, children.
■ *Secondary stakeholders* are the intermediaries in the process. These will often be distinct institutions; for example, funding, implementing, monitoring and advocacy organizations, government organizations, NGOs, politicians and local leaders. Some key individuals within institutions will have primary (personal) interests as well as formal institutional interests, and thus fall into both categories; for example, when civil servants try to acquire land in a new scheme.

At an early stage in the process a simple diagram of concentric circles of 'primary' and 'secondary' stakeholders (for each issue) can be useful to provoke debate, and provide a focus for subsequent analysis.

Further to this, the basic characteristics of both primary and secondary stakeholders can be profiled according to the following (overlapping) categories (Mayers 2001a):

- *basic demography* – men/women, rich/poor, young/old, ethnic group, etc;
- *location* – rural/urban dwellers, near to the issue/far away, region;
- *ownership* – landowners/landless, managers, staff, trade unions;
- *function* – producers/consumers, traders/suppliers/competitors, regulators, policy-makers, activists, opinion-formers;
- *scale* – small-scale/large-scale, local/international communities;
- *time* – past, present, future generations.

WAYS TO IDENTIFY STAKEHOLDERS

There are various ways to identify stakeholders; each has its advantages and risks. The analysis must recognize the risks of missing key stakeholders and work to avoid these risks. Using a combination of approaches will reduce the risks associated with any one particular approach (Borrini-Feyerabend, 1997; Higman et al 1999; Mayers 2001a):

... by different, complementary methods

- *Identification by staff of key agencies, and other knowledgeable individuals.* Those who have worked in the system for some time can identify groups and individuals that they know to have interests in the key issues and to be well informed about them. However, caution is needed about whether these individuals or groups are truly 'representative' (see below).
- *Identification through written records and population data.* Census and population data may provide useful information about numbers and locations of people by age, gender, religion, and so on. Key line agencies and officials often have useful contemporary and historical records on employment, conflicting claims, complaints of various kinds, people who have attended meetings and financial transactions, among other things. Contacts with NGOs and academics may reveal relevant surveys and reports and knowledgeable or well-connected people.
- *Stakeholder self-selection.* Announcements in meetings, in newspapers, local radio or other local means of spreading information, can encourage stakeholders to come forward. The approach works best for groups who already have good contacts and see it in their interests to communicate. Those who are in more remote areas or are itinerant (eg pastoralists), or are poor and less well educated, and those who may be hostile to other stakeholders, may not come forward in this way. There is a risk that the local elite will dominate the process of self-selection.
- *Identification and verification by other stakeholders.* Early discussions with those stakeholders first identified can reveal their views on the other key stakeholders who matter most to them. This will aid better understanding of stakeholder interests and relations. Different stakeholder groups will have different perspectives about who the key actors are, so identification, for example, just by government officials is inadequate.

STAKEHOLDER REPRESENTATION

It is important that individuals involved are 'representative' of their stakeholder group or 'constituency'. True representation will entail constituency agreement of that representation. Otherwise, the best that can be achieved is effective 'sampling'. Whether representation or sampling is done must be made very clear. Key criteria of representation are as follows:

Stakeholder groups need true representatives

- *Identity:* Does the representative share the views of the group/constituency or will the representatives bring other/multiple identities to the process; for example, tribal/class or political affinities? Where can such other identities help, and where might they hinder representation and outcomes?

■ *Accountability:* Was the representative chosen by a particular group/constituency, and does he or she consult with that group regularly? What kind of specificity and sanction has the group attached to the representative's accountability? Some individuals assume a mandate from members of a stakeholder group that is simply not backed up by processes of accountability with those people. Different people have different levels of embeddedness in their groups, and some are therefore more worthwhile representatives than others (see also Chapter 6 on representation).

Identifying stakeholder interests, relations and powers

IDENTIFYING STAKEHOLDERS' INTERESTS

Again on an issues basis, it is necessary to understand:

■ stakeholder motivations and interests in relation to the issue;
■ the rights, resources, and other means and powers that are available to them (or that are missing) to pursue their motivations and interests;
■ the external pressures on them to change;
■ their degree of acceptance of need for change – or resistance against it;
■ the constraints to making changes, such as regulatory, bureaucratic and resource constraints.

Various methods can help identify stakeholders' interests

Useful *methodologies* for identifying stakeholders' interests (as well as their relationships and powers, below) include (Mayers, 2001a):

■ *Brainstorming,* to generate analysis and ideas within a stakeholder group. This takes the form of a session in which 'anything goes', with all points recorded. Later these points can be sorted and prioritized. *Focus groups* can then be convened with particular stakeholders to discuss particular topics.
■ *Semi-structured interviews,* in which an informal checklist of issues is used to guide an interview with a stakeholder group, while allowing other issues to arise and be pursued. This approach is particularly useful for cross-checking, identification of common ground, identification of trade-offs and clarification of the decision-making frameworks that the stakeholder group prefers or uses.
■ *Digging up existing data* – a variety of recorded materials may shed light on stakeholders' interests, characteristics and circumstances. It is always worth probing and rummaging for reports and recorded information: there is almost always more of it than at first appears, sometimes found in the most unlikely places. If needs be, the other stakeholder analysis methodologies can then be used to verify data uncovered.
■ *Time lines* can be prepared with stakeholders of the history of links and impacts of particular policies, institutions and processes, with discussion of the causes and effects of specific changes. For example, time lines have been used in agricultural policy analysis to identify dates when significant events occurred and to relate these to changes in land use patterns (Gill 1998).
■ *Diagrams* help many people to get a quick idea of what is being talked about. They can work well to stimulate discussion by both non-literate and literate people. In general, diagrams and visualizations work because they provide a focus for attention while discussing an issue, represent complex issues simply, stimulate ideas and therefore assist in decision-making. Of course, some people do not think or work well in terms of diagrams and prefer verbal discussion with descriptions of real examples and stories.

■ *Sustainable livelihoods* analysis also offers a means to analyse stakeholders' livelihood interests (goals and strategies), but in the context of a broader framework for linking together such assessments with assessment of the capital assets available to stakeholders (natural, physical, financial, human and social) and assessment of the policy and institutional environment. It is described further on page 145.

ANALYSING THE RELATIONSHIPS BETWEEN STAKEHOLDERS

Particular sustainability issues are usually characterized by stakeholder conflict or, alternatively, alliances. Such relationships may need to be explored further. Simple matrices describing relations and initiatives between groups could be developed, again on an issues basis; for example, one matrix per issue. It is especially interesting to note where these initiatives might have included previous strategies such as NEAPs, NCSs, poverty reduction strategies and so on. Relationships may be analysed according to the following factors (Mayers 2001b):

Relations between groups can affect their position on issues

■ *Function of the relationship* – whether it is legal/contractual; market; information exchange; interpersonal links; or power-building, for example.
■ *Strength* of relationships, relating to the frequency and intensity of contact.
■ *Formality* of relationships – whether formal or informal relationships, and the mechanisms used.
■ *Dependence* between stakeholders: for example, a business-type dependency (with or without a 'referee'); a regulatory-type dependency (with or without incentives and sanctions); a technical dependency (with or without attitudinal changes); or a social dependency (often the most complex of all).
■ *Quality* of relationships. This could cover each stakeholder's perception of relationships with other parties – awareness, relevance and timeliness of the relationship; its accessibility; communication media used; or the ability to control the relationship. It could also include an overall assessment, for example in terms of 'good, moderate, conflictual', based on a convergence of the relevant stakeholders' opinions.

In relation to structuring an NSDS, it is useful to ascertain which stakeholders have similar positions on an issue and work together to pursue their common interests – the *'policy communities'* or *networks* that may exist in formal or informal senses (see Chapter 7, page 242) – and the kinds of initiatives they have worked on together (Box 5.5). Such policy communities can often provide much momentum for a strategy process if linked into it.

ANALYSING STAKEHOLDERS' POWERS

An assessment of the particular powers (or lack of them) of stakeholders is crucial both to an understanding of each sustainable development issue (who are the dominant and the marginalized), and to the structuring of strategy processes (who needs to be involved to remedy problems and realize opportunities). There is a limit to how far progress can be made in either the analysis or the effective change of policy without broaching issues of power differences. Ways need to be found to get some of these power issues 'out into the open' if they are going to be tackled (Mayers and Bass 1999).

Power issues must be understood and tackled

For strategy analysis, a useful first step is to identify the relative *degree* of stakeholders' power, the *source* of that power and the *means* by which power is exercised. Although both participatory and independent means of identification can work, documentary evidence of these types of power is the most effective.

Box 5.5 Policy communities in Pakistan

A 'policy community' is defined as a network of individuals and institutions with interest and expertise in a particular area, and therefore a stake in the process of decision-making regarding that area. It is based on the idea that policy-making is not a monolithic exercise located in one ministry or agency. It involves cooperation between governmental agencies as well as non-government entities. The decision-making process invariably reflects the relative political influence of these groups and involves political negotiations and compromises between them (Banuri and Khan 2000).

Analysis of the context for sustainable development in Pakistan (as part of analysing the impacts of the National Conservation Strategy) revealed six dominant communities or networks, with a seventh emerging:

(a) *Economic and trade liberalization networks*, consisting almost exclusively of economists and business interests promoting market solutions.
(b) *The poverty eradication network* which is united around community empowerment, development and institution building.
(c) *The agricultural yield improvement network* which consists of agronomists united by the green revolution's promise of dramatic yield increases.
(d) *The energy development network*, united for a long time around the unrealized potential of hydro power.
(e) *The urban agenda network*, united almost exclusively by the vision of real estate development.
(f) *The international NGOs and donor networks* which combine a multitude of visions, ranging from pure conservation, social transformation, development effectiveness, and opening up markets and business opportunities.

By and large, most of these policy communities operate at cross-purposes much of the time, with limited consideration of sustainable development. Community development and conservation/environmental NGOs – which form the backbone of the emergent (seventh) environmental *and sustainable development policy network* – still have a major role to play in bridging the gaps between other powerful policy community networks. 'This should become one of the stated core objectives of the NCS, and not an incidental one.'

Source: Hanson et al (2000)

The nature of power varies

Often the elements of 'power' will need to be unpacked. Stakeholder power is not a single 'currency' that can be expressed, like energy, in kilowatts. It is important to address the question of how stakeholders gain or lose power to influence the direction of the policy process. Filer and Sekhran (1998) identify four different types of power:

- *Managerial power*, the capacity to *control* the activities of other stakeholders, and thus to determine the quantity and quality of their outputs.
- *Executive power*, the capacity to *meet the needs* and demands of other stakeholders, thus increasing one's authority over them.
- *Bargaining power*, the capacity to *extract* resources or concessions from other stakeholders, by some combination of force and persuasion.
- *Positional power*, the capacity to *secure* the sympathy and support of other stakeholders, on the assumption of some common interest.

Since each group of stakeholders is often internally divided, it is also possible to distinguish between *external* forms of power, which are exercised by one group of stakeholders over other groups of stakeholders, and *internal* forms of power, which are exercised by some members of a stakeholder group over other members of the same group. The power of each group can then be analysed and an indication of their overall 'weight' within the policy process given – the sum of all their influences over the direction of that process.

COMPARING STAKEHOLDERS' POWERS WITH THEIR POTENTIAL FOR SUSTAINABLE DEVELOPMENT

The next challenge is to relate the power of stakeholders to their *potential* to affect, or be affected by, strategies and related policies, institutions and initiatives. Assessing which individuals and groups have power over which others will help to piece together power chains – often the potential to affect policy, institutions and initiatives is not derived through one direct link, but through a chain. Of particular concern are those stakeholders with high potential for sustainable development but little power (such as landless people). If progress towards sustainable development is to be made, some stakeholders need to be empowered to make more positive contributions, while others need to be restrained from making destructive contributions. A tabular format can be used to compare power, as illustrated in Table 5.3.

Mapping power helps in understanding the potential contribution of groups to sustainable development

Table 5.3 **Stakeholder power analysis of a particular issue (or policy or institution): suggested table for comparisons**

SD issue	Stake-holders	Main interests	Powers	Potentials	Relation with others	Net impact	Options/ways forward

An instructive example of mapping power and potential comes from Malawi where the Coordination Unit for the National Forestry Programme (NFP) recognized that stakeholders have very different levels of power to take action, and they vary in their importance or potential for good forestry and livelihoods. To provoke debate at the meetings of the multi-stakeholder Forest Forum, the Coordination Unit developed a basic 'ranking' of stakeholder groups according to power and potential (Table 5.4).

Figure 5.1 attempts to show the rankings from Table 5.4 in a more striking visual way. It shows the main stakeholder groups in Malawi's forest goods and services by circles – the larger the circle, the greater the number of people in the group. The centres of the circles are 'plotted' against the two axes – power and potential. Thus stakeholders might be grouped as follows in relation to power:

- Top LH corner – need to influence these stakeholders.
- Top RH corner – stakeholders currently matter most to the issue.
- Bottom LH corner – stakeholders marginal to the issue.
- Bottom RH corner – need to empower these stakeholders.

Another way of combining analysis of power and potential – and thereby improving the identification of which stakeholders need to be involved in a strategy – is to ask 'who counts most?' Indeed, just as it can be necessary to identify which issues are priorities (discussed on page 160), it may frequently be necessary to ask which stakeholder groups count most in relation to an issue, which are dominant, and which groups are marginalized? In other words, whose needs and opinions should have greater weight in strategy decisions? This is tricky ground, and agreement on criteria should be sought early in the strategy process. An example is presented in Box 5.6. The result can often include a definition of *'marginalized stakeholders'* – groups who are affected by an issue and should otherwise be thought of as primary stakeholders, but are marginalized from decision-making processes (eg the old and the poor, women, children and itinerant groups such as pastoralists). Such a definition can really help the strategy steering committee and secretariat to target participation and other activities.

Whose needs should have greater weight in strategy decisions? – a tricky issue

Table 5.4 **Mapping power and potential of stakeholders: Malawi's National Forestry Programme**

Stakeholder group	Size of group	Potential to contribute to good forestry	Power to contribute to good forestry
Smallholders	17	17	1
Organized users and groups at community level	16	16	2
Fuelwood and charcoal sellers and traders	15	1	4
Chiefs and traditional authorities	14	10	5
Pitsawyers	13	8	6
Small non-timber enterprises	12	9	3
Ministry of Agriculture	11	12	12
District Assemblies	10	2	9
Forestry Department	9	15	15
Other departments (wildlife, environment, energy)	8	6	11
Estate owners (tobacco)	7	3	8
NGOs	6	14	10
Wood industries	5	5	13
Plantation companies (timber, rubber and tea)	4	7	14
Investment Promotion Agency, Privatization Commission	3	4	7
Donors	2	11	16
Ministry of Natural Resources and Environmental Affairs	1	13	17

Notes: (a) 1 = smallest, 17 = highest values in each category: size, potential and power

Source: Mayers et al (2001)

Limitations of stakeholder analysis

Finally, there are limitations to stakeholder analysis. In brief, these are (Mayers and Bass 1999):

Stakeholder analysis has some drawbacks ...

- Stakeholder groups overlap – and even within one group, people take on multiple identities.
- Stakeholder groups change over time – and need the freedom to do so; 'pigeon-holing' them may restrict this.
- There are other risks to do with categorization and representation – some stakeholders may get under-represented or misunderstood.
- Differences and conflicts are based on different values – no common ground may, in fact, be apparent.
- Where sustainability analysis reveals information about less powerful groups, this can be dangerous as it might lead to manipulative, undermining and inequitable actions on the part of the more powerful groups in the process.
- Stakeholder analysis is an information tool, rather than one for decision-making. It can identify the heart of the problem – but it cannot provide easy solutions. Challenges raised are:
  - What is the common ground for compromise?
  - How to manage conflicts?
  - Which stakeholders' interests to prioritize?

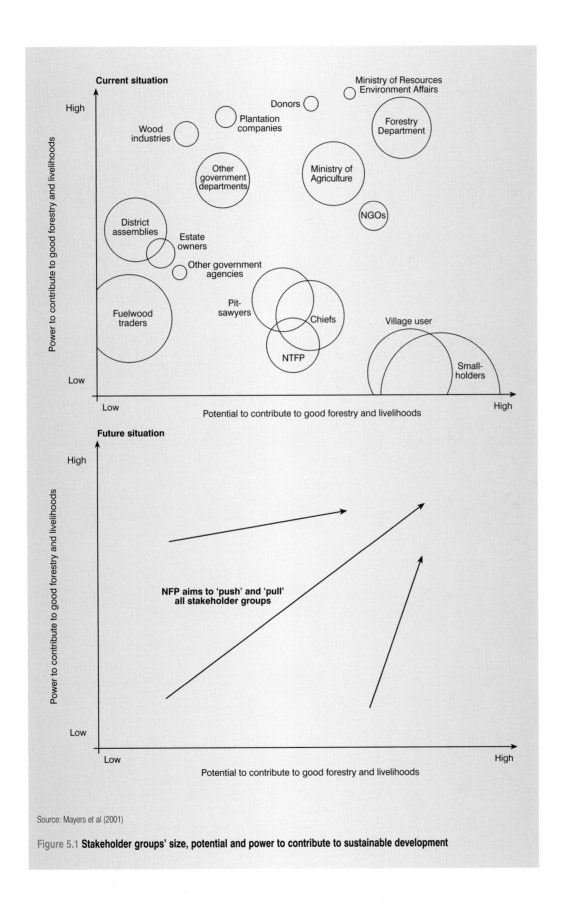

Source: Mayers et al (2001)

Figure 5.1 **Stakeholder groups' size, potential and power to contribute to sustainable development**

*... so it must be
suitably managed
and monitored*
Because of these possible drawbacks, it is important that strategy stakeholders are clear about the purpose of stakeholder analysis and agree both the desirable and the undesirable outcomes, so that the analysis can be suitably managed and monitored.

We have stressed in this section that stakeholder analysis for NSDSs should generally be organized according to sustainable development issues, rather than according to stakeholder group. In the next section, we look at how to identify and analyse issues of environmental, economic and social sustainability. The following section then addresses ways to analyse issues of policy and institutional processes.

Box 5.6 'Who counts most?' The tricky issue of stakeholder priority

In response to the challenge of redressing imbalances between stakeholders in access to forestry decisions, Colfer (1995) has developed an approach for ensuring that local forest actors are fully identified and weight is accorded to them, corresponding to their:

- *proximity* to forests, woodlands or trees on farms;
- *dependence* on forests for their livelihoods (ie where there are few or no alternatives to forests for meeting basic needs);
- *cultural linkages* with forests and uses of forest resources;
- *knowledge* related to stewardship of forest assets;
- *pre-existing rights* to land and resources, under customary or common law;
- *organizational capacity* for effective rules and accountable decision-making about forest goods and services;
- *economically viable forest enterprise* based on environmental and social cost internalization, bringing equitable local benefits.

Colfer strongly suggests that an 'inverse' criterion should also be used; that is, if a local group has a *power deficit it* should be weighted more heavily (to make up for such a deficit). Conversely, some stakeholders may have considerable levels of power and influence, as well as interests that may adversely affect the abilities of other stakeholders to pursue good forestry. In such circumstances, an approach is needed which weights stakeholders according to the degree to which their actions should be *mitigated* or *prevented*. This is, of course, difficult ground. Finally, one might also want to add an assessment of the degree to which people are risk-bearers (of risks taken by other groups).

Source: Mayers and Bass (1999)

Approaches to measuring and analysing sustainability[3]

The purpose of measuring and analysing sustainability is to answer five questions:

1 How well is the ecosystem in question?
2 How are people affecting the ecosystem?
3 How well are the people (including current and future generations)?
4 Is their well-being fairly shared?
5 How are these questions connected?

*Measuring society's
progress towards
sustainability helps
to identify priority
issues*
This information is essential for determining the progress of a society towards sustainability, its main strengths and weaknesses, and the priority issues to be addressed by the NSDS. The information equips decision-makers to focus on the priorities without losing sight of the other components of sustainable development that, if not (yet) priorities, are also crucial for its achievement. It also provides the basis for monitoring and evaluating the effectiveness of the strategy and adjusting it as necessary (Chapter 10).

---

3 This section has benefited much from material provided by Robert Prescott-Allen.

The three main approaches to measuring and analysing sustainability are:

- *accounts* (providing data) (below);
- *narrative assessments* not based on indicators (page 135);
- *indicator-based assessments* (page 135).

As Table 5.5 shows, these differ in their potential for:

- transparency (ease of detecting value judgements and construction of the assessment);
- consistency over time (comparability of successive assessments);
- participation (the more technical the method, the less scope for participation);
- usefulness for decision-making (clarity with which performance and priorities are revealed).

Sustainability analysis methods have different potentials

No approach is perfect. All can profitably be supplemented by one or more *contributing measurements and analyses* (page 138).

Accounts

Accounts are constructions of raw data, converted to a common unit (such as money, area or energy). Most cover highly important but small aspects of sustainability and are described under 'Contributing measurements and analyses' (page 138). Generally speaking, they refer to one or a narrow set of indicators and include the system of national accounts (page 141) (covering the market economy), the ecological footprint (covering resource consumption), and energy and material accounts (covering physical exchanges between the economy and the environment). The most comprehensive accounts sum many aspects of the economy, society and the environment into a single statement.

Accounts use a narrow set of indicators

The Genuine Progress Indicator (GPI), for example, starts with personal consumption expenditure (taken from the national accounts). It then makes a series of adjustments to account for the negative effects of economic activity or factors that are ignored by the GDP (such as unequal income distribution, net foreign lending or borrowing, cost of consumer durables), social costs (crime, automobile accidents, commuting, family breakdown, loss of leisure time, underemployment) and environmental costs (household pollution abatement, water pollution, air pollution, noise pollution, loss of wetlands, loss of farmlands, depletion of non-renewable resources, long-term environmental damage, ozone depletion, loss of old-growth forests). Finally it adds some benefits ignored by the GDP (value of housework and parenting, value of volunteer work, services of consumer durables, services of highways and streets, net capital investment).

The advantage of the GPI and similar comprehensive accounts is that they are directly comparable with the GDP, the most widely used measurement of national performance (Figure 5.2). But accounts have several disadvantages, particularly as a strategic tool for assessing sustainability:

Comprehensive accounts are directly comparable with GDP, but have disadvantages

- Many costs and benefits have no market value; converting them to monetary units involves assumptions, extrapolations and judgements that distort the results; and some costs and benefits, such as loss of biodiversity, are so hard to evaluate that they are omitted.
- The assumptions, judgements and omissions are difficult to detect, and the construction of the accounts is almost impossible for non-specialists to follow.
- Although values strongly influence the final outcome, calculation of the accounts is highly technical and leaves little room for wide stakeholder participation.

Table 5.5 **Three main approaches to measuring and analysing sustainability**

Approach:	Accounts (page 132)	Narrative assessments (page 135)	Indicator-based assessments (page 135)
Examples:	Index of Sustainable Economic Welfare Genuine Progress Indicator	State of environment reports World Development Report	Well-being Assessment Dashboard of Sustainability
Potential for transparency	Low	Medium	High
Potential for consistency	High	Low	High
Potential for participation	Low	High	Medium
Usefulness for decision-making	Medium	Medium	High

Although accounts produce a strikingly clear picture of overall performance – or 'genuine progress' – they do not reveal so clearly the main constituents of that performance: it is difficult to tell which priority issues to focus on to close the gap between the GPI and the GDP. This limits the usefulness of accounts for strategy development.

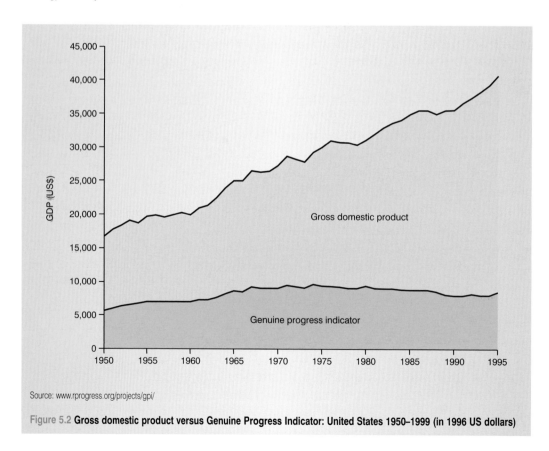

Source: www.rprogress.org/projects/gpi/

Figure 5.2 **Gross domestic product versus Genuine Progress Indicator: United States 1950–1999 (in 1996 US dollars)**

Narrative assessments

Narrative assessments combine text, maps, graphics and tabular data. They may use indicators, but are not built around them and the indicators used may change from one reporting period to another. They include standard state of environment reports (Box 10.8, the World Bank's *World Development Report*) and a wide variety of other reports, and represent the most familiar approach to measurement and analysis. Their strength is their familiarity and flexibility. The potential for participation is great, because the assessment can be tailored to the technical skills of participants. Compilers can devote their attention to topics on which they have information and choose whatever communication device they deem most suitable for each topic.

'Narrative assessments' are familiar and flexible …

However, this flexibility has pitfalls. Unsystematic choice of topics coupled with uneven treatment can mask gaps in coverage and obscure priorities: what topics have been omitted? Has a topic been left out because it is unimportant or because of lack of data? How does one topic relate to another? How can one compare the importance of a topic covered by an anecdote-rich case study with one covered by extensive statistical analysis? The topics covered, or the way they are covered, may change between reporting periods, preventing the identification of trends. Limited transparency and consistency reduce the usefulness of these assessments for decision-making, particularly for strategy development and monitoring.

… but this has its drawbacks

Indicator-based assessments

Like narrative assessments, indicator-based assessments may include text, maps, graphics and tabular data, but unlike them they are organized around indicators (see Box 5.7) – generally speaking, a broader set of indicators than accounts (page 133). A great deal of attention is paid to choosing them systematically. Indicators enable assessments to be comprehensive yet selective: because they can be selective, they are better equipped than accounts to cover the wide array of issues necessary for an adequate portrayal of human and environmental conditions. Systematic procedures for choosing indicators lay bare the selection and arrangement of issues covered by the assessment and the values involved, and make the construction of indicator-based assessment more transparent than that of accounts or narrative assessments. By employing the same set of indicators over time, later indicator-based assessments can be compared with previous ones, providing more consistent coverage from one assessment/reporting period to another. Comprehensive and consistent coverage, together with systematic organization of issues and their indicators, enable priority issues and strengths and weaknesses of performance to be clearly identified. This makes indicator-based assessments more useful than other approaches for decision-making and hence for strategy development. 'Deciding what to measure: a framework of parts and aims' on page 154 discusses the main steps in developing an indicator-based assessment.

Indicator-based assessments are more transparent …

… and can be compared over time

Participation by decision-makers and stakeholders is necessary to ensure that the assessment incorporates their values and addresses their concerns. Participants need to have a major say in what is assessed and in deciding questions of value. At the same time, the team undertaking the assessment has a responsibility to make sure that the assessment is technically sound and withstands scientific scrutiny. However, the technical demands of indicator selection impose constraints on participation. In effect, the assessment must be designed jointly by participants and technicians.

Participants should be involved in deciding what to assess

Although indicator-based assessments are potentially more transparent, consistent and useful for decision-making than other approaches, whether they fulfil their potential depends on how well they are designed and executed.

Indicator-based assessments of sustainability differ chiefly in the number of subsystems into which they divide the system (the assessment area), the number of levels between subsystem and indicator and whether they produce indices (compound indicators) of the state of the system and its subsystems (Table 5.6).

Assessments can use different numbers of sub-systems …

Box 5.7 **What is an indicator?**

An indicator is something that represents a particular attribute, characteristic or property of a system (Gallopín, 1997). More narrowly, as used here, an indicator is a measurable part of a system. For example, health is not an indicator because it cannot be measured directly, but life expectancy at birth, the child mortality rate and the incidence of specific diseases can be measured and therefore can be indicators.

An indicator that combines or aggregates several parts is called an index (plural: indexes or indices). An index may be a *compound indicator* combining several lower-level indicators. Examples are the Human Development Index, the Well-being Index, and a city's Air Quality Index. Or an index may be a *composite indicator* made up of many components that are not indicators in themselves. Examples are the gross domestic product, the consumer price index, the Dow Jones industrial average, and the ecological footprint.

Table 5.6 **Indicator-based assessments of sustainability**

Type	Number of subsystems	Number of levels between subsystem and indicator	Indices of the state of the system and subsystems?
Well-being Assessment (Figures 5.4, 5.5)	2: ecosystem, people	2–4	Yes
Dashboard of Sustainability (Figure 5.6)	3: environment, economy, society	1	Yes
Dashboard of Sustainability for CSD	4: environment, economy, society, institutions	2	Yes
CSD indicators of sustainable development	4: environment, economy, society, institutions	2	No
Global Reporting Initiative Sustainability Reporting Guidelines	4: environment, economy, society, integrated	1–3	No

The division into two subsystems ensures that assessments treat people and the environment equally and focus on the central question of sustainable development: how to achieve high levels of human well-being and ecosystem well-being together? Increasing the number of subsystems by subdividing the human side reduces the weight given to the environment from a half to a third (three subsystems) to a quarter (four subsystems) (Figure 5.3). The advantage of three subsystems is the prominence given to the economy, still the main preoccupation of decision-making. However, which aspects of human well-being are 'economy' and which 'society' can be hard to tell and depend on particular cultural perspectives. The separation of 'economy', 'society' and 'institutions' is even more arbitrary and confers no advantage other than its current acceptance by the United Nations Commission on Sustainable Development (CSD). An 'integrated' subsystem is superfluous because the 'integrated' indicators suggested by the Global Reporting Initiative (www.globalreporting.org) could be assigned to one of the other subsystems or could be generated more informatively as indices of the state of the subsystems or the system as a whole.

... and this determines their robustness and user-friendliness

The number of levels between subsystem and indicator is a major factor in both the robustness and the user-friendliness of an assessment method. Too few levels make it hard to trace the logic behind the choice of indicator – what aspect of the subsystem the indicator represents and how fully and directly it represents that aspect. Too many levels risk losing the user in a convoluted series of links between subsystem and indicator.

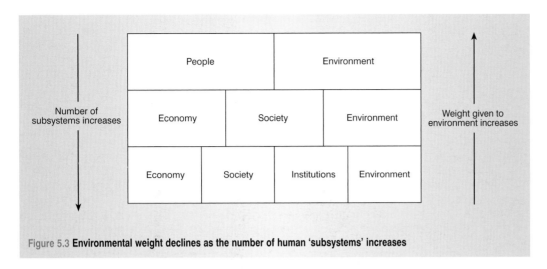

Figure 5.3 **Environmental weight declines as the number of human 'subsystems' increases**

Given the broad scope of sustainable development, a large number of indicators is inevitable but presents an enormous communication problem. The International Institute for Sustainable Development (IISD) notes the key dilemma of needing both comprehensive coverage and simple messages and presentation:

> *From those developed for rural communities to those for the United Nations, hundreds of sustainability indicator sets have been created for and presented to their respective audiences. Still, they have far to go before they can claim to be widely used. Most sustainability indicators come as large, unwieldy reports, crammed with complex charts and graphs. Although useful to policy professionals and academics, most indicator sets are not practical for the media and public. In order to build support for and an understanding of indicators, there must be a process for indicators to be legitimized through some form of public consultations or trial application.*

There are hundreds of sustainability indicator sets

The growing ranks of indicator projects and professionals worldwide face two challenges that seemingly contradict each other:

- Growing complexity. As our understanding of the complexity of sustainability grows, how do we manage the mountains of data required to monitor it?
- The demand for simplicity. Since public education and resulting political action are seen increasingly and urgently as the purpose for creating indicators, how do we present them in ways that are simple, elegant and effective, without compromising the underlying complexity?

A single indicator of sustainable development is an impossible dream (Box 5.8). The best way to overcome this problem is to combine the indicators into indices. Assessments that do not combine their indicators into indices are extremely hard to interpret. Assessments that do, can communicate their main findings very readily. When indicators are combined into indices, they can provide a clear picture of the entire system, reveal key relationships between subsystems and between major components, and facilitate analysis of critical strengths and weaknesses. No information is lost, because the constituent indicators and underlying data are always there to be queried.

Indices are more easy to understand ...

Well-being Assessment combines ecosystem indicators into an Ecosystem Well-being Index (EWI) and human indicators into a Human Well-being Index (HWI), which are then combined graphically into a Well-being Index (WI) – the intersection of the EWI and HWI on the Barometer of Sustainability (Figures 5.4 and 5.5).

Box 5.8 **The quest for a single indicator of sustainable development**

Complex problems of sustainable development require integrated or interlinked sets of indicators, or aggregations of indicators into indices. High-level decision-makers – government ministers, foundation executives, heads of corporations – routinely ask for a small number of indices that are easy to understand and use in decision-making. Many concerned with sustainable development voice their desire for a single indicator to compete with the enormous political power of the Gross Domestic Product, a single number that provides information about the total market value of production and services in a country as a single number. But many are sceptical that a single number could assess something as complex as sustainable development.

Most indicator experts believe that searching for a single indicator of sustainable development is something like the quest for the unicorn. It is a myth to think that one number – even one that vastly improved on the GDP as a proxy for overall national well-being – could have any real functional value as a policy tool. But many also acknowledge that the attempt to create an index of sustainable development may be useful because it would force a concerted effort to present the complexity of sustainable development more simply. Even a modestly successful effort by presenting a handful of aggregated indices could introduce a generation of policy and decision-makers to the goals of sustainable development.

Source: www.iisd.org

The Dashboard of Sustainability comes in two versions. The standard version combines environmental indicators into an Environment Index (EnI), economic indicators into an Economy Index (EcI) and the social indicators into a Society or Social Care Index (SI), which it then combines into a Policy Performance Index (PPI). The version for the indicator set of the CSD (Figure 5.6) combines institutional indicators into an Institutional Index (II) and then combines the EnI, EcI, SI, and II into a PPI.

... and can be shown graphically

By combining indicators into indices and displaying the indices graphically, both Well-being Assessment and the Dashboard of Sustainability show how close the society concerned is to sustainability, the state of people (socio-economic conditions) and the ecosystem (environmental conditions), and the main strengths and weaknesses of performance.

The last decade has seen considerable efforts by governments, NGOs and multi-stakeholder groups to develop indicator-based assessments of sustainable development. Some cover the full sweep of sustainability. Most tend to pay more attention either to human aspects or to the environment. IISD provides a compendium of indicator initiatives at www.iisd.org and some examples are listed in Box 5.9.

Contributing measurements and analyses

It is not the intention of this resource book to offer the complete 'how to' advice on all kinds of analytical techniques for getting to grips with particular issues. Table 5.1 lists many of them and their pros and cons. The following have been shown to be useful. The final four techniques (policy influence mapping; problem trees; strategic environmental assessment; and community-based issue analysis, see pages 147–153) are particularly useful as they: bring together several dimensions of sustainable development; help get close to an understanding of underlying causes; offer insights as to possible solutions; and are amenable to participation – or at least make the results broadly understandable to a wide group of 'non-expert' stakeholders.

Other analytical techniques are also useful

SPATIAL ANALYSIS

Spatial analysis using GIS is indispensable for strategies that deal with land use planning, coastal zone management, natural resource management, biodiversity conservation, urban planning or any other decisions about the allocation and management of land and water. Maps are by far the best way of showing the location, size, pattern, and ecological, economic or cultural values and characteristics of land areas and water bodies, and of displaying and evaluating conflicts and compatibilities between different uses.

Maps and geographical information systems are essential tools

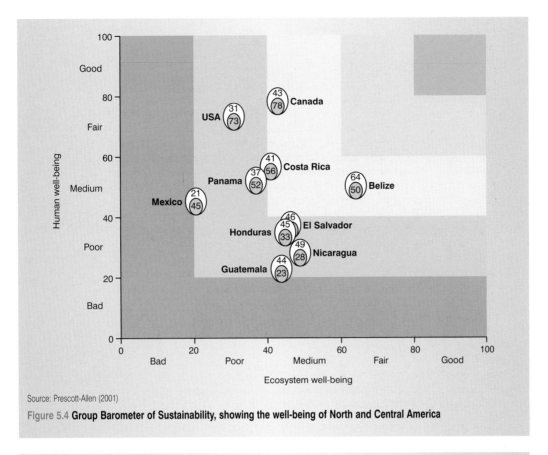

The Human Well-being Index (HWI) is in the yolk of the egg; the Ecosystem Well-being Index (EWI), in the white. (El Salvador's HWI is 36 and EWI 46.) The Well-being Index (WI) is the position of the egg – the point on the Barometer where the HWI and EWI intersect. Sustainability is the square in the top right corner. Note that the Barometer clearly shows the relationship between human and ecosystem well-being, the wide spread of performance among countries, and the distance to sustainability. Belize was assessed on fewer indicators than the other countries: a fuller assessment might move its position to between Costa Rica and El Salvador.

Source: Prescott-Allen (2001)

Figure 5.4 **Group Barometer of Sustainability, showing the well-being of North and Central America**

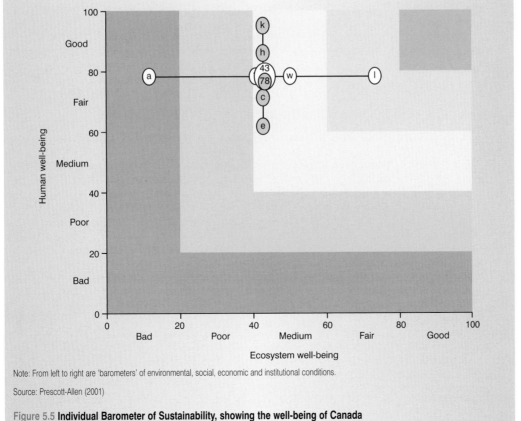

Orange circles (vertical axis) are the points on the scale of the human dimensions (major components of the HWI):

c = community; e = equity; h = health and population; k = knowledge; w = wealth.

White circles (horizontal axis) are the points of the ecosystem dimensions (major components of the EWI):

a = air; l = land; r = resource use; s = species and genes; w = water.

Some dimensions are hidden by the egg (wealth, species and genes, resource use). The dimensions that need most attention are air (reduce carbon emissions), resource use (reduce energy consumption), and species and genes (expand habitat protection for wild species, and conserve agricultural diversity).

Note: From left to right are 'barometers' of environmental, social, economic and institutional conditions.

Source: Prescott-Allen (2001)

Figure 5.5 **Individual Barometer of Sustainability, showing the well-being of Canada**

Box 5.9 **Examples of sustainable development indicator initiatives**

Worldwide

UNEP: Project to measure states of and trends in the environment and guide policy-making towards sustainable development, in implementation of UNEP Environmental Observing and Assessment Strategy. Development of indicators in specific sectors; approaches to aggregation of indicators; use of indicators in state-of-the-environment reporting. Indictor sets issued in 1997, 2000 and 2001 (www.unep.ch/earthw.html)

World Bank: (a) The Bank's annual World Development Indicators (WDI) includes 800 indicators in 75 tables, organized in six sections: world view, people, environment, economy, states and markets, and global links. The tables cover 148 economies and 15 country groups – with basic indicators for a further 58 economies (www.worldbank.org/data/wdi2000); (b) The Environmental Economics and Indicators Unit has developed indicators of environmentally sustainable development and environmental performance (for WB projects) (www-esd.worldbank.org/eei)

UNDP: Human Development Reports published since 1990, presenting the Human Development Index (HDI) as a measure of human development in individual countries (see Box 5.12) (www.undp.org)

OECD: Programme to develop a core set of (and supporting sectoral) environmental indicators initiated in 1990 (based on policy relevance, analytical soundness and measurability) (www/oecd.org//dac/Indicators/index.htm)

Dow Jones Sustainability Group: Indexes (one global, three regional and one country) based on the world's first systematic methodology for identifying leading sustainability-driven companies worldwide. (www.sustainability-index.com)

World Resources Institute: Project on highly aggregated, policy-relevant environmental indicators – developed map-based indicators of biodiversity and land use; and indicators of material flows (national, sectoral and company levels) (www.wri.org)

Hart Environmental Data: Comprehensive website with a database of indicators-related projects and resources to help people and organizations with their indicator research. Specializes in community indicators (www.subjectmatters.com/indicators/Indicators/)

National/provincial

United States: Interagency Working Group on Sustainable Development Indicators developed experimental set of 40 indicators to encourage a national dialogue towards developing a set of national indicators (www.sdi.gov/reports.htm)

Finland: Finnish Environment Institute developed sustainable development indicators for use at national level – 20–30 indicators in each of four categories: environmental, economic, social, conflict (www.vyh.fi/eng/welcome.html)

United Kingdom: Department of the Environment, Food and Rural Affairs developed core set of 150 (and 15 headline) sustainable development indicators to be central to future progress reports – take an economic-social-environmental-resource model while recognizing interactions between them (www.sustainable-development.gov.uk)

County, municipal, local area, community-based

- **Lancashire County Council, UK:** Second Green Audit incorporates 40 sustainability indicators for the county (www.la21net.com/)
- **City of San Jose, California:** The City Policy and Planning Division developed 52 quantifiable indicators of sustainability in nine categories as a step towards creating a centralized, coordinated environmental data system for performance measurement and public information (www.ci.san-jose.ca.us/esd/)
- **Hamilton-Wentworth, Ontario, Canada:** Sustainability indicators to monitor progress towards goals of city's Vision 2020 – developed through community consultation process using workbooks (www.vision2020.hamilton-went.on.ca/)
- **Sunrift Center for Sustainable Communities, Minnesota, USA:** Developed the Flathead Gauges to identify/quantify key components of sustainability in Flathead County, and to measure trends. Involved public meetings, citizen survey and feedback from individuals and organizations (cdaly@netrix.net)
- **Sustainable St Louis:** 'Measure of St Louis' project assists citizens to develop and monitor a set of community-defined indicators of sustainable development (Contact: Claire Schosser, PO Box 63348, St Louis, MO 63163, USA; Fax: +1-314-773-1940)
- **Integrative Strategies Forum, Washington, DC:** The Metro Washington Community Indicators Project is a voluntary initiative, promoting the development and use of community indicators as part of a wider sustainability planning process (jbarber@igc.org)
- **Sustainable Northern Ireland Programme:** An NGO working with communities and local authorities to promote Local Agenda 21 and sustainable development in Northern Ireland. Helped several councils to develop initial sets of indicators to raise public awareness about sustainability (Contact: Michael@snipl.freeserve.co.uk)

Source: www.iisd.org

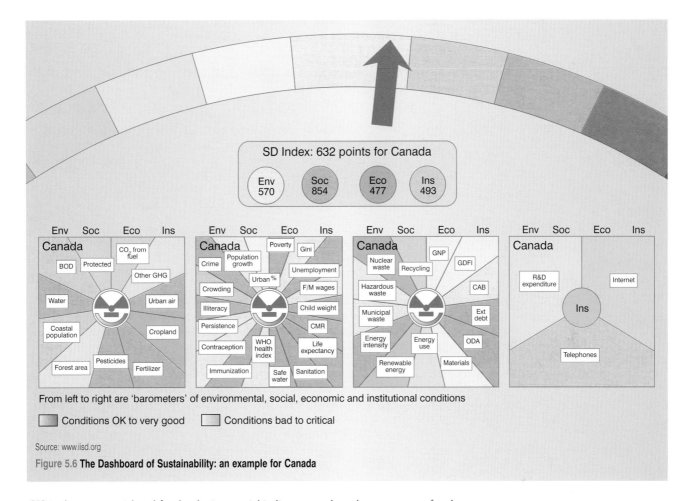

From left to right are 'barometers' of environmental, social, economic and institutional conditions

Conditions OK to very good   Conditions bad to critical

Source: www.iisd.org

Figure 5.6 **The Dashboard of Sustainability: an example for Canada**

GIS is also an essential tool for developing spatial indicators, such as the percentage of each ecosystem type that is natural, modified, cultivated or built; the status and trends of ecosystem diversity; the extent and security of ecosystem protection; the extent and severity of land degradation; the degree of conversion and modification of inland water systems; and the spread and intensity of marine pollution and habitat degradation. Because the system comprises information of different types (eg soil fertility, flood hazard), it can also be used to highlight possible correlations that may suggest significant links. It can generate scenarios by manipulating the variables.

There is an inherent danger that the aura of technical sophistication can sway some stakeholders to treat the information more seriously than information that cannot be so presented. There are also dangers that this can obscure the assumptions and uncertainties inherent in the approach. However, recent developments have made GIS more accessible to participatory approaches. Box 5.10 presents an example from Australia that illustrates the pros and cons.

SYSTEM OF NATIONAL ACCOUNTS (SNA)

National accounts are the records of asset changes, income and expenditure that governments compile routinely to track the activity of their national economy, analyse its structure and performance, decide economic policies, and compare the economies of different countries. The SNA measures the performance not of the economy as a whole but of the market economy – the production of goods and services that are owned and traded and so have a monetary value – plus certain goods and services that are not traded but for which a market value can be inferred: goods produced by farmers for their own consumption, the equivalent rental value of owner-occupied dwellings and government services.

National accounts are a source of informative and influential indicators

> **Box 5.10 The use of GIS in achieving Regional Forest Agreements, Australia**
>
> For years, stakeholder conflict had been brewing about how to use Australia's native forests – for woodchip exports or for conservation. Regional Forest Agreement processes were initiated to negotiate informed outcomes. The process offered a combination of consultative mechanisms and specialist assessments, coordinated by a task force of specialists. These included:
>
> - ecological or biodiversity assessment;
> - cultural heritage assessment;
> - indigenous heritage assessment;
> - social assessment;
> - wood resources.
>
> Geographic information systems dominated the whole phase of integrating the information from these processes. They provided a means for storing and displaying the various layers of information and creating composites of them, and a basis for various modelling exercises. They were ideal for the ecological and biodiversity aspects, which were largely driving the process, and were also quite well suited for recording the various types of heritage sites.
>
> 'Decision support models' were also developed. They endowed a high level of credibility to the content of the assessments and the technical aspects of integration. Importantly, they provided the 'language' in which negotiations were conducted, which made the inherent conflicts amenable to bureaucratic processes and thus potentially governable. However, many factors were left out of these models, and major shortcomings emerged in the attempts to ensure 'full and comprehensive integration'.
>
> Despite the availability of the highly sophisticated GIS, models and databases and attempts at all-inclusive public consultation, compromises have been difficult to reach. Two of the important sources of conflict – indigenous land rights and local economic development – are by-passed by the present process. The immediate beneficiaries are the woodchip export companies who are freed of export controls. Participatory mechanisms need to be further developed to handle genuine negotiation with community and 'middle' levels, with a similar degree of professionalism as has been accorded to the GIS.
>
> Source: Dargavel et al (1998)

It is not suggested that such accounts are compiled expressly for a strategy but, where they are available, they are a source of highly informative and influential indicators, notably gross domestic product (GDP: the total value-added of enterprises operating in the country concerned, regardless of whether owned by residents or non-residents) and gross national product (GNP: the total value-added of enterprises owned by residents of the country concerned, regardless of whether the money comes from domestic or foreign operations).

National accounts also provide basic data for broader accounts such as the Genuine Progress Indicator (page 133) and recalculations of specific aspects of the economy such as genuine saving (below).

GENUINE DOMESTIC SAVINGS

'Genuine domestic savings' show what is happening to national wealth

Genuine saving, a measurement devised by the World Bank, attempts to show whether the stock of national wealth is growing or shrinking. It starts with conventional measures of saving (from the national accounts), adds investment in education and deducts estimates of resource depletion and environmental degradation (Table 5.7). It can help to show whether, for example, the level of government expenditure is sustainable, tax and monetary policies encourage saving, resource royalties are consumed or invested (and if invested, how), and saving is sufficient to offset any cumulative effects of pollution.

ECOLOGICAL FOOTPRINT

The ecological footprint sums the quantities of energy and renewable resources – minerals excluded – that a society (at any level from country to community), household, sector or business consumes by converting

Table 5.7 **Genuine domestic savings: accounting for depletion of human, physical and natural capital. An example from Pakistan**

Pakistan	Percentage of GDP in 1997
Gross domestic savings	**10.4**
Consumption of fixed capital	6.4
Net domestic saving	**4.0**
Education expenditure	1.9
Energy depletion	1.1
Net forest depletion	1.6
CO_2 damage	0.8
Genuine domestic savings	**2.5**

Source: World Bank (1999)

them to a common unit of area: the area of productive land and sea required to supply the same resources and absorb the carbon dioxide from fossil fuels. This area is a society's ecological footprint, a vivid indicator of consumption pressure (Box 5.11).

Ecological footprints indicate consumption pressure

There are two approaches to calculating ecological footprints. The *'compound' approach*, which is the more comprehensive method, is composed of three parts:

- The first consists of consumption analysis of over 50 biotic resources such as meat, dairy produce, fruit, vegetables, grains, tobacco, coffee and wood products. Consumption is calculated by adding together the amount imported and produced, and subtracting exports. Consumption quantities are divided by FAO estimates of world average yield, to give the area of arable, pasture, forest land or sea necessary to sustain this consumption (Table 5.8). Where necessary, adjustments are made to avoid double counting across categories. For example, grain-fed animals are accounted for by grain consumed (ie as arable land), rather than grazed pasture land.
- The second part determines the energy footprint – usually the amount of forested land necessary to sequester the carbon dioxide emissions – considering both locally generated energy and that embodied in over 100 categories of traded goods.
- The final part summarizes the footprint in different ecological categories to give the overall footprint per capita, which is multiplied by the population to give the total footprint of an area. This is then compared with an estimate of how much biocapacity exists within the area or country to give the external footprint.

Box 5.11 **Ecological footprints: some examples**

- The land area or ecological footprint required to supply London's environmental needs is 120 times the size of London.
- An area three times the size of the UK's productive forests is more or less permanently taken up in providing wood products for the UK.
- In Colombia, the footprint of a semi-intensive prawn farm is between 35 and 190 times the size of the farm.

Source: IIED (1995)

Table 5.8 **Calculating annual consumption of biotic resources: Costa Rica (1995)**

Resource	Global yield (kg/ha)	Production (t)	Import (t)	Export (t)	Apparent consumption (t)	Net imported, manufactured products (t)	Footprint component (ha/cap)	Land category
Beef/buffalo	32	92,232	400	21,410	71,222		0.6529	Pasture
Sheep/goat	72	22	3	180	−155		−0.0006	Pasture
Other meat	764	87,746	564	3,270		−2706	−0.0010	Arable
Milk	458	539,000	0	12,968	526,032		0.3355	Pasture
Cheese	46	6,000	250	189		61	0.0004	Pasture
Butter	22	4,000	0	81		−81	−0.0011	Pasture
Eggs	573		0	0		0	0.0000	Arable
Marine fish	35				6		0.1846	Sea
Cereals	2,752	206,000	588,400	7000	787,400		0.0836	Arable
Fruit/vegetables	8,136	3,297,000	12,396	2,461,512	847,884		0.0304	Arable
Animal feed	2,752		0	0		0	0.0000	Arable
Roots/tubers	12,814	209,000	1,600	330	210,270		0.0048	Arable
Pulses	802	28,000	16,000	3,675	40,325		0.0147	Arable

Source: Chambers et al (2000)

In the *'component-based' approach*, footprint values for certain activities, such as car travel, primary energy use, waste production and food consumption, are pre-calculated using data appropriate to the region under consideration. The aim is to account for most consumption with a series of component analyses. For example, to calculate the impact of car travel on fuel consumption, manufacturing and maintenance energy, data on land take and distance travelled are used to derive an average ecological footprint per kilometre travelled. This can then be used to calculate the impact of vehicle use at individual, organizational or regional level. Because this method indicates impacts by activity, it is useful for policy-making and education. However, it is data intensive and the results will vary depending on the source and reliability of data (Chambers et al 2000).

Looking at ecological footprints from a Southern perspective, the late Anil Agarwal of the Centre for Science and Environment in India estimated that the total biomass currently exported from the developing world to industrial countries is ten times greater than during the colonial period (Weizsacker 1994). These exports of carrying capacity do not necessarily pose a problem if they are drawing on true ecological surpluses, and if enough remains for meeting local needs. Currently, there is no guarantee that trade flows are based on these principles.

NATURAL RESOURCE, MATERIALS AND ENERGY ACCOUNTS

Measuring physical exchanges between the economy and the environment

Natural resource accounts and material/energy balances measure physical exchanges between the economy and the environment. Natural resource accounts record changes in the stocks of raw materials such as minerals or timber. Material/energy balances record the flows of materials and energy from the environment to the economy, through the economy, and back to the environment as pollution and wastes.

'Total material requirement' (TMR) has been calculated for the United States, Austria, Germany, The Netherlands and Japan. It includes the natural resources that enter the economy as commodities for further processing, such as grain used in food manufacturing, petroleum sent to a refinery, minerals that go into metal products and logs for lumber. It also includes materials that are displaced in the course of resource production or construction: for example, soil erosion from agriculture, the rock and soil removed to reach an ore body, the portion of ore that is discarded to concentrate it, and material moved to build a highway or dredge a channel. The weight of all these materials is added up to obtain a country's TMR. For example, the TMR of the United States is 22 billion metric tons, and Japan's TMR per person is 45 metric tons (Adriaanse et al 1997; Fischer-Kowalski et al 1997). Another study has calculated the 'total domestic output' (TDO) of these countries: the amount of TMR that is returned to the national environment as pollutants of air, land and water. For example, the TDO of the United States is 19 billion metric tons, and Japan's TDO per person is 14 metric tons (Matthews et al 2000). Calculation of TMR and TDO is highly data-intensive.

HUMAN DEVELOPMENT INDEX

The Human Development Index, developed for the United Nations Development Programme's *Human Development Report*, combines indicators of longevity (life expectancy at birth), education (adult literacy rate and combined gross enrolment rate) and standard of living (real GDP per capita). It is the most widely accepted alternative to GNP and can be used as a stand-alone index of human conditions or together with other socio-economic indicators as part of a sustainability assessment. In the latter case, however, care should be taken to avoid double counting indicators of longevity, education and income that may already be included. Box 5.12 provides further details.

Using socio-economic indicators to measure human conditions as an alternative to GNP

SUSTAINABLE LIVELIHOODS ANALYSIS

The sustainable livelihoods (SL) framework (Figure 5.7) groups particular components of livelihood – the capital assets, vulnerability/opportunity context – and all the institutional structures and processes that may transform livelihoods.

This framework is a useful diagnostic device for assessing the use of capital assets, and the outcomes at the level of individuals', households' or communities' livelihoods in given policy contexts. As Shankland (2000) points out, there has tended to be a wide gap between bottom-up local level analysis and top-down policy analysis. Local level analyses have frequently not been fully aware of how policy is made and how it interacts with and impacts on local groups (it is presented as a remote part of the 'context' rather than something in which people can engage). In contrast, policy analysis has tended to focus on the motivations and initiatives of policy elites and bureaucrats, rather than the perspective of those ultimately affected by policy choices; where it does include local stakeholders, it is in terms of 'impacts on people' rather than their participation in policy.

A diagnostic for assessing capital assets for …

The sustainable livelihoods framework offers a number of elements that can help to bridge the gap between policy and livelihoods:

… helping to bridge the gap between policy and livelihoods …

- as an illustration of how policy is a part of livelihoods and how local people engage in both formal and informal policy;
- by emphasizing the importance of 'social and political capital' within people's lives and how it is within these asset groups that power to influence policy generally lies;
- as a means to 'ground-truth' policy analyses – checking that they are capturing what actually happens on the ground, rather than what is supposed to happen;
- as a means to develop sustainable development indicators at the sustainable livelihoods level (which may help improve understanding at the policy level);
- by providing a structure to merge the findings of policy and livelihoods analyses such that the links can be discerned.

Box 5.12 **The Human Development Index**

Whereas the well-used measure of national wealth – gross national product (GNP) – is measured by money, the Human Development Index (HDI), introduced by the UNDP Human Development Report (1990) measures national progress through the indexation of three socio-economic indicators:

- *Longevity* – measured by life expectancy at birth.
- *Knowledge* – measured by a combination of adult literacy (two-thirds weight) and combined secondary and tertiary school enrolment ratios (one-third weight).
- *Standard of living* – measured by real GDP per capita (purchasing power parity dollars, PPP$) – after adjusting for purchasing power.

It sets a minimum and maximum for each dimension and then shows where each country stands in relation to these scales – expressed as a value between 0 and 1. The scores for the three dimensions are then averaged in an overall index between 0 and 1.

The HDI offers an alternative to GNP for measuring the relative socio-economic progress at national and sub-national levels. Comparing HDI and per capita income ranks of countries, regions or ethnic groups within countries can highlight the relationship between their material wealth and income on the one hand and their human development on the other. A negative gap implies the potential of redirecting resources to human development.

The HDI facilitates the determination of priorities for policy intervention and the evaluation of progress over time. It also permits instructive comparisons of the experiences within and between different countries. A country's overall index can conceal the variation in living standards within it. Hence, where a country has great internal inequality, the best solution would be to create separate HDIs for the most significant groups, for example, by gender, by income groups, by geographical region or by ethnicity. These 'disaggregated HDIs' are arrived at by using the data for the HDI components pertaining to each of the groups into which the HDI is aggregated, treating each group as if it were a separate country. Disaggregated HDIs at the national and sub-national levels help to highlight the significant disparities and gaps: among regions, between the sexes, between urban and rural areas and among ethnic groups. The analysis made possible by the use of the disaggregated HDIs should help to guide policy and action to address gaps and inequalities.

Nevertheless, it can be difficult to use HDI to monitor changes in human development in the short term because two of its components, namely life expectancy and adult literacy, change slowly. To address this limitation, components that are more sensitive to short-term changes such as the rate of employment, the percentage of the population with access to health services, or the daily caloric intake as a percentage of recommended intake, can be used.

The usefulness and versatility of the HDI as an analytical tool for human development at the national and sub-national levels would be enhanced if countries chose components that reflect their priorities and problems and are sensitive to their development levels, rather than rigidly using the three components presented in the HDI of the global Human Development Reports.

Assuming income to be proportionally related to life expectancies and literacy and inverse-proportionally related to infant and child mortality rates can be misleading. These correlations can break down in many societies, where the maximization of wealth and the enrichment of human lives need not move in the same direction.

Source: UNDP: http://www.undp.org/hdro/anatools.htm

... and to develop key questions

Thus the framework can be employed to develop the following kinds of questions (Shankland 2000). These might be answered through sampling or through community-based issue analysis (page 153):

- *Livelihood priorities:* Who and where are the poor? What are their current livelihood priorities – traditional and emerging areas (see page 124)? What types of policy sector are relevant to those priorities?
- *The policy context for the livelihoods of the poor:* What is current policy in those sectors? Who makes that policy? What is the macro context for that policy?
- *Policy instruments affecting livelihoods:* What measures or instruments have been put in place to implement each policy? What are their characteristics? Through what institutions are these measures implemented and reviewed?

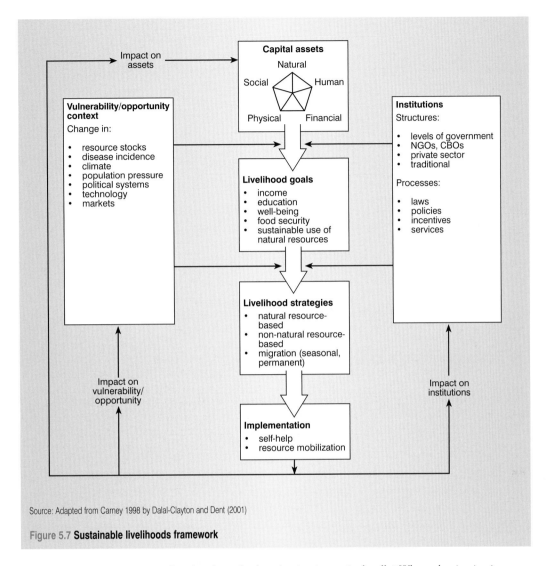

Source: Adapted from Carney 1998 by Dalal-Clayton and Dent (2001)

Figure 5.7 **Sustainable livelihoods framework**

- *Policy in the local context:* In what form do these institutions exist locally? What other institutions (formal or informal, such as labour-sharing arrangements and caste systems) affect local responses to policy? And what other institutions might be affected by policy? How do existing development strategy processes fit with the reality of local livelihoods?
- *People and policy:* What resources can poor people draw on to influence policy? What opportunities exist for poor people to influence policy, directly or indirectly? To what extent does government believe that inequality is a constraint to sustainable development?

These questions will give rise to information on local stakeholders (see page 120) and likely promising policy processes and mechanisms (see page 161) for the strategy to use, as well as providing broad information to enrich and verify the picture of the national context.

POLICY INFLUENCE MAPPING

This visualization method can be used to gradually map out the potential underlying causes of an identified problem, beginning with the more obvious proximate causes. Policies send signals to different actors and encourage certain types of reaction. Some signals are strong and compelling, while others are weak and almost subliminal. In a way, they can be viewed as consecutive layers of influence. Indeed, this is often a

Policy mapping – visualizing the causes of problems

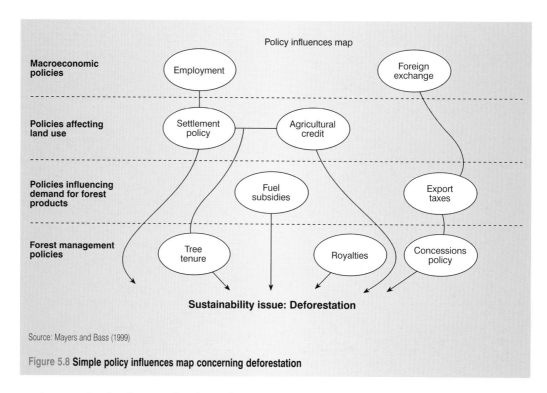

Figure 5.8 **Simple policy influences map concerning deforestation**

good way to visualize them – and such visualization can help in discussing policy as a mixed group of stakeholders.

The example in Figure 5.8 reflects a multi-stakeholder discussion about the policy influences on deforestation. Some stakeholders were more immediately concerned about the influence of forest management policies (the inner circle of influence). But others pointed to the increasing power of less proximate policies, such as foreign exchange policies. Not only did these influence forest management policies as such, but they also had an effect on forests and forest stakeholders by increasing the price of cash crop exports and, therefore, deforestation. Thus, chains of influence can be mapped out. More sophisticated versions can show the effect of non-formal policies and of private sector policies.

PROBLEM TREES AND CAUSAL DIAGRAMS

Problem trees allow a multi-stakeholder/disciplinary team to pool their analyses of several problems and map the linkages between them. This is akin to a more complex version of policy mapping, but considers a wider range of variables than policy, and tries to be more exact about tracing specific causes and effects. It can be developed in a participatory way by using the ZOPP ('Objectives-Oriented Project Planning') method.

Arranging causes and effects in a logical sequence

Through ZOPP, problem trees can be developed by multidisciplinary teams. They identify the problems and interests of the people affected by a sustainability issue, write down each problem on a separate card and pin it onto a board in a logical sequence. The first step is to identify a 'core problem', which appears to be of central importance for the affected persons, through group discussion. The causes of this problem are then arranged in logical sequence underneath it, while the effects of the core problem are arranged above it. The problem tree gradually builds up, allowing complex relationships to be clearly portrayed (Figure 5.9.). Recent advances in problem tree software (eg MINDMANAGER, 3.5) have resulted in the routine use of problem trees for displaying complex cause and effect linkages. For example, visual 'Mind Maps' can display the logical progression from the key problem or 'effect' (for example, poverty) to the underlying causes of poverty by asking the question 'Why?'

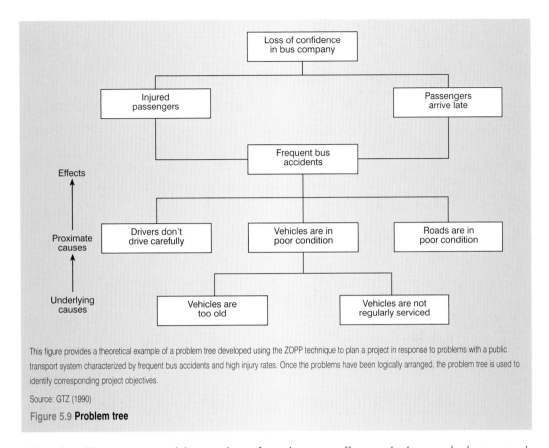

This figure provides a theoretical example of a problem tree developed using the ZOPP technique to plan a project in response to problems with a public transport system characterized by frequent bus accidents and high injury rates. Once the problems have been logically arranged, the problem tree is used to identify corresponding project objectives.

Source: GTZ (1990)

Figure 5.9 **Problem tree**

Although problem trees or causal diagrams have often taken a one-off approach, they can also be structured around standard sustainability criteria. The advantage here is that they can then be compared or ranked in different ways. For example, they can be structured around five causes of poverty which equate to low levels of the five capital assets within the sustainable livelihoods approach (Figure 5.10) (Macqueen 1999). Obviously, each of the causes in Figure 5.10 can also itself be treated as a problem, and analysis can proceed even further through more detailed causal diagrams.[4] In addition, it is possible to weight each of the branches, for example to allow prioritization. This may be done through some form of participatory ranking exercise where a score is given to each constraint by a representative sample of key informants.

STRATEGIC ENVIRONMENTAL ASSESSMENT

Environmental impact assessment (EIA) has conventionally been applied at a project level. It represents a limited response to the challenges of sustainable development discussed on page 7. It is also increasingly evident that many of the environmental problems associated with development projects arise because insufficient attention is given to environmental issues at higher levels of policy-making. Strategic environmental assessment (SEA) has emerged in the last decade as a response to the need to adopt more proactive, integrated approaches that address the causes of unsustainable development, which lie in government macro-economic policies, investment, trade and development programmes, energy and transport plans, and so on.

Sadler and Verheem (1996) have defined SEA as:

SEA – environmental assessment at the policy, plan or programme level ...

---

4 Ultimately, branching will cease where the tips represent, for example, fixed states (such as climatic constraints), basic laws (eg of free market economics) or links to other branch tips (leading to loops, eg 'poverty trap spirals').

A systematic process for evaluating the environmental consequences of proposed policy, plan or programme initiatives in order to ensure they are fully included and appropriately addressed at the earliest appropriate stage of decision-making on par with economic and social considerations.

Table 5.9 **Comparing SEA and EIA**

Strategic environmental assessment (SEA)	Environmental impact assessment (EIA)
Is proactive and informs development	Usually reacts to a specific development proposal
Assesses the effects of a proposed policy, programme or plan on the environment; or the effect of the environment on development needs and opportunities	Assesses the effects of a proposed specific development on the environment, and is not well linked to policy decisions
Assesses cumulative impacts and identifies implications for SD	Assesses direct impacts and benefits
Focuses on maintaining a chosen level of environmental quality	Focuses on the mitigation of (negative) impacts
Is a continuing process aimed at providing information at the right time	Has a well-defined beginning and end
Creates a framework against which many (negative) impacts can be measured	Focuses on specific project impacts
Has a broad perspective and low level of detail	Has a narrow perspective and a high level of detail
Driven by need for vision and overall framework for policy (as in an NSDS)	Driven by need for watertight legal process requirements (as in lawsuits)

Source: Adapted from CSIR (1996)

... offers a flexible tool for forward planning

SEA should therefore be seen as a decision-aiding rather than a decision-making process; it is a 'tool for forward planning' to be flexibly applied at various stages of the policy-making cycle (Sadler 1997). Under this broad perspective, SEA encompasses assessments of both broad policy initiatives and more concrete programmes and plans that have physical and spatial references. With this scope of coverage, the methodologies to be applied at the opposite ends of the decision-making spectrum differ markedly, but the principles of EIA should apply at all levels. Because SEA is driven by the need for a clear vision for environmental mainstreaming and an overall framework for policy development (as in a strategy for sustainable development), it is more suitable than EIA for preparing analytical material for such strategies (see Table 5.9).

To date, formal provision and guidelines for undertaking SEA are confined largely to industrial countries (eg Australia, Canada, The Netherlands, New Zealand, UK, USA). Experience with SEA appears to be very limited in developing countries (except for the requirements of lending and donor agencies, particularly the World Bank) although there is increasing experimentation with the approach.

There is no standard method, but three broad approaches

There is no standard or universal methodology for SEA. Processes vary considerably,[5] but some basic principles for the steps in SEA can be identified (Box 5.13). SEA processes may be either formal or informal, comprehensive or focused, and closely linked with or unrelated to either policy or planning instruments. In general, three broad approaches to SEA have been adopted to date:

5 Useful reviews of SEA approaches and case studies can be found in Sadler and Verheem (1996); de Boer and Sadler (1996); Therivel and Partidario (1996) and the World Bank (1996).

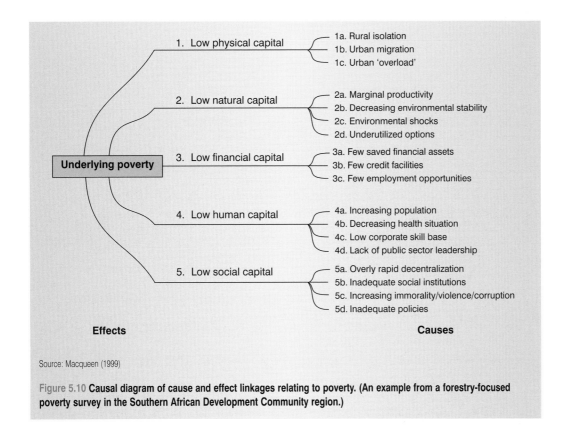

Source: Macqueen (1999)

Figure 5.10 Causal diagram of cause and effect linkages relating to poverty. (An example from a forestry-focused poverty survey in the Southern African Development Community region.)

1 It has been introduced as a relatively separate, distinct process – typically as an extension of EIA.

2 It has been established as a two tier system (eg in The Netherlands) with formal SEAs required for specific sectoral plans and programmes and an environmental 'test' applied to strategic policies.

3 It has been incorporated into environmental policy appraisal (eg in the UK) and regional and land use planning (eg in Sweden). Recently, there has been growing recognition of the importance of integrating EA with other policy and planning instruments.

A particularly promising form of SEA (in the context of strategies for sustainable development) is Strategic Environmental Analysis (denoted by the acronym SEAn). This experimental methodology has been developed and tested by the Dutch group AIDEnvironment, in cooperation with SNV (Netherlands Development Organization). It is designed for use at the earliest possible stage of policy-making to allow the relevant environmental issues and options to be fully integrated into policy, plan and programme design and priority setting. The methodology is based on experiences with EIA, environmental profiles and environmental planning, monitoring and evaluation within the project cycle, and comprises ten steps (Box 5.14) 'which are executed in a participatory manner, with systematic attention for the views and opinions of 'insiders' (local actors)' (Kessler 1997b).

Initially, the primary aim for SNV was to apply the methodology for formulating (new or adjusted) country policy plans. It has been applied under various conditions in Zimbabwe (to prepare district development plans), in Ghana (for SNV regional planning), in Benin and Nicaragua (for strategic planning purposes of donor agencies, local government or NGOs) and in Benin, Bolivia, Honduras and Zambia. Most have been carried out in collaboration with The Netherlands Development Organization SNV. Lessons from the experiences in Benin and Nicaragua are documented in Box 5.15.

Testing a 10-step planning tool for sustainable development

Box 5.13 **Some principles for strategic environmental assessment**

An SEA process should ensure:

- *Screening:* responsible agencies carry out an appropriate assessment of all strategic decisions with significant environmental consequences.
- *Timing:* results of the assessment are available sufficiently early for use in the preparation of the strategic decision.
- *Environmental scoping:* all relevant information is provided to judge whether: (i) an initiative should proceed, and (ii) objectives could be achieved in a more environmentally friendly way (ie through alternative initiatives or approaches).
- *Other factors:* sufficient information is available on other factors, including socio-economic conditions, either parallel to or integrated in the assessment.
- *Review:* the quality of the process and information is safeguarded by effective review mechanisms.
- *Participation:* sufficient information of all legitimate stakeholders (including the public affected) is available early enough to be used effectively in the preparation of the strategic decision.
- *Documentation:* results are identifiable, understandable and available to all parties affected by the decision.
- *Decision-making and accountability:* it is clear to all stakeholders and all parties affected how the results were taken into account in decision-making.
- *Post-decision:* sufficient information on the actual impacts of implementing the decision is gained to judge whether the decision should be amended.

Source: Dalal-Clayton and Sadler (1998a,b) – adapted from Sadler (1998) and Tonk and Verheem (1998)

Box 5.14 **Strategic Environmental Analysis (SEAn): the AIDEnvironment approach. The main steps**

The strategic environmental analysis approach aims to be systematic, analytical and practical. Ten methodological steps create a logical structure and provide guidance to participants in clarifying the complex issues involved.

Steps 1–4: Society–environment context analysis and impact assessment:

- identification of the main environmental functions (production and regulation);
- defining stakeholders dependent upon these functions;
- assessment of current trends within the functions revealed by environmental indicators;
- assessment of consequences (impacts) of trends on stakeholders, future generations and natural values, using environmental impact chains and a trend-impact matrix;
- defining the norms, standards and thresholds involved.

Steps 5–6: Environmental problem analysis:

- definition of the main environmental problems, based on the impacts of trends and a risk analysis;
- identification of the key factors and related actors causing the problem using the action-in-context approach (underlying factors will be mainly socio-cultural, economic and/or institutional).

Steps 7–8: Environmental opportunity analysis:

- definition of the main environmental opportunities;
- identification of the main underlying factors and the actors to realize and benefit from these opportunities.

Steps 9–10: Formulation of a sustainable development policy plan with action fields and follow-up strategy:

- synthesis of the key factors and actors related to the environmental problems and opportunities;
- definition of environmental action fields;
- definition of sustainable development action fields by integrating priority issues from social and economic dimensions;
- formulation of a policy and coherent action plan for sustainable development based on the strengths and weaknesses of the relevant institutions and existing development policies;
- formulation of a follow-up strategy, including definition of coordination responsibilities, establishment of a monitoring system with relevant indicators, procedures for regular adjustments to policy using relevant strategic environmental analysis steps, institutional strengthening and capacity building.

Source: AIDEnvironment (1997); Kessler (1997a,b)

Box 5.15 **Lessons from strategic environmental analysis (SEAn) in Benin and Nicaragua**

A number of lessons can be drawn from two widely different cases of applying the SEAn methodology.

1   The resulting strategic plan is not an environmental plan, but an integrated (sustainable development) plan. The SEAn methodology takes the environmental domain (goods and services provided to human society) as a starting point to find solutions and opportunities in the areas of overlap with the socio-economic and institutional domains.
2   The process of executing the ten methodological steps is at least as important as the actual outcome in terms of a strategic plan (Benin) or thematic reports (Nicaragua). The participatory approach allows participants to exchange ideas and views on key problems underlying root causes of unsustainability and key opportunities for sustainable development.
3   Even if (as in Benin) little time is available and there is a risk of ending up with broad and general outcomes, the process facilitates the surfacing of common views among different actors involved. Participants were particularly satisfied about the methodology as a logical framework to structure discussions. For many participants it was the first time to collaborate actively with other disciplines, and for government officers to exchange views and information with NGOs.
4   One of the main differences between the strategic plan resulting from an SEAn and existing environmental action plans is the emphasis on priority themes agreed upon by participants at the meso-level (eg to support districts and local councils in making their own development plans as part of a decentralization and capacity-building process), as well as a certain level of commitment to work on agreed activities. The meso-level is the highest level at which local stakeholders can deal with concrete issues and at which they organize themselves, while it is the lowest level at which government departments are well informed and can negotiate with other stakeholders.
5   Since SEAn step 9 takes into consideration existing policies and ongoing programmes, the resulting plan is not an unrealistic ideal plan but a gradual step in the right direction.
6   The main challenge is to simplify the existing SEAn methodology and to integrate tools from other disciplines to develop an integrated sustainability analysis. It is also clear that the entire planning process requires more continuous facilitation support than has been available so far (ie over a longer period of time, not more intensive), to implement, monitor and evaluate the activities that have been agreed upon.

Source: Dalal-Clayton and Sadler (1998b)

COMMUNITY-BASED ISSUE ANALYSIS[6]

The analysis of issues by communities is fundamental to a truly participatory planning effort. Unlike traditional 'consultation' and 'auditing', which are often top-down, expert-driven information-gathering activities, community-based issue analysis uses a series of exercises to help stakeholders share knowledge, review and participate in technical assessments, set planning priorities and jointly develop options for action. In short, the functions of community-based analysis:

- initiate detailed dialogue among community groups and between the community and technical experts;
- focus planning on people's recognized interests, needs and preferences;
- inform stakeholders about the technical aspects of the problems that they wish to resolve, by engaging them in the collection and analysis of data;
- prevent uncritical and sole reliance on the assessments of (often external) experts;
- create a well-informed constituency of residents to work for empowerment and sustainability.

Community-based issue analysis follows a process of 13 steps:

13 steps to community-based analysis

6 Main source for this section: ICLEI et al (1996a)

1 Decide what level of participation will be facilitated in the issue analysis process – stakeholder representation or direct participation.
2 Determine what target communities and target groups will be recruited to participate in the process.
3 Inform the target communities and groups about the issue analysis process.
4 With the target communities/groups, decide what specific issues will be analysed.
5 Select methods and tools for the participant assessment of the chosen issues.
6 Select methods and tools for the technical assessment of the chosen issues.
7 Modify the selected technical assessment methods to permit stakeholder involvement in the technical assessment exercise.
8 Review assessment methods to ensure that they support the analysis of systemic problems.
9 Establish baseline data on key conditions.
10 Present the findings of technical assessments to the issue analysis participants before the conclusion of the participant assessment exercises.
11 Identify any issues that require further assessment.
12 Identify any proposals or options for action that should be considered in the action planning process.
13 Prepare the final issue analysis report.

Combining participatory and expert technical assessments

A comprehensive community-based issue analysis process uses both participant assessment and technical assessment methods in parallel to achieve a consensus analysis of key issues and the tools used will depend on the capacities of the community.

- *Participant assessment* exercises are used to involve local inhabitants and service users at a very basic level. Inhabitants are assisted in defining problems and identifying what services they want most and how the services can be provided sustainably. Special exercises are used to identify indigenous solutions and to apply local know-how to the analysis of problems and the development of solutions. Participant assessment methods that have been used around the world include: mapping, focus groups, SWOT analysis, logical framework and search conferences (see Box 6.28).
- *Technical assessment* methods are designed and employed to inform the participant assessment process. Technical assessment methods – such as comparative risk assessment, environmental impact assessment and systems analysis – can be modified to allow for extensive stakeholder participation.

The key to a successful community-based assessment process is to link together the use of participant assessment exercises and expert technical assessments. Specifically, an assessment process should be organized in such a way that stakeholders participate in the technical assessments; and the findings of the technical assessments are provided as final inputs into the participant assessment process.

Deciding what to measure: a framework of parts and aims
'Indicator-based assessments' on page 135 discussed the pros and cons of indicator-based assessment. The main steps in developing such a form of assessment are:

- designing a framework of parts and aims (described here);
- choosing indicators (page 158);
- generating indices (page 159);
- identifying priority issues and policy options (page 160).

A framework of parts (components, dimensions, elements, themes, etc) is an arrangement of the parts of a system that must be measured to get a clear and accurate reading of the state of that system and changes to it. A framework of aims (goals, objectives, principles, criteria, etc) is an arrangement of the aim of each part, succinctly expressing its point, the main item or items of concern, and the level or type of performance that is sought. A combined framework of parts and aims provides a checklist of the human and environmental conditions required for sustainable development. More importantly, it enables people to:

- identify the essential parts of the system;
- avoid measuring the same part more than once;
- avoid omitting an essential part;
- highlight unavoidable gaps (so that everyone knows that a part is missing if there is no suitable indicator for it);
- ensure that an appropriate weight or value is given to each part;
- show the logic underlying the selection of parts and the weight given to each;
- measure key relationships between groups of parts;
- combine the indicators to provide measurements not just of the particular parts they represent but also of major groups of parts and of the system as a whole;
- Part of a framework of parts and aims is shown in Table 5.10.

A well-designed indicator framework (able to fulfil all the above functions) is systemic, hierarchical, logical and communicable. *Systemic* means that the parts are organized to facilitate analysis of key properties of the system and relationships between subsystems and major features. In Figure 5.11, for example, the division of the system into two subsystems (people and ecosystem) reflects the fact that human societies exist within ecosystems. It also facilitates analysis of the relationship between human and environmental conditions. The division of the human subsystem into major groups of human concerns and of the ecosystem into major compartments facilitates analysis of (for example) the relationship between resource use and the state of the rest of the ecosystem (land, water, air, biodiversity), resource use and wealth, and wealth and the state of the rest of the human subsystem.

The indicator framework should be systemic, hierarchical, logical and communicable

Hierarchical means that the parts are organized into a series of levels. Lower levels are narrower in scope and more specific than higher levels. Components on the same level are roughly equal in scope and overlap as little as possible. For example, land diversity and land quality (Figure 5.12) are intended to be equally important parts of land; conversion, modification and protection to be equally important aspects of land diversity; and forest quality and soil quality to cover roughly equal aspects of land quality.

Logical means that the levels form a series of means and ends. The level below is a means of achieving the level above. The level above is the end or purpose of the level below. For example:

- What we must measure (*means*): We measure *ecosystem well-being*, by measuring the condition of the *land*, which we do by measuring *land diversity*, which we do by measuring *conversion*, which we do by measuring *the percentage of each ecosystem type converted to non-forest or plantation.*
- Why we measure it (*ends*): We measure *the percentage of each ecosystem type converted to non-forest or plantation* to measure *conversion*, which we do to measure *land diversity*, which we do to measure the condition of the *land*, which we do to measure *ecosystem well-being*.

Table 5.10 Illustrative framework of parts and aims for indicator-based assessment (human subsystem only)

Parts (increasing specificity) ➡   Aims

Element group	Element	Sub-element	Objective
Health and population	Health		People enjoy long lives in good health
	Population		Populations are stable, with a balance of age groups, and within the bounds of human and natural resources
Wealth	Individual and corporate wealth	Needs	Individuals and households meet their needs
		Income	and obtain the income to secure their material well-being
		Business	Businesses are profitable and competitive
	Societal wealth	Capital and productivity	The society has the resources to promote enterprise and maintain prosperity,
		Inflation and employment	providing a stable climate for investment and decent livelihoods,
		Debt	while living within its means
Knowledge and culture	Knowledge	State of knowledge	People have the knowledge to innovate and cope with change, live well and sustainably, and fulfil their potential
		Education	Education levels are high and the society has well-developed and widely shared systems for transmitting knowledge formally through education
		Communication	and informally through communication
	Culture	Belief	Belief systems meet spiritual needs and promote human and ecosystem well-being
		Spirit and nature	Links between spirit and nature are strengthened and maintained
		Expression	Creative expression flourishes
Community	Freedom and governance	Freedom	The rights of all members of society are fully respected, and individuals are free to choose how decisions are made and who should make them
		Governance	Decision-making bodies are open, clean and effective
	Peace, order and solidarity	Law	Communities and citizens respect the rule of law,
		Crime	protect their members from crime and violence,
		Peace	coexist peacefully
		Solidarity	and provide a helping hand to those who need it
Equity	Gender equality		Benefits and burdens are shared equally between males and females
	Societal equity		and equitably among societal groups

Source: Robert Prescott-Allen, (personal communication)

Communicable means the parts and aims are simply expressed and readily understood by decision-makers and are not abstract or highly technical.

The Rio Declaration, Agenda 21 and some of the international convention texts have been used as frameworks with limited success because they were not designed for this purpose (see, for example, Box 5.16). The United Nations Commission on Sustainable Development started with Agenda 21 as its

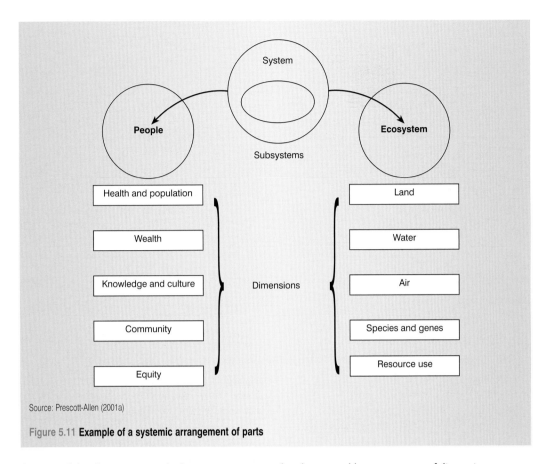

Source: Prescott-Allen (2001a)

Figure 5.11 **Example of a systemic arrangement of parts**

framework but has since switched to a more structured and manageable arrangement of dimensions, themes and sub-themes, cross-referenced to the appropriate sections of Agenda 21 (UN DESA 2001b)

Sets of principles and criteria that are expressly intended as indicator frameworks have been somewhat more useful. These tend to be devoted to particular sectors, notably forest management, such as the Forest Stewardship Council's principles and criteria (FSC 2000); the Montreal Process's criteria for the conservation and sustainable management of temperate and boreal forests (The Montréal Process 1999); the Pan-European criteria for sustainable forest management (Ministerial Conference on the Protection of Forests in Europe and Pan European Forest Certification Council 1998); and the International Tropical Timber Organization's criteria for sustainable management of natural tropical forests (ITTO 1998).

However, none of these frameworks is fully systemic, hierarchical or logical. Consequently, indicator sets derived from them suffer from one or more of such flaws as an inability to produce clear pictures of socio-economic conditions and the state of the environment, omission of essential aspects of sustainability, overlapping components and consequent redundancy and double-counting, confusion about what is being measured and why, unmeasurable indicators, and distortion of assessments through an emphasis on documenting procedures rather than achieving results.

The most useful frameworks are offered by indicator-based assessment methods because they are cross-sectoral and designed for the measurement of sustainability (page 153). They include Well-being Assessment (Prescott-Allen 2001a) (Figures 5.4 and 5.5), the Dashboard of Sustainability (Figure 5.6), the CSD's indicators of sustainable development (UN DESA 2001b), and the Sustainability Reporting Guidelines for businesses and other organizations (Global Reporting Initiative 2000).

Sector-based indicator frameworks show promise, but have flaws

Indicator-based assessment methods are often the most useful

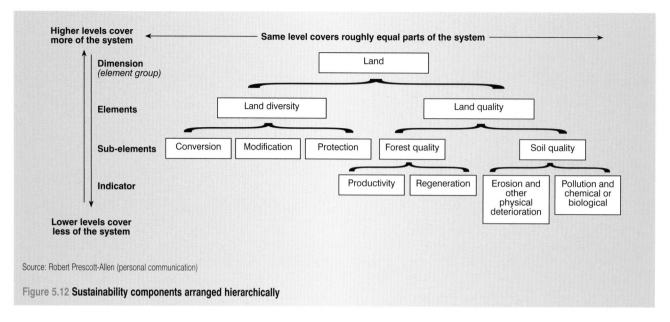

Source: Robert Prescott-Allen (personal communication)

Figure 5.12 **Sustainability components arranged hierarchically**

These frameworks can help in structuring analyses and developing checklists of questions, but their most important function is to facilitate the selection of a cost-effective set of high quality indicators for sustainability assessment.

Box 5.16 **Agenda 21 as a basis for analysis**

Agenda 21 was not designed as a framework for measurement and analysis. Consequently, efforts to use it for this purpose have met with variable success.

Costa Rica carried out a comparative analysis of its national development plan with Agenda 21 as a prelude to a comprehensive sustainable development programme. Swaziland conducted a careful, participatory review of Agenda 21 to decide how to integrate principles of sustainability into a revised national development plan. Both Ecuador and El Salvador conducted similar analyses – but also made efforts to separate the process of analysis from any political agenda, so that important principles identified by the process could be adopted by the winner of a subsequent election.

Given the absence of numerical data, Agenda 21 analyses have been subjective, usually involving people coming together to identify what is currently impeding the long-term progress of the country. In Kenya, the problem was seen to lie in a centralized planning system that did not cater to the development needs of communities. In El Salvador, the problem lay in the continuing lack of trust among factions that had fought a civil war. In Morocco, the underlying concern was population growth and employment. In Niger, the principle problem was desertification and land degradation.

Source: UNDP (2000)

Deciding how to measure: choosing indicators

Select representative, reliable and feasible indicators

Because indicators cost money to measure, the ideal is to choose one high quality indicator for each element, sub-element or indicator group (depending on how far down the hierarchy one must go to identify a measurable component). A high quality indicator is representative, reliable and feasible, and indicator selection is often a matter of balancing these qualities (Box 5.17).

A practical procedure is to:

1   Define a representative and reliable indicator for each component (element, sub-element or indicator group). More than one indicator may be necessary if one is insufficiently representative.

2 Review data sources to determine the availability of data for each indicator.

3 If data are not available for an indicator, identify one or more alternative indicators for which data are available (as determined by the data review).

4 If data are not available for the alternatives and a component lacks an indicator, decide whether to develop a programme to obtain the data or to exclude the component from the assessment.

5 If no suitable indicator is available and funds are lacking to provide one, exclude the component concerned from the assessment – but clearly note its exclusion.

Seeing the big sustainability picture: generating indices

As noted on page 132 assessments that combine their indicators into indices can communicate their main findings instantly, providing a clear picture of the entire system, revealing key relationships between subsystems and between major components, and facilitating analysis of critical strengths and weaknesses.

The problem with indices is that a typical set of indicators is a mess of incompatible measurements: pollution in milligrams per litre, ecosystem conversion in hectares, species diversity in species numbers, genetic distance and population change, and so on. Combining such different indicators mixes apples and oranges. To do this successfully requires converting the measurements to a common unit that does not

Combining indicators can distort their qualities

Box 5.17 **Selecting indicators**

An indicator is fully representative if it:

- covers the most important parts of the component concerned;
- shows trends over time and differences between places and groups of people.

For example, the indicator *percentage of each ecosystem type converted to non-forest or plantation* fully represents the sub-element *conversion,* whereas the indicators *percentage of each ecosystem type converted to agriculture, or percentage of each ecosystem type converted to built land, or percentage of each ecosystem type converted to plantation* do not because they represent only one type of conversion. *The indicator percentage of* **forest** *converted is less representative than percentage of each* **ecosystem type** *converted* because it is less likely to show differences between one place and another.

An indicator is likely to be **reliable** if it:

- is accurate;
- is measured in a standardized way with sound and consistent sampling procedures;
- is well founded;
- directly reflects the objective of the element or sub-element concerned.

'Well founded' means that the indicator's relationship to the component it represents is well established, scientifically valid or is a defensible and testable hypothesis. For example, the indicator *percentage of each ecosystem type in a natural or old growth state* derives from the view that a number of species and biotic associations are more likely to persist if an adequate part of the ecosystem remains in a natural state – a view that some would regard as scientifically established and others as at least a defensible hypothesis.

An indicator directly reflects the objective of the element or sub-element concerned if it measures its actual achievement rather than factors that could advance or impede its achievement. For example, the indicator *eroded area as a percentage of converted and modified area* measures the actual achievement of part of the objective, 'Soil degradation on modified or cultivated land is close to degradation rates on natural land.' The indicator *area of erosion prone land that is logged* measures a factor that could impede achievement of the objective, and the indicator *area and percentage of forest land systematically assessed for soil erosion hazard* measures a factor that could advance it; but neither measures its direct achievement, and the area and severity of erosion could change regardless of either factor.

An indicator is feasible if it depends on data that are readily available (as maps, statistics or both) or obtainable at reasonable cost. 'Reasonable cost' varies with the indicator. A highly representative and reliable indicator is likely to be cost-effective even if it is expensive. Unrepresentative or unreliable indicators are worthless, no matter how cheap.

distort their qualities as apples or oranges. The common unit may be a physical unit (such as area or toxicity), money or a performance score. Since many indicators are severely distorted when converted to a physical unit or money, Well-being Assessment and the Dashboard of Sustainability (in common with narrower indices such as the Human Development Index and Ecological Sustainability Index) use performance scores.

Instead, performance scores can be used

Indicator measurements are converted to a performance score, much as one currency is converted to another, by defining the rate of exchange between the indicator data and a performance scale. In the Dashboard of Sustainability one end of the scale is set by the best performance (of the societies being assessed) and the other end by the worst performance. For example, in the indicator *life expectancy at birth*, Japan's 81 years is best and defines the top of the scale; Sierra Leone's 34 years is worst and defines the bottom of the scale. So a society with a life expectancy of 57.5 years (half way between best and worst) would get a medium score (50 on a scale of 100 to 0).

In Well-being Assessment's Barometer of Sustainability five bands of 20 points each are defined (good, fair, medium, poor, bad). Performance criteria are chosen for the top point of each band and the base (0) of the scale, on the basis of the range of actual performance, the objective of the element or sub-element that the indicator represents, and factors such as estimated sustainable rates, background rates, observed thresholds, standards or targets (international, national, sub-national), expert opinion, the performance criteria of related indicators and the judgement of participants. Illustrative performance criteria for *life expectancy at birth* and the basis on which they were chosen are given in Table 5.11. Defining bands rather than just the ends of the scale allows the scale to be non-linear: a society with a life expectancy of 57.5 years would get a poor score of 37.

Once the indicators have been given scores, they can be combined back up the hierarchy from indicator to subsystem using standard combining procedures: unweighted average, weighted average or lower/lowest score, whichever is judged to be most appropriate.

Table 5.11 **Illustrative performance criteria for the indicator, life expectancy at birth**

Element: Health			Objective: People enjoy long lives in good health
Band	**Top point on scale**	**Years of life expectancy at birth**	**Basis**
Good	100	85	Encompasses projected high of 84 years by 2050
Fair	80	75	Matches UN target of >75 years by 2015
Medium	60	70	Matches UN target of >70 years by 2005
Poor	40	60	Matches UN target of at least 60 years by 2000
Bad	20	45	
Base	0	30	Encompasses current low of 34 years

Identifying priority sustainability issues: using a rigorous, routine system

A comprehensive indicator-based assessment of sustainability that generates indices – if produced rigorously and systematically – will clearly reveal the priority issues for an NSDS. What is more, it will do so in the context of a well-rounded picture of sustainable development, covering all essential elements, and a measurement of overall performance (eg the Policy Performance Index of the Dashboard of Sustainability; or the Well-being Index, Human Well-being Index, and Ecosystem Well-being Index of the Barometer of Sustainability). For example:

■ The Barometer of Sustainability (Figures 5.4 and 5.5) shows that Canada needs to pay most attention to air, resource use, and species and genes. Further interrogation of these dimensions would show that the priority issues are carbon emissions, energy consumption, habitat protection for wild species and agricultural diversity.

■ The Dashboard of Sustainability (Figure 5.6) shows a slightly different set of priorities – protected areas, cropland, carbon emissions, renewable energy, nuclear waste and recycling – but nonetheless it shows them clearly.

The next stage is to explore relationships between these issues and other ecological and socio-economic factors and to analyse the motivations, values, behaviours, policies and institutional factors that are behind the issues and need to be addressed to make progress. Policy options can then be developed on the basis of this analysis and associated scenarios. Stakeholder analysis, covering motivations and values, is discussed on page 120, analysis of policy and institutional processes on page 162, scenario development on page 171 and decision-making on policy options in Chapter 8.

Analysing sustainable development mechanisms and processes

We have stated that a strategy is as much a set of continuing *mechanisms or processes* – that provide the facility to debate, plan, experiment, monitor and review sustainable development – as it is an agreed *vision or set of goals*. The kinds of mechanisms that lead to sustainable development are illustrated in Figure 5.13 and are expanded in Table 5.12. The challenge, then, is to develop an inventory of the 'mechanisms and processes that work' and their links, and to improve these links in the context of an NSDS. Such mechanisms may include both long-standing and recent introductions, both formal and informal mechanisms, and both routine and one-off approaches.

Develop an inventory of mechanisms and processes that work …

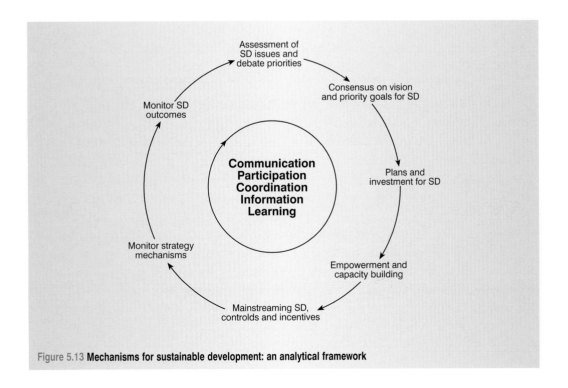

Figure 5.13 **Mechanisms for sustainable development: an analytical framework**

Steps in analysing the component mechanisms

As Table 5.12 implies, component mechanisms need first to be listed, and then assessed:

1 *List the mechanisms that currently contribute to the NSDS, or list candidate mechanisms if an NSDS is not yet in place.* Assessors must be open to the variety of sources of such mechanisms. For example, while an existing NSDS might have a formal communications programme, changes in awareness about sustainable development might actually result from other mechanisms that are not connected to the strategy.

2 *Describe each mechanism in terms of:* its legal setting/mandate; the principles followed; responsibilities for the mechanism; the main 'users' of the mechanism; resources actually applied to it in practice; and any contentions or major dilemmas associated with it.

3 *Assess the quality of component mechanisms:* Table 5.13 presents the questions that were asked by the OECD DAC review of NSDSs. A variety of methods will be found useful in answering these questions. Many are listed in Table 5.12. Desk review and key informant interviews will usually prove suitable. A participation intensity map (Figure 5.14) can be drawn up by key informants to express the quality of participation in each of the strategy mechanisms listed in Table 5.12. A SWOT analysis (Box 5.18) can help to reveal which strategies/mechanisms are effective.

4 *Assess the legal framework for sustainable development* in which key mechanisms operate: the substance of the law, the application of the law and constraints (see page 162).

5 *Assess the economic context and conditions* which will determine how any mechanism affects the motivations and behaviour of producers and consumers, and thus to a large extent, its ultimate effectiveness (see page 169).

6 *Assess how all the mechanisms fit together:* their gaps, overlaps and coordination, especially if the task is to bring together promising mechanisms into an NSDS (see page 170).

The secretariat may undertake some of these tasks itself; but it will more likely need to commission and coordinate others to carry out the assessments.

Analysing the legal framework for sustainable development[7]

In recent years, growing attention has centred on the role of law and legal institutions in sustainable development. This has coincided with a profound shift in thinking about the role of the state, and a reorientation of governance strategies towards the creation of suitable enabling environments for greater private and local initiative in sustainable development. Good laws and functioning legal institutions are essential contributors to the predictability, security and flexibility needed to define such environments. Conversely, poorly designed and implemented laws can constrain and inhibit effective action, distort economic incentives and discourage appropriate interventions by government and civil society stakeholders.

A close analysis of the applicable legal framework, therefore, is an important part of assessing the viability of any sustainable development strategy or its components. The scope of such an analysis will vary, of course, depending on the context. The following analytical steps are likely to be applicable in a wide range of situations.

---

7 This section is based on material prepared by Jon Lindsay, derived from FAO Development Law Service (2000).

Table 5.12 **Component mechanisms in NSDSs and how to analyse them**

1 Communications and awareness of sustainable development issues	**Market research/polls** with the public, to assess changing awareness of sustainable development issues, and where that awareness came from (NSDS, education, media, etc)
	Review media and educational curricula for changing level of sustainable development contents and the changing kinds of narratives on sustainable development
	Key informant interviews on: direct influence of NSDS documents/activities; level of understanding of current sustainable development goals and provisions
2 Participation in sustainable development debate and action	**Analyse committees and records of decisions** to assess who is contributing to debate and decisions locally and at macro level; assess representation (identity, accountability to group); assess the links between committees – especially between central and decentralized levels, regularity and degree of consensus/conflict
	Map '**policy communities**' around different sustainable development issues – how are they formed (eg informal, or through involvement in a formal initiative, by local interests or influenced by external agencies); how are they linked (eg poverty alleviation and biodiversity conservation 'policy communities') – do they work together, or clash?
	Sample **key informant interviews** on changes in representation, transparency, accountability, political commitment. Ask 'whose strategy is it?' to ascertain 'ownership'
	Participation intensity mapping (Figure 5.14) on informant's perception of level of participation in each component 1–12 here
3 Assessment/analysis of sustainable development issues	**Desk and key informant interviews of recent analyses:** Who identified the authors, the questions asked, and the methods used? What were these, and how locally relevant? What is the extent of new (and recycled) information? Are assumptions being tested? Is there a component of consultation in the analysis or is it all expert-led?
4 Consensus, conflict management and negotiation on sustainability	**Desk and key informant interviews** to assess provisions made for reaching agreement and handling disagreements. Are structures and processes emerging with which stakeholders are happy? Or are issues being forced through? What opportunities and constraints are there to improving cross-sectoral and top–bottom linkages?
5 Prioritizing goals for sustainable development	**Identify criteria, systems and procedures** that are being used to choose between options; the extent to which they are informed by social, environmental and economic dimensions and their integration, and whether priorities are clearly presented
	Analyse shifts in actual decisions by key bodies (government, private sector) and attempt to correlate them with the above and with other mechanisms 1–12
6 Financial mobilization, allocation and investment in sustainable development	**Desk analysis of government policies, plans, allocations and disbursement;** categorizing changes in these in relation to agreed sustainable development goals (or to generic sustainable development criteria if no formal SD goals yet established)
	Interview business sector people on investment in sustainable development and which of mechanisms 1–12 this might be correlated with (or whether entirely spontaneous or correlated with international and market demands)

7 Mainstreaming sustainable development concerns by sector activities	**Desk review and key informant interviews** with key sectors on recent policies and programmes for sustainable development; coherence between them; and how this has changed over time
8 Coordinating sustainable development activities	**Key informant interviews** on what sustainable development steering mechanisms have been established, their gaps, duplication and coherence of current sustainable development activities; and on the quality of NSDS process management – its coherence, pacing, adaptability, and so on
9 Capacity building in sustainable development	**Interviews** on changes in attitudes and skills that promote sustainable development and the sources for this; correlation with training/technology development, and with other mechanisms 1–12
10 Empowerment for sustainable development	**Desk review** of provisions for devolution of rights and powers to take responsibility for sustainable development locally **Interview stakeholders** on the practice of the above – particularly regarding opportunities and constraints they face for sustainable development responsibility
11 Information systems on sustainable development	**Desk review of the coverage and use of sustainable development information:** coverage of, for example, pressures/driving forces, current state and changing responses; how information flows and who is involved; links to decision-making; evidence of changing demand for sustainable development information from decision-makers; problems of data availability, reliability, and so on **Multi-stakeholder workshop** can reveal key issues on information and its use
12 Monitoring, learning and accountability mechanisms for sustainable development	**Desk assessment and key informant interviews on monitoring systems (internal and external) used** by key bodies and their links to policy, planning, investment and management systems. Assess coverage of strategy implementation and impact monitoring, procedures for data quality assurance, including adequate participation in monitoring. Assess evidence of changing demand/use of information generated; quality and regularity of updates; sanctions applied. Ask where learning on sustainable development has come from – own experience, other strategy-organized experience, or from external constructs and initiatives

Four steps to assessing how the legal environment enables sustainable development – or not

STEP 1 IDENTIFY THE COMPONENTS OF A COUNTRY'S LEGAL FRAMEWORK THAT ARE RELEVANT TO SUSTAINABLE DEVELOPMENT

The first step is simply a matter of defining the 'legal playing field' – what is the relevant legal framework? The answer to this is often wider than is assumed. For example, a country's sectoral legislation on forestry cannot be understood in isolation from numerous other sectoral or general laws, including the constitution; laws on taxation, investment, transport, credit, companies and associations; laws on environment, land use and tenure, soil conservation, water, wildlife and plant protection; and international agreements to which the country may be a party. Various customary laws may also apply. Even where (as in many countries) the official status of customary law is ambiguous, it often continues as a matter of practice to shape people's behaviour, and therefore needs to be included.

STEP 2 ANALYSE THE SUBSTANCE OF THE LAW

The overarching issue here is: to what extent do the laws identified in Step 1 allow, encourage, constrain or prevent the types of activities on which a sustainable development strategy is focused?

- *Is the law relatively free of unnecessary regulatory constraints that could inhibit activities essential for achieving sustainable development?* Regulatory obstacles can take many forms: for example, bureaucratic procedures that increase the transaction costs of a particular activity, without a corresponding public benefit. Every legal system contains examples of well-intended laws surrounded by excessive procedural hurdles that make them extremely difficult to use.
- *Does law provide an appropriate positive regulatory environment for activities in support of sustainable development?* While over-regulation or inappropriate regulation can stifle initiatives, the absence of a suitable regulatory framework can be equally debilitating. Many of the more important activities that flow from a particular strategy choice will need to be supported or guided by a body of predictable, understandable and enforceable rules. Issues that frequently come up in connection with the promotion of sustainable development include whether there are appropriate rules:
  - for ownership of property – as Hernando de Soto (2000) has noted, many people in developing countries face multiple legal and bureaucratic hurdles which make property ownership impossible, so that they cannot use their potential capital assets;
  - governing access to and management of public goods;
  - concerning the externalities of public and private actions;
  - governing the behaviour of government officials, to ensure basic limits on the exercise of discretion, and to support transparency and accountability;
  - ensuring a right of meaningful participation, including access to information.
- *Are the mandates for different institutional actors clear, coordinated and desirable?* Laws may leave it unclear, for example, which agency has the power to make certain decisions. The result could be that a key government stakeholder whose action is critical to the success of a particular strategy component may find that its authority is open to challenge. In other contexts, the legal allocation of authority may be fragmented among different sub-agencies that do not function well together.
- *Does the law enable the formation and empowerment of appropriate stakeholder organizations?* The question for legal analysis is whether there is a legal basis for the creation or recognition of such institutions, and for the vesting in them of real rights, powers and responsibilities. If the law treats them essentially as non-entities, their capacity and incentive may be significantly constrained.
- *Does the legal framework provide mechanism(s) by which people can obtain meaningful and secure rights to the assets essential for sustainable livelihoods?* Many national legal frameworks fall far short of supporting sustainable access to and secure rights over land, trees, water and other resources for rural stakeholders, and in fact may criminalize the exercise of locally recognized rights.

STEP 3 ANALYSE THE LAW-IN-ACTION

The substantive content of law is, of course, only part of the story. It is also important to try to assess the actual *effect* that relevant laws have on the ground – in what ways do they influence the behaviour of individuals and institutions? A particular law may fall short of its intended purpose or have quite unintended secondary effects, for a number of reasons, such as:

- *Lack of political will:* Many good laws are simply not implemented.
- *Failure to anticipate the costs of effective implementation:* Many ambitious laws lie unimplemented or under-implemented.
- *Failure to recognize the limitations of legal reform in bringing about social and economic change:* Laws that require sudden changes in deeply ingrained behaviour may prove difficult to implement.
- *Lack of understanding or acceptance of the law by various stakeholders:* As a result, there is insufficient support for the law among those stakeholders most directly affected.

Table 5.13 **Questions asked about strategy quality by the OECD DAC initiative**

Topic	Issues to be explored
1 Political and institutional enabling conditions	What are/have been the **priorities of present and past governments**? What key policies, strategies and initiatives have been put in place? What are the historical, political and administrative contexts in which **previous attempts at integrated strategies** have originated and been developed and implemented?
	Is there **political commitment** to the objectives, processes, plans and budget requirements of all strategic initiatives concerned with sustainable development? In what political fora? Is the political commitment partisan or broad-church? What are the sticking points?
	Is it clear where **responsibilities** lie for building on existing strategies and their activities, for formulating new strategies where relevant, for implementing them and for monitoring them? Do the institutions concerned have sufficient **rights, resources and effective relationships** to undertake this? (The 4Rs.)
	Is there effective **coordination**: ■ between these institutions; ■ between strategic initiatives, for example NCS or social action plans; ■ between these institutions and those central to planning and investment; ■ between institutions and donors?
	How do **national, local and regional strategies relate** to each other and how do existing strategies link into the planning and decision-making systems?
	What **cross-boundary, regional and global** issues have been considered? (eg conflict, free trade areas, legal agreements, cross-border ethnic groups, development aid and debt)
2 Quality of analysis	Is there adequate **understanding of the state of resources**, trends in their quality and quantity, and the pressures upon them?
	Is there adequate analysis of the **state of the main sectors and livelihood systems**, their interactions with resources (as above), and consequent winners and losers?
	Has full use been made of **existing studies on poverty and environment**, and the opportunity taken to strengthen the body of knowledge in concerned areas?
3 Quality of participation	Is there **continuing identification and participation** of concerned stakeholders – including government, civil society and market players at different levels, and representatives of global environmental interests – in strategy preparation, planning, implementation, monitoring and review? Do the fora and mechanisms suit the stakeholders? Does representation meet acceptable criteria of identity-with-group and accountability-to-group?
	Have **proactive mechanisms** been used to engage otherwise marginalized stakeholders in the above processes – such as women and landless poor groups?
	What role did public awareness campaigns have in encouraging stakeholder involvement in the process and how has the process strengthened people's participation in, and influence over, the decision making process?
	How were difficulties and problems addressed and consensus reached?
4 Quality of policies and plans	Have clear **policies, plans, principles, standards and/or targets** been derived from the strategy, in forms which can best elicit positive responses from those various institutions (government, market and civil society) which are supposed to implement the strategy?
	Are there **systems for defining priorities** in environmental, economic and social terms, so as to keep the number of strategy objectives (at any one time)

	manageable? And are these systems compatible with those for analysis and participation?
	Have **opportunities for win–win** activities supporting poverty alleviation, economic growth and environmental conservation been well defined with those institutions best placed to act on them? For example, have conservation and poverty alleviation strategies been brought together?
	Are there **systems for addressing the hard trade-offs** – identifying them, debating them, planning action or compensating for the costs of inaction?
	Has there been **early and tactical implementation of promising initiatives** which will both help build support for the strategy process and test its principles and ideas?
5 Effectiveness of regulations and incentives	Do fiscal and regulatory frameworks **internalize social and environmental costs** in order to correct for market failure, and open doors to best-practice investment?
	Are these frameworks efficiently **monitored and enforced**, by government or private bodies as appropriate?
	Have measures been included to ensure **compliance with international** environmental and human rights agreements?
	Are measures taken to increase public awareness of sustainable development and thus encourage the development of **consumer- or civil society-driven incentives**?
6 NSDS process management and effectiveness of capacity	What key factors assisted the development of the strategy (eg a past strategy, public pressure, government commitment) and what were the key issues to resolve (eg land tenure, resource depletion, poverty)?
	From what perspective has the process been driven (environmental, economic, interdisciplinary)?
	What tools/methodologies were useful in enhancing understanding (eg poverty assessments, SEA)? How is progress being monitored?
	Is capacity being efficiently and equitably utilized, and improved, to: ■ develop strategies with strong local ownership; ■ coordinate existing sectoral or issues-based strategies to improve their coherence and efficiency in achieving SD; ■ encourage institutions to make their responses to relevant strategies; ■ implement strategy-related activities, in a way that is consistent with the broader strategy goals; ■ monitor the impact of strategic mechanisms and activities; ■ maintain the 'big picture' of strategy evolution; ■ review and continuously improve the strategy?
7 Evidence of impact	What areas do stakeholders believe are being influenced – positively or negatively – by the strategy, for example: ■ Ecological processes conserved? ■ Biodiversity conserved? ■ Resource quantity/productivity maintained? ■ Economic efficiency improved? ■ Poverty and inequity reduced? ■ Pollution prevented? ■ Human health improved? ■ Culture conserved?
8 Donor roles	What has been the role of donors in these mechanisms and was their role useful?
	Is there effective coordination between government and donors?

Note: These questions complement those of Table 5.12, by offering questions on enabling conditions, quality of resulting plans, policies, regulations and incentives, and strategy process management. As such, it can also be useful in monitoring strategy implementation (page 320).

Source: IIED (2000)

■ *Weak judicial institutions and underpowered alternative fora:* In many countries, the resolution of legal disputes is the responsibility of a court system that is over-burdened and under-financed.

This part of the legal analysis cannot rely entirely on a review of written instruments and cannot be undertaken only by legal experts. It needs to be nested within a multidisciplinary effort to assess the perceptions, activities and interactions of the main stakeholders.

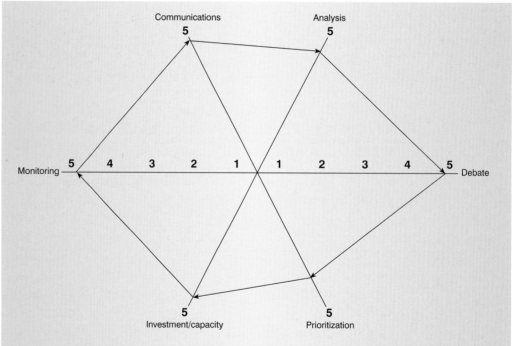

Method: The strategy mechanisms are each accorded a 'spoke' in the 'wheel', eg six mechanisms are considered in the above. Focus groups or interviewees assess the type of participation on each 'spoke' starting from the centre. Five types/intensities of participation can then be suggested:

1 **Compliance:** tasks are assigned; outsiders decide agenda and direct the process

2 **Consultation:** local opinions are asked, outsiders analyse and decide the course of action

3 **Cooperation:** local people work with outsiders to determine priorities; joint responsibility with outsiders to direct the process

4 **Co-learning:** local people and outsiders share knowledge, create new understanding and work together to form action plans; outsiders facilitate

5 **Collective action:** local people set their own agenda, mobilize in the absence of outside initiators

The reasons for different participation types/intensities, and problems and opportunities arising, can then be discussed.

Source: Adapted from Kanji and Greenwood (2001)

Figure 5.14 **Mapping the type/intensity of participation in strategy mechanisms**

STEP 4 ASSESS THE FEASIBILITY AND PRIORITY OF ADDRESSING THE LEGAL CONSTRAINTS

Once the constraining features in the legal framework have been identified, the next step is to analyse how to correct those features, or at least to mitigate their impact. A key question is how high a priority to assign to any particular legal deficiency: to what extent can they be, or will they have to be, 'lived with'? To what extent are they such fundamental threats to strategy goals that they will need to be addressed in a forthright fashion? Here, two somewhat countervailing considerations should be kept in mind:

- On the one hand, it is important to be realistic in analysing the importance of a law. No legal system is flawless, and it is often possible to achieve promising development results in a less-than-ideal legal environment.
- On the other hand, although it may be possible to side-step legal problems for the time being (especially where there is a lot of powerful, high-profile support), there may well be difficulties in sustaining and mainstreaming early successes, unless the more significant problems are dealt with in a forthright manner. A basic rule of thumb is that when the initial wave of enthusiasm for a particular activity begins to wane, legal weaknesses are more likely to come to light and to be exploited.

Analysing the economic context

One important factor that will determine the feasibility of legal reforms, or the viability of investment, is the wider economic context. As noted above, laws need to be designed with an eye to their cost and their impacts on different groups, as well as their clarity, coherence and consistency with social norms. Similarly, investments will only succeed if they work with, not against, the underlying economic forces that lead people to behave in particular ways.

Two tasks for assessing the wider economic context for sustainable development

TASK 1: IDENTIFY MAJOR TRENDS THAT ARE LIKELY TO AFFECT SUSTAINABILITY

Developing sustainable development strategies requires a clear vision of where the world, the nation, and the community are headed. One of the most important factors is population growth, which will determine the overall level of demand for goods and services, and thus the pressure on natural resources and the environment. Closely related to this is human migration and urbanization, which will affect the pattern of settlement and employment, the available mix of skills, links to other communities and nations and, of course, the nature of environmental problems (eg urban transport and waste management versus rural land degradation and deforestation).

In addition to the size and geographic distribution of the population, consumer demand also depends on the level and distribution of income. This is both a policy target – something to increase or equalize – and also a determinant of sustainable development strategies. Rising incomes will increase demand for consumer goods, but also for environmental amenities. This may create new opportunities for more sustainable enterprise, such as ecotourism; although, if everyone seeks to take advantage of such opportunities at once, the market will quickly become saturated. Another, less desirable feature of many developing economies is rising inequality in income, which may influence political priorities and the relative feasibility of alternative environment and development options. The same applies to other broad economic trends such as the liberalization of trade and investment regimes, or the spread of modern information technologies.

TASK 2: WORK WITH, RATHER THAN AGAINST INDIVIDUAL INTEREST AND MARKET FORCES

Mechanisms to facilitate the transition to sustainability will have a greater chance of success when they work *with* individual interests and market forces, rather than trying to restrain or obstruct the activities of producers and consumers. Of course, people do not always behave according to economic theory; that is, as atomistic, purely self-interested, rational calculators. Nevertheless, it is unwise to expect people to undertake actions that impose significant costs on themselves, on an ongoing basis, without clear and commensurate benefits. Likewise, where there are opportunities to secure significant gains at minimal personal risk, even where this involves behaviour that is illegal, immoral or imposes costs on others, it is highly likely that someone will take advantage, sooner rather than later. In short, while people are not all completely self-centred, they are not entirely altruistic either, and public policy needs to reflect human frailty.

In recent years, this simple insight has led to increasing reliance on the motivating force of self-interest, as expressed in the market place, as the main engine of economic development. Thus, the more 'liberal' economic policies governing international trade and investment have been widely embraced, increasing reliance on private firms to provide public services, and similar reforms. In the environmental sphere, the same trend can be seen in the growing reliance on 'market-based instruments' (MBIs) to reduce pollution and waste, or to improve the management of natural resources. Such instruments take advantage of self-interest, as well as differences among producers in the relative costs of meeting environmental aims, in order to reduce the overall costs of environmental protection. Well-designed MBIs can also help to stimulate ongoing innovation and further cost reductions over time, through the competitive pressure of market forces. MBIs include not only punitive measures to discourage environmental 'bads', such as pollution taxes, but also positive incentives to encourage the production of environmental 'goods', such as payments for watershed protection in upland areas, or the premium paid for organic food that protects wildlife and water resources.

Describing how the mechanisms link up

Two tasks for assessing how the mechanisms hold together in a decision-making system for sustainable development

TASK 1: DESCRIBE HOW THE INDIVIDUAL MECHANISMS LINK IN PRACTICE

The analyses suggested in the previous sections may reveal a number of promising mechanisms as well as problems with gaps, inconsistencies and overlaps. If the task is to pull together a coherent strategy system, however, it may not simply be a task of arbitrarily assembling the best components. Some analysis is required of what holds the mechanisms together – a conception of the overall policy process towards sustainable development.

A flow diagram could be constructed using Figure 5.14 as an example. If done by a small, multi-stakeholder focus group, it could both produce a picture of the current decision-making system for sustainable development and provide a useful learning exercise – some of the stakeholders may perceive the process differently, or not be aware of all the aspects of the system. The flow diagram should describe the actual situation – which may bear little relation to the provisions of any (paper) strategy or procedure.

TASK 2: DESCRIBE THE OVERALL INSTITUTIONAL LANDSCAPE FOR SUSTAINABLE DEVELOPMENT

A sustainable development strategy aims to change the norms and behaviour of groups, and their relationships, so that sustainable development can be achieved – in other words, to develop the overall institutional landscape (the 'meta-institution') of sustainable development, and to help other institutions to play their role within it.

The analyses above will have begun to clarify which institutions are central both to the sustainable development discourse and to the mechanisms required for sustainable development. Stakeholder power analysis (page 127) will also have revealed both the dominant institutions and those who are excluded from decision-making but have potential for sustainable development.

Institutions may then be profiled in relation to the sustainable development strategy. This entails identifying which specific government, civil society and private sector institutions have been playing a part in all or many of the sustainable development mechanisms identified through Task 1; why they play these roles; and with whom they play them – the main alliances. Furthermore, it can go on to identify the strengths and weaknesses of individual institutions in contributing to these strategy mechanisms. This work is best started as a focus group exercise, adding the details through interviews. It will begin to show which institutions are dominant in the discourse and the emerging institutional landscape. It could be expressed as:

- *a flow/process diagram* showing information flows between institutions and what happens to the information (joint decisions, alliances, conflicts, joint work, etc) (Figure 5.15);
- *a Venn diagram* showing the nature of the links between actors: for example, membership in informal 'policy communities' or formal 'NSDS committees';
- *a matrix* (with the same institutions on both x and y axes and the synergies, clashes and joint initiatives in the 'cells' – see section on identifying stakeholder interests, relations and powers, page 127).

Scenario development

The purpose and limitations of scenarios

The construction of scenarios can play an important role in strategic planning and policy-making. In effect, scenarios are a form of SEA (page 149). They are powerful tools for addressing what is both fundamentally significant and profoundly unknowable – the future (WBCSD 1997). Whereas forecasts predict patterns extrapolated from the past into the future, scenarios present plausible, pertinent, alternative 'stories'. They rely on imaging the future, rather than extrapolating from the past. Yet they are not predictions, but are means to explore options and test their robustness or sensitivity. As such, they can help to build the capacity to assess change, to look for major shifts rather than assume continued trend, and to build creativity and resilience to deal with such shifts. The assumptions behind each scenario are as important as the scenario itself and need as much discussion.

Scenarios imagine the future and explore options ...

Scenarios might regularly be developed to assist in NSDSs by considering the likely environmental, social and economic consequences of trends in key variables such as demographics, political risk, consumption and production, and/or the consequences of taking particular actions or policy options. Different scenarios can be constructed to maximize, minimize or optimize the environmental, social and economic consequences as appropriate.

... and help consideration of the consequences of trends

Different scenarios are often developed for the near future (less than 5 years hence), the medium-term future (10–15 years) and the longer-term future (25 years or more).

However, the longer the period for which projections are made, the more problematic the task since a lot can happen over that time, and the unexpected is always likely to happen, as experience from India shows (see Box 5.19). As such, scenarios should not be treated or communicated in ways that make stakeholders perceive them either as forecasts or as strategy visions.

Organizing scenario development

Scenarios depend on good knowledge of the past and present, and good judgement about the issues that may matter. Scenario approaches can be expert-based (in which case multiple disciplines are desirable, to be able to assess the multiple dimensions and access/interpret data) or participatory in the sense that stakeholders get together to develop an exercise (in which case professional facilitation is desirable).

Box 5.19 Futurology: experience from India

In 1970, a group of Indian scholars produced an eight-volume report (the *Second India Study*, see Ezekial 1975) assessing the implications of the doubling of India's population that demographers in 1970 had considered inevitable. The study predicted a range of scenarios, some of which have materialized, and others which have not. A follow-up study compared the predicted scenarios with actual developments (Repetto 1994) and showed how the authors of the original study *failed to include some significant events:* oil price changes; the globalization of the economy; and India's move away from a centrally planned regime.

As a result, the capital and resource requirements and environmental impacts of India's growth were substantially less than predicted. Indeed, neither technology nor resources were the main problem – where development has faltered, the stumbling blocks have usually been institutional and policy-related.

Scenario descriptions must be useful …

The descriptions of alternative scenarios need to be useful to many people involved in strategy debate and decision-making. Thus they should be (Brown 2001):

- understandable to the layperson;
- distinct from one another;
- possible and realistic;
- clear;
- substantiated by existing information where possible.

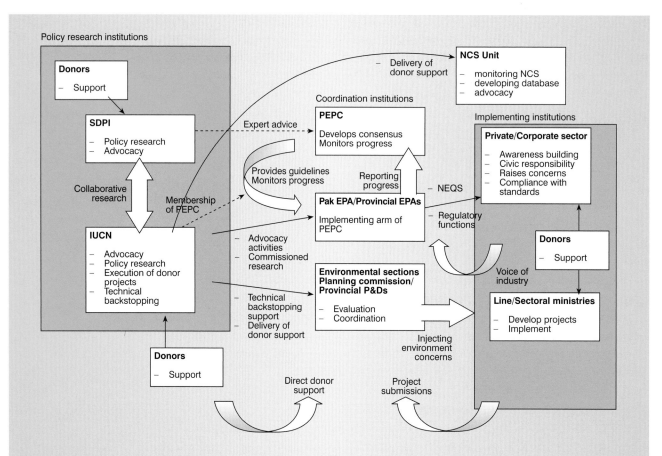

Figure 5.15 **Institutional mapping: relationship chart of the entities involved in the implementation of the Sarhad Conservation Strategy**

For an NSDS, the scenarios should reflect general societal values within the nation but with a very strong component of global coverage. Usually three scenarios will be enough to be able to think through alternative courses of action. These may often be:

- 'no change' or trends continued;
- 'much better' or a picture based on positive societal change to deal with problems;
- 'much worse' or a negative societal picture where problems are not dealt with and possibly spiral out of control.[8]

Each scenario can be described in narrative (and sometimes map-based) terms, but such a description should also be summarized in terms of key dimensions: for example, levels of GDP, population or poverty indices. The effects of the scenario may then be judged in terms of sustainability criteria, such as those suggested in 'Approaches to measuring and analysing sustainability' on page 131. It may then be possible to rank the scenarios according to such sustainability effects (environment, social and economic – or human and ecosystem well-being). Finally, good communication of the scenarios and their analyses is all-important, both so that they can be used by policy-makers (or business managers) and to avoid misperceptions.

Some illustrations of sustainable development scenarios

There is considerable experience in the use of scenario planning in the private sector. For example, Shell International (still considered by many to be a leader in the field) has developed global scenarios for 1995–2020 to help prepare for discontinuities and sudden change, to create unifying themes and images, and to help foster cohesion within the company (Shell International 1996). The scenarios envisage two possible futures (Box 5.20) built on a recognition that 'There Is No Alternative' (TINA) to adapting to three powerful forces: liberalization, globalization and technology. They consider the political, social, business and economic systems best able to exploit the forces of TINA. Shell has also drawn up scenarios for individual countries, such as China, Russia, South Africa and Nigeria. The Nigerian scenarios were presented to a government audience in Lagos as a non-controversial way of introducing potentially unpalatable ideas.

In 1997, the World Business Council for Sustainable Development (WBCSD) also experimented with a set of three global scenarios that explore and aim to stimulate broad discussion on possible responses to the challenge of sustainable development (WBCSD 1997) (Box 5.20). The WBCSD recognized that scenarios have various applications:

- to enrich debate and widen the 'strategic conversation' in an organization, with the aim of bringing new concepts and understanding to users and, ultimately, to change mental maps;
- to search for corporate resilience, including making risky decisions more transparent by identifying threats and opportunities and the creation and assessment of options;
- to trigger a formal strategic planning process, including the assessment of existing strategies and plans.

---

8 Extreme scenarios are often presented to provoke reaction. For example, in an exercise aimed at land use planning and resources protection in Gaza, three different socio-economic development scenarios were formulated. Each of them was based on a set of quite extreme assumptions 'to ensure that real development in the future will be at least somewhere in between the extreme conditions considered' (EPD 1996).

Box 5.20 **Global scenarios**

(i) Shell Global Scenarios 1995–2020

In the first scenario – *Just Do It!* – success comes to those who harness the latest innovations in technology to identify and take advantage of quick-moving opportunities in a world of hyper-competition, customization, self-reliance and ad hoc informal networking. This world allows the fullest expression of individual creativity and offers a large stage for exploring visions and for new ways of doing business and solving problems.

In the second scenario – *Da Wo ('Big Me')* – countries and companies discover that success calls for a committed investment in relationships, where relationships of trust and the enabling role of government provide the long-term strategic advantage. In this world, Asia already has an advantage because its societies and businesses are at home in a world in which the individual – the 'small me' – understands that individual welfare is inextricably linked to the welfare of the whole – Da Wo ('Big Me').

Source: Shell International (1996)

(ii) World Business Council for Sustainable Development: Global Scenarios 2000–2050

- In **FROG** (First Raise Our Growth) the responses are inadequate – the human social systems are unable to meet the challenge of sustainable development, a challenge made more difficult by a vulnerable natural system.
- In **GEOpolity** the response is to build an interlocking governance structure coordinated at the international level.
- In **Jazz** (diverse players form alliances and work together; there is innovation, experimentation, rapid adaptation and much voluntary inter-connectedness; high transparency; dynamic reciprocity) markets are harnessed for finding solutions to sustainable development.

Source WBCSD (1997)

(iii) Stockholm Environment Institute: Global scenarios

A taxonomy of scenarios is set out based on a two-tier hierarchy: classes distinguished by fundamentally different social visions and *variants* reflecting a range of possible outcomes within each class. Three broad scenario classes are depicted:

- **Conventional Worlds** – essential continuity with current patterns. Envisages the global system of the 21st century evolving without major surprises, sharp discontinuities or fundamental transformations. The future is shaped by the continued evolution, expansion and globalization of the dominant values and socio-economic relationships of industrial society.
- **Barbarization** – fundamental but undesirable social change. Envisages the grim possibility that the social, economic and moral underpinnings of civilization deteriorate, as emerging problems overwhelm the coping capacity of both markets and policy reforms.
- **Great Transitions** – fundamental and favourable social transformation. Explores visionary solutions to the sustainability challenge, including new socio-economic arrangements and fundamental changes in values. These scenarios depict a transition to a society that preserves natural systems, provides high levels of welfare through material sufficiency and equitable distribution, and enjoys a strong sense of social solidarity. Population levels are stabilized at moderate levels and material flows through the economy are radically reduced through reduced consumerism and massive use of green technologies.

Source: Gallopin et al (1997)

Other work on the process of global and regional scenario development, and associated policy analysis and public education, has been carried out by the Global Scenario Group of the Stockholm Environment Institute. Reporting on this work, Gallopin et al acknowledge that the forces of globalization take many forms – stresses on the biosphere, far-reaching cultural impacts of communications technology, expansion of worldwide commerce, and rise of new geo-political tensions (Gallopin et al 1997). They argue that, as a consequence of these forces, the world is at an uncertain *branch point* from which a wide range of possible futures could unfold in the next century. These are explored and their implications considered (see Box 5.20).

In the European Union, such strategic analysis is an important step in the process of strategic planning. Here there has been an increasing interest in the use of scenarios as a way of dealing with the inherent complexity of sustainable development at the European level, and for pinpointing gaps, inconsistencies and dilemmas in existing policy-making. Box 5.21 describes two examples of such scenario-based planning: one undertaken by European Partners for the Environment (EPE), a grouping of representatives of business, trade unions, public authorities, research organizations and environmental groups; the other by Consultative Forum, established by the European Commission to bring together 'wise people' from similar groups to provide advice on how to progress towards sustainable development.

Scenarios can help to deal with the complexity of sustainable development at the regional level

---

Box 5.21 European scenarios

European Partners for the Environment (EPE)

Set up in 1993, EPE brings together business, trade unions, public authorities, research organizations and environmental groups, to catalyse common action for sustainable development. One of its first outputs was a workbook, *Towards Shared Responsibility*, which includes a scenarios module (EPE 1994). Its aim is to encourage participants to take a more experimental approach to the sustainability agenda, to consider the likely evolution of this agenda under different social, political, economic, technological and environmental conditions, and to examine the implications for action. The module puts forward three contrasting scenarios for a generation in the future:

- Scenario 1 – *No Limits:* Characterized by rapid change, technological innovation, adaptation to environmental problems, cultural diversity and focus on individual quality of life. This is essentially a liberal free market vision of the future.
- Scenario 2 – *Orderly Transition:* Characterized by an emphasis on stewardship, managerialism, scientific expertise and balancing environment and the economy. This is more or less the vision of the European Fifth Environmental Action Programme.
- Scenario 3 – *Values Shift:* Characterized by a stress on prevention, the urgency of environmental problems, participation, decentralization and a focus on equity and community.

Consultative Forum on the Environment

The Consultative Forum was set up by the European Commission to bring together 32 'wise people' from business, trade unions, local government, research and environment organizations to advise the EC on how to progress towards sustainable development. After drawing up a range of policy statements, the Forum carried out a scenario exercise, Vision 2020, using a similar methodology to EPE (Robins et al 1996):

- Scenario 1 – *Opening Opportunities:* Environmental problems are addressed through innovation and market-friendly policies and a drive towards a dematerialized information economy. The Rio logic of resolving environmental problems through regulation and public spending is discredited.
- Scenario 2 – *Managing the Transition:* The market alone is seen as unable to solve society's problems and a stronger government role is taken to steer the economy to achieve jobs and environmental improvements.
- Scenario 3 – *Transforming Communities:* Societal tolerance for social and environmental decline reaches its limit and a new approach is taken to development, focused on stronger communities, quality of life and simpler lifestyles.

The Forum used these scenarios to draw up a set of recommendations for future EC action, including setting up a sustainability task force to develop new and innovative solutions; publishing a regular sustainable development report; establishing a 'House of the Future' to stimulate thinking; preparing a strategy on the EU's foreign policy and sustainable development; and supporting a larger role for local communities in EC policy-making (EC 1997). Commenting on the initiative, the EC's Environment Commissioner, Ritt Bjerregaard, concluded that 'the scenarios paper shows very clearly that sustainability needs more and more to take centre stage in policy-making'.

Sources: EPE (1994), EC (1997)

Another excellent example of scenario planning comes from work undertaken in South Africa preceding the end of apartheid. A group of people, supported by the Anglo American Corporation, conducted pioneering scenario work to help examine post-apartheid South Africa's choices for the future, embracing political, social, economic and environmental issues. Their analysis (Huntley et al 1989) provided a powerful argument to end apartheid and join with the rest of Southern Africa to face the environmental challenges of the 21st century (see Box 5.22).

Box 5.22 South African scenarios

Analyses undertaken in South Africa by Huntley et al (1989) considered 'both global and regional trends in environmental health, from the potential holocaust of a 'nuclear winter' to the insidious invisible threat of the 'greenhouse effect' and the ozone hole'. Against this background of possible global environmental issues, the boundary 'rules of the game' for South Africa were analysed. These included:

- its basic geography;
- the diversity of landscapes, habitats, fauna and flora;
- the climate and weather cycles;
- population dynamics and settlement patterns;
- distribution of key natural resources – minerals, water and arable land;
- agricultural and forestry resources;
- homeland (communal land) poverty;
- marine resources;
- economic growth and consumption patterns.

Two key uncertainties were identified:

- the different socio-economic paths that the country might adopt;
- the different environmental management ethics that might emerge.

These were used to derive four possible environmental scenarios in the early 21st century:

1 'Paradise Lost' associated with a regional wasteland.
2 'Separate Impoverishment' resulting from continuing down the 'Low Road' (stagnation of the political reform process, big government, more centralized economy and siege mentality).
3 'Boom and Bust' where the nation's natural resources were plundered to achieve maximum short-term economic gains resulting from the 'High Road' (negotiated political settlement, multi-party political system, decentralized power, free enterprise, mass education, etc).
4 'Rich Heritage' where sustained development was pursued along the 'High Road'.

Taking this process further, Sunter (1992) looked at the future South Africa in relation to Southern Africa and the greater world. Here, he saw the 'High Road' as potentially closing the gap between the rich and the poor nations, and the 'Low Road' as allowing that gap to increase with 'dire consequences for the stability of the world'.

Source: Huntley et al (1989); Sunter (1992)

CHAPTER

6

Participation in strategies for sustainable development[1]

Introduction

This chapter reviews past theories and current thinking on the nature and use of participation, issues and requirements to ensure effective participation, and methodologies for participation in sustainable development strategies.

There is a high degree of consensus on the need for participation of stakeholders in order to progress towards sustainable development. However, what precisely is meant by the term 'participation' is less clear and there are considerable differences in the way that participation is perceived and understood. 'Understanding participation' on page 178 explains the *multiple types* of participation, and the many different perspectives on it.

'Why participation is needed in strategies for sustainable development' on page 186 explores the *rationale for participation*. Sustainable development is essentially a political process, and political structures can tend towards top-down systems of governance. But sustainable development requires the consensus and commitment of society as a whole; experience shows that this cannot be delivered by government planning and acting alone. So participation processes are needed to involve the private sector and civil society, as well as government, in a partnership – processes that will transform governance approaches and facilitate multi-stakeholder involvement in the development and implementation of NSDSs.

The basic *requirements* for effective participation are examined in 'Ensuring effective participation – issues and planning requirements' (page 193), including: agreed principles for participation; a proper understanding of what participation means; using catalysts for participation; using specific activities and events; following a phased approach; selecting appropriate participatory methods; securing adequate resources, skills and time; and developing learning environments. An effective NSDS process requires that stakeholder interest in participation be built and carefully sustained. Practical guidance is given on the costs

Participation drives the whole NSDS process; its many tasks must be agreed and planned

1 This chapter has benefited from review comments and additional material provided by Duncan Macqueen, IIED, and Carol James, Trinidad. It also draws extensively on two existing reviews of experience of participation in strategies for sustainable development: Bass et al (1995), Dalal-Clayton et al (2000).

and benefits of participation, the importance of carefully selecting representative stakeholders, and clarifying roles and expectations. The structures, organization and legal framework needed for effective participation are discussed.

Practical guidance on *participatory methodologies* is provided on page 193, distilled from a wide range of field experiences. Concrete examples of their application are included and participatory mechanisms relevant to particular levels of decision-making are identified – ranging from experiences at rural/community levels, through decentralized planning systems to multi-stakeholder partnerships.

Understanding participation

Multiple perceptions, expectations and definitions of 'participation'

Participation traditions can be found in all societies ...

Participation is nothing less than the fabric of social life. People have always participated in survival strategies and in the development of their own cultures. Whether through formal or informal organizations, autocratic or democratic means, a variety of participatory structures and procedures has evolved to define and address collective needs, to resolve conflicts and to make plans and take the steps necessary to implement them, (see, for example, Box 6.1).

The term 'participation' pervades the literature, everyday language and rhetoric of sustainable development. The World Bank's Learning Group on Participatory Development (1994) has defined participatory development as: 'A process through which stakeholders influence and share control over development initiatives, and the decisions and resources which affect them.' Prior to this, Adnan et al (1992) observed: 'It is often difficult to understand whether those talking about people's participation mean the same thing or simply use the phrase as a kind of magical incantation.' And Rahnema (1992) noted: 'people are dragged into participating in operations of no interest to them, in the very name of participation'.

... although the term 'participation' is being captured by some groups for narrower purposes

The term 'participation' is now used by different people to convey quite different meanings (Box 6.2) and has created several paradoxes. It has been used on the one hand to justify the extension of control of the state and, on the other, to build local capacity and self-reliance. It has been used to justify external decisions, as well as to devolve power and decision-making away from external agencies. It has been used for data acquisition by experts and for interactive analysis. The varied perceptions of participation are illustrated by the opinions voiced during the development of the Bangladesh Flood Action Plan and by comments on rural planning in Tanzania (Box 6.3).

Typologies of participation – and associated dilemmas

The many ways in which the term 'participation' is interpreted and used can be resolved into seven clear types that range from manipulative and passive participation, where people are told what is to happen and implement pre-determined tasks, to the stage where communities take initiatives on their own (Table 6.1).

Box 6.1 Participation traditions in Central and South America

Indigenous communities in Central America and the Andean region of South America have developed quite effective ways to identify, plan and carry out activities that meet their collective needs. Community issues are discussed and decided in organized meetings, which are run by elected community leaders and attended by representatives from all households. It is expected that all participants provide input in the discussions, where options are assessed and decisions for action taken. Decisions are made by consensus, or near consensus, and are binding for all. Culturally sanctioned means of carrying out plans include labour pooling (known as *minga* in the Andes and *tequio* in Oaxaca, Mexico) and cash or in-kind contributions by each household in the community. Enforcement takes the form of social recognition for households that consistently fulfil their duty, and ostracism, fines or incarceration for those who do not contribute their labour to the community's well-being.

Source: Zazueta (1995)

Box 6.2 Participation – a loaded term

Participation is clearly a 'good idea' that nobody from any position will want to say they are against. But they could often be talking about very different things. To some it will be a *goal or aspiration*, to others a *demand*, and to others a *description* of the way things are. There are too many simplistic exhortations to 'get everyone participating and democratize the process'. Agenda 21 called for the 'maximum possible participation'. But if we consider why participation is needed it is clear that it is not going to be an easy business. Participation is needed because current inequities, bad land management, stakeholder stalemate or other problems persist, due to misunderstandings or lack of knowledge among stakeholders of each other's perspectives, powers and tactics, and the potential for change in these. Participation processes are fundamental to NSDSs – to understand multiple perspectives, negotiate and cut 'deals' between the needs of wider society and local actors, form partnerships and to maintain NSDSs as 'alive processes', not 'dead papers'.

Thus everyone agrees that participation is both a right and a practical necessity. But its form, mechanisms and functions need to be carefully shaped. Participatory mechanisms such as a national sustainable development forum, steering group, working groups and local-level learning groups need to be explicitly designed to tackle particular problems.

Source: Adapted from Mayers et al (2001)

Consultation is only one form of participation along the spectrum in Table 6.1, but the terms 'consultation' and 'participation' are frequently used interchangeably. Rahnema (1992) concludes that passive, consultative and incentive-driven forms of participation marginalize groups, which have no recognized stake in decision-making. They have often been used more as a vehicle for gathering information and to ensure implementation of pre-conceived plans than for shared decision-making. The 'superficial and fragmented achievements have no lasting impact on people's lives'. If the objective is to achieve sustainable development, then consultative forms of participation alone will not suffice. Sustainable development requires broader participation in governance, to deal with multiple trade-offs and uncertainties. Many of these tasks are so complex that decisions imposed by elected bodies that do not carry the consensual support of society – even though they might be enforced through legislation and the

Consultation helps to gather information for a strategy, but does not broaden the basis for decision-making

---

Box 6.3 Some perceptions of participation in the Bangladesh Flood Action Plan and in rural planning in Tanzania

Villagers:

- 'Participation is about doing something for everyone's benefit' (villager).
- 'Oh yes, the foreigners were here one day, last month. But they only went to school and spoke in English. We are not educated. We could not understand' (a poor peasant).

Government officials:

- 'Yes, we're doing people's participation. We have had people working in Food for Works programmes since the seventies' (top official in Bangladesh Water Development Board).
- 'Your idea regarding women's participation is not correct for the overall national interest.'
- 'But what will be our role if we are to have complete participation?'
- 'True participation is too expensive.'
- 'Participation takes too long and is wasting time.'
- 'There are limits to participation because somebody ultimately has to decide.'
- 'I did the work plan myself on behalf of the district staff' (District Planning Officer, Tanzania).

Foreign consultants

- 'Another idea from the social scientists. Only slogans! First "poverty alleviation". Then "women" and "environment". Now "people's participation"! It's just a new fad!' (Engineer).
- 'You have to consult my socio-economist, not me. I have no time for this participation. I'm working 12 hours every day on the project' (FAP Team Leader).

Source: Adapted from Adnan et al (1992), and Kikula and Pfliegner (2001)

Table 6.1 **Types of participation in local-level development**

Type	Characteristics
1 Manipulative participation	Participation is simply a pretence
2 Passive participation	People participate by being told what has been decided or has already happened. Information shared belongs only to external professionals
3 Participation by consultation	People participate by being consulted or by answering questions. No share in decision-making is conceded and professionals are under no obligation to take on board people's views
4 Participation for material incentives	People participate in return for food, cash or other material incentives. Local people have no stake in prolonging practices when the incentives end
5 Functional participation	Participation is seen by external agencies as a means to achieve project goals, especially reduced costs. People may participate by forming groups to meet predetermined project objectives
6 Interactive participation	People participate in joint analysis, which leads to action plans and the formation or strengthening of local groups or institutions that determine how available resources are used. Learning methods are used to seek multiple viewpoints
7 Self-mobilization	People participate by taking initiatives independently of external institutions. They develop contacts with external institutions for resources and technical advice but retain control over how resources are used

Source: Adapted from Pretty (1997)

official machinery of government – will not lead to sustainable development. However, once key issues have been explored and debated, and some consensus on the ways forward negotiated by stakeholders, a final decision will often need to be taken/endorsed by elected representatives in the fora of government.

In industrialized countries, government agencies often follow what Walker and Daniels (1997) call the 3I model: inform (the public), invite (comments) and ignore (opinions). In countries where livelihoods depend more directly on the land and power differences are great, participation is often limited to community consultation, thereby limiting the influence of local initiatives.

In developing countries, there is often incompatibility between the policies of donors about participation and on-the-ground reality. Local people frequently have no genuine say in how and where donor money is spent (unless within specific defined budget lines). The problem is often compounded by the clear incompatibilities between, on the one hand, donor spending cycles and development fashion and, on the other hand, enabling and allowing adequate time for a truly participatory process.

A study of 230 rural development institutions employing some 30,000 staff in 41 countries of Africa (Guijt 1991) found that, for local people, participation was most likely to mean simply having discussions or providing information to external agencies. Government and non-government agencies rarely permitted local groups to work alone, some even acting without any local involvement. Even where external agencies did permit some joint decisions, they usually controlled the funds.

Another study of 121 rural water supply projects in 49 countries of Africa, Asia and Latin America (Narayan 1993) found that participation was the most significant factor contributing to project effectiveness and subsequent maintenance of water systems. The best results were achieved when people were involved in decision-making through all stages of the project from design to maintenance.

The authorities' dilemma is that they both need and fear people's participation. They need the agreement and support of diverse groups of people – development is not sustainable otherwise – but they tend to fear that greater involvement is less controllable, less predictable, likely to slow down decision-

Participation in decisions can bring better results – but is more challenging to authorities than mere consultation

making, and may challenge the existing distribution of wealth and power. Thus local participation has usually been sought without any meaningful reform of the power relations between government and local communities. Degnbol (1996) argues that it is naive to expect governments to redefine their roles, and that genuine participation will only come about with the emergence of a strong and representative civil society.

Governments therefore need to work out how to take a leadership role in developing strategies for sustainable development – in terms of making the commitment and setting the agenda, creating an open and participatory 'environment' for the processes involved, inviting civil society and others to participate in all strategy tasks, and providing support where needed. Such leadership means moving towards the right in Figure 6.1. For example, Box 6.4 illustrates how the government of Trinidad fostered a community-based conservation programme and then reduced its own direct involvement.

Governments can organize participation ...

Most countries include some element of public participation in their policy processes. In an analysis of many actual policy processes, Bass et al (1995) developed a typology analogous to Table 6.1. They found that the greatest degree of public participation was achieved in reaching consensus on the elements of a strategy (level 5 in Table 6.2). Fundamental decision-making on national policies and strategies (level 6) has remained the prerogative of the national decision-making process, democratic or otherwise.

Care is needed to avoid participation being seen or promoted as an alternative to established democratic processes. Rather the approaches and methods available can bolster and support such processes and help to improve their quality and effectiveness. In theory, governments are elected because they have an acknowledged representation function and have the capacity to make difficult decisions. In practice, however, the democratic process is not always as good or effective as electorates would wish. But care is needed, when external agencies promote and sponsor participatory processes, not to undermine the credibility of established local and national governance structures. The legitimate governments of countries hold different political or philosophical development preferences (eg USA versus Cuba), and these may change over time (eg with changes in government). Also sustainable development may take different forms depending on the prevailing religious, social, environmental and social value systems – which set the boundary conditions shown in Figure 2.1.

... as complements to local democratic means – not as substitutes

A key NSDS principle (Box 3.1) is that strategies need to be developed as continuous (cyclical) learning processes, which build and improve systems for multi-stakeholder participation – not as one-off exercises. Experience shows that the first cycle necessitates considerable effort to secure commitment and buy-in from different stakeholders, and build trust and confidence to work together. This requires patience, time and resources. It will involve considerable investment in identifying, strengthening and introducing new participatory structures and methodologies. The first full cycle (Figure 4.2) might require as much as 3–5 years. Once in place, however, the participation structures can be employed in subsequent strategy iterations and other exercises, such as sectoral plans.

An initial period of investment in participation will be needed

Table 6.2 **Levels of participation in policy processes**

1	*Participants listening only* – receiving information from a government public relations campaign or open database
2	*Participants listening and giving information* – through public inquiries, media activities, 'hot-lines'
3	*Participants being consulted* – through working groups and meetings held to discuss policy
4	*Participation in analysis and agenda-setting* – through multi-stakeholder groups, round tables and commissions
5	*Participation in reaching consensus on the main strategy elements* – through national round tables, parliamentary/select committees and conflict mediation
6	*Participants directly involved in final decision-making on the policy, strategy or its components*

Source: Bass et al (1995)

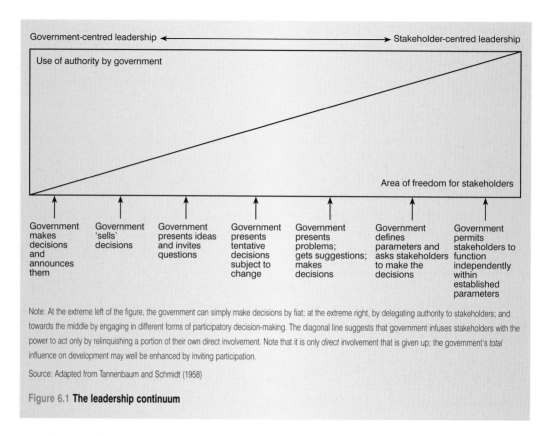

Government-centred leadership ← → Stakeholder-centred leadership

Use of authority by government

Area of freedom for stakeholders

| Government makes decisions and announces them | Government 'sells' decisions | Government presents ideas and invites questions | Government presents tentative decisions subject to change | Government presents problems; gets suggestions; makes decisions | Government defines parameters and asks stakeholders to make the decisions | Government permits stakeholders to function independently within established parameters |

Note: At the extreme left of the figure, the government can simply make decisions by fiat; at the extreme right, by delegating authority to stakeholders; and towards the middle by engaging in different forms of participatory decision-making. The diagonal line suggests that government infuses stakeholders with the power to act only by relinquishing a portion of their own direct involvement. Note that it is only *direct* involvement that is given up; the government's *total* influence on development may well be enhanced by inviting participation.

Source: Adapted from Tannenbaum and Schmidt (1958)

Figure 6.1 **The leadership continuum**

'Horizontal' and 'vertical' channels for participation – and associated dilemmas

Participation is inadequate if confined to the national level ...

In a study of participation in strategies for sustainable development, Bass et al (1995) distinguish between horizontal and vertical channels for participation (see Figure 6.2). Horizontal participation refers to the interactions needed to ensure that issues are dealt with across sectoral interest groups, ministries and communities in different parts of the country. Vertical participation is required to deal with issues throughout the hierarchy of decision-making from national to local levels, or from leaders to marginalized groups. The deeper the vertical participation within a given institution or nation, the better the understanding and support for the strategy is likely to be. Table 6.3 illustrates the wide range of institutions and actors that are likely to be involved in decision-making at different levels and in different sectors. Box 6.5 lists the kinds of structures available.

In respect of recent *national* conservation strategies, any participation at national level has tended to be restricted to government, academics and a few favoured NGO circles. The private sector has generally had a less overt influence – although there may have been significant lobbying and other means of influence. However, even when all views have been sought and consensus achieved, it may remain difficult for politicians to make an honest response and for the establishment to change its ways. This may be because there is no link to local level sustainable development realities.

... or the local level alone ...

In contrast to the situation at the national level, there is ample evidence of interactive participation of communities and sectoral interests at the *local* level – resulting sometimes in impressive work on the ground, with generation of much local information and some localized institutional change (eg Box 6.4). Particular progress has been made in:

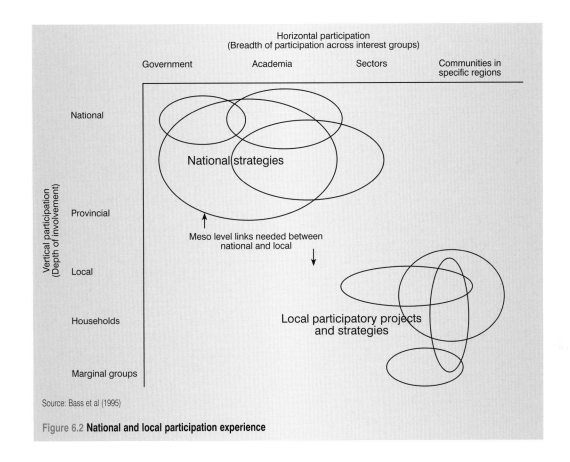

Source: Bass et al (1995)

Figure 6.2 **National and local participation experience**

Box 6.4 **Community-based Turtle Conservation Programme, Trinidad**

Exhaustive government efforts have been made to prevent the slaughtering of turtles and poaching of their eggs on nesting beaches at Matura Bay, Trinidad. In early 1989, frustrated by the failure of these efforts, Wildlife Section Officers began a process of engaging community members to assist in the conservation of this endangered species. There was genuine dialogue between the government and the local community for several months around issues of concern and interest to each group of participants: youth, women, teachers, political activists and ordinary villagers. This was followed by two years of information sharing, education and training which resulted in the formation in 1990 of a dynamic community-based organization (CBO), Nature Seekers Inc. This transformed matters, allowing villagers to develop an ecologically sustainable turtle management programme with strong potential for social and economic benefits for the community.

    Prior to formation of the CBO, the government was heavily involved, initially in fostering an understanding of the basics of biological conservation and benefits to be realized from sustainable use of the resource; training the community in ecologically sensitive tour-guiding around turtle nesting sites; facilitating the establishment of a legally designated protected area; developing basic research and resource assessment programmes in collaboration with the community; and fostering buy-in by the wider national and international communities – including encouraging support from scientific, NGO and academic bodies.

    After 18 months, the government's direct involvement was reduced to merely responding to community needs for guidance on terms determined entirely by the community, and enabling implementation of new policy measures as they evolved.

    Twelve years later, the socio-economic and conservation benefits resulting from effective community participation and their exercise of rights over the use of their resources, continue. Nature Seekers Inc. is now internationally renowned as a successful community-based natural resource institution. Its expertise for guiding similar processes in other countries has been tapped on several occasions by international NGOs and academic institutions.

Source: James and Fournillier (1993); UNDP (2001c)

Table 6.3 **Examples of institutional channels for decision-making and action, by sector and level**

Levels	Sectors		
	Governmental/ quasi-governmental	**Voluntary/ collective action**	**Private/quasi-private**
International	Bilateral and multilateral donor agencies	Society for International Development	Multinational corporations; external NGOs
National ministries	Central government ministries; parastatals; corporations	National cooperative federation	National corporations; national NGOs
Regional	Regional administrative bodies; regional development authorities	Regional cooperative federation; watershed consultative assembly	Regional companies; regional NGOs
District	District council; district administrative offices	District supply cooperative; soil conservation; educational forum	District firms; charitable organizations
Sub-district	Sub-district council; sub-district administrative offices	Sub-district marketing cooperative	Rural enterprises; private hospital
Locality	Division council; health clinic; secondary school; extension office	Wholesale cooperative society; forest protection association	Businesses in market town; service clubs
Community	Village council; post office; primary school; extension worker	Primary cooperative society; village dyke patrol; parent-teachers association	Village shops; committee for village welfare; religious institutions
Group	Caste; panchayat; ward or neighbourhood assembly	Tubewell users' association; mothers' club; savings group	Micro-enterprises
Household/ individual	Citizen; voter; taxpayer; partaker of services	Member	Customer; client; beneficiary

Source: Uphoff (1992)

- ■ Joint community/business/local government initiatives in urban or peri-urban areas, often facilitated by local governments and NGOs – for example, Groundwork UK, Local Agenda 21s in many local authorities North and South – as well as corporate–community partnerships in farming, forestry and tourism.
- ■ Buffer zones (economic support zones) around national parks, with joint government/community management. There are many well-documented examples: for example, in India, Nepal and Zimbabwe (IIED 1994) and several Man and Biosphere Reserves worldwide.
- ■ Rural development projects based on social organization and/or environmental protection, often at river catchment level, again facilitated or managed by NGOs.

Although most did not start as 'local strategies', many of these successful local projects have had to evolve strategic approaches to thrive – notably linking with national policy and institutional initiatives.

In spite of individual successes, the problem of 'scaling up' such local participatory initiatives and the channels/mechanisms open to them remains plagued by policy and institutional inertia. Often, 'successful' local projects have been identified by the policy actors (or by academics who inform them) with little more than anecdotal evidence, and these are then replicated in other areas, frequently without success. This is

---

Box 6.5 Structures for 'horizontal' and 'vertical' participation

Horizontal links between sectors/resources/communities

- *Different sectors:* central planning system with associated procedures, for example, planning inquiry, SEA and EIA; local authority development control and environmental health; round tables; environmental core groups; conflict mediation organizations; participatory inquiry groups.
- *Living/working communities (household, work place, neighbourhood):* housewives' associations; neighbourhood associations; commuter groups; unions; participatory inquiry groups.
- *Different claims on the environment and resources:* legal system; local authority planning and development control; lands commission; conflict mediation organizations.
- *Different social groups:* traditional fora; local authority social services; religious groups; conflict mediation organizations; participatory inquiry; NGOs.
- *Supply chains (producers/consumers/sufferers of pollution):* industry associations; trade associations; consumer groups; rights groups; round tables; conflict mediation organizations; certification schemes.

Vertical links between national and local interests

- *Top-down and bottom-up decision-making:* planning and development control systems; decentralization of government, private sector and civil society operations; local authorities; NGOs; fora (local, national or tiered).
- *Party politics:* parliamentary system; party membership and representation.

Source: Bass et al (1995)

---

because the precise policy, institutional and physical conditions surrounding 'successful' local activities need to be identified and assured before replication is possible. In general, the genesis and implementation of national strategies and local participatory efforts have tended to be separate, and there appear to have been few efforts to unite them to their mutual advantage.

In other instances, government structures cannot deal with participation. It may then be necessary for government departments to sort out their own differences – using interdisciplinary approaches – before embarking on full-scale participation. In the UK, this approach appears to have dominated the first strategy for sustainable development in the UK (HMSO 1994) – different wings of government felt the need to get together to sort things out first, and only limited consultation outside government could be countenanced. In Australia, the very different approaches of federal, state and municipal strategies necessitated a legal Intergovernmental Agreement on the Environment to ensure consistency between them; this had the effect of putting the federal strategy in the ascendancy.

A number of approaches have managed to link participation at local levels with participation at national level. For example, Gestion de Terroir, in the Sahel, has always addressed the administrative and legal constraints to local resource management, and gradually builds up a larger, national-level picture. The success of the Aga Khan Rural Support Programme (AKRSP) in Northern Pakistan led to a major government-led National Rural Support Programme. AKRSP staff played key roles in the Pakistan National Conservation Strategy.

Essentially, a good information 'cycle' is needed between local and national levels, driven by participatory exploration of sustainable development needs and options. Key to doing this in future will be:

... Links are needed, so that policy and local realities are mutually informed

1 building on existing participatory structures, methodologies and projects, including successful informal approaches;
2 mobilizing many of these at local level to influence national policy;
3 capacity building for participation and partnerships;
4 securing financial flows to support these steps.

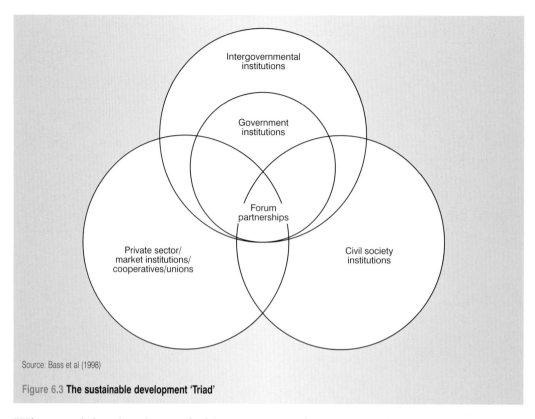

Source: Bass et al (1998)

Figure 6.3 **The sustainable development 'Triad'**

Why participation is needed in strategies for sustainable development

The 'sustainable development triad' of government, business and civil society ...

In recent years, the roles and relations of the three 'sustainable development triad' sectors (government, civil society and business) have begun to change significantly (Figure 6.3). For example (Tennyson and Wilde 2000):

- Civil society-led popular movements more or less peacefully overthrowing undemocratic governments in South Africa, the former Soviet Union and central Europe, with many of the civil society activists forming the new governments; and with a subsequent lack of faith placed in centralized government planning systems.
- The South-east Asian so-called 'economic miracle' having come and gone within a decade, reminding governments and international organizations that business investment alone will not bring the needed development they (perhaps naively) hoped it would.
- Many international businesses, previously entirely focused on maximizing shareholder value, rethinking their responsibilities to the societies in which they operate – as the gulf between rich and poor widens and threatens social stability and economic growth.

These and other events have opened up new possibilities for a greater interdependence between sectors and have led to innovation and creative collaboration. So world events have, in a sense, encouraged sectors to work together more closely. Now that they have begun to do so, it is becoming clear that each sector brings to the collaboration different but potentially complementary skills, experiences and attributes:[2]

2 See also Table 6.10

- The public sector (government) is rights-driven – it provides information, stability and legitimacy.
- The private sector is profits-driven – it is inventive, single-minded and fast.
- Civil society is value-driven – it is responsive, inclusive and imaginative.

... works by bringing their different attributes together in partnership

It must also be acknowledged that individuals are often the key catalysts/champions for initiating action within each of these sectors. Individuals are driven by many agendas (personal, community, country) but, once motivated, their energies can contribute effectively to development.

But there is still a need to define better the respective roles of these three sectors in national processes as well as international negotiations concerning sustainable development. Mechanisms for their effective participation need to be developed. For example, civil society often needs to be enabled to prepare properly for meetings (governments and the private sector can do this as part of their jobs), and supported financially.

Collaboration – fostered through the participation of the three sectors in strategy processes – can draw together and build on the drivers of each sector (rights, profit and values) and can achieve far more than any of the sectors acting alone. Increasingly, successful sustainable development initiatives are resulting from partnership between organizations from two (or all three) sectors in which the organizations commit themselves to working together. Partnerships involve sharing the risks as well as benefits, and reviewing (and revising as necessary) the relationship regularly. Genuinely sharing or seeking to achieve mutual benefits (as opposed to one-directional benefits) are often described as delivering a 'win–win' scenario – perhaps more accurately 'win–win–win' where all three sectors are involved. NSDSs will clearly involve an exploration of different forms of partnership.

However, such collaboration does not necessarily imply equal rights in determining the outcomes. All key stakeholders need to have a role in strategy development and implementation. Some will be involved directly (eg government), while others will be represented through interest groups (eg resource user associations). Limited companies by their nature (ie established to generate profit, operating under limited liability) will have fewer rights and, in any case, their shareholders will be able to represent their views and positions through civil society institutions.

Centralized planning allows for certain economies of scale; for example, professional skills can be 'efficiently' employed and databases maintained. But it excludes or marginalizes many groups. Half a century of professional development planning has demonstrated that plans drawn up by outsiders, with little or no reference to the priorities of the people who have to implement them, are not implemented. Or, if they are implemented, they turn out very differently from what was intended by their architects. The need for greater stakeholder participation in strategic planning is becoming increasingly well recognized – at least it is now well espoused in the literature and development agency documentation. But experience with existing country-level strategic planning frameworks shows that practice still lags behind. The formulation of most national strategies remains dominantly top-down (Box 6.6) or suffers from problems with participation. Essentially, planning structures remain the same but there are attempts to graft on participatory methods.

Top-down systems of planning can be efficient, but ...

There are various equity-based reasons for bottom-up components in the strategy process: stakeholder rights of recognition, and equitable sharing of benefits, costs and risks. Furthermore, effectiveness and efficiency can be improved by bringing local knowledge on board, tailoring activities to local conditions and structuring local incentives for sustainability. Credibility can be improved by incorporating the values, ideas and perspectives of the many groups in society – government, non-government, the private sector and the general public.

... a combination with bottom-up systems improves equity, effectiveness and credibility

Participatory planning is now promoted as an alternative to top-down planning – but it still faces problems of undefined lines of authority, a weak information base and an institutional culture both at

---

Box 6.6 Why existing strategies continue to be mainly top-down

The term 'top-down' implies that a strategy is conceived by an authority (usually government) and is developed by professional staff, with no or limited involvement of those likely to have a legitimate interest or be affected by the outcomes (stakeholders). It also implies goals and approaches which are set by that authority – but which are not necessarily those of stakeholders. Implementation is also typically the responsibility of such authorities. Such top-down approaches to strategies are not restricted to national governments but are also found at decentralized levels. 'Bottom-up' approaches are characterized by the opposite approach and involve the active participation of stakeholders, and are often initiated by them. Top-down strategies persist even today, for many reasons.

- Many of the earlier sustainable development strategies emanated as ideas from *development cooperation agencies*, who are increasingly being held accountable for sustainability dimensions of their interventions – but who find it easier to employ their own frameworks rather than to work through and encourage local frameworks.
- Others have been the result of *international accords* (eg conventions) and tend to assume the pre-eminence of global stakeholders' interests.
- There is often *weak capacity* in governments, the private sector and civil society to articulate interests, build alliances, seek compromises, accept different perspectives, formulate and implement long-term goals and strategies and manage participatory and pluralistic processes (although admittedly, the private sector and civil society are not set up to undertake all these tasks – they are primarily the role of governance).
- *Professional arrogance:* Civil servants and others in positions of authority (often those in the middle ranks) have behaved as if they know best and have seen moves towards more bottom-up approaches as a threat to their status and power.
- *Mechanisms and methodologies* for organizing appropriate participation at different levels and at different stages of the planning cycle often do exist but are not commonly used, supported by laws and policies, or are unfamiliar and unclear to those usually involved, or the transaction costs and time requirements are excessive.
- *It is difficult to achieve effective participation in a single exercise* (eg poor people are forced to emphasize their immediate priorities, and also lack resources, capacity and power to engage in decision-making for the longer term).
- *It is also difficult to ensure continued commitment* and engagement of those outside government, when their past involvement in participatory processes has been shown to be mainly cosmetic and their opinions have not been taken into account.

It is important, however, to note that top-down approaches are not always synonymous with failure, nor are bottom-up approaches always successful.

Source: OECD DAC (2001b)

---

policy level and within organizations that is not conducive to participatory processes. Generally applicable participatory methods of information gathering (eg natural resource surveys) and planning have yet to evolve. They need both local legitimacy and recognition by central authorities. In many developing countries, public demand for participation has often been ignored. Sometimes such demands have been countered by state repression. In a few cases, as a last resort, the lack of opportunities to further their interests pushes communities to use violence. As Zazueta (1994) notes, 'the costs of violence – in terms of human lives, economic losses, and environmental damage – must be always accounted for when assessing the benefits of participation'.

Zazueta illustrates the negative and costly impact of exclusionary, non-participatory development strategies with an account of the bloody uprising of Indian peasants (of Mayan descent) in Chiapas State in Mexico in January 1994. The peasants rebelled against the North American Free Trade Agreement (NAFTA) – being officially celebrated at the time – and the process of modernization that had clearly passed them by, on top of the neglect and exploitation that they had endured for over 400 years. The government at first bombed the area but, on noting the swift and widespread social support for the peasants, it quickly acknowledged their grievances and shifted to a negotiated solution.

The different objectives of society – social, economic and environmental – need to be integrated where possible, and traded-off where they are incompatible (see Chapter 2, page 25). Institutional and individual roles and responsibilities have to change – in government, the private sector and civil society – so that new patterns of behaviour will foster sustainable development. State-dominated policy and legislation for central control needs to give way to subtler mixes with enabling legislation, and civil society and private sector checks and balances. The range of policy instruments developed through sustainable development principles in the 1990s – voluntary codes, standards and certification – as well as new forms of participatory democracy using electronic media, point away from a state-dominated model. A strategy needs to be able to accommodate them. Thus it is clear that strategies should not merely be a technocratic planning process: the political dimensions of strategies are also key (Box 6.7).

It has long been understood that a *multidisciplinary approach* is needed to handle the analysis of social, economic and environmental dimensions and their interactions; and *coordination* is required among the various authorities and interests. And, furthermore, it is broadly agreed that strong *educational efforts* are needed to demonstrate to the various actors the complexities of developmental and environmental issues, and to encourage sustainable responses.

Realization of these needs during the 1980s led to a proliferation of national strategic planning approaches for dealing with environment and development. NCSs and NEAPs, for example, were built around a multidisciplinary, coordinated approach to planning (see Chapter 3, pages 50–52).

However, these strategies contained few provisions for *participation*, beyond consultation among a few select groups. The strategies were essentially led by a small group (usually government, and often with a significant donor input in developing countries). Successes were mixed. Even so, people closely involved in preparing and implementing such strategies and plans describe the most practical benefits in terms of, for example: enhanced understanding of sustainable development issues; improved communications and consensus on the main issues, and what to do about them; networks of committed individuals and institutions; agreements on new roles and responsibilities; and greater commitment.

As experience of past strategies shows (page 180 and Chapter 3), the more successful ones appear also to have been more participatory. Conversely, those strategies that appear to be going nowhere, even though the documentation may look good, frequently have been characterized by a lack of participation and consequently resilience, 'ownership' and commitment (Carew-Reid 1997; Wood 1997).

But a participatory approach is rarely associated with quick decisions. Participation along with ensuring a cyclical approach (ie periodic revision and adjustment to take account of learning from implementation and feedback from monitoring – rather a one-off effort) are two key, linked requirements for effective strategies for sustainable development (Boxes 3.1 and 3.2). In effect, a successful strategy is one in which the capacity is built up to think and work strategically, as a product of all appropriate groups in interaction. Successful strategies and policies have tended to evolve over time. Rarely have they been integrated deliberately in a single, supreme planning effort (although sometimes, perhaps, they should be). Indeed, deliberate strategic planning has always been difficult. Rather, transformations in development patterns tend to have been made through incremental responses to general economic and societal trends, political awareness and public opinion (Grayson 1993). Hence the OECD DAC approach to NSDSs – not a master plan, but a *set of continuing mechanisms that keep sustainable development on the national agenda and are able to deal with change.*

As Bass et al (1995) note:

It would be a counsel of perfection to suggest that policies have to be integrated from the outset, since not all possible fields of conflict can be foreseen, nor may it be politically apt to raise potential sources of conflict. It is in implementation that any strains become obvious.

Linking 'top-down' and 'bottom-up' has many political implications

Successful strategies have been characterized by their participation ...

... especially if participation is not one-off, but is continued and refined over time

Box 6.7 **The political dimensions of participation**

Any significant increase in the degree of participation in strategies is likely to face a number of key political dilemmas (Bass et al 1995):

- the political dimensions of the great structural constraints and inequalities which face sustainable development (local, national and international power structures);
- whether participation is a complement to, or substitute for, political processes of democracy;
- ways of defining values and making societal choices, which are strategy tasks, but also overwhelmingly understood to be in the political domain;
- the corollaries of empowerment and participation.

These dilemmas are perceived variously – a function of which groups are pushing for participation; which groups are threatened by the professional and institutional changes required for a participatory approach; who perceives that they will be the winners, and who the losers, of a sustainable development strategy; and the existing politicization of the issues dealt with by the strategy.

The drive for a greater degree of participation in national sustainable development strategies has come from:

- *Development cooperation agencies*, which have become frustrated with the lack of implementation of past plans; which are convinced – for rural development at least – of the practical benefits of participation generally; and which aim to further foreign policy aims of increasing democratization.
- *Strategy teams* (largely government professionals and administrators and their advisers), which have become aware that technical analyses of sustainable development issues cannot, by themselves, provide an adequate picture of needs; and which have similarly become frustrated with a lack of implementation of their 'top-down' plans.
- *Governments*, particularly of newly independent countries, which are struggling with trying to replace policies and procedures set up by (colonial) authorities with those which are meaningful to the population; and those of ex-communist countries, which are aiming to replace centralized planning with approaches which motivate and sit well with people.
- *Non-governmental and citizen's groups*, which are demanding a greater role in decision-making (generally, as well as for strategies).
- To an extent, the *private sector*, which is identifying a number of opportunities for joint action in sustainable development projects.

Moreover, there are more general societal and foreign policy moves towards democracy and greater human rights, which appear to call for participation. Given the confusion over different meanings of participation, it is not surprising that there is great confusion between participation as a populist political movement and the more functional aspects of participation as applied to a strategy, irrespective of politics. As Dalal-Clayton et al (1994) note, at an ambitious extreme, the long-term goal of an NSDS could be seen as creating an alternative national consensus through the NSDS process. Participation in such a strategy would clearly amount to a political process. It should be clear that the arguments for greater local-level empowerment, and the arguments for participation, have common roots and often the same protagonists, but they are not identical.

It is sometimes held that significant progress towards sustainable development can be achieved only in a democratic society, where stakeholders have reasonable opportunities to engage in planning and decision-making processes (Banuri and Holmberg 1992). However, this contention does not address the issue in its entirety. The answer to the question 'is democracy necessary for a successful strategy?' really depends on how democracy is defined. If it means building on the best and most representative systems for participation, then democracy is certainly needed. However, the answer is 'no' if democracy means the supremacy of an individual's rights to produce and consume irrespective of the effects on others. It may also be 'no' if the electoral cycle means politicians push short-term goals to win votes from individuals with strong aspirations to consume more resources, as opposed to doing what is sustainable in the long term:

Current political incentives are such that politicians have to be more concerned with generating policies that secure the short-term goal of re-election, rather than tackling the inevitably fraught transition towards more sustainable development. Ironically, it is probably democracy itself that is the greatest political barrier to a truly sustainable future.
(Pearce 1994)

It is clear that the politics of democracy need to be supplemented by longer-range participatory structures, such as local authorities, interest groups and traditional associations.

Many would argue that more radical change is necessary for sustainable development, because of the prevalent inequality in distribution of resources and in the costs and benefits of their use, and because of entrenched behaviour patterns (at least in the rich North), which threaten social/environment balances. This need for radical change does not necessarily have anything to do with democracy. Indeed, democracy has tended to lead to a slow incrementalism, and is not particularly good at introducing radical change. Furthermore, the *market* has not yet offered a strong mechanism for sustainable development. Alternative means of participation – based on new professionalism, voluntary approaches, participatory methodologies and supportive institutions – are required, at least as a strong complement to political processes. These can be instituted irrespective of political positions.

Party politics, as a relatively narrow value system, should not therefore provide the main forum for strategy formulation. Party politics tends to polarize the issues: sustainable development, in contrast, may be more easily negotiated with a committed 'middle ground' of interest groups.

Source: Bass et al 1995

Strategy experience has made it clear that science-based and interdisciplinary approaches are helpful for identifying social, environmental and economic problems and options, but are not sufficient. They cannot address all the issues nor provide access to all necessary and useful information. Much of this is held by individuals and communities. Moreover, the decisions needed are value judgements. They need to be made with the participation of both 'winners' and 'losers', so that some sort of agreement and commitment is reached on the outcome. A people-centred approach is needed as a complement to the science-based approach. Recognizing this, many early conservation/environment strategies built in some elements of participation, albeit often in an ad hoc manner.[3] Even without adequate resources and professional skills, such efforts tend to have paid off (Bass et al 1995; Carew-Reid 1997; Lopez Ornat 1997; Wood 1997), and invariably strategies have recommended greater participation in their implementation and further iteration.

Science-based decisions cannot handle the value judgements needed for sustainable development

There is, therefore, a clear role for both technical inputs by individual experts and the broader involvement of many people in participatory exercises – but at the same time not overburdening these people, resulting in 'participation fatigue'. It is very important that a balance be struck between these two approaches.

The need for the 'widest possible participation' in working towards sustainable development is noted in a number of chapters of Agenda 21 (Box 6.8), although there is little clarity about how to assure it. This is a tremendous challenge, without precedent. National laws (as in Bolivia – Box 6.14) and international conventions (such as the Aarhus Convention – Box 7.1) have been emerging to support a routine participatory approach in key decisions and actions.

Participation is increasingly enshrined in both international obligations and national laws

It is also important to set participation in strategy processes in an international context. Every year, there are numerous international meetings and conferences organized by UN organizations and other international bodies, which are concerned with a broad range of issues connected to sustainable development. In many cases, these events involve debate and negotiations, which will affect individual countries and even place obligations upon them (ie through conventions, treaties and the like). In some cases, such meetings are concerned with cross-sectoral and interdisciplinary matters. In other cases, they are concerned with single issues or sectoral concerns, but ought to take into account linkages with, and impacts in, other sectors.

Experience shows that, in many cases, those selected to represent their country are ill equipped for the task. Often, they have inadequate knowledge of the subjects being discussed, or are poorly briefed

---

3 Few strategies, however, have been entirely participatory on the one hand, or completely non-participatory on the other. Most strategies have had to incorporate existing participation structures and methodologies, improve them or even create new ones, to get close to their declared objectives.

Box 6.8 Agenda 21 on participation

Agenda 21 refers to the need for broad participation in various chapters. For example:

In **Chapter 8** (*Integrating environment and development in decision-making*): an adjustment or even a fundamental reshaping of decision-making, in the light of country specific conditions may be necessary if environment and development is to be put at the centre of economic and political decision-making, in effect achieving full integration of these factors.

In **Chapter 23** (*Strengthening the role of the major groups*), Agenda 21 requires, in the *specific context of environment and development, the need for new forms of participation* and notes *the need of individuals, groups and organizations to participate in decisions, particularly those which affect the communities in which they live and work.*

In **Chapter 26** (*Recognizing and strengthening the role of indigenous people and their communities*), active participation is called for to incorporate their 'values, views and knowledge'.

In **Chapter 33** (*Financial resources and mechanisms*): *priorities should be established by means that incorporate public participation and community involvement providing equal opportunity for men and women ... In this respect, consultative groups and round tables and other nationally-based mechanisms can play a facilitative role.*

In **Chapter 37** (*National mechanisms and international cooperation for capacity-building*): *as an important aspect of overall planning, each country should seek internal consensus at all levels of society on policies and programmes needed for short- and long-term capacity building to implement its Agenda 21 programme. This consensus should result from a participatory dialogue of relevant interest groups and lead to an identification of skill gaps, institutional capacities and capabilities, technological and scientific requirements and resource needs to enhance environmental knowledge and administration to integrate environment and development.*

It is notable that Agenda 21 calls, effectively, for participation in all the elements of a strategy cycle.

Source: UNCED (1992)

---

beforehand about them. Sometimes (particularly in small or poor countries), staff resources are so limited that a particular individual finds him or herself having to cover an array of responsibilities and tasks, and therefore to represent their country at many international conferences and meetings – even though they may lack sufficient understanding of the issues concerned, or of the domestic relevance and consequences of agreements reached. In other cases, they might be a delegate because no one else is available, or perhaps just because it was merely their turn to travel. As a result, countries (particularly poor ones) are not able to participate effectively in international meetings, or represent and defend their country's interests during debate.

Local participation can also improve a country's ability to involve itself effectively in international processes

An effective strategy process will involve debate about the international dimensions of development (eg the impacts on the country of globalization and its possible responses, regional concerns, harmonizing commitments under treaties and conventions, etc). This will enable countries better to prepare for participation in international fora. It will help those charged with attending such meetings to be more conversant with, and better prepared on, a wide array of linked issues concerning the sustainable development of their country and the international dimensions of the issues concerned. Participation in strategy processes will also indicate those individuals who might be the most able and appropriate persons to attend particular international events.

Ensuring effective participation – issues and planning requirements

Scoping the basic requirements

Requirements will depend on the scope and goals of the strategy and the likely participants, as well as on political and social circumstances. In general, the needs are:

- *Agreed principles for participation*. These need to be the subject of early discussion, based on the diagnostic of previous and existing strategies (see Tables 5.12 and 5.13). They are likely to include: promotion of diversity, equity, representation, transparency, learning, time to consult and inclusiveness (see also Boxes 6.10, 6.16 and Box 3.1 on principles). National legislation and international conventions may offer further principles.
- *A proper understanding* of all the strategy stakeholders – those with a legitimate interest in the strategy – with a considered and concrete approach to include the more vulnerable and disenfranchised among them.
- *Catalysts for participation*, for example NGOs and local authorities, to start participation and to link decisions that need to be taken centrally with those appropriate to more local levels.
- *Specific activities and events* – around which to focus participation.
- *A phased approach* – that is, start modestly, building on existing participation systems; then deepen and focus participation with each iteration of processes.
- *Appropriate participatory methods* for appraising needs and possibilities, dialogue, ranking solutions, forming partnerships, resolving conflicts and reaching solutions.
- *Adequate resources, skills and time* – effective participation tends to start slowly and requires early investment; it becomes more cost-effective with time.
- *Learning environments*, for example policies, laws and institutions that encourage, support, manage and reward participation in the planning/development process – including specially formulated groups where appropriate institutions do not exist – and which allow participants and professionals to test approaches. Their presence will greatly support the above requirements.
- *Demonstrable results and benefits, especially in the early phases* – stakeholders need to be convinced that their investments of time and other resources will have impact.

Consideration of costs and benefits of participation

In principle, all who have a stake in the strategy, or the outcomes that flow from it, should be part of the processes relating to its development and implementation. This would realize some of the benefits of participation noted in Box 6.9. But this potentially means the whole population of a country. However, very extensive participation is clearly neither possible nor necessarily desirable – it would be extremely costly. Injudicious or excessive participation will help no one, and may engender reactions against participation. Box 6.10 sets out the financial and other costs of participation. In addition, in any country or situation, there will be a range of constraints to participation, as illustrated by the case of Joint Forest Management in India (Box 6.11).

Stakeholders need to talk through the costs and benefits of participation ...

In designing a strategy, the benefits of high or low degrees of participation need to be weighed against the associated costs and weaknesses. Equally, the means to overcome the weaknesses should be identified, as summarized in Table 6.4.

Clarity of expectations

Involvement in a broad-ranging process such as an NSDS is likely to raise expectations, as it deals with so many issues and takes so much effort: involving people in setting targets and agreeing social objectives uses

... so that they can be clear on expectations

Box 6.9 The benefits of participation in strategies

Strategy information and analysis tasks:

- Basing the strategy on a broad knowledge base and spread of opinion; offering the best informed judgement on issues, trade-offs and options in the time available.
- Improved communications within and between interest groups.
- Increased debate, mutual education, understanding of major issues both within and between different groups.
- Tackling issues that cannot be identified, properly defined or dealt with by any other means (eg changing values, local conditions, rights and claims and lifestyles, and particularly issues such as poverty which otherwise may be submerged).
- Application of the potentials of group dynamics.

Strategy policy formulation and planning:

- Application of consensus-building and conflict-resolution potentials to major societal decisions.
- Practicality and realism of objectives, targets and standards, which are negotiated so that they are locally acceptable, meaningful and practicable; this avoids the risk of 'imposing' approaches, or blanket solutions.
- 'Ownership' of, and commitment to, the strategy can be built up by groups actually working on it (essential if the strategy is to result in social mobilization).
- Political credibility of the strategy is higher than when it is just a product of technicians and bureaucrats.
- Accountability and transparency – people can see what 'government' does.
- Greater equity. Every policy or market decision has a redistributive effect (involving who gains and who loses, over time, space or social group); participation can link decision-making back with groups that have become marginalized through previous decisions and so help an equitable definition of trade-offs.

Strategy implementation and monitoring:

- Increased, and more relevant, capacity (learning by exposure and debate; learning by doing).
- More extensive networks for tasks, such as monitoring.
- Through utilizing networks, others buy into the process.
- Efficient mobilization and management of resources and skills.
- Greater likelihood of change to more appropriate behaviour by different groups.
- Greater likelihood of self-mobilization for sustainable development.

Source: Bass et al (1995)

---

their time and energy, which can leave them with high expectations of rewards for the results of their labours. Most 'raised expectations' should be welcomed – they are generally a driving force for people's motivation and capabilities for organization and collaboration.

However, if improperly managed, participatory processes can result in expectations being raised too high among certain groups. And the increased diversity of participation makes conflict more likely. For example, there can be expectations (that cannot be necessarily met) that:

- whatever problems or issues are raised will automatically become priorities for action or can be solved in the very near future;
- all stakeholders will be required to agree completely (full consensus) before the process can move forward;
- tangible rewards or incentives for participation will continue through all stages of the iterative process;
- things will change rapidly or an immediate boost to development will come to a particular locality (eg development projects, new or revamped infrastructure or services, investment and new jobs);

Box 6.10 The costs of participation

The value of participation in strategic planning and decision-making is now generally accepted. However, it is sometimes assumed that the maximum participation of all of the people all of the time is necessary and a good thing. It is not. Complete participation may actually lead to complete inertia, due to the costs involved and practical difficulties such as transportation, reaching a quorum, time and energy. The costs of participation depend on various factors (below). However, while initially high, the costs can reduce with each iteration of the strategy as the scope, purpose and methodologies for participation of each group become clearer and better focused.

Cost of communication and providing access to information: If people are to be actively involved in strategic planning, they need to have a thorough understanding of the process as it unfolds and decisions that are being made. This requires effective and timely feedback, the sharing of reports and a recognition of the contribution of different groups and individuals. The many institutions and individuals engaging in debate will need to have access to – and understand – key information important to the issue(s) being discussed. This requires communication through the medium appropriate to the groups in question (telecommunications, mass or traditional media, various fora) which has cost implications (Chapter 7).

The cost of raising expectations: Participation may generate considerable excitement, and expectations may be raised. If there is no follow-up to early discussions, disillusion may set in and jeopardize people's willingness to continue to participate. This can be minimized by cautious initial discussions that focus on problem identification and provide all stakeholders with clear ideas of what is possible and what is not, given the resources that are available (see page 193).

The costs of specialist skills. Skills in participatory enquiry, communications, education and media activities are all essential in order to establish the right linkages and ensure quality of participation and communications. Open and frank discussions over key issues (eg resource allocation and use) can lead to conflict that needs to be addressed through specialist skills.

Transaction costs of developing and maintaining institutional mechanisms for local participation, including the non-market costs involved in conflict resolution, time spent in meetings and time spent on resource management. There are also costs for food and accommodation, and the potential of political and social disputes that surface or are generated by the intervention of outsiders.

The costs to stakeholders of being actively involved: The costs of participation depend on the types and numbers of participants, their location and the opportunity costs of their participation. Many stakeholders will be able to engage through their existing jobs and roles. Others will need to take time from their livelihood activities (eg those in civil society and particularly those from local communities where involvement can mean, for example, time lost to harvesting crops). Some women may find it particularly difficult to engage in participatory processes due to the multiplicity of tasks they otherwise perform. So ways of compensating for this, or for providing assistance, may need to be found if they are to participate effectively. The example of New Zealand is outlined in Box 6.25.

Time requirements – it takes time to establish trust, especially at some local levels, and a framework within which people may be encouraged to collaborate with outsiders. It has often taken between 18 months and five years to set up and undertake the more comprehensive participation exercises associated with national strategies.

Source: Adapted from IIED (1998c)

- government officials and politicians will always be available and supportive, even when recommended actions or outcomes are not politically expedient or palatable;
- sufficient effort will also be devoted to lower group priorities which are nonetheless important to a minority of stakeholders;
- respect for the views of grass-roots participants, and the levels of trust achieved during the initial stages of participation, will be ongoing;
- all stakeholders will be involved in every stage and activity of the strategy process;
- the same stakeholder groups will be represented at all activities of the strategy process.

> **Box 6.11** **Key constraints to participation: the experience of Joint Forest Management, India**
>
> - *In the initial phases, participation requires considerable time and extra effort in development of human resources*, for which few incentives are provided. Individuals, institutions and programmes may feel constrained in making such investments, as they are currently evaluated primarily by the criteria of achievement of physical and financial targets.
> - *Participation requires major reversals in the role of external professionals*, from a 'management' role to a facilitating one. This requires changes in behaviour and attitudes, and can only be gradual. To do this will entail significant retraining for which, usually, inadequate resources are devoted.
> - *Participation threatens conventional careers*; professionals feel a loss of power if they have to deal with local communities as equals and include them in decision-making. This discourages professionals from taking risks and developing collaborative relationships with communities.
> - *Participation and institutional development are difficult to measure*, and require quantitative and qualitative performance indicators together. Existing monitoring and evaluation systems cannot measure these well. Thus, physical and financial indicators, which are easier to measure, dominate performance evaluation and impact analysis.
> - *Programmes tend to retain financial decision-making powers for themselves.* While many programmes initiated by external agencies tend to use participatory methods for planning, they do not make corresponding changes in resource allocation mechanisms to local institutions. This hampers the growth of local institutions and leads to poor sustainability of the programmes.
> - *Participation is a long, drawn-out process and needs to be iterative in the initial period before being scaled up and replicated.* Most development programmes tend to blueprint the process of participation and institutional-building in the early phases, without enough experimentation and iteration. The institutional form thus evolved is ineffective.
> - *Participation is also directly linked with equity, which threatens elites.* This political dilemma is addressed on pages 178–186.
>
> Source: Bass and Shah (1994)

If these expectations are not managed, it can lead to disillusionment and anger. It is important, at the outset, that the strategy participants know just how far up the decision-making 'hierarchies' their recommendations can and will reach. One of the failures of participation has been disillusionment resulting from unrealistic expectations about how far-reaching, and how quickly, the results of participation will make a difference to policies and plans.

One solution is to openly debate the costs and benefits (above). Further, to ensure continuing good communication and willingness to develop collaboration between stakeholders. This helps get expectations and realities out in the open, and allows realistic goals, standards and targets to be hammered out with key stakeholders. Other ways to deal with unrealistic expectations include (Higman et al 1999):

- At the outset, *clarify what might be possible* in the short-, medium- and long-term.
- Hire/work with *people who understand local issues.*
- Ensure that key strategy staff have *a consistent picture* of the scope of the strategy. Widely differing views among staff will lead to confused perceptions among other stakeholders.
- *Respect different positions* and keep communication channels open.
- Maximize *regular face-to-face contact* with stakeholders.
- Ensure *continuity of approaches* and stability of staff in positions which involve collaboration with stakeholders.
- Try to *solve problems while they are still small.*
- Give consultation processes *plenty of time*, and get stakeholders to focus on priorities.
- In developing initiatives aimed at improved stakeholder benefits, *start with small experiments* in one area first, ensuring that stakeholders are part of the plan.
- *Allow adaptation and flexibility* in operations involving stakeholders.

Table 6.4 **Illustrative comparison of strategies with high and low intensities of participation**

Low participation	High participation	Overcoming participation weaknesses
Participation only up to level 3 of Table 6.2; that is, listening, giving information and consultation only Few groups involved	Participation up to Level 5 of Table 6.2; that is, also participation in agenda-setting, analysis and consensus Many groups involved	
Pros ■ Low costs of participation ■ Few local expectations raised ■ Relatively quick ■ Technical detail ■ Technical rigour ■ Clear leadership of process ■ Strategy management easy ■ Gives strong directions ■ High involvement at top ■ Few conflicts during preparation ■ Understood by donors ■ Can be quick political impact ■ Done with routine procedures	**Cons** ■ Higher costs ■ Can raise expectations ■ Slower (depends on systems used) ■ Less technical detail ■ Trustworthiness problems ■ Shared/changing leadership ■ Complex strategy management ■ Directions more devolved ■ Less control at top ■ Many conflicts exposed ■ Difficult for donor cycles ■ Political impact slower/surer ■ Incentives needed to participate ■ Participation fatigue in actors ■ Participation skills needed	■ Share costs among actors ■ Phase participation process ■ Quick first iteration; then deeper ■ Bring in expertise (eg in participatory inquiry) ■ Framework for judging ■ Institutionalize this ■ Hire personnel with experience ■ More monitoring and coordination ■ Strengthen top–bottom links ■ Deal with them in phases ■ Focus donors; flagship projects ■ Major, phased strategy events ■ Incentives early in participation plan ■ Only appropriate participation ■ Hire and train early
Cons ■ Limited understanding by public ■ Limited 'energy source' for ideas ■ Limited commitment to implement ■ Have to 'sell' to implementers ■ Undue influence of external experts ■ High (cross-sectoral) technical skills needed ■ Much relevant information missing ■ Analysis/policy may not reflect reality ■ Weak processes for sustainable development trade-offs ■ Judgement of a few 'experts' only ■ Only government implements	**Pros** ■ Strong public understanding ■ Release much energy for ideas/inputs ■ Strong implementation commitment ■ Strategy not a surprise to actors ■ External experts used appropriately ■ Does not depend on high science; participation offers analogues ■ Uncovers information that matters ■ Analysis/policy checked with reality ■ Strong processes result ■ Gives best informed judgement ■ Much more local/private implementation	

Source: Bass et al (1995)

Consideration of scale and links

A strategy process is likely to require several strands or layers of stakeholder collaboration. This might involve, for example, core groups surrounded by larger 'sounding boards' and groups who (initially) address separate parts of key issues. Provision also needs to be made to enable additional stakeholders to be invited into the process if gaps become clear. Feedback loops between different levels (local to national, and international) and between different strategies (such as sectoral strategies for biodiversity and forestry and the NSDS) can help to inform dialogue and decision-making. In identifying options and models for implementing outcomes, the involvement of groups likely to be involved in actual implementation is critical.

Representation, selection and intermediaries

The proper *selection of participants* is perhaps the most critical step in establishing a strategy process. The composition of participants will determine both the legitimacy of the strategy and its ability to develop new ideas, insights and consensus for action. Issues of representativeness, sampling and appropriate degrees of participation are important. A balance needs to be struck between involving as wide a range of participants as possible to forge a broad-based and durable consensus, and avoiding overloading the facilitating and managerial capacities of those who are organizing the strategy process.

Early efforts to ensure wide, balanced representation – especially redressing power imbalances ...

It is very important to establish *transparent criteria by which to identify relevant stakeholder groups*, and to select bodies to invite to represent such groups in the strategy process. Information about these criteria should be provided to all participating and non-participating stakeholder groups as well as the general public. Key criteria include:

- the degree to which representatives identify primarily with the group in question (rather than with other interests);
- the legitimacy and accountability of stakeholder representatives within and towards their own defined interest groups;
- equitable arrangements within the represented stakeholder interest groups concerning the participation of their representatives; for example, democratic processes to elect/appoint representatives and requirements to report back;
- the expertise that particular bodies/individuals can bring to the process;
- commitment to the strategy process;
- track record of involvement in multi-stakeholder processes.

Communities have a fundamental right to self-determination, which needs to be respected. In cases where a potential agreement affects the future lives of a stakeholder group, they need to have the right to say 'no' even if they are in the minority. They should, however, hear all arguments and actively participate in discussions before they make a decision.

It is very important to ensure the inclusion of service user *representatives*, and representatives of interest groups who are traditionally under-represented in planning efforts. In its planning guide for Local Agenda 21s, ICLEI (1996a) suggests a matrix exercise to help in the identification of partners for stakeholder and working groups (Figure 6.4) and a checklist to verify that representation is inclusive for effective sustainable development planning (Box 6.12).

The representativeness and legitimacy of stakeholder representatives has been the focus of considerable discussion. As UNED Forum (2001) notes, attention has tended to focus on NGOs:

> *many of which, particularly those collaborating in NGO networks, have been developing mechanisms of self-governance to ensure democratic, transparent and truly participatory processes as a basis of their mandate. Certification schemes would be another option; yet the question of who should govern or control certifying bodies remains unsolved. One should keep in mind, however, that these questions not only apply to NGOs but other sectors of civil society as well, such as the business community, trade unions, local authorities, women, and so on.*

Potential partners	Components of sustainable development		
	1.Community development ■ Housing ■ Social services ■ Public safety	2. Economic development ■ Transportation ■ Employment ■ Tourism	3. Ecosystem development ■ Pollution control ■ Green space ■ Waste management
A. Community residents ■ Special groups of people (women, youth and indigenous people) ■ Community leaders ■ Households ■ Teachers			
B. Community-based Organizations ■ Coalitions ■ Church groups ■ Formal women's groups ■ Special interest groups			
C. Independent sector ■ NGOs ■ Academia ■ Media ■ Political parties ■ Trades unions and workers' organizations			
D. Private/Entrepreneurial sector ■ Environmental service agencies ■ Small business/ cooperatives ■ Banks			
E. Local Government and Associations ■ Elected officials ■ Management staff ■ Field/staff operations ■ Regional associations			
F. National/Regional Government ■ Planning Commission ■ Utilities ■ Service agencies ■ Financial agencies			

Source: Adapted from ICLEI (1996)

Figure 6.4 **Identifying partners for stakeholder and working groups**

Where particular stakeholder interest groups are not organized, one approach to ensuring their involvement is through *intermediaries or surrogates*. Surrogates may be any group, organization (eg an NGO) or individual that has close links with the concerned stakeholders and is capable of representing their views and interests during the strategy process. For example, in Nigeria, female extension agents served as surrogates for farm women at a national planning workshop on women in agriculture (World Bank 1996).

A key issue is the *voluntary participation* of stakeholders. It is vital that stakeholders are informed adequately, and sufficiently early, to enable them to make a decision about participating. Such information should include the role that they can play in the strategy process or in a particular group, the amount of

---

Box 6.12 Checklist for partner selection in Local Agenda 21s

Ensure representation of:

1   under-represented groups;
2   service-users – those people who use and are affected by services;
3   service providers – those people who control and manage services or service systems;
4   parties with a particular expertise related to the relevant services or issues;
5   parties whose interests are affected by the service and the service system.

In selecting partners, consider:

1   the scope of work to be undertaken by the partners;
2   the need to develop a critical mass of organizations and individuals who have the political will to take action;
3   the degree of inclusiveness it is hoped to achieve;
4   the skills, knowledge, and experience that different individuals or organizations can contribute;
5   the inclusion of parties who will need to be involved in the implementation of any plan;
6   the inclusion of organizations or individuals with credibility within their own constituencies.

Source: ICLEI (1996)

---

time they will be expected to commit and the amount of work, travel and so on involved. They should have the right to decline if they are unhappy about arrangements (see Box 6.13).

Often it is only during the process of raising awareness during the advocacy stages of strategy formulation that potential partners become aware of their stake in the process. This is illustrated by the case of Guyana's National Biodiversity Action Plan when, during its formulation stage, potential partners were made aware, in concrete terms, of their potential interests and role in biodiversity conservation and realized that they too had a stake in biodiversity conservation (Table 6.5).

... will be rewarded with a credible, enduring strategy process

The legitimacy of a strategy process is strongly associated with clarity among stakeholders on the strategy's purpose and scope, how they will be involved and how they will interact. It will suffer if key stakeholders distance themselves from the process, if they are marginalized or if they *feel* marginalized. If this begins to occur, it might be better to review the design of the process and/or to carefully work out what kind of legitimacy it can claim, and conduct it clearly within those limitations.

Box 6.13 Transparency in the selection of stakeholder representatives

Stakeholder groups need to be transparent about their procedures of selecting representatives to the strategy process, within and without the process itself. Stakeholder groups should also be transparent to others about their elections or appointment criteria, and about criteria being used to identify individuals with expertise on the respective issues at hand. The process of identifying individuals to represent groups is helped by regular election or appointment processes within stakeholder networks and associations – eg caucus coordinator elections among NGOs, appointments of representatives to particular processes by stakeholder groups such as industry, trade unions, and so forth. Other participants should be allowed to bring to the floor any problems they might have with criteria other stakeholders are using.

It is important to balance the numbers of participants from each stakeholder group, and, in some cases, with regard to which views they are likely to represent. Stakeholder groups should be required to meet certain balance criteria within their delegations, such as regional and gender balance. Preferably, representatives of stakeholder groups should remain the same persons over the course of a strategy cycle. If representatives have to be replaced, they need to be briefed and be introduced to the group.

Source: UNED Forum (2001)

Table 6.5 **Stakeholder interests and roles: the case of Guyana's National Biodiversity Action Plan**

Stakeholder group	Interest in biodiversity	Role in biodiversity
General public	As part of national patrimony biodiversity is an asset to each citizen	Taking action at the local and other levels to conserve and wisely use biodiversity; support various actions in the Plan
Natural resource public agencies	Granting of access to biodiversity and other resources that affect biodiversity	Conservation of biodiversity resources; minimizing impact of use activities on biodiversity; national level planning
Environmental regulatory agency	Monitoring impact of development activities on biodiversity; regulating access; developing policy, legislation, and administrative mechanisms; promoting public awareness	Establishing framework for sustainable biodiversity use and conservation; improving public knowledge and attitudes towards biodiversity; national level planning
Regional and local administrative authorities	Maintenance and use of biodiversity resources	Conservation of biodiversity; local and regional planning; promotion of public awareness
Private sector entities	Utilization of biodiversity and other resources; supporting research and planning	Implementing conservation and sustainable use of biodiversity; supporting various actions in the Plan
Local communities	Subsistence and commercial use of biodiversity	Conservation of biodiversity; provision of information and sharing of knowledge
Academic community	Research, training and public awareness on biodiversity	Providing scientific information on biodiversity; improve public awareness
Funding agencies	Conservation, research and sustainable use of biodiversity	Providing financial and technical support for biodiversity action
Media entities	Information on biodiversity as natural resource and national patrimony	Improving public awareness on biodiversity
Non-governmental organizations	Promoting action towards conservation and use of biodiversity; public awareness	Supporting action on biodiversity; conservation advocacy; improving public awareness

Source: GEPA (1999)

Infrastructure, organization and legal framework for participation

For effective participation, the basic infrastructure of involvement needs to be in place (see pages 186–194).

Use of existing structures: The more well developed and regularly used the existing participation structures and mechanisms (see Table 6.6), the more cost-effective they are likely to be. If managerial capacities are weak and participatory mechanisms are poor, the number of participants may be limited at first – but this should be increased with the development and reiteration of specific strategy tasks.

However, where such participatory structures are lacking, weak or ineffective, it has usually been found necessary to establish new structures – even if informal or one-off. In practice, if they work, they are likely to survive into subsequent cycles or iterations of the strategy. Examples include:

- special committees;
- focus groups on particular subjects/issues;
- round tables to discuss specific common or cross-sectoral issues;
- core groups to take issues forward;

Where participatory structures are weak, several emerging new types of approach can be tried

Table 6.6 **Examples of likely existing structures/institutions and methodologies for participation**

Participation structures/institutions	Participation methodologies
■ Planning system	■ Participatory learning and action (PLA)
■ Traditional structures, eg village-based systems, religious systems	■ Resource surveys
■ Education/academic system	■ 'Green' audits
■◘Extension system	■ Planning methodologies, environmental impact assessment, etc
■ Arts/theatre	■ Consensus-building and negotiations
■ Media	■ Traditional methods, eg of conflict resolution
■ Political system	■ Communications and information techniques, eg 'phone-ins' and e-mail networks
■ National Councils for Sustainable Development	■ Participatory dialogue
■ Discussion forums (formal/informal, professional, etc)	■ Focus groups
■ Women's' groups	■ Roundtables
■ Unions	■ Seminars/workshops/working groups
■ Cooperatives	■ SEA and SEAn (see pages 149–152)
■ Formal multi-country political bodies or negotiating machinery	

■ sectoral and professional associations, for example, agricultural or horticultural societies, or associations of engineers or planners.

A legal framework for participation may already be in place ...

The legal framework for participation is fundamental to all the above. Public participation rests on the principles of free speech, and rights to a healthy environment and secure livelihood. A clear legal framework is needed within which to exercise such rights. It tends to be more fully developed within the urban and rural planning systems of most countries, and in some EIA legislation. Specifically, the legal framework needs to sanction: public access to information held by public authorities; participation in decision-making processes; and involvement in judicial and administrative review. Such sanctions, if they are to be more than symbolic, require backing up by effective procedures, notably the requirement of prior informed consent, due notice of impending decisions, and channels to object and make appeals. Successful strategies tend to have developed ad hoc procedures where legislative procedures are absent or not fully exercised (REC 1994b).

... or can be developed – perhaps through the strategy process itself

Recognizing that participation must be assured, some countries have introduced laws to actively promote greater participation, particularly of those groups often marginalized from decision-making. In recent years, many developing countries have introduced participatory mechanisms in decentralizing their planning systems (see Box 6.21). For example, the Popular Participation Law in Bolivia promotes decentralized government and aims to allow municipalities and their citizens (particular in remote areas) greater control over social services and basic infrastructure (Box 6.14).

An innovative and useful approach adopted by member states of the Organization of Eastern Caribbean States (OECS) benefited from the synergies of intergovernmental collaboration. OECS member states are all small, and suffer limitations of human resource and institutional capacities. In a very involved and lengthy participatory process spanning a period of over three years, the OECS fashioned a legally binding Eastern Caribbean Environmental Charter formally adopted in 2001 which enshrines commitment

Box 6.14 **The Popular Participation Law, Bolivia**

Prior to 1995, 42 per cent of the Bolivian population, all of them indigenous groups or peasants, lived in dispersed rural communities, without any official mechanism of governance, and without access to the resources necessary to meet basic human needs. Besides those residing in these isolated communities, many more Indians and peasants had moved into urban areas, principally La Paz, Santa Cruz and Cochabamba, where they faced overwhelming unemployment and poverty, often receiving little or no support from municipal governments.

The Popular Participation law (1994), implemented in 1995, is a decentralization programme that divided the country's provinces into 314 sections, each with a local-elected municipal government. Many of the municipalities had to be created from scratch. They were given control over the physical infrastructure in their jurisdiction (eg health, education, culture, sports, local streets and local irrigation efforts). To ensure greater possibilities for participation than occasional elections, the new law formally recognizes in each community a grass-roots organization to represent civil society (*Organización Territorial de Base*, OTB) and affords these OTBs specific rights and obligations within their municipalities (Table 6.7). The members of the OTB must be representative of a given community, and each OTB must elect one representative to serve on the municipality's *Comité de Vigilancia* (surveillance committee). The latter elaborates proposals from the villages and controls the municipal budget and is thus planned as a form of 'social control' of 'good governance' of municipal government.

Table 6.7 **Rights and obligations of OTBs**

Rights of OTBs	Obligations of OTBs
1 Propose, control and supervise the delivery of public services in accordance with the needs of the community	1 Identify, prioritize, participate and cooperate in the execution and administration of public works for the collective well-being
2 Participate in and promote actions related to the growth and preservation of the environment, the ecological equilibrium, and sustainable development	2 Contribute to the maintenance and protection of public, municipal and community goods
3 Represent the community in forcing the modification of actions, decisions, public works or services undertaken by the municipal governments	3 Make available to the communities their records regarding their actions in the territory
4 Propose the removal or ratification of education and health authorities within the municipality	4 Introduce administrative and judicial resources in defence of the rights they have under the law
5 Have access to information regarding the resources destined for popular participation efforts	5 Promote equitable access for women and men to the various levels of political representation

The law includes allocation of 20 per cent of the republic's revenues to the municipalities (85 per cent for projects and 15 per cent for administration) on a per capita basis, so that the 42 per cent of the population living in remote areas now have more control over social services and basic infrastructure (previously large cities received most of the government disbursements).

In parallel, the Education Reform Law specifies eight different 'popular participation mechanisms' or councils, which the municipalities create and control. Two of them are directly created by OTBs, giving these civil society representatives access to the planning, development and supervision of educational activities and services. Other councils, made up of private citizens, government representatives and educational professionals, are charged with ensuring that the goals of the reform process are met. There are even councils of Indian groups to oversee the introduction of bilingualism and multiculturalism into the education system. These mechanisms ensure that, within national guidelines for standards and objectives, the new education system in each municipality will be built and monitored by a partnership between citizens and local governments.

The municipal councils are functioning, but in many municipalities it has been the town elite who have been elected as councillors and they do not represent the majority of the rural population. The surveillance committees are functioning sub-optimally in many municipalities. Distances are great so that it is difficult for members of the surveillance committees to meet. But, more importantly, they are an artificial construction that have little to do with realities in many rural areas and have no natural role to play – there are long-standing councils of authorities at the village level (elected village councils). These commonly operate by consensus, so it is not unusual for all members of the council of authorities to turn up at meetings of the municipal council, the members of which are town dwellers and get annoyed by the villagers' presence to ask for particular projects/actions to be taken, and they invoke the law to conduct their operations. The difference between the two social systems shows.

The Popular Participation Law intended to change national and local power structures and, in theory, acknowledge the indigenous rural population and its social organizations which had been marginalized for centuries. The new law has yet to achieve its goals. The political parties are still the main power holders in Bolivia, nationally and locally, and this still tends to exclude the indigenous population.

Source: Andersson (1999); IADB (1996)

to introduce participatory planning systems and structures (Box 6.15). Participants included all ministers with responsibility for environmental policy and management of each member state, governmental and intergovernmental institutions, NGOs and donors. They collaborated under the mandate of the OECS Ministers of the Environment Policy Committee (EPC).

Obligations by each member state are explicit and implementation is monitored at EPC meetings. This sub-regional approach enabled eight countries with limited legal infrastructure and other resources to fashion an instrument that can be adapted easily to suit national conditions. Using this strategy OECS countries are seeking to achieve collectively what would have been difficult or impossible (for some member states) to achieve individually.

Government-civil society relations will determine what kinds of participation can proceed in practice, and how much participation will achieve. Where relations between government and civil society are good, the conditions for effective strategies for sustainable development are good. The converse is also true. It is vital that the interaction between government and non-governmental groups be strengthened – the strategy process itself can gradually improve this. Also central to the pursuit of sustainability is the need to strengthen a country's democratic institutions and elected bodies, particularly parliamentary assemblies.

The NSDS secretariat (Chapter 4) or others organizing meetings, events or other gatherings need to consider and make known information about meeting times and locations, transport, and even arrangements for such matters as childcare and access for the handicapped, etc. There are always likely to be barriers to the effective participation of some stakeholders, whether for cultural, religious or other reasons, and special activities may be required if their inputs are to be assured. The secretariat should avoid taking unilateral decisions that limit the range or number of participants or compose groups in certain ways. Rather this challenge should be referred to the steering committee, which should be representative of the main stakeholder groups involved.

The state of government–civil society relations helps or hinders participation

The strategy secretariat should coordinate the participation processes ...

Planning for participation in strategies

... including planning for participation

Experience of strategic planning over the past two decades indicates a number of requirements for effective participation (page 193). All of these requirements will need to be well planned if the benefits of participation are to be realized. Otherwise, interest groups can be left out of the process, the complex organizational tasks of participation can be underestimated, and the many prerequisites required may not be in place in time. This entails various tasks, which might be coordinated by the NSDS secretariat with a broad proto-group of stakeholders:

(a) *Mapping out the themes* that may need to be worked on during the strategy process and by different groups of stakeholders: for example, sectoral, cross-sectoral or comprehensive sustainable development issues.

(b) *Identifying the main levels* at which policy and institutional changes will be needed to address the above themes/issues – usually: national, provincial and local.

(c) *Stakeholder analysis:* (see page 120) to determine representativeness, interests, dynamics and power relations.

The initial definition of strategy themes, levels and stakeholders (tasks a, b and c) can be tackled together. For effective participation, this should not be done entirely by a government department or a development cooperation agency. It is important to get the local 'ownership' right, for tasks a, b and c will determine the choice of participation structures and methodologies, and incentives required for participation.

Box 6.15 **Enshrining participation in legislation: principles of the Eastern Caribbean Environmental Charter**

Several of the Charter's principles bind member states to enshrine participation in domestic legislation:

Principle 4: Ensure meaningful participation by civil society in decision-making

Each Contracting State agrees to:

1   establish, strengthen and promote institutional structures and procedures for the broad participation by civil society in the design, implementation and evaluation of decision-making processes and programmes;
2   uphold the right of everyone to seek, receive and disseminate clear and timely information on environmental matters, and on all development plans and activities in which they have an interest, and which are likely to affect their lives;
3   guarantee the right of everyone with an interest, to transmit comments on proposed activities to the competent authority, before any formal decision is taken;
4   provide opportunities for the expression of ideas, and the exchange of information and traditional knowledge on environmental management between organizations, communities and individuals, as well as facilitating their effective participation in the formulation, adoption and execution of decisions affecting their lives.

Principle 18: Implementation

Each Contracting State agrees to:

1   adopt the Eastern Caribbean Environmental Management Strategy (hereinafter called the ECEMS) of the contracting states to guide the implementation of the Principles contained in this Charter;
2   cooperate in good faith with each other to achieve optimal results from their environmental policies and actions relating to the use of transboundary natural resources, and in the effective prevention or abatement of transboundary environmental problems;
3   communicate timely and relevant information on all aspects of the Charter's Principles to other interested States and persons likely to be affected by planned or actualized development activity;
4   undertake to apply equal standards at all times, in respect of addressing issues concerning the impact or adverse effects of transboundary natural resources, on the environment;
5   work concertedly together to implement the Principles enunciated in this Charter;
6   ensure that the requisite actions outlined under the heading of Commitments, and contained in the annex to this Charter, are strenuously pursued.

Principle 19: Obligations of Contracting States

Each Contracting State shall recognize the objectives, commitments and the interrelated Principles enshrined in this Charter, and shall take the necessary steps to adopt such legislative or other measures as may be necessary, to give effect to the provisions of this Charter.

Source: OECS (2001)

(d) *Choice of participation structures and methodologies.* The precise participation structure or methodology used at any time within a strategy will depend upon:

■ the *specific strategy task* (information collection, analysis, decision-making, implementation, monitoring, etc);
■ the *maturity of the strategy* (the number of cycles or revisions the strategy has been through);
■ the nature of *horizontal/vertical* links and the actors involved.

Box 6.5 lists some *participatory structures* that are often best suited to specific groups. Based on experience so far, for most strategy tasks, the promising participation structures appear to be: the planning system; traditional structures (eg village-based systems, religious systems); the existing avenues for people's participation in specific sectors (eg public health, adult education, agricultural extension); and specially

Table 6.8 **Examples of participatory methodologies for strategy tasks**[4]

Tasks	Methodologies
Survey, analysis and monitoring	Participatory enquiry, including participatory resource surveys and 'green' audits
Decision-making	Consensus-building, negotiations and traditional methods, eg of conflict resolution
Implementation	Voluntary agreements (eg covenants) and joint management
Communications, information, education and monitoring	Seminars, workshops, interviews, phone-ins, websites, e-mail networks, exhibitions and plays

constituted committees, round tables and other groups formulated to take advantage of group dynamics. For communications, information, education and monitoring tasks, the useful structures so far have been: the education system, extension system, workshops and conferences, the arts/theatre and the media.

It is likely that the government planning and administration structure, and the political system will largely determine how a strategy for sustainable development can use both strategic planning frameworks and other local initiatives, and how far it can use existing decentralization structures. It will also partly determine what kind of mix of participatory and multidisciplinary approaches can be taken.

Some useful *participation methodologies* are listed in Table 6.8, and are described on pages 207–224. In most countries, the use of many of these methodologies in strategic planning processes will be relatively new, and skills in using them will be limited. So planning for capacity building will be important.

(e) *Communications, information and education*
The participatory aspects of a strategy require an ethically motivated, educated and socially aware public. However, in many areas, the public may not understand, or simply may not be interested, in the issues of 'sustainable development' as currently discussed in many national-level fora. Clearly, a two-way process of education and consultation is needed so that the sustainable development concept is understood in local terms. Chapter 7 discusses the considerable challenge of communicating 'sustainable development', and effective processes of communication, information and education which are essential complements and precursors to participation in a strategy.

(f) *Phasing and coordination*

Participation takes time, and government agencies may need to participate among themselves first before being able to interact with others

It is inevitable that a strategy process will be slower with participation than without, but experience shows that a participatory process is likely to be much better (Bass et al 1995; Carew-Reid 1997; Lopez Ornat 1997; Wood 1997). We should expect an NSDS to progress in a manner and over a timescale set by the main participation processes, and by the pace at which stakeholders consult with their constituencies and reach agreements. Consensus building and conflict resolution can take a considerable time; and past experience indicates that these processes usually have to be phased to deal with the *least* contentious issues first.

Sustainable development will entail quite radical changes in institutional roles. In some circumstances, governments might best focus on integration across ministries and departments first, before going on to a

---

4 A good resource book on methods of participation geared for use by corporate clients is provided by Spencer (1989). It critically examines the technology of participation and offers useful guidance at the practical level.

Box 6.16 Sectoral collaboration for environmental management in Trinidad and Tobago

The Environmental Management Authority (EMA) is required to facilitate cooperation and to manage the environment in a way which fosters participation and promotes consensus. It has signed over 30 Memoranda of Understanding (MOU) with a range of governmental and parastatal agencies that have environmental functions. Routine meetings with designated sectoral Environmental Officers (EOs), and special reporting requirements enable formal cooperation and collaboration within the official sector. EOs have been appointed as representatives of those agencies which have signed MOUs and act as the liaison between the agency and the EMA.

Much of the work of the EMA is done through advisory and other committees, the composition of which is drawn from various sectors as well as from NGOs and community-based groups.

Source: Trinidad EMA Annual State of Environment Reports; http://www.ema.co.tt/main.htm

---

wider, participatory process with many civil society and private sector stakeholders. This may well be the case for government systems, which recognize the risks of moving from centralized, sectoral norms towards more experimental, integrated, participatory modes of operating. For example, Box 6.16 summarizes the situation in Trinidad and Tobago, where formal memoranda of understanding have been signed between the coordinating body and sectoral agencies to formalize collaboration.

It follows, therefore, that a phased approach to participation will be required, beginning with the use of participation structures and methodologies with which the majority of participants are familiar, and which are acceptable scientifically and politically. It will probably not be possible to both focus and get adequate detail from all the stakeholder groups in the initial strategy cycle. As with the scope of the strategy, it can be best to build up to greater ambitions in participation. The capacity for participation can be built throughout the process – indeed, it is participation capabilities that have been the subject of much of the capacity building of many successful (local) strategies.

Methods for participation in strategies

Participatory learning and action

The natural sciences have developed a wide range of objective methods to gather and analyse data. But the situation is different when it comes to management, social issues and determining opinions: you can't stick a meter into a farmer to find out what he thinks.

Social scientists have usually used *extractive* techniques such as household surveys and questionnaires, where large numbers of people can be surveyed and statistical techniques can be applied to determine the reliability of the results. However, these methods do not reveal local complexities: many of the contextual grounds for understanding the data are systematically removed or ignored, there is a tacit assumption that the respondent and researcher hold the same values, and cultural divisions affect the types of response. Multiple perspectives are lost. Gill (1993) has captured a real problem with interview and questionnaire approaches:

The stranger then produces a little board and, clipped to it, a wad of paper covered in what to the respondent are unintelligible hieroglyphics. He then proceeds to ask questions and write down answers – more hieroglyphics. The respondent has no idea of what is being written down, whether his or her words have been understood or interpreted correctly ... The interview complete, the enumerator departs and is probably never seen again.

It is difficult to uncover diverse stakeholder perspectives and needs ...

Box 6.17 Principles of participatory learning and action

The term *participatory learning and action* (PLA) is now used to encompass a suite of techniques for diagnostics, planning, implementing and evaluating development activities. The key principles are:

- *Cumulative learning by all the participants.* Interaction is fundamental to these approaches and a visual emphasis enables all people to take part on an equal basis.
- *Seek diversity* rather than attempt to characterize complexity in terms of average values. Different individuals and groups make different evaluations of situations, which lead to different actions. All views of activity or purpose are laden with interpretation, bias and prejudice. Therefore there are many possible descriptions of any activity.
- *Group learning.* The complexity of the world will be revealed only through group enquiry and interaction which requires a mix of investigators from different disciplines, from different sectors, outsiders (professionals) and insiders (local people).
- *Context-specific.* The approaches are flexible enough to be adapted to suit each new set of conditions and participants, so there are many variants.
- *Facilitating role of experts.* The goal is to bring about changes that the stakeholders regard as improvements. The role of the 'expert' is to help people in their particular situation carry out their own study and make their own plans.
- *Sustained action.* The learning process leads to debate about change. Debate changes the perceptions of the participants and their readiness to contemplate action. Action is agreed, so implementable changes will represent an accommodation between different views. The debate and/or analysis both defines changes which would bring about improvement and seeks to motivate people to take action to bring about those changes. This action includes strengthening local institutions, so increasing the capacity of people to initiate action on their own.

Source: Pretty et al (1995)

... but PLA approaches are filling the gap; they are strongly compatible with NSDS principles

There are alternatives to extractive techniques that have won wide acceptance and considerable credibility. In the 1980s and 1990s, there was a blossoming of participatory approaches – accompanied by a babel of acronyms. Some focus on problem diagnosis; for example, AEA (agro-ecosystems analysis), DRR (diagnostico rural rapido), RRA (rapid rural appraisal) and MARP (*methode acceleré de recherche participative*). Others are oriented towards community empowerment; for example, PAR (participatory action research) and TFD (theatre for development). Some facilitate on-farm or user-led research, such as FPR (farmer participatory research). Others are designed simply to get professionals in the field listening to resource users; for example, SB (*samuhik brahman* – joint trek). Some have been developed in the health context, for example RAP (resource assessment procedure); some for watershed development, for example PALM (participatory analysis and learning methods); some in government extension agencies and others in NGOs. The diversity of names, derivations and applications is a sign of strength because each variation is, to some extent, dependent on its local context. However, they are underpinned by some common principles (Box 6.17), principal among which is the new learning path that needs to be followed.

Participatory learning and action is the antithesis of teaching and technology transfer, both of which imply transfer of information from one who knows to one who does not know. Its assumptions are completely different from those of conventional surveys, and have grown more distinct as the techniques have evolved. For example, early work in farming systems analysis and rapid rural appraisal was essentially extractive. Researchers collected data and took it away for analysis. There has been a significant shift towards investigation and analysis by local people, who then share their insights with outsiders. Methods such as participatory mapping, analysis of air photos, matrix scoring and ranking, flow and linkage diagrams, and seasonal analysis are not just means for local people to inform outsiders. Rather, they are methods for local people to undertake their own research (Chambers 1992). Local people using these

Table 6.9 Techniques of participatory learning

Group and team interaction	Sampling	Dialogue	Visualization and drawing
■ Team contracts ■ Team reviews and discussions ■ Interview guides and checklists ■ Rapid report writing ■ Energizers/ activators ■ Work sharing (taking part in local activities) ■ Villager and shared presentations ■ Process notes and personal diaries	■ Transect walks ■ Wealth ranking and well-being ranking ■ Social maps ■ Interview maps	■ Semi-structured interviewing ■ Direct observation ■ Focus groups ■ Key informants ■ Ethnohistories and biographies ■ Oral histories ■ Local stories, portraits and case studies	■ Mapping and modelling ■ Social maps and wealth rankings ■ Transects ■ Mobility maps ■ Seasonal calendars ■ Daily routines and activity profiles ■ Historical profiles ■ Trend analyses and time lines ■ Matrix scoring ■ Preference or pairwise ranking ■ Venn diagrams ■ Network diagrams ■ Systems diagrams ■ Flow diagrams ■ Pie diagrams

Source: Bass et al (1995)

methods have shown a greater capacity to observe, create concepts and undertake analyses than most outsiders had expected and are, also, proving to be good teachers (see, for example, Box 6.4 on community turtle conservation in Trinidad).

The techniques of participatory learning fall into four groups (Table 6.9): group and team interaction, sampling, dialogue, visualization and drawing. One of the strengths of participatory learning has been the emphasis on pictorial techniques. By creating and discussing a diagram, model or map (see, for example, Figure 6.5), all who are present – both insider and outsider – can see, point to, discuss and refine the picture, sharing in its creation and analysis. Non-literates are not excluded; everyone who can see has visual literacy which allows them to participate actively – although, admittedly, not everyone may be able to speak up in such gatherings.

Early approaches (notably rapid rural appraisal) emphasized speed, and the label 'quick and dirty' has sometimes been applied. As the discipline has evolved, the emphasis has moved from quick exploitation of local people's labour or knowledge (to push through projects or facilitate research) towards sharing over a longer period, with contributions from both sides and patient iteration (Box 6.18).

This avoids some of the biases of rapid rural appraisal: spatial (emphasis on valuable land or sites undergoing construction), personal (led by leaders, entrepreneurs, professionals, English-speakers, males), often undertaken only in the dry-season (when access is easiest/possible), politeness and timidity (eg outsiders not shown the worst conditions and will not ask searching questions).

It is not simply the techniques themselves, but the combination and sequence in which they are used, that makes PLA particularly useful for understanding the myriad issues and values at the local level. For example:

Source: Denniston (1995)

Figure 6.5 **Land use map made by an indigenous surveyor and villagers of the Marwa sub-region, Panama**

Box 6.18 **RRA and PRA compared**

Among the various approaches of participatory learning and action, perhaps the best known are rapid rural appraisal (RRA), which emerged in the late 1970s and evolved a decade later into participatory rural appraisal (PRA).

RRA developed as a response to a growing awareness that conventional planning approaches failed to meet the needs of the rural poor. It was introduced as a planning approach to help minimize existing investigation biases, to provide an alternative to the limitations of questionnaire surveys, and to give timely information for externally driven planning.

PRA built on the principles and methods of RRA but placed added emphasis on empowering local people to undertake their own appraisals, to analyse and act on them, and to monitor and evaluate local changes.

Both approaches use similar methods (see Table 8.3) but differ in their purpose and process. RRA is used mainly to collect information and enable 'outsiders' to learn. By comparison, PRA is more relaxed and creative and places emphasis on facilitating local processes of learning and analysis, sharing knowledge and building partnerships among individuals and interest groups for local-level planning and actions. Consequently, it is a much longer and open-ended process.

Source: Guijt and Hinchcliffe (1998)

- Social mapping and well-being ranking can identify diverse socio-economic groups within a community, enabling data collection to be better targeted, to understand how wealth and social aspects affect people's dependence on resources.
- Seasonal calendars and timelines can be used to understand how the use and importance of natural resources varies over time.
- Maps, models and transects can be used to locate and appreciate the spatial relationships of particular resources. When developed with elders, these can aid understanding of historical changes in resource status.
- The values of natural resources can be elicited using a variety of matrix scoring and ranking techniques. These reveal not only how valuable different resources (eg tree species) are to different people, but also the ways in which they may be important, including non-financial values, and their relative importance compared with other resources and activities.
- Product flow diagrams and tenure maps can be used to understand how resources and access to them are controlled, and to clarify who is and is not involved in their use and management.

The usefulness of participatory learning approaches is also determined by the attitude of mind and behaviour of the professionals towards the people with whom they work. Success comes from rapport, dialogue and fair sharing of information and ideas – which means that the professionals too must have attractive 'trade goods' and must appreciate what they are getting in return.

Community-based resource planning and management

Progress on the ground seems to occur best where there is an equal and long-standing partnership between local land users, planners and technical (natural resources) specialists. In a review of experience of rural planning in developing countries, Dalal-Clayton et al (2000) provide examples of a range of approaches to community-based participatory planning (Box 6.19), many of which can be built on in developing local strategies for sustainable development.

Community-based programmes have used many purposeful participatory approaches; these also can be strong contributors to NSDSs

Such initiatives have usually been most successful when they have supported local capacity utilization and development, stakeholder organization, information and education. They share the characteristic of being strongly outcome-oriented; that is, participation helps to achieve agreed local ends, rather than being treated as a (political) end in its own right.

Brown (1997) describes how the authority of state agencies to control coastal and marine resources was devolved to community stakeholders in St Lucia. This resulted in more efficient management of these resources. Mechanisms to address conflict and competition were developed with full participation of all stakeholders. Problems remain, but there is genuine community commitment to engage in the multi-stakeholder process formalized within the framework of the Soufriere Marine Management Area.

One community-based methodology for participation in planning offers several lessons for strategies. In Planning for Real in the UK (Box 6.20), communities are involved fully in interactive participation for neighbourhood planning. The tendency for outside professionals to dominate is held in check by several agreed norms for group behaviour. These norms take time to develop, and are critical for successful participation and collaboration.

Participation in decentralized planning systems

It is often only at the local level that a people-centred approach to sustainable development becomes truly evident – for at this level, decisions are taken daily by individuals and groups of people that affect their livelihoods, health and often their survival. Concepts have to become realities. In a local context, individuals

Decentralized planning systems offer new opportunities for participation

Box 6.19 **Some examples of participatory rural planning**

Local-level resource planning

- community-based natural resources management (CBNRM) initiatives such as CAMPFIRE in Zimbabwe (see PlanAfric 1997);
- Aga Khan Rural Support Programme in India and Pakistan (see World Bank 1995b);
- Participatory reforestation in Baruch District, South Gujarat, India (Shah 1995)
- Village-level planning, for example, the HIMA programme in Tanzania (Kikula et al 1999)

Attempts to scale-up and link bottom-up and top-down planning

- the Regional Rural Development (RRD) approach (GTZ 1993);
- rapid district appraisal – a broader-scale application of RRA used in Indonesia (see Kievelitz 1995);
- participatory approaches in large-scale projects (eg North Western Province Dry Zone Participatory Development Project, Sri Lanka, see Backhaus and Wagachi 1995);
- the catchment approach to soil and water conservation in Kenya (Harding et al 1996);
- water catchment planning in Zimbabwe (PlanAfric 2000);
- the *Gestion de Terroir* approach to land use planning in francophone West Africa (Winckler et al 1995);
- responsibility for planning and programme implementation delegated to independent sectoral organizations, as in the Mexican Programme for the Protection of Tropical Forests (PROAFT) (Zazueta 1995);
- community forest programmes, for example, in Nepal (Fisher 1995);
- The community-based Landcare movement in Australia, concerned with conservation and management of land (Campbell et al 1996; Lockie and Vanclay 1997).

Case studies of these and other approaches to participatory rural planning are provided in Dalal-Clayton et al (2000).

Box 6.20 **Planning for real: neighbourhood planning in urban Britain**

In community development, there is a need for all views to be accounted for, yet the talkers nearly always win. At public meetings and consultations, local planners tend to sit on a platform, behind a table, maintaining their superiority. When only a few people turn up, and only a few of them speak up, they blame local indifference. Planning for Real attempts to bridge this gap, to identify local needs and resources, and to do it without endless talk.

The focus is a physical model of the neighbourhood. Unlike an architect's model, this should be touched, played with, dropped and changed around. At the first meeting, the neighbourhood model is constructed, using houses and apartment blocks made from card and paper on a polystyrene base. The model then goes into the community (to the launderette, the school foyer, the local shops, etc) so that people see it and learn about the second consultation. At the second meeting, the objective is to find out: 'have we got it right?' There is no room for passivity, not many chairs, no platform, with the model in the middle of the room. People spot the landmarks, discuss, identify problems and glimpse solutions. They move around, and can put down pieces of paper with suggested solutions written on them at particular locations. They are permitted to put more than one on the same place – so allowing conflicts to surface. Often, people who put down an idea wait for others to talk first about it. The process permits people to have first, second and third thoughts – they can change their minds. The model allows people to address conflicts without needing to identify themselves. It depersonalizes conflicts and introduces informality where consensus is more easily reached.

The professionals attend too. The local planners, engineers, transport officials, police, social workers and others wear a badge identifying themselves. *But they can only talk when they are spoken to.* The result is that they are drawn in, and begin to like this new role. The 'us and them' barriers begin to break down. The priorities put on the model have 'disagree' written on the reverse side. Anyone can turn these over, again remaining anonymous. The priorities are assessed as Now, Soon or Later, and also on the basis of whether they can be done solely by local people (with the help of outsiders, with some money and advice) or only by outsiders. Obligations are negotiated and made explicit. People are able to negotiate compromises.

The next stage is a local talent survey conducted by local people. The form is pictorial and does not look like a government form. The human resources are documented, and planning can then capitalize on these hitherto hidden resources. Participation in this alternative planning process acts as a demonstration of local capacity, from which larger things can grow.

Source: Gibson (1991)

and communities are best placed to identify the major trends, challenges, problems and needs, and to agree their own priorities and preferences and determine what skills and capacities are lacking. Hence, some strategies are now beginning to concentrate particular issues at the most appropriate level; for example, the approach followed by the Ministry of Planning in Bangladesh in the early 1990s to develop the Participatory Perspective Plan, or the emerging 'hierarchy' of strategies in Pakistan – Box 4.12.

A combination of top-down and bottom-up approaches is emerging in district planning in some countries. For example, in Tanzania, ward planning in Rungwe District involves top-down decisions on certain matters (eg setting ward bank rates) but stakeholder participation is encouraged on other aspects of development (eg education, agricultural production and communication).

Strategies need to consider which *mechanisms* can achieve this balance between top-down and bottom-up approaches. The new planning systems in a number of countries provide examples of how decentralization can contribute to this (Boxes 6.21 and 3.21). Such balance needs to be accompanied and supported by mechanisms that ensure good dialogue, ongoing monitoring information flow and learning within and between all levels. The challenges of decentralization are discussed on pages 20–22 and examples of sub-national strategic planning approaches are provided on pages 63–66.

Multi-stakeholder partnerships

Increasingly, multi-stakeholder partnerships are being used to address development issues and to negotiate solutions. But, as with participation, the term 'partnership' can be used to mean different things (Box 6.22).

An NSDS itself is, primarily, a multi-stakeholder partnership

A recent review of multi-stakeholder processes by UNED Forum (2001) describes them as being:

akin to a new species in the ecosystem of decision-finding and governance structures and processes ... [that] have emerged because there is a perceived need for a more inclusive, effective manner for addressing the urgent sustainability issues of our time.

The review notes that such multi-stakeholder processes include a broad body of approaches:

The term multi-stakeholder processes is used to describe processes which aim to bring together all major stakeholders in a new form of decision-finding (and possibly decision-making) structure on a particular issue. They are also based on recognition of the importance of achieving equity and accountability in communication between stakeholders, involving equitable representation of three or more stakeholder groups and their views. They are based on democratic principles of transparency and participation, and aim to develop partnerships and strengthened networks between stakeholders. MSPs cover a wide spectrum of structures and levels of engagement. They can comprise dialogue (statements, exchange and discussion), or grow into processes encompassing consensus-building, decision-making and implementation. The exact nature of any MSP will depend on the issue, the participants, the time-frame, etc.

It suggests a range of key principles of such processes (Box 6.23) – which are entirely consistent with those for strategies for sustainable development given in Box 3.1.

A good example of a multi-stakeholder partnership at the national level is the Canadian *Projet de société* – one of the most participative national strategy processes to have been undertaken (Box 6.24). Many such multi-stakeholder processes include special efforts to involve particular groups; for example, the development of New Zealand's Resource Management Act (Box 6.25).

Box 6.21 Decentralized planning systems

Bolivia introduced a decentralized, participatory planning system in 1994 with the adoption of the Law on Popular Participation and Administrative Decentralization (Box 6.14). This transferred significant political and economic power to regional and local levels. Twenty per cent of national tax revenue is passed directly to 314 municipalities and is allocated according to their five-year development plans. These municipal plans are developed under the guidance of the five-year Global (ie national) Plan for Economic and Social Development and on the basis of priorities identified by territorial organizations representing communities in particular areas. In addition, accountability committees, comprising municipal officers and civil society representatives, have been established to monitor the activities of municipal governments and their adherence to development plans. In parallel, regional government departments receive 40 per cent of national revenue allocated according to regional five-year development plans developed on the basis of the national indicative plan and municipal plans.

Nepal. The 1998 Local Self-Governance Act transferred power and responsibility to development committees in districts, municipalities and villages – these now undertake participatory planning and the sustainable management of resources in their areas. The district planning committees are seen as autonomous bodies, responsible for bringing stakeholders together and for harmonizing/balancing local needs and national policies.

Thailand. In the past, all projects and budgets for local and provincial authorities were set by central government. Now, stakeholders, through participatory planning processes, produce information, ideas and proposals – which are channelled to the Budget Bureau. This is responsible for financial allocations to local, municipal and provincial authorities. Under the new law on decentralization, government authorities at these levels are allocated a fixed percentage of the total government budget to enable them to implement the plans and projects determined by stakeholders.

For decentralized planning in **Ghana**, see Box 3.21.

Source: OECD DAC (2001a)

Stakeholder energies can be united by discussing major trends and searching for desirable 'futures'

One of several methods to promote participation in policy-making is the 'future search conference', a multi-stakeholder forum introduced by the Australian systems thinker Fred Emery (Emery and Emery 1978). It has been used throughout the world for a wide range of purposes: for example, to help develop a nature tourism strategy in the Windward Islands (Box 6.26), Pakistan's National Conservation Strategy and Colombia's energy sector policy. As described by Baburoglu and Garr (1992):

The conference [usually 35–40 participants, 2–3 days] uses a systematic process in which groups design the future they want and strategies for achieving it. The 'search' is for an achievable future. This may be a future that is more desirable than the one that is likely to unfold if no action is taken, or a future that is totally unexpected. Designing a future collectively

Box 6.22 Partnerships – a loaded term

Like 'participation' nobody will disagree that 'partnerships' are a good idea – but this agreement in itself will not change players' relationships overnight. Indeed, some argue that working in partnership is a deeply unnatural form of behaviour. The word can imply 'business partners' and/or the more difficult 'partners as equals'. Taking the notion of a business partnership beyond its origin in the private sector, and using it to mean a relationship which allows the business at hand to be dealt with, it begins to make more sense. Taking it a step further, the term 'deal' may be more useful for 'business transactions', which are mutually acceptable (or bearable) to the parties. Striking such deals within an NSDS may or may not move the relationship towards a partnership of equals – but it will at least engender the need for 'give and take' to build partnerships that can address some of the NSDS's core concerns. Partnerships may start as small catalytic actions by a couple of people or partner organizations, demonstrating something tangible and attracting others to join the action.

Source: Adapted from Mayers et al (2001)

Box 6.23 **Principles for multi-stakeholder processes**

These principles are based on experience and common lessons from a detailed review of a wide range of national and international multi-stakeholder initiatives. They reflect those characteristics of the processes that have been effective and represent best practice. They show close links with the principles of participatory learning and action (Box 6.17) but are distinct.

Accountability: Employing agreed, transparent, democratic mechanisms of engagement, position-finding, decision-making, implementation, monitoring and evaluation.

Effectiveness: Providing a tool for addressing urgent sustainability issues; promoting better decisions by means of wider input; generating recommendations that have broad support; creating commitment through participants identifying with the outcome and thus increasing the likelihood of successful implementation.

Equity: Levelling the playing field between stakeholder groups whose 'traditional' lobbying activities largely depend on their resources and are therefore imbalanced; applying principles of gender and regional balance; providing equitable access to information.

Flexibility: Covering a wide spectrum of structures and levels of engagement, depending on issues, participants, linkage into decision-making, timeframe and so on.

Good governance: Further developing the role of stakeholder participation and collaboration in (inter) governmental systems as supplementary and complementary vis-à-vis the roles and responsibilities of governments, based on clear norms and standards.

Inclusiveness: Allowing all views to be represented increases the legitimacy and credibility of a participatory process.

Learning: Taking a learning approach throughout their design; requiring participants to learn from each other.

Legitimacy: Requiring democratic, transparent, accountable, equitable processes in their design; requiring participants to adhere to those principles.

Ownership: People-centred processes, allowing ownership for decisions, thus increasing chances of successful implementation.

Participation and engagement: Bringing together the principal actors; supporting and challenging all stakeholders to be actively engaged.

Partnership/cooperative management: Developing partnerships and strengthening networks between stakeholders; addressing conflictual issues; integrating diverse viewpoints; creating mutual benefits (win–win rather than win–lose situations); developing shared power and responsibilities; creating feedback loops between local, national or international levels and into decision-making.

Societal gains: Creating trust through honouring each participant as contributing a necessary component of the bigger picture; helping participants to overcome stereotypical perceptions and prejudice.

Strengthening of (inter) governmental institutions: Developing advanced mechanisms of transparent, equitable and legitimate stakeholder participation strengthens institutions in terms of democratic governance and increased ability to address global challenges.

Transparency: Bringing all relevant stakeholders together in one forum and within an agreed process.

Voices, not votes: Making voices of various stakeholders effectively heard.

Source: UNED Forum (2001)

Box 6.24 **The multi-stakeholder approach of Canada's *Projet de société***

The Projet de société recognized several necessities: that the transition to sustainability is a collective responsibility of all Canadians; that all levels and sectors of society must be engaged in identifying and implementing the necessary changes; and that new institutional models and processes are needed to achieve a common purpose and course of action. These involve partnerships and networks.

Five Canadian organizations came together to organize a First National Stakeholders meeting in November 1992: the Canadian Council of Ministers of the Environment (CCME); Environment Canada; the International Institute for Sustainable Development (IISD); the International Development Research Centre (IDRC); and the National Round Table on the Environment and the Economy (NRTEE). Representatives from over 40 sectors of Canadian society attended the meeting, including business associations, community organizations and indigenous peoples.

Each of the five 'sponsoring' organizations, acting as a Working Group, contributed Can$50,000 to establish a secretariat and hire a research director. Two sub-committees (Documentation and Information; and Vision and Process) assumed responsibility, respectively, to analyse Canadian responses to Rio, and to draft a concept paper on sustainability planning. The NRTEE facilitated and chaired the process and provided the secretariat. Most of the tasks were undertaken by volunteers and committees which met monthly. There were those who wanted to 'develop strategic plans' and others who wanted 'do specific projects'. It was therefore decided to do both.

A progress report and recommendations were presented to a Second National Stakeholders meeting in June 1993. At the Third Assembly in December 1993, the NRTEE was asked to assume a larger management role for the next phase of the Projet, rather than merely acting as a facilitator, and to move towards preparing a draft strategy. The NRTEE worked closely with a volunteer working group to develop, revise and critique a strategy document. A draft was tabled at the Fourth Assembly in November 1994, entitled 'Canadian Choices for Transitions to Sustainability'. Minor changes were suggested and the document was endorsed. A revised document was published in January 1995. The NRTEE then organized a series of 12 meetings across the country to determine how useful such a document might be in engaging various constituencies in discussions about sustainability. A final revised draft, based on the feedback received, was published in June 1995. The Working Group, which had been reconstituted in early 1995, in addition to completing the strategy document, developed a work plan involving, among other things, the compilation of a directory of sustainability tool kits for communities. Sustainable livelihoods was selected as a focus for Working Group activities, with a forum on this subject in 1996.

Principles of the Projet de société:

- The process was designed to be transparent, inclusive and accountable.
- Each partner and sector was encouraged to identify and take responsibility for its own contribution to sustainability.
- Dialogue and cooperation among sectors and communities were key elements of problem-solving.
- A shared vision and agreement on key policy, institutional and individual changes were seen as necessary for the transition to sustainability.
- It was stressed that strategy and action must be linked, and must build on previous and ongoing initiatives.
- Canada's practice of sustainable development and its contribution to global sustainability should be exemplary.

Sources: Projet de société (1993, 1994, 1995)

unleashes a creative way of producing organizational philosophy, mission, goals and objectives enriched by shared values and beliefs of the participants. This process is especially useful in times of social, economic and technological turbulence [characterized by unexpected changes, uncertainty, unintended consequences and complexity].

In recent years, periods of upheaval in social and political conditions have provided fertile ground for forging tri-sector (government, civil society and private sector) partnerships for change. For example, in South Africa, the ANC government has established the National Economic Development and Labour Council with a membership drawn from business, government and civil society, and with labour organizations effectively making up a fourth sector. This forum is charged with making multilateral decisions to impact on policy, economic growth and social equity (Box 6.27). In Grenada, the Prime Minister chairs a regular tri-partite forum involving representatives from government, business and labour.

Box 6.25 **Involving the public, and particularly Maoris, in developing New Zealand's Resource Management Act**

The resource management act (RMA) was a major piece of reforming legislation, which aimed to rationalize severe inequities in the way environmental management operated across different sectors, to integrate national planning and decision-making, to address the plethora of legislation that dealt with natural resources, and to provide a single objective – namely, the sustainable management of natural and physical resources. In developing the act, a massive attempt was made to involve the public through meetings, seminars, free phone-ins and written submissions. All papers submitted to government on the RMA highlighted where stakeholder views accorded or differed from proposals being made. A special stream for Maori consultation was established. This involved traditional-style meetings (*hui*) with Maori organizations throughout the country to explain the RMA process and to secure views and opinions. Funds were made available to enable NGOs to engage in the process and some NGOs undertook commissioned work.

Source: Dalal-Clayton (1996)

The benefits of the tri-sector partnership to individual partners may differ, but can still be complementary (Tennyson and Wilde 2000):

- Public sector partners are viewed as more responsive and accessible through their engagement with the partnership.
- Private sector partners become more stable and successful, and therefore profitable.
- Civil society partners gain a wider reach and have greater impact.

Sustainable development partnerships bring different advantages to each partner

Each sector can bring its own set of resources to the partnership, and these are not just money (Table 6.10).

Focusing on consensus, negotiations and conflict resolution

The early establishment of consensus on key issues such as the purpose of the NSDS and, subsequently, its vision and priorities, is a source of strength – both for the strategy's durability and for its ability to lead to change for the better. Consensus is a best-bet principle for strategies, but particular issues will also need negotiation and conflict resolution. These decision-making tasks depend on sound participation. They are considered in detail in Chapter 8 on decision-making (pages 270–276).

Table 6.10 **Potential resources from organizations in the development triad**

Public sector	Private sector	Civil society
■ Access to information ■ Skilled staff with a public interest focus ■ Surplus of accommodation and transport capacity ■ Authority to mobilize resources from other public sector sources ■ Budget process ■ Stability	■ Management and technical skills ■ Equipment ■ Dissemination and distribution capacity ■ Contacts and sphere of influence ■ Innovation ■ Financial resources/rigour ■ Fast-acting	■ On-the-ground know-how ■ Development experience and knowledge ■ People skills ■ Imaginative, low-cost responses to challenges ■ Social mobilization and public advocacy skills ■ Associated credibility ■ Values-driven

Source: Tennyson and Wilde (2000)

Box 6.26 Search conferences and nature tourism strategies in the Windward Islands

Search conferences were held in four Windward Island countries in the Eastern Caribbean during 1991/92 as part of a process to develop nature tourism strategies. The stimulus was the threat to banana exports in the face of an impending change in trade relations with the UK in 1992. This was expected to lead to increased economic dependence on tourism. Limited potential for expanding traditional tourism resulted in a growing interest in nature tourism (also called ecotourism).

The search conference process was initiated by senior officials in government agencies with a direct interest in tourism (planning/economic development, tourism and forestry). The Canada-based 'Adapting By Learning Group' acted as facilitators. In each country, key stakeholders were brought together by the government body acting as the lead agency – either tourism or planning. Stakeholders included: government agencies (economic development, planning, tourism, agriculture, fisheries, finance, forestry), environmental and heritage groups, community organizations, women's and youth groups, farmers' cooperatives and private business. Their initial task was to form National Advisory Groups to direct the process.

The search conference process allowed the political implications of nature tourism to be addressed by the full range of interests involved: for example, environmentalists examining the validity of nature tourism as an economic development strategy; hotel associations incorporating environmental conservation into tourism strategies; and finance officials working with agricultural ministry personnel to support small businesses in the provision of local produce for tourist consumption.

The objectives of the conferences were to:

- develop comprehensive national perspectives on nature tourism;
- examine the potential of an integrated nature tourism strategy as a basis for future economic development that is environmentally sustainable;
- discuss the planning, design and management needs of such an approach;
- connect this alternative approach to existing tourism initiatives;
- advise on ways in which the search conference initiative could assist in creating an integrated and ongoing planning capacity both nationally and regionally.

Each conference involved alternating plenary and small group sessions with presentations (by local participants with special skills and experience) to provide a basis for discussions. The small groups generated issues and concerns, which were reported in plenary. Key issues were selected to focus subsequent group sessions, during which constraints and opportunities were identified. Ideas and concerns were then integrated into a set of recommendations for action, and submitted to the National Advisory Groups to be carried forward into further planning and implementation.

Source: Franklin and Morley (1992)

Working in groups

A majority of strategy tasks depend on the quality of group work

Strategies will need to employ a variety of approaches to engage different stakeholders. Many approaches involve group work (in meetings, seminars, focus and cross-sector groups, collective analysis, workshops, round tables, etc). For example, in many Local Agenda 21s, a working group:

> is typically a small body of 10 to 20 stakeholder representatives who have a particular interest or expertise in a specific issue or problem ... Working groups undertook the distinct tasks of issue identification, problem analysis, technical research, priority setting, action planning and impact analysis, implementation and monitoring, and evaluation and feedback. Some structures were used to collect and analyse information or to develop action proposals; others were used to integrate action proposals; others were used to develop performance indicators and to evaluate progress in achieving targets (ICLEI 1996a).

Box 6.27 **National Economic Development and Labour Council (NEDLAC), South Africa – an example of a public sector-led partnership initiative**

History

NEDLAC had its origins in the struggle against apartheid and unilateral decision-making, as well as in calls from all sectors of society for decisions to be taken in a more inclusive and transparent manner. It is a statutory body established under the NEDLAC Act, 1994, and was launched by President Mandela in 1995. NEDLAC provides a unique forum for multilateral decision-making to impact policy, economic growth and social equity in South Africa. It is an agreement-making body, not an advisory organization. Administrative costs are met by government.

Objectives

The NEDLAC Act enshrines the following objectives for the Council:

- Promote economic growth, participation in economic decision-making and social equity.
- Seek consensus and reach agreements pertaining to social and economic policy.
- Consider all proposed labour legislation.
- Consider all significant changes to social and economic policy.
- Encourage coordinated policy-making on social and economic matters.

Structures

National summit – (annual meeting of 300 people from all sectors) – receives inputs from and gives feedback to the affiliated organizations.

Executive Council – meets quarterly with up to 18 delegates from each 'constituency' (sector). Reviews progress, reaches consensus and concludes agreements.

Management Committee – meets monthly to oversee and coordinate activities.

Chambers – are issue-based (eg trade and industry; public finance and monetary policy; labour market and development). They meet frequently with six delegates from each constituency/sector to draft reports and make recommendations to the Executive Council.

Secretariat – supports all NEDLAC's activities and has 19 staff members.

Intermediary or partnership promotion role

A partnership of business, government, labour and civil society, NEDLAC acts as an intermediary between the partners, in addition to promoting partnership and consensus as its principal operational focus.

Main activities

NEDLAC focuses on building consensus between all constituencies/sectors in formulating policy for the South African government. All recommendations are presented in parliament and become the basis for new or revised legislation. Secretariat activities include:

- building the capacities of the representatives from each constituency to negotiate effectively;
- supporting the different structures (see above) in their work;
- making links with other public bodies;
- conducting research and undertaking investigations to ensure that all parties are kept informed of national and international developments in social and economic policy;
- drafting NEDLAC's annual report – tabled for discussion in parliament;
- communicating all agreements, reports and findings to the general public;
- monitoring implementation.

Source: Adapted from Tennyson (1998)

Box 6.28 The dynamics of group work

Some general observations:

- Groups generally produce fewer ideas than individuals working separately, but they often generate more appropriate ideas as each is discussed and thought through more deeply.
- Groups are more likely to identify errors of judgement before action is taken.
- Discussion stimulates more careful thinking and leads to consideration of a wider range of ideas. Rather surprisingly, good groups tend to take more adventurous decisions than the individuals comprising them would have done if acting independently.
- Groups that are too cohesive can also create their own problems. Religious sects, military groups, sports teams and political groups all show a tendency towards a dominant group identity. In extreme cases, the individual's conscience and principles are sacrificed for group loyalty, harmony and morale.
- Full consensus is not always desirable (see 8.3.3).
- Seeking a consensus at all costs can bring the group into a blind spot when it becomes highly selective in the facts it sees, sorts and accepts.
- Maintaining an open agenda, creating a sense of self-critical awareness and preventing secrecy within these types of groups is essential if group 'delusions' are to be prevented.

Stages in group functioning:

Several people brought together to work on a single research or development activity do not necessarily make a productive *team* of investigators (Handy 1985). Before a group of people can function well as a team, they tend to pass through a series of stages.

First, various individuals come together, sometimes as strangers, sometimes as colleagues, to create a new group for some stated purpose. In this early *forming* stage, they are still a collection of individuals, each with his or her own perspectives, agenda and expertise, and little or no shared experience.

As these individuals become more familiar with one another, the group will enter a *storming* phase. There is a good reason for giving this name to the second phase of group formation, because it is during this stage that personal values and principles are challenged, roles and responsibilities are taken on and/or rejected, and the group's objectives and mode of operating will start to be defined more clearly. If there is too much conflict and discord within the group, it will collapse. If, however, some common ground can be found, the group will gain greater cohesion and a sense of purpose.

As the group members begin to understand their roles in relation to one another and establish a shared vision or goal, they will develop a clearly discernible identity and group-specific norms of behaviour. At this *norming* stage, the group has settled down. People know each other better, they have accepted the rules and probably developed subgroups and friendships.

Once these norms have been established, the group will be ready for action and will enter into the *performing* phase. It is in this phase that they will work most effectively as a team. This team has a life of its own; its power to support learning may be considerable. The confidence level of the team members will have reached the point where they are willing to take significant risks and try out new ideas on their own.

It is important that the secretariat and facilitators are skilled in managing the dynamics of group working (Box 6.28). For a group to perform effectively, achieve its goals and build consensus, the individuals present should contribute to a wide mix of roles and functions (eg some individuals will be creative and spark ideas; some practical and able to turn ideas into practical actions; others more sober and analytical and capable of deep analysis, etc). They should also be reasonably compatible (although some conflict between members can avoid complacency).

FACILITATION

Facilitation skills are a basic requirement to ensure active participation and meaningful exchanges during workshops and other group activities (Box 6.29). Facilitators should have been involved in the strategy design process (where possible) or at least be fully briefed to ensure their full understanding of the process and their commitment to how it was decided to conduct the process.

It is worth investing in good facilitators to kick off the strategy – and then spreading facilitation capacity through the strategy process

Box 6.29 Facilitation skills

The **key role** of a facilitator is to:

- ensure the effective flow of communication within a group so that the participants can share information and arrive at decisions;
- pose problems and encourage group analysis;
- provoke people to think critically and motivate them towards action;
- not change or ignore any decisions reached by the participants through consensus;
- be sensitive, to both the verbal and the non-verbal communications that occur in the group;
- be sensitive to the feelings, attitudes, culture, interests and any hidden agenda that may be present in a group.

To **resolve conflict(s)**, a facilitator should be able to:

- sense where agreements should be explored;
- sense where disagreements should be respected;
- identify any irrelevances so that the focus will be on reaching an agreement;
- in exploring differences, ask problem-solving questions, not judgmental ones – and encourage all participants to do so.

A **good facilitator** will:

- have a good grip of the subject(s) being discussed (so as to keep things moving and to the point);
- closely track the direction and flow of discussion, noting everybody's contributions to draw out aspects of common ground when summarizing what has been said at regular intervals;
- when summarizing, state differences clearly, and not allow pressure to conform;
- be prepared with contingency plans (eg in case a speaker does not turn up);
- encourage an open atmosphere, conducive to learning and sharing ideas, making everyone feel welcome, important and recognized as part of the group;
- encourage everyone to speak freely, share and participate (including drawing out quieter participants);
- know his or her own limits and assess those of participants;
- have an idea of what is achievable and what is not;
- be sensitive regarding issues on which participants will need to consult with their constituencies;
- be aware of the condition and contribution of participants: who is responding, who is sleepy, who is not listening or frequently leaves the room, etc; this will signal when to change or adjust the discussion;
- manage the available time effectively, keeping to agreed timetables and speaking times – which need to be the same for everybody (with obvious exceptions for participants operating in another language and the like); Ttis means balancing being too tight or rigid and being too lax or liberal;
- be flexible and responsive to different situations (hence, they need considerable diagnostic skills to enable them to assess a given situation correctly);
- use creative approaches and techniques to encourage participation;
- judge when to call a halt to discussion, wait or carry on;
- be humble, respectful and recognize everyone's contributions;
- make sure the participants evaluate/assess the meeting, to provide feedback (whether formally or informally, quantitatively or qualitatively, orally or in writing – as appropriate).

Ways of working

- The group needs to agree on how to deal with possible substantive contributions from the facilitator. Alternating the role of the facilitator is an option.
- In some cases, it might be worth considering working with special facilitators to be the link into particular stakeholder groups.
- Using flip charts, meta-plan or other facilitation techniques is recommended in order to transparently keep track of what is being said, enable summarizing and help decision-making. Other group work techniques are worth considering and experimenting with. These include scenario workshops, future labs and citizen juries (depending on the situation, the issue, the cultural context and the group).

Source: Walker and Daniels (1997); UNED Forum (2001)

For guidance on facilitation and managing group meetings, see Pretty et al (1995).

Facilitators can help participants to avoid arguing for their favourite proposals but to make innovative suggestions; challenge them to be creative and integrative; not allow them to agree just to avoid conflict; and highlight differences as helpful. When decisions become stalled, the facilitator can point out where there is agreement to build on. When it is not possible to reach agreement on an issue, it can be agreed to revisit it at a later stage.

PARTICIPANTS' RESPONSIBILITIES

It is also important for participants to agree on, and observe, some basic ground rules if group work is to be effective. Box 6.30 suggests some based on a recent UNED survey of successful approaches.

RAPPORTEURS

Rapporteurs (persons responsible for reporting on the group's activities) need to be agreed by the group and assigned at the outset of meetings, as does the documentation process (minutes, reports, etc). Rapporteuring needs to be done in the most neutral fashion possible, reflecting the breadth and depth of discussions. It should usually concentrate on recording group-generated or -endorsed findings, ideas and decisions – rather than statements attributed to individuals.

Box 6.30 Illustrative ground rules for group working

From a recent survey, the following rules have proved to be effective tools in group working:

1   During discussion, participants must make every effort to be as frank and candid as possible, while maintaining a respectful interest in the views of others. An atmosphere that cultivates directness, openness, objectivity and humility is important.
2   Participants need to be honest and trustworthy.
3   Participants should refrain from personal attacks.
4   All participants and their contributions should be treated equally.
5   To help understanding and clarify perceptions, participants and facilitators should be encouraged to restate one another's views in their own words ('active listening').
6   Participants should refrain from presuming motives of others and rather be encouraged to ask direct questions.
7   Participants are asked to address the group as a whole, while showing concern for each point of view, rather than confronting and criticizing individuals.
8   Participants must argue on a logical basis, giving their own opinion while seeking out common ground as well as differences.
9   Brain-storming can be helpful: conducting a session of putting forward ideas and collecting them without judgements for later discussion can create a larger pool of ideas. When an idea is put forward, it becomes the property of the group.
10 Participants should consider conducting a learning exercise, to draw out the success of other processes and agreements and use the outcomes to deepen the pool of ideas.
11 All participants need to be open to change when embarking on a communication process as outlined above. A true dialogue cannot be entered into with the goal of 'getting one's way'.
12 Allow space and time for various modes of communication, socio-emotional as well as strictly task-oriented.
13 If participants feel that others are not playing by agreed rules, they need to put that to the group and the group needs to address the problem.

Source: UNED Forum (2001)

MEETING AGENDAS

The possibilities for the programme of any working group meetings or workshops are many and include:

1   Introductory activity:
    ■ participant introduction, giving names, organizational backgrounds, brief expectations of meeting outcomes (taking care not to take too much time);
    ■ scene setting – by local people (if in a particular locality) and/or the organizers;
    ■ summary of key issues – from different perspectives;
    ■ objective-setting exercise, to clarify the agenda.

2   Group work:
    ■ in sector groups;
    ■ in focus groups (perhaps each group discussing a different theme or issue);
    ■ in task groups (each group taking a specific task);
    ■ using perhaps 1–3 questions per group.

3   Plenaries:
    ■ feedback/presentation of group work to all participants;
    ■ case studies – national, from a particular locality or even from other countries;
    ■ presentations on problems or options from specialists;
    ■ audio-visual input;
    ■ outcomes from any background research.

4   Planning action and closing:
    ■ summary of the outcomes of the workshop/event;
    ■ proposed enhancements to existing policies, institutional arrangements, investments, programmes or projects, and so on;
    ■ identified new policies, institutional arrangements, investments, programmes or projects;
    ■ agreement on priorities;
    ■ creation of an action plan in small groups or together with all participants, ending with an agreement on who/what/when;
    ■ resource commitments in support of further action.

5   Appropriate breaks:
    These are essential for a variety of reasons – to:
    ■ enable group participants to get to know each other on a more personal level;
    ■ reduce/diffuse rising tensions;
    ■ foster opportunities for sub-group negotiations;
    ■ reduce boredom;
    ■ re-energize participants with refreshments;
    ■ avoid physical fatigue and emotional overloading.

Facilitators must be sensitive to group dynamics and should be sufficiently flexible to introduce breaks even when not timetabled.

Box 6.31 suggests a model timetable for a cross-sectoral workshop.

Box 6.31 **Example timetable for a cross-sectoral workshop**

Session 1 Welcome and introduction to workshop agenda

- Outline of workshop objectives
- Introduction to organizers and facilitator

Session 2 Sectoral groups

Separate sector discussions on:

- strengths and weaknesses of the sector;
- views of other sectors;
- benefits to each sector of cross-sector partnerships.

Break

Session 3 Plenary session

Brief feedback on each question in turn from each sector, followed by reactions and discussion

Session 4 Core value/principles

Identification of core values/principles underpinning any potential partnership initiative

Break (lunch)

Session 5 Case studies/issues

Guest speaker presentations of relevant examples of successful partnerships (local, national, regional or international as appropriate)

or

Key issues for the group – brainstorm on general sustainable development issues (eg developing integrated planning processes, building capacity for cross-sector partnerships) or a specific theme (eg youth unemployment, crime, enterprise development)

Session 6 Task group on action planning

Mixed-sector discussions on development of parallel aspects of the planning process

Session 7 Plenary session

- Brief feedback on action planning and implementation of integrated development strategy
- Agreement on who will do what

Feedback

- On how the workshop process was conducted
- On how happy participants feel about the outcomes

End

Note: This timetable can be spread over 1 to 3 days

Source: Adapted from Tennyson (1998)

Market research, electronic media and other remote methods

Telecommunications and the internet are providing ever-greater channels to elicit participation of the general public, as well as special interest groups. Strategy development by the UK's Forestry Commission, for example, has frequently made use of telephone surveys of the public's perception of forest values and their own needs. The UK and Belgian NSDSs received significant reactions to draft strategy papers placed on websites. But such 'market research' is not confined to the richer countries. It is being used in many countries where planners are becoming aware of the power of stakeholders to encourage change towards sustainable development, as in Grenada (Box 6.32).

The internet can keep participation going at little cost and high convenience to many stakeholders

---

Box 6.32 Market research clinches participatory forest policy, Grenada

In Grenada, a small nation in the Eastern Caribbean, a new era in forest policy – a participatory one –emerged in the late 1990s. To concerned individuals, the increasingly evident failure of previous forest policies – based on the preoccupations of foresters, politicians and foreign consultants – made it clear that a turn-around was needed, linked strongly to stakeholders' values. A consultative process was designed locally, reaching every parish.

However, the Grenadian Forest Dept (FD), which organized the process, was constrained by the fact that there were few traditional or governmental systems for consultation and participation. Indeed, 'participation' was a concept that had been strongly associated with the previous Communist regime.

Hence, the participatory methodologies used for the process had to be specially introduced: strings of meetings of various types, one-off studies linked to consultative groups, questionnaires, radio phone-ins and school lessons. While written material often had less impact than expected, meetings, workshops and interviews (many questionnaires were filled in through structured interviews eg with farmers) and other oral means worked well. Senior FD staff became alert to the fact that few women had been attending the local meetings, and responded with a meeting for representatives from women's groups. Building on the national predilection for TV and radio, a mix of awareness-raising broadcasts, phone-ins and surveys was carried out.

Most revealing (indeed of a very wide range of opinions) was the newspaper-based market research. This public opinion survey of the public's 'forest priorities' may be an artificial construct – a nation-wide view from the more highly educated classes rather than the specific local views of *different* groups. But its quantitative results were very significant in changing policy: the public ranking of forest priorities was almost precisely the reverse of what the FD had been doing – soil and water conservation and recreation coming top of the list, instead of wood supplies.

This was such a stark contrast that the FD had no choice but to: (a) thoroughly revise policy; and, perhaps more significantly, (b) make policy implementation a continuation of the participatory approach. The next stage of the forest strategy will be identifying and strengthening the local forms of governance, such as community, social and resource-user groups, as a basis for future planning, implementing and monitoring policy.

To sum up, much is revealed by the contrast between the previous FAO-supported Tropical Forest Action Plan (which was neither widely known, nor accepted as valid by those who did know it) and the new participatory policy. The new policy has been perceived – including by the Prime Minister – not only as a milestone towards a more viable and equitable use of forests, but also as a model for all country-driven policy development in Grenada.

Source: Bass (2000)

CHAPTER

7

Communications[1]

Introduction

On the assumption that previous chapters have made the NSDS philosophy and principles clear, this chapter focuses on practical ideas on the methods and channels for communication and information, as well as outlining some of the shifts required to unblock some of the all too frequent barriers to communications for, and about, sustainable development.

Effective communication is the 'lifeblood' of a sustainable development strategy

A strategy for sustainable development involves a long-term process of change. Capacity to manage this process is required at the individual, institutional and systemic levels. To be effective, a strategy needs to be participatory and interactive. Representatives of government, civil society and the private sector should be enabled to get to know each other, discuss challenges and perspectives, identify problems and needs, agree new objectives and roles, make transitions towards these ends, be kept up-to-date on progress and problems, and correct course when needed. These tasks depend critically on awareness, trust, coordination and mechanisms for dialogue. Conversely, misunderstanding and unrealistic expectations make a coordinated approach to sustainable development very difficult. In a world where all initiatives have to compete for attention, the strategy needs to be presented as an attractive initiative with clear opportunities and clear limits, to excite relevant stakeholder input and to ensure public support for its implementation.

Effective communication is the principal vehicle for the above tasks. It is no wonder that it has been called the 'lifeblood' of a strategy (Carew-Reid et al 1994). Indeed, without clear two-way communication, engaging all key stakeholders, a strategy will not succeed because cooperation and collaboration – which depend on it – are compromised (Figure 7.1).

The information, education and communications (IEC) strategy and action plan will influence the purpose and objectives of the NSDS, who is involved, what gets discussed, and what actions are taken and their outcomes. Its philosophy, rationale, methods, style and reach are, therefore, critical considerations. The NSDS principles and elements (Boxes 3.1 and 3.2) should be used to help develop the IEC strategy and action plan – they apply as much to communications as to the NSDS itself.

---

1 This chapter has benefited from review comments and additional material provided by Dafina Gercheva, Bulgaria; Saneeya Hussain, Panos, Nepal; Penny Stock, UNDP Capacity 21; and Lilian Chatterjee, IIED.

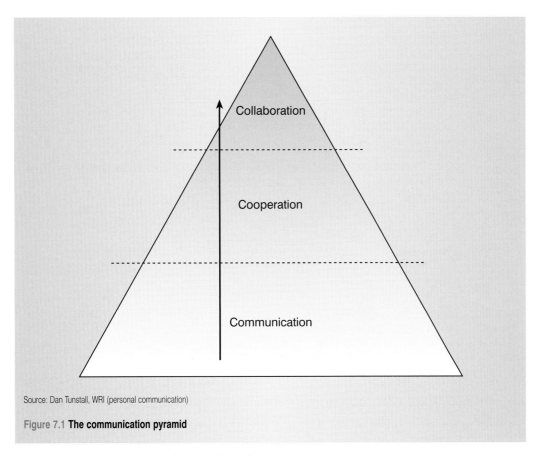

Source: Dan Tunstall, WRI (personal communication)

Figure 7.1 **The communication pyramid**

Shifting values, attitudes and styles

Experience from previous strategic planning frameworks reveals difficulties in:

- *Information management:* Accessing and generating information and knowledge to support the preparation and implementation of strategies.
- *Information use:* using information effectively once available.
- *Language:* Sharing information with participating stakeholders, and with the general public, on sustainable development in everyday and easily comprehensible language.
- *Targeting:* Providing information that is tailor-made and relevant to the needs and interests of different target groups.
- *Access:* Providing equal access to the information for all parties involved in the strategic planning.

Currently, information is provided without sufficient explanation or elucidation, and this is insufficient for the demands of modern strategic governance.

To overcome these difficulties there is a need for a coherent shift in values, attitudes and styles. The following requirements should be discussed early on in developing the IEC strategy:

- An 'easily understood' *conceptual basis or model* for sustainable development as a social construct, involving institutional change.
- A commitment to *disclosure of, access to, and provision of information* as an essential element of accountability and transparency. At the international level, Principle 10 of the Rio Declaration stressed the need for 'citizen's participation in environmental issues and for access to information on the environment held by public authorities'.[2] In some regions and countries, this has been

Strategy stakeholders need to agree on a commitment to good information access and provision

> **Box 7.1 The Aarhus Convention**
>
> The Aarhus Convention binds governments to make environmental information publicly available within a specific timeframe through national legislation.
>
> *'In order to contribute to the protection of the right of every person of present and future generations to live in an environment adequate to his or her health and well-being, each Party shall guarantee the rights of access to information, public participation in decision-making, and access to justice in environmental matters in accordance with the provisions of this Convention.' (Article 1)*
>
> Convention on access to information, public participation in decision-making and access to justice in environmental matters. Objective. Aarhus, Denmark, 25 June 1998.
>
> Source: http://www.unece.org/env/pp/treatytext.htm

followed up by conventions and legislation outlining civil rights in environmental and social issues; for example, the Aarhus Convention of the UN Commission for Europe has three 'pillars': access to information, public participation in decision-making and access to justice (see Box 7.1).

The Access Initiative is a global coalition of public interest groups that seeks to promote public access to information, participation and justice in environmental decision-making (Box 7.2).

- Acknowledgement that *information and power are inextricably linked* and that a realistic IEC strategy and action plan needs to be shaped by local as well as national realities. This will help to strengthen the NSDS process by promoting informed decision-making (Powell 1999). There is a need to analyse access to information by key stakeholders, taking account of age, gender, socio-economic status, culture or geographic location.
- A shift from just didactic ways ('us teaching them') to *more inclusive methods of communication, learning and dialogue* (eg round table discussions, seminars, negotiations, establishing strategic partnerships, etc). Strategy processes open up opportunities for innovative and two-way communication which enable the stakeholder groups to talk and listen actively to, and be informed by, each other (Howard and Scott-Villiers 2000). It is important to foster a *culture of dialogue* (across levels, sectors, borders), supported by networks (human and electronic) of practitioners, stakeholders and other change agents. These networks are essential to sustain the growth of (and linkages between) institutions and individuals, as well as to generate learning dynamics. The establishment of feedback mechanisms for learning is essential.
- *Empowering individuals and communities to take part in leaning, knowledge creation, sharing and use* through and for the strategy. It is useful to encourage stakeholders to prepare and bring their own information into the process rather than solicit new studies by external consultants.
- Recognition that communication can be an ill-defined discipline, misunderstood, under-valued and often ignored for its contribution (actual or potential) to development (Rockefeller Foundation 1999). This requires a shift from communicating often glossy, dull and uninspiring project and programme data to *understanding the information and communication needs* of stakeholders, enabling their *learning* through the strategy development process, and encouraging their *involvement in its implementation*.
- *Capitalizing on traditional, indigenous knowledge and culture.* Indigenous knowledge systems, as growing bodies of locally relevant experience and means for resilience, can make positive contributions. Institutional processes need to be able to value and encourage them.

---

2 Kofi A. Annan, Secretary-General of the United Nations. http://www.unece.org/env/pp/

Box 7.2 The Access Initiative

Launched in November 2000, the Access Initiative is led by the World Resources Institute (USA), Environmental and Management Law Association (Hungary), Corporación Participa (Chile) and the Thailand Environment Institute. To implement public access to information, participation and justice in environmental decision-making requires national policies, legislation, institutions and practices for *public access to*:

- information in emergencies and monitoring information about the quality of the environment and natural resources;
- information about the environmental performance of industrial facilities and/or pollution release and transfer registries (PRTRs);
- opportunity for review and comment on decisions on sectoral policies, programmes, plans with potential environmental impacts;
- opportunity for review and comment on environmental impact assessment (EIAs) and decisions on site-specific activities with environmental impacts;
- redress and remedy for infringement of rights to access to information and participation.

By proposing and assessing *benchmarks of performance in the above areas*, the Access Initiative aims to promote their establishment as good practices and common standards for all countries.

The Access Initiative will build on the momentum created by Europe's Aarhus Convention (see Box 7.1), and will provide support to civil society organizations in other regions seeking to promote similar norms of environmental governance. It is pursuing a two-track approach involving parallel strategies:

- A short-term strategy targeting the World Summit on Sustainable Development in August 2002 as an opportunity to assess progress towards implementation of Principle 10 in the Rio Declaration.
- A long-term strategy designed to develop an inclusive, decentralized and sustainable institutional framework to accelerate the implementation of Principle 10 in the years following the Summit.

In implementing its short-term strategy, the Access Initiative works at three levels:

At the national level in nine pilot countries (Chile, Hungary, India, Indonesia, Mexico, South Africa, Thailand, Uganda, USA), the Initiative will support local groups to conduct assessments and monitor the extent to which structures and practice of government agencies are consistent with commitments to access to information, participation and justice in environmental decision-making.

At the regional level, the Initiative will promote the adoption of best practices and implementation of regional instruments and/or commitments to access to information, participation and justice in environmental decision-making. Examples of such commitments include the Aarhus Convention and the Organization of American States' Inter-American Strategy to Promote Participation in Sustainable Development.

At the global level, the Initiative will support a coalition of organizations to collaborate on the development of indicators of implementation, and provide a platform for institutionalization of the Initiative over the long term. To achieve this long-term outcome the Initiative will:

- raise awareness among government, civil society and private business actors regarding existing commitments to principles of openness in environmental decision-making, and forge consensus on what these principles mean in practice;
- strengthen the capacity of public interest groups both to assert access to information, participation and justice in environmental decision-making, and to identify and monitor gaps between stated commitments and actual performance on the part of public authorities.

Source: The Access Initiative Summary, www.accessinitiative.org

- Supporting *advocacy and awareness-building* on sustainable development issues and options among parliamentarians, journalists and decision-makers at all levels.
- Incorporating sustainable development dimensions into *formal educational curricula* at all levels.
- Developing *partnerships with media actors* at the local, national and international levels. These are important as part of an overall effort to inform public opinion and key decision-makers about the strategy process and sustain momentum.

Box 7.3 **Principles of effective communication**

The Communication for Social Change initiative of the Rockefeller Foundation defines such communication as a process of public and private dialogue through which people define who they are, what they want and how they can get it. Social change is defined as change in people's lives as they themselves define such change. This initiative seeks particularly to improve the lives of the politically and economically marginalized, and is informed by principles of tolerance, self-determination, equity, social justice and active participation for all. It attempts to rebalance strategic approaches to communication and change by emphasizing what can, in practice, be regarded as principles for effective communication. These principles take the emphasis:

■ away from people as the objects for change ... and on to people as agents of their own change;

■ away from designing, testing and delivering messages ... and on to supporting dialogue and debate on the key issues of concern;

■ away from the conveying of information from technical experts ... and on to sensitively placing that information into the dialogue and debate;

■ away from a focus on individual behaviours ... and on to social norms, policies, culture and a supporting environment;

■ away from persuading people to do something ... and on to negotiating the best way forward in a partnership process;

■ away from technical experts in 'outside'' agencies dominating and guiding the process ... and on to the people most affected by the issues of concern playing a central role.

Source: Rockefeller Foundation (1999)

■ A shared understanding that communication to influence behavioural change is a *slow process* (it needs time to gestate). It requires a judicious balance between *longer-term commitment to social interaction and learning*, and communications *activities with more immediate impacts*.

■ *Clear understanding of the principles for effective communication* in strategies for sustainable development. These are laid out in Box 7.3. There are some particular challenges in communicating sustainable development issues, set out in Box 7.4. Some of the means to overcome these difficulties and effectively put across sustainable development messages are suggested in Box 7.5.

There are special challenges to communicate what 'sustainable development' is – but plenty of 'tricks' on how to do it

Establishing a communications and information strategy and system

Government alone cannot develop a high quality NSDS. It needs analytical and other inputs from civil society stakeholders such as NGOs and policy research groups, to ensure that the strategy process has access to and takes account of a broad body of information and views. Access to information and communication is a precondition for sustainable development, and can help stakeholders to break out of their isolation, exchange ideas and learn from the experience of the others. Fortunately, this is a task that is being made much easier by technology. Telephones, fax machines, computers, television and radio have transformed the ability of ordinary people to become informed, and thus to liberate their creative potential. Each technology has contributed to breaking down barriers to information exchange.

Therefore, as indicated in Box 4.1, a key step in the strategy process is for the secretariat to establish a *communication and information strategy and system* to ensure regular, two-way flows of information concerning both the strategy process itself and sustainable development, and effective dialogue between stakeholders and between fora (see Box 7.6). This, in turn, will help build the necessary national consensus, create transparency and facilitate public participation in the elaboration and implementation of the NSDS. Communication should be an ongoing task through successive cycles of the strategy process. Effective communication will promote wider participation – horizontally, by linking different sectors, and vertically, by bringing local to global, and global to local. This would require:

Box 7.4 **Sustainable development – a communications challenge**

Whilst the concept of sustainable development recognizes the interdependence of environmental, social and economic dimensions, it does itself not provide a clear vision of where we go and how we get there. Nor does it address the issue that these dimensions are connected, but with unequal power and interests, and therefore, sustainable development is very much a long-term political project that requires deep changes in governance. Sustainable development is justified in the long-term, but most of our political and economic systems function on a short-term basis. Sustainable development does not itself provide mechanisms to bargain about trade-offs between long- and short-term considerations, and between the three pillar dimensions. The point is that sustainable development is a paradigm that leaves it to people and countries to interpret and take forward, without directly addressing the underlying structures that make it so difficult. It is, therefore, difficult to 'sell'. An NSDS is an approach to overcome some of these problems, but must be seen in the context of real structures. (Stephan Paulus, GTZ, personal communication)

The term 'sustainable development' is often seen as a communications failure. Respected journalists and communicators have recognized this:

- 'Any attempt by a journalist to do a story on sustainable development per se is almost doomed to failure.' (former BBC environment editor)
- 'It's grandiose and vague – as good as bad television for sending you to sleep.' (Jonathan Dimbleby, broadcaster)

Many NGOs avoid using the phrase, believing it has little resonance with the public:

- 'Sustainable development means absolutely nothing to most people and never will.' (WWF-UK campaigns director)
- 'People see it as loose, undefined words.' (Greenpeace)

Indeed, *there's a strong consensus amongst those engaging with the public that the term sustainable development is a turn-off* (report for the UK Commission for Sustainable Development). The general public certainly does not understand the term, as a 2001 survey by Forum for the Future found.

However, the concept is not difficult to grasp, and it should not be presented as 'too difficult' for the ordinary person. Once prompted by Forum for the Future, most people interviewed could talk about sustainable development as it affects their life, work, investment, shopping and leisure. They could then express sustainable development as being of central importance, especially in their neighbourhood. Of course, it is also inherent in a wide range of important global, national and business initiatives as well as neighbourhood concerns. Indeed, it is being used as the strategic organizing concept for key government, education and business decisions.

Perhaps that is part of the problem. Those who have been using the phrase 'sustainable development' most commonly are government agencies and, increasingly, corporations. They use the term promiscuously but vaguely – implying that they are merely justifying current policies, especially if those policies have not yet changed. This can increase the 'turn-off' factor.

Even though journalists and environmentalists have pointed out the difficulties of the *term* sustainable development, their leading practitioners are convinced of the concept's value:

- 'The words are boring. The subject isn't.' (Geoffrey Lean, journalist)
- 'Sustainable development is the only intellectually coherent, sufficiently inclusive, potentially mind-changing concept that gets even half-way close to capturing the true nature and urgency of the challenge that now confronts the world. There really is no alternative.' (Jonathan Porritt, environmentalist)

Principal source: *Green Futures* No 30 (2001) Forum for the Future, London

---

Box 7.5 How can sustainable development be communicated successfully?

- By recognizing that it is *specific issues that interest people*, rather than the whole of the SD agenda: 'If you replaced all the various eco-labels with one saying "certified sustainable" it might on the surface be simpler and more rigorous, but a lot of enthusiasm would collapse.' (Corporate social responsibility consultant)
- In other words, breaking SD down into *manageable pieces that make sense to people in their context*. Not forbidding the words 'sustainable development' but adding the message that 'this idea/initiative contributes to sustainable development'.
- By using opportunities to *demonstrate links between the issues that matter to people* – for example trade terms and environment, fuel use and flooding through climate change.
- *By presenting the positive side, not just the negative.* Too often, problems are presented, implying that SD is about what you *cannot* do. In contrast, SD communications should emphasize opportunities, ideas and innovations that excite people about the future, and show what roles people can play in it.
- This will often mean *focusing on the doable and immediate* – recycling and local environmental clean-ups – and adding messages on the broader, longer-term context for these activities.
- It will also mean *illustrating options for the future that interest people*: for example, low-energy housing and transport, community action to remove homelessness, farmers' markets that strengthen rural economies and provide healthier food.
- By *using good communications practice*: asking people what concerns them, and what they can do, and not just telling them what to do; spinning stories about what has worked, and not just presenting abstract 'recommendations'; using straightforward language rather than jargon; knowing the audiences and their concerns and not just the subject and its complexities. This approach works for the 'specialists', too.
- By *opening up workshops and conferences to other stakeholders* who will be comfortable with the above, and not feel obliged to talk about SD among 'insiders' only. SD does not need 'dumbing down' to do this: it needs 'opening up'.

Principal source: *Green Futures* No 30 (2001) Forum for the Future, London

---

- putting in place, within the secretariat, appropriate information, education and communication (IEC) staff with a broad range of skills (see Box 4.6) and a clear mandate;
- identifying, through an initial scoping exercise, the precise information and communications needs of the secretariat itself, and of the key participants;
- preparation of a promotional strategy about the NSDS;
- commissioning a sectoral paper on the current state of information, education and communication to provide baseline information for the preparation of an IEC strategy and action plan;
- after a multi-stakeholder consultation process, preparing a longer-term IEC strategy and action plan that addresses the communications needs of each stage in the NSDS process.

Prior to the preparation of an IEC strategy, the team might wish to establish an IEC Roundtable (see Boxes 3.20 and 7.11 for examples from Pakistan's national, provincial and district conservation strategies) with

---

Box 7.6 Communication strategy for the Pakistan National Conservation Strategy

To ensure that a planned, comprehensive, coordinated approach using the most appropriate medium is used to generate awareness of the NCS, it was thought necessary to draw up a strategy for communications. It was hoped that this strategy would help avoid the traditional ad hoc focus on reactive publicized solutions to environmental problems, and instead create a systematic support for effecting behavioural change. Adil Najam of the NCS secretariat makes recommendations for this behavioural change in his prescriptive study, *Communicating Conservation*. According to him, behavioural change does not just support the NCS environmental awareness campaigns—it is the NCS. In order for the communication process to be truly effective, it must empower individuals and communities by educating them on the issues of sustainable development.

A communication strategy is therefore an essential prerequisite to intelligent planning and implementation. It does not preclude mistakes; it simply improves the chances of success.

Source: Final Report. Mid-Term Review of National Conservation Strategy. Mass Awareness Initiatives. HBP Ref.: D0B01NCS. February 16, 2000. IUCN Pakistan Islamabad

multi-stakeholder representation from the broadcast and print media, the performing arts, IT, education and NGO sectors. This would, in particular, ensure inputs into and ownership of the communications strategy upon its completion and implementation.

An information, education and communications strategy and action plan

An *IEC strategy* acts as the principal policy and intellectual framework for planning education and communications activities. It should envisage the establishment of a general and enduring mechanism for consulting civil society concerning all important decisions and initiatives towards sustainable development, in order to allow wider public participation, to build consensus and to ensure ownership and support. It should include the steps that are needed to promote and develop continuing education about sustainable development (see Box 7.7).

At an operational level, the IEC strategy requires translation into an *action plan* that identifies key

---

Box 7.7 Educating for sustainable development

The overall success of any sustainable development strategy will depend on the involvement of the people and their willingness to take responsibility. They need relevant *information* in forms that they can understand and use, as well as *skills* and *motivation*, which will facilitate change.

Over time, it has been demonstrated that education is the most efficient and cost-effective means to change people's thinking towards a particular problem, which then produces the desired attitudinal change. As Albert Einstein once said, 'We cannot solve the problems we have created with the same thinking that created them'.

Awareness raising and education are important tools in moving towards sustainable development, and should be used as complements to legal, regulatory and economic tools. Knowledge leads to greater understanding which, in turn, helps to foster sustainable development practices. However, understanding is only one element that can generate changes in behaviour. Other ingredients which can stimulate change include motivation, access to skills and opportunities, relevance and self-interest, and recognizable and tangible benefits. The advantage of an NSDS process is that it can combine these factors.

Education for sustainable development needs to meet three important goals (adapted from the Tbilisi Declaration, UNESCO 1977):

- To foster awareness and *understanding of the interdependence* of the economic, social and ecological dimensions of development, in both urban and rural areas, and the need to deal with these holistically as well as with political, technological, legislative, cultural and aesthetic concerns.
- To provide every person with *opportunities to acquire* the knowledge, values, attitudes, commitment and skills needed to contribute to sustainable development.
- To create *new patterns of behaviour* among individuals, groups and society as a whole towards the environment, society and the economy.

To meet these three goals, education initiatives should:

- evolve within the existing education system;
- focus on sustainable development at all levels in the formal education system;
- adopt interdisciplinary methods;
- take a global perspective while also having regard to regional differences;
- promote the value of local, national and international cooperation in making progress towards sustainable development;
- focus on both current and future situations;
- centre on practical problems that relate directly to the students' immediate environment;
- aim to instil an ethic of conservation;
- include comprehensive non-formal education programmes to provide information about sustainable development to a wider segment of the population than is possible through formal means;
- be a continuous, life-long process, both in school and beyond;
- emphasize active stakeholder participation in preventing and solving development problems.

The goals are especially important in many developing countries where the literacy rate is low, formal education infrastructure needs to be improved, and NGOs have started playing an important role through non-formal communication and education channels.

Source: Ali Raza Rizvi, IUCN Pakistan (personal communication)

participants/audiences, the kinds of behavioural change required, appropriate messages and means of communicating them, responsibilities and resources, and the most difficult aspect of them all – indicators for monitoring behavioural change. It will need to include activities with short-, medium- and long-term timeframes. Activities to promote cultural, attitudinal and behavioural change will most likely be of a long-term nature (3+ years) and will require sufficient resources to see them through. The action plan should be regularly revised throughout the strategy process.

Skills in developing and implementing an IEC strategy and plan with government, civil society and private sector players will be vital; as will training in such skills where they are in short supply. The IEC team will need to understand the conceptual basis, genesis and dynamics of the NSDS, as well as the technical issues; and thus will need to be involved (as a core element) in the NSDS process from the start – not be seen as a supplementary activity to be added down the line (as has so often been the case in the past). It is very important that they understand how the various stakeholders communicate, learn and change behaviour. A priority task for the team will be to set up a network of principal communications agents and media contacts for different localities, topics and groups.

Box 7.8 provides a set of questions to help guide the design of the IEC strategy.

Box 7.8 Key questions for developing an information, education and communications plan

The National Institute of Design in India has defined a sequence of eight questions, which it follows in the field when developing communications strategies for national or local development programmes. This approach has been tested and refined through more than a decade of field experience:

- **Target audience:** whose behaviour must communication attempt to change?
- **Target response:** what is the behaviour change that is needed?
- **Research involved:** what do we need to know about existing knowledge, attitudes and practices before planning our messages?
- **Target message:** what messages can be exchanged between planners/activists and target audiences to help achieve the desired response?
- **Media:** what media are best suited to the exchange of the target message?
- **Media resource institutions and individuals:** what skills and talent can be drawn on to help develop and implement media decisions?
- **Budget:** what will be the cost of communication plans to reach each target audience?
- **Evaluation criteria:** what goals and indicators will be used to monitor the intended behaviour change?

Evaluation should lead to reviewing each step in a sequence, and reactivating the sequence in the next phase of the communications strategy.

Source: Carew-Reid et al (1994)

Coordination of information

The various agencies responsible for the NSDS will need to ensure that partners and stakeholders are informed about new developments and are encouraged to respond. The mass media should be encouraged in its role as critic and monitor. To service these different needs, an IEC 'clearing house' may be needed to ensure that information is disseminated effectively to the appropriate audiences (within and outside government) and fed back into the strategy. This may be best managed by the IEC team.

The coordination of information can be seen from two perspectives: *internal* (within government or the core strategy stakeholders) and *external* (between the government/core strategy stakeholders and other stakeholders):

INTERNAL COORDINATION – FOCUS ON CREATING A SHARED INFORMATION BASE

There is a need for effective internal cooperation and coordination between individuals and institutions within government – breaking down traditional barriers and attitudes which defend areas of influence and control ('turf') – in support of strategy development and implementation.

The development of a common information base on sustainable development – to make relevant information readily accessible and to enable information to be manipulated to useful ends – is therefore a priority task at the beginning of a strategy process and needs to be maintained throughout the process. Such an information base does not need to be in one place, but all information needs to be accessible to everyone. See Chapter 10 on monitoring, and Chapter 5 (pages 133–162) on sustainability assessment. Electronic approaches can enable an information base to be put together by many stakeholders efficiently (page 246).

A common information database can unite strategy stakeholders – as well as bringing all helpful information together

EXTERNAL COORDINATION – USING A WIDE RANGE OF METHODS

There is also a need for effective external communication between government and other stakeholders (donors, the private sector, civil society), as well as with other interested parties (eg donors), and for stronger partnerships with key media actors in support of the strategy process.

Communicating with the general public is very important, since strategies for sustainable development are of concern to everybody. Strategies must be open and transparent to the wider public concerning their objectives, structure and processes. So information should be released throughout all stages of the process and not just published as a final strategy document. The general public also needs to be encouraged to play roles in pushing for, and monitoring, standards and indicators of sustainability. All participants should be free to share information about the strategy with the public and present it from their perspective. To avoid public confusion, however, communication on the strategy process as a whole should be coordinated by the secretariat. The secretariat should clarify how and when it plans public inputs and reactions will be sought throughout the process. The challenge of making issues understandable to the general public will need to be addressed.

Mass media channels are generally relied on for communicating with the public in layman's language, though so-called 'alternative' media may also be appropriate at times with particular groups (Table 7.1).

Communications with the public may be divided into the following:

Non-technical, 'everyday' language can help the 'experts' as much as the general public

- *Public relations activities* (short-term impact): these are usually conducted through the mass media and advertising, and are principally a one-way means of communications.
- *Market research:* this elicits one-way communications in the opposite direction, that is, from the public. Chapter 6 (page 225) gives details. Work on NSDSs has included:
    - *Opinion polls.* A regular and large-scale poll of the general public can elaborate an independent view on the strength of public feeling and awareness on different issues. This can be a very powerful tool in the strategy policy formulation and associated debates.
    - *Phone-ins.* In developing New Zealand's Environment 2010 strategy (1995), free phone-in facilities were provided to encourage public participation. All comments made were added to the written submissions and entered into a database to prepare a profile of issues.
- *Public awareness activities* (medium-term impact): these work by consulting groups in the strategy process, through traditional and mass media and government/NGO participation structures; involving them in the debate on sustainable development; and keeping them informed about all aspects of the outcomes (Box 7.9 provides an example from Burkina Faso).
- *Public participation* (longer-term impact): this takes much longer and depends on incentives, formal and informal education and training, and results in behavioural change. Mass media activities are much less significant here. Active participation and experience are key, particularly in setting and monitoring indicators of sustainability. Participation is discussed in detail in Chapter 6.

Table 7.1 **Examples of mass and alternative media forms**

Mass media:

Newspapers	Weekly magazines (programmes and news spots)
Radio	Commercial journals
Newspaper and magazine advertisements	Cinema
Television	Web-based publishing

Alternative media:

Printed/written media	Local publications
Annual reports	Newsletters
Banners	Pamphlets and brochures
Children's books	Pins and badges
Comic books	Poems
Information kits	Specialized reviews
Labels and stickers	Teaching materials
Letters	T-shirts

Audio-visual media:

Advertising panels	Posters
Documentary films	Public announcements
Exhibitions	Songs
Photographic exhibitions	Video and slide presentations

Interactive media:

Competitions – art, debating, farming	Parades
Presentations	Participation in existing events
Press conferences	Prizes and recognition awards
Public debates	Public meetings
Site visits	Puppet shows
Symposia in universities	Religious programmes
Telephone	Round tables
Demonstrations	Special days (World Environment Day ...)
Face-to-face (neighbour-to-neighbour, child-to-child, etc)	Street/community theatre (beaches, public places, medina or souk)
Expert conferences	Visits
Internet	Youth clubs
Religious fora/activities	

Source: Adapted from Mehrs (1998)

Choosing the medium, and developing complementary information products

In order to improve awareness, change attitudes and encourage action on sustainable development, various information products will be required, notably: documents and audio-visual (page 238), events (page 240), networks (page 242), databases (page 245), electronic media (page 246) and mass media (page 249).

Box 7.9 **Sustainable development and desertification: a public awareness campaign in Burkina Faso**

In Burkina Faso in the late 1990s, nearly 47,000 people took part in a nationwide campaign to spread the word about sustainable development and its key role in combating desertification. While communicating information and raising awareness at the village level, teachers and trainers also listened to the people, finding ways to convey the people's priorities to planners and policy-makers in the capital. Many citizens were involved in the process.

With support from UNDP's Capacity 21 programme, the National Council of Environmental Management (CONAGESE) created a decentralized mechanism to facilitate national-to-local information sharing through a pyramid of steering committees. Comprising representatives from all sectors, these covered the national, regional, provincial, department and village levels. For two years, the committees held discussions with citizens at every level on how to combat desertification through sustainable development.

The programme focused on enabling local communities to take responsibility for managing natural resources sustainably. In some cases, this meant correcting widely held misconceptions that had led to the failure of past attempts to combat desertification. For example, tree-planting campaigns had not worked. So efforts were made to explain how trees could provide more than just firewood; that planting trees could protect and improve the soil, and improve agricultural production.

The pyramid of committees functioned as a cascade of information sharing, focusing especially on strengthening development planning and resource management at the village level. The national committee trained the regional committees, which trained provincial committees, which, in turn, trained departmental committees, which then trained village committees. The latter consisted of 5 to 10 people, one of whom was literate and acted as secretary. The committees constituted the nucleus of the system of local governance and local action plans on which the country's rural development strategy is based.

Advocating an integrated approach to development was central to the programme's communication strategy, which was designed to provide information about sustainable development to all stakeholders, rural and urban, educated and illiterate, from the general public to the national school system to the private sector.

Booklets, posters, music and a quarterly environmental magazine were produced, and journalists were trained in environmental reporting. Rural radio programmes on sustainable agriculture were launched, as well as 'theatre-fora', in which travelling actors put on plays to highlight development issues.

People learned that fighting desertification is more than one isolated activity and that it is necessary to integrate activities such as planting trees, building little stone walls, using fertilizer, conserving water and soil and working together cohesively.

The campaign led to clear changes in people's thinking and behaviour. Fewer trees were cut down to make new fields and people stopped burning brushwood. Compost heaps were prepared in most villages. Villages began to develop their own integrated development plans to make changes happen.

A key player in the multi-level process of awareness raising and information sharing was COPODE (Committee for NGOs Fighting Desertification), which trained 114 NGOs from around the country in ways to promote dialogue on sustainable development at the village level. With support from Capacity 21, COPODE produced thousands of copies of simplified, illustrated versions of the Convention to Combat Desertification in Burkina Faso's four national languages. This helped ordinary people to take ownership of the country's response to the convention.

Source: UNDP Capacity 21 (www.undp.org/capacity21)

In order to establish which media provide the most effective communications channels for each stakeholder group, it is important to do the following:

- *Undertake a comprehensive needs analysis:* The IEC action plan should identify specific stakeholder groups, the most suitable media to reach these groups, and ways to link them together. In developing the plan, reliance should not be placed on assumptions. A stakeholder analysis and associated 'needs analyses' will help to validate initial assumptions, identify gaps in information flows and suggest innovations that encourage stakeholders to actually use the information.
- *Ensure that the media empower stakeholders and enable strategy improvement:* Effective communications will empower individuals and groups, enabling them to use their skills and resources and identify new ways of working together. The media selected should, therefore, be of a type that best enables participating groups to communicate what they feel, what they know and what they want – as

well as to best understand what the strategy is all about. When using the print, electronic and traditional media, and in the education system, it will be important not to restrict the role of these various media to delivering strategy 'messages'. As far as possible, media roles should encompass those of strategy critic, monitor and solicitor of opinions.

- *Multiple media will be needed:* Stakeholder groups may exhibit different attributes, from hierarchical to egalitarian in nature, and from task-orientation to people-orientation. Information will flow in and out of such groups in different ways. Each group will also have its preferences and dislikes for media. Thus the diverse stakeholders of a strategy will require diverse communication media, according to country and locality circumstances, topic, audience/participant group and cost considerations. Many of these media may be new to strategy staff.
- *Cost/benefit analysis of media:* The costs and benefits of alternative media need to be assessed. Hidden benefits should be included, especially on the user side. For example, e-mail can appear very cheap, but some users – particularly in remote areas in developing countries – may have to travel to an urban centre to use a computer charged on an hourly basis with a poor connection. In such cases, a letter, a telephone call, or a community meeting, entertainment and performing arts, and involvement of extension agents and NGOs, may be the most appropriate approach.

All materials should be available in local languages (where appropriate) and should develop and promote the strategy's identity. The latter is important if an 'umbrella' approach is taken; that is, products produced by many government departments and other stakeholders through the NSDS process.

Documents and audio-visual material
These can include:

- The strategy prospectus and summaries based on it – setting out such matters as the aim of the strategy, the processes involved, how to participate or the schedule of steps/events. An outline of such a prospectus is given in Box 7.10.
- Briefing documents (on issues, options, and initiatives; some of a general nature, others for particular target groups; both regular and one-off).
- 'State of environment and development' reports and maps.
- Regular newsletters and news releases.
- News releases.
- Videos and multimedia presentations.
- Training and resource packs (for participants and others).
- An overall strategy document setting out the broad vision, rationale, objectives, system to address them and outline plans.

The strategy is not a 'document' – but documents are useful tools for the strategy

Although it is commonplace to refer to a strategy document as 'the strategy', this is misleading and encourages people to expend excessive efforts in preparing papers instead of establishing the mechanisms to develop the strategy and its outcomes. Documents are only intermediate products or 'milestones' of the process – the means to an end. Nevertheless, documents (whether hard copy or electronic) are essential tools for the effective preparation and implementation of a strategy. They enable (literate) participants and others, and especially policy-makers and decision-takers, to understand the vision and objectives, know what is happening, what has been agreed and what is expected of them. Without documents, a strategy may quickly lose coherence and fragment into ad hoc decisions dictated by the immediate needs of the government department and other national agencies concerned. Some NCSDs, for example, have suffered

Box 7.10 **Outline of the prospectus for the Canadian *Projet de société***

The Canadian *Projet de société* was initiated in 1992 as a Canadian response to UNCED and Agenda 21. It was coordinated by the National Round Table on the Environment and the Economy (NRTEE) and was concerned with sustainable development issues at national (not just federal) level, resulting in a strategy document, *Canadian Choices for Transitions to Sustainability* (Projet de société, 1995).

A prospectus was issued in 1994. This introduced the initiative, described its work and invited the participation of interested parties in future activities. It described the initiative as a multi-stakeholder partnership of government, indigenous, business and voluntary organizations, committed to promoting Canada's transition to a sustainable future, and set out its primary role as a catalyst for change, recognizing that sustainable development is a collective responsibility of all Canadians.

The prospectus explains that the first year involved an assessment of Canada's progress since UNCED, the drafting of a framework and process for a national strategy for sustainable development, and the initiation of a series of practical actions to advance various elements of this approach. The prospectus marked the movement of the process into a more substantive programme of activity, including communication, planning and demonstration components to foster sustainability as a national mission. The documents issued an invitation to all interested institutions and individuals to participate in the work of the *Projet de société* and to invest ideas, skills and contributions to the task of planning for a sustainable future. The prospectus was set out in various sections:

- The Earth Summit and beyond – why we must act.
- *Projet de société*: Planning for a sustainable future – what we want to achieve.
- Towards a National Sustainable Development Strategy – how we are approaching the challenge of changing course (includes principles and characteristics of the initiative).
- Progress to date – describes work already undertaken (see previous paragraph) (includes chronology of the *Projet de société*).
- Next steps – where we are going (describes the broader process and opportunities for collaboration and initiatives by existing stakeholders and other interested parties; and discusses building public awareness, information sharing and networking, outreach and facilitation, designing a strategy, convening a national dialogue, catalyzing preparation of sustainability strategies in sectors and communities and learning from experience).
- Resource requirements – what we need for the task ahead.
- Strategic alliance – who should join the *Projet de société*.

Source: Projet de société (1994)

from the lack of strategy documentation: this has made them appear opaque to some groups; and the lack of a clear plan may have contributed to rather passive or reactive approaches to their work.

However, information overload must be avoided. Although analyses, records and investment portfolios will require detailed documentation, the key strategy documents should not be too lengthy. Coherence, consensus and clear direction are important features of a strategy and the key documents will need to express these features. Everyday language, charts, maps and illustrations will help.

To be most effective, the central strategy document needs to be published and widely available in final approved form. Government agencies, local authorities, major NGOs and many businesses will need the full document. But highly technical reports are not useful for politicians, busy decision-makers, community interest groups and the general public. The main strategy documents may need to be presented in different forms, each targeted to a particular audience.[3] However, it will be important to ensure that the different documents do not send contradictory messages.

Condensed information can be made available to the public – in local languages where appropriate – and to schools and universities where it can promote debate about issues to be addressed by the strategy –

---

3 There is often a shortage of people with the skill to write well and clearly. It may be necessary to engage communications specialists with the appropriate writing and presentational skills, to develop products that adequately meet their purpose and serve their target audiences well.

helping to strengthen the key competences of students, tomorrow's leaders (eg innovation, questioning, communication, change management, strategic thinking/planning and leadership).

Short documents tend to be best, but stakeholders also need access to the full information sources

Electronic versions could usefully be made available on the strategy website and periodic CD-ROMs (see page 246) and audio and video versions could also be produced (for example, as done for the Pakistan NCS and Local Agenda 21s for UK authorities). With a premium being placed on concise documents, complementary access to the full strategy knowledge base, perhaps through the strategy website, would both contribute to improved transparency and enable stakeholders to engage further.

Events

Events can be powerful – but are expensive and so need careful justification and planning

During the development and implementation of the strategy, the secretariat will need to organize various events that aim to improve communication of concerns, issues and ideas among stakeholders, and to disseminate strategy objectives. Meetings often form milestones in a strategy process – and thus need to be judiciously timed and planned, especially as they can form a large proportion of the strategy costs.

- *Briefing meetings for decision-makers* on strategy issues, recommendations, progress and remaining issues. Equal attention should be given to conceptual clarity and good and timely local case material. Costs, risks and benefits should be outlined.
- *Briefing meetings for the mass media and traditional media.* Here, the challenge is to create a newsworthy story from what can seem to be a large and heavy agenda, and to be able to complement this with good contacts to enable the media to pursue the story further and thus contribute to debate, analysis and ideas. Once sensitized, the media can also help to promote dialogue between stakeholders (letters to the editor, opinion pieces, etc) and increase accountability. Journalists have played strong roles in some strategies, such as one of the provincial strategies under the Pakistan NCS (see Box 7.11).
- *Public meetings.* These can surface widespread concerns – as illustrated in the case of St Helena concerning the environment (Table 7.2). Here, clarity on the purpose of the meetings and strategy organizers' expectations is key, as is good notice for the events, accessibility by stakeholders, and follow-up reporting and its dissemination. Care is needed in organizing the agenda; this and the political framework for the event can often dictate the outcome and restrict honest debate. It is important to consider how the results of public meetings can be effective and have an impact on the development of the strategy, on policy-making and decision-taking, and to explain this.
- *Training workshops.* Some training workshops will be directly the concern of the strategy (providing training, for example, on what the strategy process is all about and how particular interest groups

---

Box 7.11 Support services for journalists and NGOs, Sarhad Provincial Conservation Strategy, Pakistan

One of the challenges for the Sarhad Provincial Conservation Strategy (SPCS) has been to help its constituency to grow outside the government system, as well as within it. Both the Frontier Forum for Environmental Journalists (FFEJ) and the Frontier Resource Centre for NGOs and CBOs (FRC) were given considerable strategic boosts by the SPCS. FFEJ holds courses for journalists in the province to familiarize them with environmental issues (for which the journalists pay) and is resulting in an increasing body of stories on sustainable development being placed with the media. The Urdu press in particular is being targeted. FRC offers training, research and documentation and networking services, with a concentration on practical local sustainable development. The work of these support services, plus the SPCS issues roundtables, is building up expectations of improved government–civil society partnerships in decision-making, and expectations of improved transparency – which will help to drive the SPCS. Something similar is needed for the private sector and banks, individual members of which have been expressing interest through the roundtable.

Source: Hanson et al (2000)

Table 7.2 Public concern survey on the environment in St Helena

Rank/issues raised	Forum 1	2	3	4	5	6	7	8	9	10	11	12	13	14	15	Total
1. Government closed shop	–	*	*	*	*	–	*	*	–	*	*	*	–	–	*	10
2. Agricultural/food security	–	–	–	–	*	*	*	–	*	*	*	*	–	*	*	9
2. Research/education	*	*	*	*	–	*	–	*	–	–	*	–	–	*	*	9
2. Soil erosion	*	–	*	–	*	–	*	*	*	–	*	–	–	*	–	8
2. **International pollution**	*	*	*	–	*	*	–	*	–	–	*	–	–	*	–	8
2. Apathy among populace	–	*	*	–	–	*	*	*	–	–	–	*	*	–	*	8
3. Water shortage	–	*	*	*	–	–	*	*	*	*	–	–	–	–	–	7
3. Living costs	–	–	–	*	*	*	*	*	*	*	–	–	–	–	–	7
3. **Too many consultants**	*	*	–	*	*	–	*	*	–	–	–	–	–	*	–	7
3. No cash for environment work	*	–	–	*	*	–	*	–	–	*	*	*	–	–	*	7
4. **Unemployment**	–	–	–	–	*	–	*	*	*	*	–	–	–	–	*	6
4. **International overfishing**	*	–	–	*	*	*	–	–	–	*	*	–	–	–	–	6
4. **Lack of continuity**	*	–	–	*	*	–	*	–	–	*	–	–	–	*	–	6
5. Increased water cost	–	–	–	*	–	–	*	*	*	*	–	–	–	–	–	5
5. Cactoblastus killing Opuntia	–	*	–	*	*	–	*	–	–	–	–	–	–	–	–	5
5. Organic matter	*	–	*	–	–	*	–	–	*	*	–	–	–	–	–	5
6. Increase in number of pests	–	*	*	–	–	–	*	–	–	–	–	*	–	–	–	4
6. Local pollution	–	–	*	–	*	–	*	–	–	–	*	–	–	–	–	4
6. Flax mulch/soil conditioner	–	–	*	–	–	–	*	–	*	*	–	–	–	–	–	4
6. Land use strategy	*	–	–	–	*	*	–	–	–	–	–	*	–	–	*	4
7. Lack of fishing fleet	*	–	–	*	–	–	*	–	–	–	–	–	–	–	–	3
7. Recreational facilities	–	–	–	–	–	*	–	*	–	–	–	*	–	–	–	3
7. 3-day labour	*	–	*	–	*	–	–	–	–	–	–	–	–	–	–	3
7. Natural regeneration	–	–	*	–	–	*	*	–	–	–	–	–	–	–	–	3
7. Taxes, esp land tax	*	–	*	–	–	–	–	–	–	–	*	–	–	–	–	3
7. **Global climate change**	–	*	–	–	–	–	*	–	–	*	–	–	–	–	–	3
8. Water quality	–	–	–	*	–	–	–	*	–	–	–	–	–	–	–	2
8. Building heritage	–	–	–	*	–	–	–	–	–	–	–	*	–	–	–	2
8. Nature trails	–	–	*	–	*	–	–	–	–	–	–	–	–	–	–	2
8. Legislation	–	–	*	–	*	–	–	–	–	–	–	–	–	–	–	2
8. **Videos**	*	–	–	–	–	–	*	–	–	–	–	–	–	–	–	2
8. Drought	–	*	–	–	–	–	–	–	–	–	*	–	–	–	–	2
9. Absentee landowners	*	–	–	–	–	–	–	–	–	–	–	–	–	–	–	1
9. Road condition	–	–	–	–	–	*	–	–	–	–	–	–	–	–	–	1
9. School closure	–	–	–	–	–	*	–	–	–	–	–	–	–	–	–	1
9. Lack of finance	–	–	–	–	–	–	–	–	–	–	–	*	–	–	–	1
9. Removing historical remains	–	–	–	–	–	–	–	–	–	–	–	*	–	–	–	1
9. Spear fishing	–	–	–	–	–	*	–	–	–	–	–	–	–	–	–	1
Number present	7	13	8	16	11	7	7	9	6	14	6	4	3	5	15	131
Sex – male	2	7	3	11	7	3	2	6	5	12	6	1	3	3	10	81
– female	5	6	5	5	4	4	5	3	1	2	0	3	0	2	5	50
Age <30	0	2	1	3	2	2	2	2	0	2	0	0	0	1	0	17
30–60	6	7	7	10	8	2	4	5	5	9	6	2	1	4	14	90
60+	1	4	0	3	1	3	1	2	1	3	0	2	3	0	1	25

Notes: Bold items are, or are influenced by, international affairs. The fora listed above are detailed below

The small island of St Helena (population 5000) is an Overseas Territory of the UK, located in the remote southern Atlantic Ocean. It has a rich endemic fauna and flora, but suffers from severe land degradation, limited development options, and is highly vulnerable to external actions and decisions.

A process was started in 1993 towards developing a Sustainable Environment and Development Strategy (SEDS). Initially, a six-week scoping exercise was conducted, facilitated by a team from the Royal Botanic Gardens, Kew and IIED. The exercise was cross-sectoral and inclusive of all government departments, the private sector, NGOs and the public. It involved a wide range of surveys and data-gathering exercises and consultations; for example, numerous official meetings and 13 public meetings (listed below), visits to farmers and smallholders, phone-ins, school painting competitions and seminars, and ad hoc discussions.

The following public meetings and other activities were organized – as numbered in the table:: (1) Alarm Forest (the Briars) Community; (2) Half Tree Hollow Community; (3) Longwood Community; (4) Kingshurst (St Pauls) Community; (5) Levelwood Community; (6) Blue Hill Community; (7) Jamestown Community; (8) Sandy Bay Community; (9) Farmers Association; (10) Smallholders; (11) Fishermen's Association; (12) Heritage Society; (13) Church Group; (14) Radio Phone In; (15) SEDS Seminar. The issues raised were both national and international in scope. The team ranked them after placing them in context together with information from the diversity of other methods used to assess islanders' opinions and attitudes, for example, questionnaires

Source: Royal Botanic Garden Kew and IIED (1993)

can engage effectively in it and present their views, on sustainable development concepts and key issues, and on methods for analysis). But there will be many other training workshops organized elsewhere, which also present opportunities for improving understanding of sustainable development and the strategy. As they are all focused on change, they present opportunities for contributing to the NSDS process.

■ *Share fairs.* These are where various stakeholders display their outputs and information in a type of information 'market'. The meeting is open to all and people are encouraged to discuss and share their work in a non-formal manner. This can help to build consensus on priority areas of action. It also supports a growing body of valuable information about approaches that can be adopted by others facing similar challenges.

■ *Formal and informal exchange visits and study tours.* These often work well with mixed groups from a particular region or strategy and encourage learning and building of trust relationships. Such visits enable the participants to see how strategy processes have been organized elsewhere; to compare issues, challenges, solutions, and so on, and to learn from strategy experience in other countries/areas with the aim that the individuals will be able to engage better in their domestic processes.

Some events are often expensive to run, can include relatively few people and therefore should be balanced against maintaining cheaper information activities. Often meetings are held in major capitals and urban centres; locating events equitably across the country will encourage greater participation and 'ownership'. So also could integration with events held for other purposes. Alternatives may be considered if they are suitable to stakeholders and to the task in hand: for example e-mail conferences and the other media described in this section.

MANAGING DIALOGUE AND CONSENSUS-BUILDING DURING MEETINGS

Ground rules for strategy meetings can get better strategy results – and contribute to an improved climate for stakeholder participation

Many of the strategy tasks involve meetings. The way in which communication is conducted within those meetings will have significant implications for the success of the strategy. For working groups to be effective, it has been found useful to agree ground rules of communication, especially for the purpose of dialogue and/or consensus building. Participants must assume that no one has all the answers. In its study of multi-stakeholder processes, UNED Forum (2001) suggests some ground rules for meetings (Box 7.12).

Establishing networks, or making links with existing networks

The term 'network' is frequently used to describe different types of organizational or individual relationships. Networks are primarily formed by individuals from different organizations or from departments within large organizations and can often be confused with other types of organizational relationships such as alliances, coalitions, associations and federations. The structure of these forms depends to a large degree on the basis of unity, that is, to what degree the organizations and individuals share common aspirations and challenges. Alliances, for example, are often short-lived, as they form around a particular issue and then dissolve, whereas coalitions and federations create more permanent secretariats with sophisticated information and communication channels. If such groupings start to support the strategy, they are able to bring with them their own organizational members, branches, political influence and technical knowledge as well as their multiple information channels (Wilson 1993).

Existing 'policy communities' and professional networks provide ready channels for NSDS communications – many of them welcome the broader NSDS strategy process

Networks may be both formal and informal in nature. There are a number of types of 'network' that it may be helpful to involve in the strategy:

■ *Policy communities* that focus on specific subjects for specific reasons (see Box 5.5), and work through an established medium (eg e-mail) can be very supportive. Such 'communities' will exist both

Box 7.12 **Ground rules for meetings**

In a study of multi-stakeholder processes, UNED Forum (2001) noted that the following communications 'rules' have proved effective:

1 During discussion, participants must make every effort to be as frank and candid as possible, while maintaining a respectful interest in the views of others. An atmosphere that cultivates **directness, openness, objectivity, honesty, trust and humility** is important.
2 All participants need to be open to change when embarking on a communication process as outlined above. A true dialogue cannot be entered into with the goal of 'getting one's way'.
3 To help understanding and clarify perceptions, participants and facilitators should be encouraged to restate one another's views in their own words ('**active listening**').
4 Participants should refrain from presuming motives of others and rather be encouraged to **ask direct questions**.
5 Participants are asked to **address the group as a whole**, while showing concern for each point of view, rather than confronting and criticizing individuals.
6 Participants must argue on a **logical basis**, giving their own opinion but also seeking different views.
7 **Brain-storming** can be helpful: conducting a session of putting forward ideas and collecting them without judgements for later discussion can create a larger pool of ideas. When an idea is put forward, it becomes the property of the group.
8 Participants should consider conducting a **learning exercise**, to draw out the success factors of other processes and agreements and use the outcomes to deepen the pool of ideas.
9 Allow space and time for **various modes of communication**, socio-emotional as well as strictly task-oriented.
10 If participants feel that others are **not playing by agreed rules**, they need to put that to the group and the group needs to address the problem.

These points are all well and good but other factors are often overlooked – meeting location, style of location and the culture of the various participants. As much as possible, meetings should be spread equitably across the country in locations that encourage the full participation of the participants and not just cater to the vanity of important personalities. As one author notes (Barnard 1995), 50 per cent of time spent in meetings is wasted but the difficulty lies in determining which 50 per cent!

Furthermore, rules might be developed on **recording and reporting** – for example, where to attribute opinions (after major consultation exercises, responses need to be classified according to specific groups) and where not to (for example, public reports of round table meetings). In some cases, this may require a high degree of confidentiality. The Chatham House rule is one such tradition and is widely used in other settings.

The Chatham House rule

Meetings of the [Royal Institute for International Affairs, London] may be held 'on the record' or under the Chatham House rule. In the latter case, it may be agreed with the speaker(s) that it would be conducive to free discussion that a given meeting, or part thereof, should be strictly private and thus held under the Chatham House rule.

When a meeting, or part thereof, is held under the Chatham House rule, participants are free to use the information received, but neither the identity nor the affiliation of the speakers, nor that of any other participant may be revealed; nor may it be mentioned that the information was received at a meeting of the Institute.[4]

A similar tradition was used by Filipino community development workers from different political persuasions under the Marcos dictatorship to allow for debate and building consensus while providing self-protection and confidentiality.

formally (see, for example Box 7.13 for Bolivia) and informally (many advocacy groups which come together now and then to pursue their interests).

4 Royal Institute of International Affairs (RIIA): www.riia.org/meetings/rule.html

---

Box 7.13 Some existing networks in Bolivia

In Bolivia, there are networks and associations on strategy-related issues, which provide information, promote capacity strengthening, mobilize joint initiatives, and act as fora for discussion and focal points for dialogue with the central government and other actors. These can be useful assets for a strategy. There are two key networks:

The Federation of Municipal Associations of Bolivia (FAM-Bolivia) comprises all the Municipal Associations in each region. It represents the municipalities and their interests, requests and needs. Its goal is to consolidate the decentralization process, strengthen representative and participatory democracy, and bring about a multi-ethnic, efficient, transparent, participatory state – largely by promoting municipalities' institutional development. As a result of the DAC dialogue workshops on NSDSs organized in Bolivia, networks for strategic planning have been established in two regions and in La Paz, and are being developed in other regions, with support from FAM, NGOs and others.

National Environmental NGO Network: LIDEMA – League for Defence of the Environment – aims to improve the quality of life for Bolivians and promote citizen participation in identifying and addressing environmental problems. Members promote a policy of coordination with government and other civil society organizations. This has resulted in their broad participation in the development of environmental laws, the National Environmental Action Plan, the environment dialogue and the National Dialogues I and II. LIDEMA played an active role in voicing environmental concerns, encouraging more concerted government action for environment and sustainable development (including legal and institutional aspects), raising public awareness and building capacity. It has promoted the establishment of a Forum for Environment and Development and an information centre for industry.

■ *Communities of practice* or networks, which comprise a range of people and institutions from different practice areas, such as knowledge networks,[5] education specialists, 'extension' agents and business representatives, who keep each other more loosely informed about development in a range of areas can also be useful.

Chapter 5 (Analysis) looks at how to identify them and bring them into the strategy process (see pages 120 and 170). We must be wary of creating alternatives to these, but this may be necessary where none exist or where change is required because of, for example, entrenched positions or inertia.

The Roundtables established in Canada for the *Projet de société* are good examples of effective networks in a country with sophisticated communication facilities (see Box 6.24); Box 7.14 lists some of the benefits and problems of networks.

Care should be taken to identify each network's information and communication needs (whether formal or informal, national or local) as well as building rapport and trust with the key contacts in such groupings. In each, information and knowledge is shared in different ways depending on the levels of interdependence and trust, so a different strategy to work with different groupings will often be required. Unfortunately, there remains relatively little documentation of working with, and maintaining, such networks and partnerships.[6,7,8]

---

5 *Knowledge networks* are engaged in moving knowledge into practice and to broad audiences (see Creech and Willard 2001). Examples include: Pan Asia Networking (PAN) and Bellanet of the International Development Research Centre; Global Knowledge Partnership and Global Development Network of the World Bank; Sustainable Development Communications Network hosted by the International Institute for Sustainable Development; and the Regional and International Networking Group (RING) hosted by the International Institute for Environment and Development.
6 For example see Starkey (1998); Edwards and Gaventa (2001); Keck and Sikkink (1998).

7 The International Institute for Sustainable Development in Canada has supported much research into how to increase network members' impact on policy and practice: http://iisd1.iisd.ca/networks/
8 See Cala and Grageda (1994) for an interesting review of national level networks in the Philippines, which provides an insight into the dynamics of alliances and coalitions from the views of the members themselves.

Box 7.14 Benefits and problems of networks

Benefits of networks

- Networks facilitate exchanges of information, skills, knowledge, experiences, materials and media, through meetings, workshops, publications and cooperative programmes.
- Network information exchange and coordination leads to less duplication of work and effort.
- Networks link people of different levels, disciplines, organizations and backgrounds who would not otherwise have an opportunity to interact.
- Networks can create an awareness that others have similar concerns and developmental problems.
- Networks can provide the critical mass needed for advocacy, action and policy change.
- Networks can help to address complex development problems and issues that seem overwhelming to those working at only one level.
- Networks can bring together funding and technical cooperation agencies and those in need of resources and support.
- Networks can provide members with a source of peer support, encouragement, motivation and professional recognition.

Problems of networks

- membership disparity;
- thus a potential lack of clear objectives;
- domination and/or competition;
- donor interference;
- centralization and bureaucracy;
- lack of resources, or manipulation of resources;
- difficult monitoring and evaluation.

Source: Adapted from Starkey (1998)

Finally, network capacity can be enhanced and interest and motivation promoted by sharing experience with those involved in other strategy processes. There is much to gain from South–South and South–North learning between networks of strategy practitioners. There is a growing number of such networks interested in NSDSs and similar strategic approaches (Box 7.15). A number of them have established websites to facilitate information sharing (eg www.nssd.net).

The Sustainable Development Networking Programmes in Pakistan and China (Box 7.19) are good examples of how, through using internet technology, developing countries can access information and share good practices, lessons learned and know about sustainable development. This is a growing area, with huge potential to stimulate lasting change (for further information, see www.sdnp.undp.org/).

The international networks of strategy practitioners are useful resources for a strategy secretariat

Establishing databases, or making links with existing databases

Databases are computer programmes that can retrieve and manipulate data, text and other forms of electronic elements such as graphics. Electronic databases, which can come in many diverse forms and sizes, are invaluable tools to support the development of strategies. Properly structured and updated, they can provide accurate and up-to-date information to the user.

Databases commonly hold information such as contact data, financial and statistical information and geographical information (see, for example, the case of China's Sustainable Development Information website, Box 7.19). Some databases hold meta-data ('information about information'), with details of important information sources including other databases and resource centres, as a 'sign post' to other sources of information. Apart from the costs of software and training, databases can be very expensive to maintain owing to the human cost of data maintenance, so it is imperative to maximize their use by increasing access to strategy stakeholders as much as possible.

Many useful sustainable development databases are becoming available internationally

Box 7.15 **Some examples of strategy practitioner networks**

IUCN: In the early 1990s, IUCN organized several informal regional networks for strategy practitioners and experts. These served well to share experience and generated many of the basic lessons on best practice that form the OECD DAC principles (Box 3.1).

RedLat: For example, the RedLat (Red Latinoamericano de Estrategias para el Desarollo Sostenible) was helped by IUCN. It has met five times since 1994. A core group of practitioners involved in some 25 sub-national and local strategies in 14 countries discuss common issues and share lessons learned. These lessons are maintained on a website and there is a lively electronic network with over 1200 users in Spanish-speaking countries. RedLat has organized thematic workshops on tools for sustainable development, and organized South–South visits to exchange field experience.

The Network for Environment and Sustainable Development in Africa: NESDA was established in 1992 with World Bank sponsorship and assists African governments, institutions, the private sector, NGOs and local communities in capacity building for strategic planning and implementation. Initially focused on NEAPs, its remit is now much broader.

Earth Council: Based on resolutions of the International Forum for National Councils for Sustainable Development (NCSDs) (April 2000), the global network of NCSDs is undertaking a multi-stakeholder assessment of the Earth Summit commitments. Various regional NCSD groups meet regularly to share experiences. They vary in their effectiveness as well as in their adherence to the principles of NSDSs. Nevertheless, they are a useful first point of contact to support and help NCSDs to evolve.

Capacity 21: UNDP has also developed extensive networks of people involved in sustainable development strategies around the world through its work on Capacity 21.

The International Network of Green Planners: INGP was founded in 1992 as an informal network of practitioners from around the world involved in developing and implementing plans, strategies and policy frameworks for sustainable development. In April 1998, the INGP was converted into a formal membership association. A global conference is organized every 18 months with intermediate regional meetings (www.greenplanners.org).

Source: www.nssd.net

This can be done by putting material extracted from the databases on websites, distributing them on CD-ROMs or sending lists of updated information to potential users through newsletters and e-mail.

An example of a relatively simple and straightforward on-line database is that of the International Collective in Support of Fishworkers' on-line documentation centres (www.iscf.org). Another more complex and very powerful example is ELDIS (www.eldis.org), maintained by the Institute of Development Studies, UK. By October 2001, ELDIS had reviewed over 6400 documents, listed 3423 organizations and had over 120,000 web pages.

Whatever the database strategy adopted, it remains critically important to provide high quality and up-to-date information.

Use of electronic media

Improving internet connectivity can be a valuable investment for strategy stakeholders

Once information is in digital format, it can be very cheaply manipulated into various media, for example e-mail and attachments, websites and CD-ROMs. This may include not only text-based information but also graphics, video and sound. Depending on the target groups, technological capacity and access, a variety of these forms can be used (see Table 7.3).

If useful, the IEC team might establish and operate a *website* at a reasonable cost. This can be used both as an information source for all interested parties and as a communication tool. A frequently updated website allows the strategy to be open to input from stakeholders who are not able to participate directly in the process. It could be complemented by regularly updated *CD-ROMs* containing key information on the

Table 7.3 **The choice of electronic media will be determined by access costs and speeds to the internet**

Choice electronic media	No internet connectivity	Poor internet connectivity	High internet connectivity
CD-ROM	✔	✔	✔
E-mail		✔	✔
Internet browsing of web-based information			✔

✔ = suitable medium

strategy process and its products. The CD-ROM could simply duplicate the most useful website material.

To date, most websites associated with particular strategies have tended to be used mainly to post brief descriptions or the full text of strategy documents (some examples are listed in Box 7.16). Only a very few websites have been used actively to aid communication and involve stakeholders during the strategy development process itself – a good example is the website of the National Assembly for Wales (Box 7.17).

The IEC team can also use the other electronic means to encourage and enable debate and information exchange; for example, e-mail discussion lists/groups (moderated or not) or e-mail newsletters. But, in using such electronic forms of communication, it needs to be borne in mind that many stakeholders (particularly the poor and those in remote areas) may have limited or no access to computer equipment and the internet (Box 7.18). Table 7.4 shows how use of the internet varies according to regions, with least use in Africa and the Middle East.

In developing countries, the best approach might often be to link the narrower information needs for coordinating an NSDS with a broad-based internet resource that serves many pro-sustainable development purposes; for example, improving stakeholder interconnectivity and improving access to sustainability information. UNDP's Sustainable Development Networking Programme has helped to play such a role in several countries (Box 7.19).

ELECTRONIC DEMOCRACY

Electronic democracy and *electronic governance* describe new forms of citizen communication and popular participation in government. These concepts are heralded as means to use communications media to democratize information and participation in decision-making. 'Electronic governance is not about putting data on websites, but about changing the political and institutional structure so citizens can access needed information' (Susana Finquelievich, University of Buenos Aires).

'Electronic democracy' is on the rise; a communications strategy needs to think through its many implications

Table 7.4 **Users of the internet (February 2000)**

Region	Numbers (millions)
USA and Canada	135.06
Europe	71.99
Asia/Pacific	54.90
Latin America	8.79
Africa	2.46
Middle East	1.29
Total	274.49

Source: UNDP (2001b)

Box 7.16 **Some examples of strategy websites**

Bulgaria

A site for local Agenda 21 and regional sustainable development strategy: www.Capacity21-bg.com

Canada

Each ministry in Canada has a website dedicated to its own strategy for sustainable development (see also Box 4.11). For example:

Environment – www.ec.gc.ca (French/English)
Citizenship and Immigration – www.cic.gc.ca
Industry – www.ci.gc.ca/SSG
Fisheries and Oceans – www.dfo-mpo.gc.ca/sustdev/sust_e.htm
Natural resources – www.nrcan.gc.ca/dmo/susdev

There are also regional sustainable development strategies. For example:

The Athabasca Strategy in Alberta, Canada – www3.gov.ab.ca/env/regions/

China's Agenda 21

National report and White Paper on China's Agenda 21: www.acca21.edu.cn/

India

A useful site is that of the Sustainable Development Networking Programme (India) operated as a joint initiative of the Ministry of Environment and Forests, UNDP and IDRC: http://sdnp.delhi.nic.in/

Scotland

The sustainable development strategy for rural Scotland is held on a site maintained by the Scottish Office: www.scotland.gov.uk/library/

Switzerland

The sustainable strategy of the Federal Council is available on www.buwal.ch/publikat/d/

United Kingdom

The site on the UK sustainable development strategy is maintained by the Department for Trade and Industry: www.dti.gov.uk

Uzbekistan

A site for the National Biodiversity Strategy and Action Plan: http://bpsp-neca.brim.ac.cn/books/actpln_uzbek/index.html

Cities and towns

Some cities and towns have also developed their own strategy websites, many of them connected to Local Agenda 21; for example, that for Sandwell in the UK: www.sandwell.gov.uk/smbc/susstrat.htm

Strategy initiatives in multiple countries

Information of a range of strategic planning frameworks is held on sites maintained by international organizations. For example, information on progress with poverty reduction strategies and the text of Poverty Reduction Strategy Papers can be found on the IMF website; for example, for Senegal, see www.imf.org/external/np/prsp/prsp.asp

According to UNDP (2001b), promoting information communications technology (ICT) as part of a social vision requires: the formulation of relevant public policy; new approaches to knowledge, learning and evaluation; and sensitive approaches to differential access, use and appropriation of ICTs. An ICT strategy that promotes equitable access to information could have the following objectives:

Box 7.17 **The website of the National Assembly for Wales**

The National Assembly for Wales is one of the few with a statutory responsibility for sustainable development (others include Estonia and Tasmania). It aims to add value to work done at the UK level on sustainability, building on the UK NSDS, and reflecting the needs of Wales. In January 2000 the Assembly launched its major consultation document *A Sustainable Wales – Learning to Live Differently* which sets out how it will meet its legal obligations on sustainable development.

The Assembly has actively used its website (www.wales.gov.uk/themessustainabledev/) to promote the development of a Welsh *Sustainable Development Scheme* (strategy) and to involve stakeholders in the process. The website gives information about sustainable development, what it is, the Assembly's duty to promote it and the action that is being taken to fulfil that responsibility.

The Assembly initiated a wide and proactive consultation process, which lasted for 3 months until April 2000. Several different ways of reaching people were used, aiming to persuade as many as possible to contribute. These included sending out 2000 copies of a consultation document and 1000 copies of its summary to a wide range of organizations and community groups. The consultation document, a leaflet about the proposals and other documents were placed on the Assembly's website which was also used for a moderated discussion forum. Braille, audio and large print versions are available from the website.

An important part of the consultation process were public meetings or 'Roadshows' held by the Assembly's four Regional Committees in February 2000. Organizations representing all sections of society attended and gave presentations and many members of the public gave their views to Assembly Members.

The Assembly received 161 responses to the consultation exercise: 80 by post, 52 through presentations at the Regional Committee Roadshows, 21 by post and presentation, 3 by e-mail to the Assembly's Sustainable Development Unit, and 5 via the website discussion forum. All of the individual responses and an analysis of them are presented on the website. Some of the key issues in the Analysis include:

■ the relationship between the Sustainable Development Scheme and the Assembly's Strategic Plan – www.Better Wales.com;
■ the main issues to be tackled to achieve a sustainable Wales;
■ the need for a Sustainable Development Forum.

Most of the Assembly's Subject Committees considered a paper on the responses, and there was a Plenary debate in July 2000. Following this, the Assembly's Sustainable Development Unit redrafted the Scheme in the light of Members' wishes. The Scheme was subsequently debated and endorsed by the Assembly in November 2000. An action plan was launched in March 2001 and a first annual report on progress against commitments has been released for the financial year 2001–2002.

An important element of the draft Sustainable Development Scheme is the emphasis it places on finding ways to measure success in delivering a sustainable Wales and the need for monitoring and reporting on progress. The consultation process had sought views on a set of national sustainable development indicators for Wales, as well as on a broader framework for reporting on sustainable development.

Source: www.wales.gov.uk/themessustainabledev/

■ Collaboration between private, public and civil society, with a transparent agenda and an informed strategy that draws on local knowledge.
■ Strengthening of new skills and processes in order to transform public policy.
■ Development of methodologies to produce and adapt information to convert it to knowledge.
■ Documentation, communication and analysis of both positive and negative results.

Mass media

The local, national and regional mass media should be engaged as key stakeholders in the NSDS process. They can serve not only as reporters of news about strategy progress and sustainable development issues, but also to help set the agenda and promote dialogue. The media is no longer just an observer, but an actor for sustainable development.

Box 7.18 Some benefits and limitations of electronic communication

Focuses on the message content, not participant personality: Switching from face-to-face to electronic communication can provide a good basis for neutralizing differences in status and personality, as related to gender, age and ethnicity. Non-verbal stimuli like personal characteristics, such as charisma, mimic and gesticulation can be displayed less effectively in the process of communication and thus be less successful in preventing others from contributing/contradicting (Kiesler et al 1988; Hiltz and Turoff 1993). Representatives of groups with less status, such as women or members of ethnic minorities would benefit primarily from this filtering of personal characteristics. Without participants being physically present, more attention can be given to the contents of the communicative act (Turkle 1995; Geser 1996).

Supports diversity: Research suggests that IT-supported communication is more suitable for producing heterogeneity. Thus, the internet could be the ideal tool for collecting suggestions to a given problem in a brainstorming or for getting an overview of the diversity of opinions on a given subject matter. If the goal is to convince others or to generate unanimity, the internet would not be the most useful tool (Geser 1996; Kerr and Hiltz 1982; Sproull and Kiesler 1993).

Speed, low cost and global reach: Some multi-stakeholder processes have operated with massive use of the internet or even complete reliance on web-based information, including the channels for participants to provide input. There are numerous and significant advantages of internet-based information dissemination and communication. These include speed, low costs and the ability to inter-connect a theoretically unlimited number of people and stakeholder groups.

Access and equity problems: However, in countries with limited internet connectivity and disadvantaged social and linguistic groups (eg ethnic minorities, women, poor people), there are huge gaps regarding access to web-based information. These gaps cross traditional divides: between South and North, between women and men, between poor and rich, ethnic minorities and majorities, and so on (UNDP 1999; Paul 2000).

Source: UNED Forum (2001)

We have become accustomed to thinking of mass media as prime agents of change. They can and do contribute to change, and they have importance in raising the awareness of the general public and in influencing key decision-makers and opinion-formers. Yet, the transition to sustainable behaviour must take place at the local, community and individual level – and here 'mass' approaches have their limitations. That is not to say mass approaches cannot be adapted at the local level – feeding news and information to existing local newspapers and radio stations is often much appreciated. (See also page 240 on media events.)

Monitoring the communication process

The quality of communications is indicative of the vitality of the strategy process itself; regular reflection on it can help

Monitoring and evaluation in the field of information and communications is notoriously challenging. Those responsible for managing and implementing such programmes are often distant from those at the 'user' end of the communication 'chain'. The changes in the knowledge, awareness and behaviour of the target group will be influenced by many factors other than the communications activities undertaken by the IEC team, so it is difficult to attribute those changes only to the information and communications strategy. In the context of multiple objective and process-orientated NSDSs, the requirement to support and adapt to rapidly shifting needs, expectations and requirements will be even more demanding and will need the establishment of mechanisms to monitor the progress of the communications process. The challenges of, and approaches to, monitoring and evaluation are discussed in Chapter 10.

If the IEC action plan has well-defined objectives and targets that are set in collaboration with the target groups themselves, then it is possible to prepare verifiable and informative indicators of impact and process towards the goal. It may not be necessary or indeed sensible to monitor all activities continuously, but without a predetermined system of some kind, little adjustment and verification will be possible.

Indicators can either be quantitative or qualitative, as well as process-oriented or impact-oriented (see Table 7.5).

In some circumstances, traditional readership surveys and resource centre visitor user forms still remain potent reactive measures for monitoring information impact. But in most others, more participatory approaches to monitoring and evaluation will be more appropriate (especially where the communication involves face-to-face meetings and conferences with groups and individuals who do not have access to adequate facilities).

Mechanisms will be needed to enable stakeholders to reflect on the process of communication itself – the procedures, choice of media, framing of messages and their participation (meta-communication).[9] Mechanisms for meta-communication have been rare components of strategies to date, but it has sometimes happened spontaneously in an informal manner.

The IEC team can set up a process for meta-communication through feedback loops; for example, by facilitators asking for reflections on the process in meetings. All participants need to be included in such feedback exercises, and they need to be transparent and agreed on by the participants. Problems that might be identified then need to be collectively addressed in the fora to which they apply.

Table 7.5 **Examples of possible indicators to use in monitoring and evaluating a strategy website**

	Quantitative indicators	Qualitative indicators
Process-oriented	Return rate of users to website Time spent by users on site Monthly visitor numbers Number of documents downloaded Number of other websites linking to the strategy website Number of individuals requesting further information about the strategy after visiting website	Users' comments on navigability and web design Range of types of other sites linking to the main site Users voluntarily offer information to place on website
Impact-oriented	How often the documents were used by the users Number of times the documents were used in training packs	User views on the impact of website information

Note: Web management software packages are available that can track the process-oriented quantitative indicators. For other indicators, measurement processes will need to be developed including surveys and direct contacts with users

9 Meta-communication (from Greek 'meta' = higher) is communication about communication: exchanging information, views, opinions about the way we communicate in a given situation and structure. An important tool in communication processes, particularly where there is a high diversity of language, culture and background.

Box 7.19 The internet for communication, awareness raising and problem solving: UNDP's Sustainable Development Networking Programme. Examples from Pakistan and China

Pakistan

The information revolution accompanying the establishment of the World Wide Web and introduction of e-mail can be successful within countries only if there was good connectivity available at a reasonable cost. Most organizations require a shift in corporate culture in order to make the transformation. In 1992 the Sustainable Development Networking Programme (SDNP) was established in Pakistan through UNDP support. SDNP quickly became the country's leading advocate for maintaining internet access under reasonable financial terms, and itself established the early networks. It pioneered the pathway to electronic information networking within Pakistan, especially for development organizations. SDNP presents much potential as a communication tool about NCS objectives and implementation.

Today, the large private sector internet service provider (ISP) capacity has drawn attention away from SDNP's original roles. Now SDNP is beginning to concentrate on how to ensure better access to information on sustainable human development, for example, by creating a major website relevant to Pakistan's needs, and by building a within-Pakistan internet backbone that will reduce the costs of purchasing expensive international bandwidth. In the process, SDNP is seeking to become financially self-sufficient through the sale of various services. None of this is easy, particularly since there are formidable obstacles to reaching out to client groups who live well away from established data-ready telecommunication systems and who are hampered by low literacy rates and poverty. Thus SDNP, judged a great success for what it has already done in creating awareness and actual connectivity, faces a future where it must re-invent itself in a fashion that will serve sustainable development information needs in a much more equitable way. Its future role could be an extremely valuable adjunct to the devolution initiative now underway in Pakistan, and also to backstop state-of-environment reporting and other information dissemination needs of the NCS.

Source: Hanson et al (2000)

China

Each month, some 4 million people visit China's new Sustainable Development Information Website (www.sdinfo.net.cn). It contains 9 gigabytes of information, never before stored electronically, about China's natural resources, environmental protection and natural disasters, as well as demographic, economic, agricultural and meteorological data. With support from Capacity 21, in partnership with UNDP's Sustainable Development Networking Programme (SDNP), the Information and Networking Division of China's Agenda 21 (known as ACCA21) has coordinated the transfer of this data from government documents, and developed integration technologies that enable users to link and compare data from different sources.

Not only has the data been digitized; value has also been added through matching the digital data to Geological Information Survey spatial location data. Five thousand people access this map-based data every month. In addition, a standard template has been created so that data from a number of sources can be accessed simultaneously. Thus, for example, a user can compare forestry data with data on land use, water supply and weather patterns.

It is estimated that 40 per cent of users are private individuals, students or businesspeople, including NGO members. Another 30 per cent are from government agencies and academia, and the remaining 30 per cent are from overseas. One group that appears to be benefiting from the website is Chinese farmers – at least those with access to the internet. Farmers frequently seek information on inputs such as improved seeds.

Source: UNDP Capacity 21 (www.undp.org/capacity21)

CHAPTER

8

Strategy Decision-Making[1]

Strategies have to be grounded in the politics, the policies, the programs, the practices, the paradigms, the performance measures, and the pathologies that preoccupy both the populace and the policy-makers. (Tariq Banuri 1999)[2]

A great many 'low key' decisions need to be taken on a daily basis throughout a sustainable development strategy process – from where best to hold a meeting, to how to encourage an important person to become involved. But these day-to-day decisions, although important, are not the concern of this chapter. Rather the focus here is on how to arrive at major decisions that can determine the overall purpose and approach of a sustainable development strategy. The chapter addresses:

A strategy is fundamentally about making choices: the art and the science of decision-making is central to it

- the *scope* of major strategy decisions – from agreed visions and policy goals to decisions on implementation of strategy action programmes, is discussed next;
- possible *values, principles and frameworks* which can guide strategic choices (page 258);
- *institutional and procedural* arrangements for making strategy decisions (page 270);
- factors to consider when deciding on which *instruments* will be best for implementing the strategy (page 283).

There are many links between this chapter and others concerning the 'strategy cycle' (Figures 4.2 and 5.13). In particular, good strategy decisions cannot be made without the right 'inputs', particularly relevant analysis and stakeholder participation, which are described in detail in Chapters 5 and 6.

The scope of strategy decisions[3]

The typical set of major strategy decisions covers vision, objectives, targets, triggers, action plan and

---

1 This chapter has benefited from review comments and additional material provided by Ralph Cobham, UK; and Professor Michael Carley, Herriot Watt University, Scotland.
2 Cited in Hanson et al (2000).
3 Material for this section has drawn from Hagen (n.d.); ICLEI (1996a); and Carew-Reid et al (1994).

institutional roles. Table 8.1 illustrates these, using examples from The Netherlands and North West Frontier Province (Sarhad), Pakistan. The following describes each type of decision in turn:

Strategic vision

A vision tells us where we want to go

The *strategic vision* describes the long-term aspirations which stakeholders agree should guide all other aspects of the development of the strategy. This may describe, for example, what kind of society is envisaged; and/or what types of major changes in production, consumption, or societal organization and behaviour are desired. It can be accompanied by a statement reflecting stakeholder consensus on key problems and issues that should receive priority. A 20–30-year period is commonly used for visioning, such as the Vision 2020 exercises in Malaysia, Ghana, Malawi and many other countries. The process of developing and agreeing the vision has to be a multi-stakeholder, multi-level effort and will be a valuable learning exercise. Consensus should normally be sought throughout the process, or key stakeholders will not be 'on board' in later steps (see page 272). Scenarios can form useful inputs (page 171).

Strategic objectives

Objectives describe how we might get there ...

Strategic objectives, taken together, describe how the vision might be achieved. The principles and values inherent in the vision can be applied to priority issues to establish particular objectives for each issue. Each objective should cover a given issue (problem or opportunity), address the main changes required to make the transition to sustainable development, be expressed in a way that is broad enough to encompass all aspects of the issue and ensure 'buy-in' by all relevant stakeholders, but also specific enough to allow measurable targets to be defined. The strategy should cover sufficient objectives to address the main economic, social and environmental concerns of sustainable development, but few enough to be achievable and comprehensible. Some objectives may be agreed as priorities, to be accorded targets (see below) and implemented within a short timeframe. Other objectives, which are not current priorities, may come into effect only when progress has been made with the priorities, or if triggers (below) reveal they have become of higher priority.

Targets

... some to be achieved by target dates ...

Targets for each objective describe specific and measurable activities, accomplishments or thresholds to be achieved by a given date. These form the core of any action plan, and serve to focus resources and guide the selection of options for action. Because targets imply concrete actions and behaviour changes by specific stakeholders, they should be the product of negotiation. For example, The Netherlands Environmental Policy Programme and the Egyptian NEAP both negotiate local targets with local authorities and other stakeholders.

Triggers

... with action on others to be triggered in the future ...

Triggers are commitments to take a specified action at a future date. Where agreement cannot currently be reached on a particular target due to lack of information, or where a target may not yet be realistic given the extended timeframe of a strategy, it may instead be 'triggered' when specific conditions develop. This could include reaching a specified threshold for population growth or environmental damage, or when resources become available, or a given target is achieved. In addition, if a strategy has established first- and second-priority objectives, targets can be set for the first priorities and triggers for the second priorities. For example (ICLEI 1996a):

Strategic Objective 1: To promote technologies, products and practices that reduce the creation of wastes.

Target 1.1: By 2015, reduce the generation of household solid waste by 50 per cent from 2000 levels.

Trigger 1.1: If household solid waste is not reduced by 25 per cent of 2000 levels by 2010, volume-based waste collection charges will be instituted.

In short, both targets and triggers need to relate specifically to the strategy objectives.

Action plan

An *action plan* is a framework of actions for achieving strategy objectives and targets. It states clearly how each action contributes to one or more given strategy objectives, and may suggest a relative priority rating (eg high, medium or low; or essential, important, desirable). The following types of actions and their sequencing may be outlined in broad detail:

... and all set out in the framework of an action plan, comprising existing and new activities ...

- new policies, policy changes and links for improved coherence (page 280);
- new and changed legislative, economic or other instruments which assist implementation of policies or build capacities (page 283);
- major programmes and pilot projects for sustainable development and change management;
- sustainability guidelines and standards for sector activities and institutional roles.[4]

The strategy action plan/framework would, therefore, comprise existing activities as well as specifying new ones. It would note where existing resources are adequate for implementation, and where extra (outside) investment is needed. However, it would not offer a step-by-step blueprint for each action.

Institutional plan

An *institutional plan* covers the roles, partnerships and systems required to implement the strategy. This may include linkage between the NSDS and other strategic plans and between plans at different spatial levels: national, sub-national, local, or for different sectors or geographical regions. It would identify which institutions are responsible for which parts of the strategy action plan, their degrees of freedom and where they have an obligation to defer to other stakeholders or strategy coordinators. It might also signal a rationale for streamlining institutions (especially where responsibilities overlap or conflict) or even propose the establishment of new institutions as necessary.

... with clear institutional roles

For all of the above, there is a need for clarity on the *geographical boundaries* to which the strategy decisions apply. Chapter 4, page 107 addresses the distinction between international, national and local needs, with an example from Pakistan given in Box 4.12. This is important because a weakness that has undermined previous attempts at strategy development has been the omission of key spatial levels of decision-making, or weak links between levels.

There should also be a *clear and logical path from vision to action plan and institutional roles*. Many previous strategies have missed one or other of these components. For example, many NCSs did not develop shared stakeholder visions, at best 'borrowing' visions direct from the World Conservation Strategy, without their

---

4 Sometimes *sustainability guidelines* and standards may be articulated in detail in a strategy, especially where strategic objectives emphasize voluntary actions and common principles for institutional and legal change.

Table 8.1 Examples of the framework of linked strategic decisions

A: Netherlands 4th National Environmental Policy Plan (NEPP)

Strategic vision	A new, broader and more future-oriented vision is needed. A **broader vision**, so that we can look across national boundaries and realize that surfeit and scarcity are unequally distributed and ecological equilibrium is being distributed transnationally. A more **future-oriented vision**, because reaching a sustainable equilibrium in the long term – for instance, thirty years – demands that we make choices today. This rationale has brought about a **policy plan** which is different because it extends much further into the future, with a policy horizon extending to 2030, and a desired situation to be reached in 30 years' time described as: ■ A healthy and safe life: *The land, water and air, as well as food, products and drinking water are all so healthy and safe that there is a negligible risk that people will become ill or die from them. The risk of serious accidents is socially accepted.* ■ Within an attractive living environment surrounded by dynamic nature: *The daily living environment is perceived as clean and attractive. Everywhere the quality of the air, the land and the water is in keeping with the function of that area and this quality does not pose any obstacles to the nature functions. Water availability is not a problem anywhere and the rural areas are of high quality. Biodiversity and soil fertility are used sustainably.* ■ Without damaging global diversity or depleting natural resources: *The availability of natural resources is safeguarded; both current and future generations can fulfil their needs. The demand for renewable resources is in balance worldwide with the supply. Non-renewable resources are available long enough to allow for the development of good alternatives. Biodiversity is such that the supply of genetic material remains adequate.*
Strategic objectives	There are '**tenets**' and '**objectives**' stipulated for each theme. Interestingly the rhetoric used to elaborate on the objectives of each theme is not uniform: for 'External safety policy innovation', 'tenets' are stipulated, whereas for 'Chemical substances policy innovation', 'objectives' are set.
Targets	The strategy is given a **30-year timescale.** The targets are said to be **negotiated locally** in light of national objectives. As a member of the **European Union**, The Netherlands also complies with the environmental targets set for EU member countries.
Triggers	Funding is a major crux of the institutional plan for The Netherlands. If the possibilities for **internalizing environmental costs** turn out to be limited in practice, the phased implementation of the proposed set of instruments for the policy document will be modified.
Action plans	These are decided **per theme**: 'Emissions, energy and mobility', 'Biodiversity and natural resources', 'Environment, nature and agriculture', 'Chemical substances policy innovation' and 'External safety policy innovation'. For example, under 'Biodiversity and natural resources', specific tasks such as: ■ to take international initiatives to combat deforestation; ■ to work towards translating the concept of sustainable agriculture into concrete guidelines for developing countries.
Institutional plan	There is considerable emphasis on coherence, coordination and the significance of local government: ■ greater cohesion between environmental and spatial policy; ■ greater cohesion between the policies at the various levels of government. Additional responsibilities for the local living environment, and greater freedom, for 'lower' tiers of government.

B: Sarhad Provincial Conservation Strategy (SPCS), Pakistan

Strategic vision	The SPCS is a statement of **commitment** by the Government and people of North West Frontier Province (NWFP) to move towards an effective programme of sustainable development. There is no explicit 'vision' – instead a goal and principles. The fundamental **goal** is to secure the economic, social and ecological well-being of the people of the NWFP through the conservation and sustainable development of the province's natural resources. The **principles** to guide the implementation of the SPCS are: ■ The conservation and sustainable development of the NWFP's resources are essential for human survival. ■ Essential ecological processes and life-support systems must be maintained. ■ The genetic and biological diversity of plants, animals and ecosystems should be conserved and promoted. ■ Economic development and environmental management must be designed together. ■ Community and development organizations and the private sector are essential in finding solutions to sustainable development. ■ Religious and cultural values must be respected and used as a resource in the design and implementation of the SPCS. ■ Each individual citizen has a responsibility to the environment and can have a positive impact on environmental conservation. ■ The NWFP has a role to play in national and international efforts for sustainable development and global environmental protection.
Strategic objectives	Treatment of the fundamental social problems that are the underlying cause of environmental degradation. Conservation, rehabilitation and sustainable development of natural resources. Protection of the living environment from air, water and soil pollution. Development of high-quality environmental protection mechanisms including appropriate legislation, development planning mechanisms, environmental quality standards, and participatory and regulatory institutional arrangements. Improvement of the institutional and financial capacity of the Government for sustainable development of natural resources. Protection and conservation of the cultural heritage of the NWFP. Improvement of community and individual involvement in decision-making about natural resources and the environment. Raising of public awareness and understanding of conservation and sustainable development issues.
Targets	All action plan commitments (below) are given a three-year time horizon.
Triggers	No triggers are apparent.
Action plans	These are phrased as **'commitments'** under **broad theme headings** such as 'Urban Environment and Sustainable Cities' and 'Sustainable Industrial Development'. Although these headings do not correspond exactly to the objectives as above, the commitments appear designed to fulfil these objectives. They are listed in a **financial plan**, are budgeted for, and form part of the **'Greening' of the Annual Development Programmes.**
Institutional plan	Key responsibilities are noted in the **financial plan.** **Focal points** have also been created in different organizations, brought together in **thematic roundtables.**

articulation for local conditions. Lacking targets and clear lines of responsibility as well as clear ownership by stakeholders or society at large, such NCSs became viewed as little more than a 'wish-list' of old and new proposals, or as set of generic technical guidelines ('encyclopaedias of desirable actions', in the opinion of the Pakistan NCS Mid Term Review Team – Hanson et al 2000). Some of the Vision 2020 exercises lacked institutional plans, and so had no clear link to implementation. And many strategies lack triggers – framing all aspirations in terms of unprioritized and unlinked targets, which are prone to failure in their entirety.

However, as noted in Chapter 4 (page 82), a strategy that concentrates on basic visions, core societal goals and mechanisms – rather than getting wrapped up in the details of individual targets – can be more desirable from one political regime to the next.

Challenges, principles and useful frameworks for making strategy decisions

Challenges for decision-making

GETTING A GOOD GRASP OF THE PROBLEMS BEING FACED

It isn't that they can't see the solution, it is that they can't see the problem. (G K Chesterton)
A problem well stated is a problem half solved. (Charles Kettering)
The problem, not a theory nor a style, determines the solution. (Karl Gerstner)

Understanding the problem is the first step to action on sustainable development

Although it seems obvious that decision-makers should have a clear understanding of the nature of the problems to be addressed as the fundamental first step towards action on sustainable development, it is not always the case. How this can be achieved is addressed in Chapter 5 (Analysis) and Chapter 6 (Participation). If problem definition is done well, half the battle of arriving at sensible decisions has been won:

DEALING WITH A WIDE RANGE OF INTEGRATION AND TRADE-OFF CHALLENGES

If our decisions are going to be made in the conventional, one-dimensional way, how can we hope to better a world that is entirely made up of complex linkages? (Ashok Khosla 2001)

It is difficult to bring the complexity of different objectives, levels and stakeholders together in ways that help decision-making ...

Even given good inputs, it can still be very difficult to integrate a variety of different objectives, dimensions, hierarchical levels, stakeholders and the interests of different generations or societal groups – much less to make informed trade-offs between them – where integration proves impossible. The challenges include the following:

- Making trade-offs between very *different objectives and dimensions*: This is the common problem of a lack of a commonly accepted 'scale' on which to compare and make choices between options which are as different as 'apples and oranges'. A good example is decisions for options for poverty reduction as opposed to biodiversity protection. Economic analysis attempts to use money as that scale, but there are very different degrees of willingness to trust prices, particularly when monetary values are estimated for non-marketed environmental or social values, or to interfere with markets to produce a given outcome.
- Making trade-offs between *different spatial levels*: Many issues tend to be complicated by differential effects at different scales. For example, a decision to open up mining in a wild landscape may reduce biodiversity at a local level. But it could also open up beneficial paths for national development and alleviate regional structural employment problems. However, such a trade-off may not be simply

between local environment and national development. At the global level, the mineral being produced may permit a technology to take off, resulting in widespread energy efficiency and reduction of global greenhouse gases.

- Making trade-offs between the interests of *different stakeholders*: Some stakeholders may be affected more than others by a particular decision, or one stakeholder may bear more risk than another. This suggests the importance of identifying key stakeholders, and for government to lead in multi-stakeholder negotiation. It may also be necessary to weight decisions in favour of those who bear costs and risks involuntarily, as opposed to those who do so for entrepreneurial gain.
- Making trade-offs between *generations*: From the very definition of sustainable development, future generations are important stakeholders who, however, cannot speak for themselves. Protecting their interests is fundamental to the achievement of sustainability. This may require decision systems and procedures, from forecasting and modelling to legislation and agreed discount rates on investments, to make their case.

This complexity gives rise to both institutional and methodological challenges. An early one is to determine which value set should take preference in strategy decisions, who should do what in the process and what capacity they need to participate effectively. The methodological challenges concern how to make the decisions, or – preferably – how to negotiate them. There is no universal formula – decisions processes need to reflect a society's accepted values and cultural norms, and various socially acceptable procedures for negotiation and working towards consensus. There also needs to be an adequate awareness of decision processes at different spatial levels. For example, if a national strategy is being developed, it will need to be sensitive to values and consensus decisions, which have been taken in the international framework, and in local areas.

DEALING WITH 'REAL-WORLD' ISSUES AND AVOIDING 'PLANNERS' DREAMS'
Strategies to date have often made decisions in a political, commercial or social vacuum. Current guidelines on strategy development often fail to address problematic aspects of decision-making, even when these guidelines cover most aspects of participation and information requirements (eg GEF guidelines for National Biodiversity Strategies and Action Plans; Carew-Reid et al 1994 on NSDSs). Overall, they give the impression that major decisions can and will be made through brainstorming, provided good information is available and enough stakeholders are involved. At best, they tend to assume that decisions are arrived at through a 'rational' process of expert assessments, a series of workshops, document finalization and final government approval (Box 8.1). Such an approach to decision-making has been common in many strategies to date. But it suffers from two major drawbacks:

- The different values held by stakeholders and team members are rarely made explicit.
- Their power bases operate unchecked by outcomes of the strategy process.

In other words, NSDS processes have tended to use decision-making processes that are too technocratic, and often politically naive. In most, if not all, countries, many of the 'real' decisions that profoundly affect society and steer the direction of development are essentially and fundamentally political, not technical, decisions. They reflect overtly or implicitly some value sets over others, and they involve many obvious or subtle mechanisms to make the voices of some stakeholders count for much more than others. They may involve 'behind the scenes' negotiations, and may use consensus-building processes to particular ends (eg trades union negotiations and making deals with business in privatizing public functions).

> ### Box 8.1 Flaws in the conventional route of strategy decision-making
>
> (i) 'Expert' assessments and technical tools have dominated the provision of information for decision-making, notably economics and modelling tools. However, the relevance of these tools and their power to influence decisions are often taken as given and are not open to criticism. Yet it could be argued that:
>
> *Every tool carries with it the spirit by which it has been created.' (Heisenberg, 1901–1976).*
>
> (ii) **A series of 'workshops'** has been a common procedure to reach 'decisions' – the notion being that getting as many stakeholders as possible around a table will produce the best ideas about how to deal with issues. Whether workshops actually make the best decisions is also open to question. In practice:
>
> *Those who show up and shout loudest usually get their way.*
>
> 'Consultation' and 'consensus-building' are inherently different activities that should not be confused. Both are part of the decision-making and decision-taking processes but, in themselves, do not ensure that decisions, compatible with the principles of sustainable development, will be taken.
>
> (iii) **'Document finalization'** results, ultimately, in one person or a small team effectively becoming obliged to make the final decision. Again, this reality is not always questioned, in spite of:
>
> *He who controls the pen controls everything.*
>
> (iv) **Final 'government approval'** and decision to proceed with the strategy. There tends to be an assumption that the strategy as a whole should be submitted to the highest levels of government, in spite of increasingly common observations that:
>
> *A decade after Rio … faith in the ability of governments to shift the direction of development through their collective power of decision appears a bit quaint. Governments are no longer expected to take decisions that will 'bring about' sustainable development.* (Halle 2001)

There are no easy answers on how to ensure that political decision processes support sustainable development objectives. On the one hand, strategy processes must make use of the 'real' decision-making processes of politics, business and investment, and input mainstream sustainability objectives into them more effectively. People involved in strategy processes need to be constantly aware of the social values that could both guide trade-offs and promote sustainability. On the other hand, there is often a bad legacy of rotten decision-making 'procedures', frequently masked by a technocratic approach, intended to protect the status quo of the powerful. These may need to be dismantled or subtly altered. Similarly, there are anti-sustainability 'values' which need to be challenged – especially by ensuring good communications and promoting the value of transparency.

… and work towards long-term changes in governance that will bring sustainable development into the mainstream

The long-term implication of this problem is the need for changes in patterns of governance through the continued exercise of strategy decision-making, rather than decision-making perceived simply as efficient multi-factorial 'project design'. The strategy process may typically start off by being hampered by inadequate decision-making structures and value systems and by the exclusion of marginalized groups from decision-making. But the strategy itself should be seen as a principal means to develop governance processes that bring sustainability and relevant social groups into the mainstream of decision-making. At the national level, this implies recognition that the strategy will experiment with new approaches to decision-making. Here, one role for both states and multilateral organizations is to encourage discussion and eventual adoption of a universal, normative framework of rights and sustainability principles that should guide future decisions (page 261).

ACHIEVING CONSENSUS ON THE VAST RANGE OF SUSTAINABLE DEVELOPMENT ISSUES

According to the Earth Council (2000), a major constraint to evolving strategies being developed by the NCSDs in Burkina Faso, Canada, Honduras and Uganda, was an inability to achieve consensus on sustainability issues. Part of the problem is that sustainable development covers such a multiplicity of interrelated topics that practically no one can get a grasp of (or even cares about) the whole agenda. It is easier to be clear about the values being brought to bear in a very specific case; for example, a development decision to remove natural forest for pulp plantations or a decision to introduce carbon taxes. If people do have a broad grasp of the agenda, their positions may be extreme, such as a 'cornucopian' approach, which believes in the potential for technological triumph versus a 'doomsday' belief in inevitable ecological and societal collapse.

In the absence of consensus, knowledge about what can possibly and practically be achieved is an essential ingredient in the decision-making process. For example, while it may be sensible to explore the inconsistencies between a government's existing sectoral policies and sustainable development principles, this may be counter-productive as a result of being perceived as negative/critical. Investment in the development of a replacement strategy that bypasses the deficiencies of the existing arrangements may, at times, be the only way forward. This was witnessed directly in the conduct of a strategic environmental assessment in the North–West Region of Botswana, which focused on the minimization of risk in controlling major cattle diseases (Ralph Cobham, personal communication).

Principles and frameworks for decision-making

GOOD DECISIONS SHOULD BE BASED ON ACKNOWLEDGED VALUES

Values invariably condition strategy decisions, whether expressed overtly (eg in constitutional rights, principles or codes of practice) or implicitly in the decision. Those values that predominate not only determine the outcome of decision processes, but also the acceptability of the decisions to various stakeholders, and thus the likelihood of their implementation. Arriving at a workable consensus on a value system to underpin sustainable development is one of the most challenging areas of NSDSs and one where considerable further attention is required.

Society's values condition strategy decisions and their acceptability …

There are two broad dimensions to the issue. First, given the trans-border and regional nature of many tasks of sustainable development and the global reach of multinational corporations (for good or bad) and international agreements, there is the need for a shared ethical system which transcends national boundaries and cultures, and yet can also find resonance and expression in local cultural systems (the latter is discussed in the next section). Second, there is a need to consider issues of international equity, which, for example, currently bedevil debate over implementation of the Kyoto Accord.

These are large issues that can only be touched on here. The first is addressed by Carley and Christie (2000b):

> *Underpinning organizational and institutional constraints to sustainable development … is the failure to develop a consensual philosophy of resource conservation that enables us to devise workable solutions to the challenges of managing 'the commons'. By consensual, we mean a philosophy which bridges nations and cultures and, perhaps more difficultly, which links the interests of the world's rich, poor and middle-income residents in a common concern for resource conservation. Such a philosophy would also have to link ethical concerns about intergenerational equity and social justice to quantitative and qualitative systems for allocating opportunities for resource harvesting on the basis of scientific assessments of the carrying capacity of ecosystems.*

… so seeking consensus and addressing ethical concerns is very important

The second aspect of the issue is pinpointed by Cable (1999):

Perhaps one of the most difficult of all the ethical issues is international inequality. It is also one of the most pressing since some important international agreements, notably those related to the environmental 'commons', hinge upon achieving a shared sense of a fair distribution of obligations and benefits. This issue has lurked at the back of international relations throughout the post-war era.

STRATEGY DECISIONS SHOULD REFLECT LOCALLY ACCEPTED VALUES

A strategy process must reflect local values and work through existing national and local decision-making frameworks

Local value systems are also vitally important as a basis for a national strategy. If the strategy does not reflect local values, it is unlikely to be 'owned' or implemented, even if its decisions appear logical, interesting or scientifically sound. Consequently, a strategy process needs to identify and articulate, where necessary, the normative framework for decision-making. It should begin with the existing national/local value basis on which decisions may be made. This will include formal and informal values expressed through, for example:

■ constitutional guarantees;
■ property rights;
■ democratic rights;
■ major provisions of economic, environmental and social legislation;
■ existing sustainable development programmes (if actually implemented);
■ related political values, especially those held in common by major parties;
■ local knowledge frameworks embodying uncertainty, experience and values;
■ traditional cultural systems;
■ religious beliefs.

A good starting point is to review which existing public policy goals have helped sustainable development

Conflicts over values cannot always be completely resolved – the strategy should not hide this reality

It will not always be easy to capture the 'spirit' with which strategic decisions have been made locally. Participatory approaches can offer both politically desirable and analytically rigorous means of uncovering the more informal values (ESRC 1998). The most reliable basis would be to identify a *hierarchy of existing public policy goals*, each with a precedent, which can be shown to have helped sustainable development. For example, in many countries, certain human rights tend to come first. This has helped in reaching decisions by excluding development options that deny the rights of some groups in society, even if they might help to fulfil those of others.

Mediating between conflicting value systems is a major challenge. For example, in some countries, the tradition is that local people freely cut trees, but this practice, which may or may not be sustainable depending on the regeneration capacity of the ecosystem, may run counter to national legislation. In other countries, legislation may allow livestock to freely graze, or fishing in all waters, but local custom may impose some restrictions on who can do what and when. Multi-stakeholder strategy processes may help to overcome such conflicts, but there are always likely to remain some situations where conflicts over values cannot be totally resolved, where some individuals maintain intransigent positions with immovable views.

---

5 A major challenge is that definitions/interpretations of justice differ. The continuing conflicts in many areas of the world (eg in Northern Ireland and between the Israelis and Palestinians) suggest that even the basic right of self-determination is problematic.

STRATEGY DECISIONS SHOULD REFLECT GLOBAL VALUES

This is necessary partly because there is an international 'footprint', or impact, of national actions, and the means to address these impacts need to be decided in ways which are universally just and sound, or in accord with some ethical framework, as discussed above.[5] But it is also necessary because a given society's value set itself may need to *evolve* – or at least be *challenged* – to promote sustainable development. Precedent and the existing hierarchy of local values offer an expedient basis for decision-making, but they may not reflect what should be modernizing aspirations of contemporary society.

However, there also needs to be clarity, transparency and widespread participation in any process by which 'new' values are introduced into decision-making frameworks. It is, therefore, instructive and necessary for future-oriented NSDSs to consider the *universal normative framework* which is emerging internationally (Box 8.2) – particularly so because its emergence is, in large part, a response to issues of environment, development and equity.

It is not surprising that there are a number of alternative sets of principles to guide decisions, both local and international, but how are 'meta-decisions' taken on which set or sets to guide subsequent decision-making processes? A diagnosis of the current hierarchy of public policy objectives (above) might reveal areas that need strengthening. The decision-making framework used by the World Commission on Dams – based on rights, risks and negotiation – is highly instructive in this regard as it pulled together a coherent set of principles from international practice (Boxes 8.5 and 8.13). The fact that the World Commission on Dams has provided this framework reflects the widespread dissatisfaction over several strategic decisions taken concerning the development of large dam projects, including several in China, India and Pakistan.

Decisions should consider the impact of national decisions

Strategies need to address new global values introduced by the emerging universal normative framework

The framework used by the World Commission on Dams is instructive

Box 8.2 The emerging universal normative framework

Human rights, expressed in the 1947 Universal Declaration of Human Rights (www.un.org/Overview/rights). This covers rights to: self-determination; consultation; democratic representation; remedy; and an adequate standard of living. It also covers freedom from arbitrary deprivation of property and from violence; and freedom of thought, conscience, religion and expression. It promotes the right to a social and international order in which these rights can be fully realized. Being expressed in law, human rights offers, as the report of World Commission on Dams (2000) has put it, 'a principled basis for mediating development choices among competing interests'.

Development rights, expressed in the 1986 Declaration on the Rights to Development (www.unhcr.ch). This moves beyond the sphere of individual human rights to address relationships between actors and the state, and specifies responsibilities in applying a human rights approach to development. It promotes the right of people to exercise full sovereignty over their resources, rights to participate actively, freely and meaningfully in national development, and rights to fair distribution of the benefits. It promotes certain good governance criteria, such as the rule of law, accountable bureaucracies and freedom of information. It defines limits to state authority (ie through adherence to the framework of international conventions). A number of development agencies have expanded on this rights framework to suggest the need for a rights-based approach to development, where civil, political, economic, social and cultural rights are, in effect, indivisible. They promote rights to education, health care, livelihood, and so on.

The Rio Principles on integrating environment and development, expressed in the 1992 Declaration on Environment and Development (www.unep.org/Documents). This accepted that the environment was fundamental to human well-being, and that its management for advancing human goals was a central task of governments and the international community. The 27 principles include: the notions that people are at the centre of concerns for sustainable development (Principle 1); the right to development provided that it is met in an equitable way that considers future generations (2); the importance of integrating environmental concerns into the development process, but also forming a central feature of that process (4); participation in decision-making (10); state compensation for victims of environmental damage (13); the precautionary principle to be adopted by states according to their capabilities (15); and the importance of indigenous people and local communities in environmental management and development (22). The effect of these principles has been strengthened further by their inclusion in various UN agreements, from the legal to the operational, including Agenda 21.

'Integrating environment and development in decision-making' is particularly significant for NSDSs. It is a key principle of the UN Commission for Sustainable Development, and progress is regularly addressed in CSD sessions in two broad areas: development of integrated NSDSs (the lack of progress in which has regularly been cited as a major problem); and valuation, natural resource accounting and other forms of integrated economic/environmental accounting.

The International Development Goals – an integrated set of economic, social and environmental goals for sustainable development, selected by the OECD DAC (see Box 2.7, OECD DAC 1997 and www.developmentgoals.org).

The Millennium Development Goals – set out in the Millennium Declaration, signed by 187 world leaders at the UN General Assembly on 8 September 2000. Among these is the goal 'to integrate the principles of sustainable development into country policies and programmes and reverse the loss of environmental resources', for which NSDSs are an acknowledged mechanism (www.un.org/millenium/declaration/ares552e.htm) (see Box 2.10).

Other sustainable development principles are becoming established in international law, principally through the framework of Multilateral Environmental Agreements. These include (see also Chapter 5):

■ *The precautionary principle* – if there are threats of serious or irreversible environmental damage, lack of full scientific certainty should not be used as a reason for postponing measures to prevent environmental degradation.[6]
■ *Polluter pays* – those who generate pollution and waste should bear the costs of avoidance, containment and/or abatement.
■ *User pays* – the users of goods and services should pay prices based on the full life cycle of costs, including the 'externalities' connected with use of non-marketed natural resources and assets and the ultimate disposal of wastes.
■ *Inter-generational equity* – the present generation should maintain or enhance capital and keep development options open for future generations (see 'strong and weak sustainability' below).
■ *Intra-generational equity* – the lessening of inequality in the current generation as a primary goal of development. However, this is often interpreted differently – usually as elimination or alleviation of poverty (as in the International Development Goals, see Box 2.9) but also as equal shares for all (as in calls by many developing nations for equal 'eco-space' rights in carbon emissions).
■ *Free, prior and informed consent* of groups to changes such as development plans. This has been given legal standing in the Draft Declaration on the Rights of Indigenous Peoples and in Conventions 107 and 169 of the ILO.
■ *Helping (involuntary) risk-bearers to participate in decisions as well as risk-takers (government, investors)* – precedents in this area are just starting to emerge through the work of the World Commission on Dams (Box 8.4).

International comprehensive sets of sustainable development principles: To the above growing list may be added sets of principles associated with particular international initiatives. These have been promoted precisely because they offer a comprehensive set of principles to aid decision-making for sustainable development. They may include many of the above. Key examples are:

■ the IUCN/UNEP/WWF 'Caring for the Earth' principles (IUCN/UNEP/WWF 1991);
■ the Earth Council's Earth Charter (www.earthcharter.org);
■ the UN Global Compact principles (three principles from each of Human Rights, UNCED and ILO labour convention) (www.unglobalcompact.com);
■ the OECD DAC principles for Strategies for Sustainable Development (Box 3.1); this offers key principles on the institutions, processes and systems required for sustainable development (transparency, accountability, comprehensive, integration, participation, consensus, capacity, demand-driven from bottom-up, etc).

Constitutional commitments to protecting the environment and for sustainable development. Already, more than 60 national constitutions in the world recognize at least some responsibility to protect the environment (Box 8.3 provides examples from Southern Africa). Enshrining such rights in constitutions is one thing; guaranteeing them is more difficult.

6 Blanket use of the *precautionary principle* has tended to obscure a range of very different levels of uncertainty. Unless used in a way which distinguishes between low and high probability risks, there is a danger that the principle will be seriously devalued or will result in unwarranted discrimination, for example, in trade terms.

STRATEGY DECISIONS SHOULD REFLECT RISK AND UNCERTAINTY

Decision-makers need to be able to cope with the long-term horizon of sustainable development, with unknowns in stakeholder reactions to decisions, with unknowns in science and with unforeseen changes in social and market systems. Different political systems, livelihood systems and businesses have their own ways of dealing with uncertainty and will exhibit different attitudes to risk. Many of them will have developed useful sources of resilience. These provisions need to be identified, discussed and assessed in relation to the frequently increasing levels of uncertainty. Existing approaches may not be adequate. They may be supplemented by a number of approaches that have helped in strategies elsewhere:

Sustainable development is a long-term business ...

- *Assessment and ranking of risk.* Comparative risk assessment was developed in the USA as a tool to help decision-makers rank priorities among many risks. It involves the collection of data, use of statistical techniques and presentation of relative risks to stakeholders (see first paragraph in Box 8.5). Often, however, it has tended to focus on current risks rather than emerging trends. The risk assessment is a separate process from the priority setting (which then brings together risk-based and non-risk based criteria and can use a variety of methods from negotiated consensus, to formulae, to voting).
- *Involve research and information networks.* As noted in Chapter 5, it is remarkable how much policy is made without an informed approach to science and market/social trends. Support to research institutions and 'think tanks' and to their interaction with strategy stakeholders can help to generate an informed approach. It may also be necessary to agree a formal role for such institutions in providing best judgement on emerging issues.

... and the risks and uncertainties need to be assessed

FORMAL METHODOLOGIES FOR DECISION-MAKING CAN HELP, BUT HAVE LIMITATIONS

Many *analytical* methods, which can provide useful information for good decisions, were discussed in Chapter 5, such as strategic environmental assessment. Here, we introduce a few formal *decision-making* methods and frameworks. On the one hand, they have an important role to play in fostering intelligent treatment of complex issues – through structuring information, presenting possible options and highlighting issues for which trade-offs may need to be made. On the other hand, no formal method can be relied on as the primary means to assess choices and make trade-offs for sustainable development, not least because:

Formal approaches can be used to make decisions ...

- each type of formal method is based on series of assumptions, which themselves represent value judgements about the way in which development ought to unfold, and about what priorities ought to hold;
- each method represents a simplification, or model, of a complex, highly interactive reality and is only a partial representation.

Decision theory   Decision theory tends to be highly complex. However, at its basic level, it involves a few, simple steps:

... from the theoretical, with assumptions that need careful assessment

- an intelligence phase, collecting information to understand a problem;
- a design phase in which alternatives are explored by building models and assessing possible consequences by altering variables in the model;
- a choice phase, in which the alternatives are weighed up against given criteria.

Box 8.3 **What some Southern African constitutions say about the environment**

Malawi: Article 13 of Chapter III (Fundamental Rights) commits the State to actively promote the welfare and development of the people of Malawi by progressively adopting and implementing policies and legislation aimed at, inter alia, managing the environment responsibly in order to 'accord full recognition to the rights of future generations by means of environmental protection and the sustainable development of natural resources'.

The State also has an obligation to prevent the degradation of the environment; provide a healthy living and working environment for the people of Malawi; and conserve and enhance the biological diversity of Malawi.

While the new constitution is not specific about environmental rights per se, Article 30 (2) states that the:

State shall take all necessary measures for the realization of the right to development. Such measures shall include, amongst other things, equality of opportunity for all in their access to basic resources, education, health services, food, shelter, employment and infrastructure.

Mozambique: The constitution obliges the State to promote efforts to guarantee the ecological balance, and the conservation and preservation of the environment, seeking to improve the quality of life for citizens. Article 72 (Fundamental Rights, Duties and Freedom) states that Mozambican citizens

shall have the right to live in a balanced natural environment and shall have the duty to defend the same.

Article 80 further provides an opportunity to citizens to compel the state to protect their environmental and other rights. It states that

all citizens shall have the right to present petitions, complaints and claims before the relevant authority to obtain the restoration of rights that have been violated, or in defence of the public interest.

Namibia: Article 95 (Promotion of the Welfare of the People) refers to the maintenance of ecosystems, essential ecological processes and biological diversity of the country, and utilization of living natural resources on a sustainable basis for the benefit of all Namibians, both present and future. In particular,

the Government shall provide measures against the dumping or recycling of foreign nuclear and toxic waste on Namibian territory.

South Africa: Widespread provisions are aimed at ensuring a healthy environment. The constitution stipulates that 'every person shall have the right to an environment which is not detrimental to his or her health or well-being'. Section 175, Sub-section 3, extends this right to local governments:

A local government shall, to the extent determined in any applicable law, make provision for access by all persons residing within its area of jurisdiction to water, sanitation, transportation facilities, electricity, primary health services, education, housing and security within a safe and healthy environment, provided that such services and amenities can be rendered in a sustainable manner and are financially and physically practicable.

The constitution also provides for the restitution of land rights.

Source: Adapted from Chenje (1995)

Taking these steps requires a standardization of values in order to compare options on a single scale (commonly money or probability of events). The standardized values are then aggregated to form the basis for a judgement – through decision support tools such as factor analysis or multi-criteria analysis (below). A favourable decision is advocated if the aggregate values exceed a given threshold. While decision theory can help in some engineering or land use planning decisions, for example, it is also based on assumptions that may not hold in consideration of complex issues of development and social change. Among the problematic areas are: poor measurability of variables, lack of knowable relations between variables, the difficulty of objectivity in calculation, and the utility of aggregation.

Box 8.4 **The decision-making framework of the World Commission on Dams: 'Recognition of rights and assessment of risks as the basis for negotiated decisions'**

The mandate of the World Commission on Dams (WCD) is highly pertinent to NSDSs – balancing local environment and development needs, and balancing these in turn with needs at the national and regional levels. The WCD recognized the dilemmas that governments face when trying to satisfy urgent national development needs and, at the same time, advance the realization of fundamental rights. It noted how, in the face of these dilemmas, the 'public interest' is shifting from one which placed a premium on economic growth interests to one that places more weight on the rights and interests of people and communities affected by development, and the risks they (often unwillingly) bear. The WCD judged that the value basis for making decisions needed to broaden accordingly:

The traditional balance sheet approach of assessing costs and benefits is inadequate for effective development planning and decision-making ... Such trade-offs neither capture the complexity of considerations involved nor can they adequately reflect the values societies attach to different options in the broader context of sustainable development ... [Furthermore], traditional practice is to restrict the definition of risk to the developer or corporate investor. By contrast, a far larger group often have (sic) risks imposed on them involuntarily and managed by others ... [In] the case of future generations and the ecosystem ... these 'risk bearers' cannot speak for themselves, even if the risks they face are acknowledged.

As a recent initiative, the WCD sought to assess the growing range of international normative frameworks now available to address these issues. It proposed a framework that would be consistent at the global level but allow for local differences. Consequently, the WCD decision-making framework is based on 'a rights based approach where recognition of rights and assessment of risks (particularly rights at risk) provides the basis for negotiated decisions on dams'.

The WCD suggests that demonstrable public acceptance of key decisions is essential, and that this acceptance emerges from recognizing rights, addressing risks, safeguarding the entitlements of all groups of affected people, and ensuring agreements are negotiated in an open and transparent process conducted in good faith, with informed participation and free, prior and informed consent. It notes how a multi-stakeholder forum can facilitate this. For actually making decisions, the WCD proposes five values of equity, efficiency, participatory decision-making, sustainability and accountability. It applies the precautionary principle in relation to risk.

Source: World Commission on Dams (2000)

Where there is difficulty in modelling decision-making processes – which is frequently the case for sustainable development issues – there is a tendency to rely on particular individuals to take the necessary judgements (what those involved in decision theory dress up as 'human-based decisions', as if there were any other). In some, simpler cases, a small number of people may have the capacity to weigh alternatives and recognize a good outcome, even if they cannot articulate the reasons for it. However, everyone embodies some value system which they apply to sustainable decisions. Where people from many backgrounds need to work together to arrive at consensus, conflicting values need to be made apparent, and agreed value sets defined (above) (Hall, undated).

Decision support tools   Decision support tools can help with some aspects of sustainable development decisions, particularly if it is recognized that they support, or help with, decisions, but do not make those decisions. For example, regulators and planning inspectors act as referees and face a series of repeated decisions in which issues of consistency and uniform criteria arise. Consistency should be based on relevant values and principles, and should be transparently applied. But decisions can also be aided by 'off-the-peg' tools that are scientifically respectable, professionally justifiable and socially acceptable. Some of these are software-based:

... to standard planning tools, which often simplify reality ...

- *Computer-aided design (CAD) and geographic information systems* (GIS, Box 5.10) have proved to be of value for spatial planning.

Box 8.5 **Risk-based priority setting**

Risk ranking

In risk ranking (environmental) problems are assessed on the basis of three types of risk: human health risk, ecological risk and quality of life risk, including adverse economic and social impacts. Environmental problems are assessed and ranked within a common framework that allows for comparisons between problems. Specific steps and formulas for assessing risk have been developed for each of the three types of risk.

Priority setting

In the priority-setting step, the information gathered through risk analysis is presented to stakeholders and decision-makers to augment, but not to replace, people's values, concerns and judgements in setting priorities. Stakeholders are invited to set priorities based on an analysis of both risk and non-risk factors. Priorities may ultimately differ from the risk ranking, owing to such non-risk factors as cost-effectiveness, technical feasibility, public perception and resources available.

Three activities are commonly used in risk-based priority setting: negotiated consensus, voting and formulas. These tools range from being relatively unstructured to being very systematic.

Negotiated consensus is the least structured priority-setting method and involves open discussion to analyse and discuss data, values and uncertainties. The following steps are generally followed: review data; solicit proposals for how individual problems should be prioritized; discuss objections or alternatives to proposals; discuss and debate unresolved objections; and establish final priorities.

Voting to establish the majority's will is the approach used if there are unresolved disagreements about problems or projects. The majority can be defined by the decision-making group (eg 51 per cent, 66 per cent, and so forth). There are at least three voting methods – secret ballots, open voting and multi-voting.

Formulas are used to break environmental problems into parts, evaluate each of these parts mathematically and recombine the parts to produce an output. Priorities are determined based on resulting scores assigned to each problem. There is a wide variety of formulaic approaches to priority setting. Weighted scoring is commonly used in comparative risk and involves five steps:

Step 1	Identify criteria for evaluating risk.
Step 2	Score each problem for each criterion.
Step 3	Assign weights to each criterion.
Step 4	Multiply the criteria scores by the weights and add the results to produce a total score.
Step 5	Rank problems according to total scores.

Source: ICLEI (1996a)

- *Life cycle analysis* can help link particular production systems with multiple sustainability issues and different institutional responsibilities.
- *Risk assessment* can help with planning major developments (point (d) above).
- *Knowledge-based systems* can 'capture' expertise and turn data into useful information for decision-makers.
- *Multi-criteria analysis* (MCA) is widely thought to be more conducive to an approach that hinges on stakeholder participation as much as technical analysis, as it emphasizes political decisions.
- *Decision trees* (Figure 8.1) provide a structure in which alternative decisions and the implications of taking those decisions can be laid down and evaluated. They assist the formation of an accurate, balanced picture of the risks and rewards associated with each choice. The objective should be to make the choices and degree of uncertainty explicit at each stage, as a way to improve stakeholder input and transparency into the decision. Where possible, numbers might be allocated to each of the arrows in the diagram (cost-benefit ratios, ranking, etc). See Chapter 5, page 149 for more information on causal diagrams, problem and decision trees.

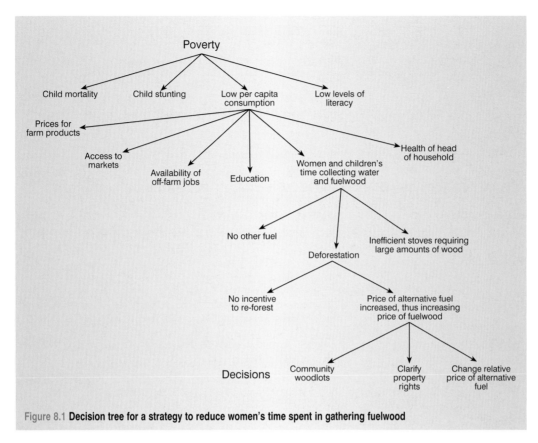

Figure 8.1 Decision tree for a strategy to reduce women's time spent in gathering fuelwood

However, all of these tools tend to side-step the challenge of assessing trade-offs and making difficult choices. Even MCA basically 'passes the buck' to the stakeholders who are expected to decide how to trade off progress on one criterion against negative change in other criterion. In effect, it is cost-benefit analysis without monetization. These approaches are more or less reductionist in that they simplify reality with more aggregated approaches losing information as aggregation proceeds.

... and avoid making hard choices ...

Not surprisingly, there remains a continued search for decision support systems for sustainable development that can bring these disparate tools and associated information together, especially if it is also conducive to a stakeholder-led approach. A recent conference organized by the Canadian-based International Development Research Centre to assess needs for decision support systems concluded that the most useful kind of system should comprise knowledge-based systems, GIS and modelling, with multiple language capabilities (Hall, undated). The Economic and Social Research Council (ESRC) agrees that an integrated system would be useful, but stresses that we should not become slaves to it (ESRC 1998).

'Strong' and 'weak' sustainability   Making use of a concept of *'strong' sustainability* can help with certain decisions, by restricting the range of options that need to be considered. For example, its principles forbid trade-offs involving certain forms of 'critical natural capital', which it demands are passed undiminished to succeeding generations. This capital might include, inter alia, national parks or other lands of high biodiversity value, wetlands and other ecosystems providing vital life-supporting functions such as nutrient recycling. The rationale is that these values are irreplaceable. The difficulty comes, of course, in identifying the boundaries of 'critical' natural capital: which biodiversity, for example, is 'critical' as opposed to merely 'valuable'? Another difficulty is that denying the possibility of substitution implies that certain types of capital have 'absolute' value, greater than any other objective or consideration. This is often hard to reconcile with a people-centred approach to sustainable development.

... to limiting the range of choices to be considered

The alternative concept of *'weak' sustainability*, on the other hand, allows substitution of different forms of capital – natural, physical, financial, human and social. Its principles demand that equivalent or increasing amounts of capital are passed to subsequent generations, but allow the form of this capital to be interchangeable (still a very hard test for most existing societies to meet!). Thus, potentially the concept allows the removal of, say, tropical rainforest on the basis that it might provide farmland for sustained food production or financial accumulation that would permit improved education. The difficulty here is in comparing these 'apples and oranges' and in ensuring that technically feasible substitutes for natural environmental benefits actually emerge in practice.

Institutional roles and processes for strategy decisions

The strategy's institutional framework must help and support decision-making

Enabling institutional frameworks are needed to be able to undertake and coordinate the broad scope of decisions required (page 253), and to apply the principles of sustainability to all such decisions (page 258).

Five institutional initiatives are required, namely:

- establishment of multi-stakeholder structures (discussed below);
- the provision of facilitated workshops (page 272);
- the pursuit of full/partial consensus (page 272);
- the development of guidelines for negotiating sustainable outcomes (page 276);
- the adoption of a step-wise, evolutionary approach towards achieving coherence between sectoral policies (page 280).

Those who develop and take decisions have different roles

To begin with, however, a clear distinction needs to be made between two groups involved in the whole process of strategy decision-making, and their respective responsibilities:

- The *decision-developers* are normally groups of professionally and technically experienced people (eg members of a sustainable development secretariat or council), who collectively have the responsibility to reflect and coordinate the needs and aspirations of the full range of legitimate interest groups. Their roles are usually *advisory*. While, for the most part, the organizations involved are likely to be nationally or locally based, there are clear examples of external bodies that have had an important impact on the decision-making process: for example, international and regional banks, multinational aid agencies, bilateral donors and international NGOs.
- The *decision-takers*, usually recognized as being central and local government politicians and members of the boards of large national and multinational companies, bear *ultimate responsibility* not only for the decisions that are taken, but also for the ensuing impacts.

Close interaction and cooperation between the decision-developers and decision-takers is essential to ensure that the interests of all stakeholders are both recognized and balanced. Otherwise there is a risk that decisions will be 'skewed' to reflect one or more special interest group. A primary function of the decision-developers is to exclude bias from the decision-taking process, thereby easing the task of the decision-takers.

Multi-stakeholder structures for decision-making

Some form of multi-stakeholder structure, with linked tiers at decentralized levels where appropriate, is essential to strategy decisions, as discussed in Chapter 4. Such a structure needs to operate over a longer term as a basis for exploration, development and normative clarification of both *the values and the procedures* that will be brought to bear in decisions. Useful guidance on multi-stakeholder processes has been produced by the UNED Forum (2001) (described in Chapter 6).

Box 8.6 **Diverse mandates, structures and composition of National Councils for Sustainable Development (NCSDs)**

Mandates

Most NCSDs have been assigned multiple functions and have varying degrees of authority to implement their tasks. Consistent themes in most mandates include:

- providing forums for debate on development issues which render advice and recommendations to decision makers;
- developing (and sometimes implementing) national policies and plans;
- coordinating and harmonizing action plans;
- capacity building of key bodies;
- monitoring broad progress towards sustainable development;
- raising public awareness as an important activity.

The NCSD may also have a significant regulatory and supervisory mandate, as in Uganda and Uzbekistan. However, the scope may be somewhat more limited than the broad sweep of sustainable development: for example, Romanian and South African NCSDs focus on environmental issues.

There are nearly as many procedures for creating NCSDs as there are NCSDs, ranging from legislation to government decrees to private sector initiatives. The first NCSDs were set up in the Philippines and Dominican Republic, and their experiences soon proved that legislative support was necessary for NCSD continuity, to ensure clarity in the competence of the NCSD vis-à-vis other governmental agencies and civil society organizations, and thus to avoid duplication of efforts and clashes. NCSDs in Canada, Cuba, Malawi, Mexico and Uganda are also functioning through legislation.

Organizational structures

The organization of NCSDs varies widely and is still evolving to meet the changing needs of the sustainable development agenda:

- The most important and common component of an NCSD is its *multi-stakeholder assembly*, which includes representatives of different groups and sectors and usually meets at regular intervals.
- Several countries have adopted a flexible approach that provides for the formation of *specialist committees or working groups* and the employment of outside experts as the need arises. These committees undertake most of the technical work of the NCSD, such as preparing documents and reports for consideration of the multi-stakeholder assembly. For example, the Dominican Republic's NCSD has eight thematic committees.
- Some countries also have *regional councils or branches*. For example, Mexico has four regional councils, which have authority to create separate regional structures.
- A *secretariat* often serves as the administrative or technical support to the NCSD. These can be either part of the ministry in which the NCSD is based, such as in Estonia, or independent as in Belgium, Finland, Nicaragua and Canada. In the Philippines, the NCSD is served by a secretariat made up of two independent components, one to coordinate government activities and give overall technical and administrative support, and another to coordinate activities and inputs from civil society. In El Salvador, an executive committee exists to oversee the execution of the activities by the secretariat, as agreed by the stakeholder assembly. Uganda has developed a unique multi-tiered structure involving a secretariat-like implementing body, which receives work from an environmental policy committee and board of directors. These bodies in turn receive advice from technical committees and environmental liaison units within government departments, NGOs and the private sector. This encourages greater collaboration with the NCSD. In this way, the Uganda NCSD meets many of the NSDS process principles (Box 3.1).

Membership

The *chair* of the NCSD is a significant position. She or he usually reports to a high-level position in government. The chair is also usually at a very high level:

- The NCSDs of Burkina Faso, Estonia, Finland, Honduras, Kyrgyzstan, Mongolia, Panama, Philippines, Uganda and the USA are chaired by, or report directly to, the head of state.
- Many countries have chairpersons holding government positions at ministerial level or higher. NCSDs in the Dominican Republic and El Salvador are chaired by the vice president, and in Uzbekistan by the deputy prime minister. A state minister (often of environment) chairs in Cuba, Hungary, Mexico, Niger, Norway, Philippines, Russia and Senegal.
- Other NCSDs are chaired by a well-respected independent person.

The composition of *members* varies. In most countries, the stakeholder groups represented in the NCSD are determined by an executive or legal mandate.

- A balance between government, civil society and the private sector is often required, as in Belgium, Finland, Indonesia, Nicaragua, Malawi, Mexico, the Philippines, Senegal, Slovak Republic, the United States and El Salvador.
- The NCSDs in Canada, Switzerland and the UK differ in that they do not have any government representatives. Members include opinion leaders from different regions and sectors of society; business, labour, academia, NGOs and (in Canada) indigenous peoples.
- In contrast, in Uzbekistan and South Africa, the NCSD is composed entirely of government representatives.

The procedure for *selecting representatives* varies among countries. For approximately a third of NCSDs, the head of state appoints all NCSD members. In many cases, the government representatives are appointed by the government and non-government representatives by their own groups or constituencies. In El Salvador, representatives of the NGO sector are appointed by the president, based on candidates nominated by the different groups represented in the council. Representatives are usually expected to consult with and speak for their constituencies.

Source: Earth Council (2000)

National Councils for Sustainable Development take many forms

The last ten years has seen much experience of the national fora loosely termed NCSDs. However, NCSDs have taken many different forms (Box 8.6, see also Box 3.14 and Table 3.2). Box 8.7 brings together some best practice from the last ten years.

Facilitating decision-making through workshops

Workshops can be key milestones in the process of reaching decisions

In multi-stakeholder processes for sustainable development, workshops are inevitably important for explaining the basis for, and agreeing, key decisions. Recognizing also that they have limitations – all too frequently short-cutting good decisions (page 258) – the UNDP-GEF Biodiversity Planning Support Programme has developed useful guidance (Box 8.8).

Consensus

Consensus processes are integral to most strategy decisions …

The term 'consensus' is increasingly being used in the context of sustainable development but is interpreted in many different ways (Box 8.9).

… as a valuable basis for agreement …

A strategy with a broad base of support requires consensus among all participants. Consensus needs to be built concerning the strategy's objectives, principles, issues, vision, priorities, policies and actions. Consensus can be a particularly valuable basis of agreement for strategies, because no participant can be outvoted. All participants are therefore obliged to do their best to accommodate each other's interests, to compromise, to reach agreement where possible and to identify issues remaining contentious to be resolved later.

As Box 8.7 on NCSDs suggests, working to achieve full consensus is desirable in NSDS multi-stakeholder fora, because the power of these fora derives not from their executive or legislative roles, but from the unique opportunity to create agreements by bridging what may be deep divisions in society.

> **Box 8.7 Best practice decisions in NCSDs**
>
> It is not easy for a multi-stakeholder NCSD to achieve agreement on the difficult and important issues of sustainable development. Often it is the divisions on those very issues among the stakeholders that have prevented good decisions in the past. It is inevitable – and necessary – that NCSD members bring those differences to the council table. It is also essential that they find means to resolve those differences. The 1999–2000 review of NCSDs pointed to common approaches that have built trust and created the basis for agreement:
>
> *Operating by consensus* (see page 272): Broad agreement (but not necessarily unanimous consensus) has been found to be slower and more difficult than resolution of issues by majority vote. But – since NCSDs are neither executive nor legislative bodies – divided decisions are relatively meaningless because they simply replicate the disputes that divide society as a whole, without offering resolution. Indeed, where this has occurred, it has sometimes hardened that division. The power of the NCSD is derived not from the power to require others to act, but from its unique opportunity to create agreements that enable and persuade others to act – and which would not otherwise have occurred. Consensus is needed to cross the boundaries of old disagreements that have obstructed sustainability. Where NCSD members may have a history of mistrust and conflict, consensus building is also an effective means for building understanding, trust and an emerging set of values conducive to sustainability. It treats each member as equally important, and requires all members to understand one another.
>
> *Fair process:* Members must be assured that they have an equal opportunity to express their views, to participate in meetings, to review drafts, to have access to information and to contribute to decisions. For those without adequate resources, they should have access to staff support and financial assistance. Thus, a clear and agreed set of rules is needed to ensure that the NCSD's proceedings are fair and balanced.
>
> *Transparency:* Part of fairness is assuring that the NCSD's own practices are transparent, both internally and externally. All members need to know what is being said and agreed, and the public need the opportunity to learn about and comment on the NCSD's activities (some NCSDs have provision for public participation).
>
> *Engagement and problem solving:* Disagreements stem from strongly held values and ideas and significant sectoral interests. Resolving them requires engagement, persistence, good faith and – often – dispute resolution skills. Members need to show up for meetings and need to see that there is real benefit for them in overcoming disagreement. Access to group facilitation, negotiation and dispute resolution skills has been useful.
>
> Source: Earth Council (2000)

Consensus processes are also a good means for building understanding, trust and an emerging value set for sustainability, and for developing commitment to implementation of the strategy. The real differences between stakeholder consultation and consensus building need to be well understood from the outset. The former can never be a surrogate for the latter, as was only belatedly recognized in the process chosen to formulate the NCS in Botswana. The process addressed major sustainability issues and was partly responsible for an additional 12 months being required before the Government of Botswana was ready to approve the NCS.

... and for building understanding, trust and commitment ...

The consensual approach is quite different from the typical adversarial approach of parliamentary politics and law, the latter usually being based on majority rule – which often leaves a significant minority both dissatisfied with the outcome and potentially alienated from the decision-making process. It is also different from top-down administration, which tends to impose decisions (Carley and Christie 2000a).

Consensual approaches may be unfamiliar to many people, and there may be unrealistic or unclear expectations about both the 'broader interest' they are seeking and the methods they employ. So it is important to agree a set of rules concerning the process of working towards consensus early in a strategy process. For example, there are big differences between 'unanimous' consensus and 'majority' consensus, each with significant implications for strategy decisions. In Canada, for example, the Negotiated Rule-Making Act defines consensus as 'unanimous concurrence among the interests represented on a negotiated

Consensual approaches may raise unrealistic or unclear expectations, so process rules are needed

---

Box 8.8 Workshops as a means to find decisions, not pre-determine them

Even though much of the information collection, analysis and consultation will have been done by a relatively few people, the way that it can be presented to stakeholders will help them to play a significant part in strategy decisions. Workshops are helpful mechanisms here, to involve stakeholders directly in translating findings into objectives. A typical presentation that can be put by the NSDS secretariat/facilitator to a *multi-stakeholder workshop on the initial analysis and consultation* would cover the following:

- These are the criteria that we think are important for determining priorities ...
- These are the key findings from the information gathered about problems and (underlying) causes of problems ...
- These are the key gaps or weaknesses in the information base ...
- Our preliminary application of criteria to the findings suggests that these should be the (national) priorities ...
- Our reasoning is ...
- This is our degree of (un)certainty about the findings/recommendations ...
- Do you agree/disagree with our findings and recommendations?
- Is there key information that we have overlooked?

Where there is good consensus, the work of the strategy team in developing options based on the generally agreed recommendations is relatively straightforward. These can then be put to subsequent *multi-stakeholder workshops focusing on finalizing strategy options*. A typical presentation to such a workshop would cover:

- This is a reminder of the agreed priorities from the first workshop ...
- This is what work we have done to develop the priorities ...
- These are the strategy options ...
- Here is a summary of what we think each option's pros and cons, costs and responsibilities could be ...
- This is how we might wish to compare and rank the options ...

Source: Hagen (undated)

---

rule-making committee'. An NSDS may need to be flexible, as it will be dealing with a wide range of issues; it is therefore important to be clear about when unanimity is desired (say for immediate priority objectives) and when it is not necessary (such as for future options or triggers). The pros and cons of unanimity for different situations are addressed in Box 8.10.

UNED Forum (2001) recommends that:

- Participants need to agree at the beginning of any multi-stakeholder process what will constitute consensus.
- In general, participants should seek a solution that incorporates all viewpoints.
- Sometimes a majority vote can help to bring a consensus process to closure.
- However, there are considerable risks of forcing consensus and, more generally, making decisions that are premature.
- The latter can be avoided by a challenge to be creative and integrating, rather than arguing for favoured existing positions; and to view differences as helpful.

Both consensus views and dissenting views need to be recorded. During the development of the Botswana NCS in the late 1980s, for example, when issues were too contentious, or effectively non-negotiable (at the time), it was (eventually) found to be necessary to state this clearly, and to agree when and how the issue would be revisited.

> **Box 8.9 Consensus – a loaded term**
>
> The term 'consensus' has slipped easily into the rhetoric of dialogue, along with 'win–win', 'participation', and so on. In general, it means agreement – a condition in which all participants can live with the result, although not all (and maybe none) of them may embrace it with great enthusiasm. But consensus does not mean wholehearted agreement or unanimity: differing views, values and perspectives are a fact of life. Nor does consensus mean majority agreement, whereby minority concerns are effectively excluded.
>
>   Many multi-stakeholder processes assume that consensus is possible (although they may grossly underestimate the time, goodwill and money needed to produce it). But there are dangers in achieving a fragile consensus. Apparent agreements between ministries or key politicians may be worth little if those same powers continue to make decisions without reference to it, but at the same time use the agreement to rationalize these same decisions. Rushed consensus does not allow all parties to get what they want out of it, but can still produce language that appears acceptable (eg 'consensus' over 'co-management' which serves only powerful interests, or consensus over adopting 'foreign' solutions before local ones have been developed). Consensus can thus be an illusion, and forcing its formation may impede equity as well as innovation.
>
> Source: Adapted from Mayers et al (2001)

Consensus is not necessary at all stages of a strategy process. Indeed, given the value-laden and uncertain nature of many of the issues and the enormous interests at stake, strong and persistent disagreements are likely. Fundamental differences of value are probably immune to consensus. But consensus is achieved very gradually, through joint enquiry and action focused on (shared) problems. An exploration and understanding of the diversity of concerns and opinions is very important, and wide participation in the strategy process provides a continuing vehicle for this.

The use of multi-stakeholder consensus-building mechanisms, particularly roundtables, has been central to many of the strategic initiatives in Canada during the last decade (Box 8.11). They have been used to develop broad strategies and to tackle the institutional constraints facing strategy development (ie some of the barriers to 'horizontal' and 'vertical' participation); to implement or monitor those strategies; to prepare principles or action plans which may then be 'self-implemented'; to prepare policy options for government (for temporary or permanent issues); or to carry out public consultation phases in the development of public policy.

In 1993, the Canadian National Round Table on the Environment and Economy (NRTEE) issued a set of *consensus principles*, which have been very widely distributed across Canada and many other countries. In brief, these principles (NRTEE/ParticipACTION 1994) are:

10 consensus principles

  1 Purpose-driven (people need a reason for participation)
  2 Inclusive, not exclusive (as long as parties have a significant interest)
  3 Voluntary participation
  4 Self-design (the parties design the process)
  5 Flexibility
  6 Equal opportunity (in access to information and participation)
  7 Respect for diverse interests (and different values and knowledge)
  8 Accountability (to parties both within and outside the process)
  9 Time limits (realistic deadlines)
10 Commitment to implementation and monitoring

Consensus building is an iterative activity that can proceed either through mediation or through facilitation, the latter being more usually applicable to NSDSs. *Mediation* is formal and carefully structured, focuses on clearly defined and contentious issues and makes use of trained mediators. It is a form of assisted

> **Box 8.10 100 per cent consensus, or less – which is better?**
>
> A negotiated consensus may be the most likely way to reach many strategy decisions.
>
> **Full consensus:** This knits the multiple stakeholders together into a group with a common goal – developing a mutually acceptable outcome. Although they may not agree with all aspects of the outcome, all participants are willing to live with the total package. At its best, this creates a climate of 'if any one of us has a problem, we all have a problem, so let us focus on resolving the particular problems of every participant'. Yet this means that all stakeholders then also have a veto – which can engender considerable waste of effort, good ideas and goodwill if full consensus is not reached. If minority parties effectively control a linchpin component to the agreement, this vests extraordinary power in them and the majority parties (and the mediator/facilitator) will be stymied.
>
> **The '80 per cent' option:** The dynamics of the process change markedly if the definition of consensus is modified to require less than unanimity. It may make procedures easier, because difficult interest groups can be 'ignored' – they will never be fully ignored, however, as they will have recourse to other processes such as courts and means of compensation. But it can also result in parties adhering to fixed public positions, as opposed to being encouraged to develop their underlying interests and finding creative alternatives.
>
> Source: Harter and Pou (1997); Sigurdson (1997); Katz (1997)

dispute resolution. *Facilitation* (see page 220 and Box 6.29) is more useful when issues are ill defined or when stakeholders may be suspicious of the implications of a consensus process. It also tends to take longer, because it uses approaches of mutual self-discovery, or learning processes (Carley and Christie 2000a).

It has been found that consensus-building and decision-making processes can be significantly advanced through the appointment of teams of independent consultants, recruited from a combination of international and national experts.[7]

Negotiations and conflict resolution

NEGOTIATIONS

Negotiation is particularly important in setting decentralized targets

The aim of negotiations is to tackle the trade-offs inherent in sustainable development, to reach compromise in policy-making or setting responsibilities and plan objectives. It is important at the overall strategy level, but especially in setting decentralized targets. Agreed objectives and targets have a better chance of being implemented than those that are imposed.

In The Netherlands, there has been an emphasis on negotiation processes for target setting (Box 8.12). In contrast, UK recycling targets, German carbon dioxide targets and EC sulphur dioxide and NO targets were set without negotiation and, although the targets made a powerful political impact, they have not been met in practice.

> *Where rights compete or conflict, negotiations conducted in good faith offer the only process through which various interests can be legitimately reconciled ... Where no process for good-faith adjudication among competing interests exists, the result is often protracted conflict, escalation and, eventually, 'win-lose' outcomes in which less privileged groups are further disadvantaged ...*
> (World Commission on Dams 2000)

---

7 Examples where the decision-making process has been enriched in this way include the Victoria Falls SEA, the Ngamiland SEA, the environmental enrichment of the Jordanian Energy Strategy, the mechanisms for strengthening sustainable development policies and plans in Russia, and the strengthening of all institutions involved in implementation of the Kenya NEAP.

Box 8.11 **Experience of multi-stakeholder mechanisms to build consensus in Canada**

In Canada, multi-stakeholder mechanisms have been used extensively during the last decade to build consensus on policy issues. These have included:

- roundtables (many hundreds have been organized by the National Round Table on the Environment and Economy (NRTEE) at national, provincial and local levels) such as the Forest Round Table and the connected Pulp and Paper Dialogue;
- multi-stakeholder task groups (eg the Climate Change Task Group and the task Force on Economic Instruments and Disincentives to Sound Environmental Practices);
- commissions, councils and collaboratives (eg the Economic Instruments Collaborative).

These all attempted to bring together a broad range of competing interests to work on solutions, and they usually relied on consensus for decision-making and a neutral chair or facilitator.

A review of Canada's experience with roundtable processes (NRTEE 1995) highlighted some clear lessons and dilemmas:

1   When designing the multi-stakeholder process, it is important to distinguish consultation from consensus. The former meets the needs of the initiating party, but the latter should be participant-driven, which requires a neutral facilitator. The role of a multi-stakeholder process is different in each case, but *many of the frustrations of past efforts have resulted from a lack of clarity on this ... or from an attempt to blend the two approaches. They do not blend easily... You can't have the buy-in and other advantages of a consensus process until you're willing to ... allow the participants to design and manage the process.* Specific examples are not, however, given.
2   Neutral facilitation is needed to achieve roundtable objectives, as people with very different value systems and even different vocabularies naturally find it hard to agree.
3   The involvement of NGOs is essential, but many cannot afford to participate, especially to get involved in research and go beyond mere attendance. Yet government funding for NGOs compromises their independence and means that some NGOs are fully taken up with government-driven agendas. In other words, roundtables could be seen as a way for governments to neatly 'contain' participation to a limited part of the whole policy process, and indeed to coopt some groups. This has been a real problem in some roundtables.
4   In many circumstances, roundtable approaches are not appropriate, because of subject matter, lack of timeliness or lack of commitment from key stakeholders. In particular, firm political commitment to act on possible outcomes is needed initially. Roundtable processes are *still in the development stage, and it is wrong to see them as a mature phase of the policy process.*

Yet, as current institutions are not coping well with the transition to sustainability, in part because of their jurisdictional fragmentation, roundtables have forced the government to take more seriously what they call the 'horizontality problem'; that is, cross-departmental cooperation. Ronald Doering, the former Executive Director of the NRTEE, assessed that multi-stakeholder processes:

have been important experiments in policy-making and public administration. Their role is essentially transitional and catalytic; they support rather than replace elected bodies. With all their flaws, and while still generally marginal to core policy-making, Canadian roundtables are common sense partnerships.

Another commentator addressed the political aspects, acknowledging that multi-stakeholder processes have helped environment, consumer and aboriginal interests to be better represented in the 'policy marketplace'. But these processes may result in *politically compelling consensus which constrains the ability of elected politicians to make decisions'*. In other words, 'bargaining' through this marketplace is replacing the search for the common good. The better bargainers get the best deal or, perhaps, *organized interests bargain amongst themselves, cut up the pie and invite elected representatives to serve the helpings.*

In effect:

> the utility of multi-stakeholder exercises should reflect both how and how well they assist elected representatives in their core task – searching for and defining the common good, and incorporating it in public policy.

A further commentator suggests that it is essential to have a neutral forum such as NRTEE; no one stakeholder could bring together the right group without raising suspicions.

The NRTEE examined the issues of representativeness, governance and democracy. The kinds of dilemmas raised include: the notion of the flourishing of a stakeholder elite at the expense of the broader public's involvement in decision-making; stakeholder representation (stakeholders should be able to state who they are and who and what they represent); the need to make participation more transparent and involve more than an elite, and a broader network of stakeholders would reduce the burden on the 'over-consulted'. One commentator suggested that 'multi-stakeholder processes mask significant imbalances in power over resources and considerable ... differences in influence on government among the participants'.

Further dilemmas present themselves when it comes to implementing roundtable agreements and action plans. Dana Silk proposed the notion of 'sustainability mediators' – individuals in the various institutions whose job it is to liaise with other institutions and work on further consensus, joint management, and so on. He sees such people as specialists in working across different sectors, recognizing that this is a special skill which not all people have.

This approach has been used in some NCSs and NEAPs. Under the Pakistan NCS, for example, environment contact officials are appointed in key government agencies. However, it is not known whether the Pakistan Government selected these contact officials on the basis of their aptitude.

Source: NRTEE (1995)

All relevant stakeholders should be involved ...

Negotiated outcomes need to involve all stakeholders with rights related to an issue, both risk-takers and risk-bearers (Box 8.13). The appropriate negotiation process will depend to some extent on the type of issue, the political and cultural setting, and other constraints relating to the urgency of need and the likelihood of negative impacts. A process that is too complex can needlessly delay decisions and deprive beneficiaries of the early fruits of options under consideration.

... using recognized negotiating procedures where possible ...

It is notable that there are many international procedures for negotiation (eg for agreeing trade tariffs through WTO, for international conventions through the UN) and local procedures (eg over labour rights

Box 8.12 Target setting in The Netherlands

The Netherlands has prepared a series of National Environmental Policy Plans (NEPPs) – the fourth was published mid-2001 (see Boxes 4.3 and 4.5). The NEPPs are intended to link national policy with local targets and are developed by the Ministry of Housing, Physical Planning and Environment (VROM). The ministry works with provincial and municipal government and various *target groups* (eg agricultural producers, chemical manufacturers, trade unions). Each group is led by a steering committee, consisting of representatives of government and of the target group. Local targets are set by local officials based on the national plan. Provinces are obliged to do this; municipalities have the incentive of additional central government funding if they also do so. With industry, NEPPs have emphasized voluntary agreements or covenants (Box 4.5) to secure agreements with government on environmental objectives and targets. Covenants are negotiated with trades associations, and local variations are allowed for branch members. Ministry staff accept that the price to be paid for a high degree of local participation and motivation will be a certain loss of control over the direction and actions of the NEPPs. The ministry has negotiated action plans with all target groups in the NEPPs.

> Central government came increasingly to regard the target groups and the regional and local authorities as important partners in the preparation and implementation of policy. Partnership and covenants became important environmental policy instruments. The next step was for central government to incorporate deregulation, flexibilization and decentralization in environmental policy with the object of implementing joint responsibility for the solution of environmental problems. This represented a shift in the role of central government from regulator in the 1960s and 1970s to 'negotiator', contractual partner as well as regulator in the late 1980s and the 1990s.

Source: VROM (1997)

Box 8.13 Rights- and risk-based negotiation process for decision-making on dams

In view of the importance of rights-related issues in relation to dams, and the nature and magnitude of the potential risks for all protagonists, the World Commission on Dams proposed that an approach based on the recognition of the rights and assessment of risks (particularly the rights at risk) be developed as a tool for guiding future planning and decision-making (see also Box 8.4). This would also provide a more effective framework for integrating the economic, social and environmental issues at stake when assessing development options and implementing projects.

The notion of risk adds an important dimension to understanding how, and to what extent, a project may have an impact on such rights. Traditionally, the definition of risk was limited to the capital invested and returns expected by developers or corporate investors. These voluntary risk-takers can determine the level and type of risk they wish to take, and explicitly define its boundaries and acceptability. But there is also a far larger group of involuntary risk-takers, who find that their livelihoods, quality of life and very survival are at stake, and that the risks imposed upon them are managed by others. Typically, these involuntary risk-bearers have little or no say in overall policy.

Like rights and entitlements, these risks must be identified, articulated and addressed. This will involve formal recognition of the fact that governments or developers are not the only parties at risk.

A rights-and-risks approach to assessing options and implementation will provide an effective framework for determining who has a legitimate place at the negotiating table and which issues need to be on the agenda (Figure 8.2). Although this approach may be more demanding in the early stages of options assessment and project design, inclusive and transparent decision-making processes aimed at negotiated outcomes should legitimize subsequent stages of the project, thereby helping to resolve the many and complex issues surrounding water, dams and development.

Source: World Commission on Dams (2000)

though trade unions, and local plans), but rather fewer at the national level, where decisions have been made by other means dominated by government. Furthermore, negotiated outcomes do not replace government decision-making. In fact, they depend on the state actively fulfilling its role as planner and enabler, and often financier and implementing body of development decisions. If a negotiation results in full agreement among parties, the state (as one concerned party) need only endorse it.

The World Commission on Dams proposes a rights- and risks-based negotiation process; see Box 8.13 and Figure 8.2.

... focusing on rights and risks

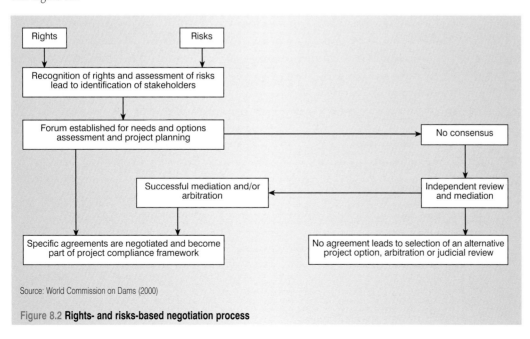

Source: World Commission on Dams (2000)

Figure 8.2 Rights- and risks-based negotiation process

The NSDS secretariat (or other appointed facilitator) will play a key role in negotiation. Indeed, it usually has to take some position in relation to negotiating a decision. If it approaches the negotiations as if it has all the answers and only seeks ratification, it may come away with no agreement and anger the participants, who will feel 'used' at best. At the other extreme, if it sits back and takes no position, the parties are not likely to reach agreement – they will talk and talk, but not converge (Harter and Pou 1997; Sigurdson 1997; Katz 1997).

CONFLICT RESOLUTION

Resolving conflicts – particularly at the local level – is essential

The number of 'win–win' possibilities in sustainable development is limited, and conflict resolution is invariably required. To date, few strategies have used such techniques, preferring to concentrate on non-contentious or win–win possibilities. However, at a local level, where several groups may depend on a single resource – such as a fishing ground, a watershed or a forest – conflict resolution is essential. For example, in the mid-1990s in British Columbia, Canada, a provincial land use strategy was negotiated by a large number of interest groups. Issues on which consensus could not be reached were reverted to government for decision. In St Lucia, the Soufriere Marine Management Area is managed by the local community, but conflicts are referred to government to resolve (Brown 1997). Box 8.14 describes a successful exercise by the Northern Lights Institute to deal with a river basin.

In Canada, 'choicework' tables have been used to help stakeholders reach innovative solutions to areas of conflict

A key feature of the Canadian *Projet de société* was conflict resolution through 'tête-à-tête' meetings, linking individuals together (brokerage on a personal level by the NRTEE – the strategy process facilitator). To assist stakeholders to reach innovative solutions, the strategy document of the Projet de société (1995) attempts to reduce the 'blinders' of sectoral bias and traditional mandates by providing innovative 'choicework'[8] tables around basic human needs, such as air, water, food and mobility. An example of a choicework table is provided in Table 8.2. These tables attempt to 'compare expert and public perceptions of various issues in order to find a method to bridge the gap between experts and the general public on a range of sustainability issues'.

The tables also identify areas of conflict and levels of consensus in order to show where immediate progress can be made and where more consensus building is needed.

Policy coherence – a step-wise approach

'Mainstreaming' sustainable development needs procedures for policy coordination, consistency and coherence

If the key principle of 'integrating environment and development' is perhaps the most germane of all the Rio Principles (and Millennium Development Goals) to an NSDS, more investment is needed in procedures to achieve such integration (see Chapter 4, page 102). In its 'policy coherence checklist for poverty reduction', the OECD DAC discusses three different terms which are used to describe what most governments do to integrate their policies better (usually with respect to new policies, rather than existing policies). These are: coordination, consistency and, more rarely, coherence:

Most governments, and certainly all of those in the OECD, have institutions and management mechanisms for policy **coordination***. Officials will have familiarity with the inter-ministerial or inter-agency machinery in which an entity with primary responsibility for a policy decision will bring together others that could be affected by or have an interest in it, to iron out a common position. Such coordination often involves whittling down an original proposal to obtain consensus, in lowest-common-denominator fashion.*

Policy **consistency** *has more to do with the design and implementation of policies of several ministries or agencies to support an overall objective, usually defined and articulated at a high political level. Poverty reduction is such an objective. The key idea behind consistency lies in the*

---

8 'Choicework' is defined as sorting out choices, weighing pros and cons and beginning to make the difficult trade-offs.

Box 8.14 **Conflict resolution and mediation in a river basin strategy, USA**

Historically, the use of the water of the Clark Fork River, Montana, USA, has been contentious. Ranchers, environmentalists, mining companies, recreational fishing groups and electricity companies are all critically dependent on the river for their operations. The huge demand for water, particularly in times of drought, has reduced some tributaries to dry streambeds. In other parts, they are loaded with chemicals, threatening some user interests. The different interest groups have – until recently – been waging increasingly bitter battles in courtrooms and legislatures.

The Northern Lights Institute, a group that encourages the use of conflict mediation techniques in environmental disputes, offered a participatory approach, which it termed 'river basin citizenship' as a more sustainable alternative to litigation and advocacy. The state's attempt to claim rights to a part of the river's waters to protect fishing interests offered an opportunity to test this approach.

Northern Lights attempted to answer the question: could local citizens with competing interests, along with federal and state water managers, come together to develop a watershed management strategy that would support both irrigation and environmental protection, and reduce conflict? The uncertainty and 'battle fatigue' helped to open the door for conflict mediation. Collaborative decision-making has been shown by the Institute to work particularly well when all parties feel it is their last resort; people have to feel they have little to lose, and perhaps something to gain.

Early meetings of the various groups dealt with the issue slowly – spending time getting to know one another and particularly the river. Key was learning about the river together – through field trips, where different groups' perspectives were put forward. Gradually, the 'symbols and demons' that dominated the debate and participants' views of each other gave way to a broader understanding. From agreements on common ground, agreement towards more contentious issues could begin to be mapped out. Eventually, a multi-interest Clark Fork Basin Steering Committee was formed to prepare the water management strategy – the first consensus-based water plan developed in Montana. This was particularly successful in addressing 'the gap between water law and policy, and how the resource is actually used' – in other words, it addressed realistic needs and situations.

Source: Maughan (1994)

Table 8.2 **Choicework table for mobility**

Some examples of choices that could be considered	Timing Duration Impact	Costs: $ Environ. Social	Benefits $ Environ. Social	Some consequences	Partnerships	Responsibilities	Consensus levels
Replace vehicle registration fees with 'feebates': rebates for efficient vehicles; fees for inefficient vehicles	months years xx	$ ss	$ eeee sss	Would increase efficiencies and ensure that the polluter pays	Car dealers	P	?
Negotiate covenants with insurance industry to facilitate car pooling and sharing and pay-at-pump insurance	months years xx	$$ ss	$$ eee sssss	Higher vehicle occupancy; more jobs in car leasing industry; fairer distribution of insurance costs	Commuters and insurance industry	F P B	?
Reduce the deficit through dedicated increases in excise taxes on fossil fuels	months decades xxxxxx	$ sss	$$$$$ eeeeee ssss	Would take advantage of concern over deficit to reduce CO_2 emissions and respect UNCED commitments	Public transport and car servicing industry	F	?

Note: **Timing**: Time it would take to implement choice. **Duration**: Period during which the impact is felt. **Impact**: x = low impact; xxxxx = high impact. **Cost**: $ = low monetary cost; eee = medium environmental cost; sssss = high social cost. **Benefits**: $$$$$$ = high monetary benefits; eee = medium environmental benefits; s = low social benefit. **Responsibilities**: F = federal; P = provincial; M = municipal; B = business; C = civil society

Source: Projet de société (1995)

avoidance of policies that conflict in reaching for the defined goal.

*Policy **coherence** aims still higher. It too operates to achieve politically defined goals, but looks beyond the removal of policy contradictions to a more creative enterprise that harnesses all relevant policy actions to enhance the achievement of an objective. It stresses a notion of cumulative value added from the contributions of different policy communities, thus moving beyond mere consistency to a more positive, stronger vision of how objectives can be achieved.* (OECD DAC 2001c)

The OECD DAC goes on to offer a checklist of steps to go through to work towards the 'higher' aim of coherence, and a checklist of policy issues to guide the search for coherence (in this case, specifically related to poverty). The mechanisms and facilities that governments tend to have in place to improve coherence can be key assets for strategies.[9] The OECD DAC cites the UK as being most advanced in ensuring policy coherence for its poverty reduction interest in developing countries. The UK initiatives are illustrated in Box 8.15.

It can be useful to develop a framework for assessing and planning coherence for sustainable development. The Shell International Petroleum Company has developed a diagnostic that all its divisions are encouraged to use (Table 8.3), in order to formulate and monitor annual plans for integrating sustainable development into business (Figure 8.3). These are available on its website (www.shell.com).

A challenge: strengthening relations between decision-developers and the ultimate decision-takers

Despite progress since Rio, there is a large gap between published strategy documents and results ...

This chapter has concentrated on the design and operation of good decision-making processes. It is appropriate now to refer to what does and does not happen in practice, in order to provide some insights into the ways whereby improvements might be achieved.

Great progress has been made since the 1992 UNCED in Rio de Janeiro. Most nations have engaged in preparing documents in support of sustainable development. Some have published what can only be described as exemplary suites of vision statements, strategies, policies, action plans, awareness programmes, and so on. Yet, in reality, a huge gap exists between words, actions and the achievement of beneficial results. To many, the sceptics in particular, the documents are regarded as adding to the pile of 'paper tigers' and the words read as just more rhetoric. The challenge lies not just in narrowing the gulf between words and actions, but in raising knowledge about what initiatives are working and why.

... in both the North and the South

The gaps and contradictions between principles and practice, words and actions, are not confined to countries that are seriously poor or are in transition. They also apply to richer economies where, surprisingly, some policies have proceeded directly contrary to the advice of multi-sectoral advisory committees appointed by government; likewise where developments have been permitted without reference either to NSDSs or to EIAs. 'Government by double standards' is not only counter-productive in relation to the issues at stake, but sours the goodwill of stakeholders upon which all successful sustainable development initiatives are founded.

Many initiatives can strengthen relationships between decision-developers and decision-takers

In looking ahead we need to return to the distinction that was made between 'decision-developers' and 'decision-takers' at the beginning of 'Institutional roles and processes for strategy decisions' on page 270. While the need for improvements in procedures to develop decisions is beyond doubt, the decision-taking processes require just as much, if not more, attention. In this respect, attention needs to focus on effective ways of strengthening relationships between the decision-developers and -takers. Again, while there are no panaceas, much can be achieved through the following types of initiative:

---

9 That said, the pursuit of policy coherence alone is no panacea. It needs to be accompanied by a parallel exercise relating to the supporting mechanisms. Thus the integration of laws and regulations, of enforcement measures, of economic instruments and of public awareness initiatives (to mention but a few) is also required.

Box 8.15 Promoting policy coherence in the United Kingdom

The United Kingdom has taken far-reaching initiatives to promote policy coherence:

- The Government made a clear *political commitment*. It established a *new, separate department* (Department for International Development, DFID) and gave its Secretary full cabinet status.
- Following extensive discussions between government departments, the Government elaborated a *White Paper on Poverty Reduction*, presented it to Parliament and widely *publicized it*.
- *Resources were committed* to policy coherence. DFID secured capacity to analyse independently or commission research on the development implications of non-development issues and to debate them within the Government. Four sets of issues received the most attention: (i) the environment, (ii) trade, agriculture and investment, (iii) political stability and social cohesion, and (iv) economic and financial stability.
- *Mechanisms for policy coordination* were strengthened. This included creation at the ministerial level of an *Inter-departmental Working Group on Development* to deal with cross-cutting issues.
- DFID strengthened its *links with multilateral organizations*, such as the WTO, UNCTAD and the World Bank, which deal with fields needing more policy coherence.
- DFID moved to *build developing-country capacity* to prepare for and participate in international negotiations.

Source: OECD DAC (2001c)

- *Employing expertise in institutional development and good governance* to work with NCSDs and strategy secretariats.
- *Vesting appropriate powers in NCSDs*, such that they are not perceived to be just advisory pawns of the governments and their cabinets.
- *Developing a strong relationship between the NCSDs and cabinets* in the recognition that the former is one (possibly the only) non-political body providing an impartial forum for the objective resolution of complex multi-sectoral issues.
- *Strengthening the relationship between the strategy secretariat and the NCSD*, such that jointly they are able to influence (and change) single-sector organizations.
- *Increasing the levels of trust and professional understanding* between the strategy secretariat/NCSD and sector organizations (especially line ministries); for example, through Sustainable Development Liaison Officers in each of the sector organizations.
- *Harnessing policy research skills* – political scientists and historians, in addition to the normal array of professional skills – to identify the lessons from past and contemporary events, and the successes and failures of particular packages of instruments (as happens in national defence establishments).
- *Mandating consistency and coherence audits* of all government policies, programmes and instruments, by strategy secretariats and/or audit commissions – who should report their findings to cabinet via NCSDs.
- *Working with the media* to ensure that the reporting of issues is based on accurate facts, objective analysis and balanced debate.

Selecting instruments for implementing strategy decisions

The core instruments that may be used within the strategy process itself (ie participation, analysis, information systems, communication, etc) are covered in other chapters. Here, we introduce the wider range of instruments for implementing sustainable development – the means by which the strategy objectives might be achieved. Every one of these instruments deserves a 'resource book' in itself, and detailed guidance on them is outside the scope of this strategy guide. The instruments described below are not intended to represent an exhaustive set, but provide a flavour of those that are available and can be utilized in implementation.

Table 8.3 **Diagnostic for alignment of business processes with sustainable development principles**

Chart breakdown	Level 1 Minimal alignment	Level 2	Level 3	Level 4 Full alignment
Degree of integration	Decision-making is based overridingly on financial or economical considerations	Decision-making takes account of wider economic and environmental considerations	Decision-making incorporates economic, environmental and social considerations, but each element is managed independently	Decision-making is based on a systematic process that manages the interrelationships between economic, environmental and social issues
Scope of engagement	Local, internal focus	Some internal engagement and use of special external advisers	Well-developed engagement programme	Advanced engagement activity integrated into cross-functional decision-making processes
Time horizon	Predominantly short term	Short term with some recognition of longer-term needs	Short-term priorities managed with context of longer-term needs	Short-term priorities managed as enablers of long-term value growth

Note: A self-assessment tool comprises a series of statements describing the degree of alignment of strategy and planning processes with the three key principles of sustainable development. Note that other information could be added; for example, institutional responsibilities in each 'cell'

Source: www.shell.com/royal-en/content

The range of sustainable development instruments

These instruments can be categorized in various ways. Given that sustainable development may require changes to ownership, investment, production and consumption, one approach is to group instruments according to their economic *role*; that is, supply-side management, demand-side management and redistribution. Instruments can also be distinguished according to whether they serve as measures of persuasion ('carrots') or as command-and-control interventions ('sticks').

Four sets of instruments – categorized by their means of operation

The approach used below is to categorize instruments according to their *means of operation*, mainly because the different means share similar pros and cons. Many instruments, of course, overlap such categories. Some of the instruments are well known, while others have been designed specifically to promote sustainable development, and may be in experimental stages.

LEGISLATIVE/REGULATORY/JURIDICAL INSTRUMENTS[10]

- Constitutional guarantees on sustainable development and its elements (see Box 8.3).
- Laws, by-laws and regulations set standards governing ownership, production, consumption, trade, environmental liability, association and contracts.
- Conventions – national and international agreements on social, environmental and economic behaviour.

Legal instruments have advantages in that they can set absolute limits and provide clear sanctions. This is desirable where clear consensus obtains in society about certain goals. They also have an educational role if information on legal instruments is made widely known. However, legal instruments can quickly become

---

10 Refer to chapter 5 (page 162) for guidance on analysing the legal framework for sustainable development.

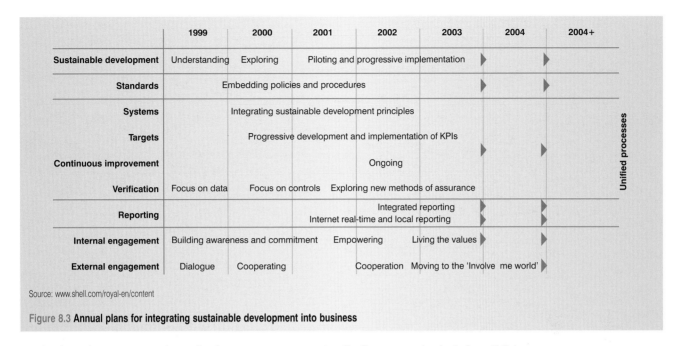

	1999	2000	2001	2002	2003	2004	2004+
Sustainable development	Understanding	Exploring	Piloting and progressive implementation			▶	▶
Standards	Embedding policies and procedures					▶	▶
Systems	Integrating sustainable development principles						
Targets	Progressive development and implementation of KPIs						
Continuous improvement				Ongoing		▶	▶
Verification	Focus on data	Focus on controls	Exploring new methods of assurance				
Reporting			Integrated reporting / Internet real-time and local reporting			▶	▶
Internal engagement	Building awareness and commitment		Empowering	Living the values ▶		▶	
External engagement	Dialogue	Cooperating		Cooperation	Moving to the 'Involve me world' ▶	▶	

Unified processes

Source: www.shell.com/royal-en/content

Figure 8.3 Annual plans for integrating sustainable development into business

outdated in relation to society's rapidly changing aspirations, scientific discovery, technological possibilities and economic conditions; for instance, inflation can erode the power of fines. The 'mandate, regulate and litigate' approach can become very costly to implement, in financial terms, in the hostilities it has produced, in locking in outmoded or irrelevant technologies and in the innovation that it may have stifled. In addition, regulation can be 'captured' to serve the interests of powerful groups. Finally, public sector capacity to enforce legal instruments may be weak.

Setting legal limits and providing clear sanctions

FINANCIAL/MARKET INSTRUMENTS[11]

- *Property rights-based approaches* – generally preferred by economists – including tradable pollution permits, ecotourism concessions, tradable fishing licences, allowing liability claims for environmental damages.
- *Price-based approaches* including pollution taxes, payments for environmental amenities (eg to farmers), auctioning publicly owned resources rather than selling them at administratively determined prices, user fees, tax credits for socially responsible investment funds, deposit refund schemes, performance bonds.
- *Reform of perverse subsidies* to reduce environmental degradation, for example, by intensive farming, and to encourage more efficient use of resources (basically the reverse of price-based approached).
- *Market-enabling measures* including information disclosure requirements, product certification and labelling, procurement policies.

Most economic instruments work by influencing behaviour through price signals. The advantages of economic instruments centre on their ability to benefit from the existence of competition and efficiency in the market. They can produce a desired outcome at much lower cost than regulation – by encouraging innovation and continuous improvement, by finding solutions that fit the local situation well, and by reducing enforcement and administration costs below those associated with legislation.

Market instruments produce a desired outcome more cheaply than by regulation

Two types of cost-saving are generally recognized: 'static' efficiency which results from the fact that compliance is mainly undertaken by those for whom it is currently cheapest, and 'dynamic' efficiency

11 Many of these instruments are introduced in more detail in Chapter 9, as they are central to the financial basis of a sustainable development strategy.

which results from innovation by firms to reduce the costs of compliance even further. The costs of enforcing market-based instruments (MBIs) are **not** necessarily less than command-and-control instruments (C&C)![12] As such, they end up with the beneficial effect of incorporating social and environmental costs into product and service prices. This can also be true of C&C instruments, but with the distribution of costs and benefits less transparent and generally less efficient. MBIs can, therefore, also be an efficient means to raise revenue for environmental management and social provision. However, considerable capacity is needed to develop and implement efficient MBIs. Introducing market-based instruments without careful preparation and negotiation may lead to severe economic dislocation, perhaps favouring richer economic groups with greater capacities to deal with change. Economic instruments that involve the imposition of charges for previously 'free' use of natural resources may not be politically feasible or even desirable where poor groups are significantly affected.

EDUCATIONAL/INFORMATIONAL INSTRUMENTS

- Accessible information on resources, stakeholders and their performance, sustainability problems and opportunities to improve performance (eg discriminating markets).
- Consumer information on production processes and the environmental/social content of goods and services (also a market instrument).
- Research and pilot projects on sustainable development issues, especially where stakeholders are themselves involved.
- Demonstration projects, especially where run by 'real' stakeholders facing actual business environments.
- Public awareness campaigns (eg through the media), training and extension on best practice and means of improving sustainability.

Raising awareness, encouraging self-regulation and inducing positive peer pressure – but few 'sticks' and 'carrots'

Advantages of educational instruments include the ability to raise awareness, encourage self-regulation and bring about positive peer pressure. They can also reinforce other instruments, by improving understanding of the latter's rationale and benefits. Like most persuasion instruments, the performance of public awareness initiatives relates to the ability of the designers to make them fashionable and thus irresistible. However, on their own, they tend to lack adequate 'sticks' and 'carrots', except perhaps in publicly minded societies with high educational levels.

INSTITUTIONAL INSTRUMENTS

- Fora and facilities for dialogue.
- Partnerships (public–private) and associations (corporate or mixed).
- Environmental management systems.
- Corporatization (of resources, rights, service provision) to parastatals.
- Full privatization (of resources, rights, service provision) to private companies and communities.
- Decentralization of rights and responsibilities.
- Codes of conduct by individual corporations and associations.
- Citizens' actions.
- Contracts/agreements on access, management, service provision.
- Common property regimes.

---

12 Market-based instruments and command-and-control instruments are both grounded in law and may require specific legislation. The main difference is that C&C takes no account of differences in the costs of compliance across producers/consumers, while MBIs are designed to achieve specific environmental targets at minimum cost. C&C typically makes little use of market incentives (although simple sticks and carrots may be used), while MBIs rely almost entirely on market prices and incentives to achieve their aims.

Institutional instruments tend to rely on self-interest and the innovation that can be generated in multi-stakeholder approaches. However, there are real limits to what can be achieved through voluntary approaches. Partly because real change in behaviour may be less evident than the words produced (especially in the absence of 'sticks and carrots'). And partly because they can be too successful, leaving government behind and producing a climate of neglect by the state, in which weaker groups may become vulnerable.

Relying on self-interest and innovation

Guidance on selecting instruments

The vision of the strategy, and the precise strategy objectives, are the major criteria by which to select a candidate instrument, or set of instruments. The decision-making frameworks discussed on pages 261–269 can similarly help to screen potential instruments. The following criteria may help to make a final selection from alternatives that have been screened to meet the above requirements.

1 *Effectiveness* in delivering environmental and social outcomes and/or in tackling root causes of problems (extent of geographical coverage, 'stretch' beyond current performance, multiplier/extension effects, and consistency between stages of, for example, a production/processing/use/recycling cycle).

2 *Efficiency* (low marginal costs in financial, information, resource, transaction and administrative cost terms; incentives for innovation and improvement; ease of understanding).

3 *Administrative feasibility* (building on what's on the ground already that works well, where there is good precedent, understanding and capacity).

4 *Equity* in cost-benefit distribution (at different levels).

5 *Acceptability* to groups who will be affected, and degree of controversy.

6 *Timeliness and 'bite'* in relation to major political/economic/social issues and stakeholder concern about them.

7 *Level of risk and uncertainty* especially in relation to possible perverse impacts.

8 *Reliability and replicability* across different groups and regions.

9 *Innovation and learning potential*; that is, the ability to make progress through tests and trials and to feed learning back into the policy process.

10 *Credibility* to stakeholders in general (which can be secured by good attention to the above).

11 *Balance* between the instruments being applied to address a given need.

Criteria for selecting instruments for sustainable development …

The last criterion, balance, is particularly important. No society will respond well to instruments based solely on coercion, persuasion or incentive. A balance is needed to address a range of stakeholder motivations and interests. And the instruments themselves need integration to ensure that they are mutually reinforcing. Indeed, some can be ineffective in the absence of others. Without education, no one will know of legislation, or of the means to change behaviour at low cost. Without economic or legal instruments, education can merely raise awareness and foster real pressure to achieve practical change. Without clear assignment of liability and property rights, or publication of relevant information (eg on emissions), many economic instruments will not work. The instruments need to be considered and designed collectively (ie as a bespoke package) rather than just individually. A specific package needs to be chosen for each of the strategy objectives. The packages should, as far as possible, be designed to consist of measures that, at best, complement and reinforce each other and, at least, are supplementary.

… and for getting balance between them

CHAPTER

9

The financial basis for strategies[1]

Introduction

No strategy for sustainable development can succeed without financial backing. This is borne out by the experience of Agenda 21, which lost credibility as the gap between what was required and what was available became more apparent.

> *The pronouncements and programmes of Agenda 21, though individually reasonable and compelling, when taken together and without a reference to sources of financing, appear little more than a wish list of things good to have but beyond our reach.* (Panayotou 1994)

Earlier strategies focused on costing long 'shopping lists' of projects ...

Earlier national conservation strategies (NCSs), national environmental action plans (NEAPs), tropical forestry action programmes (TFAPs) and other strategies also quickly lost momentum, as a crucial part of the system needed for sustainable development – finance – was barely considered. Strategy 'finance' tasks were often limited to adding up the cost of recommended actions and proposing increases in the government budget. While it is important to mobilize finance for a sustainable development strategy, in particular to get the formulation process started, this is not sufficient. As the concept of a sustainable development strategy has moved away from a focus on producing a plan document (often, in developing countries, containing or accompanied by a suite of proposed projects) to a more process-oriented approach, so the financial challenges have changed.

... but now the challenge is to ensure the finance system in general supports sustainable development ...

It is no longer simply a case of mobilizing funds for such projects or activities, with the government in the lead implementing role. A strategy is now seen as being more about setting a vision with broad directions, agreeing the attributes of a path towards sustainable development, and putting in place the key mechanisms. So attention must be given also to the financial mechanisms needed to internalize environmental and social costs in order to achieve the necessary changes in direction (see Chapter 8, which integrates financial or market mechanisms into the list of strategy instruments). Responsibility still lies

---

1 The first draft of this chapter was prepared by Maryanne Grieg-Gran of IIED. It has also benefited from review comments and additional material provided by Tariq Banuri (Stockholm Environment Institute, Boston Center) and Nicola Borregaard, Germany.

primarily with government to introduce the required measures, but the aim is also to change financial behaviour, particularly within the private sector; for example, to make polluters and beneficiaries of environmental services pay.

By 1997, most governments had realized the importance of the financial viability of new sustainable development policies. In its 'Five Years after Rio' Report, the World Bank highlighted the need to remove perverse subsidies, impose environmental taxes and apply more adequate user charges as policy instruments that could ensure financial sustainability. These instruments can be complemented by a range of others that can strengthen the financial base for sustainable development strategies: for example, markets for environmental services. Governments need to place less emphasis on financing project implementation and more on establishing frameworks or enabling activities; for example, designing the necessary policy mechanisms or helping certain groups to adjust to the changes required for sustainable development. This means that governments may have to concentrate less on prescriptive regulation and more on catalyzing initiatives, channelling resources or fostering cooperation between actors.

In addition, the decisions made by institutions concerned with finance and investment must be coherent with the goals and directions of the strategy; otherwise the whole strategy process will be undermined. To achieve this, sustainable development must become an integral part of the objectives and operations of investors and financial institutions, and these institutions need to be fully involved in the strategy process from the outset. For example, through providing 'seed funding', financial institutions can play a role in redirecting industry into more sustainable production.

It could be argued that if mechanisms were established to internalize the environmental and social costs of development, the decisions of financial institutions would be aligned automatically with the direction of the strategy. In practice, this is unlikely to happen smoothly because of information failures, transaction costs and problems of enforcement. For this reason, it is necessary to target financial institutions directly, and work with them on analysing the constraints to sustainable investment.

A greater focus on private financial decision-making is essential in both industrialized and developing countries, especially given the trends in capital flows to many Southern countries. For developing countries as a whole, private capital flows were more than four times official flows in 2000 (World Bank 2001a).

The financial basis of a strategy for sustainable development has three dimensions:

- *Mobilizing finance for specific activities* such as strategy formulation, review and framework activities, as well as specific components of the strategy that require specific funding. This is addressed in 'Mobilizing finance' on page 290.
- *Using market mechanisms to align incentives* with the strategy directions (page 298).
- *Mainstreaming sustainable development* within the decision-making and operations of financial and investment institutions, in both the public and the private sectors (page 303).

Scale issues are also important, as strategies for sustainable development can be developed at various levels: national, sub-national and local. At the local level, financial resources are often limited, there are fewer financial options for developing and implementing a strategy and the types of financial institution involved are likely to be different compared with the national level. For example micro-finance institutions may be key players in sustainable livelihoods and small enterprises at the local level. The balance between the three dimensions may also be different depending on the level. At the local level, the emphasis may need to be more on mobilizing finance given the limits on tax setting power that often apply to local government.

This chapter considers the challenges involved in addressing these different dimensions, in both the short and long term and at different levels (national to local).

… which means involving private investors in the strategy process, as well as government

Mobilizing finance

Under the old paradigm (strategies as plan documents, with portfolios of activities), most finance was allocated for project implementation. In the past, in developing countries, considerable donor support has been provided to assist the formulation of strategic plans, but it has proved more challenging to secure finance for implementation. Even where donor support has been secured for specific projects, it has usually been restricted to investment costs, and donors have rarely made a commitment to cover recurrent costs over a long period. Consequently, many projects have not contributed to sustainable development.

The Agenda 21 approach emphasized the need for a substantial flow of new and additional resources to developing countries. The UNCED Secretariat estimated that the average annual costs (1993–2000) of implementing Agenda 21 in developing countries would be over US$600 billion, including about US$125 billion/year in grant or concessional finance from the international community (Agenda 21, Chapter 33; www.un/org/esa/sustdev). In reality nothing like this amount was raised.

This experience shows that reliance on the mobilization of large amounts of additional finance, particularly donor finance, for the implementation of a sustainable development strategy is unrealistic. While there is growing pressure on developed countries to increase their official development assistance and, in particular, to meet the target of 0.7 per cent of GDP, there will still be a financing gap. Even if the focus were only on the provision of global public goods, the situation would not be much different. The UN High Level Panel on Finance for Development has recently estimated that 'beginning to address this need will probably require at least US$20 billion' – a sum, which, it states, is about four times the current spending level (UNHLPFD 2001) For this reason, there have been calls to find other ways of mobilizing finance and to rely more on realigning incentives.

The concept of strategies for sustainable development now focuses on processes and systems. The effect of this is to blur the traditional distinction made between strategy formulation and implementation and, by implication, the financial requirements. The processes established for strategy formulation must now be viewed as activities to be maintained indefinitely. The focus of implementation now needs to shift to setting potentially self-financing activities in operation, meeting adjustment costs and only in a minor way funding activities on a long-term basis.

Financial requirements of the strategy

FORMULATION AND REVIEW

Finance is needed to invest in effective strategy formulation processes

If a strategy is to be participatory, country-led and based on comprehensive and reliable analysis (ie meeting the principles and elements for effective strategies set out in Boxes 3.1 and 3.2), then financial resources will be needed in the early stages for research, analysis, consultation, communication, and for the development and maintenance of monitoring and evaluation mechanisms. The kinds of resources required for the strategy processes are set out in Chapter 4, pages 94–95. The costs of these processes should not be underestimated, given the amount of time involved and the need to keep processes going, as the case of Pakistan's NCS shows (Box 9.1). Nevertheless, the extent to which the strategy is building on previous activities and processes will have an important influence on cost. It is to be expected that the costs of the first strategy iteration will be relatively high, but that the costs and preparation time required for subsequent strategies will be lower.

Moreover, it is not just the government that needs financial resources; other stakeholders also need support so that they can make an effective input. While the costs involved may not always be an issue for the private sector, they may prevent other stakeholders such as NGOs and labour unions from participating. NGOs may need financial assistance to meet the time and travel costs of attending consultation meetings

---

Box 9.1 Financing the Pakistan National Conservation Strategy

The widely acclaimed Pakistan National Conservation Strategy had a nine-year gestation period. Over three years from 1988, during which the strategy document was prepared, more than 3000 people were involved through workshops and consultation. This level of participation was possible because it attracted donor funding from the outset (from the International Bank for Reconstruction and Development (IBRD), the Canadian International Development Agency (CIDA) and UNDP).

Some concern has been expressed that the product (the NCS strategy document and, subsequently, the portfolio of projects) took precedence over the continuing multi-stakeholder participatory processes, and monitoring and evaluation mechanisms were neglected.

Donors came to believe that the 'process' investment had largely been completed once the strategy document had been approved. Implementation of projects assumed a higher priority for them. Yet this shift dramatically reduced the potential impact of the projects, as there was no longer a strong coordination, monitoring, communications and dialogue facility at the 'centre' of the strategy to keep it on the right path and enable it to evolve.

Source: Hanson et al (2000)

---

and to conduct the necessary preparation such as independent research. For example, the New Zealand Government made funds available to assist NGOs to take part in the discussion on the 1991 Resource Management Act and also funded some NGOs to undertake commissioned work (Dalal-Clayton 1996).

Expenditure on ensuring effective participation may be costly but may pay off later in ensuring credibility of the strategy (see Chapter 6, especially pages 193–208). This is also shown by experience in New Zealand where public response to the Resource Management Act was much more favourable than to the Environment 2010 strategy which had been formulated in a less participatory manner (Dalal-Clayton 1996). The communication of the strategy (see Chapter 7) is part of the participatory elements and should not be forgotten when designing the budget for the participatory process.

Many of the financial requirements will be, therefore, to build and use strategy mechanisms such as participation and communications. Apart from funding these strategy mechanisms, two other financial tasks are relevant to strategy formulation:

First, the potential environmental, economic and social impacts of strategy recommendations will need to be assessed, including those of proposed new policies and any new financial mechanisms. A key aspect of such impact analysis will be an assessment of the financial sustainability of any new policy tools (analytical tools required for the strategy process are listed in Table 5.1). Some countries have made it obligatory to undertake socio-economic analyses of environmental regulations (although rarely introducing this requirement for other policy areas as well). The case of Chile provides a recent developing country example (Box 9.2).

There is a need to assess the financial implications of all policies and activities recommended by the strategy ...

Box 9.2 Assessing the impact of new environmental regulations

Economic analysis of new environmental regulations was introduced in Chile in 1996. After developing the methodological system for these analyses, by 2001, about ten such analyses had been completed. The studies are carried out directly by the National Commission on Environment or by external consultants, and identify the costs and benefits of the respective new regulation, including the financial requirements falling into the private and the public sector. Very often, the studies have concentrated on the economic valuation of the environmental impacts. However, a change towards more pragmatic indications concerning, for example, the financial sustainability of the regulation, would be useful and policy-relevant, and would not require additional resources.

Source: Borregaard et al (2001)

... and to assess the environmental and social implications of financial instruments

Second, the design of financial mechanisms needs to be informed by research on their potential impact on economic growth, the environment and income distribution. In particular, their likely impact on specific groups should be examined and projects developed to help those affected to adjust in the transition period. Before these mechanisms are fully implemented, they will need to be tested in pilot schemes to improve understanding of how they will work in practice.

IMPLEMENTATION

The search for self-financing approaches to implementing a strategy will often suggest market-based mechanisms – but there are limits to what can be self-financed

Strategy implementation implies different types of financial activity. In spite of the shift to a process approach, there will still be some activities which will require long-term funding and for which there is limited scope for self-financing: for example, social safety nets or protected areas. Other activities may need financial support in the initial stages but have the potential to be self-financing in the longer term. Examples include fuel switching and the promotion of cleaner production. It is easier to make a case for financing such activities if they are shown to form part of a programme which, in the long-term, will become self-financing. Finally, the implementation of market mechanisms is likely to be self-financing – depending on the balance struck between using them as a means to change behaviour and as a source of revenue. Funds will need to be set aside to monitor the impact of these mechanisms and to redesign them if necessary. Nevertheless, there will still be activities which will require long-term funding and which have limited scope to be self-financing, such as the management of protected areas.

Sources of finance

DONOR FINANCE

Donor finance can help – but the implications of donors' favoured 'brands' of strategy process, and their associated conditionalities, should be well understood

To date, most strategy processes in developing countries have been supported by donors, or have been set in motion to meet donor conditions for further support to other activities (eg NEAPs in the mid-1990s). An advantage of donor support is that sufficient funds can be made available that would not normally be provided from the recurrent budget of the ministry leading the strategy, especially for activities not normally funded fully, such as participation. But the downside is where there is pressure (from the donor) to produce a strategy document within a rigid timeframe in order to justify the support provided or to secure future development assistance. This can seriously affect the quality of participation, as in Pakistan (Box 9.1). The Highly Indebted Poor Countries (HIPC) initiative provides for debt relief, subject to the approval of a Poverty Reduction Strategy. It has been noted that there is a tension between securing quick debt relief and preparing a quality strategy with civil society participation (US General Accounting Office 2000). While donors have been willing to support the initial formulation of a strategy document, it has proved more difficult to secure donor funds for monitoring and review. The challenge is to persuade donors to provide financial support for a recurrent process with no predetermined outputs. The trust fund model (see page 296) may be a solution to this problem.

Another issue is that donors have different agendas and priorities, so they have tended to finance different activities or types of strategy. For example, the GEF has concentrated on funding biodiversity action plans in a number of countries. The IMF and World Bank have been promoting PRSs for low-income countries as a condition initially for debt relief under HIPC and, from July 2002, for IDA assistance. The transaction costs involved are considerable – Uganda's PRSP, for example, took over five years to prepare (US General Accounting Office 2000). This is not helped by the fact that donor priorities also change over time as a result of changes in government, or personnel or development fashions. The challenge is to integrate or streamline these various strategies and make more efficient use of donor funds.

Two important aspects need to be kept in mind: timely donor support, correctly provided, can be important for specific issues, and can trigger the mobilization of resources several times greater than the initial amounts; and a clear indication of potential multiplier effects might help to convince donors of the benefits of their contribution.

Very often, donor finance is channelled through NGOs and does not pass through the government – as with the preparation of many NCSs, which were coordinated by IUCN. There are no estimates of the overall amount of private donor/recipient finance for sustainable development. Rather than regarding NGOs as competitors or 'environmental police', governments can benefit by adopting a more positive approach to the contributions of NGOs, such as innovative policy proposals and sustainable development projects.

GOVERNMENT

Government funding of strategies usually entails a reallocation of expenditure from other activities. It is, therefore, necessary to make a good case for government support to a strategy process, particularly in poor countries where government revenue is often constrained by the small size of the tax base and problems of tax evasion. Here, there is a stronger chance of justifying framework activities which eventually might lead to self-financing mechanisms, than there is of projects which require sustained financial inputs.

Government financing of strategies may be justified by efficiency and equity reasons …

Frequently, government funding will consist of a commitment of the necessary human resources for strategy and policy formulation and implementation. However, reliance on government funding for strategy formulation involves the risk that the government, and hence 'ownership' and priorities, may change in the course of the process. Funding may be cut off before significant progress has been made. This is a problem that can occur even in Northern countries – for example, Canada's *Projet de société*, which started in November 1992 with money from Environment Canada and other government agencies, suffered a serious setback when the government changed a year later. The new government was concerned to reduce budget deficits and would make no funds available for the process, even though the new environment minister was supportive of the concept (Dalal-Clayton 1996).

… but a dominance of government funding can produce credibility problems for the strategy

Government funding for implementation can be – and will have to be – quite significant. In Chile, the development of an institutional framework for environmental management was financed (originally in 1992) one-third by World Bank sources and two-thirds by Chilean counterparts. When the system started consolidation in 1999, government spending on environmental issues had risen to approximately US$300 million annually, against a total contribution of donors and bilateral agencies of US$105 million over a span of eight years (World Bank 2001b).

Governments often channel available donor funds to NGOs. NGOs also need information on private and public donor programmes, the availability of funding and contacts. Such a channelling and information role can be developed by government relatively easily, by using existing or very marginal additional resources. However, governments can go further and work to strengthen social capital which eventually will help in the formulation and the implementation of an NSDS. But this role requires more substantial resources. An NSDS might therefore include a revision of the existing policy and incentives for donations. In many developing countries, donations to environmental or sustainable development objectives have not yet been recognized as eligible for tax credits, which are, in general, applicable to humanitarian aid, education or cultural programmes (Fund of the Americas 2000). The Inter-American Development Bank has recently been involved in several country strategies aimed at strengthening civil society.

Governments can create incentives to increase voluntary donations for sustainable development

OTHER IN-COUNTRY SOURCES OF FINANCE

It is not realistic to expect much direct financial contribution to strategy processes from civil society, except where NGOs are the conduit for donor funds (see previous section). However, in-kind contributions may be considerable as consultation processes involve time input and the provision of information by various stakeholders. But some groups have more financial capability than others, such as large companies and, to a lesser extent, international NGOs. The challenge is to ensure that the less powerful groups are not prevented from participating because of financial constraints.

Private sector organizations – transnational companies in particular – have the most potential to make direct financial contributions for both strategy formulation and implementation. The corollary is the need to ensure that the strategy processes are not compromised in any way. Financing the strategy should not mean 'buying influence'. Channelling private sector contributions through an independently managed trust fund (see page 296) may be a way of resolving this.

INTERNATIONAL TRANSFER PAYMENTS

These are transfers made by Northern countries to Southern countries in recognition of, or as a payment for, providing global public goods such as biodiversity conservation and carbon sequestration. Transfers are made by multilateral agencies on behalf of contributing countries or by NGOs, or in some cases by the private sector. The three most important types are discussed below.

GEF can fund activities that provide global environmental services and are consistent with local sustainable development needs

Global Environment Facility   The GEF was set up to fund projects which protect the global environment in the area of climate change, biodiversity and international waters. Its contribution to projects is based on the 'agreed incremental cost' to developing countries of providing global benefits. It also finances enabling activities like biodiversity action plans. While the incremental cost principle sounds simple in theory, it has proved extremely difficult to apply – hence the emphasis on 'agreed'. The basic approach adopted by the GEF is to distinguish between actions that provide global benefits and those that are in the national interest as defined by a national sustainable development baseline. If there is a gap between the current situation and the national sustainable development baseline, the necessary activities to bridge the gap have to be funded with other sources of finance. GEF will not finance these, as they are not considered incremental.

Partly because of the need to distinguish incremental costs, GEF projects are associated with heavy transaction costs, with projects taking from nine months to four years to prepare. In view of the remit of GEF, projects are focused on environmental benefits, rather than development. While community participation is emphasized in GEF project criteria, it is projects with global environmental benefits rather than community benefits that get funded.

The GEF has recently been moving to further engage the private sector at both project and strategic levels by using 'contingent finance mechanisms'. These aim to increase the effectiveness of GEF fund use, maintaining the performance incentives for the private investor while reducing investment risks (eg for new technologies or for technologies so far not applied in developing countries). They are expected to leverage other (public or private) capital in high-risk markets. At the same time, these mechanisms reduce the need for direct grants.

The NSDS process may reduce the transaction costs involved in GEF projects because it will provide clarity about the sustainable development baseline. However, by definition, GEF will not be able to finance activities that form a direct part of the strategy, as these will be considered to be in the national developmental interest. The potential contribution of GEF funding to a strategy for sustainable development will, therefore, be primarily through the financing of enabling activities such as biodiversity action plan formulation – the challenge being to ensure that these are consistent with the strategy process. At the implementation stage, GEF funding may have an indirect effect in that it may serve to catalyse other financial support from donors or from the government required as co-funding. GEF contributions to trust funds are also important (see 'National environmental funds', page 296).

Carbon offsets and the Clean Development Mechanism[2]   The Clean Development Mechanism of the Kyoto Protocol will allow developed countries to implement projects in developing countries that reduce net greenhouse gas emissions. It has the additional goal of assisting developing countries to achieve sustainable development. Developed countries may use 'certified emission reductions' (CER) generated by project activities in developing countries to contribute to compliance with their own emission commitments. A share of the CER will be withheld by the CDM executive to assist developing countries in meeting the costs of adaptation to climate change (see www.unfccc.de/text/issues/mechanisms).

As there are believed to be more opportunities for low-cost greenhouse abatement in developing countries than in developed countries, this mechanism can reduce the cost of meeting commitments and thus provides a powerful incentive for the involvement of the private sector. However, analysts have indicated that, due to an oversupply of carbon credits (in the absence of US participation) and thus low prices, the high transaction costs implied by the CDM may make it an unattractive instrument to some investors (CAEMA 2001). Critics of the CDM have also pointed out that costs may be low in developing countries because of low social and non-climate related environmental standards – rather than because of any difference in carbon abatement efficiency.

After most operational details were confirmed in Marrakech in November 2001, Parties have indicated their willingness to ratify the treaty before the WSSD. This will help to provide more certainty to the private sector regarding the recognition of the Protocol's mechanisms, especially the CDM. The projects carried out after January 2000 will be eligible for carbon credits under the CDM. Previous 'carbon offset' initiatives will have to be regarded as public relations benefits or as learning exercises in preparation for when the CDM comes into force (Landell-Mills et al, forthcoming).

The extent to which the CDM and other similar carbon offset initiatives can promote activities that contribute to sustainable development and promote poverty reduction will depend on how they are implemented. It will, in particular, be determined by the framework put in place to assess projects according to their sustainable development impact and the scope for stakeholder participation in project design and approval (Baumert and Petkova 2000). It is up to the host government to define the sustainable development criteria to which CDM projects must conform. The NSDS can therefore be very important in providing the key reference point for such initiatives. In turn, the actual contribution of these carbon offset initiatives to wider sustainable development will be enhanced if procedures for assessing their sustainable development impact are development through the strategy process. The US$410 million fund that is being made available as financial assistance to developing countries in the context of the Protocol (see 'Funding Mechanisms' in the Marrakech agreement) can help developing countries in this task.

Debt swaps   This is a mechanism introduced in the 1980s, by which debt or currency claims against a developing country are cancelled in exchange for environmental or social development commitments (see Box 9.3). Until recently the most common type was debt-for-nature swaps. More recently, the HIPC initiative has linked debt relief with poverty reduction strategies for selected low-income countries.

As a source of finance for an NSDS, debt swaps have two main drawbacks:

- They may not necessarily be additional, as the agencies cancelling or reducing the debt may offset this by reducing other forms of aid.
- They may be unduly focused on developed country priorities. This has been the main criticism of debt-for-nature swaps, particularly where these have concentrated on protected areas rather than sustainable use (eg Panayotou 1994).

An NSDS offers the local sustainable development criteria needed for CDM project design ...

... and also increases the likelihood that CDM projects will actually contribute to sustainable development

Independent local funds for sustainable development can be capitalized by debt swaps ...

---

2 See www.cdmcapacity.org (a joint initiative of IIED, EcoSecurities and Edinburgh Centre for Carbon Management) for more details.

Box 9.3 Examples of debt swaps

Peru

In 1994, Canada cancelled 75 per cent of the Can$22.7 million face value of debt owed to it by Peru. In return, the Peruvian Ministry of Economics and Finance paid 25 per cent of the debt amount in local currency to a Poverty Fund, UNICEF and a Nature Fund.

Philippines

A bilateral debt of US$32.3 million was converted at a 50 per cent redemption rate; that is, half of it was forgiven. In exchange, the Philippines government paid US$16.1 million in local currency to a private foundation established to finance environmental and social projects.

Jamaica

The Jamaica Environmental Foundation was set up to administer funds from a US government debt swap. These funds are targeted at non-governmental actors' activities that promote local sustainable development policy initiatives.

Principal source: Kaiser and Lambert (1996)

The PRSPs required for debt relief under HIPC have also come in for criticism, as discussed in Chapter 3. But if a way can be found to align the interests of the creditor country with the directions of the strategy, then they may prove useful.

NATIONAL ENVIRONMENTAL FUNDS

... they can be set up by government itself ...

In some countries, particularly in Eastern Europe, governments have earmarked revenue from pollution charges and fines for environmental funds. These funds can finance environmental projects through grants and soft loans. These can also operate at regional level (eg in Poland; Zylicz 1994) and at municipal level (eg in Bulgaria; Klarer et al 1999). Such funds have played a significant role in helping enterprises adjust to stricter environmental requirements and in accelerating environmental improvement. In Poland, these funds accounted for 30–40 per cent of total national pollution abatement and control investment expenditures during 1993–1996 (Klarer et al 1999). Some countries have set up forestry funds, financed by forestry-related charges such as stumpage fees, area taxes and taxes on timber. For example, in Slovenia, the government uses a 10 per cent sales tax on timber to finance a subsidy programme supporting forest management (Landell-Mills and Ford 1999). Both types of fund have the advantage of providing more stable finance for activities such as pollution control and forest management which are typically low on governments' lists of priorities (Landell-Mills 2001).

Such funds could play an important role in the implementation stage of a strategy by providing temporary assistance to companies to help them make the far-reaching changes necessary to move towards sustainability, for example, through giving concessional loans for clean technology.

TRUST FUNDS

... as well as by private organizations

Most of the trust funds that are relevant to sustainable development have been set up for environmental purposes, but there are some with social objectives such as poverty reduction. They draw in funds from a number of different sources, typically donor funding but also debt swaps and revenues from environmental taxes or fees (see page 295). For example, the Protected Area Conservation Trust of Belize raises US$500,000 per year through a tax on tourists entering the country by plane or ship (GEF 1999). But trusts are often created and managed by private organizations or NGOs. For this reason, they are discussed separately here from national environment funds (see 'National environment funds' above) which tend to be created as

---

Box 9.4 PROFONANPE – Peru's Conservation Trust Fund

The National Fund for Natural State Protected Areas (PROFONANPE) is a private not-for-profit entity, established in 1992 with the aim of supporting the conservation and management of protected areas. It started with grant finance but, in 1995, received US$5.2 million from GEF to operate as an endowment fund. By 2000 it had attracted a total of US$28.8 million from various sources, principally bilateral and multilateral donors and the Macarthur Foundation. It has also received funds from the Peruvian Government as part of debt-swap arrangements. PROFONANPE now plans to broaden its funding base to include more multilateral and regional organizations as well as the private sector. Together with the Nature Conservancy Council, it is currently exploring how to access the debt swap possibilities opened up by the Law on Tropical Forest Conservation approved by the US Congress in July 1998.

The trust fund operates endowment funds, sinking funds and mixed funds as well as earmarked and contingency funds and grant finance.

The board of directors of PROFONANPE includes government representatives from the Ministry of Economy and Finance, as well as the National Institute for Natural Resources and civil society representatives and an international donor representative.

Source: www.profonanpe.org.pe

---

autonomous government agencies. Typically, trust funds are governed by a board of directors drawn from the private sector, NGOs, government and academia while management of their assets is handed over to professional fund managers. Trust funds are most appropriate when the issues being addressed require financing over a number of years, that is, long-term, stable financing is required. Three types of trust funds are usually distinguished:

- endowment funds, where only income from the fund's capital (ie investment income) is spent;
- sinking funds, which disburse their entire principal and investment income over a fixed period;
- revolving funds, which receive new income from taxes or fees on a regular basis.

In practice, trust funds can involve a combination of these different modalities. Profonanpe, the conservation fund of Peru, has both endowment funds and sinking funds (Box 9.4).

An evaluation conducted by the GEF found that successful environmental funds were the product of broad consultative processes, involved people from different sectors in their governance, and had credible and transparent procedures. It also found that active government support was necessary, even if the fund was operating beyond its direct control (Smith 2000).

In many poor countries, trust funds could provide a mechanism for financing the development and implementation of NSDSs through successive cycles over many years. The Funds of the Americas (see Box 9.5) provide an example of how trust funds can be an important innovative element in NSDSs, especially when they are managed by a multi-stakeholder committee.

Mobilizing finance at the local level

Through decentralization, sub-national authorities (eg districts and municipalities) are increasingly assuming responsibility for sustainable development and are preparing their own development strategies and action plans. However, formal decentralization is seldom backed by adequate financial allocations from the central government (see 'Sub-national strategies', page 63). Local authorities in many developing countries have little or no revenue-raising power and this makes it difficult to formulate and implement credible strategies for sustainable development. Even where they do have such powers, there might not be political will to seek alternatives to dependence on national governments for resources.

Ghana offers an example of one approach to dealing with this problem. Each of Ghana's 110 districts has responsibility to develop and implement medium-term and annual District Development Plans, which

Independent funds offer a long-term, sustainable source of funding – and thus have potential to keep strategy processes alive over many years

> **Box 9.5 The Funds of the Americas**
>
> 'Funds of the Americas' were established in four Latin American countries in the 1990s: Argentina, Chile, Colombia and Peru. These Funds were created on the basis of debt swaps between the United States and the countries concerned. They are private–public entities directed at strengthening civil society response to sustainable development. The Funds have developed different sustainability strategies and have made significant contributions to sustainable development in their respective countries.
>
> In Chile, for example, the Americas Fund has financed 198 projects as well as 14 strategic studies that were steered by stakeholder committees and accompanied by communication strategies. Additionally, it has developed three cooperative programmes with private and public sector actors in order to promote sustainable management of the country's natural resources. Between 1995 and 2000, the Fund contributed more than US$16 million to these projects and initiatives.
>
> Source: www.fdla.cl

should address sustainable development. At least 5 per cent of internal government revenue is allocated by parliament to the District Assemblies Common Fund. A formula for distribution between districts is agreed each year based on population and development status indicators. District assemblies are able to use these funds for capital expenditure on development activities (see Box 3.21).

Innovative approaches are needed to bring local stakeholders together for mobilizing finance

Initiatives that bring the local actors together, while potentially promising for the future financial sustainability of a local sustainable development strategy, do require seed funding to enable trust to be built and a basic institutional framework to be set up. Subsequently contributions from local stakeholders, especially private companies, can be sought. One such attempt is currently being pursued in the Region of Antofagasta, Chile (see www.cipma.cl/bolsambiental/). In Thailand, tax concessions given by the national government were an important incentive for multinational companies to participate in the Thailand Business in Rural Development initiative to promote rural livelihoods (Grieg-Gran 2001).

Using market mechanisms to create incentives for sustainable development

More needs to be learned from where the private sector has adopted sustainable practices spontaneously – learning the lessons of effective policy and market signals that match with producer motivations. (Hanson et al (2000) commenting on the Pakistan National Conservation Strategy)

Market mechanisms can capture funds from users and polluters of environmental resources

Market mechanisms can create powerful incentives to achieve the objectives of the strategy and can have a more lasting effect than mobilizing finance for specific projects. For example, it is pointless to finance a wastewater treatment plant if companies are not charged sufficiently for discharging waste into it. While market mechanisms may generate some revenue, their most important effect is to capture more resources from polluters or resource users or from the beneficiaries of environmental services, and to change their behaviour.[3] The use of these mechanisms may thus result in less expenditure on the part of the government and in a more efficient use of resources. However, the distribution of resources is likely to change. The introduction of an industrial pollution emissions charge means that companies have to pay for their use of the assimilative capacity of the environment whereas, previously, they accessed this at no charge. For this reason, finance may be needed in the short term to help certain groups to adjust.

---

3 The distinction between financial mechanisms and policy instruments to achieve sustainable development can become a little blurred. The emphasis here is on policy measures that can be classified as financial.

A number of reports have addressed the issue of financing mechanisms for sustainable development: for example, Panayotou (1994) on Agenda 21, and Landell Mills (2000) and Richards (1999) on sustainable forest management. The literature on market mechanisms for sustainable development is extensive. In the *Five Years after Rio* report by the World Bank (1997), a policy matrix describes different market mechanisms and provides concrete examples of their implementation. In recent years, several initiatives have addressed how market mechanisms can be adequately implemented in the face of very slow adoption, especially in developing country contexts. One ongoing initiative is UNEP's Expert Group on the Introduction of Economic Instruments, run by its Economics and Trade Unit. Market mechanisms can operate at the national level (see next section) and, to a lesser extent, at the local level (page 302).

Market mechanisms at the national level

There are three basic approaches:

- Remove existing financial mechanisms that work against sustainable development, such as energy subsidies.
- Adapt existing market mechanisms.
- Introduce new financial mechanisms that internalize environmental or social externalities.

The three types of measure will have winners and losers and their impact and effectiveness will vary depending on the nature of the sector, or the environmental or social issue being addressed. For this reason, a study of their potential impact is needed first – as discussed on page 291.

REMOVING PERVERSE INCENTIVES

For a number of reasons, key productive inputs such as energy, water and pesticides are often priced below private marginal cost. This may be because of government subsidies or price controls which aim to encourage industrial productive activity. Alternatively, the rationale may be to protect the interests of low-income groups or to provide services considered to have public health benefits. In some cases, it may be considered administratively simpler to have less precise charging policies. WRI (1996) estimated that, on average in developing countries, consumers pay only 35 per cent of the costs of water provision. This under-pricing results not only in economic losses but also in environmental costs, because it encourages activities which use natural resources or degrade the environment. For example, in the case of Poland, it was estimated that the removal of energy subsidies would have reduced emissions of particulates and sulphur oxides by more than 30 per cent between 1989 and 1995 (World Bank 1992).

Removing subsidies for energy and resource use can benefit sustainable development …

As Panayotou (1994) notes, the removal of distorting subsidies has a number of positive effects. It frees up financial resources which can then be deployed in activities more conducive to sustainable development. It improves the environment. It encourages economic efficiency. And it is likely to improve income distribution. The OECD (1998), drawing from case studies in several member countries, has shown how the removal of subsidies in agriculture, energy, industrial activities and transport can lead to win–win situations.

Even where subsidies have the aim of protecting the interests of the poor or providing public health benefits (eg free or subsidized water supply), they may be counter-productive for sustainable development objectives. Many of the problems in providing water and sanitation stem from inadequate cost recovery. At the same time, it is the poor that are least likely to be connected to subsidized municipal water supply and sanitation systems (Johnstone 1997). Instead of providing poor quality urban services at subsidized rates, it would be better to charge the full rate for a service that is more reliable and more tailored to the needs of low-income communities (Panayotou 1994). Involving communities in the provision of such services may

… including for the poor

> **Box 9.6 Integrating sustainable development objectives into the tax system – Belgium**
>
> Belgium has prioritized the mainstreaming of sustainable development principles into the fiscal system in its Federal Plan for Sustainable Development 2000–2004. It aims to review the tax base, abolish preferential fiscal regimes for products and production processes which pollute, introduce a (supplementary) tax on patterns of production or consumption which are undesirable for social or ecological reasons, and/or introduce preferential regimes for desirable ones.
>
> An interdepartmental working group, chaired by the Ministry of Finance, will prepare a report on the green reform of taxation. The group will first draw up an inventory of all the exemptions and reductions which exist within the fiscal system and which militate against sustainable development, and then formulate proposals to amend this situation. It will also look at various proposals for green taxes.
>
> Source: Federal Plan for Sustainable Development 2000–2004, Belgium

also reduce the overall financing needs. In the context of development projects in Pakistan, it has been estimated that a service that costs US$1 when delivered by the local community, costs between $3 and $5 when it forms part of a government project and between $7 and $30 if it is a component of a World Bank-funded project (Hassan 2001).

Identifying and addressing such perverse incentives requires the participation of the Ministry of Finance or equivalent authority as well as other line departments since it may involve a radical rethinking of standard tax policy – as the case of Belgium shows (Box 9.6).

ADAPTING EXISTING MARKET MECHANISMS

Many existing market mechanisms have potential for sustainable development – if they can be 'retuned' towards sustainable outcomes

In order to create an incentive for sustainable development, it is often a better to adapt existing policies so that they more adequately take account of sustainable development objectives, rather than remove them or introduce new mechanisms. A study of adaptable existing instruments in Chile called them 'pseudo economic instruments for environmental policy-making' (ECLAC 2001), emphasizing that, while the instruments appear to be market mechanisms for environmental policy-making, they were, in fact, originally designed on purely economic grounds. The study provides examples of such instruments, including:

- A subsidy for reforestation activities which originally included exotic as well as native species. This is now being redirected at native species and small- and medium-sized owners only, taking account of environmental and social considerations.
- A system in which the rights to use water have been allocated free of charge, with no restrictions concerning hoarding of the rights.

An important point is that adaptations of existing market mechanisms are relatively easy to implement and no new administrative system is required to introduce them. So they might be perceived as a more viable option than introducing entirely new mechanisms.

NEW MARKET MECHANISMS

New market mechanisms can be designed to produce multiple benefits for sustainable development ...

Market mechanisms may penalize companies or individuals for adverse environmental or social impacts. Or they may make them pay for natural resource use. Or they may reward them for providing environmental or social services. These approaches have three main advantages:

- They can reduce the costs of achieving the objectives set out in the strategy for sustainable development.

- They provide continuing incentives for innovation and improvement.
- They provide a source of revenue which can be used for the purposes of the sustainable development strategy – whether through earmarked funding of specific activities, a contribution to an environmental or social fund, or offsetting other taxation (eg on labour). In Eastern Europe, environmental funds created from the various environmental charges introduced are playing a key role in the move to address environmental problems.

There is now experience of a wide range of mechanisms which have been introduced in both developed and developing countries, from which considerable lessons can be drawn (see Box 9.7).

Box 9.7 Market mechanisms for meeting sustainable development objectives

- Emission charges such as effluent charges, and SO_2 and NO_x taxes – to encourage firms to reduce their emissions through process-integrated and end-of-pipe measures in order to avoid charge payments.
- Waste taxes (eg landfill tax) to make final waste disposal more expensive and so promote recycling and waste reduction.
- Product taxes on, for example, energy, lubricant oils, batteries, fertilizers, pesticides and packaging, and other products which have an environmental impact in manufacture, consumption or disposal.
- Tax differentiation to favour sustainability (eg leaded and unleaded petrol) to divert consumption away from a more polluting product to a less polluting product.
- User charges such as entrance fees for natural parks.
- Subsidies or preferential credits for the introduction of clean technology or other production that implies the provision of positive environmental externalities.
- Increased resource rent capture (eg for forest concessions) through competitive bidding and area-based taxes, and for water through abstraction charges (eg groundwater pricing in Thailand).
- Environmental performance bonds in mining and forestry to ensure that abandoned mine sites are reclaimed and that reforestation or sustainable forest management is carried out.
- Deposit refund schemes (eg on packaging) to encourage reuse, recycling or controlled disposal. A deposit is made on purchase of a product and refunded when the product or, in some cases its packaging, is returned to a designated point.
- Markets for environmental services: for example, tradable permits for SO_2, carbon offset trading, transferable development rights, payments for watershed protection (see Table 2.1).

The main issues associated with such mechanisms are:

- *Determining the appropriate level of the charge or payment*. Early schemes were introduced more as revenue-raising instruments than behaviour-changing approaches. Charges were therefore low. Later schemes have tried to put more emphasis on the incentive effect.
- *Enforcing payment and dealing with evasion* without increasing unduly the administrative costs involved, especially where there is poor regulatory enforcement. Mexico's wastewater charge has suffered from poor enforcement (Seroa et al 2000).
- *Overcoming resistance from certain groups* who are likely to lose as a result of the introduction of the market mechanism. Fossil fuel energy taxes have been resisted by energy-intensive industry sectors with the result that they have often been watered down by the inclusion of exemptions and reductions. International cooperation can help to overcome these problems. For example, at the meeting of the UN Preparatory Committee for the International Conference on Financing for Development in October 2001, the introduction of a carbon tax on an international scale was considered as one of the principal mechanisms by which sustainable development could be promoted. While industrialized nations would have to contribute a certain proportion of the tax to

… but there are several constraints to their effective operation …

the international agency in charge of the administration, developing countries would be exempted from such obligation and could thus earmark the total amount to sustainable development strategies.

- *Dealing with regressive impacts on the poor* who are least capable of adapting to the proposed changes. Taxes on fossil fuels, for example, may have adverse impacts on the poor unless assistance can be given to these groups to adopt energy saving measures; for example, upgrading cooking and heating equipment to new, more efficient means.
- *Ensuring that the revenue raised is used appropriately*, and to provide safeguards against misappropriation. This will usually involve setting up institutional structures.

The OECD (1997b, 2001) has evaluated market mechanisms in OECD countries. The Economic Commission of Latin American and the Caribbean has recently compiled first evaluations of these mechanisms for that region (ECLAC 2001).

... which the strategy process can help to overcome

Some financial mechanisms shift the cost of controlling or monitoring from the state to companies. But such approaches are often left out of the overall 'menu' of market mechanisms because they lack the incentive element of the traditional market mechanisms. However, in a developing country context, they can be important instruments to finance environmental policy tools. In Peru, the cost of monitoring the environmental plans of mining companies is met by the companies concerned (CONAM 1998).

Market mechanisms at the local level

The extent to which the mechanisms described above can be applied by local governments depends on the extent of decentralization and the associated division of responsibility and authority. In many cases, local governments have limited tax-setting authority. But they may often have control over the provision of urban services such as waste collection, water supply and sanitation. Greater cost-recovery for services controlled at the local level will both mobilize finance and increase the efficiency of natural resource use. Brazil provides an example of a financial mechanism operating at local level to meet environmental and social objectives (Box 9.8).

Box 9.8 Financial mechanisms for environmental objectives at the local level: the ICMS Ecologico

The ICMS ecologico shows how the rules on revenue-sharing between different levels of government can affect incentives for sustainable development at the local level. The ICMS is a sales tax levied by the various states of Brazil. Under the Brazilian constitution, state governments must pass on 25 per cent of the ICMS revenue to municipalities. Of this amount, 75 per cent is distributed between municipalities on the basis of the value added they generate. The remaining 25 per cent is divided between municipalities according to criteria chosen by the state government. Traditionally, these criteria have been population, land area and agricultural production. But in some states of Brazil, an ecological criterion has been introduced. This is based on the area of land subject to protection and, in some cases, the quality of protection. This provides an incentive to municipalities to designate protected areas and to improve the management of existing ones. In the State of Parana, 2.5 per cent of the total amount passed on to municipalities is distributed according to this ecological criterion. Another 2.5 per cent is distributed on the basis of watershed protection areas. In Minas Gerais, in addition to the ecological criterion, distribution is also on the basis of the quality of urban services, sanitation and waste disposal.

Source: Grieg-Gran (2000)

Mainstreaming sustainable development into investment and financial decision-making

The success and credibility of a strategy for sustainable development depends on the extent to which key stakeholders act in accordance with it. For example, a strategy that emphasizes the promotion of renewable energy or energy efficiency is undermined if investments are made by private sector or public sector organizations in fossil fuel power plants. This means that key financial decisions have to be coherent with the NSDS, and that at the same time, the integration of sustainable development objectives into companies' decision-making should be one of the key objectives of the NSDS. To achieve this, a number of different actors must be involved, notably: government departments, the private sector and financial institutions both in-country and overseas (see Box 9.9). Given the importance of foreign investment in developing countries, the situation is complicated by the need to address foreign-owned companies and the financial institutions that support them. Most corporate decisions on foreign direct investment (FDI) involve the participation of a financial institution – either directly through the provision of a loan to cover establishment costs, or indirectly through, for example, the provision of risk insurance. Local financial institutions, which in developing countries are increasingly foreign-owned, are also important sources of finance for productive enterprise.

Investors should include local sustainable development criteria in their decision-making

To develop a coherent NSDS with the right tools, it is important to understand the motives for companies and financial institutions to address sustainable development. A key requirement is to improve the disclosure by companies and public and private financial institutions of their investment decisions – a necessary condition for channelling private resources towards sustainable investments and for monitoring the impact of their activities.

Assessing investor motivations and the investment criteria they currently use is a useful strategy task

Motives for addressing sustainable development

For all the different types of institution listed in Box 9.9, a key question is: why should they be interested in making sustainable development a core consideration for their operations?

Multilateral and bilateral development finance institutions (DFIs) and export credit agencies (ECAs) have been criticized by NGOs for the apparent conflict between their financing decisions and their respective government's policy on aid and sustainable development (or international development goals in the case of the multilateral institutions). The prime objective of the ECAs is to promote industrial development or exports of the source country. But a significant driver is the need for coherence with overall government policy. So, until recently, they have paid little attention to the impacts on the host country of the developments they fund. But pressure from NGOs is now forcing them to look at the wider impacts of their activities. This comes after some controversial projects involving ECA funding, such as the Three Gorges Dam in China and the Illisu Dam in Turkey. In late 2000, the UK Export Credit Guarantee Department published a statement of business principles. The aim was to ensure that its activities reflected the government's policies on sustainable development: environment, human rights, good governance and trade (see www.ecgd.gov.uk). ECAs in other OECD countries are developing similar policies, and the OECD is now developing guidelines for ECAs to ensure a level playing field for companies.

For the government institutions of the host country, the coherence argument is less compelling. Pressures to compete with other countries for inward investment could lead to acceptance of FDI activities which conflict with an NSDS in terms of environmental or social standards. The provision of incentives or tax concessions may also undermine financial mechanisms to drive sustainable development introduced in the strategy. Two factors may encourage this lack of interest in coherence: institutional pressure to meet certain objectives (eg the number and size of inward investment deals, or number of jobs created); and the perception that addressing sustainable development will be a net cost.

Box 9.9 **Types of institution involved in private sector investment decisions in developing countries**

Official agencies

Domestic

- Ministry of Industry or Finance and other ministries involved in negotiating with foreign investors.
- Investment Promotion Agency, or Board of Investment – at national and sub-national levels – is charged with publicizing investment opportunities in the country and attracting foreign investors.
- National development banks provide loans and equity finance for local enterprise.

Multilateral/bilateral development finance institutions

Development finance institutions (eg IFC and Swedfund) aim to promote private sector expansion in developing countries by providing loan or equity finance as well as catalysing private capital. They also invest in venture capital funds to provide start-up finance for companies.

Export credit agencies

Export credit agencies (ECAs) were originally set up to promote trade by providing government-backed cover to companies for the risks involved in exporting or by assisting buyers with finance. Nowadays, the functions of ECAs are much broader and extend to investment guarantees, political risk insurance and, in some cases, direct finance for investment through loans and equity funds. Thus, ECAs are an important player in foreign direct investment decisions, particularly regarding large infrastructure, mining and oil and gas projects. Their participation may determine whether or not a project goes ahead.

Private sector

Asset managers

Institutions that manage pension funds and mutual funds in developed countries are important investors in many transnational companies and/or companies with supply chains in developing countries. They also invest directly, but to a lesser extent, in publicly traded developing country enterprises. In some middle-income countries, local pension funds are becoming important investors.

Commercial banks support foreign direct investment and local enterprise through the corporate and project finance they provide for new facilities, expansion or company acquisition.

Private equity/venture capital is often invested in companies that are not listed on stock exchanges, and typically invested in high return, high risk activities. Such investment is particularly important for financing start-ups and restructuring of companies.

However, it has been observed that those governments which are most successful in attracting FDI are also those that meet the requirements for good governance. So, instead of using a traditional incentives approach, a rules-based approach – concentrating on the creation of more stable and transparent rules for investors – could be effective as a means of attracting FDI without necessarily weakening environmental and labour standards (Oman 2000). In order to convince those government institutions concerned with investment of the need to address sustainable development, it will be necessary for the NSDS process to address the rules governing investment.

For private sector institutions, the most effective argument is that there is a business case for addressing sustainable development issues. This is illustrated by the findings of a UNEP survey of financial institutions, which found that a significant obstacle to integrating environmental issues into credit and investment analysis was a perception that such issues are not important for profitability (UNEP/PWC 1998). However, this business case argument is also being promoted for public sector institutions, especially because of the pressures for them to operate on a commercial basis.

The business case for sustainable development can be addressed at two levels: at the company level and at the level of the supporting financial institution.

COMPANY LEVEL

It is widely claimed that companies practising corporate social responsibility have a number of financial benefits which ultimately affect the returns and risks for investors. Typical arguments include:

- *Cost savings:* Clean technologies are usually more efficient, while reducing raw materials use and increasing recycling can reduce production costs. Similarly, good working conditions can lead to higher productivity and fewer union disputes and make it easier to attract and retain employees.
- *Greater readiness:* Changes in legislation (eg tightening regulations) or changes in rules on liability for damage can imply significant costs – these are sometimes unanticipated for companies. Companies that can prepare for regulatory change, through, for example, voluntary action, will have a competitive advantage.
- *Market benefits:* Companies that can demonstrate compliance with stringent environmental and social standards can generate market benefits. They can access certain environmentally sensitive markets, or are more likely to retain their existing markets if buyers adopt stricter purchasing standards, or they may secure higher prices for their products.
- *Reputation and risk management:* Responsible business practice has a positive impact on the reputation and public perception of the company. Loss of reputation can affect sales, particularly where NGO campaigns are urging consumer boycotts. More generally, it can affect the company's social 'licence to operate'. Safeguarding reputation is important for maintaining good relationships with regulators and the local community. This has financial benefits in reducing the time required to secure government approval of, and community support for, new developments or expansion.

THE BUSINESS CASE FROM THE FINANCIAL INSTITUTION VIEWPOINT

The financial benefits to companies from addressing sustainable development issues translate into higher returns or lower risks for investors. Conversely, the increased risk facing a company from inadequate management of the environmental and social aspects of its operation can turn into risks for the supporting financial institutions.

Risk assessment is a standard part of procedure for investment decisions, but it is only recently that environmental and social issues have been considered an essential part of risk. Environmental and social risk for financial institutions can be classified as:

- *Direct risk* – where the financial institution finds itself liable for clean-up costs or third-party claims for pollution damages. This may occur where a bank forecloses on a loan and takes possession of land offered as collateral.
- *Indirect risk* – where tightening environmental regulation affects a company's cash flow and ability to repay loans or generate a return on investment.
- *Reputation risk* – where failure on the financial institution's part to give careful consideration to environmental and social impacts of a project can result in bad publicity for both the institution and the company concerned.[4]

More positively, the way a company deals with sustainability issues may provide a good indication of its management capability, which is one of the most important factors in any financial decision. Effectiveness

The business case for sustainable development needs to be explored through the strategy process, both from the company point of view ...

... and from the investor's point of view

---

4 Based on UNEP Financial Institutions Initiative Fact Sheet No. 3 'The Environment and Credit Risk' (www.unep.ch/etu/finserv/finserv/Fact-Sheet-3.htm).

in dealing with complex sustainable development challenges implies an ability to handle other management areas as well (Trevet 2000).

CRUCIAL FACTORS IN THE BUSINESS CASE

The business case argument relies heavily on the following factors:

- Governments introduce and enforce regulation on environmental and social issues.
- Markets become sensitive to sustainable development issues.
- The threat to company reputation of poor environmental and social performance, if publicized, will have an impact on the financial performance of the company.

In many developing countries, the first two factors are currently less relevant, as enforcement of legislation is weak and consumers are not so interested in issues beyond price and quality. So here the immediate argument hinges on the financial implications of impacts on company reputation at local, national and international level. Yet reputation risk is uneven in its impact, and is likely to affect large companies with high consumer visibility more than others.

The NSDS process may not necessarily make companies more visible. However, it may provide a more objective basis for judging the reputation of a company. The process can raise awareness about societal expectations of companies, and about what trade-offs between economic development and environmental and social performance are considered acceptable. Business participation in the NSDS process could also have a positive impact on reputation, both for companies and for the financial institutions that support them.

How can financial institutions mainstream sustainable development?

With some exceptions, financial institutions have traditionally approached decision-making in a narrow way, without giving much attention to environmental or social impacts. However, there are signs of change as many institutions (albeit mostly in the North) are introducing procedures for environmental and social assessment. A large number of institutions have endorsed the UNEP Statement by Financial Institutions on the Environment and Sustainable Development (see Box 9.10). In addition, some large transnational financial institutions have signed up to the Global Compact (see page 17), implying a commitment to social and environmental sustainability.

CHALLENGES FOR NORTHERN FINANCIAL INSTITUTIONS

The NSDS can guide foreign investors on the sustainability standards that make sense locally

The challenge for Northern financial institutions is to determine what standards are appropriate as a reference point, and to ensure that these take account of local perspectives and priorities. This is particularly important where host country legislation does not set or effectively enforce high environmental and social standards. There is some pressure from Northern NGOs on official financing agencies to exclude certain activities altogether (eg mining and fossil fuels) because of their environmental and social impact. But these sorts of decisions need to be made at the country or local level on the basis of an analysis of the trade-offs as in the NSDS process.

Another challenge for financial institutions is to examine impacts beyond project and company boundaries along the supply chain. Given the complexity of the network of suppliers and contractors that can be associated with a particular company, and the lack of transparency that has typically prevailed in such trading relationships, collecting the information needed for assessment can be difficult.

A number of mechanisms have been developed which can help companies and financial institutions to address environmental and social issues when evaluating investment decisions:

Box 9.10 UNEP Financial Institutions Initiative

A wide range of institutions have signed up to the UNEP Financial Institutions Initiatives (commercial banks, investment banks, venture capitalists, asset managers and multilateral development banks). They have endorsed the UNEP Statement by Financial Institutions on the Environment and Sustainable Development. This commits signatories to incorporate environmentally sound practices into their operations. A secondary objective of the Initiative is to foster private sector investment in environmentally sound technologies and services. In spite of the inclusion of 'sustainable development' in the UNEP statement, the emphasis is mainly on environmental issues, reflecting the remit of the driving organization.

So far, signatories have been primarily from Europe and North America. However, UNEP has been holding meetings in different regions to encourage financial institutions in developing countries to sign up (starting with Asia in April 2001 and Latin America in November 2001). Examples of signatories include: Philippines Land Bank, Uganda Commercial Bank, Banco Nacional de Angola and Thai Investment and Securities Public Company. In developing countries, signatories are mainly development banks and other government-owned institutions, but participation of the private sector is being promoted through the regional meetings. However, some of the largest transnational private financial institutions are also represented: HSBC, Barclays, UBS and Citigroup. These institutions are increasingly setting up affiliate companies in developing countries.

A survey was carried out in 1998 to monitor progress of the signatories to integrate environmental considerations. It found that the majority of responding organizations had an internal environmental policy and a dedicated environmental department, and had in operation, or under development, environmental policies and procedures for corporate credit and project finance. Fewer institutions had environmental policies covering investment banking or insurance.

The environmental issues most commonly considered in credit, investment and insurance transactions were:

- legal compliance;
- overall company reputation;
- the nature and extent of environmental liabilities.

Source: UNEP/PWC 1998 www.unepfi.net

- *Certification schemes* can reduce the extent of information gathering and assessment required of individual investors by offering an independent seal of approval or assessment of key environmental and/or social performance.
- *Improving the quality of company reporting on sustainability issues*, facilitating interpretation by investors and comparison with other companies. The Global Reporting Initiative (GRI) aims to standardize sustainability reporting and put it on a par with financial reporting in terms of credibility and comparability. Sustainability reporting guidelines were launched by GRI in June 2000 following multi-stakeholder discussion, and are currently being revised.
- Following the model of credit ratings and stock market indices, a number of organizations have developed *environmental and/or sustainability ratings* for companies. Given the problems of environmental and sustainability reporting mentioned above, these organizations aim to use expert analysis to interpret and assess this information and assign a rating to each company in a sector (Box 9.11).

It is unrealistic to expect that the overseas financial institutions will play a major direct role in the NSDS process. Nevertheless, it is important to consider how the strategy process can reinforce their initiatives by providing reference standards, generating information and securing stakeholder agreement on activities/sectors to be prioritized and those to be avoided.

CHALLENGES FOR NATIONAL FINANCE AND INVESTMENT INSTITUTIONS

All the national level institutions listed in Box 9.9 need to be involved in the strategy process. Government agencies concerned with inward investment and industrial development generally must broaden their remit

---

Box 9.11 Sustainability ratings for companies

The Dow Jones Sustainability Group Index (DJSGI) tracks the performance of the leading sustainability-driven companies in the Dow Jones Group Index. It aims to provide investors and industry with a neutral, rigorous and transparent measurement of sustainability performance. As of October 2001, the two component Indexes, the Dow Jones Sustainability Index World and the Dow Jones STOXX Sustainability Index, included 300 and 151 companies from 64 industries respectively. The DJSI World selects the top 10 per cent of the leading sustainability companies in the Dow Jones Group Index. The DJSTOXX Sustainability Index includes the top 20 per cent of the Dow Jones STOXX600 index in terms of sustainability. Companies are assessed according to a methodology devised by DJSGI, which assesses economic, environmental and social risks and opportunities. The criteria include general as well as industry-specific issues. Social criteria addressed include: strategies for stakeholder involvement, formulation of a social policy, corporate codes of conduct and standards for suppliers. The basis for the assessment is information supplied by the company through a questionnaire and company policies and reports as well as publicly available information (see: www.sustainability-index.com).

The FTSE4Good index series is a similar approach from the other main market player in stock market indices (see www.ftse4good.com). It was launched in 2001. The series consists of eight regionally different indices for socially responsible investment. Companies must apply for consideration and are assessed according to environmental sustainability, social issues and stakeholder relations, as well as human rights.

The NSDS process offers an opportunity for national finance institutions to address sustainable development costs, benefits and risk – and to work together on forging coherent standards

to address sustainable development issues. Financial institutions need to be persuaded of the benefits of integrating sustainable development considerations into their operations. Both types of institution must therefore be key stakeholders and participants in the NSDS process from the outset.

In developing the strategy, it is necessary to identify activities which will build capacity within financial institutions for assessing sustainable development, to generate information and agree on reference standards. This may involve new initiatives but, in some cases, it may be possible to build on or link in to existing initiatives. Box 9.12 provides examples of national and regional initiatives in developing countries which aim to provide information for investors on company environmental and social performance, and to raise awareness about the links between financial performance and sustainable development.

Box 9.12 Examples of sustainable investment initiatives in developing countries

Brazil

The Eco-financas initiative in Brazil was launched in September 2000 as a partnership between Friends of the Earth and a São Paulo business school. It aims to educate NGOs about financial institutions and raise awareness in financial institutions about environmental issues. Workshops are organized for NGOs on finance, and for financial institutions on environmental issues – notably environmental risk and environmental management systems.

Asia Pacific

The Association for Sustainable and Responsible Investment (ASrIA) was formed in 2000 to promote corporate responsibility and sustainable investment practice in the Asia Pacific region. It aims to create a community of individuals and organizations interested in sustainable and responsible investment (SRI) and, in so doing, to mobilize the capital markets in Asia so that they reward sustainable enterprise. Its basic premise is that the 'triple bottom line' approach of integrating concerns such as social justice, economic development and a healthy environment with financial considerations can bring both financial and societal benefits. ASrIA is supported by some of the key financial players in the SRI field in Europe and North America (see www.asria.org).

India

The Centre for Science and Environment in India is implementing a 'green ratings' project. It aims to analyse the relative performance of Indian industries in incorporating good environmental management principles in their management practices. The ratings are intended to provide information for investors, but will also be useful to industrial managers and regulatory agencies. Ratings have been produced for the pulp and paper sector and are under preparation for the automobile and chlor-alkali sector (see www.oneworld.org/cse/html/eyou/eyou32_old.htm).

CHAPTER
10

Monitoring and evaluation systems[1]

Introduction

Elements of a monitoring and evaluation system

How do we know that a strategy for sustainable development has been successful, or is on the right path? Not only do strategies have multiple objectives, but also strategy activities will change over time and so will social, economic and environmental conditions. This presents a considerable challenge for monitoring and evaluation, but one that must be met, since the whole point of a strategic approach is to learn and adapt. The central monitoring and evaluation requirement is, therefore, to track systematically the key variables and processes over time and space and see how they change as a result of strategy activities (Spellerberg 1991). To do this requires:

Four monitoring tasks to keep an NSDS is on the right track

- measuring and analysing sustainability;
- monitoring implementation of the strategy;
- evaluating the results of the strategy;
- reporting and dissemination of the above findings.

Measuring and analysing sustainability is necessary to determine the state of the society, the economy and the environment, the main strengths and weaknesses, the issues for the strategy to address, and underlying factors. The most productive way to approach this is to undertake an indicator-based sustainability assessment, supplemented by spatial analysis and possibly other contributing measurements and analyses. The indicators chosen for the assessment need continued monitoring to identify trends, detect (and, if possible, anticipate) change and track progress. This is covered in detail in Chapter 5, pages 132–162.

Monitoring implementation of the strategy (page 321) is necessary to ensure standard management oversight and accountability. Regular monitoring is needed of the following factors to assure that strategy activities are proceeding well:

1 This chapter has benefited from review comments and additional material provided by Robert Prescott-Allen, Canada.

- *inputs* in terms of financial, physical and human resources applied to the strategy and its related activities;
- *process quality* in terms of how strategy principles are satisfied (eg people-centred, participation, integration, commitment generation, see Box 3.1);
- *outputs* in terms of the generation of strategy products (goods, services and capacities) by agencies involved in the strategy;
- *outcomes* in terms of access to, use of, and satisfaction with strategy products (which are not necessarily under the control of agencies involved in the strategy);
- the *performance of individual strategy actors* in implementing the strategy, in terms of the effectiveness and efficiency of their service provision and management.

Evaluating the results of the strategy (page 324) is necessary to correlate actions with specific changes in human and environmental conditions, test the strategic hypotheses (choice of priority issues, analysis of underlying factors, prescription of actions), assure accountability, capture lessons and develop capacity through learning.

Reporting and dissemination (page 325) of the above findings is necessary to feed back key messages to key stakeholder groups, and thus enable them to continuously improve their behaviour, the strategy itself and its component activities. Much of the guidance from Chapter 7 (Communications) is directly relevant.

Data for the required monitoring, sources and CSD indicators are listed in tables in the Appendix

Tables A.1 and A.2 (see Appendix) illustrate the *range of data, sources and timing* for the different kinds of monitoring outlined above.

Some – or too frequently all – of these elements have been missing from many strategies in the past. Typical problems associated with the lack of a monitoring system are illustrated by Box 10.1.

Box 10.1 A strategy without regular monitoring and evaluation – Pakistan

The mid-term review of Pakistan's National Conservation Strategy (NCS) found an almost complete lack of routine monitoring of outputs, outcomes and impacts in relation to sustainability indicators, and a lack of policy links between the NCS coordinating body and NCS-inspired projects. This had meant that the possibilities for learning were far fewer than there could have been. During eight years of implementation the (quite coherent) strategic objectives had fragmented into hundreds of unconnected component activities with no feedback mechanism (except for a narrow monitoring of some inputs, notably government expenditure). The NCS review therefore tried to install a simple baseline and framework for correlating sustainability outcomes with strategic processes in future.

Good M&E likely would have changed the prevailing perception of the NCS being a static reference 'document' to appreciation of its potential as a dynamic process to improve future economic, ecological and social well-being. Finally, it would have contributed to a culture of transparency and learning.

Source: Hanson et al (2000)

Principles of successful monitoring and evaluation

Five principles for effective monitoring and evaluation

From experience, effective monitoring and evaluation can be described as follows:

- *Constructed and developed as a system* that combines the functions described in the previous section, and makes them a core part of the overall strategy management system. Very few countries, and especially developing counties, have formal monitoring and auditing capacities and procedures in place for strategic planning frameworks. However, in most, several government agencies and significant NGOs and business associations will already be conducting some of the monitoring functions required as inputs to the strategy monitoring system. As an example, Table A.1 on page 327 lists the kinds of agencies that can offer monitoring inputs on poverty-related issues. The challenge is to bring these together.

■ *A mix of internal and external exercises.* Internal approaches help with self-reflection, learning and adaptation. External exercises complement this by offering balanced judgement (by independent and/or multi-stakeholder groups). This is described in 'Formal internal and external monitoring' below, with approaches for ensuring participation on page 315.

■ *Driven by strategy objectives* rather than (as so often at present) by the availability of data. This allows the generation of focused information rather than being overwhelmed by comprehensive (and not always useful) data. Monitoring everything is impossible. It is impossible in *theory* because we do not know enough about natural, social and economic systems to know all the aspects we could record – and new techniques and approaches are being developed all the time. It is impossible in *practice* because there will never be enough resources – time, money, equipment, expertise – to record everything. Therefore, data selection is necessarily selective.

■ *Related to good baseline data* to be able to compare 'before and after' or 'with or without action' situations. Many countries already undertake regular stocktaking such as state-of-the-environment reports (see Box 10.8), which could be built on to become comprehensive sustainability assessments. Chapter 5 discusses some of the analytical methods that can be used for such stocktaking. Data quality also needs to be assured; principles for this include (Carson 2000):
  ■ integrity and objectivity in the collection, compilation and dissemination of statistics;
  ■ methodological soundness (eg following international standards, guidelines and agreed practices);
  ■ accuracy and reliability;
  ■ serviceability (timeliness, consistency and policy relevance);
  ■ accessibility (including assistance to users).

■ *Organized into a consistent framework.* The pressure–state–response framework has been used, although it is better suited to environmental monitoring than more comprehensive sustainable development needs. This is discussed further on page 318.

Further guidance is offered by the more general Bellagio principles for assessing progress towards sustainable development (Box 10.2).[2] These principles have much in common with those for NSDSs in Box 3.1.

Who should undertake monitoring and evaluation?

Formal internal and external monitoring

INTERNALLY DRIVEN MONITORING (CONDUCTED BY LOCAL STRATEGY STAKEHOLDERS)
Those directly concerned – local decision-makers and affected groups – have the most to gain from monitoring and evaluation, and should be centrally involved. By participating, they will know better what to do to achieve their objectives. Participatory approaches are important, and strategies need to make special efforts to involve affected communities (page 315).

Local strategy stakeholders should participate in internal monitoring, but there can be conflicts of interest …

2 The Bellagio Forum for Sustainable Development launched an international science and policy dialogue to improve existing sustainable development indicators so that they are user-friendly and robust. The dialogue has been carried out through the International Institute for Sustainable Development (IISD), the World Conservation Union (IUCN), the Earth Council and the Institut für Wirtschaftsforschung.

Box 10.2 The Bellagio principles for assessing progress towards sustainable development

In November 1996, an international group of measurement practitioners and researchers from five continents came together at the Rockefeller Foundation's Study and Conference Centre in Bellagio, Italy, to review progress to date and to synthesize insights from practical ongoing efforts. The following principles resulted and were unanimously endorsed.

These principles deal with four aspects of assessing progress towards sustainable development. Principle 1 deals with the starting point of any assessment – establishing a *vision* of sustainable development and clear goals that provide a practical definition of that vision in terms that are meaningful for the decision-making unit in question. Principles 2–5 deal with the *content of any assessment* and the need to merge a sense of the overall system with a practical focus on current priority issues. Principles 6–8 deal with key issues of the *process of assessment*, while Principles 9 and 10 deal with the necessity for establishing a *continuing capacity* for assessment. Assessment of progress towards sustainable development should consider the following aspects:

1   **Guiding vision and goals**
    - be guided by a clear vision of sustainable development and goals that define that vision.
2   **Holistic perspective**
    - include review of the whole system as well as its parts;
    - consider the well-being of social, ecological and economic sub-systems, their state as well as the direction and rate of change of that state, of their component parts, and the interaction between parts;
    - consider both positive and negative consequences of human activity, in a way that reflects the costs and benefits for human and ecological systems, in monetary and non-monetary terms.
3   **Essential elements**
    - consider equity and disparity within the current population and between present and future generations, dealing with such concerns as resource use, over-consumption and poverty, human rights, and access to services, as appropriate;
    - consider the ecological conditions on which life depends;
    - consider economic development and other, non-market activities that contribute to human/social well-being.
4   **Adequate scope**
    - adopt a time horizon long enough to capture both human and ecosystem timescales – thus responding to needs of future generations as well as those current to short-term decision-making;
    - define the space of study large enough to include not only local but also long distance impacts on people and ecosystems;
    - build on historic and current conditions to anticipate future conditions – where we want to go, where we could go.
5   **Practical focus – Be based on:**
    - an explicit set of categories or an organizing framework that links vision and goals to indicators and assessment criteria;
    - a limited number of key issues for analysis;
    - a limited number of indicators or indicator combinations to provide a clearer signal of progress;
    - standardizing measurement wherever possible to permit comparison;
    - comparing indicator values to targets, reference values, ranges, thresholds or direction of trends, as appropriate.
6   **Openness**
    - make the methods and data that are used accessible to all;
    - make explicit all judgements, assumptions and uncertainties in data and interpretations.
7   **Effective communication**
    - be designed to address the needs of the audience and set of users;
    - draw from indicators and other tools that are stimulating and serve to engage decision-makers;
    - aim, from the outset, for simplicity in structure and use of clear and plain language.
8   **Broad participation**
    - obtain broad representation of key grass-roots, professional, technical and social groups – including youth, women and indigenous people – to ensure recognition of diverse and changing values;
    - ensure the participation of decision-makers to secure a firm link to adopted policies and resulting action.

9   **Ongoing assessment**
  - develop a capacity for repeated measurement to determine trends;
  - be iterative, adaptive and responsive to change and uncertainty because systems are complex and change frequently;
  - adjust goals, frameworks and indicators as new insights are gained;
  - promote development of collective learning and feedback to decision-making.

10   **Institutional capacity:** Continuity of assessing progress towards sustainable development should be assured by:
  - clearly assigning responsibility and providing ongoing support in the decision-making process;
  - providing institutional capacity for data collection, maintenance and documentation;
  - supporting development of local assessment capacity.

Source: www.iisd.org

EXTERNALLY DRIVEN MONITORING AND EVALUATION (CONDUCTED BY AGREED INDEPENDENT BODIES OR BY DONORS)

Unbiased opinion and independent expert analysis can make a critical contribution to understanding, such as where special expertise is needed (air, soil and biodiversity assessment, etc) and where impartial judgement is called for. An external assessment can give stakeholders new insights and avoid or overcome conflicts of interest in self-assessment. Independent monitoring and auditing can be used to measure the performance of organizations against their mandates and to assess compliance with rights, powers and responsibilities. So far, independent auditing of government performance (at any level) in relation to strategy development and implementation is rare.

... which impartial, external expertise can avoid, while providing stakeholders with new insights

The official procedures for auditing public expenditure that exist in many countries could possibly provide a useful model, as in Canada where the Auditor General's office looks at government bodies' performance in terms of sustainable development. The model of independent commissions, both one-off and on a continuing basis, could also be useful (Box 10.3).

Box 10.3 The use of Commissions to hold government to account – Ghana and Canada

In **Ghana**, the 1992 Constitution mandated a Commission on Human Rights and Administrative Justice to act as an ombudsman, national watchdog and redress mechanism. It is a formal monitoring mechanism to ensure accountability, human rights and compliance with proper and fair procedures in the administration of state affairs.

In **Canada**, a Commissioner of the Environment and Sustainable Development holds the government accountable for the 'greening' of its policies, operations and programmes. Federal ministers must table departmental sustainable development strategies in Parliament. The Commissioner monitors and reports to Parliament on the progress of government departments in implementing their action plans and meeting their sustainable development objectives.

The role of *donors* in monitoring strategies is considered in detail in the OECD DAC policy guidance for development cooperation on NSDSs (OECD DAC 2001a).[3] In summary:

Donors can also play a role in monitoring

- *Donor agencies themselves* need to ensure that support for the monitoring of a country's strategy is not aimed at their own internal accountability needs, but is primarily for the purpose of helping a country's own learning, and improving progress towards its agreed objectives and goals. However, such indications of progress can be used to assess the contribution and possible impact of agency support.

---

3 OECD DAC (2001a) also includes guidance on monitoring the response of donors and on monitoring progress in NSSDs at the international level, issues which are outside the scope of this Resource Book.

- At the *national level*, donor agencies can play an important role in supporting and advocating the development of indicators and monitoring instruments for a country's own assessment of progress towards sustainable development. Only if such instruments are nationally owned are they likely to be successful.
- At the *operational level*, agencies can support capacity building for statistical analysis and research to monitor strategy progress towards nationally defined objectives. This could include the development of systems which ensure that national policy and programmes are reviewed and revised to reflect impact at the local level.

Box 10.4 offers 20 questions to help monitor and evaluate donor roles in relation to strategies.

Box 10.4 Development agency performance in supporting strategy processes: 20 questions

1 To what extent is the agency's country assistance strategy based on, and aligned to, the partner country's sustainable development strategy?
2 What specific programmes does the agency finance to support this strategy?
3 To what extent do they respond to the principles outlined in Box 3.1?
4 To what extent does the country assistance strategy analyse and respond to the partner's capacity for strategies (eg participation, analysis)?
5 To what extent is this done jointly with other agencies and country partners?
6 What actions has the agency taken to promote convergence, complementarity and coherence between strategic frameworks in the country?
7 When providing support in sectors, how does the agency foster relevant cross-sectoral linkages and policy coherence?
8 To what extent are activities supported by the agency coordinated with those of other bilateral and multilateral development agencies, and is this under the leadership of the partner country?
9 What support for such country-led coordination is the agency providing, and is it working?
10 How is the agency sharing experiences gained in relation to strategies?
11 How are issues relating to strategies for sustainable development, and the principles contained in Box 3.1, included in the agency's staff training programmes?
12 How are agencies learning internally from their assistance to a country's strategy process?
13 What changes has the agency made as a result of this learning? How have staff incentives changed?
14 What special efforts has the agency made to support and facilitate civil society participation in strategy processes?
15 How does the agency safeguard policies and how does the application of strategic assessment methodologies relate to a country's strategic planning framework?
16 To what extent does the agency encourage and support the application of strategic assessment methodologies when supporting sector wide approaches (SWAPs) and policy reform?
17 To what extent is the agency able to provide long-term funding for strategic planning processes?
18 If the agency is providing shorter-term funding (eg annually), how has the agency ensured that this contributes to a country's longer-term strategy for sustainable development?
19 To what extent is the agency funding clearly linked with the national budget of the country?
20 In what ways has the agency promoted a broadening of ownership and joint agreement around achievable strategy targets and outcomes?

Source: Adapted from OECD/DAC (2001a)

LINKING INTERNAL AND EXTERNAL MONITORING

Independent and internal assessments should be complementary

Independent assessments are likely to be most valuable if agreed and commissioned by multiple strategy stakeholders and if they build on internal assessments, rather than if they are imposed from outside, such as by a donor. For example, an external review of the Pakistan NCS was used to pull together and to weigh up various internal processes of monitoring and evaluation done by government and NGOs, as well as through local roundtable discussions (see Box 10.5).

Box 10.5 **The process to review Pakistan's National Conservation Strategy**

Steps: The following tasks were undertaken:

1 Agree on an analytical framework on sustainable development, for use throughout Review.
2 Focus group discussions on the changing context.
3 Review development of institutions proposed by the NCS (Secondary review).
4 Review the progress of provincial and district strategies.
5 Create a database of all projects relating to the NCS.
6 Review a sample of these projects.
7 In light of the above, review the overall NCS process and its management.
8 Produce a draft synthesis report, summarizing findings and recommendations.
9 Multi-stakeholder debate on findings and ways forward.
10 Produce and disseminate final report.

Studies: Nine component studies were prepared by government, private sector and NGO bodies, and by mixed teams, over the course of a year:

1 A report of stakeholder consultations on improvements to sustainability at federal and provincial levels, and the role of the NCS.
2 A database on public sector investments in the core areas of NCS, 1992–2000.
3 A study of resourcing for NCS implementation.
4 A study of changes to environmental legislation.
5 A study of institutional development for NCS implementation.
6 A review of progress and impacts of provincial and district conservation strategies.
7 A review of mass awareness and education initiatives.
8 A study of the contributions of the private sector and NGOs.
9 A scoping study of environmental, economic and social trends and futures for reorienting the NCS.

An overview report was prepared by an independent 'External Review Team' using this material:

10 Pakistan's National Conservation Strategy: Renewing the Commitment to Action. Report of the Mid-Term Review (Hanson et al 2000).

Prospectus: Finally, a prospectus for a revised approach to the NCS (in fact, for an NSDS) was prepared following discussions between the External Review Team and NCS stakeholders.

Applying NSDS principles to the monitoring exercise: The External Review Team noted that the review process itself succeeded by applying principles compatible with a successful NSDS:

The review 'wove a cloth' combining a complex mix of players, interests, competing sectors, federal and provincial government departments. This process was essential for building consensus on the purpose of the review and for addressing the varying perceptions and interests of key actors. It was hindered by the limited culture for a consultative approach within the government and, at various times, by the cumbersome governmental rules of business. In a sense, the review had to rekindle the spirit of participation and inquiry that had characterized the formulation of the NCS – overcoming inertia and educating many of the actors who were new to the NCS.

Source: Hanson et al (2000)

Participatory monitoring and evaluation

At the local level, participatory monitoring and evaluation (PME) has been developed over more than 20 years to 'shift emphasis away from externally-controlled data-seeking evaluations towards recognition of locally-relevant or stakeholder-based processes for gathering, analysing, and using information' (Estrella 2000). With this emphasis now having shifted effectively in many countries, it would be wrong to think of

Participatory monitoring and evaluation approaches have evolved over 20 years ...

Box 10.6 **Guidelines for participatory monitoring and evaluation**

There is now a huge literature on PME. Useful entry points are IIRR (1998), Abbot and Guijt (1998) and IIED (1998c). A news service is provided at www.mande.co.uk, focusing on developments in monitoring and evaluation methods relevant to development projects and programmes with social development objectives. A range of guidelines and manuals for aiding development practitioners in carrying out PME can be found on the ELDIS development information service hosted by the Institute for Development Studies, University of Brighton, UK (www.ids.ac.uk/eldis). Some of the PME guidelines and manuals are widely applicable. Others are relevant to specific sectors, to use by different actors, or to various aspects of either monitoring or evaluation. There are a number of broadly relevant manuals, mainly developed by the large donor agencies for use by their staff and partners. Examples include:

■ **Participatory monitoring, evaluation and reporting: online manual**, PACT (an advisory organization for NGOs) manual designed for South African NGOs.

This manual explains why participation is important and how to achieve effective stakeholder participation; the role of monitoring in sustaining progress toward better organizational effectiveness; how evaluation helps an organization to assess its capacity; and the critical role of reporting in keeping stakeholders informed. It then deals with applying the Organizational Capacity Assessment Tool (OCAT) in practice, together with examples. A step-by-step guide to designing and implementing a Participatory Monitoring, Evaluation and Reporting (PME&R) information system is included. Although it has been specifically adapted for use by South African NGOs, OCAT can be used by NGOs in other countries (see www.pactworld.org).

■ **Assessing Progress Towards Sustainability (IUCN)**

(This manual) focuses on the development and application of methods and tools for system, project and institutional assessment, including a participatory approach to engaging stakeholders in defining the key sustainability issues affecting their lives, and practical ways of measuring change in human and ecosystem condition related to these issues. This includes a way of developing and combining indicators into a sustainability index or rating, and training, capacity-building and networking for field practitioners engaged in assessment activities. (It) includes case studies from Colombia (Sierra Nevada de Santa Marta), Zimbabwe (District Environmental Action Plans) and India (Integrated Resource Management Plan, Tumkur District, Karnataka State). (The document is also available in Spanish and French, see http://iucn.org/themes/eval/index.html)

■ **Who are the Question-makers?** (UNDP)

Provides the information needed, and helps to develop the sensitivity and skills required, to support evaluations that place greater emphasis on stakeholder participation in the evaluation process. Parts one to four, which present an overview of the participatory evaluation approach, include:
– *a brief description of the evolution of the participatory approach;*
– *a comparison of participatory evaluation with more conventional evaluation approaches;*
– *a discussion of the role of participation in UNDP;*
– *a description of the framework of a participatory evaluation and a discussion of some of the practical issues involved in doing such an evaluation.*

Part five consists of a stand-alone package developed around the case study 'Money and Mambas'. It describes an attempt at undertaking a participatory evaluation of a rural water supply and sanitation project and focuses on the practical aspects of applying participatory evaluation techniques:
– *pre-planning, including negotiation of the TOR, assessing the participatory evaluation context and identifying enabling and inhibiting factors surrounding that context;*
– *collaborative planning with stakeholders;*
– *data-gathering and analysis;*
– *reflection and follow-up.*

This case study is presented as a training module, which can be the subject of a mini-workshop to introduce staff to the practice of participatory evaluation. It is suggested that this exercise can be accomplished within 3 to 4 hours.

- ■ **Mid-term Participatory Evaluation Guidelines (CARE)**

  (An) example of a detailed outline for the participatory evaluation of a development project.

- ■ **Community Toolbox (FAO)**

  Manual on methodologies for Participatory Assessment, Monitoring and Evaluation (PAME). Includes: an overview; separate chapters on participatory assessment, participatory monitoring and participatory evaluation; methods for analysing and presenting information; suggestions for 23 tools for applying this (eg handling group meetings, mapping, theatre, videos).

- ■ **Conducting A Participatory Evaluation (notes from USAID)**

  Short set of methodological tips on how to undertake a participatory evaluation.

- ■ **Participatory Impact Monitoring (PIM) (GTZ/GATE)**

  Short, simply written pamphlets explaining methods and justifications for participatory monitoring. Series includes:
  - *group-based impact monitoring;*
  - *NGO-based impact monitoring;*
  - *application examples;*
  - *the concept of participatory impact monitoring;*
  - *keywords and bibliographical abstracts;*
  - *selected reading examples.*

PME as a highly distinct category of monitoring and evaluation, with expert or external M&E as another category. First, the most useful assessments are technically sound *and* shaped by their users (decision-makers at whatever level, from households upwards), and therefore are a mixture of 'expert' and 'participatory'. Second, although some M&E methods are so technical that their potential for participation is limited, many methods are, in fact, quite open or neutral: they can be conducted by technicians alone or in highly participatory ways. Third, outside agents are usually involved in participatory assessments and often have a significant influence on them – an influence that can be masked and sometimes hidden entirely by the label 'participatory'.

Nevertheless, the term 'participatory monitoring and evaluation' is useful to describe a wide range of practices. For the purpose of sustainable development strategies, PME should be taken to mean monitoring approaches that develop partnerships of multiple stakeholders for efficient, effective and socially inclusive monitoring.

Abbot and Guijt (1998) note the many approaches to PME. They place them in three broad categories:

- ■ methodologies based on the *visualization* techniques of participatory rural appraisal (see Chapter 6 page 194);
- ■ those that use *oral testimony* to uncover patterns of environmental and social change;
- ■ those that adapt methods of *assessment* to make them more accessible to local people.

There is also much literature, and many guidelines, now available on PME (Box 10.6).

Monitoring methods and indicators often meet the needs of many stakeholder groups, but this is not always the case. This highlights the need for negotiation between stakeholders to reach consensus on the objectives, methods, indicators and end-users of the monitoring process. Reaching such agreement will

... covering a wide range of approaches – in three broad categories

increase the chances that the system will work and be supportive of the overall strategy process. Many of the national and more local PME initiatives listed in Box 10.6 have adopted such an approach.

GTZ's QUIM approach to 'Qualitative Impact Monitoring' of Poverty Reduction Strategy Papers (PRSPs) combines a *technical policy analysis* of poverty-related policies and programmes with *beneficiary assessments* based on Participatory Rural Appraisal to reveal local people's opinions of the poverty situation and government programmes. It thereby combines a hard, top-down thrust with a softer, bottom-up position and contributes to improved programme–beneficiary relationships (GTZ 2001).

More details on community-based monitoring are given in Box 10.7.

When should monitoring and evaluation be undertaken?

Assessment should commence from the outset of a strategy process to establish a baseline. But, as monitoring and evaluation are integral to a continuous improvement approach to decision-making, they should be regular and integrated activities rather than sporadic and separate events. The benefit of regular assessment is that it encourages participants to rethink priorities, reset objectives and rechart their course of action. It keeps the strategy working as a *system*, rather than an (increasingly out of date) master plan.

Table 10.2 suggests some typical frequencies for assessment, which will depend on the following:

- The work plans of component activities. Input, output and process indicators will change more frequently, and they can be monitored as part of a regular management information system (eg monthly).
- How rapidly and significantly conditions are changing. Outcomes and impacts take time to emerge and become apparent, and are relatively expensive to assess. Annual assessments, or every 3–5 years, would normally be acceptable.
- The magnitude of the risk to human or ecosystem well-being. A higher level of risk would warrant more frequent monitoring.

The 'pressure–state–response' framework for monitoring – its utility and limitations

Use in state-of-the-environment reporting

The pressure–state–response framework is an approach for linking a great number of variables that need to be monitored to assess the state of the environment. As such, it has both utility and limits – limits that are being stretched with its more recent application to the even more complex issue of the state of sustainable development.

The framework can be applied at a national level, at sectoral levels, at the level of an industrial firm or at the community level. The framework follows a holistic cause–effect–social response logic. Sustainability indicators are selected, based on variables, which signal *pressure, state and response*:

- The *pressure* that society puts on the environment; for example in the form of demands on resources (leading to resource depletion) and demands on ecological processes (leading to pollution). Pressure indicators are based on measurements or on model-based estimates of actual behaviour. Consequently, they are particularly useful in formulating policy targets and in evaluating policy performance. They can also be used prospectively to evaluate potential environmental impacts of socio-economic scenarios or proposed policy measures.

Such monitoring processes need to be negotiated by stakeholders, so they support overall strategy processes

Assessment from the outset establishes a baseline for regular monitoring

A common approach for linking many variables that can be used to signal ...

... pressure ...

Box 10.7 Community-based monitoring and indicator development

Community-based monitoring: Given the lack of coverage of trade-offs and distributional differences in national sustainability indicators, the local level is the best way to obtain, for example, equity indicators. Local communities can play critical roles in tracking the 'bottom-up' realities, which an NSDS should be addressing, and in assessing the strategy outcomes and impacts of strategy activities. Traditional community fora have been used to air views, discuss problems, monitor changes and reach decisions affecting local people, and have been an important mechanism for local monitoring and accountability. But many of them have fallen into disuse or have been replaced as governments have introduced formal administrative structures at local levels and as political parties have established local organizational units. Traditional ways still exist in many countries and local people respect these systems that could again play a useful role. In some countries, traditional chiefs continue to play a key and powerful role in local monitoring, governance and decision-making (see Chapter 6). But they often behave in unaccountable ways. Some problems of accountability can be overcome through establishing local democratic structures (which is a medium to long-term affair).

Development programmes can also catalyse action. In Nepal, for example, local communities are increasingly becoming involved in collecting baseline data for sustainable development programmes, and NGOs and CBOs have developed participatory tools for community use in monitoring their sustainable development activities. In some countries, informal citizen monitoring is on the increase. For example, during the last three years in Bangladesh, a leading NGO (Proshika) has facilitated a broad participatory process to monitor the government's poverty alleviation targets and budgets. This is quite different from, but a useful complement to, the household-level monitoring that is required on social, economic and environmental conditions which so far is best supplied through efficient survey/questionnaire approaches.

Community-based indicator development: MacGillivray and Zadek (1995) suggest that there should be three processes for community-based indicator development:

- *Outsiders* with indicator expertise can first make a list of possible indicators that might be of use to a community. Examples include: indicator species prevalence, birth weight, literacy rates and soil erosion rates. These indicators might be derived from sustainable development literature or from their own personal experience.
- *The community* should discuss the utility of indicators. A small group of people proficient in the local language and culture should agree a local word to use. In Uganda, the word chosen was 'signpost'. Everybody recognized what it was and what it was not: a signpost points to something else, but is not itself the thing it points to. The South African team used the concept of a tool to measure a child's school progress – the school report card. Next, through internal (facilitated) consultations, the community should develop its own list of indicators of sustainable livelihoods. Community indicators of sustainable livelihoods often provide useful insights into community dynamics and coping strategies, by revealing trade-offs and priorities.
- *A joint process* of indicator selection should be undertaken by both the community and the outsiders. Community-based indicators should be selected for collection by the community (thus the issue must be one in which they are stakeholders) while also being upwardly compatible with higher-level monitoring and evaluation concerns. Thus, it is necessary to find common ground between the statistician and the community, and a possible trade-off between professional standards and practicality or realism from the community point of view. If communities are involved in monitoring indicators, there needs to be motivation, and mechanism(s) for feedback into a local information system so that the process of indicator measurement is not purely extractive. It should contribute to local understanding and empowerment, and not simply aim to satisfy external needs.

- The resulting *state* of the environment (especially the incurred changes) compared with desirable (sustainable) states. State indicators cover the major characteristics of natural, physical, financial, social and human capital assets, individually or in a combined manner. They can be obtained variously from national accounts, poverty monitoring, natural resource inventories and remote sensing, sector information systems and demographic monitoring – although it is not always the case that variables pertinent to sustainability are currently collected.

... state ...

... and response

■ The *response* mainly in the form of political and societal decisions, measures and policies. Response indicators measure progress towards regulatory compliance or other governmental efforts, but don't directly tell what is happening to the environment. Response indicators need to be able to ascertain the most relevant policy or programme in relation to any given driving force or state indicators. Further investigation of any given response, of course, leads into the territory of impact assessment.

The framework is generally accepted, and many countries find it useful for state of environment reporting (Box 10.8). Core lists of environmental issues – and of relevant pressure–state–response indicators – have been, and are being, developed by several organizations to do this, building on initial work by the OECD. Italy, for example, publishes a national state of the environment report using this framework every two years, and is setting up a national monitoring system along the same lines.

Box 10.8 State of the environment reporting

State of the environment reporting (SOER) is a general term used to describe the compilation and review of data collected over a period of time, usually 2–5 years. Reports generally provide a comprehensive review of the status and trends of different natural resources and ecological processes (air, soil, water, etc) often correlated in some way with pressures arising from public issues (child health, noise, employment, training, etc) for the particular time period, noting policy responses. SOERs collate existing data from different monitoring systems and programmes. They provide analysis of this data to clarify trends in relation to some base line. GIS-generated data may be used for graphic representation.

   Sometimes, there is involvement of stakeholder institutions and the public. In Lancashire County, UK, more than 70 organizations formed an 'Environment Forum' to jointly collect and analyse environmental data for the 'Lancashire Environmental Audit'. Such network-based approaches to SOER can increase access to data and information that is not normally made public. In addition, it facilitates the interpretation of data by knowledgeable stakeholders during the process of data selection and analysis.

Use and limitations for monitoring sustainable development

Figure 10.1 illustrates how the pressure–state–response framework has been broadened to cover *'driving forces'–state–response*, covering a range of human activities, processes and patterns affecting social and economic systems as well as the environment – and thereby opening up possibilities for its application to a wide range of capital stocks necessary for sustainable development (in this case, agricultural systems). The European Environment Agency, following a proposal from Denmark, expands the approach further to a 'driving forces–pressures–state–impacts–response' model for its state of environment reports, because it also invites assessment of the adequacy of policy responses to pressures on natural resources (Baldock 1999).

   There is now a working list of 134 indicators of sustainable development developed by the CSD (Table A.2; see page 328), which is undergoing voluntary testing by countries from all regions of the world. The goal is to have an agreed set of such indicators available for all countries to use by 2002. The CSD aims to produce a flexible list from which countries can choose indicators according to national priorities, problems and targets.

   The pressure–state–response framework works well for such environmental assessments (for which it was designed). However, it is less well suited to sustainability assessment because it treats human aspirations and activities merely as environmental problems. Although the CSD tried to get round this by changing pressures to 'driving forces', users found it increasingly hard to disentangle states, driving forces and responses (eg responses are often driving forces). It was also cumbersome to identify an indicator for each state, driving force and response.

   Note also that the *sustainable livelihoods framework* (Chapter 5, page 124 and Figure 5.2) groups particular components of livelihood: their capital assets, their vulnerability/opportunity context, and all the institutional structures and processes that may transform livelihoods. As such, it can provide an analogous pressure–state–response model for (participatory) monitoring at the level of livelihoods.

Monitoring the implementation of the strategy and ensuring accountability

Despite the burgeoning efforts to monitor progress towards sustainable development, very little attention has been given to tracking the actual processes involved in strategies and their impacts. Even in PRSPs – one of the more recent frameworks to emerge, which espouses a focus on process and participation – this need is not routinely addressed. For example, in their recent review of PRSPs, Booth and Lucas (2001) note that 'the authors of many of these plans have listed a wide range of traditional indicators in a fairly indiscriminate way', many of which 'derive from routine administrative/facility returns or management information systems … and it is very difficult to identify any evidence of community involvement in the proposed indicators'. They concluded that most indicators selected have been brought together from those already agreed for separate projects, programmes and concessional loans, and are not integrated in any overall rationale.

To date, there has been little attention to tracking strategy processes …

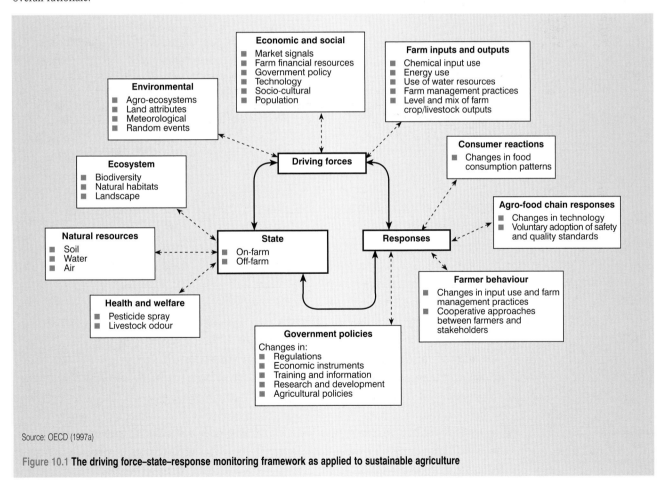

Source: OECD (1997a)

Figure 10.1 **The driving force–state–response monitoring framework as applied to sustainable agriculture**

Strategy implementation monitoring covers:

■ *Inputs*, in terms of monitoring financial, physical and human resources applied to the strategy and to its component activities. An example would be the proportion of government recurrent and

... but the components need to be monitored

investment expenditure spent on activities identified as a priority by the NSDS. Such information is frequently collected by finance or line ministries. It was collated by the Pakistan NCS, but on its own was agreed to be inadequate.

- *Process quality*, in terms of monitoring how strategy principles are adhered to and developed (eg people-centred, participation, integration, commitment generation, etc; see Box 3.1). Indicators for these process components will need to be developed. Because of the qualitative nature of strategy processes, often a questioning approach will be best for monitoring (as used by the OECD DAC dialogues), rather than an approach of assessment against indicators. Chapter 5 (pages 161–172) lays out the component mechanisms in NSDSs, possible questions to ask, and methods that can be used to answer them. Table 5.13 may be found to be particularly helpful.

- *Outputs*, in terms of monitoring which specific strategy products are generated by the agencies involved in the strategy. Examples include roundtables, workshops, publications, media events, methodologies and guidelines, for which an 'inventory' should be kept. Annual reports by the strategy secretariat are good ways of reporting on outputs.

- *Outcomes*, in terms of monitoring access to, use of, and satisfaction with strategy products. Such outcomes are not necessarily under the control of agencies involved in the strategy. For example, roundtables are an output because the strategy team can organize them; but attendance at each roundtable and the decisions made are outcomes, which depend on stakeholder behaviour. In Burkina Faso, satisfaction with reforms in government tendering procedures is seen as an important indicator of the reform programme. It is usually more difficult to assess outcomes, and special surveys (questionnaires, focus groups, interviews) may be needed so that information is collected direct from the beneficiaries.

- *Accountability for implementation* – monitoring the performance of individual strategy actors in implementing the strategy, encouraging them to report to other stakeholders and monitoring related capacity constraints. This is discussed further below.

Monitoring the performance of strategy stakeholders, and mutual accountability

Four key questions for assessing government performance ...

Monitoring stakeholder performance focuses on the actions being taken to achieve the overall goals and the specific targets established in the strategy. Key questions that need to be addressed in monitoring and evaluating performance of government include:

- Are *official statistics and data of good quality*, and the institutional and technical arrangements for coordinating data from different sources effective for routine monitoring (page 310)?
- Are the *administrative and/or sectoral management information systems* (government as well as other stakeholders involved in implementation) operating to necessary quality standards? Do they enable feedback for learning and accountability purposes?
- How do *budget allocations and releases* accord with strategy objectives and with sectoral/sub-sectoral priorities; and how do releases reach their destinations within particular sectors?
- Does the performance represent *value for money*? How do the outputs produced match up against the inputs provided, and against the outcomes in terms of stakeholder use and satisfaction with the outputs?

These questions can be addressed using standard government audit procedures, adjusted as necessary. For example, many Local Agenda 21 programmes have established internal audit procedures to review how existing procedures and practices might support or hinder the implementation of agreed action plans, and to

---

Box 10.9 Internal audits for implementing Local Agenda 21

Internal audits can be undertaken by external consultants or can be organized as participatory processes involving municipal staff. Two key elements are the audit criteria and the audit protocol. The criteria should test the consistency of current municipal practices, procedures and policies with the goals, targets and action strategies of the LA21 Action Plan. The protocol consists of a set of procedures that will be used by the auditor(s) to determine performance relative to the criteria. Based on the internal audit, a municipality can identify and define what procedures, rules and standards will need to be reformed in order to support implementation of the plan. An inter-departmental committee can serve as an internal stakeholder group to review proposals generated by staff and prepare a comprehensive proposal for procedural reform to be submitted to department heads or directly to the elected municipal council.

Following such internal audit and reforms, systems need to be established to ensure that future actions or plans are consistent with the objectives of the Action Plan. For this purpose, a variety of environmental management systems (EMSs) have been designed for both private and government application. These systems establish the organizational structure, responsibilities and procedures that will be consistently used by the municipality to achieve its goals and control its impacts. Typical EMS procedures require systematic internal reviews of proposed development activities before these proposals are submitted to decision-making bodies. These procedures identify the extent of possible impacts that a project might have and define when a detailed environmental or social impact assessment should be undertaken to help mitigate negative impacts.

Source: ICLEI (1996a)

---

provide a framework for introducing the action plan to all municipal departments and agencies (Box 10.9). In addition, a range of 'quick and dirty' approaches can provide a useful rough check on official information reported (see Box 10.10).

... can be addressed using standard government audit procedures

---

Box 10.10 The value of 'quick and dirty' monitoring

'Quick and dirty' methods of monitoring, such as participatory beneficiary assessments, implementer self-assessments, using focus-group methods, 'exit polls' and light-weight service-delivery surveys, can provide an indispensable rough check on formal information – often reported slowly and unreliably through official channels. They can also provide a more dynamic type of input into the strategy process, a means of highlighting problems while there is still time to act on them, and mobilize public interest and pressure at the same time.

Source: Booth and Lucas (2001)

Because a strategy is a multi-stakeholder affair, government accountability is only part of the requirement. A major challenge is to get all the major stakeholders and institutions to report on their own actions in a candid, consistent and regular way. This requires, in effect, the establishment of a system of accountability among all the major actors and sectors: large institutions, businesses, key interest groups and even individual households, as well as government. This approach is considerably different from traditional one-way processes in which, for example, business reports to government, government reports to society, but civil society and its organizations do not report back to either.

A system of accountability is needed for all the main stakeholders and institutions

For Local Agenda 21, ICLEI (1996a) suggests that an ideal system would accomplish the following:

- *Provide a schedule and guidelines for all actors to report to each other. The best guidelines would assure that reports from different parties can be aggregated to determine the joint progress being made to achieve a specific target.*
- *Establish a set of indicators to measure performance in achieving targets (the reporting system should provide the stakeholder group or municipal planners with the data needed to determine the present value of these indicators).*

- *Provide a periodic opportunity for all actors to meet together to review each other's performance relative to their commitments and targets, and to discuss how to better coordinate their actions.*
- *Provide an opportunity to expose local residents to the different projects and campaigns being implemented, and to inform them about how they can participate.*
- *Link the performance reporting process to relevant statutory planning cycles of the municipality, such as annual budgeting, so that the municipality can adjust its plans based on the actions taken by other sectors.*

The city of Hamilton-Wentworth, Canada, has introduced an annual Sustainability Day to accomplish the objectives of mutual accountability among many stakeholders (Box 10.11).

Box 10.11 Annual Sustainability Day: Hamilton-Wentworth, Canada

Each year, the Canadian municipality of Hamilton-Wentworth organizes a Sustainability Day to bring together all the organizations and institutions in the city that have committed to implement their Vision 2020 Action Plan. Workshops are organized for different actors to meet together to discuss implementation of the different aspects of Vision 2020. There is an exhibition for local organizations, businesses and municipal departments to distribute reports and display their activities to the general public. Educational study tours are organized for citizens to visit and learn about project sites or new municipal facilities. All members of the Regional Council are invited to attend this event and, due to public expectations, most councillors do attend. In this way, Sustainability Day offers an opportunity to inform and engage decision-makers prior to annual budget deliberations, elections or other planning activities.

Hamilton-Wentworth used its first Sustainability Day to undertake a survey on possible indicators to measure performance in implementing Vision 2020. These performance-based indicators have been used to prepare an annual 'Report Card' on Vision 2020 performance, which is presented and discussed at each annual Sustainability Day. A similar approach in Bangalore, India, called the Citizen Report Cards process, is used to evaluate the municipality's performance in the area of service delivery.

Source: ICLEI (1996a)

Monitoring and evaluating the results of the strategy

A continuous improvement approach to NSDSs requires monitoring of the 'big picture' ...

The continuous improvement approach to an NSDS necessarily puts far more emphasis on monitoring strategy results than the previous 'linear' approaches. Strategy impact assessment involves: the identification of specific changes in the well-being of people and ecosystems – from *monitoring the 'state' of sustainable development* (discussed in Chapter 5, page 171); and correlating such changes with the strategy and its component mechanisms and activities – from *monitoring strategy outputs and outcomes* (discussed on page 322). To do this well requires clarity in the strategy objectives and, hence, clarity in the indicators selected, coordination between the various monitoring and analysis tasks, a good baseline and a systematic approach to monitoring.

... but sometimes focused impact assessments will be needed

In addition to this routine, systematic monitoring, it will occasionally be necessary to undertake focused *impact assessments to evaluate* more directly the impacts of the strategy and/or key strategy products, to analyse apparent correlations that look interesting, and to assess how the strategy has impacted on institutional and governance conditions such as:

- values, habits and practices;
- knowledge;
- technologies and infrastructure;
- institutions (laws, incentive systems, organizations and their relations).

Such impact assessments will entail the collection of relevant information directly from those who are affected (households, organizations, etc), which may best be organized through specially commissioned studies.

Monitoring and evaluation of strategy impacts is complicated by the fact that there are many other influences such as markets, events and macro policies which will have significant influences – albeit the strategy will be trying to track and intervene in them. Furthermore, there is invariably no good baseline data available at the start of an NSDS, a common problem of 'umbrella' initiatives such as strategies (which are cheaper and easier to embark on without a baseline). Neither is there a control case.

This was the case in Pakistan and so the approach used to assess the impacts of Pakistan's NCS is instructive. Essentially, it triangulated information. A matrix similar to that shown in Table 10.1 was used to bring together two types of information:

■ Information from those stakeholder groups who, on a sectoral or geographic basis, had identified specific positive *sustainability impacts* (biodiversity conserved, poverty reduced, etc) but had only an idea of the reasons why (whether projects, or changed policy or other factors were the cause).
■ Information from close strategy stakeholders who were familiar with the mechanisms used and promoted by the NCS (eg how well the strategy improved awareness and participation) but had only an idea of what impacts these mechanisms led to.

Information on impacts and strategy mechanisms can be compared ...

In Pakistan, this information was generated through a mix of special studies and workshops – as no routine monitoring system had been put in place (refer back to Box 10.5). The results revealed how some of the commonly cited improvements in sustainability were the result of activities that were directly planned by the NCS. Others had been identified by the NCS as good examples to follow. Further improvements arose separately from the NCS (notably initiatives of the private sector – as it had been subject to different drivers for sustainability, eg export markets). But the conclusion was that all the successful initiatives were considered to offer lessons for how the NCS *could* evolve in the future, especially as:

... generated through studies and workshops

It is also quite evident that the NCS has not yet managed to influence the key socio-economic concerns of poverty alleviation, economic development, and environmental quality of life—in terms of policy, legislation, investment, incentives or a full set of activities on the ground. The NCS awareness work and projects have demonstrated what could be done for sustainable development: bringing this into the mainstream is the challenge for the next phase of the NCS.
(Hanson et al 2000)

Disseminating the findings of monitoring exercises and feedback to strategy decisions

Reporting and dissemination of the findings of monitoring is crucial so that key messages can be fed back to stakeholder key groups, enabling them to continuously improve their understanding and behaviour, the strategy itself and its component activities.

Key information should be fed back to stakeholders

Feedback has been one of the most overlooked and yet most valuable tools for the implementation of strategies. Governments (whether national or local) can never be in a position to monitor and guide all the actions or organizations, businesses and citizens in complex societies. For this reason, a feedback system is necessary to disseminate information so that organizations and individuals themselves can learn from progress or problems and can make wise choices. As suggested by ICLEI (1996a), such a system should provide both recognition and rewards for positive behaviours and disincentives or punishments for detrimental actions in order to guide the regulation of behaviour without the need for external control.

Table 10.1 **Example matrix for linking impacts with strategy mechanisms**

Impacts (examples): Mechanisms (examples):	Biodiversity conserved	Ecological processes protected	Poverty alleviated	Environmental health improved	Economic efficiency improved
Information management					
Communication					
Participation					
Prioritizing					
Investment					
Coordination					
Capacity building					
Empowerment					
Learning					
etc					

Note: The matrix was used in Pakistan as an aid to assessment, rather than a presentational tool. As an aid to assessment, it helps in offering a checklist of mechanism and performance categories, in organizing information and in pointing to what is important and what can be neglected. But if used to present information it would imply that very many 'cells' need to be assessed and treated equally – which would not be helpful for strategic analysis

Source: Hanson et al (2000)

The first and most fundamental requirement of a good feedback system is to disseminate appropriate information to the different stakeholders and 'audiences' in the country and in local communities. The primary information requirements are (a) the status of conditions, and (b) preferable behaviours and actions.

The impact of such information is greatly influenced by who prepares it (eg government or municipal departments, individual experts or businesses), who disseminates it (eg government offices, elected officials, NGOs, community organizations, individuals) and the vehicle used for dissemination (eg meetings, written reports, the media). Generally speaking, in designing a feedback system, the familiarity, credibility and accessibility of information sources should be optimized. Chapter 7 discusses in detail the elements of a strategy information system and optimum approaches.

The second key element of feedback is consistency (page 320) and regularity (page 318). If this is assured, people gain confidence that their actions will be appropriate, will be noticed and will be rewarded.

Appendix

Table A.1 **Data for monitoring, sources and timing: examples from a poverty alleviation strategy**

Type	Indicator	Instrument	Agency	Level	Frequency
Input	Public finance data: revenues, expenditures by category Human resources	Budget documents; expenditure data Expenditure tracking surveys Payroll data	Ministries of finance, planning and administration; sectoral ministries; public accounting and audit agencies	National and various sub-national administrative levels	Monthly or quarterly where possible; at least yearly
Output	Outputs of public expenditures: infrastructure, services provided	Administrative systems, Management Information Systems Community surveys	Sectoral ministries; project implementation units; local administrations and local service providers	National and various sub-national administrative levels; facilities (schools, clinics, etc)	Possibly every six months; at least yearly
Outcome	Access to, use of and satisfaction with services	Priority and quick monitoring surveys; multi-topic household surveys; qualitative studies	Central statistical agency; local service providers; others	Households and individuals, facilities (schools, clinics, etc); communities	Yearly where possible
Impact	Household consumption and income; living conditions; social indicators; household priorities; perceptions of well-being	Household budget/ expenditure/ income surveys, labour force surveys; living standard measurement surveys; qualitative studies	Central statistical agency	Households and individuals; communities	Every three to five years
Context	National accounts: GDP, consumption, investment, exports, imports, etc Consumer and producer prices Climatic data	System of national accounts, trade statistics Direct measurement	Central statistical agency, central bank National weather agency, others	National (largest sub-national levels in some cases) As detailed as possible	Monthly or quarterly trade statistics, price collection; yearly consumer price index basket Daily where possible

Source: Prennushi et al (2001)

Table A.2 **CSD list of indicators of sustainable development (September 1996)**

Chapters of Agenda 21	Driving force (pressure) indicators	State indicators	Response indicators
Category: social			
Chapter 3: Combating poverty	Unemployment rate	Indices of poverty: head count; poverty gap; squared poverty gap; Gini index of income inequality Female:male wage ratio	
Chapter 5: Demographic dynamics and sustainability	Population growth rate Net migration rate Total fertility rate	Population density	
Chapter 36: Promoting education, public awareness and training	Rate of change of school-age population Enrolment ratio (gross and net) in primary and secondary school Adult literacy rate	Children reaching grade 5 School life expectancy Difference between male and female enrolment Women per hundred men in the labour force	GDP spent on education
Chapter 6: Protecting and promoting human health		Basic sanitation Access to safe drinking water Life expectancy at birth Adequate birth weight Infant mortality rate Maternal mortality rate Nutritional status of children	Immunization against childhood diseases Contraceptive prevalence Proportion of chemicals monitored in food National health expenditure devoted to local health care Total national health expenditure related to GNP
Chapter 7: Promoting sustainable human settlement development	Growth of urban population Per capita consumption of fossil fuel by vehicles Losses – natural disaster	Percent in urban areas Area and population of urban settlements Floor area per person House price:income ratio	Infrastructure expenditure per capita
Category: economic			
Chapter 2: International cooperation to accelerate sustainable development	GDP per capita Net investment in GDP Sum of exports and imports as percentage of GDP	Environmentally adjusted net domestic product Share of manufactured goods in total exports	
Chapter 4: Changing consumption patterns	Annual energy consumption Share of natural-resource intensive industries in manufacturing value-added	Mineral reserves Fossil fuel reserves Lifetime of proven energy reserves Intensity of material use Share of manufacturing value-added in GDP	
Chapter 33: Financial resources and mechanisms	Net resources transfer/GNP Total ODA as a percentage of GNP	Debt/GNP Debt service/export	Environmental protection expenditures (% of GDP) New or additional funding for sustainable development

Chapters of Agenda 21	Driving force (pressure) indicators	State indicators	Response indicators
Chapter 34: Transfer of environmentally sound technology, cooperation and capacity building	Capital goods imports Foreign direct investments	Share of environmentally sound capital goods imports	Technical cooperation grants
Category: environmental			
Chapter 18: Protection of the quality and supply of freshwater resources	Annual withdrawals of ground and surface water Domestic consumption of water per capita	Groundwater reserves Faecal coliform ratio Biochemical oxygen demand in water bodies	Waste-water treatment coverage Density of hydrological networks
Chapter 17: Protection of the oceans, all kinds of seas and coastal areas	Population growth in coastal areas Discharges of oil, nitrogen and phosphorus into coastal waters	Maximum sustained yield for fisheries Algae index	
Chapter 10: Integrated approach to planning and management of land	Land use change	Changes in land condition	Decentralized local-level natural resource management
Chapter 12: Combating desertification and drought	Population living below poverty line in dryland areas	National monthly rainfall Vegetation index Extent of desertification	
Chapter 13: Sustainable mountain development	Population change in mountain areas	Sustainable use of NRs in mountain areas Welfare of mountain populations	
Chapter 14: Promoting sustainable agriculture and rural development	Use of pesticides Use of fertilizers Irrigation percentage Energy use in agriculture	Arable land per capita Area affected by salinization and waterlogging	Agricultural education
Chapter 11: Combating deforestation	Wood harvesting intensity	Forest area change	Managed forest area ratio Protected forest area as a proportion of total area
Chapter 15: Conservation of biological diversity		Threatened species as a percentage of total native species	Protected area as a percentage of total area
Chapter 16: Environmentally sound management of biotechnology			R&D expenditure for biotechnology National biosafety regulations or guidelines
Chapter 9: Protection of the atmosphere	Emissions of greenhouse gases; sulphur oxides; and nitrogen oxides Consumption of ozone depleting substances	Ambient concentrations of pollutants in urban areas	Expenditure on air pollution abatement

Chapters of Agenda 21	Driving force (pressure) indicators	State indicators	Response indicators
Chapter 21: Environmentally sound management of solid wastes and sewage	Generation of industrial and municipal solid waste Household waste disposed per capita		Expenditure on waste management Waste recycling and reuse Municipal waste disposal
Chapter 19: Environmentally sound management of toxics		Chemically induced acute poisonings	Number of chemicals banned or severely restricted
Chapter 20: Environmentally sound management of hazardous wastes	Generation of hazardous wastes Imports and exports of hazardous wastes	Area of land contaminated by hazardous wastes	Expenditure on hazardous waste treatment
Chapter 22: Management of radioactive wastes	Generation of radioactive wastes		
Category: institutional			
Chapter 8: Integrating environment and development in decision-making			NSDSs NCSDs Integrated environmental and economic accounting Mandated EIA
Chapter 35: Science for sustainable development		Potential scientists and engineers per million population	R&D employees per million population R&D expenditure as % of GDP
Chapter 39: International legal instruments and mechanisms			Ratification of agreements Implementation of ratified global agreements
Chapter 40: Information for decision-making		Telephone lines/person Access to information	Programmes for national environmental statistics
Chapters 23–32: Strengthening the role of major groups			Major groups, ethnic minorities, indigenous people on NCSDs Contribution of NGOs to sustainable development

Source: www.un.org/esa/sustdev/isd

References

Abbot, J and Guijt, I (1998) *Changing Views on Change: Participatory Approaches to Monitoring and Evaluation*, SARK Discussion Paper No 2, International Institute for Environment and Development, London

Aden, J (2001) *Indonesia's Natural Resources Under Siege: Environmental Impacts of the Economic Crisis and Decentralisation*, paper presented to the United States – Indonesia Society, 20 July, Washington, DC

Adnan, S, Barrett, A, Nurul Alam, S M and Brustinov, A (1992) *People's Participation, NGOs and the Flood Action Plan*. Research and Advisory Services, Dhaka, Bangladesh

Adriaanse, A, Bringezu, S, Hammond, A, Moriguchi, Y, Rodenburg, E, Rogich, D and Schütz, H (1997) *Resource Flows: The Material Basis of Industrial Economies*, World Resources Institute, Washington, DC

Agarwal, A, Narain, S and Sharma, A (1999) *Green Politics*, Centre for Science and Environment, New Delhi

AIDEnvironment (1997) *Strategic Environmental Analysis: A New Planning Framework for Sustainable Development*, AIDEnvironment, Amsterdam

Anderson, R and Deutsch, C (eds) (2001) 'Sustainable Development and the Environment in East Timor', *Proceedings of the Conference on Sustainable Development in East Timor, 25-31 January 2001*, Timor Aid, Dili, East Timor

Andersson, V (1999) *Popular Participation in Bolivia: Does the Law 'Participación Popular' Secure Participation of the Rural Bolivian Population?* CDR Working Paper 99/6, Centre for Development Research, Copenhagen

Baburoglu, O N and Garr, M A (1992) 'Search Conference Methodology for Practitioners' in M.R.Weisford (ed) *Discovering Common Ground*, Berrett-Koehler, San Francisco, 73-81

Backhaus, C and Wagachi, R (1995) *Only Playing with Beans? Participatory Approaches in Large-Scale Government Programmes*, PLA Notes No 24, Sustainable Agriculture Programme, International Institute for Environment and Development, London

Baldock, D (1999) 'Developing and Using Agri-environmental Indicators for Policy Purposes: OECD Country Experiences' in OECD *Environmental Indicators for Agriculture*, vol 2, *Issues and Design*, OECD, Paris

Banuri, T and Holmberg, J (1992) *Governance for Sustainable Development: a Southern Perspective*, IIED, London

Banuri, T and Khan, S R (2000) *Environmental Strategy Background Report*, Sustainable Development Policy Research Institute, for Ministry of Environment, Local Government and Rural Development, Islamabad, Pakistan and World Bank, Washington, DC

Barbier, E B (1987) 'The Concept of Sustainable Economic Development', *Environmental Conservation*, vol 14, no 2, pp101–110

Barnard, G (1995) *Cross-cultural Communication. A Practical Guide*, Cassell, London

Bass, S (2000) *Participation in the Caribbean: A review of Grenada's forest policy process*, Policy that Works for Forests and People Series, no 10, IIED, London

Bass, S (2001) *Certification in the Forest Political Landscape*. Keynote paper for the International Conference on the Social and Political Dimensions of Forest Certification, University of Freiberg, 20–22 June 2001

Bass, S and Shah, P (1994) 'Participation in Sustainable Development Strategies; with a Case Study of Joint Forest Management in India', presentation to IUCN General Assembly, Workshop 9, January 1994, Buenos Aires

Bass, S M J and Dalal-Clayton, D B (1995) 'Small Island States and Sustainable Development: Strategic Issues and Experience', *Environmental Planning Issues*, no 8, International Institute for Environment and Development, London

Bass, S M J, Dalal-Clayton, D B and Pretty, J (1995) 'Participation in Strategies for Sustainable Development', *Environmental Planning Issues*, no 7, International Institute for Environment and Development, London

Bass, S, Balogun, P, Mayers, J, Dubois, O, Morrison, E and Howard, B (1998) 'Institutional Change in Public Sector Forestry: A Review of the Issues', *Forestry and Land Use Series*, no 12, IIED, London

Baumert, K A and Petkova, E (2000) *How will the Clean Development Mechanism Ensure Transparency, Public Engagement and Accountability?* World Resources Institute Climate Notes, Washington, DC

Bergeson, H O, Parmann, G and Thommessen, O B (eds) (1999) *Yearbook of International Co-operation on Environment and Development, 1999/2000*, Fridtjof Nansen Institute, Norway and Earthscan, London

Bernstein, J (1995) *The Urban Challenge in National Environmental Strategies*, Environmental Management Series Paper no 012, Environment Department, The World Bank, Washington, DC

Booth, D and Lucas, H (2001) *Initial Review of PRSP Documentation. Desk Study of Good Practice in the Development of PRSP Indicators and Monitoring Systems*, Overseas Development Institute, London

Borregaard, N, Ladrón de Guevara, J, Leal, J and Ramirez, J A (2001) *El Análisis Económico en la Gestión Ambiental. Lom Ediciones*, CIPMA, Santiago

Borrini-Feyerabend, G (ed) (1997) *Beyond Fences: Seeking Social Sustainability in Conservation*, IUCN, Gland, Switzerland

Bressers, H and Coenen, F (undated) *Green Plans: Blueprints or Statements of Future Intent for Future Decisions*, Center for Clean Technology and Environmental Policy, CSTM, University of Twente, Enschede, The Netherlands

Bretton Woods Project (2001) 'PRSPs just PR', *Bretton Woods Update*, no 23, June/July, Bretton Woods Project, c/o Action Aid, London

Bretton Woods Project (2002) 'Limitations of Asian PRSPs Revealed', *Bretton Woods Update*, no 27, March/April, Bretton Woods Project, c/o Action Aid, London

Bromley, D W (1995) *Natural Resource Issues in Environmental Policy in South Africa*, Land and Agriculture Policy Centre, Witwatersrand, South Africa

Brown, L (2001) *State of the World 2001*, Worldwatch Institute in association with Earthscan, London

Brown, N (1997) *Devolution of Authority over the Management of Natural Resources: The Soufriere Marine Management Area, St Lucia*, Caribbean Natural Resources Institute, St Lucia

Cable, V (1999) *Globalisation and Global Governance*, Royal Institute of International Affairs, London

CAEMA (2001) *Instrumentos Económicos y Medio Ambiente*, Boletín vol 1, no 3, Centro Andino para la Economia en el Medio Ambiente, Bogotá

Cala, C P and Grageda, J Z (eds) (1994) *Studies on Coalition Experiences in the Philippines*, Bookmark, Manila

Campbell, B, Byron, N, Hobane, P, Matose, F, Madzudzo, E and Wily, L (1996) 'Taking CAMPFIRE beyond Wildlife: What is the Potential?' paper presented at the *Pan African*

Symposium on Sustainable Use of Natural Resources and Community Participation, Harare, Zimbabwe, 24–27 June, Centre for Applied Social Sciences, University of Zimbabwe, Harare

Carew-Reid, J (ed) (1997) *Strategies for Sustainability: Asia*, IUCN in association with Earthscan, London

Carew-Reid, J, Prescott-Allen, R, Bass, S and Dalal-Clayton, D B (1994) *Strategies for National Sustainable Development: A Handbook for their Planning and Implementation*, IIED, London, and IUCN, Gland, in association with Earthscan, London

Carley, M and Christie, I (2000a) *Managing Sustainable Development*, 2nd edn, Earthscan, London

Carley, M and Christie, I (2000b) 'The World's Commons: The Challenge of Governance', in *Governance for a Sustainable Future*, World Humanity Action Trust, London

Carson, C S (2000) *Toward a Framework of Assessing Data Quality* IMF, Washington, DC

CEC (2001) *European Governance: A White Paper*, Com (2001)428, 25 July, Commission of the European Community, Brussels

Chambers, N, Simmons, C and Wackernagel, M (2000) *Sharing Nature's Interest: Ecological Footprints as an Indicator of Sustainability*, Earthscan, London

Chambers, R (1992) 'Methods for Analysis by Farmers: The Professional Challenge', paper for the *12th Annual Symposium of Association for Farming Systems Research and Extension*, Michigan State University, Ann Arbor, Michigan

Chenje, M (1995) 'Environmental Rights are Human Rights', paper presented at the *Seminar on Human Rights and Justice, 1–2 August 1995*, SARDC, Harare

Cobham, R (1990) *Towards a National Conservation Strategy for Barbados – Preparation Guidelines*, IUCN, Gland

Coenen, FHJM (1996) *The Effectiveness of Local Environmental Policy Planning*, CSTM Studies and Reports, University of Twente, Enschede, The Netherlands

Colfer, C J P (1995) *Who Counts Most in Sustainable Forest Management?* CIFOR Working Paper No 7, October, Centre for International Forestry Research, Bogor, Indonesia

CONAM (1998) *Sistema Nacional de Gestión Ambiental*, report prepared by Dames & Moore Consultants, Comisión Nacional del Medio Ambiente, Lima

Creech, H and Willard, T (2001) *Strategic Intentions: Managing Knowledge Networks for Sustainable Development*, International Institute for Sustainable Development, Winnipeg

CSIR (1996) *Strategic Environmental Assessment: A Primer*, Council for Scientific and Industrial Research, Stellenbosch, South Africa

Dalal-Clayton, D B (1996) *Getting to Grips with Green Plan: National Level Experience in Industrial Countries*, Earthscan, London

Dalal-Clayton, D B (1997) 'Southern Africa Beyond the Millennium: Environmental Trends and Scenarios to 2015', *Environmental Planning Issues* no 13, IIED, London

Dalal-Clayton, D B and Bass, S (2000) *National Strategies for Sustainable Development: A Guide to Key Issues and Methods for Analysis: A Prompt for Status Reviews and Dialogues*, June 2000, IIED, London (www.nssd.net)

Dalal-Clayton, D B and Dent, D (2001) *Knowledge of the Land: Land Resources Information and its use in Rural Development*. Oxford University Press

Dalal-Clayton, D B, Bass, S, Sadler, B, Thomson, K, Sandbrook, R, Robins, N and Hughes, R (1994) 'National Sustainable Development Strategies: Experience and Dilemmas', *Environmental Planning Issues*, no 6, IIED, London

Dalal-Clayton, D B, Dent, D and Dubois, O (2000) 'Rural Planning in the Developing World with a Special Focus on Natural Resources: Lessons Learned and Potential Contributions to Sustainable Livelihoods', *Environmental Planning Issues*, no 20, IIED, London

Dalal-Clayton, D B and Sadler, B (1998a) 'Strategic Environmental Assessment: A Rapidly Evolving Approach', in A Donnelly, D B Dalal-Clayton and R Hughes (eds) *A Directory of Impact Assessment Guidelines*, 2nd edn, IIED, London, pp 31–42

Dalal-Clayton, D B and Sadler, B (1998b) 'The Application of Strategic Environmental Assessment in Developing Countries: Recent Experience and Future Prospects, including its Role in Sustainable Development Strategies', unpublished draft

Dargavel, J, Guijt, I, Kanowski, P, Race, D and Proctor, W (1998) *Australia: Settlement, Conflicts and Agreements*, Study for IIED 'Policy that works for forests and people' project

de Boer, J J and Sadler, B (eds) (1996) *Strategic Environmental Assessment 54: Environmental Assessment of Policies: Briefing Papers on Experience in Selected Countries*, Ministry of Housing, Spatial Planning and the Environment, The Netherlands, and the International Study of Effectiveness of Environmental Assessment, The Hague

De Soto, H (2000) *The Mystery of Capital: Why Capitalism Triumphs in the West and Fails Everywhere Else*, Basic Books, New York

Degnbol, T (1996) *The Terroir Approach to Natural Resource Management: Panacea or Phantom? – the Malian Experience*, working paper no 2/1996, International Development Studies, Roskilde University, Denmark

Denniston, D (1995) *Defending the Land with Maps*, PLA Notes no 22, Sustainable Agriculture Programme, IIED, London

DFID (2000) *Achieving Sustainability: Poverty Elimination and the Environment*, Department for International Development, London

Dobie, P (2000) *Models for National Strategies: Building Capacity for Sustainable Development*, thematic study, Approaches to Sustainability Series, Capacity 21, United Nations Development Programme, New York

Dorm-Adzobu, C (1995) *New Roots: Institutionalizing Environmental Management in Africa*, World Resources Institute, Washington, DC

Dubois, O, Gueye, B, Moorhead, R and Ouali, F (1996) *Etude des points forts et faibles des projets forestiers financés par les Pays-Bas en Afrique occidentale sahélienne*, Etude préparée pour les Ambassades des Pays-Bas de Bamako, Ouagadougou et Dakar

EAP Task Force (1998) 'Evaluation of Progress in Developing and Implementing National Environmental Action Programmes (NEAPs) in CEEC/NIS', paper produced for *Environment for Europe, Aarhus, 23–25 June 1998*, OECD, Paris

Earth Council (2000) *NCSD Report 1999–2000: National Experiences on Multi-Stakeholder Participatory Processes for Sustainable Development*, Earth Council, San José, Coasta Rica

Earth Council (n.d.) *Guidelines for NCSD Rio+10 assessment*, Earth Council, San José

EC (1997) *Vision 2020: Summary and Recommendations*, XI/121/97, European Commission, Brussels

ECLAC (2001) *Desafios y propuestas para la implementacion mas efectiva de instrumentos economicos en la gestion ambiental de America Latina y el Caribe*, Serie Seminarios y Conferencias, CEPAL, Division de Medio Ambiente y Asentamientos Humanos, Economic Commission of Latin America and the Caribbean, Santiago de Chile

Edwards, M and Gaventa, J (eds) (2001) *Global Citizen Action*, Lynne Rienner, Boulder, Colarado

Emery, M and Emery, F E (1978): 'Searching', in J W Sutherland (ed) *Management Handbook for Public Administrators*, Van Nostrand Reinhold, New York

EPD (1996) 'Gaza Land Resources: Land Use Planning and Resources Protection', *Focus on Environment in Palestine*, no 2, Environmental Planning Directorate, Ministry of Planning and International Cooperation, The Palestinian Authority, Gaza

EPE (1994) *Towards Shared Responsibility*, European Partners for the Environment, Brussels

ERM (1994) 'Developing Plans and Strategies', paper II prepared for the Ministry of Housing, Spatial Planning and Environment in The Netherlands and presented to the *First Meeting of the International Network of Green Planners, 30 March–1 April 1994, Maastricht, The Netherlands*, Environmental Resources Management, London

ESRC (1998) *Strengthening Decision-making for Sustainable Development*, report of a workshop held at Eynsham Hall, 15–16 June 1998, Global Environmental Change Programme, Economic and Social Research Council

Estrella, M (2000) 'Tracing the History of Participatory Monitoring and Evaluation' Institute of Development Studies/The Participation Group, www.ids.ac.uk

Ezekiel, H (1975) *Second India Study: Overview*, MacMillan, Delhi, India

Falloux, F and Talbot, L (1993) *Crisis and Opportunity: Environment and Development in Africa*, Earthscan, London

Falloux, F, Talbot, L and Christoffersen, L (1990) *National Environmental Action Plans in Africa: Early Lessons and Future Directions*, AFTEN, Technical Department, Africa Region, World Bank, Washington, DC

Falloux, F, Talbot, L and Larson, J (1991) *Progress and Next Steps for National Environmental Action Plans in Africa*, The World Bank, Washington, DC

FAO Development Law Service, Legal Framework Analysis for Rural and Agricultural Investment Projects: Concepts and Guidelines. FAO Legal Papers, Online #12, September 2000 (FAO, Rome).

Fernández, J J G (1998) *Guide for the Preparation of Action Plans within the Framework of the Convention on Biodiversity*, Global Environment Facility and United Nations Development Programme, New York

Filer, C and Sekhran, N (1998) *Loggers, Donors and Resource Owners: Papua New Guinea Country Study*, Policy that Works for Forests and People Series, no 2, IIED, London

Final Report *Mid-Term Review of National Conservation Strategy. Mass Awareness Initiatives* HBP Ref.: D0B01NCS, 16 February 2000, IUCN Pakistan, Islamabad

Fischer-Kowalski, M, Haberl, H and Payer, H (1997) in Moldan, B and Billharz, S (eds) *Sustainability Indicators: Report of the Project on Indicators of Sustainable Development*, SCOPE 58, John Wiley & Sons, Chichester

Fisher, R J (1995) *Collaborative Management of Forests for Conservation and Development. Issues in Forest Conservation*, IUCN, Gland, Switzerland

Forum for the Future (2001) *Green Futures* No 30. Forum for the Future, London

Franklin, B and Morley, D (1992) 'Contextual Searching: Cases from Waste Management, Nature Toruism, and Personal Support', in M R Weisford (ed) *Discovering Common Ground*, Berrett-Koehler, San Francisco, 229–46.

FSC (2000) 'FSC Principles and Criteria', Document 1.2, revised February 2000, Forest Stewardship Council, www.fscoax.org

Fund of the Americas (2000) *Developing a Strategy to Foment Philanthropy*, Fondo de las Américas, Santiago

Gallopín, G C (1997) 'Indicators and their Use: Information for Decision-making. Part 1: Introduction', in Moldan, B and Billharz, S (eds) *Sustainability Indicators: Report of the Project on Indicators of Sustainable Development*, SCOPE 58, John Wiley & Sons, Chichester

Gallopin, G, Hammond, A, Raskin, P and Swart, R (1997) *Branch Points: Global Scenarios and Human Choice*, PoleStar Series Report no 76, Global Scenario Group, Stockholm Environment Institute, Stockholm

GEF (1999) *Experience with Conservation Trust Funds*, Global Environment Facility, The World Bank, Washington, DC

GEPA (1999) *Guyana National Biodiversity Action Plan: A Programme for Action by Stakeholders towards the Conservation and Sustainable Use of Biodiversity*, Guyana Environmental Protection Agency, Georgetown, Guyana/ Global Environment Facility/United Nations Development Programme, New York

Geser, H (1996) *Auf dem Weg zur "Cyberdemocracy"? Auswirkungen der Computermetze auf die oeffentliche politische Kommunikation* (Towards 'Cyberdemocracy'? Effects of Internet on Public Political Communication), http://www.unizh.ch/~geserweb/komoef/flezt.html

Ghana NDPC (1994) *Vision 2020: The National Development Policy Framework*, National Development Planning Commission, Accra

Ghana NDPC (1995) *Planning Guidelines for the Preparation of Sectoral and District Development Plans*. National Development Planning Commission, Accra, Ghana, December

Ghana NDPC (1997) *Vision 2020: The First Medium-Term Development Plan (1997–2000)*. National Development Planning Commission, Accra, Ghana

Gibson, T (1991) 'Planning for Real', *RRA Notes* 11, IIED, London, pp29–30

Gill, G (1993) *OK, the Data's Lousy, But it's All We've Got (Being a Critique of Conventional Methods)*, Sustainable Agriculture Programme, Gatekeeper Series SA38, IIED, London

Gill, G (1998) 'Using PRA for Agricultural Policy Analysis in Nepal: The Tari Research Network Foodgrain Study', in J Holland and J Blackburn (eds) *Whose Voice: Participatory Research and Policy Change*, Intermediate Technology Publications, London pp9–41

Global Reporting Initiative (2000) 'Sustainability Reporting Guidelines', www.globalreporting.org/GRIGuidelines/June2000/June2000GuidelinesDownload.htm

Government of Balochistan and IUCN Pakistan (2000) *Balochistan Conservation Strategy*, IUCN Pakistan and GOB, Karachi

Government of Canada (1995) *A Guide to Green Government*, Catalogue no En21-136/1995E, Ministry of Supply and Services, Canada

Grayson, A J (1993) *Private Forestry Policy in Europe*, CAB International, Wallingford, UK

Grieg-Gran, M (2000) *Fiscal Incentives for Biodiversity Conservation: The ICMS Ecológico in Brazil*, EEP Discussion Paper 00-01, IIED, London

Grieg-Gran, M (2001) 'Investment in Sustainable Development: The Public–Private Interface', in *The Future is Now*, vol 2, IIED, London

GTZ (1990) *Objectives Oriented Project Planning*, Deutsche Gessellschaft für Technische Zusammenarbeit (GTZ) GmbH, Eschborn, Germany

GTZ (1993) *Regional Rural Development RRD Update: Elements of a Strategy for Implementing the RRD Concept in a Changed Operational Context*, Deutsche Gesellschaft für Technische Zusammenarbeit (GTZ) GmbH, Eschborn, Germany

GTZ (2001) 'Presentation of Products for Poverty Reduction Strategies: Instruments, Methods and Approaches', www.gtz.de/forum_armut

Guijt, I (1991) *Perspectives on Participation. An Inventory of Institutions in Africa*, IIED, London

Guijt, I and Hinchcliffe, F (1998) *Participatory Valuation of Wild Resources: An Overview of the Hidden Harvest Methodology*, Sustainable and Rural Livelihoods Programme, IIED, London

Hagen, R T (undated) *A Guide for Countries Preparing National Biodiversity Strategies and Action Plans*, Biodiversity Planning Support Programme, United Nations Development Programme, New York

Hall, P A V (undated) 'Decision Support Systems for Sustainable Development: Experience and Potential, Paper for the Humus Network, http://unganisha.idrc.ca/humus/macau.html

Halle, M (2001) 'What Does Sustainable Development Mean?' draft contribution to IIED project, Mining, Minerals and Sustainable Development, IIED, London

Handy, C (1985) *Understanding Organisations*, Penguin Books, Harmondsworth, UK

Hanson, A J, Bass, S, Bouzaher, A and Zehra, M (2000) *Pakistan's National Conservation Strategy – Renewing Commitment to Action*, Report of the Mid-Term Review, Government of Pakistan, Islamabad

Hardi, P and Pinter, L (1995) 'Models and Methods of Measuring Sustainble Development Performance', revised draft discussion paper prepared for the Sustainable Development

Coordination Unit, Executive Council, Government of Manitoba, International Institute for Sustainable Development, Winnipeg

Harding, D, Kiara, J K and Thomson, K (1996) 'Soil and Water Conservation in Kenya: The Development of the Catchment Approach and Structured Participation Led by the Soil and Water Conservation Branch of the Ministry of Agriculture, Kenya', paper prepared for the *OECD/DAC Workshop on Capacity Development in the Environment, 4–6 December 1996, Rome,* OECD, Paris

Hardy, J E, Mitlin, D and Satterthwaite, D (2001) *Environmental Problems in an Urbanizing World,* Earthscan, London

Harter, P J and Pou, C, Jr (1997) 'Negotiating Environmental Policies: Upfront Planning is Vital to Success', *National Institute for Dispute Resolution News,* vol IV, no 5, Canada

Hassan, A (2001) 'Working with Communities, Karachi, Pakistan', City Press cited in *Financing for Sustainable Development,* IIED, London

Higman, S, Bass, S, Judd, N, Mayers, J and Nussbaum, R (1999) *The Sustainable Forestry Handbook,* Earthscan, London

Hill, J (1993) *National Sustainability Strategies: A Comparative Review of the Status of Five Countries: Canada, France, The Netherlands, Norway and the UK,* The Green Alliance, London

Hill, J (1996) *National Sustainability Strategies: A Guide to Drafting and Ensuring Participation,* 1st edn, The Green Alliance, London

Hiltz, S R and Turoff, M (1993) *The Network Nation: Human Communication via Computer,* MIT Press, Cambride, Massachusetts

HMSO (1994) *Sustainable Development: The UK Strategy.* Cm 2426. Her Majesty's Stationery Office, London.

Howard, J and Scott-Villiers, P (2000) *They are Shouting it Whenever they Can. Beyond Invited Participation: The Power of Popular Communications,* PLA Notes no 39, IIED, London

Hughes, R, Adnan, S and Dalal-Clayton, D B (1994) *Floodplains or Flood Plans? A Review of Approaches to Water Management in Bangladesh,* IIED, London, and Research and Advisory Services, Dhaka

Huntley, B, Siegfried, R and Sunter, C (1989) *South African Environments into the 21st Century,* Human & Rouseau Tafelberg, Cape Town

IADB (1996) *Participation Initiatives in Latin America, Section V in Resource Book on Participation,* Inter-American Development Bank, Washington, DC

ICLEI (1996a) *The Local Agenda 21 Planning Guide,* International Council for Local Environmental Initiatives, World Secretariat, City Hall, Toronto

ICLEI (1996b) *Economic Instruments to Improve Environmental Performance: A Guide for Local Governments,* International Council for Local Environmental Initiatives, Toronto

ICLEI (1997) *Local Agenda 21 Survey: A Study of Responses by Local Authorities and their National and International Associations to Agenda 21,* International Council for Local Environmental Initiatives, Toronto, in cooperation with the United Nations Department for Policy Coordination and Sustainable Development, New York

ICLEI (2000) *Second Local Agenda 21 Survey,* Background Paper No 15, submitted by International Council for Local Environmental Initiatives, Toronto, to the *Preparatory Committee for the World Summit on Sustainable Development, Second Preparatory Session, 28 January–8 February 2002,* United Nations, New York

IIED (1994) *Whose Eden? An Overview of Community Approaches to Wildlife Management,* IIED, London

IIED (1995) *Citizen Action to Lighten Britain's Ecological Footprints,* Report to the UK Dept of the Environment, February 1995

IIED (1998a) *Participatory Valuation of Wild Resources in Agricultural Systems: A Summary,* Sustainable Agriculture Programme/Environmental Economics Programme, IIED, London

IIED (1998b) *The Hidden Harvest – The Value of Wild Resources in Agricultural Systems: A Summary*, Sustainable Agriculture Programme/Environmental Economics Programme, IIED, London

IIED (1998c) *Participatory Monitoring and Evaluation*, PLA Notes no 31, Sustainable Agriculture and Rural Livelihoods Programme, IIED, London

IIED (2000) 'National Strategies for Sustainable Development: A Guide to Key Issues and Methods for Analysis: A prompt for Status Reviews and Dialogues', Rolling Draft, www.nssd.net

IIRR (1998) *Participatory Monitoring and Evaluation: Experiences and Lessons. Workshop Proceedings*, International Institute for Rural Reconstruction, Y.C. James Yen Center, Silang, Cavite, Philippines

IMF (2001) *Poverty Reduction Strategy Papers – Progress in Implementation*, prepared by the Staffs of the International Monetary Fund and the World Bank, Washington, DC

IMF/OECD/UN/World Bank (2000) *A Better World For All: Progress Towards the International Development Goals*, report prepared by the staffs of the International Monetary Fund, Organisation for Economic Cooperation and Development, United Nations and World Bank, Washington, DC

IPCC (2001) *Third Assessment Report. International Panel on Climate Change* Cambridge University Press, Cambridge

IPF (1997) *Proposals for Action. Programme Element 1A – National Forest and Land Use Programmes*, Inter-governmental Panel on Forests, ECOSOC, United Nations, New York

IPIECA (1996) *Long-Range Scenarios for Climate Change Policy Analysis*, report of workshop held in Brighton, 8–10 January 1996, International Petroleum Industry Environmental Conservation Association, London

IPPF, UNFPA and IUCN (1993) 'Strategies for Tomorrow's World', *People and the Planet*, vol 2, no 4, p6–29

ITTO (1998) *Criteria and Indicators for Sustainable Management of Natural Tropical Forests*, International Tropical Timber Organization (ITTO), Yokohama, www.itto.or.jp/Index.html

IUCN (1984) *National Conservation Strategies: A Framework for Sustainable Development*, Alden Press, Oxford

IUCN (1997) *An Approach to Assessing Progress Towards Sustainability: Overview – Approach, Methods, Tools and Field Experience*, IUCN International Assessment Team, Gland, Switzerland

IUCN/UNEP/WWF (1980) *World Conservation Strategy*, IUCN, Gland, Switzerland

IUCN/UNEP/WWF (1991) *Caring for the Earth: A Strategy for Sustainable Living*, IUCN, United Nations Environment Programme and Worldwide Fund for Nature, Gland, Switzerland

James, C and Fournillier, K (1993) *Marine Turtle Management in North-East Trinidad: A Successful Community-based Approach Towards Endangered Species Conservation*, Caribbean Natural Resources Institute, St Lucia

Jänicke, M and Jörgens, H (1997) *National Environmental Policy Plans and Long-term Sustainable Development Strategies: Learning from International Experience*, Forschungsstelle für Umweltpolitik, Berlin

Johnstone, N (1997) *Economic Inequality and the Urban Environment*, EEP Discussion Paper 97-03, IIED, London

Jones, B T T (2001) *Integrating Environment and Sustainability Issues into the Development of Namibia's National Development Plan 2. A Participatory Process for Developing a Sustainable Development Strategy*, paper prepared for the OECDDAC project on Donor-Developing Country Dialogues on National Strategies for Sustainable Development, available on www.nssd.net

Kaiser, J and Lambert, A (1996) *Debt Swaps for Sustainable Development: A Practical Guide for NGOs*, IUCN/SCDO/EURODAD, IUCN Gland, Switzerland and Cambridge, UK

Kanji, N and Greenwood, L (2001) *Participatory Approaches to Research and Development in IIED: Learning from Experience*, Policy and Planning Processes Series, IIED, London

Katz, J W (1997) 'The Consensus Debate: The 80% Solution', in *National Institute for Dispute Resolution News*, vol IV, no 5, Canada

Kaufmann, D, Kraay, A and Zoido-Lobaton, P (1999) *Governance Matters*, Policy Research Working Paper 2196, World Bank, Washington, DC

Keck, M E and Sikkink, K (1998) *Activists Beyond Borders*, Cornell University Press, New York

Kerr, E and Hiltz, S R (1982) *Computer-Mediated Communication Systems: Status and Evaluation*, Academic Press, New York/London

Kessler, J J (1997a) *An Introduction to Strategic Environmental Analysis: A Framework for Planning and Integration of Environmental Care in Development Policies and Interventions. Application for SNV -Netherlands Development Cooperation*, AIDEnvironment, Amsterdam

Kessler, J J (1997b) *An Introduction to Strategic Environmental Analysis: A Framework for Planning and Integration of Environmental Care in Development Policies and Interventions. Application for SNV -Netherlands Development Cooperation. Reader with Theoretical Background and Application Guidelines*, AIDEnvironment, Amsterdam

Khosla, A (2001) *The Road from Rio to Johannesburg*, Millennium Paper Issue 5, UNED Forum, London

Kiesler, S, Siegel, J and McGuire, T (1988) 'Social Psychological Aspects of Computer-mediated Communication', in I Greif (ed) *Computer-supported Cooperative Work: A Book of Readings*, Morgan Kaufman, San Matei, California

Kievelitz, U (1995) *Rapid District Appraisal: An Application of RRA on District Planning Level*, Kurzinfo Nr 21, 8–12, Sektorúnberg Städtische und Ländliche Programme, GTZ, Eschborn, Germany

Kikula, I S and Pfliegner, K (2001) 'The Long Pursuit to Sustainable Development in Tanzania', draft paper prepared for publication by UNDP

Kikula, I S, Dalal-Clayton, D B, Comoro, C and Kiwasila, H (1999) *A Framework for District Planning in Tanzania*, vol 1, report prepared for the Ministry of Regional Administration and Local Government and UNDP, Institute of Resource Assessment, University of Dar es Salaam and the IIED, London

Klarer, J, Francis, P and McNicholas, J (1999) *Improving Environment and Economy, Sofia Initiative on Economic Instruments*, The Regional Environmental Center for Central and Eastern Europe, Budapest

LACCDE (1990) *Our Own Agenda*, Report of the Latin American and Caribbean Commission on Development and Environment, Inter-American Development Bank, Washington, DC and United Nations Development Programme, New York

Lampietti, J A and Subramanian, U (1995) *Taking Stock of National Environmental Strategies*, Environmental Management Series Paper no 010, Environment Department, The World Bank, Washington, DC

Landell-Mills, N (1999) *Defining a Strategy for Financing Sustainable Forestry in Malawi: A Review of International Experience*, report prepared for the Working Group on Financial Flows and Mechanisms in support of Malawi's National Forestry Programme, PROFOR, UNDP, New York

Landell-Mills, N (2001) *Forestry in the Public Interest: Regulation and the Market*, paper for Commonwealth Forestry Conference, Perth, Australia, April 2001

Landell-Mills, N and Ford, J (1999) *Privatising Sustainable Forestry: A Global Review of Trends and Challenges*, Instruments for Sustainable Private Sector Forestry Series, IIED, London

Landell-Mills, N, and Porras, I T (2002) *Silver Bullet or Fool's Gold? Developing Markets for Forest Environmental Services and the Poor*, IIED, London

Lockie, S and Vanclay, F (eds) (1997) *Critical Landcare*, Key Papers Series no 5, Centre for Rural Social Research, Charles Sturt University, Wagga Wagga, New South Wales

Lopez Ornat, A (ed) (1997) *Strategies for Sustainability: Latin America*, IUCN in association with Earthscan, London

MacGillivray, A and Zadek, S (1995) *Accounting for Change: The Role of Sustainable Development Indicators*, Global Environmental Change Programme Briefing no 4, New Economics Foundation, London

Macqueen, D (1999) *Causal Diagrams: A Prioritisation Tool for Poverty Eradication within the Sustainable Livelihoods Framework*, paper for DFID's Forestry Research Programme, Natural Resources International, Chatham, UK

Manitoba Environment (1997) *State of the Environment Report for Manitoba 1997 – Moving Toward Sustainable Development Reporting*, Manitoba Environment, Winnipeg

Matthews, E, Amann, C, Bringezu, S, Fischer-Kowalski, M, Hüttler, W, Kleijn, R, Moriguchi, Y, Ottke, C, Rodenburg, E, Rogich, D, Schandl, H, Schütz, H, van der Voet, E and Weisz, H (2000) *The Weight of Nations: Material Outflows from Industrial Economies*, World Resources Institute, Washington, DC

Maughan, J (1994) *Taming Troubled Waters*, Ford Foundation Report, Washington, DC

Mayers, J (2001a) *Stakeholder Power Analysis*, Power Tools Series no 2, IIED, London

Mayers, J (2001b) *The 4Rs*, Power Tools Series no 3, IIED, London

Mayers, J and Bass, S (1999) *Policy That Works for Forests and People: Series Overview*, IIED, London

Mayers, J, Ngalande, J, Bird, P and Sibale, B (2001) *Forestry Tactics: Lessons from Malawi's National Forestry Programme*, Policy that Works for Forests and People Series no 11, IIED, London

MBPRAC (1988) *The Blue Plan: Future of the Mediterranean Basin*, Executive Summary and Suggestions for Action, Mediterranean Blue Plan Regional Activity Centre, UNEP

Mehrs, G M (1998) *Environmental Communication Planning Handbook for the Mediterranean Region*, International Academy for the Environment, Geneva, Switzerland

Ministerial Conference on the Protection of Forests in Europe and Pan European Forest Certification Council (1998) 'Pan-European Criteria, Indicators, and Operational Guidelines for Sustainable Forest Management', www.minconf-forests.net; www.pefc.org

Muduuli, M C (2001) 'Uganda's Poverty Eradication Action Plan: National Sustainable Development Strategy Principles Tested', presentation to *International Forum on National Sustainable Development Strategies, Accra, Ghana, 7–9 November 2001*, available on www.johnnesburgsummit.org

Munemo, M (1998) *The Zimbabwean District Environmental Action Plan (DEAP) as a National Strategy for Sustainable Development*, paper presented at the donor-developing country scoping workshop on national strategies for sustainable development, 18–19 November, Sunningdale, England

Najam, A (1999) 'World Business Council for Sustainable Development: The Greening of Business or a Greenwash?' in H O Bergeson, G Parmann and O B Thommessen (eds) *Yearbook of International Co-operation on Environment and Development, 1999/2000*, Fridtjof Nansen Institute, Norway, and Earthscan, London, pp65–75

Narayan, D (1993) *Focus on Participation: Evidence from 121 Rural Water Supply Projects*, UNDP-World Bank Water Supply and Sanitation Program, World Bank, Washington, DC

Neefjes, K (2000) *Environments and Livelihoods: Strategies for Sustainability*, Oxfam Development Guidelines, London

NRTEE/ParticipACTION (1994) *SustainABILITY: A National Communications Program in Support of Sustainable Development*, presented to the Government of Canada, December, National Round Table on the Environment and the Economy, Ottawa, and ParticipACTION, Toronto

NRTEE (1995) *Newsletter*, vol 1, no 4, April, National Round Table on the Environment and the Economy, Ottawa, Canada

ODA (1995) *Guidance Note on how to do Stakeholder Analysis of Aid Projects and Programs*, Social Development Division, Overseas Development Administration, London

OECD (1992) *Good Practices for Country and Environmental Surveys and Strategies*, OECD Development Assistance Committee, Guidelines on Environment and Aid, no 2, OECD, Paris

OECD (1995a) *Planning for Sustainable Development: Country Experiences*, OECD, Paris

OECD (1995b) *OECD Environmental Performance Review of The Netherlands*, OECD, Paris

OECD (1997a) *Environmental Indicators for Agriculture*, OECD, Paris

OECD (1997b) *Evaluating the Use of Economic Instruments*, OECD, Paris

OECD (1998) *Improving the Environment through Reducing Subsidies*, OECD, Paris

OECD (2001) *Environmentally Related Taxes in OECD Countries – Issues and Strategies*, OECD, Paris

OECD DAC (1997) *Shaping the 21st Century*, OECD - Development Assistance Committee, Paris

OECD DAC (2001a) *The DAC Guidelines: Strategies for Sustainable Development: Guidance for Development Cooperation*, Development Cooperation Committee, OECD, Paris, available on www.SourceOECD.org

OECD DAC (2001b) 'Development Cooperation Report 2000', *The DAC Journal*, vol 2, no 1, Development Assistance Committee, OECD, Paris

OECD DAC (2001c) 'Policy Coherence Checklist for Poverty Reduction', room document no 5, Development Assistance Committee Working Party on Development Co-operation and Environment, 22nd Meeting, Paris, 8–9 March 2001, OECD, Paris

OECD DAC (2001d) 'Report on the Informal Workshop on Poverty Reduction Strategies, Comprehensive Development Framework and National Strategies for Sustainable Development: Towards Convergence', Document DCD(2000)13, OECD, Paris

OECS (2001) *The Eastern Caribbean Environmental Charter*, Organisation of Eastern Caribbean States, Secretariat, St Lucia

Oman, C P (2000) *Policy Competition for Foreign Direct Investment: A Study of Competition Among Governments to Attract FDI*, OECD Development Centre, Paris

Panayotou, T (1994) *Financing Mechanisms for Agenda 21 (or How to Pay for Sustainable Development)*, Harvard Institute for International Development, Massachusetts

Paul, M (2000) *Global Internet Connectivity. Status, Indicators and Use in Developed and Developing Countries*, UNED Forum, London, www.unedforum.org/publi/connectivity/connreport.htm

Pearce, D W (1994) *Blueprint 3: Measuring Sustainable Development*, London, Earthscan

Pearce, D (1999) 'Measuring Sustainable Development: Implications for Agri-environmental Indicators', in OECD *Environmental Indicators for Agriculture*, vol 2, *Issues and Design*, OECD, Paris

PlanAfric (2000) 'Rural Planning in Zimbabwe: A Case Study, Report Prepared by PlanAfric, Bulawayo', *Environmental Planning Issues*, no 23, IIED, London

Poapongsakorn, N, NaRanong, V, Ayudhaya, A I N, Kaothien, U and Tremmakird, A W (2001) *The Process of Formulating Poverty Reduction Strategies in Thailand*, Thailand Development Research Institute, in cooperation with National Economic and Social Development Board and Ministry of Science, Technology and Environment, Bangkok, available on www.nssd.net

Powell, M (1999) *Information Management for Development Organisations*, Oxfam, UK

Prennushi, G, Rubio, G and Subbarao, K (2001) 'Monitoring and Evaluation', draft chapter, *World Bank PRSP Sourcebook*, www.worldbank.org/poverty

Prescott, J, Gauthier, B and Nagahuedi Mbongu Sodi, J (2000) *Guide to Developing a Biodiversity Strategy from a Sustainable Development Perspective*, Institut de l'Énergie et de l'Environnement de la Francophonie (IEPF), Ministère de 'l'Environnement du Quèbec, United Nations Development Programme (UNDP), United Nations Environment Programme (UNEP), Quèbec, Canada

Prescott-Allen, R (2001a) 'Well-being Assessment', www.altarum.org/SST/

Prescott-Allen, R (2001b) *The Well-being of Nations: A Country-by-Country Index of Quality of Life and the Environment*, Island Press, Washington, DC, and International Development Research Centre, Ottawa

Pretty, J (1997) 'The Sustainable Intensification of Agriculture: Making the most of the Land', *The Land*, 1,1, 45-64

Pretty, J N, Guijt, I, Thompson, J and Scoones, I (1995) *A Trainer's Guide for Participatory Learning and Action*, IIED, London

Projet de société (1993) *Overview of the Projet de société*, vol 1, *Towards a National Sustainable Development Strategy for Canada*, December, Round Table on the Environment and the Economy, Ottawa

Projet de société (1994) *Planning for a Sustainable Future: Projet de société – A Partnership for Change. Prospectus*, May, Round Table on the Environment and the Economy, Ottawa

Projet de société (1995) *Canadian Choices for Transitions to Sustainability*, vol 5, *Towards a National Sustainable Development Strategy for Canada*, June, Round Table on the Environment and the Economy, Ottawa

Rahnema, M (1992) 'Participation', in W Sachs (ed) *The Development Dictionary*, Zed Books, London

REC (1994a) *Summary of the Environmental Action Programme for Central and Eastern Europe*, document endorsed by the Ministerial Conference in Lucerne, Switzerland, 28–30 April 1993, Regional Environmental Center for Central and Eastern Europe, Budapest

REC (1994b) *Manual on Public Participation in Environmental Decision-Making: Current Practice and Future Possibilities in Central and Eastern Europe*, AQUA Press, Budapest

REC (1995a) 'Report on the Stage of Advancement of the Central and Eastern European Countries in Development and Implementation of the National Environmental Action Programs (NEAPs)', draft, Regional Environmental Center for Central and Eastern Europe, Budapest

REC (1995b) *Status of National Environmental Action Programs in Central and Eastern Europe*, Regional Environmental Center for Central and Eastern Europe, Budapest

REDDA-NESDA (1993) *Proceedings of the Fourth Regional Workshop on National Strategies on Environment and Sustainable Development*, Network for Environment and Sustainable Development in Africa, Abidjan, Cote d'Ivoire, 15–19 May

Repetto, R (1994) *The 'Second India' Revisted: Population, Poverty and Environmental Stress Over Two Decades'*, World Resources Institute, Washington DC

Rhodes, R A W (1997) *Understanding Governance, Politics and the State*, Macmillan, Basingstoke, UK

Richards, M (1999) *Internalising the Externalities of Tropical Forestry: A Review of Innovative Financing and Incentive Mechanisms*, European Union Tropical Forestry Paper 1, Overseas Development Institute, London

Robins, N Trisoglio, A and Van Dijk, F (1996) *Vision 2020: Scenarios for a Sustainable Europe*, SustainAbility and International Institute for Environment and Development, London

Robins, N (forthcoming) 'Profit in Need? Business, Sustainable Development and the Great Transformation', in N Cross (ed) *Evidence for Hope*, IIED and Earthscan, London

Rockefeller Foundation (1999) 'Communication for Social Change', a position paper and report on the *Rockefeller Foundation Cape Town Conference, 6–10 October 1998*, Rockefeller Foundation, New York

Royal Botanic Garden Kew and IIED (1993) *Report on Sustainable Environment and Development Strategy and Action Plan for St Helena*, vol 1, *Sustainable Environment and Development Strategy: A Proposed Approach*, Government of St Helena

Sadler, B (1997) 'Recent Progress in Strategic Environmental Assessment', unpublished manuscript

Sadler, B (1998) 'Institutional Requirements for Strategic Environmental Assessment', paper to Intergovernmental Forum, organised by the Ministry for the Environment, Christchurch, New Zealand, 25 April 1998

Sadler, B and Verheem, R (1996) *Strategic Environmental Assessment 53: Status, Challenges and Future Directions*, the International Study of Effectiveness of Environmental Assessment, International Association for Impact Assessment, and Ministry of Housing, Spatial Planning and the Environment, The Hague, The Netherlands,

SARDC (1994) *State of the Environment in Southern Africa*, a report by the Southern African Research and Documentation Centre (SARDC) in collaboration with the World Conservation Union Regional Office for Southern Africa (IUCN-ROSA) and the Southern African Development Community (SADC), SARDC, Harare, Zimbabwe

Seroa da Motta, R, Contreras, H and Saade, L (2000) 'Wastewater Effluent Charges in Mexico', in J Rietbergen-McCracken and H Abaza (ed) *Economic Instruments for Environmental Management*, Earthscan, London

Shah, M K (1995) 'Participatory Reforestation Experience from Bharuch District, South Gujarat, India', *Forests, Trees and People Newsletter*, no 26/27

Shankland, A (2000) *Analysing Policy for Sustainable Livelihoods*, IDS research report 49, IDS, Brighton

Shell International (1996) *Global Scenarios: 1995–2020*, Shell International, London

Sigurdson, S G (1997) 'The Consensus Debate: 100% or Less – Says Who?' *National Institute for Dispute Resolution News*, vol IV, no 5, Canada

Smith, S (2000) 'What is an Environmental Fund and When is it the Right Tool for Conservation?' in R A Norris (ed) *The IPG Handbook on Environmental Funds*, www.geocities.com/shores_system/ef/ef_handbook_chap_2.html

Spellerberg, I F (1991) *Monitoring Ecological Change*, Cambridge University Press, Cambridge, UK

Spencer, L J (1989) *Winning Through Participation*, Institute of Cultural Affairs, Washington, DC

Sproull, L and Kiesler, S (1993) 'Computers, Networks and Work', in L M Harasim (ed) *Global Network. Computers and International Communication*, MIT Press, Cambridge, Massachusetts

SSESD (2000) *Federal Plan for Sustainable Development, 2000–2004*, Secretary of State for Energy and Sustainable Development, Belgium

Starkey, P (1998) *Networking for Development*, ITDG Publishing, London

Stoker, G (ed) (2000) *The New Politics of British Local Governance*, Macmillan, Basingstoke, UK

Sunter, C (1992) *The New Century: Quest for the High Road*, Human & Rouseau Tafelberg, Cape Town

Tannenbaum, R and Schmidt, W H (1958) 'How to Choose a Leadership Pattern', *Harvard Business Review*, March–April

Tennyson, R (1998) *Managing Partnerships: Tools for Mobilising the Public Sector, Business and Civil Society as Partners in Development*, The Prince of Wales Business Leaders Forum, London

Tennyson, R and Wilde, L (2000) *The Guiding Hand: Brokering Partnerships for Sustainable Development*, the United Nations Staff College and The Prince of Wales Business Leaders Forum, London

The Montréal Process (1999) 'Criteria and Indicators for the Conservation and Sustainable Management of Temperate and Boreal Forests', 2nd edn, www.mpci.org/meetings/rep2000/rep2000_e.html

Therivel, R and Partidario, M R (1996) *The Practice of Strategic Environmental Assessment*, Earthscan, London

Tonk, RAMN and Verheem, R A A (1998) 'Integrating the Environment in Strategic Decision-making: One Concept, Multiple Forms', paper presented at the *Annual Meeting of the International Association for Impact Assessment (IAI98), 19–26 April 1998, Christchurch, New Zealand*

Toulmin, C (2001) *Lessons from the Theatre: Should this be the Final Curtain for the Convention to Combat Desertification*, Opinion paper for the World Summit on Sustainable Development, International Institute for Environment and Development, London

Trevet, P (2000) '(Innovest) Maximising Environmental and Financial Performance', presentation to the *Forest Trends Conference, Vancouver BC, 4 October 2000*

Turkle, S (1995) *Life on the Screen*, Simon & Schuster, New York

UN DESA (2001a) *Commission on Sustainable Development Indicators of Sustainable Development*, www.un.org/esa/sustdev/isd.htm

UN DESA (2001b) *Indicators of Sustainable Development: Guidelines and Methodologies*, Department of Economic and Social Affairs, United Nations, New York

UN DESA (2002a) *Report of an Expert Forum on National Strategies for Sustainable Development*, meeting held in Accra, Ghana, 7–9 November 2001, Department of Economic and Social Affairs, United Nations, New York, available on www.johnnesburgsummit.org

UN DESA (2002b) *Guidance in Preparing a National Sustainable Development Strategy: Managing Sustainable Development in the New Millennium*, background paper no 13 (DESA/DSD/PC2/BP13), submitted by the Division for Sustainable Development, Department of Economic and Social Affairs, United Nations, to the Commission on Sustainable Development acting as the preparatory committee for the World Summit on Sustainable Development Second Preparatory Session, 28 January – 8 February 2002, New York, available on www.johnnesburgsummit.org

UN General Assembly (2001) *Recommendations of the High Level Panel on Financing for Development*, 55th Session of the General Assembly, 25 June 2001

UNCED (1992) *Agenda 21*, United Nations Conference on Environment and Development (UNCED), United Nations General Assembly, New York

UNDP (1997) *Caribbean Capacity 21 Project Terminal Report*, United Nations Development Programme, New York

UNDP (1999) *Human Development Report*, United Nations Development Programme, New York

UNDP (2000) '"Walking the Talk": Capacity 21's Global Experiences with Participatory Planning', final draft, 27 June, United Nations Development Programme, New York

UNDP (2001a) *Making New Technology Work for Human Development*, The Human Development Report, United Nations Development Programme, New York

UNDP (2001b) *Getting Connected: Information and Communications Technology for Development*, Cooperation South, No 1, United Nations Development Programme, New York

UNDP (2001c) *Proposal to Advance The Sea Turtle Tagging Programme 2001 on the East Coast (of Trinidad)* (Tr1/98/G52/2101/007), UNDP GEF Small Grants Programme, UNDP, New York, www.undp.org/sgp

UNED Forum (2001) 'Multi-Stakeholder Processes: A Methodological Framework', draft dated 10 April 2001, UNED Forum, London

UNEP (1994) *Government Strategies and Policies for Cleaner Production*, UNEP IE, Paris

UNEP (1999) *Global Environmental Outlook 2000*, United Nations Environment Programme in association with Earthscan, London

UNEP (2002) *Global Environmental Outlook 3*, United Nations Environment Programme/Earthscan Publications, London

UNEP/PWC (1998) *UNEP Financial Institutions Initiative 1998 Survey*, UNEP, Paris/ Price Waterhouse Coopers, www.pwcglobal.com/environment

UNESCO (1997) 'Final Report – Tbilisi', paper presented at the *Inter-Governmental Conference on Environmental Education, Tbilisi, Republic of Georgia, 14–26 October 1997*, UNESCO, Paris

UN General Assembly (2001) *Report of the Secretary General: Road Map Towards the Implementation of the United Nations Millennium Declaration*, A/56/326, 6 September 2001, United Nations, New York

UNSO (1999) *A Preliminary Overview of National Action Programme Processes of the United Nations Conventions to Combat Desertification and Drought*, report prepared as a contribution to the deliberations at COP II, UNDP Office to Combat Desertification and Drought (UNSO), New York

Uphoff, N (1992) *Local Institutions and Participation for Sustainable Development*, Gatekeeper Series SA31, International Institute for Environment and Development, London

US General Accounting Office (2000) *Developing Countries: Debt Relief Initiative for Poor Countries Faces Challenges'*, Chapter Report, 06/29/2000 GAO/NSIAD–00–161, US General Accounting Office, Washington, DC

van Keulen, W F and Walraven, S J E (1996) *Negotiations in Participation: Improving Participatory Methodologies with Insights from Negotiation Theories*, Thesis Report, department of Communication and Innovation Studies, Wageningen Agricultural University, The Netherlands

Vodoz, L (1994) La Prise de Décision par Consensus: Pourquoi, Comment, à Quelles Conditions *Environnement et Société*, FUL, 55–66

von Weizsacker, E (1994) *Earth Politics*, Zed Books, London

Vordzorgbe, S D and Caiquo, B (2001) *Report on Status Review of National Strategies for Sustainable Development in Ghana*. Submitted to IIED and the National Development Planning Commission, Ghana, Devcourt Ltd. Accra, June 2001

VROM (1997) *The Netherlands' National Environmental Policy Plan 3*, Department for Information and International Relations, Ministry of Housing, Spatial Planning and the Environment (VROM), The Hague

VROM (2001) *4th National Environmental Policy Plan – Summary*, Ministry of Housing, Spatial Planning & the Environment (VROM), The Hague

Walker, G B and Daniels, S E (1997) 'Rethinking Public Participation in Natural Resource Management: Concepts from Pluralism and Five Emerging Approaches', paper prepared for the *FAO Workshop on Sustainable Forestry and Rural Development in Pluralistic Environments, Rome, Italy, 9–12 December 1997*, FAO, Rome

WBCSD (1995) *Eco-Efficient Leadership – for Improved Economic and Environmental Performance*, World Business Council for Sustainable Development, Geneva

WBCSD (1997) *Exploring Sustainable Development: WBCSD Global Scenarios 2000–2050. Summary Brochure*, World Business Council for Sustainable Development, Geneva

WCED (1987) *Our Common Future. Report of the World Commission on Environment and Development*, Oxford University Press, Oxford

Wilson, D (1993) *Campaigning. The A–Z of Public Advocacy*, Hawksmere, London

Wilson, D (2000) 'Towards Local Governance: Rhetoric and Reality', *Public Policy and Administration*, vol 15, no 1, pp43–57

Winckler, G, Rochette, R, Reij, C, Toulmin, C and Toé, E (1995) *Approche gestion des terroirs au Sahel: analyse et évolution. Mission de dialogue avec les projets GT/GR du Club du Sahel au Burkina Faso, au Niger et au Mali, 1994–95. Rapport de mission*, Comité Permanent Inter-Étatsde Lutte Contre la Sécheresse dans le Sahel (CILSS) and Club du Sahel, Ouagadougou, Burkina Faso

Wood, A (ed) (1997) *Strategies for Sustainability: Africa*, IUCN in association with Earthscan, London

World Bank (1992) *World Development Report 1992 Development and the Environment*, Oxford University Press

World Bank (1994) *Report of the Learning Group on Participatory Development*, third draft, The World Bank, Washington, DC

World Bank (1995a) *National Environmental Strategies: Learning from Experience*, World Bank, Washington, DC

World Bank (1995b) *Pakistan: The Aga Khan Rural Support Programme. A Third Evaluation*, OED, World Bank, Washington, DC

World Bank (1996) *The Impact of Environmental Assessment: Second Environmental Assessment Review*, Environment Department, The World Bank, Washington, DC

World Bank (1997) *Five Years After Rio – Innovations in Environmental Policy*, The World Bank, Washington, DC

World Bank (1999) *World Development Indicators*, World Bank, Washington, DC

World Bank (2000) *Comprehensive Development Framework Country Experience: March 1999 – July 2000*, World Bank, Washington, DC

World Bank (2000) *World Development Report 2000/2001: Attacking Poverty*. World Bank, Washington DC

World Bank (2001a) *Global Development Finance 2000*, The World Bank, Washington, DC

World Bank (2001b) *Implementation Completion Report (Loan 3529-CH) on a Loan in the Amount of US$11.5 Million to the Republic of Chile for an Environmental Institutions Development Report*, report no 20652, World Bank, Washington, DC

World Bank (2001c) *Comprehensive Development Framework: Meeting the Promise? Early Experiences and Emerging Issues*, 17 September, CFD Secretariat, The World Bank, Washington, DC

World Bank (2002) *Participation in Poverty Reduction Strategy Papers: A Retrospective Study*, report by the Participation and Civic Engagement Group, Social Development Department, World Bank, Washington, DC

World Commission on Dams (2000) *Dams and Development: A New Framework for Decision-making*, Earthscan, London

WRI (1996) *World Resources 1996–1997*, World Resources Institute, Washington, DC, in association with Oxford University Press, Oxford

WRI/IIED/IUCN (1996) *World Directory of Country Environmental Studies: An Annotated Bibliography of Natural Resource Profiles, Plans, and Strategies*, World Resources Institute (WRI), IIED and the IUCN, Washington, DC

WRI/UNDP/UNEP/World Bank (2000) *The World Resources Report*, World Resources Institute, Washington, DC

Zakharov, V M (ed) (1999a) *Priorities for Russia's National Environmental Policy: Summary*, Center for Russian Environmental Policy, Moscow

Zakharov, V M (ed) (1999b) *Priorities for Russia's National Environmental Policy*, Center for Russian Environmental Policy, Moscow

Zakharov, V M (ed) (1999c) *Priorities for Russia's National Environmental Policy: Projects Portfolio*, Center for Russian Environmental Policy, Moscow

Zazueta, A (1994) *A Matter of Interests: Participation, Equity and Environment in Policy-making*, World Resources Institute, Washington, DC

Zazueta, A (1995) *Policy Hits the Ground: Participation and Equity in Environmental Policy-making*, World Resources Institute, Washington, DC

Zylicz, T (1994) 'Environmental Policy Reform in Poland', in T Sterner (ed) *Economic Policies for Sustainable Development*, Kluwer Academic Publishers, Dordrecht

Index

Page numbers in *italics* refer to boxes, figures and tables

3I model 180
4Rs *see* rights, responsibilities,
    returns/revenues and relationships
Aarhus Convention (UN) 228, *228, 229*
ACCA21 (China) *248, 252*
Access Initiative 228, *229*
accounts 133–5
accountability
    of development cooperation agencies 27–8
    government 19, 21, 22, 27–8, 38, 165, 323
    NSDSs *78, 79,* 81, 87, 112, 132, *134, 163,*
        321
    of private sector 27–8
    of stakeholders 124, 198, *200, 215,* 321–4
advocacy 17, 81, *101, 103,* 124, *172,* 200, *217,*
    229, 245, 281
aid flows *23*
Africa 44, 50, 52, 96, 113, 170–1, 185, *212*
Aga Khan Rural Support Programme
    (Pakistan) 68, *101–2,* 185, *212*
Agarwal, Anil 144
Agenda 21
    background 24, 36, 115, 156, 157, *158*
    finance 18, 288, 290
    Local Agenda 21 (LA21) 63, *64, 140,* 184,
        200, 322, 323, *328–30*
    and NSDSs *13, 23,* 24
    participatory approach *179,* 191, *192*
agriculture 5, 8, 9, *11, 16,* 28, *67, 322*
AIDEnvironment (The Netherlands) 151, *152*
AIDS 5, 8, *25,* 40
Albania 58
Andean Biodiversity Strategy 110
Anglo American Corporation 176
Angola *307*
Annex 1 Parties (UNFCC) *see* developed
    countries
Argentina *298*
Armenia *41*
Asia
    economic crisis 7, 18, 23, 186

existing planning frameworks 50, 56, *62*
    Financial Institutions Initiative *307*
    National Councils for Sustainable
        Development 52
    NSDS analysis methods *174*
    participation 178–80, 186
assessment
    indicator-based 135
    narrative 135
    participant 154
    risk 265, 305
    technical 153–4
Asia Pacific region *308*
Association for Sustainable and Responsible
    Investment (ASrIA) *308*
attitudes 21, 66, 76, 92, 105, 164, 196, 201,
    211, 221, 227, 233–236, 241, 265
audits 153, *202, 206,* 310, 313, *323*
awareness building/raising 37, *101, 103,* 200,
    229, 233, 235–6, 237, *250, 252,* 286, 306
Australia *20,* 141, *142,* 185, *212,* 214

Balochistan 65, 81, *82*
Bangladesh *40, 41, 62, 101, 179,* 213
Bangladesh Flood Action Plan 40, 178, *179*
Barbados *80*
barometer of sustainability 119, 137, *139,*
    160–1
Basel Convention on the Transboundary
    Movements of Hazardous Wastes (1989)
    14
behavioural models *121*
Belgium *19, 29,* 225, *271, 272, 300*
beliefs 156, 216, 262
Belize *139,* 296
Bellagio principles 311, *312*
Bellanet (IDRC) 244
Benin *41,* 151, *153*
biodiversity 5, 9, 10, *14,* 28, 42–4
Biodiversity Planning Support Programme
    (UNDP-GEF) 42, 272

Bolivia
    decentralized planning systems 66, 202,
        203, 214
    existing planning frameworks *41, 46,* 55, 58,
        66, *106,* 244
    governance *12*
    networks *244*
    NSDS analysis methods 151
    participation 66, 202, *203, 214*
    sustainable development strategies *1*
Botswana *45,* 67, 84–5, 108, *111,* 261, 273
bottom-up approaches *67,* 107, *188, 212,* 213
brainstorm 126, *224, 250,* 259
Brazil *20, 41, 302,* 308
Brundtland Commission (1987) 11, *12, 83*
budgets/budgetary capacity 33, 36, 38, 94,
    214, 288, 314, 322, 324, 327
Bulgaria *248,* 296
Burkina Faso *1, 45, 53, 54,* 58, *106,* 237, 261,
    272, 322
business
    environmental services *16,* 289
    in existing planning frameworks 38, *46,*
        54–5, *57*
    in Global Compact 17
    leadership 17
    NSDS involvement *80,* 88
    in partnerships 54–5, *57*
    sustainable development strategies 16–17,
        27–8, 37–8, *281, 284, 285,* 305–6
    see also financial institutions; industry;
        private sector

calendar for strategy process 112
Cambodia *41, 62*
Cameroon *41*
CAMPFIRE (Zimbabwe) *212*
Canada
    communications strategy *239, 248*
    debt swaps *296*
    decision-making 261, 273, 273–5, *277–9, 279*

existing planning frameworks *54*, 83, 108, *109*, *111*
governance *19*, *20*
monitoring 313, 324
multi-stakeholder partnerships *216*, 218, *239*, 244, 273–5, *277–8*, 280, 293
National Council for Sustainable Development *271*
NSDSs analysis methods *139*, *140*, 161
Canadian Council of Ministers of the Environment (CCME) *216*
Canadian International Development Agency (CIDA) *291*
capacity 22, 34, 36, 64–67, 70–73, 167, 188, 259, 308, 312, 313
capacity-building/strengthening 31–34, 49, 75, 92, 93, 101, 161, 164, 192, 271
Capacity 21 (UNDP) 1, *36*, *40*, 52, 93, 115, *237*, *246*, *252*
Cape Verde *45*
carbon offsets 16, 295, *301*
CARE *317*
Caribbean 69–70, 72, 202, *205*, *218 225*, *302*
Caring for the Earth (1991) 10, *264*
causal diagrams *121*, 148–49, *151*
CD Roms 240, 246, *247*
Central America 18, 110, *139*, *178*
Central American Forest Convention 110
Central Europe 70, 186
Centre for Russian Environmental Policy 90
Centre for Science and Environment (India) 144, *308*
certification schemes *185*, 307
certified emission reductions (CERs) 295
challenges
  for analysis 115, 130, 137
  for communication 230
  for decision-making 258–260
  for finance and investment institutions 306–308
  of sustainable development 2, 5–23, 28, 31, 33, 108, 114, 115, 149, 306
Chatham House rule *243*
Chile *46*, *229*, 291, 293, *298*, 300
China *39*, *46*, 173, 245, *248*, *252*, 303
choicework 280, *281*
CIS *41*
CITES (1973) *14*
citizens' organizations 2, 64, 100, 190

city development strategies (CDSs) 56
civil society
  commitment 87, 88, 90
  in existing planning frameworks 38, 39, *40*, *45*, *52*, *53*, 54–5, 58, *59*
  financial contributions 293–4
  financial help 93–4, 290
  opposition to poverty reduction strategies *62*
  participatory 186, 207, 292
  role of *92*, 98, 100
Clean Development Mechanism (Kyoto Protocol) 295
cleaner production 17, 292
climate change 5, 9, 28, *14*, 46–7, *73*, 294–5
coherence 104–10, *283*
coherence of strategy frameworks 34, 36, 46, 69, 70, 78, 104–110, 164, 167, 314
collaboration 48, 49, 58, 75, 106, 183, 186, 187, 194, 196, 197, 202, 207, 211, 215, 226, 227, 239, 249, 250, 271
Colombia *143*, 214, *298*, *316*
Commission on Human Rights and Administrative Justice (Ghana) *313*
Commissioner of the Environment and Sustainable Development (Canada) 108, *313*
Committee for NGOs Fighting Desertification (COPODE, Africa) *237*
commitment to a strategy 23, 31, 33, 34, 36. 50, 64, 76–78, 82–91, 163, 166, 167, 194, 257
communications
  access to information *36*, 8, 165, *195*, 227–8, *229*
  challenge 226
  information strategy 226–250
  electronic 246–7
  information, education and communications (IEC) strategy 226–8, 233–51, *252*
  market research *122*, *163*, 225, 235
  mass media *91*, 234, 235, *236*, *240*, 249–50
communities 66–70
community-based analysis *124*, 153–5, *319*
community-based organizations (CBOs) *40*, 53, 66, *82*, *86*, 101, *183*, *186*, *319*
community-based resource planning 211
comprehensive development frameworks

(CDFs) 54–6, 58, *57*, 105
computer-aided design (CAD) 267
conflict
  management 78, *91*, *103*, 107, 111
  resolution *92*, *194–5*, 206, 217, 276, 280, *281*
consensus 33, 41, 75, 79, 161, 163, 194, 202, 206, 217–221, 242, 259–261, 268, 272–281
conservation 50, *65*, 80, 82, 110, *172*, *183*, 232, *240*, 291, 297, *316*
continuous improvement approach *32*, 74–5, *75*, 82, 94
Consultative Forum on the Environment (EC) 175
consumption 5, 8–9, 10, 16, 18, 24, 27, 100, 171
Convention Concerning the Protection of the World Cultural and Natural Heritage (1927) *14*
Convention for the Preservation of Animals, Birds and Fish (1900) *14*
Convention on Biological Diversity (1992) *14*, 42–3
Convention on International Trade in Endangered Species (CITES, 1973) *14*
Convention on the Conservation of Migratory Species (1979) *14*
Convention on Wetlands (1971) *14*
Convention to Combat Desertification (1994) *14*, 44–5, *238*
coordination 32, 34, 49, 75, 77–81, 102–110, 161, 166, 167, *172*, 206, 234, 235, 280
Corporación Participa (Chile) *229*
corruption 8, *61*, *151*
cost-benefit/cost-effectiveness analysis *121*, 236, 269
costs
  of strategies 94–96
  of participation 193
Costa Rica *53*, *139*, 144, *160*
Côte d'Ivoire 55
country assistance strategies 52, *413*
covenants 88, *89*
cross-sectoral plans and strategies 42, 56
CSD (UN) 133, *136*, 157, *264*, 320
Cuba *271*, *272*
cultural issues 10, *14*, 261

DAC *1, 24,* 25, 31, 35, 95, *106, 264,* 313

Danish International Development Agency (DANIDA) *57, 68*

dashboard of sustainability 136, 138, *141,* 157, 160–1

data
baseline data 154, 311, *319,* 325

decision developers 270, 282

decision-making
ethical issues 262, *263–4, 267, 279*
strategy 253–87

decision theory 265–7

decision support tool 266–7

decision takers 270, 282

debt swaps 295, *296, 297, 298*

decentralization 18–23, 56, 105, 151, 213, 286, 297, 302
defined 20–2
and sustainable development 18, 20, 29, *34*

decentralized development planning/planning systems 66, 67, 211, 214

decision trees *121,* 148–50, *151,* 268, *269*

deconcentration 21

Declaration on the Rights to Development (1986) *263*

deforestation 5, 9, *48,* 148, *269, 329*

delegation 21

Denmark 18, *68, 228,* 320

deposit refund schemes 285, *301*

deregulation *21, 278*

DESA 1, 27, *36*

desertification *14,* 44–5, *46,* 158, *237, 329*

developed countries
financial institutions 306–7
international transfer payments 295
official development assistance 18, 290
resource consumption 5, 8–9, *89*
UNFCC compliance 46–7

developing countries
debt swaps 295, *296*
development challenges 5, 7–8, *11,* 22–3, *24,* 27
ecological footprints 142
environmental challenges 9, 10, *11*
foreign investment 18, *23,* 90, 303
international transfer payments 294, 295
overseas aid 18, 90, 95, 100
planning frameworks 33, *34,* 35, 38–41
sustainable development 18, 22–3, 28

UNFCC compliance 46–7

Development Assistance Committee (OECD) *see* DAC

development cooperation agencies
accountability 27–8
sustainable development strategies 27–8

development finance institutions (DFIs) 35, *86,* 303, *304*

development triad 186, 217

devolution 21, 22

Department for International Development (DFID) *283*

diagrams *121,* 124, 126, 148–50, *151,* 170–2, 208–211

dialogue(s) 1, 52, 55, 58–60, 90, 100, 102, 153, 202, 209, 228, 242

disease 5, 8, *11, 41*

district council *68, 184*

district developmental plans 67, 297

district environmental action plans (DEAPs) *46, 63*

Dominican Republic 55, *271, 272*

donor finance 100, *166,* 180, *184, 290, 291,* 292–3, *297*

donors 100, 292, 313

Dow Jones Sustainability Group Indexes *140, 308*

Draft Declaration on the Rights of Indigenous Peoples *264*

drugs 8

Earth Charter (Earth Council) *264*

Earth Council *36,* 52, *53, 246,* 261, *264*

Earth Summit (1992) 5, 13, 15, 17–18, 23, 115

East Timor 28, *29*

Eastern Caribbean Environmental Charter (2001) 72, 202, *205*

Eastern Europe *41,* 46, 70, 296, 301

eco-efficiency 18

Eco-financas initiative (Brazil) *308*

Eco Management and Audit Scheme (UK) 88

ecological footprint 133, 142–4, 262

Ecological Sustainability Index 160

Economic and Social Research Council (ESRC) 269

economic development
disparity of income 5, 7, *23*
and sustainable development 10, *12, 24,* 27, 28, 169

economic growth 8, 27, 99, 186, 292

economic instruments 15–16, 90, 285–6 *see also* market mechanisms

economic migrants 8

economic reform 15, 27, 62, 285, 300

ecosystem damage 5, 9, 10, *14*

Ecuador *158*

education *24, 59, 60, 163,* 189, 205–6, 229, *234,* 235

educational instruments 286

Egypt *41,* 88, 90, 108

El Salvador *103, 139, 158, 271, 272*

ELDIS 246, *316*

electronic democracy 247

electronic media 189, 225, *236,* 237, 238, 246–9, *250, 251, 252,* 267

emission charges *301*

endangered species *14, 43, 183*

energy consumption 9, 28, *89*

Environment 2010 (New Zealand) *111,* 235, 291

Environment Canada *216,* 293

environmental action plans 25, 35, *40,* 50–52, *63, 87, 97, 101,* 153 *see also* Netherlands; South Africa; UK

Environmental and Management Law Association (Hungary) *229*

environmental impact assessment (EIA) *121,* 149, 151, *150,* 202, *291*

environmental issues
assessments 84, 120, *122,* 149–2, *152, 153,* 172, 261, *291, 292,* 313, 320
costs 27, 133, 167, 256, 281, 286
in developing countries 9, 10, *11*

environmental agreements 14–15, *264*

environmental degradation/deterioration 5, 6, 9–11, 16, 22, 23, 63, 80, 142, 257, 264, 266, 285, 299

environmental management 17, 54, 72–74, 205, 207, 263, 286

environmental performance 15, 89, 140, 229, 306–308

environmental services *16,* 42, 289

environmental sustainability 224, 25, 39, 61, 218, 306, 308

environmental taxes 16, 289, 296, *301*

government strategies *16,* 42, 289

market mechanisms 15–16, 27, 169, 170

monitoring 15, 311, 318–20, *320*

in national development plans 38, *40*
  private sector involvement *16*, 17–18, 307
  and sustainable development 10, *12*, 14–15,
    24, 28
Environmental Management Authority (EMA,
    Trinidad) 207
environmental performance bonds 285, *301*
Eritrea *45*, 55
Estonia *54*, *271*, *272*
ethical issues 10, *14*, *24*, 262, 263–4, *267*, *279*
Ethiopia *45*, 55
Europe 18, 186, *247*, *307*
European Commission 70, 175, *175*, 276
European Environment Agency 320
European Partners for the Environment (EPE)
    175
European Union *19*, 175–6, *256*
events 79, 94, 95, 177, 193, 197, 204, 236, 238,
    240, 242, 322
evaluation *see* monitoring
exchange visits 242
Expert Group on the Introduction of
    Economic Instruments (UNEP) 299
export credit agencies (ECAs) 303, *304*
extension agencies 208

facilitation 80, 91, 101, 122, 123, 153, 171,
    220–222, 239, 273, 275–277
FAO *48*, 49, *51*, *317*
Federal Plan for Sustainable Development
    (Belgium) *29*, *300*
Federation of Chambers of Commerce and
    Industry (Pakistan) 90
Federation of Municipal Associations (FAM-
    Bolivia) *244*
Finance
  contingent finance mechanisms 294
  mobilising finance/sources of finance 32,
    75, 90, 94, 103, 163, 185, 289, 290,
    292–295, 297, 298, 302
  financial institutions 62, 86, 289, 303–308
  financial instruments 285
  financial mechanisms 18, 288, 291–293,
    298, 299, 302, 303
  financial requirements of a strategy 58,
    289–291
  financial resources 13, 15, 19, 21, 22, 33, 34,
    46, 78, 103, 106, 107, 192, 217, 289, 290,
    299, 321, 328

Financial Institutions Initiative (UNEP) 305,
    307
financing sustainable development 288–308
Finland *54*, *140*, *271*, 272
fiscal policies *see* economic instruments
fishing 9, *11*, *241*, 262, 280, *281*, 285
Flood Action Plan, Bangladesh *40*, *179*
focal points 24, 45, 79, *110*, 244, *257*
focus groups *122*, *201*, *202*, *209*, *223*
food production 8, 270
food security/insecurity 42, *147*, *241*
foodstuffs 8
foresighting *122*
Forest Stewardship Council (FSC) 157
forests *see* deforestation; national forestry
    programmes
France *19*, *20*
Frontier Forum for Environmental Journalists
    (FFEJ, Pakistan) *240*
Frontier Resource Centre for NGOs and CBOs
    (FRC, Pakistan) *240*
FTSE4Good index *308*
Funds of the Americas 293, 297, *298*

Gaza 55, 173
genuine domestic savings 142, *143*
Genuine Progress Indicator (GPI) 133–4, *135*,
    143
GEO–2000 7
geographic information systems (GIS) 138,
    141, *142*, *269*, 320
German Agency for Technical Cooperation
    (GTZ) 93, *212*, *317*, 318
Germany *19*, *20*, 93, 276
Gestion de Terroir approach (Africa) 185, *212*
Ghana
  analysis methods 151
  decentralized planning systems *67*
  environmental problems *11*
  existing planning frameworks *55*, 66, *67*, 83,
    84, 105, *106*, *107*
  finance 297
  monitoring *313*
  sustainable development strategies *1*, *36*, 84
global assessment 7
Global Development Finance 2000 report
    (World Bank) 18
Global Development Network (World Bank)
    244

Global Environment Facility (GEF) 42, 272,
    292, 294, *297*
Global Environment Outlook project 7
Global Knowledge Partnership 244
Global Reporting Initiative (GRI) 158, 307
globalization 10, 18, 22–3, 29, 97
governance 18, 28, 156, 162, 177, 214
  defined *19*
  electronic governance 247
  good governance 12, 19, 36, 55, 60, 71, 77,
    203, 215, 263, 283, 303, 304
  local governance 19, 23, 66, 225, 137
  structures 19, 20, 181, 213
  and sustainable development 18–23, 27–8,
    66, 82, 261
  systems 18–20
  see also decentralization; globalization
government
  accountability 21, 22, 27–8, 38, 321
  economic instruments 15–16, 27
  environmental issues *16*, 40–1, 289
  industry relationship 17, *89*
  monitoring 314, *315*, 325, 326
  role of 98–100
  in partnerships *36*, 54–5, 99
  sustainable development strategies 27–8,
    37–8, 82, 83, 96, 106, 108–9, *166*, 289
  typologies *19*, *20*
  see also local government
Green Plan (Canada) 83, *111*
green taxes 16, *300*
greenhouse gas emissions 9, 28, 46, 295
Grenada 50, 216, 225
gross domestic product (GDP) 133, 142, 143,
    290, *327–30*
gross national product (GNP) 18, *80*, *141*, 142,
    145, *146*, *327–30*
Groundwork UK 184
GTZ 93, *212*, *317*, 318
Guatemala *139*
Guide to Green Government (Canada) 108, *109*
Guyana 44, 200, *201*

habitats 5, 9, 28
Hamilton-Wentworth Sustainability Day *324*
Hart Environmental Data *140*
hazardous waste 10, *14*
health care provision *24*, *60*
heritage issues 10, *14*, 262

highly indebted poor countries (HIPCs) 55, 292, 295

HIMA (Tanzania) 66, 68, 212

HIV/AIDS 5, 8, 41

Honduras 58, 139, 151, 261, 272

human development 24, 41, 41, 72, 145, 146, 263, 264

Human Development Index 42, 136, 145, 147, 160

Human Development Report (UNDP) 41, 145

human rights 24, 41, 61–2, 247, 264, 265

Hungary 54, 229, 272

ICMS Ecologico (Brazil) 302

IMF 56, 58–61, 61, 87, 292

incentives
    for innovation and improvement 287, 301
    for participation 194, 196, 197, 204, 235
    market incentives 286, 298
    performance incentives 294
    perverse incentives 119, 299, 300
    sustainable development 15, 75, 87, 88, 90, 100, 147, 161, 167, 302–304

index
    air quality 163
    consumer price 163
    economy 138
    environment 138
    generating indices 159
    Human Development 145
    society or social care 138
    policy performance 138
    well-being 138

India
    communications strategy 229, 248
    environmental management 308
    existing planning frameworks 38, 39, 41, 42, 43
    governance 19, 20
    human development reports 41
    monitoring 316
    participation 184, 196, 212
    scenario development 171, 172

indicators 133, 136, 137, 158–160, 327
    choice/selection of indicators 158, 159
    comunity-based indicators 319
    compound indicator 135
    CSD indicators of sustainable development 136, 157, 310, 328

genuine progress indicator 133, 142

governance indicators 19

human development indicators 21 (see also Human Development Index)

indicator-based assessments 134–138, 156, 157, 160

indicator framework 155, 157

indicator initiatives 140

indicators of implementation 229

indicators for monitoring/evaluating a strategy website 251

indicator sets 137, 138, 157, 159, 323

integrated indicators 136

performance indicators 80, 196, 218, 324

single indicator of sustainable development 137, 138

spatial indicators 141

sustainable development indicators 28, 52, 79, 140, 145, 235, 249, 311, 318–320

indigenous knowledge 92, 228

Indonesia 21, 22, 212, 229, 272

industrial economies 8

industrialized countries see developed countries

industry 16, 17–18, 89, 90, 289

information
    access to 36, 165, 202, 203, 215, 217, 227–230, 245, 247, 248, 273, 275, 326, 330
    baseline information 117, 232, 235, 274
    consumer information 286
    communications technology 248
    informational instruments 286
    management 227, 326
    mechanisms 34, 75
    products 79, 236
    sharing 61, 127, 153, 171, 180, 183, 204, 205, 208, 211, 221, 227, 235, 237, 239, 245
    technology 169
    local information 182, 319
    statistical information 122, 245

information, education and communications (IEC) strategy 226–8, 233–51, 252

Institute for Development Studies (UK) 246, 316

Institutional capacity 50, 59, 61, 63, 66, 313

institutional instruments 286

intellectual property rights 10

intensive agriculture 89

integrated frameworks 30

Inter-American Development Bank 293

Inter-American Strategy to Promote Participation in Sustainable Development 229

inter-generational equity 264

Intergovernmental Agreement on the Environment (Australia) 185

Intergovernmental Panel on Climate Change (IPCC) 9, 46

Intergovernmental Panel on Forests (IPF) 47

International Bank for Reconstruction and Development (IBRD) 291

International Collective in Support of Fishworkers 246

International Council for Local Environmental Initiatives (ICLEI) 64

international development assistance (IDA) 87, 292

international development goals (IDGs) 24, 264

International Development Research Centre (IDRC) 216, 269

international development target xxii

International Institute for Environment and Development (IIED) 1, 11, 25, 51, 96, 244

International Institute for Sustainable Development (IISD) 137, 138, 216, 244

International Monetary Fund see IMF

international transfer payments 294

International Network of Green Planners (INGP) 246

International Tropical Timber Organization 158

internet 225, 236, 247, 248, 249, 250, 252

interviews 103, 122, 123, 163

intra-generational equity 264

investment 303–8

Ireland 140

islands 72, 214

ISO 14001 88

Italy 19

IUCN 1, 15, 25, 35, 50, 63, 94, 172, 246, 316

Jamaica 42, 47, 54, 296

Japan 144–5, 160

Joint Forest Management, India 196

journalists 229, 231, 237, 240, 240

juridical instruments 284

Kalpavriksh (India) *43*
Kaunda, Kenneth 83
Kazakhstan *46*
Kenya *45, 101,* 108, *158, 212*
key informant interviews *122, 163, 209*
key tasks
    for secretariat 77, *78,* 79–81
    for steering committee 45, *63,* 81, *82*
knowledge
    indigenous knowledge *92,* 228
    networks 244
    system 69, 76, *92,* 228
    traditional knowledge *205*
Kyoto Protocol 295
Kyrgyz Republic 55, *272*

land suitability classification *121*
land use 22, 48, *68,* 96, 126, 138, 164, 210
Landcare movement (Australia) *212*
Lao PDR *62*
Latin America *46,* 50, 52, 70, 180–1, *298, 307*
Latin American and Caribbean Commission
    on Development and Environment
    (LACCDE) 70, 302
laws 14, 29, 54, 89, 105, 112, 132, 147, 149,
    156, 162, 164, 165, 169, 284, 324
law on popular participation, Bolivia 202, 203,
    214
Law on Tropical Forest Conservation (US,
    1998) *297*
leadership continuum *182*
League for Defence of the Environment
    (LIDEMA, Bolivia) *244*
legal
    analysis 165, 168
    constraints 169, 185
    principles 14
    framework/system 45, 48, 72, 73, 92, 162,
        164, 165, 169, 178, 185, 201, 202, 284
    instruments/tools 13, 91, 106, 233, 285,
        287, 330
    mandate 162, 272
    measures/requirements 43, 66, 70, 105, 150
    reforms 76, 105, 165, 169
legislative instruments 284
Lesotho *45,* 84
life cycle assessment (LCA) 18, 268

Lithuania *41*
Local Agenda 21 37, 63, *64, 200, 323*
local capacity 212
local government 20, 21, 22, 62, *64,* 92, 184,
    270, 289, 302
local government organization (LGO) *64*
local level planning 69, 210, 212
local strategies 69, 70, 76, 91, 184, 207, 246,
    262, 297, 311
Luangwa Integrated Resource Development
    Project (Africa) 113

Madagascar *41*
Madhya Pradesh, India *41*
malaria 5, 8, *25*
Malawi
    environmental issues *266*
    existing planning frameworks *45, 49, 51,* 84
    National Council for Sustainable
        Development *271, 272*
    NSDS analysis methods 129, *130*
Mali *46*
Man and Biosphere Reserves 184
mandates *78,* 85, *271*
mapping 147, *163, 168, 172,* 204, 208, 211
    institutional mapping 172
    participatory maps 208, 209, 317
    intensity of participation 86, 162, 163, 168
    policy communities 163
    power 129, 130
    strategy processes 45, 58, 59., 62, 76, 78, 93,
        102, 105, 113
    policy influence mapping 138, 147, 148
    social maps 211
marginalization 7, 8, 23
market instruments 285
market mechanisms 27, 37, 90, 169, 288, 292,
    298–302, *301 see also* economic
    instruments
market research *122, 163,* 225, 235
mass media *91,* 234, 235, *236, 240,* 249–50
Mauritania 58, *61*
media
    in communications strategy *163,* 233, *237,
        239,* 249–50
    environmental campaigns *16*
    sustainable development campaigns *80*
    see also electronic media
mediation 101, 181, 185, 275, 279, 281

Mediterranean Blue Plan (1988) 70
Mexico *19, 46, 53, 54,* 188, *139, 229, 271, 272,*
    301
micro-finance institutions 289
migration 8, *11, 147, 151,* 169
migratory species 14
Millennium Declaration (2000) 24, *25,* 264
Millennium Development Goal 264, 280
Millennium Ecosystem Assessment 15
Moldova *59*
Mongolia *54, 272*
monitoring
    communications strategy 250–1
    community-based *319*
    data 310, 311, *327–30*
    in developing countries 310
    environmental 15, 38, 307, 311, 318–20, *320*
    externally-driven 311, 313–14
    feedback 310, 325–6
    by government 314, *315,* 325, 326
    ground rules 112
    implementation *33, 36, 91,* 309, 320–2, *327*
    internal audits 323
    internally-driven 311, 314
    limitations 320, *321*
    by NGOs 310–11, 314, *315,* 326
    pressure-state-response framework 311,
        318–20
    principles 310–11
    results 310, 324–5
    stakeholders 322–4
    timing 318, *327*
    'quick and dirty' 323, *323*
Montreal Process (1999) 157
Montreal Protocol on Substances that Deplete
    the Ozone Layer (1987) 14
Morocco 39, *40,* 55, *158*
Mozambique 58, *266*
multi-criteria analysis (MCA) 269, 268
multi-sectoral *64,* 81, 82, 87, 282–3
multi-stakeholder
    assessment 246
    approaches 34, 94, 177, 181, 198, 215, 216,
        243, 262, 274, 275, 277, 278,
    forums 52, 54, 78, 129, 214, 267, 271, 272
    groups 118, 138, 170, 181, 311
    partnerships 178, 213. 239
    structures for decision making 270
multi-stakeholder integrative sustainability

planning 53

Multilateral Agreement on Investment (OECD) 23

multilateral/bilateral development finance institutions (DFIs) 86, 303, 304

multilateral environmental agreements (MEAs) 14–15, 263

Namibia 1, 41, 84, 266

narrative assessments 132, 135, 139, 142, 143

national action programmes (NAPs) 44–5, 46, 106

national biodiversity strategies and action plans (NBSAPs) 41–4, 107, 200, 201, 292, 294

National Commission for the Environment (Chile) 291

national conservation strategies (NCSs) 30, 32, 50, 52, 63, 65, 66, 83, 88, 182, 315

National Council of Environmental Management (Africa) 237

National Councils for Sustainable Development (NCSDs)
communications strategies 238
decision-making strategies 261, 272, 271–2, 273
as existing planning frameworks 52–3, 53, 85, 90, 261

national development 55, 6, 30, 32, 51, 53, 55, 98, 258, 259, 263, 267, 294, 304

national development plans 30, 32, 38–40, 40, 53, 55

National Economic and Social Development Plan (Thailand) 40

National Economic Development and Labour Council (NEDLAC, South Africa) 219

national environmental action plans (NEAPs) 35, 40, 50–2, 87, 101, 189

National Environmental Policy Plan (Netherlands) 29, 37–8, 83, 89, 118, 254, 256, 278

national environmental funds 296

national forestry programmes 47–50, 49, 51, 129, 130, 133, 225

National Fund for Natural State Protected Areas (PROFONANPE, Peru) 297

National Human Development reports (HDRs) 41

national planning commission 38,79

National Institute of Public Health and Environmental Protection (RIVM, Netherlands) 118

National Round Table on the Environment and the Economy (NRTEE, Canada) 216, 239, 275, 277–8

National Strategy for Sustainable Development (Netherlands) 38

national sustainable development strategy 5, 23–5, 38, 69, 104

national visions 53–4, 55, 69

natural resources 5, 9–10, 94, 144, 169, 170, 217

Negotiated Rule-Making Act (Canada) 273

negotiating 217–8, 276–80, 279
rights- and risk- based 263, 279, 285

Nepal 1, 66, 184, 212, 214

Netherlands
donor finance 18
environmental strategies 29, 37–8, 83, 84, 89, 118, 254, 256, 278
governance 19
strategic environmental analysis 150, 151, 152
sustainable development strategies 29, 38, 88, 89, 97

Network for Environment and Sustainable Development (NESDA) 246

networks 228, 242–5, 246, 262

New Zealand 67, 111, 216, 217, 235, 291

NGOs
biodiversity strategies 43
commitment 90
in communications strategy 230, 232, 237, 239, 240
on decentralization 21
and donor finance 293, 303
in existing planning frameworks 35, 40, 46, 52, 61, 62, 80, 244, 293
financial help 94, 290–1
government relationship 204, 290–1
international transfer payments 294
local participation involvement 67, 184
monitoring 310–11, 314, 315, 326
NSDS involvement 86
participatory 182, 184, 186, 190, 198
private sector relationship 303–4, 306, 308
role of 95, 97, 100, 101–2
trust funds 296–7

Nicaragua 58, 139, 151, 153, 271, 272

Niger 45, 58, 272

Nigeria 41, 85, 97, 108, 173, 199

nitrogen loading 9

non-Annex 1 Parties (UNFCC) see developing countries

non-governmental organizations see NGOs

non-renewable resources 133, 256

North see developed countries

North American Free Trade Agreement (NAFTA) 188

Northern Lights Institute (USA) 280

Norway 18, 272

nutrition 8, 39, 328

OECD 1, 23, 24, 140, 302, 303

official development assistance (ODA) 18, 290

Organisation for Economic Co-operation and Development see OECD

Organization of Eastern Caribbean States (OECS) 72, 73, 202, 205

'Our Own Agenda' (LACCDE, 1990) 70

ownership of a strategy 21, 40, 43, 50, 76, 78, 85, 87, 105, 117, 118, 189, 194, 215
by civil society and private sector 88
country/national ownership 31, 35, 36, 54, 56, 87, 95, 106
by government, ministries and agencies 787, 87, 88
local ownership 167, 204

ozone 14, 28, 133, 176, 329

ozone depletion 14

Pacific Islands 72

PACT 316

Pakistan
analysis methods 143
communication strategy 232, 240, 252
desertification 46
development projects 300
existing planning frameworks
finance 291, 300
government involvement 84, 84, 88, 105, 108, 111
monitoring 310, 315, 325
National Conservation Strategy 50, 52, 63, 65–6, 70, 82, 84, 105 see also Sarhad Provincial Conservation Strategy
national vision 55

NGO involvement 69, *101–2*, 185, *212*, *241*
    participation *65,* 69, 105, *107,* 185, *212,* 213, *291,* 292
    private sector involvement 90
    stakeholder involvement *128,* 217
    sustainable development strategies *1,* 49, *52,* 119
Pan Asia Networking (PAN) 244
Pan European Forest Certification Council (1998) 157
Panama *139, 210, 272*
participation 34, 36, 60, 75, 117, 163, 166, 177–181, 192, 204–6, 312
    benefits of participation 186–97
    constraints to participation 123, 180, 196–7
    costs of participation 193–5, 197, 291
    in decentralized planning systems 211–4
    definitions of participation 178
    horizontal participation 182–5, 275
    intensity of participation 168, 197
    legal framework for participation 201–4, 205, 228–9
    levels of participation 181–3
    methodologies for participation 117, 121–3, 202 206–225, 315–8
    perceptions of participation 178–9, 181
    political dimensions 116–7, 182, 190–1
    popular Participation Law, Bolivia 203
    selection of participants 198–9
    structures for participation 97–8, 178–80, 184, 201–5
    types of participation/typology 178–180
    vertical participation 182–5, 275
    voluntary participation 199, 275
participatory inquiry *185*
participatory learning and action 69, 207, 208, *209*
participatory learning techniques 69, 207, 208, *209*
participatory planning *55,* 66, 122, 153, 187, 204, *214*
participatory rural appraisal *68,* 208, 209, *211,* 317, 318
participatory rural planning *212*
People's Forum on Development Priorities (Thailand) *55*
Permanent Committee for Drought Control in the Sahel (CILS) 44
Peru *46,* 296, 297, 298, 302

Philippines *41, 53,* 244, *271, 272,* 296, *307*
pilot
    programmes *45*
    projects *45, 91,* 112–3, 286
Pilot Analysis of Global Ecosystems (PAGE) 15
planning 102–4, 193–225
Planning for Real (UK) 211, *212*
Poland *41,* 296, 299
policy
    analysis 120–5, 145–51, 163–4
    coherence 280, 282–3
    communities 90, 128, 242–4
    development 6, 17, 87, 97, 150, 225
    framework 48, 55, 59, 60, 71, 105, 246
    guidance on NSDSs 33–34
    instruments 13, 146, 189, 278, 289, 298
policy mapping 148
political instability 7
politicians 98
polluter pays principle 14, *264,* 289, 298
pollution 10, *11,* 28, *264,* 289, 298
Popular Participation Law (Bolivia) *203, 214*
population 8, 10, 25, 38, 87, 94, 125, 143, 156, 159, 173, 254, 298
population growth 5, 8, *11, 24,* 169
poverty 5, 8, *24, 39, 40, 41, 151*
poverty eradication action plan (Uganda) *71*
poverty reduction strategies 30, 32, 56–63
poverty reduction strategies papers (PRSPs) 52, 56, *59–61,* 61–2, *71,* 87, 106, 292, 296
    civil society opposition *62*
    full PRSP 56, *59,* 61, *106*
    interim PRSP 58, *59*
    sourcebook 58
precautionary principle 14, *263*
pressure-state-response framework 311, 318–20
principles
    for analysis 116–8; 162
    for assessing progress towards sustainable development 311, 312
    for comprehensive development frameworks 54, 56
    for communication 230
    for consensus 275
    for decision-making 258, 261–70
    for governance 19
    for monitoring and evaluation 310, 311
    for multi-stakeholder processes 215

for national councils for SD 53
    for national forestry programmes 48
    for participation 193, 202, 205
    for participatory learning and action 208
    projet de société, Canada 216
    for strategic environmental assessment 152
    for sustainable development strategies 25, 30, 32–5, 45–6, 48, 54, 58, 63, 64, 70–73, 112, 310
    for sustainable development 263–4, 269–70, 284
    Rio principles on integrating environment and development 263, 280
prior informed consent principle 14, 202
private sector
    accountability 27–8
    company reports 307
    environmental strategies *16,* 17–18, 307
    NGO relationship 306, *308*
    NSDS involvement *86*
    see also business; industry
problem trees *see* decision trees
professional associations *86,* 100, 101, 202
Programme for the Protection of Tropical Forests (PROAFT, Mexico) *212*
project cycles 151
Projet de Société (Canada) *216, 239,* 244, 280, 293
property rights 10, 27, 168, 262, 285
prospectus *78,* 94–5, 112, 238, *239, 315*
Protected Area Conservation Trust (Belize) 296
provincial conservation strategies (PCSs) 65, *66*
PRSP Sourcebook 58
public
    authorities *21,* 98, 100, 175, 202, 227, *229*
    awareness *80, 91, 140, 166*–7, *201,* 235, *237, 271,*286
    information *140*
    participation 181, *192,* 202, 228, 230, 233, 235, *273*
    relations 21, *181,* 235, 295
public awareness campaigns 229, 233, 235–6, 237, 250, *252,* 286

QUIM approach (GTZ) 318

Ramsar Convention (1971) *14*

rapid rural appraisal 208–9, *210*

Rawlings, Jerry *55, 83*

RedLat *246*

refugees 8, 109

regional action programmes (RAPs) 44

Regional and International Networking Group
(RING, IIED) 244

regional approaches 70–3

Regional Environment Centre (REC),
Budapest *27, 202*

regional strategies 70–3

religious groups *86, 185*

renewable resources *21, 89, 109,* 133, 142, *256*

rent capture *312*

resource boards/agencies 99

resource consumption 5, 8–9, 37, 68, 89, 144–5

Resource Management Act (1991, New
Zealand) 213, *217,* 291

resource management acts *217, 291*

resource users 69, 86, 99, *101,* 107, 187, *225,* 289

rights
development rights *16, 263, 301*
human rights 17, *24, 41,* 70, *167, 190,* 262,
263–4, 303, 308, 312, 313

rights, responsibilities, returns/revenues and
relationships (4Rs) 96, *166*

rights- and risk- based negotiation *263, 279,*
285

Rio Declaration (1992) 156, 227*see also* Earth
Summit

Rio+5 xxii

Rioplus Programme (Germany) 93

risk assessment *121,* 154, 265, *268,* 276, 278,
279, 305

risk-based priority setting *268*

roles
civil society 100
donor agencies 100
NGO *101*
politicians' 98
private sector 99
public authority 98
resource board 99
sub-national authority 99

Romania *54, 55,* 56, *271*

round tables *54, 65, 66, 86, 91,* 94, 107, 108,
110, 181, 185, 192, 201, 206, 228

Russia 45, 90, 173, *272*

Sahel region 44, *45–6,* 185

Sarhad Provincial Conservation Strategy
(Pakistan) 108, *107, 110, 172, 240, 257*

scaling up 63, 184

scenario development 171

scoping 77, 193

Scotland *248*

secretariat 77–81

sectoral analysis 50

Senegal *45, 54, 272*

Shaping the 21st Century (OECD) 24

share fairs 242

Shell International 173, *174, 282, 284, 285*

Sierra Leone *41,* 160

skills 91–3, 117
facilitation skills 221
education skills 234, 239

Slovak Republic *272*

Slovenia 296

small island developing states (SIDS) 50, *47*

social development 10, *12, 24,* 28

social impact assessment *323*

social services 8, *185, 199,* 202, *203,* 300

Society for International Development *184*

soil erosion 8, 9, *11*

solid waste management 10, *11*

Soufriere Marine Management Area (St Lucia)
211, 280

South *see* developing countries

South Africa
access to information *229*
analysis methods *151, 173, 176, 176*
environmental strategies 15, *266, 271*
existing planning frameworks *51*
monitoring *316*
National Council for Sustainable
Development *271, 272*
participation 186, 216, *219*

South America 18, 110, *178*

South Korea 54

South Pacific Regional Environmental
Programme (SPREP) 72

Southern Africa *116, 151, 176, 266*

Southern African Development Community
(SADC) 15

Southern African Research and
Documentation Centre (SARDC) 15

Soviet Union *see* Russia

Spain *19, 20*

Sri Lanka *212*

St Helena 240, *241*

St Lucia 85, 211, 280

St Vincent 50

stakeholders
accountability 124, 198, *200, 215,* 321–4
analysis 120
costs 91–4, *195,* 199, 290–1
in existing planning frameworks 35, 44, *45,*
51, 52–3
expectations 193–6
identifying *124*
monitoring 321–4
multi-stakeholder partnerships 214–20, 241,
243, 262, 270, 272, 273, 274–5, *277–8,* 323
'ownership' 85, 87, 88, 93, *215*
policy communities 90, 97, *128, 163,* 242
in partnerships 56, *57,* 213
power issues 127
primary 124–6, 129
relationships 127
representation 125–6
secondary 124–5
see also participation

State of the Environment in Southern Africa
15

state-of-the-environment reports 15, 311,
318–20, *320*

state of the world reports 15

steering committee 45, 81, *82,* 85

Stockholm Environment Institute *174*

strategic assessment *32, 75, 106*

strategic environmental assessment (SEA) 149,
152, 153, 171

strategic planning frameworks
as basis for NSDSs 30–1, 32, 35–72, 75–6,
85, 87–8, 102–10
business involvement 38, *45,* 54–5, *57*
capacity-building programmes 49, *51*
civil society involvement 38, *40,* 41, *45,* 52,
53, 54–5, *60,* 61
cross-sectoral approach 42, 50
finance 288, 292–3
government involvement 42, *41,* 54–5, 60
local level 66–70
national level 30, 32, 38–62, 69–70
NGO involvement 35, *40, 45,* 52, 61, 63, *80,*
244, 293
participatory approach *43, 51, 52, 53,* 60, 61

private sector involvement 38, *45*, 54–5, *57*

regional level 70–3

sector-based approach 42

shortcomings 38–41, 42–3, 44, *48*, 58

stakeholder involvement 38, 44, *45*, *51*, 52–3

sub-national level 63–6, 69–70

successful 41, 44, 47–9, 50–2, 54–6, *64*, *71*

strategy document 28, 81, 95, 28, 239, 247, 292

strategy objectives *34*, 103, *240*, 255, 283, 287, 311, 324

strengths, weaknesses, opportunities, threats (SWOT) 154, *168*

structural adjustment *11*, *23*, *62*

sub-national strategies 63–9, 99

sub-Saharan Africa 8

sub-regional action programmes (SRAPs) 44

subsidies 16, 285, 289, 299, *301*

Sudan *45*

surveys *41*, *68*, *97*, *118*, *122*, 125, *151*, *202*, *206*, 207, 208, 225, *241*, 251, *319*, *322*, *323*, *327*

sustainability 6, 11, 12, 24–5

　barometer of sustainability 140

　dashboard of sustainability 142

　strong and weak sustainability 269–70

　sustainability analysis 114, 130, 153

　sustainability assessment 114, 119, 132–161, 309, 311, 316, 320

　sustainability indices 18

　sustainability ratings for companies 307–8

Sustainability Day (Canada) 324, *324*

Sustainability Reporting Guidelines 157

sustainable development

　analysis 114

　Bellagio principles 311, *312*

　business strategies 16–17, 27–8, *284*, *285*, 305–6

　challenges 7–10, *11*

　civil society strategies 96–7

　and decentralization 18, 20, 29, *33*

　defined 5, *12*

　in developing countries 18, 22–3, 28

　and economic development 10, *12*, *24*, 27, 28, 169

　and environmental issues 10, *12*, 14–15, *24*, 28, 37

　financing 18, 289

　and globalization 22–3, 29, 98

　and governance 18–23, 27–8, 66, 82, 261

　indicator-based assessment 135

international initiatives 11–18, *24*, *25*, *264*, 301

mainstreaming 289, 303–8

market mechanisms 15–16, 27, 299

measuring 132–61, 309

participatory approach 23, 27–8, 72, 177

private sector strategies 16–17, 96–7, 289, 308

scenario planning 171

and social development 10, *12*, *24*, 28

sustainability ratings 307, *308*

Sustainable Development Communications Network (IISD) 244

sustainable development instruments

　educational 286

　financial 285

　guidance on instrument selection 287

　informational 286

　institutional 286

　juridical 284

　legislative 284

　market 285

Sustainable Development Networking Programmes (UNDP) 245, *252*

sustainable development triad 186

sustainable investment initiatives *308*

sustainable livelihoods

　analysis 119, 145

　framework 127, 146–8, 320

Swaziland *45*, *158*

Sweden 16, 18, *19*, 151

Switzerland *20*, *248*, *272*

SWOT analysis 162, *168*

System of National Accounts (SNA) 141–2

Tajikistan *59*

Tanzania

　existing planning frameworks *45*, 55, 56, 60–61, 66, *68*

　NSDSs *101*, 107

　participation *179*, *212*, 213

　sustainable development strategies *1*

taxes

　carbon 261

　environmental 289, 296

　'green' 16

　NSDS 10, 100, 142, *148*, *184*, 214, *241*, 289, 293, 300–3

　pollution 170, 285

technology 17–18, 246

TFAP *see* tropical forestry action plans

Thailand *1*, *12*, 40, *55*, 88, 214, *229*, 298, *306*

Thailand Environment Institute *229*

time lines 126

Tobago *207*

Togo *45*

top-down approaches *188*

total material requirement (TMR) 144–5

tradable permits 285, *301*

trade 8, *23*, *59*, 169, 170, 190

trade offs *12*, 28, 31, *38*, 41, *78*, *101*, 110, 115, 126, 179, 194, *197*, 258, 265, 269, 276, 306, *319*

trade protectionism 8

trade unions 100, 125, 198, *200*

traditional knowledge *205*

training 87, *92*, 101, *164*, 234, 235, 240

transparency *see* accountability

trends 7–11, 18, 169

　environmental 116, 140

　governance 19

triggers 253–5, *256*, *257*, 258

Trinidad 181, *183*, *207*

tropical forest action plans (TFAPs) 33, 47, *48*

trust funds 294, 296–7, *298*

Turkey *41*, 303

Turkmenistan *45*

Uganda

　existing planning frameworks *45*, *53*, *54*, 55, 56, 70, *71*, *106*, 292

　Financial Insitutions Initiative *307*

　National Council for Sustainable Development *53*, *271*, *272*

　NSDSs *229*, 261

UN Commission for Europe 228, *228*

UN Commission on Sustainable Development (CSD) 136, 138, 157, 158, *264*, 320

UN Conference for Financing for Development (2001) 301

UN Conference on Environment and Development (1992) *see* Earth Summit

UN Conference on the Human Environment (1972) 11

UN Convention on the Law of the Sea (1982) *14*

UN Department of Economic and Social Affairs 1, 27

UN Development Programme *see* UNDP

UN Environment Programme *see* UNEP
UN Framework Convention on Climate
    Change (UNFCC, 1992) *14,* 46–7
UN General Assembly Special Session (1997)
    24, *25, 263*
UN Global Compact (1999) 17, 88, *264,* 306
UN High Level Panel on Finance for
    Development 290
UNCED *see* Earth Summit
uncertainty 74, 76, 96, 265, 287
under-nourishment 8
UNDP 1, *36, 40, 41, 63, 140, 291, 316*
UNED Forum (2001) 214, 270, 274
UNEP *7,* 11, 17, *48, 140,* 299, 304, 306, *307*
United Kingdom
    analysis methods *140, 143,* 150
    communications strategy 246, *248*
    economic instruments 16
    environmental strategies 88, 151, 276
    governance *19, 20*
    participation 184, 185, 211, *218,* 225
    policy coherence 282, *283*
    see also Ireland; Scotland; Wales
United States
    analysis methods *140,* 146
    communications strategy *229*
    debt swaps *296, 297, 298*
    decision-making strategies 265, *281*
    governance *20*
    National Council for Sustainable
        Development *54, 272*
Universal Declaration of Human Rights (1947)
    263
universal normative framework 263, *263–4*

urbanization 10, *11,* 169
USAID *317*
user pays principle *264,* 298
Uzbekistan *46, 248, 271, 272*

values *see* ethical issues
Vienna Convention for the Protection of the
    Ozone Layer (1985) *14*
Vietnam 55, 56, *57, 62*
village level planning I21, 39, 43, 49, 52, *66*
village strategies 66, *68, 86*
Vision–2020 (Ghana) *55,* 83, *84,* 105, *106*
Vision–2025 (Tanzania) *55*
voluntary agreements 90, *206, 278*
voluntary organizations 6, 38, *86*

Wales *249*
waste management 10, *11, 91,* 301
watershed management *11, 16, 281*
water supply 10, *11,* 299
websites 206, 240, 246–7, *248, 249, 251, 252*
well-being index 138
West Bank and Gaza 55, 173
wetlands 9, *14*
Windward Islands 214, *218*
Wolfensohn, James D. 54
women 24, *25, 39, 41, 42, 62, 68,* 93, 125, 129
    166, 179 183, 192, 195, 198–9, *250, 269,*
    312, 328
work plan *68,* 88, *216,* 318
working in groups 218
Working Party on Development Cooperation
    and Environment *1*
workshops 207, *232,* 270, *274*

World Bank
    donor finance 292, 293
    on governance *19, 21*
    networks *246*
    NSDSs 1
    planning frameworks involvement 35, *48,*
        50, 54, 56, 59–61, 87
    sustainable development involvement *140,*
        142, 289
World Business Council for Sustainable
    Development (WBCSD) 17, 18, 88, 173,
    174
World Commission on Dams 263, *267,* 276,
    279
World Commission on Environment and
    Development 11
World Conservation Strategy 11, 50, 83, 255
World Conservation Union *see* IUCN
World Directory of Country Environmental
    Studies 15
World Economic Forum (1999) 17
World Resources Institute (USA) *48, 140, 229*
World Resources Report 2000–2001 15
World Summit for Sustainable Development
    (2002) 6, 27, *36,* 229
World Trade Organization (WTO) 15, 278
Worldwatch Institute 15

Yearbook of International Co-operation on
    Environment and Development 15

Zambia 56, 80, 83, 88, 113, 151
Zimbabwe *45, 51, 63,* 151, 184, *212, 316*